Photoshop 4
COMPLETE

· · · · · · · · · · · · · · · · · · ·

Kate Binder, Ted Alspach, et al.

Hayden
Books

Hayden Books

President
Richard Swadley

Associate Publisher
John Pierce

Publishing Manager
Laurie Petrycki

Managing Editor
Lisa Wilson

Marketing Manager
Stacey Oldham

Acquisitions Editor
Rachel Byers

Development Editor
Beth Millett

Copy/Production Editor
Kevin Laseau

Technical Editor
Catherine Benante

Publishing Coordinator
Karen Flowers

Cover Designer
Jay Covers

Illustrator
Eric Lindley

Book Designer
Ann Jones

Manufacturing Coordinator
Brook Farling

Production Team Supervisor
Laurie Casey

Production Team
Maureen Hanrahan,
Linda Knose, Elizabeth
SanMiguel, Scott Tullis

Indexer
Ginny Bess

Photoshop 4 Complete

©1997 Kate Binder, Ted Alspach, et al.

Library of Congress Catalog Number: 96-078097

ISBN: 1-56830-323-8

Copyright © 1997 Hayden Books

Printed in the United States of America   2 3 4 5 6 7 8 9 0

Warning and Disclaimer

TRADEMARK ACKNOWLEDGMENTS

ABOUT THE AUTHORS

Ted Alspach is the author of several books, including the best-selling *Illustrator Filter Finesse, Macworld Illustrator 6 Bible, 2nd Edition, KPT Studio Secrets, The Complete Idiot's Guide to Photoshop,The Complete Idiot's Guide to QuarkXPress*, and *Internet E-mail Quick Tour*. Considered one of the leading experts on computer graphics and vector-based drawing software in particular, Ted has given hundreds of seminars in the areas of graphic design and illustration. In addition, Ted is a forum consultant on America Online, where disguised as AFC Touls he cohosts the Adobe Illustrator special interest group.

Joined by his four unruly and quite furry sidekicks, Ted runs Bézier, a graphics and desktop publishing training company located somewhere in the untamed desert of Arizona. He occasionally writes for various magazines, inlcuding *Adobe Magazine* and *Mac Addict*. Ted has also edited several other books, including *The Macintosh Bible* and the *Mac Internet Quick Tour, 2nd Edition*.

Ted wrote the chapters covering system calibration, color correction, and automating Photoshop with actions.

Kate Binder, owner of Ursa Editorial Design, is a production artist and writer living on Massachusetts' North Shore. Also a contributor to Hayden Books' *Maclopedia* and *The Whole Mac*, her publishing experience ranges from magazine editing and design to textbook page composition. Her favorite use for Photoshop is changing beer cans into soft drink cans in photos destined for publication in respectable alumni newsletters. She can be reached at UrsaDesign@aol.com, and her Web site is at http://members.aol.com/ursadesign.

Kate wrote the chapters on importing; selections, paths, and masks; editing images; type; saving and exporting; third-party plug-ins; and contributed to the appendix covering plug-in vendors.

Howard Ehrenfeld has worked as a photographer for over 16 years. During much of that time he worked on multi-image slide production. He has maintained his own photography studio since 1987. His photowork has concentrated on complex studio setups and photos manipulated in the darkroom. Howard's work has found it's natural progression to the computer where he has been creating photo-illustrations for a number of years. Howard teaches Photoshop workshops for EPI Computer Training in Rockville, MD and has taught Photoshop at Maryland Institute College of Art in Baltimore, MD. He has a Master of Fine Arts degree. His client list includes MCI, National Public Radio, Time-Life Books and Westinghouse. Howard can be reached at Studio H, 1250 Key Highway, Baltimore, MD 21230 (410-685-3686) or at HEhrenfeld@aol.com.

Howard wrote the chapters on channels, layers, and accelerating Photoshop.

Rich Evers, a Photoshop lover (though that probably goes without saying since this is a Photoshop book) is a graphic designer and developer/programmer of Web sites. He's been know to double-over with laughter at the sight of a rotating high heel shoe. Scandalous!

Rich wrote the chapter on Photoshop for the World Wide Web.

Steven Frank is an independent computer consultant, trainer and author. He is the co-author of *Kai's Power Tools Studio Secrets*. Steve has also contributed to *The Macintosh Bible* and numerous industry periodicals. In addition to his writing, Steve is an accomplished game designer, and has created several well-received games including *Quest!* and *Sword for Hire*. His next project is Oathbreaker, a multi-player, computer strategy game of clan warfare in ancient times.

Steve wrote the chapter on printing.

Allan Gibbs is the founder and president of DiskCovery Technologies, a Massachusetts-based computer consulting/training organization. He obtained his B.S. in Education and M.A. in Mathematics from Salem State College, and has effectively combined fifteen years of experience on the teaching faculty of the University of Massachusetts with another twelve years directing the training, service, and support programs for one of Boston's leading computer retailers to develop his own unique skill set that is the cornerstone from which he created DiskCovery Technologies' teaching philosophy. Allan is recognized nation-wide as the "guru" of QuarkXPress, Illustrator, and Photoshop and has traveled extensively throughout the U.S. and internationally to provide custom-designed on-site training and consulting services to many of our nation's elite businesses. He resides in Massachusetts with his wife and business partner, Lorraine, and daughter Heather.

Al wrote the chapter on setting Photoshop's preferences.

Mike Lee is a Baltimore-based graphic artist and consultant. His company, VisualLee, specializes in internet development. Mike works with his partner Amy Kilgallon Lee to develop strategies for web site design and implementation. Their clients include NASA, IBM InfoMarket, McCormick & Co., Baltimore Gas & Electric, and Radio City Music Hall. Before discovering computer graphics, Mike worked as a photo-retoucher and airbrush artist.

While he is resting, Mike teaches Intermediate Computer Graphics and Web Design at The Maryland Institute College of Art.

Mike wrote the quick reference and online resources appendices and contributed to the appendix covering plug-in vendors. He also contributed to compiling the CD content.

Sherry London has been working with computer graphics applications since the days of "Paint" on the Atari 800. She has used Adobe Photoshop since version 1.0 appeared.

Since 1989, Sherry has been reviewing graphics software and writing how-to articles for a number of publications. She is currently a contributing editor for *Computer Artist* magazine and is quite active on CompuServe as one of the Mac Photoshop Section Leaders in the Adobe Photoshop forum. She has also been a Section Leader on the CompuServe Crafts forum and a sysop on Ziff's Download and Support forum.

Professionally, Sherry has used Photoshop both as a graphic artist and as a fiber artist. She has been doing needlework design since 1973, and has used Photoshop as the basis for several needlepoint works that are currently in a traveling exhibit sponsored by the Embroiderer's Guild of America.

Sherry London has a background in education and has worked as an instructional systems designer. She has taught classes in management information systems at Drexel University in Philadelphia, PA, and now teaches Photoshop and Pre-Press at Moore College of Art and Design. She is the author of *Photoshop Special Effects How-To* and *A Certified Course in Photoshop*, both published by the Waite Group Press.

Sherry wrote the chapter on filters.

Steven Moniz is the Director of Training at Graphics Express in Boston, Massachusetts and teaches regularly scheduled courses in everything from Macintosh Basics to Advanced Photoshop, QuarkXPress, HTML programming and Web Design. On the cutting edge of Desktop Publishing and Electronic Prepress technology since its inception in the early 80's, Steve's background includes traditional offset printing, prepress and typesetting. Steve often lectures on Digital Prepress topics and provides customized training for corporate clients on both Macintosh and Windows computers.

Steve wrote the chapters on scanning, painting, working with color images, and custom colorization.

ACKNOWLEDGMENTS

Hayden Books would like to thank each of the authors for their commitment and contribution to *Photoshop 4 Complete*, and especially Kate Binder for going above and beyond the call of duty.

Special thanks also to Beth Millett, Kevin Laseau, and Catherine Benante for managing the whole process and keeping it on track. Their dedication to the book should not go unnoticed.

HAYDEN BOOKS

The staff of Hayden Books is committed to bringing you the best computer books. What our readers think of Hayden is important to our ability to serve our customers. If you have any comments, no matter how great or how small, we'd appreciate your taking the time to send us a note.

You can reach Hayden Books at the following:

Hayden Books
201 West 103rd Street
Indianapolis, IN 46290
317-581-3833

Email addresses:

America Online: Hayden Bks
Internet: **hayden@hayden.com**

Visit the Hayden Books Web site at **http://www.hayden.com**

CONTENTS AT A GLANCE

TABLE OF CONTENTS

Introduction

WELCOME TO *Photoshop 4 Complete*

Our goal in this book is to increase your productivity and to give you the answers to the problems you encounter in your work. The headings in the chapters will help you quickly find the solutions you are looking for, and all the information you need is close at hand. The modular structure of the *Complete* series means less flipping between chapters in order to find all the coverage of a topic; instead, everything you need is in one location.

This is a cross-platform book. Where keyboard shortcuts are mentioned, the Macintosh combination appears in parentheses (Command-J) and the Windows combination in brackets [Control-J]. We've made every attempt to cover differences clearly and completely.

Here's a review of the icons you'll encounter as you read *Photoshop 4 Complete*.

Tip

This icon represents a tip, a useful piece of information that helps you get the most out of Photoshop.

Trick

Tricks reveal something extra or a hidden technique to make your life a little easier.

Note

Notes include helpful extra information from the author, such as background information not directly related to the topic at hand but is interesting or useful to know.

Warning

Warnings suggest you stop and think about what you're going to do because it may cause problems later on. A common warning suggests you save a backup copy before attempting the process described.

This icon indicates features, commands, or tools that are new to Photoshop 4.0.

The CD-ROM icon notes sample documents or software demos that are on the *Photoshop 4 Complete* CD-ROM.

We hope that you find this book the most exhaustive resource on its topic and also the easiest to use and navigate. We've tried to put all the information you need right at your fingertips.

C h a p t e r 1

SETTING PHOTOSHOP PREFERENCES

Preference settings permit you to customize the Photoshop environment to suit your needs. Some of the settings affect final printout, others affect performance, and still others are purely cosmetic. In some cases you have to compromise between "pretty" and "performance." If experience tells you a certain effect causes a certain output, you are encouraged to pick the settings that enable you to see and create changes faster. Other times the need to display a more accurate representation of the finished product encourages you to select "slow boat to China" settings. At any rate (pun intended), enjoy the fact that Photoshop lets you have it your way. Except where noted, the procedures for configuring Mac, Windows 95, and Windows 3.11 are the same. When the general term "Windows" is used, Windows 95 and Windows 3.11 are implied.

After you install Photoshop, a set of preferences is already in play. These settings are referred to as the *default* settings (or preferences). Don't be afraid to change any of the preferences settings because you can return to these defaults at any time.

THE PHOTOSHOP PREFERENCES FILE

The Photoshop Preferences file is the storage bin for your customized preferences. These preferences control things such as general display options, tool options, ruler units, options for exporting information from the clipboard, palette settings, and palette placement. Each time you start up Photoshop, it queries the settings in this file. Photoshop then creates the look and feel you have requested for your Photoshop environment.

The preferences settings for Photoshop on MacOS are stored in the file "Adobe Photoshop 4.0 Prefs." This file can be found in the Preferences folder within the System Folder.

The preferences settings for Photoshop on Windows are stored in the file "Photos40.PPS." This file can be found in the Prefs folder within the Photoshop folder.

Replacing the Preferences File

There are two reasons why you might want to revert to the factory defaults. After you have used Photoshop for a while you may decide that you want to clean house and start from scratch now that you have a better idea of how things work. I can't explain specifically what leads up to this decision, but I do know that I went through this transition myself.

The other reason is one that is much clearer to define: a corrupted preferences file.

You will be using Photoshop one day and it will start behaving strangely. This is not a slur on Photoshop; this is a general truism regarding all applications. Some people say, "I wonder if my application will ever screw up?" What they really should be saying is, "I wonder *when* my application will screw up?" Computers—gotta love 'em.

So what does this have to do with your preferences file? It is the nature of your preferences file to be on the lookout for settings and standards regarding how your Photoshop program should operate. It is this open door, constant surveillance policy that causes your preference file to pick up everything that is going on in your environment. This includes the fact that something went haywire in memory and caused your Photoshop to crash. Your preference file quite often notes this interesting occurrence and assumes that that is an enhancement to the way you want Photoshop to run. That's right. The preferences file establishes a setting that says, "Whenever this person starts up this machine, begin the kamikaze routine."

How do you fix this?

1. Throw away the preferences file

2. Restart Photoshop.

When Photoshop starts up it looks for the preferences file. If it does not find one, Photoshop creates a brand new one using the factory default settings. This fresh copy is not disposed to the evil ways of its predecessor and therefore functions normally. This is the quickest and easiest troubleshooting trick you will ever learn. No guarantees with this, but it sure beats reloading Photoshop as a first step.

Backing Up Your Preferences File

An enormously clever thing to do is to locate and backup your preferences file onto a second hard drive, file server, disk, or removable media. The key here is that the backup of your preferences file should be on media other than the one on which your copy of Photoshop resides. You do this for the same reason that you back up any file on a separate drive (in case of hard disk failure). This can be a very strategic move when you encounter behavioral problems with Photoshop. Tossing your corrupted preferences file (as described earlier) can get you out of the immediate jam, but it is a little irritating when you have to reset all those favorite settings.

If you have a backup of your preferences file, you have an interesting alternative to the factory fresh option. You simply replace the current (possibly corrupted) version of your preferences file with the older (but tried and true) preferences file and restart Photoshop. Your problems may disappear and you are able to keep all of your settings.

The time to make a backup of your preference file is any time you make changes. Hopefully this backup coincides with a time when everything is functioning correctly. There is nothing more frustrating than replacing a corrupt version of the preferences file with another corrupt version of the preferences file. For the ultimate in protection, alternate your backups of this key file between two disks. (You could put them both on one disk. It is just simpler to have Disk A and Disk B.) This way if you should make a backup of a corrupted preference file, you have another (hopefully not corrupted) backup of your preference file in reserve. If you are unfamiliar with the techniques for backing up and copying files, consult the user's guide that came with your computer (Macintosh User's Guide, Windows User Guide, and so on).

Protecting Your Preferences File

Both the Mac and Windows environments offer the capability to lock a file so that no changes can be made. If you do this to your Photoshop preferences file, you protect it from all changes, accidental or otherwise, until the preferences file is unlocked. I recommend this option only after you have used Photoshop for a while. To exit Photoshop and unlock the preferences file to save a new preference setting is fairly annoying. On the other hand, after you use Photoshop for a while, you may decide you are working with optimal settings. Locking the file at this time insures these settings won't change until you want them to change. This includes adding corrupt information.

Changes you make to preferences while Photoshop is running are stored in RAM as a temporary setting. This setting is used as long as Photoshop is running. When you quit Photoshop the preferences file is updated with these latest changes unless the preferences file is locked. In that case the changes are discarded and you are returned to your locked preferences settings the next time you launch Photoshop. Now that you know all the pros, cons, and strategies, the following is how to lock your preferences file.

For a Mac follow this procedure:

1. Locate your preferences file using the following path: System Folder: Preferences Folder: Adobe Photoshop 4.0 Prefs.

2. Click the file and select Get Info from the File menu (see Figure 1.1).

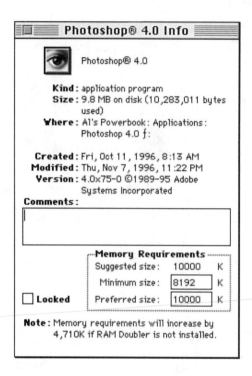

Figure 1.1

The Macintosh Get Info window.

3. Check the "Locked" box in the lower right of the window.

4. Close the Get Info window.

To lock your preferences file on a Windows machine:

1. Quit Photoshop

2. Open the hard drive on which you installed Photoshop.

3. Follow this subdirectory path: Adobe: Photoshop: Prefs

4. Click the file called "Photos40"

5. Select Properties from the File menu.

6. Under Attributes check Read-Only.

    Windows 95 users should see Figure 1.2. Windows 3.11 users should see Figure 1.3.

Figure 1.2

Photos40 Prefs Properties–
Windows 95.

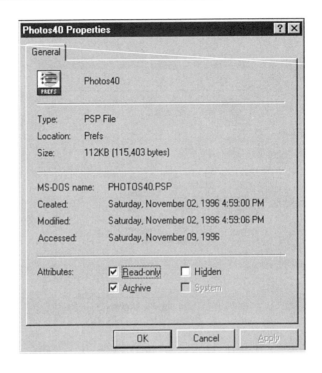

Figure 1.3

Photos40 Prefs Properties–
Windows 3.11.

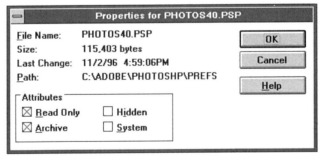

7. Close the window and re-launch Photoshop.

Your preferences are now protected from any change.

ACCESSING THE PREFERENCES

All the Preferences dialog boxes are accessed from the File menu. The keyboard shortcut for General Preferences is (Command-K)

[Control-K]. The other preferences subsets can be accessed using keystrokes, but not directly. You must first get yourself into the "preferences neighborhood" by selecting any one of the specific preferences (General, Saving, and so on). Then you can use the (Command) [Control] key followed by numbers ranging from 1 to 8. (You could, for example, access the Saving preferences dialog box by Command-K then Command-2.) You can see these specific keystrokes when you click and hold the pop-up found at the top of any preferences dialog box.

GENERAL PREFERENCES SETTINGS

This collection of preferences is a catch-all for settings and controls that did not fit under any of the other preferences categories (see Figure 1.4).

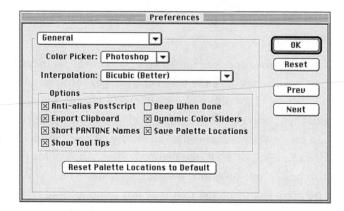

Figure 1.4

The General Preferences dialog box.

Choosing a Color Picker

Photoshop offers two options for choosing color on Mac and Windows machines (Mac System 7.5 users actually get a third option—more information on this later) called color pickers. Color pickers are the means by which an individual selects colors to use for a background or foreground color. They are also used to select colors for masks and out-of-gamut visual display.

Note

Photoshop lets you install and use other color pickers that are plug-ins. A color picker plug-in you install appears in the General submenu of the Preferences menu under the File menu. For more information about plug-ins see the section "Plug-Ins and Scratch Disk Preferences" later in this chapter. For additional information regarding plug-ins see Chapter 20, "Third-Party Plug-Ins" and Appendix B.

The General Preferences Color Picker pop-up on a Mac lets you select Photoshop or Apple. On a Windows system the choices are Photoshop or Windows. To switch between these choices follow these steps:

1. Select File➤Preferences➤General.

2. Select Photoshop, Apple, or Windows from the Color Picker pop-up.

   The Windows and Macintosh color pickers are standard to those platforms. (See the following sidebar for more information about Mac color pickers.) Photoshop's color picker offers you many ways of looking at and choosing your colors. You can create your colors using the following color models: RGB, CMYK, LAB, or HSB (see Figure 1.5). Adobe's color picker also has an out-of-gamut warning indicator to tell you when you are selecting colors that may not print accurately. (For more information on gamut, see Chapter 11, "Color Correction.")

Figure 1.5

Photoshop's color picker.

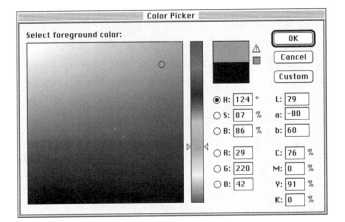

If you are using a Windows version of Photoshop, the clear choice for a color picker would be the Photoshop color picker. The Windows option, shown in Figure 1.6, is more of a hassle because the ability to select from a field of color is two levels away from your grasp every time you want to pick a color. Furthermore, even if you are using only a few colors and this subset would suit your needs, Photoshop has a much slicker option called the Swatches palette (accessed through Photoshop's Windows menu) that surpasses the offerings of this color picker. The Swatches palette is also handier because it can be displayed as a floating palette for direct access. For more specific information regarding the use and adding of colors to this color picker, see the Windows user guide.

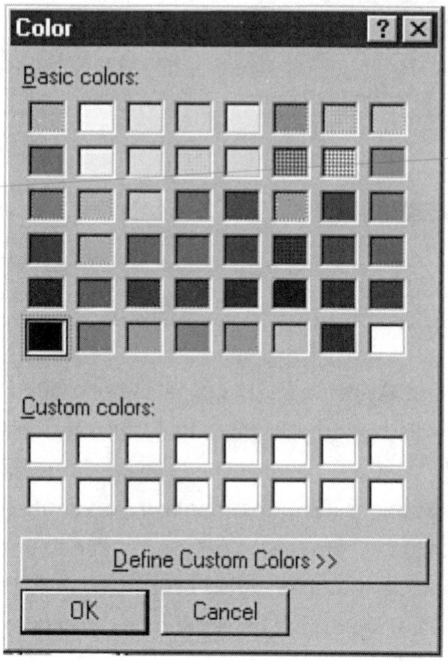

Figure 1.6

Window's color picker.

3. Click OK.

The Mac Color Pickers

If you have selected the Apple color picker in Preferences, when you do anything in Photoshop to set a color, you will see the traditional **Apple color wheel and brightness bar** (a Hue, Saturation, and Brightness approach to color selection) shown in Figure 1.7. You would use this option if you prefer to think about color in terms of hue, saturation, and brightness. Apple calls this Hue, Saturation, and Lightness (HSL).

Figure 1.7

Apple's HSL Color Picker.

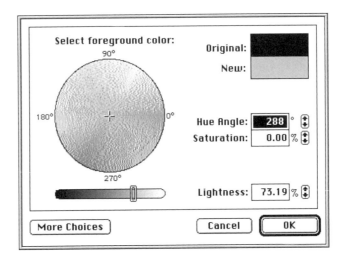

You can also use **Apple's RGB color picker** (see Figure 1.8). In order to use this option you must have system 7.5 Color Picker control panel activated. You can check to see if the Color Picker is loaded by choosing Extensions Manager, or another third-party extensions manager, from the list of Control Panels under the Apple menu. See your computer or utility user manuals for more details. Apple's RGB color picker is a better choice if you prefer working in the Red, Green, Blue color space.

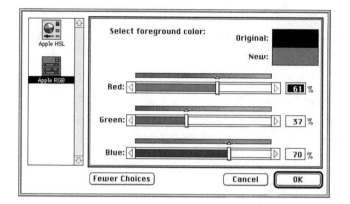

Figure 1.8

Apple's RGB Color Picker.

To choose RGB or HSL follow these steps:

1. In Photoshop's toolbox, click color background, foreground, or some other color selection option.

2. Click the More Choices button.

3. Click one of the icons on the left of the dialog box (HSL or RGB).

4. Click OK.

Setting Interpolation

Webster's *New World Dictionary* defines interpolation as follows: "to estimate (a missing functional value) by taking a weighted average of known functional values at neighboring points." In the case of Photoshop, the functional values are dots and interpolation refers to the art of guessing where and what kind of dots to use to fill in the gaps in your image.

So what causes gaps? When you enlarge an image, the dots that comprised the original image spread apart. (To visualize this effect, look at a newspaper photograph under a magnifying glass.) If nothing is done, the image may suffer from "swiss-cheese-itis": gaps between dots. Photoshop may also have to guess where and how to place dots when you rotate, skew, or change an image's perspective. As you become more familiar with the tricks of the trade, you learn to control projects so that the need for Photoshop to participate in these guessing games can be minimized. In any event, Photoshop offers three different methods of interpolation.

If you select **Nearest Neighbor,** in general, Photoshop simply copies the nearest pixel when creating a new one. This is the fastest but least helpful setting. Nearest Neighbor can generally be spotted by the jagged edges that result. The jagged edges are less obvious on some "squared-off" shapes.

Bilinear creates a softer look. The Bilinear option smoothes the transitions between pixels by creating intermediary shades. It accomplishes this by rounding off the transition between neighboring colors. Bilinear takes more time, but the softened effect is worth it.

Still more time intensive is the default setting, **Bicubic,** which boosts the amount of contrast between pixels in order to offset the blurring effect that generally accompanies interpolation. When you choose this option, Photoshop uses a much more complex mathematical algorithm to create better transitions between the original pixels. The Bicubic setting adds special color and grayscale adjustments the Bilinear setting leaves out. This difference accentuates contrast and prevents over-blurring. Bilinear and Bicubic derive their names from the complexity of the polynomial used to calculate their interpolations—Bicubic being the more complex of the two. After observing the output, one clear message should prevail: All these methods are guesses. Chapter 3 shows you techniques used when scanning that can provide you with more usable information and thus decrease the need for Photoshop to generate as much fictitious dot information (see Figures 1.9 and 1.10).

Figure 1.9

A comparison of interpolation methods on grayscale images.

Nearest Neighbor
Notice the rough edges and lack of detail in the interior. There is little or no contrast.

Bilinear
This method provides much smoother edges and transitions. Contrast is better but still leaves room for improvement.

Bicubic
Silhouette is smoother. Interior edges are better defined. Better overall contrast.

Figure 1.10

Comparison of interpolation methods on solid colors.

Nearest Neighbor
The original image was a solid gray box with a solid black border. Nearest Neighbor leaves you with fewer transitions of grays and clearly defined edges.

Bilinear
This offers an interesting average between the other two approaches. More gray levels than Nearest Neighbor but fewer than Bicubic.

Bicubic
Many gray levels. In an attempt to transition smoothly there has been a loss in definition where black meets gray. An interesting 3-D illusion has surfaced.

Whichever method you choose for your preference becomes the default method. You can, however, override this default on an individual file basis when selecting Image Size from the Image menu. This dialog box offers you the option of altering the interpolation method.

Setting the Options

The following is a wide range of options for controlling your Photoshop environment. Their extreme diversity is what makes the word "general" such a suitable choice for the name of this collection of preferences.

◆ **Anti-alias PostScript**—Select this option if you want Photoshop to improve the quality of a rasterized image being pasted into Photoshop. This smoothes the "stair step" look that edges of pasted images so often inherit. Use this feature when you want to make a more subtle transition between a pasted object and the surrounding pixels (which is almost always). There is a slight performance hit for this option because Photoshop must calculate and then implement mathematical smoothing algorithms. See Chapter 4 for more information on importing files as it relates to the Anti-alias PostScript option.

◆ **Export Clipboard**—Select this option when transporting information on Photoshop's clipboard to a format acceptable to the Macintosh or Windows system clipboard for transport to other programs. This permits pasting an image in part or as a whole from Photoshop into other applications. On a Mac computer, if this option is selected, it saves and converts the contents of Photoshop's clipboard upon quitting. On Windows based computers, this setting prompts Photoshop to ask you if you want to save the changes when you quit Photoshop. Remember that this is generally not a desirable method for moving high-resolution image information between applications because some of the information may be compromised or lost. It is better to save the document in a format that can be imported by the other application. For more information on moving files between applications refer to Chapter 16, "Saving and Exporting."

◆ **Short PANTONE Names** should be used when you're using PANTONE colors in images that you plan to export to other applications, such as Adobe Illustrator, Adobe PageMaker, or QuarkXPress.

This insures that the PANTONE color names match the naming conventions used in other applications. The colors in your images are properly separated when brought into the destination program. See the instruction manual for your page layout programs to get additional information on issues regarding color separation.

◆ **Show Tool Tips**—This is a new feature for Photoshop 4.0. Click and hold (approximately two seconds) any tool. If you have this option turned on in your General Preferences, a one- or two-line description of the tool pops up. Note that the pop-up also indicates the letter shortcut that can be used to quickly select the given tool. Figure 1.11 illustrates the Eyedropper tool tip.

Figure 1.11

The Eyedropper tool tip.

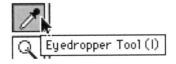

◆ **Beep When Done**—This option signals you when longer tasks are completed. If you have a slower computer and enjoy reading novels while waiting for special effects and calculation-intensive filters, this could be helpful in bringing your attention back to the task at hand.

◆ **Dynamic Color Sliders**—This option affects the appearance of the color bars in the color palette. If this feature is turned on, color within the Red, Green, and Blue bars changes as you drag the sliders. This can be a helpful visual effect because you can look at the bars to know which way to drag them to achieve the color you want. If this feature is turned off, the sliders bars remain a constant color. In this case you receive no color hints as to which way to drag the sliders, which is much more of a guessing game. The additional time needed to produce this refresh is minuscule. I would leave this setting on at all times.

◆ **Save Palette Locations**—When selected Save Palette Locations asks Photoshop to remember the status of the palettes when you quit. By status we mean which palettes were open and precisely where they were positioned on the screen. If you do not check this box, the default palettes (Toolbar, Layers, Channels, Paths, Navigator, Info, Color, Brushes, Swatch, Selection Tool Options, and Actions) open in their default positions.

◆ **Reset Palette Locations to Default**—When checked, Photoshop is directed to open the default palettes and place them in their default locations on the screen.

SAVING FILES

The Saving Files preferences give you choices with regard to image previews and naming options and control what additional information, beyond the normal image data, is stored with the files.

Setting Image Previews Save Preference

This section explains your choices for saving the Image Preview Preferences discussed in the next section. Photoshop offers the same saving options for Mac (see Figure 1.12) and Windows (see Figure 1.13), but the way in which they affect the appearance of your Save dialog box is different.

Figure 1.12

Preview options in the Mac Save dialog box.

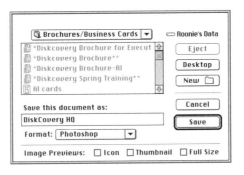

Figure 1.13

Preview options in the Windows Save As dialog box.

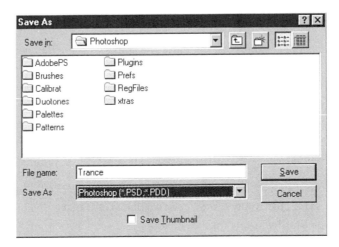

If you are a Mac user your options include:

◆ **Always Save**—Selecting this option from the Image Previews pop-up indicates that you want Photoshop to include the image preview choices you have checked with every saved file. If, for example, you checked Thumbnail and Full Size, every file saved from that point on would be saved with a Photoshop preview thumbnail, which is used in Photoshop's Open dialog box; and a full size preview, which is displayed in the Open dialog box of many page layout programs.

◆ **Never Save**—Selecting this choice indicates that you do not want to save any previews. Never Save is for those who want to conserve disk space and feel that their filenames alone serve as adequate information for differentiating between files without the added visual aid. Interestingly enough, you can achieve the same results by specifying Always Save and unchecking all the Image Preview options. With this option selected, Windows users find the Save Thumbnail checkbox in the Windows Save dialog box unchecked when the Save dialog box is opened.

◆ **Ask When Saving**—This places additional checkboxes onto the bottom of the Save dialog box on a Mac. This lets you decide what previews you want to save as you save the document. As with the Always Save option, Windows machines check the Save Thumbnail checkbox as the default when you save a file.

For Windows users the Image Preview Save preference determines the initial state of the Save Thumbnail checkbox in the Save dialog box (if it is checked or not). In all instances, Windows users can change the initial status of the Save Thumbnail box by checking or unchecking the box before clicking the Save button.

◆ **Always Save**—This option checks the Save Thumbnail checkbox of the Save dialog box by default. This is a good choice if you feel that most of the time you want to preview files before opening. Remember that a preview adds bulk to the file's size.

◆ **Never Save**—This is the choice for those who want to conserve hard disk space and feel that their file name structure serves as an adequate clue for identifying specific files. This option leaves the Save Thumbnail checkbox unchecked by default.

◆ **Ask When Saving**—This option offers the same initial setting as Always Save (Save Thumbnail checkbox checked).

Setting Image Previews Preferences

Macintosh users are offered three types of image previews. You select the combination of previews you want (see Figure 1.14).

Figure 1.14

Saving Files preferences on the Mac.

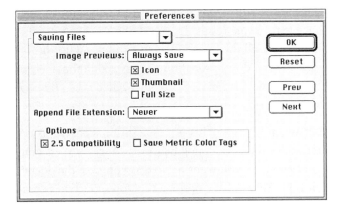

Selecting **Icon** tells Photoshop to create a miniature snapshot of your image and use it as the icon for the file. It is often helpful to be able to recognize a file by looking at its icon. The downside of this is that it does make the file size slightly larger. If this is a regular practice and you save many files, you fill up your free hard disk space more rapidly.

Thumbnail stores a picture of the file with the file that can be used to view the thumbnail in Photoshop's open dialog box. This makes life a little nicer if you are somewhat forgetful with filenames. This is also helpful if you have saved many versions of a file and need to do a quick visual comparison rather than commit to the time required to open each file. Trying to look at miniature file icons (utilizing the former setting) in an attempt to detect minute differences between files is a practice that should be relegated to those who are cramming for an upcoming eye exam.

Full Size stores a full size, 72 dpi screen image with the file. This preview is intended to be used by page layout programs and other programs that accept Photoshop files and offer their own preview options (such as QuarkXPress).

Windows users are automatically offered the option of including Thumbnails (previously described) using the Save Thumbnail checkbox in the Save dialog box (see Figure 1.15).

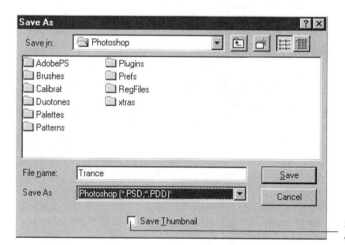

Figure 1.15

The Save Thumbnail option in the Save As dialog box (Windows).

Save Thumbnail checkbox

Windows 95 users can create icon previews for a file in the following manner:

1. Save the file normally.

2. Choose Save As from the File menu.

3. Select the file in the file list window (see Figure 1.16).

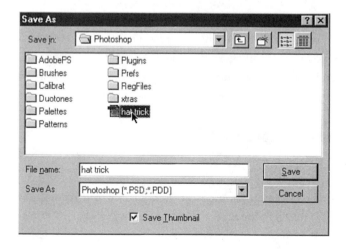

Figure 1.16

Selecting a filename from the file list.

4. Click the right mouse button.

5. Choose Properties from the pop-up menu that appears.

6. Click the Photoshop Image tab.

7. Select one of the four choices for your icon preview (see Figure 1.17).

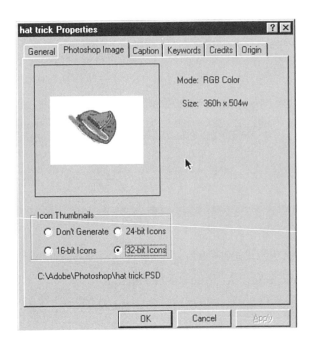

If you choose an option other than Don't Generate, you create an icon that looks like the image in your file with a resolution corresponding to your choice. Understand that this icon preview can only be viewed when you choose to view files in the large icon view.

Append File Extension (Mac Only)

The primary reason for adding filename extensions to Mac filenames is to structure files so that they can be exchanged with Windows users. If this box is checked, a period followed by a three letter extension corresponding to the type of file you are saving (.PSD, .JPG, and so on) is added to the end of the file name. In addition you should design your filenames not to exceed eight characters (not including the suffix) to comply with all versions of Windows file naming conventions. The Windows version of Photoshop does not offer this option in the preferences but instead inserts the appropriate suffix automatically when you save. There are two choices with this option—you either don't want it or you do.

Never means that under no circumstances should a three character extension be added to filename. **Always** puts an extension on the end of every filename. **Ask When Saving** adds an additional checkbox to the bottom of the Save dialog box that gives you the option to save the file with an extension or not (see Figure 1.18).

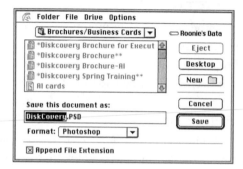

Figure 1.18

The Append File Extension checkbox automatically gives the filename and extension.

Setting Compatibility Options

Generally speaking, 2.5 Compatibility should be turned off unless the file is being sent to an individual using Photoshop 2.5. When this setting is turned on, a saved file stores a non-layered version of the file along with the layered version, thus increasing the size of the file. If you need to save files using this setting, see Chapter 16 for more information.

Check Save Metric Color Tags only if you use EFI color tables to create separation tables in Photoshop. You can save TIFF and EPS Adobe Photoshop files with metric color tags for use with QuarkXPress 3.3.x.

DISPLAY & CURSORS

These preferences affect two visual aspects: how CMYK colors and tool cursors are displayed on your monitor (see Figure 1.19).

Figure 1.19

*The Display & Cursors
preferences box.*

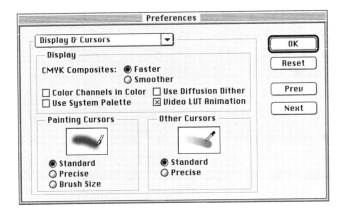

Setting Display Preferences

RGB is the color mode used by your monitor to display images. It is the only color mode your monitor can display because it makes color onscreen by projecting and mixing red, green, and blue light. You may recall the first projection TVs that had three huge eyeballs—red, green, and blue. CMYK, on the other hand, is a color mode used to blend colors in a printing process. No matter which of Photoshop's many color modes you choose, Photoshop must try to figure out how to convert the color you choose into a color that is a combination of percentages of pure red, green, and blue light. To make this a little more complicated, there are some colors that can be produced using printing inks that are not reproducible using a mix of red, green, and blue light. For more detailed information on the various color models and their use see Chapter 10.

The following is an explanation of the display options that can be controlled through preferences:

◆ **CMYK Composite Options**—When Photoshop attempts to display your image in CMYK mode it can use one of two techniques: Faster or Smoother.

Faster CMYK Composites takes a shortcut to the conversion by converting the colors in an image to their nearest RGB equivalents according to a color lookup table (CLUT). This method speeds up the process significantly but at the expense of image quality.

Smoother CMYK Composites preserve the actual CMYK color values in an image and converts them on the fly to your RGB display. The good news is that this option offers a display that emulates the CMYK color space. The bad news is that the screen refresh rate is extremely slow when this option is selected.

◆ **Color Channels in Color**—Color channels contain only 8 bits of information per pixel, which means that they display grayscale images in 256 levels. Photoshop provides you with the option of coloring the channel according to the primary color it represents or levels of gray. When this option is turned on, for example, the red color channel looks like a grayscale image viewed through red acetate. Though this makes it easier to identify a color channel at a glance, it is usually easier to distinguish tonal differences with shades of the color gray.

◆ **Use System Palette**—This option applies specifically to using Photoshop in an 8-bit mode (256 colors or grays at one time). If your machine supports thousands of colors or more, you might still want to read this information, particularly the last paragraph.

By default, Photoshop selects the closest set of 256 colors best suited for the file in the foreground and uses those colors for the temporary palette. Each time you bring a different file to the foreground (activate a new window or open another file), Photoshop must switch color palettes to select the new set of colors for that file. This can be a problem if you are trying to view two separate files

---

Speeding Up CMYK Composites and More

There is another possibility that appeals to the professional or anyone who won just a little too much money in the lottery—a graphics accelerator card. Adding a graphics accelerator card is like hiring your own private screen refresh gopher who owns a turbocharged paint sprayer and knows how to use it. Specifically, installing such a board enables you to use the Smoother option from CMYK Composites yet get the same performance (or better) than you would from the Faster setting with no graphics accelerator. In addition to this, you benefit from increases in processing speed when performing any tasks involving screen refresh including exotic filter application. We already gave you a hint about the downside. These puppies can be expensive. As you might guess, the more money you spend the better the performance. This makes it tough to know where to draw the line unless you have no money, in which case drawing the line is easy (though noticeably slower). For more information regarding graphic acceleration and other performance enhancing techniques, see Chapter 18, "Accelerating Photoshop."

onscreen at the same time; the inactive window is viewed through the eyes of a temporary color palette that is supporting the active window. This explains why, when viewing a grayscale image in the foreground, all color images are displayed as grayscale as well.

Use System Palette offers a workaround with a concession. If you want all open documents to conform to the same color palette, the one built into the system software, select the Use System Palette option. If you turn this on to view documents not created using the system palette, you may get some color shifting. In this case you must weigh the options of seeing two or more images close to their original appearance against seeing one image faithfully reproduced and the other one completely distorted. If you create documents using the system palette, you never have this problem, but you are limited to the system palette colors for your color display choices. (There is another possibility—ask Santa for a VRAM or video board upgrade and this becomes a non-issue. You would be able to display as many as 16 million colors at one time so that each image can display its entire original palette at the same time and without compromise.)

If you are creating images for display on other users' video screens, you may want to limit yourself to the system palette even if your machine can display millions of colors. A circumstance that might dictate restricting your color palette is when you are preparing images for the Internet. For more information regarding this topic see Chapter 17, "Photoshop for the World Wide Web."

♦ **Use Diffusion Dither**—Images with more than 256 colors that are being displayed on a machine that supports only 256 colors must use some form of trickery to accomplish the task. One method is dithering. Dithering adjusts adjacent pixels of different colors to give the illusion of a third color, which simulates the display of colors that are not in the current color palette. By default, Adobe Photoshop uses pattern dithering to display colors not in the current color palette, which can result in a distinctive pattern of darker or lighter areas in the image. The diffusion dithering option spreads out the inaccuracy in representing a pixel's color to the surrounding pixels and eliminates distinctive patterning. Diffusion dithering can cause temporary visual inconsistencies when only part of a screen is refreshed. This occurs when you are scrolling, editing, or painting. When you print the image, however, the onscreen dithering inaccuracies aren't printed. As long as you are aware of the temporary contraindications, this feature can improve visual accuracy.

Keep in mind that no video display is 100 percent accurate, but if you are striving to get an image that looks as close to the finished product as possible, a hardware investment that increases the number of onscreen colors beyond 256 is a good option.

◆ **Video LUT Animation**—LUT stands for LookUp Table. The lookup table refers to the part of your video hardware (VRAM or graphic card) that controls the set of color values your monitor can use to draw the screen. When you make changes to a color image using any of the color correction dialog boxes, Photoshop tells the video hardware to make changes to the color values in the LUT in response to your changes. Though Photoshop is responsible for sending the hardware the initial information about your changes, the hardware is in control of the actual changes to the display. Video LUT Animation can speed up the exchange of the information in these color tables to permit faster video refresh in response to your color adjustments. For more in depth information regarding graphic acceleration see Chapter 18, "Accelerating Photoshop."

When you are making changes that affect the entire image (not a selected portion) this approach is faster and generally visually correct with only a few exceptions that are explained later. To enjoy the speed advantage, make sure that the Preview checkbox in the color correction dialog box is unchecked.

To change only a selected area of the picture, check the Preview box. This temporarily turns off Video LUT Animation and displays the color corrections only within the selection area. If you select an area of your image and do not turn on Preview, the entire image adjusts to your changes (using Video LUT animation), even though the selected area is the only area affected when you click OK. The situation that presents the greatest discrepancies is when you are working in CMYK or Duotone mode. In these cases it would be better to select the area of your image that you want to adjust and turn on Preview in the Color Correction dialog box.

Note

For most systems running under Windows, color table animation works only if the monitor is set to 256 colors. For color table animation to work in 24-bit mode with Windows, you must install a color table animation extension in the PLUGINS directory. You should be able to obtain such an extension from your video card manufacturer. Turn off Video LUT Animation until you install this extension.

On the Mac, certain 24-bit and 32-bit cards not specifically designed for Photoshop acceleration may have color QuickDraw routines built into the ROM of the card that could cause problems when Video LUT Animation is turned on. Turn off Video LUT animation in the Display & Cursors preferences and contact the manufacturer of your video card for information regarding your options.

Choosing Painting Cursors

The Painting Cursors options control the pointers for the Airbrush, Paintbrush, Eraser, Pencil, Rubber Stamp, Smudge, Blur, Dodge, Burn, Sharpen, and Sponge tools in three ways: Standard, Precise, and Brush Size.

Standard painting cursors let you use the cute little distinct icons associated with each drawing or special effects tool. When you are using these tools the cursor looks just like the tool in the toolbar. With this option, it is tough to forget what tool you are using (see Figure 1.20).

Figure 1.20

The Painting tools standard cursors.

The Precise painting cursor takes on the appearance of a plus sign (crosshair) regardless of which tool is selected (see Figure 1.21). This option makes it easier to determine the center of the tool's "hot spot," than with the standard painting cursors. The precision cursor, however, gives no advanced indication of how wide the stroke of the tool is (a distinct advantage of the Brush Size painting cursors). There are moments when you want to know precisely where the center of your stroke is and that is when the precise painting cursor is handy.

Figure 1.21

The Painting tools precision cursor.

Tip

Pressing Caps Lock key temporarily converts all tool cursors to the precision cursor. Since it is so quick and easy to switch to the precision cursor, it is better to set your defaults to brush shape or standard. This gives you more options for quick switching between cursors.

Brush Size painting cursors shape your cursor to correspond to the brush shape defined in the tools brush shape tab. This is true for both the shape and the size up to a maximum diameter of 450 pixels at 100% view. Above that the cursor converts back to the standard cursor for that tool.

Choosing Other Cursors

These options control the pointers for the Lasso, Polygon Lasso, Marquee, Magic Wand, Crop, Eyedropper, Pen, Gradient, Line, and Paint Bucket tools.

The Standard option here works the same as the Standard option for painting tools: Photoshop displays a unique cursor for each tool you select. Though a little tougher to distinguish the location of the hot spot, you never forget what tool you are using if you select the Standard option. See Figure 1.22 to see what we mean.

Figure 1.22

Other tools' standard cursors.

The precise painting cursor is an icon similar to a printer's registration mark regardless of which tool you are using (see Figure 1.23). This makes it easier to determine the tool's "hot spot" and thereby makes it easier to use and more precise. As mentioned in the Painting Cursors section, I usually do not set my defaults for Precise.

Figure 1.23

Other tools' precision cursor.

TRANSPARENCY & GAMUT

This section offers three distinct adjustment options. The first deals with the ability to control the look of areas of your image intended to be transparent. The second setting involves the ability to extract alpha channel information from Photoshop and transfer it to video editing software using 32-bit video cards. The third setting lets you adjust the display color and opacity of the Gamut color (see Figure 1.24).

Figure 1.24

The Transparency & Gamut preferences box.

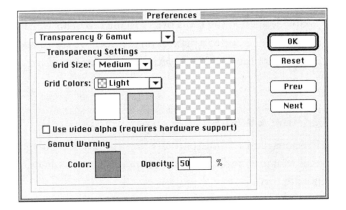

Selecting Transparency Options

Transparency & Gamut selections have not changed in Photoshop 4.0, but they are now grouped within the same preferences dialog box. Photoshop's transparency settings offer a good set of options you can use to designate regions of the artwork that are to be considered transparent. The default is a light black and white checkerboard pattern.

- **Grid Size**—These options enable you to choose various checkerboard patterns to designate areas of a layer that are transparent. There are four basic choices. Small, Medium, or Large set the size of the squares in the pattern. None is selected when you want the transparent areas displayed as white. With this setting it is impossible to distinguish between areas that are suppose to be white and areas that are suppose to be transparent. For this reason, this is not desirable when creating art that has white areas and transparent areas. In other instances it can be less distracting than the checkerboard as long as everyone remembers that it represents areas that are transparent and not opaque. I have found it much easier to see how the edges of an image appear when I set the background to white. White might also be preferred if your artwork incorporates patterns similar to a checkerboard pattern. Working with a solid white can also be easier if you are using grids and guides to align things in your image. Grids and guides are discussed in their own section in this chapter.

- **Grid Colors**—This option offers several cosmetic options that fall into two categories. For B&W options you can choose Light, Medium, or Dark. Color options are Red, Orange, Green, Blue, or Purple. Your choice depends upon your own aesthetic whims. But as with the grid pattern, there may be a certain color or gray in your image that dictates a need for greater contrast between image and transparent areas. This situation is when controlling the pattern color could be helpful. If none of these options fulfill your needs, you can select Custom from the Grid Color pop-up to select your own combination of colors for a checkerboard pattern. When you choose this option you are swept away to the color picker and given the opportunity to select background and foreground colors for the checkerboard pattern.

◆ **Use video alpha (requires hardware support)**—Do not select this option unless you have a genuine 32-bit graphics card such as Raster-Ops 364, Raster-Ops ProVideo32, or TrueVisions NuVista. These cards are specifically designed to work with Photoshop and video editing packages that have the capability to accept information from Photoshop and parse it to the video editing software. (Interestingly, Adobe Premiere is not one of these applications.) If you have one of these cards, you have the ability to extract alpha channel information from a Photoshop image, park it in the upper 8-bits of your video card, and use it as a mask of a video source. The black areas of the alpha channel completely block the underlying video, gray areas are translucent, and white areas are completely transparent. By the way, Adobe Premier can accomplish the same sort of thing without the hardware.

Displaying a Gamut Warning Color

The gamut or color space is the collection of colors that can be represented by an output device. The output device can be a monitor, laser printer, or a phototypesetter. Colors that are not reproducible within a specific color space (the colors that can be represented by CMYK process color, for example) are referred to as out-of-gamut. There are display options throughout the Photoshop program that enable you to delineate (and correct) these out-of-gamut colors in different ways. For more information on this and related topics see Chapter 11, "Color Correction."

You can set the color you want displayed as the warning color telling you, "You're not in Kansas anymore!" in the Preferences. Let's say you set your Gamut Warning color for lime green. The area of your display that would not print correctly based on the selected color mode would display as lime green.

To set a color for your Gamut Warning following these steps:

1. In the Transparency & Gamut preferences box click the color field to the right of the word Color.

2. Choose the color you want using any of the available color systems and options.

3. Select the desired level of opacity by typing in a whole number from 0 to 100.

   You could, for example, choose a 50% opacity if you wanted to see the details of the image through the lime green "acetate." This lets you see more detail of the parts of your images that will not print correctly.

UNITS & RULERS

This is the part of the preferences where you designate the metrics for your document. You can start by selecting your favorite unit of measure (inch, point, picas, and so on). From there you can designate information about the page layout into which your image is dropped to make it easier for you to specify dimension information in terms of columns instead of absolute measures. You can even opt to choose the traditional ratio of points to inch over the accepted PostScript ratio (see Figure 1.25).

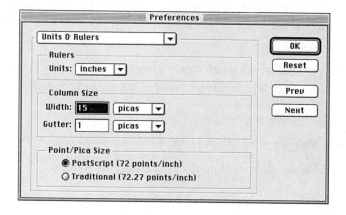

Figure 1.25

The Units & Rulers preferences box.

Choosing Your Ruler Units

If you choose Rulers from the Window menu, rulers are placed along the top and left edge of your file window. Here in Preferences, you choose the unit of measure you want to work with and have displayed by your rulers. Your choices are pixels, inches, centimeters, points, or picas. Your choice is used as the default unit of measure for the Image Size dialog box, Canvas Size dialog box, and Info palette.

Tip

You can quickly access the Units & Rulers preferences box by double-clicking the ruler. Changing the units on the Info palette also changes the unit of measure used by the rulers.

Designating a Column and Gutter Size

Some layout programs such as QuarkXPress use column and gutters for specifying page geometry. Photoshop can "think" in terms of columns when determining image size and canvas size widths. This is a two part process: setting column sizes in the Preferences dialog box and then setting the canvas size to the number of columns you need.

To set up your preferences so Canvas Size and Image Size dimensions can be created using columns as the unit of measure:

1. Type the width and unit of measure for a column in your page layout file under Width in the Column Size part of the Units & Rulers preferences box.

2. Type the gutter width (space between columns that is used in your page layout file) and unit of measure under Gutter.

3. Click OK.

4. Open Canvas Size (or Image Size) from the Image menu.

5. Choose columns from the Width pop-up options.

If you select columns from the Width pop-up in the Canvas Size dialog box, you can designate the width of your canvas in terms of the number of columns you need to span.

6. Type in the number of columns.

Here is a quick example: In the Units & Rulers preferences box, you specified 2.25 inches for the column width and 0.25 for the gutter width. Next, under the Image menu you entered 3 columns for the Image Size width or Canvas Size width. Photoshop would create a canvas width (or image width) that is just right—7.25 inches ($3 \times 2.25 + 2 \times 0.25$).

Choosing a Points to Inch Ratio

The Traditional Ratio between points and inches is 72.27 points = 1 inch. The reason for this strange decimal ratio is that neither points nor inches were originally created with the other in mind. The inventors of the PostScript language (Adobe) dropped the decimal portion of the ratio to make the math simpler when converting between the units (72 points = 1 inch). This discrepancy is pretty small potatoes when considering that the difference is less than 3 tenths of $^1/_{72}$ of an inch. If you are doing drawings that must be dead accurate when viewed under the microscope *and* measured in points *and* printed on a device that can hold that level of precision and handles graphic images while avoiding PostScript, you might be interested in this setting. If the printing device you use for output is "talking" PostScript, you might want to cave in to the desire for a little nostalgia in favor of output certainty by selecting the PostScript ratio.

GUIDES AND GRID

This set of preferences deals with positioning, aligning, and page sectioning techniques that assist you in getting things on the page where you want them (see Figure 1.26). What is the difference between the grid and guides? They are both guides by nature, but the grid lines are much more structured.

Figure 1.26

The Guides & Grid preferences box.

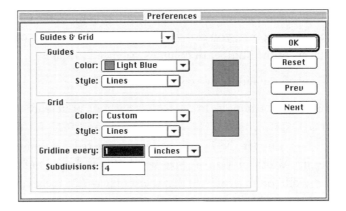

Setting Up Guides

Photoshop offers you guidelines that can be used to visually align items on the page. They can be laid down wherever you want to put them. You can place just one or a hundred as needed. You can also give these lines a little magnetism by turning on Snap to Guides under the View menu. When this choice is checked, tools gravitate (perhaps leap is a better word) toward these guidelines on the page when you get close to them. This distance is referred to as the snap distance, which we define when we describe the grid system. For now, here are the steps for setting up your guides.

1. Select File➡Preferences➡Guides & Grid.

2. Choose one of the nine preset color choices from the Color pop-up menu.

3. Optionally, you can select Custom from the Color pop-up choices or click the square of color immediately to the right of the pop-up menu.

   This takes you to your color picker where you can select a color for your guides using your choice of color systems and options.

4. Choose the Style pop-up menu.

   This lets you choose between two appearances for your guides—solid lines or dashed lines. See Figure 1.27 for a better idea of the effects of these two options.

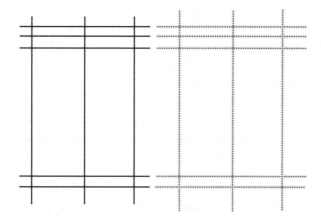

Figure 1.27

Guideline options.

Setting Up the Grid System

Grid lines fill the playing field with evenly spaced vertical and horizontal lines, spread out in whatever configuration you designate using Gridline Positioning and Subdivisions. After you deliver the specifications for the grid system, Photoshop does the math and figures out just how many grid lines (and subdivisions) it can lay down within the bounds of your designated canvas size. After you have set the options for the metrics and appearance of your grid lines, you can control them with several options from the View menu. The gridlines can be displayed (Show Grid) or hidden (Hide Grid). They can also be assigned magnetic properties (Snap To Grid checked) or used strictly as a visual aid (Snap To Grid unchecked). It is in Preferences where we designate the grid line color, style, positioning, and subdivisions.

◆ **Color**—Set the color for your gridlines using the Color pop-up menu. You have the same nine default color options for your grid lines plus the option to create a custom color guide by clicking the color square.

◆ **Gridline every**—Establish the gridline spacing by entering a value in the Gridline every box. You are designating the space Photoshop places between the main grid lines.

◆ **Subdivisions**—Here is where you designate into how many parts you want the main grid broken. This creates a secondary grid system comprised of even smaller units.

Note

If you do work that can benefit from this sort of grid layout feature and appreciate the smaller subdivisions, you may want to use white as the background for transparent areas. It is difficult to see the grid against the checkerboard background. (See the section on Transparency & Gamut earlier in this chapter.) Photoshop does, however, offer some assistance in this area. As you are snapping an object to the grid, the subdivisions temporarily become noticeably more visible.

◆ **Style**—We left Grid Line Style for last because once you understand grid lines and subdivisions, you can have a better appreciation for the style choices. Choosing Lines enables you to clearly see the differences between the main grid lines and the subordinate grid system. Dashed Lines fade into the subordinate lines. The net result is a smaller grid for aligning objects. Use Dots to designate the corners of the main grid system. The subordinate system disappears from view. (If Snap To Grids is turned on, Photoshop still insists that objects jump to these subordinate "ghosts of grid lines past.") For a clearer delineation of these differences see Figure 1.28.

Figure 1.28

Examples of the three grid line styles: Lines, Dashed Lines, and Dots.

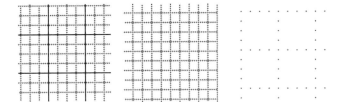

MANAGING PLUG-INS AND SCRATCH DISK

What are plug-ins? Photoshop has created an environment that permits the adding of mini-programs (plug-ins) that work in conjunction with Photoshop and add select functionality. The user can add plug-ins, made by Adobe or other software companies, that provide features a user wants. In turn a user can choose to reject plug-ins that are not needed. The incentive for adding plug-ins is obvious. The incentive for removing them is a little more subtle. Each plug-in you use adds the following overhead to your working environment: additional hard disk space consumed; increased startup time (each plug-in must be loaded at startup); and additional RAM because plug-ins reside in memory.

When you first install Photoshop it creates a folder called "Plug-ins" in the Photoshop folder (Mac) or a folder called "PLUGINS" in the Photoshop folder within the Adobe folder (Windows). Within this folder are folders containing plug-ins. These files are grouped based on the types of specialized functionality they perform for Photoshop. Plug-ins added to this folder or its subfolders are loaded when Photoshop is launched.

Note

Other applications offer similar functionality using their own plug-ins, add-ons, or XTensions as QuarkXPress calls them. Some programs actually support the use of many of the Photoshop plug-ins.

This section also explains how to set up a Photoshop scratch disk to compensate for inadequacies in the RAM department (see Figure 1.29).

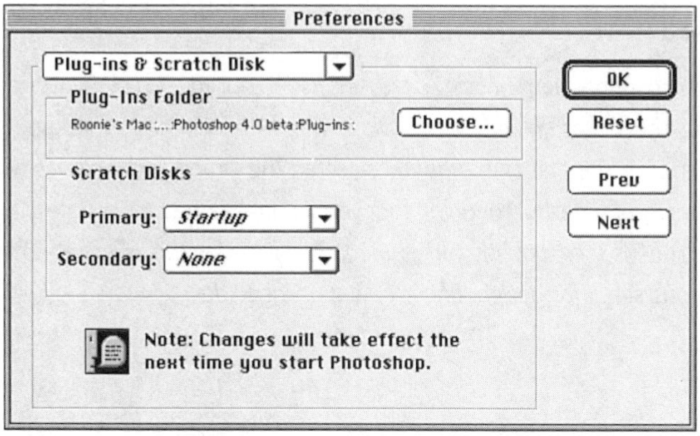

Figure 1.29

The Plug-ins & Scratch Disk preferences box.

Designating a New Plug-Ins Folder

The Plug-ins & Scratch Disks preferences box is the best way to tell Photoshop where the plug-ins folder is. When you first venture into this dialog box you find the default Plug-ins folder as the selected plug-ins folder. One possible reason to use this preference would be to designate a temporary plug-in folder different from the one you normally use. If you have a collection of memory intensive plug-ins that work particularly well for a specific project, you might want to have them loaded on an interim basis separate from the normal stock with the intention of reinstating your normal collection after the project is completed. Follow these simple steps:

1. Choose File➡Preferences➡Plug-ins & Scratch Disk.

2. Click the Choose button.

3. Locate and select the designated plug-ins folder (subdirectory) in the same way you would locate or open any folder (or subdirectory).

4. Click the Select button (Mac) or the OK button (Windows).

5. Restart Photoshop.

For more information on plug-ins and their use read Chapter 20, "Third-Party Plug-Ins," and Appendix B.

Note

Be very careful when choosing a plug-ins folder that you do not inadvertently select the wrong folder (say a folder within the folder you intended to designate). The first clue that you selected the wrong folder comes when you restart Photoshop and find that you do not seem to have access to all the plug-ins you thought you loaded. The cure for this is to repeat the previous steps for designating a new plug-ins folder.

Tip

If you launch Photoshop on a Mac and realize that you want to switch to another plug-ins folder, hold down the Command and Option keys. A dialog box appears onscreen enabling you to locate and select the new plug-ins folder. After you do, click OK and Photoshop continues its startup.

Choosing a Scratch Disk

First off, what is a scratch disk? Is it a CD with rough edges attached to a long handle for reaching those hard to get areas in the small of your back? Good guess, but no. A scratch disk is a hard disk you select in Preferences as a storage device that Photoshop is permitted to use to temporarily store information needed in memory. What information does it store? Necessary data that needs to take a back seat to more pressing information. Scratch disks are used only when there is inadequate RAM to handle the current memory needs. If you have more than one hard drive at your disposal, you can designate a primary and a secondary scratch disk.

The primary scratch disk designates the drive that Photoshop should use as its first choice for swapping information in and out of memory. The default choice is your system startup drive. Your primary scratch disk should be your fastest hard disk and should have plenty of defragmented space available. Use a utility program such as MacTools or Norton Utilities to defragment your file and clear up continuous blocks of hard disk space. Follow these steps to select the Primary Scratch Disk:

1. Select File➡Preferences➡Plug-ins & Scratch Disk.

2. Click the pop-up menu to the right of the word Primary.

    This reveals a list of candidates for the Primary Scratch Disk.

3. Select your choice and click OK.

The secondary scratch disk is the second hard drive that could be used if the Primary scratch disk becomes full. Do not use removable drives for scratch disks because they are too slow. There is also the possibility that a removable disk might not be in place when needed. The procedure for secondary scratch disk selection is identical to selecting a primary scratch disk with one substitution.

1. Select File➡Preferences➡Plug-ins & Scratch Disk.

2. Click the pop-up menu to the right of the word Secondary.

This reveals a list of hard drive candidates for the Secondary Scratch Disk.

3. Select your choice and Click OK.

See Chapter 18, "Accelerating Photoshop," for more information on strategies for using a scratch disk in conjunction with other settings to improve performance.

IMAGE CACHE

Photoshop uses a scheme called image caching to help speed the redraw of high-resolution images. With image caching, Photoshop uses lower resolution versions of an image to update the image onscreen when performing basic operations such as compositing, layering, and applying color adjustments. On the Macintosh the Preference is called Image Cache as shown in Figure 1.30. On Windows it is called Memory & Image Cache as shown in Figure 1.31.

Figure 1.30

The Image Cache preference box (Mac).

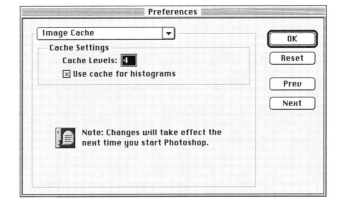

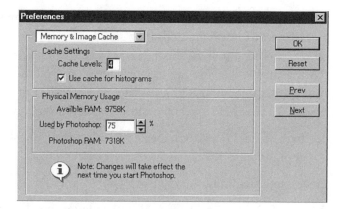

Figure 1.31

*The Memory & Image Cache
preference (Windows).*

◆ **Adjust Cache Levels**—Enter a value between one and eight. A
higher value results in greater image caching and quicker screen
redraw. Making these adjustments has no effect on final output
and is strictly a setting that offers increased screen refresh
performance at the expense of a more accurate display.

◆ **Using Cache for Histograms**—The histogram gives you a
picture of the pixel value distribution for an image. It also
indicates whether the image contains enough detail in the
shadows, midtones, and highlights. To increase the speed of
histogram displays, select Use Cache for Histograms. Selecting
this option produces a faster, though slightly less accurate,
histogram display. See Chapter 11 for more information
regarding the use of the histogram in making color corrections.

◆ **Adjusting Windows Memory Settings**—As its name suggests,
this option is in the Windows dialog box but not in the
Macintosh dialog box. See the following bullet, Adjusting
Macintosh Memory Settings, for more information on that
procedure.

The memory allocated to Photoshop for Windows can be set in
the Memory & Image Cache. By default, 75 percent of available RAM is allocated to Photoshop. Available RAM refers to
RAM not needed for the operating system or general disk-
caching. You can make this number larger to allocate more
memory to Photoshop or set it for less to make more memory
available for other applications or tasks.

◆ **Adjusting Macintosh Memory Settings**—Photoshop running on a Mac is set to a default application size determined by the type of Mac you have (68k based or Power Mac). If you have more RAM available that you can use for Photoshop, you can increase the amount of RAM allocated to Photoshop in the Finder. To change the memory allocation for Photoshop:

1. In the Finder (Desktop), locate and select the Photoshop application icon.

2. Choose Get Info from the File menu.

3. Specify Minimum Memory Size (the minimum value that you would permit Photoshop to load under) and Preferred Memory Size (the amount of memory that you would prefer to have Photoshop use if it is available).

IMPROVING PERFORMANCE

This book contains a significant amount of information with regard to performance strategies. Some of this information can be used to help you set preferences more effectively or in some cases help your existing preferences work better for you. Be sure to read Chapter 18, "Accelerating Photoshop," to gain valuable tips to get the best performance out of your equipment and the Photoshop application.

Chapter 2

CALIBRATING YOUR SYSTEM

You spent hours tweaking the photo of your prize red rosebush as it intertwines through a brilliantly white lattice column. Backed by a cloudless sky and luscious pine-covered mountains in the distance, the image screams perfection. You pop the file into your PageMaker document and send off the files to your printer. He calls you in to look at a Chromalin to make sure everything is hunky-dory. You've never been so excited to see something, which is why the concerned expression on your printer's haggard, ink-stained face has you momentarily befuddled.

You glance down to the table where your publication sits. There, in a clever layout you designed, sits your image, with vividly orange roses intertwining through yellowed lattice in front of an unearthly purple sky, which is cut off at the bottom by what is surely a forest full of blue spruce. As you run screaming out of your printer's office, you vow to always let specialized color separation houses handle your color work from start to finish.

It doesn't have to be this way. Maintaining color from an original image to onscreen display to final printout can be achieved with a little foresight. The key is found in *calibration*, the process of adjusting your computer hardware, from input (possibly a scanner) to display (monitor) to printout (usually done on an imagesetter). After this equipment is properly calibrated, the original image appears accurately onscreen, and the adjusted onscreen image appears accurately when printed.

Because of Photoshop's extensive color-correction capabilities, the input isn't nearly as important as display or printing. And depending on who is doing the printing (hopefully an experienced color professional), the display might be the *only* thing you have to change. This chapter deals with fixing your monitor so that what you see really is what you get when the image prints.

WHY THE WORLD NEEDS CALIBRATION

Kind of weird, isn't it? Although you seemingly have complete control over your image in Photoshop, it still manages to look different than its eventual printout. There are several reasons for this (although none of them really make up for the fact that the whole thing *should* work correctly):

- ◆ RGB and CMYK are unequaled inverses; inverting the values of RGB does *not* result in a CMYK value and vice versa.

- ◆ Your monitor isn't the highest possible quality.

- ◆ The lighting in your work area is either inconsistent or consistently incorrect.

- ◆ The scanner you use isn't the highest possible quality.

- ◆ Your output device isn't properly maintained (or was purchased secondhand from a little old lady who only printed on Sundays).

- ◆ The computing gods are angry.

Fortunately, there are ways to compensate for all of these things (including the gods, which are easily satisfied with offerings of unusable 256K RAM SIMMs).

Consistency is key here. If you know how your monitor is set, the condition of your scanner, and the results of imagesetter output, you can go a long way to improving the quality of printed images.

RGB versus CMYK

Your monitor uses red, green, and blue lights at various brightness levels to represent colors for each pixel it displays. Paper uses cyan, magenta, yellow, and black (the K in CMYK). To make matters worse, 100 percent of red, green, and blue is white on a monitor; 100 percent of cyan, magenta, yellow, and black is black on paper. RGB is *additive;* the more color added, the brighter the image is. CMYK is *subtractive;* the more color added, the darker the image is.

Studies have shown that the human eye probably sees primary colors and then merges them together to form other colors. Those primary colors are red, green, and blue, the same as your computer monitor. Because CMYK works on a subtractive basis, each of the colors being laid down on paper subtracts one of the primary colors. Magenta, for instance, prevents green from appearing, cyan prevents red light from appearing, and yellow prevents blue light from appearing. Black is laid down mainly as a darkening mechanism but is also used to make edges sharper and richer.

Oddly enough, cyan, magenta, and yellow can be used to display red, green, or blue; red, green, and blue cannot accurately form cyan, magenta, or yellow. Unfortunately, it's the best system we have right now.

Monitor Quality

Particularly important to your computer system's penchant for properly displaying colors and image is the type of monitor you have. There's an incredible diversity of monitors and manufacturers from which to choose, and all too often a monitor with a cheaper price and lower quality becomes the monitor of choice. With color correction, however, there are few things as important as the quality of your monitor's display.

There are two main types of monitor tubes available: Hitachi and Sony Trinitron. Ninety percent of all monitors have one of these two tubes. The difference is noticeable even to the novice: Hitachi screens are more rounded (towards the user) while Trinitron screens are quite flat. Quite a bit goes on behind the screens as well to differentiate the two monitor types. In short, Sony Trinitron monitors have the best color reproduction and shape retention. But that doesn't mean you have to buy a Sony brand monitor; many monitor manufacturers use Sony Trinitron tubes in their monitors. Unfortunately, if you only have one monitor, which type it is isn't always that apparent.

The Hitachi monitors work fine for most applications, but their effectiveness in color correction is limited.

Consistent Lighting

The lighting around your monitor is incredibly important. Here are some things to avoid:

- Natural light (Windows, skylights, and so on)
- Bright commercial fluorescent lighting
- A pitch black room
- Standard "yellow" incandescent lights
- Lights directly behind a monitor
- Lights that reflect into your eyes from the monitor

Any of these lighting conditions can change the way your image appears onscreen. Viewing your image on a monitor in a pitch black room, for instance, gives you a tendency to darken the image. A room with natural light presents the problem of different levels of brightness during different times of day and even different times of the year (think of the bright blue glow cast by sun shining on snow).

The best environment in which to work with images is by using artificial "white" light. Many color professionals recommend standard incandescent "soft white" lighting, whereas others swear by fluorescent tubes designed specifically for color correction.

Of course, although the color of the light is important, the amount, or intensity, of the light is equally important. The best amount of light is the amount needed to comfortably read newspaper text (which is by nature slightly difficult to read in low light).

When positioning light sources, try to avoid shadows and bright spots in your immediate viewing area when using the computer. If you have a desktop or work area in the same location, be sure that the lighting is the same there as it is in front of your computer.

Scanner Quality

Low-end desktop scanners can provide accurate color representation to a certain point, but for the best quality and consistency, you need to use a drum scanner. Desktop drum scanners are now available for less than $20,000, which sounds like a lot but is well worth the time and materials saved. Many color separation houses will scan images for you at a reasonable rate and then provide the image on the media of your choice (Zip, SyQuest, and so on).

The majority of users want the convenience and low cost of a desktop scanner, however. The catch is, very few desktop scanners can come close to the quality of a drum scanner, and the ones that do cost as much as (or more than) a desktop drum scanner. The low- to mid-range scanners (600 dpi) end up being the best decision for most users. Chapter 3, "Scanning," discusses scanners and scanning in great detail.

Imagesetter Blues (or Greens, or Reds)

Imagesetters come in all shapes, sizes, and qualities. How do you know if your service bureau uses a quality machine? How do you know how they maintain it? Well, you can ask. Most service bureaus who have good equipment and maintain it properly tell you often without you even asking. Note as well how often they change the chemicals in their processors; irregular and inconsistent changes can result in poor quality output.

If you own an imagesetter, *you* need to do the maintaining, which seems like a full-time job. There are parts to clean, density tests to run, and smelly, stinky, staining chemicals to change at least once a day.

Make the Computing Gods Happy

All sorts of theories abound on this one, but those same deities that cause system crashes, corrupted files, "lost" email, and other computing atrocities are also responsible for mangling your output. My advice is to refrain from calling your computer profane names (at least wait until you're out of the room and it can't hear you), keep your mouse ball free of dust and lint, and never reminisce about "the good ol' days" when there was no such thing as desktop publishing.

WHAT NEEDS TO BE CALIBRATED

Even after you've tried to compensate for all the potential problems listed above, odds are what you see onscreen still isn't the same as the original scanned image or the final output. This is where calibration comes into play.

There are three important areas within calibration:

◆ Correct the appearance of your monitor

◆ Correct the input of your scanner

◆ Correct the output of your output device

The following section focuses mainly on correcting the appearance of your monitor. After that is accomplished, you can correct your scanner's flaws using various color correction techniques within Photoshop (see Chapter 11, "Color Correction"), and talk to your service bureau about adjusting their imagesetter.

The process of calibrating your monitor is quite involved. Once you do it, however, you only have to make minor adjustments in the future to keep the monitor consistent.

Tip

Fortunately, you can save several different settings, so if you need to work in two different lighting conditions you can have a calibration set for each condition.

Calibrating Your Monitor on the Macintosh

Photoshop 4.0 includes a control panel called Gamma that adjusts your monitor each time you start up (see Figure 2.1). Of course, in order to get it to adjust your monitor you need to set it up correctly. The following instructions explain how this is done, from installing the software to adjusting the settings to making minor changes later.

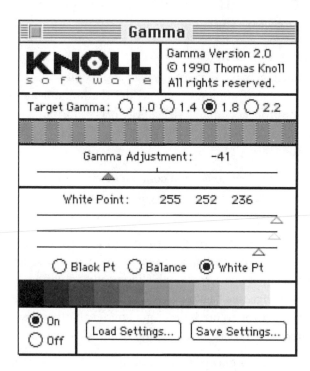

Figure 2.1

The Gamma control panel.

Warning

If you have a monitor that supplies calibration software, do not use the software with Photoshop's software. Doing so miscalibrates your monitor. Although most third-party calibration software works adequately, Photoshop's calibration was specifically designed for Photoshop, so I recommend you use it.

Installing Photoshop's Calibration Software

1. Drag the Gamma control panel (located in Photoshop application folder➡Goodies➡Calibration) onto the System folder.

2. A message appears stating that Control Panels need to be installed in the Control Panels folder, and so on. Click OK to install the control panel.

3. Restart your Macintosh.

   The software is now installed. If you haven't made any changes to the control panel yet, you probably won't see much of a difference onscreen at this point.

Calibrating Your Monitor

Before starting, make sure your system and monitor have been turned on for at least 20 minutes; this enables the monitor ample time to display the proper colors and sizing. Also make sure the light conditions are the same as they will be when you're working with images in Photoshop.

1. Adjust the brightness and contrast controls of your monitor. Make sure the settings look good at this point; changing them results in having to recalibrate your monitor entirely.

2. Change your desktop pattern to gray by opening up the Desktop Patterns control panel in your Control Panels folder. Then choose pattern #4, which is a solid 55 percent gray. You can change this back after you're done calibrating, but a darker or lighter (or colored) desktop pattern can often skew your interpretation of the calibration window's grays and tints.

3. Open the Gamma control panel from the Control Panels window.

4. Click the On button in the lower left of the control panel.

5. Select a Target Gamma at the top of the Gamma window. Use one of the following gammas:

   ◆ 1.8—For CMYK printing, Web graphics, or multimedia images

   ◆ 2.2—For video or display with an NTSC monitor (television set compatible)

6. Hold a piece of paper similar to stock your images will be printed on next to the monitor. You might want to tape it there so your hands are free to work the keyboard and mouse.

7. Click the White Point button.

8. Drag the three sliders until the white in the monitor matches the white of the paper. Typically, monitors have a bluish cast to them; lowering the blue slider (dragging it to the right) often corrects this.

9. Drag the Gamma Adjustment slider left or right until the boxes in the gray bar above it all look the same tone of gray. This is kind of strange because they never match perfectly, but they can be adjusted to be very close.

10. Click the Balance button.

11. Drag the three sliders until the gray under the word Balance is a neutral (mid-tone, 50%) gray.

12. If the boxes above the Gamma Adjustment slider have become more differentiated, drag the Gamma Adjustment slider to compensate.

13. Click the Black Point button.

14. Drag the three sliders until the black box under Black Pt is a neutral black and there is a distinct variation between each of the 11 boxes along the gradation strip.

15. If the boxes above the Gamma Adjustment slider have become more differentiated, drag the Gamma Adjustment slider to compensate.

16. Click the Save Settings button.

17. Name your settings and save them in an easy-to-find location such as your Photoshop application folder.

18. Close the Gamma control panel.

Figure 2.2

The top bar is improperly calibrated. The bottom bar is properly calibrated.

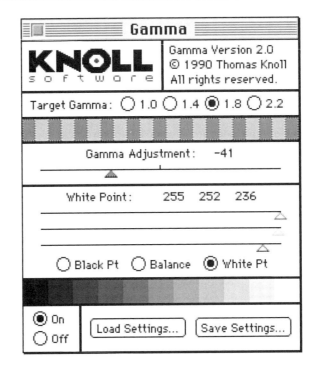

Calibrating a Second Monitor

Many Macintosh users use more than one monitor; especially users of programs such Photoshop that have tons of palettes. I use a 21-inch monitor alongside a 14-inch monitor (which holds my palettes).

1. Drag the Gamma control panel to the second monitor.

2. Adjust the settings as previously described, focusing on making your second monitor appear like the first.

3. Save the settings.

Note

Each monitor has its own settings, so when you load saved settings you have to place the Gamma control panel on each monitor and load the appropriate settings for that monitor. Name your settings differently to indicate which monitor they are for. If, for instance, you have two monitors, place the Gamma control panel window on the first one, load your settings, and then place it on the second one and load your settings.

Unless you're working with drastically different images or paper stocks, you shouldn't have to reload your settings after you initially set them.

Calibrating Your Monitor on Windows

Photoshop 4.0 for Windows incorporates calibration directly into Photoshop. This means that your calibration setting works only when you're in Photoshop (unlike the Macintosh, which calibrates the entire system). For Photoshop to adjust your monitor automatically you need to adjust the Monitor Setup. The following instructions explain how this is done.

Warning

If you have a monitor that supplied calibration software, do not use that in tandem with Photoshop. This miscalibrates your monitor. Although most third-party calibration software works adequately, Photoshop's calibration was specifically designed for Photoshop, so I recommend you use it.

Calibrating Your Monitor

Before starting, make sure your system and monitor have been turned on for at least 20 minutes. Also make sure the light conditions are the same as they will be when you're working with images in Photoshop.

Tip

Fortunately, you can save several different settings, so if you need to work in two different lighting conditions, you can have a calibration set for each condition.

1. Adjust the brightness and contrast controls of your monitor. Make sure the settings look good at this point; changing them results in having to recalibrate your monitor entirely.

2. Close any open images and palettes within Photoshop so that the screen is the standard gray background.

3. Choose Monitor Setup... from the Color Settings submenu in the File menu (see Figure 2.3).

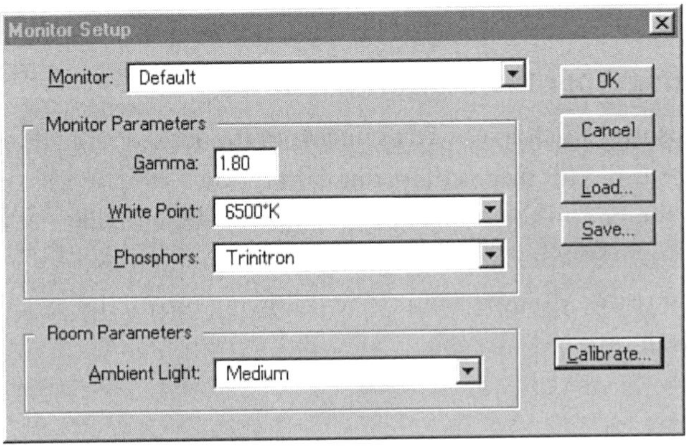

Figure 2.3

The Monitor Setup window.

4. Enter a Target Gamma at the top of the Gamma window. Use one of the following gamma values:

   ◆ 1.8—For CMYK printing, Web graphics, or multimedia images

   ◆ 2.2—For video or display using an NTSC monitor (television set compatible)

5. Hold a piece of paper similar to the stock your image will be printed on next to the monitor. You might want to tape it there so your hands are free to work the keyboard and mouse.

6. Click the Calibrate button. The Calibrate window appears (see Figure 2.4).

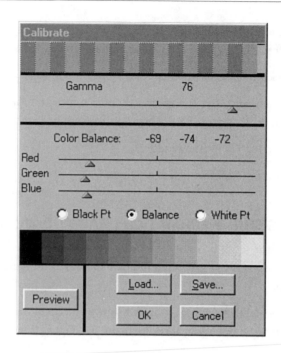

Figure 2.4

The Calibrate window.

7. Click the White Pt button.

8. Drag the three sliders until the white box under the words White Pt match the white of the paper. Typically, monitors have a bluish cast to them; lowering the blue slider (dragging it to the right) often corrects this.

9. Drag the Gamma slider left or right until the boxes in the gray bar above it look the same.

10. Click the Balance button.

11. Drag the three sliders until the gray under the word Balance is a neutral gray.

12. If the boxes above the Gamma slider have become more differentiated, drag the Gamma slider to compensate.

13. Click the Black Pt button.

14. Drag the three sliders until the black box under the words Black Pt is a neutral black and there is a distinct variation between each of the 11 boxes along the gradation strip.

15. If the boxes above the Gamma slider have become more differentiated, drag the Gamma slider to compensate.

16. Click the Save... button.

17. Name your settings and save them in a location that's easy to find, such as your Photoshop application directory.

18. Close the Calibrate window.

19. Close the Monitor Setup window.

MONITOR SETUP INFORMATION (MAC AND WINDOWS)

The monitor setup box contains additional controls used to maintain color consistency between your monitor display and eventual full color printouts.

1. Choose File➧ColorSettings➧Monitor Setup... from the Color Settings submenu in the File menu (see Figure 2.5).

Figure 2.5

The Monitor Setup window (Macintosh).

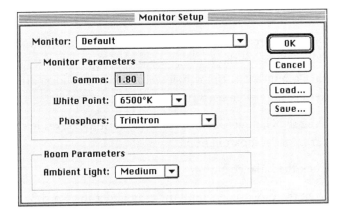

2. Macintosh users should enter the Gamma value from the Gamma control panel in the dialog box; Windows users have already done this step.

3. Make sure the White Point is set to 6500K.

4. Select your monitor type in the Phosphors pop-up menu.

5. Select the Ambient light type in the Room Parameters section; High if the room is very bright, Medium if it is the same as the monitor, and Low if the light level is less than the monitor.

6. Save your settings by clicking the Save button and entering a name and location for the settings to be saved.

FINAL STEPS

At this point, you're ready to see how well your scanner scans and your printer prints. By scanning an image and comparing the result to the original image, you can quickly see if you need to be compensating for your scanner each time you scan. After printing to an imagesetter, you know how closely your monitor is displaying what is being printed.

At this point, it is a wise idea to recalibrate your monitor based on the final output, matching the image as closely as possible. After doing this and testing the output again with your service bureau, determine what changes need to be made to scanned images to obtain the corrections you need (see Chapter 11 for more details).

Tip

Keep all things consistent after you make your final adjustments. Changing lighting conditions, monitor settings, service bureaus, and so on results in different output quality.

Chapter **3**

SCANNING

Scanning is the term used to describe the process of digitizing flat art and photography. Prior to the arrival of desktop publishing and personal computers, scanning was performed exclusively by color professionals at traditional prepress companies and printers. Today, a large majority of scanning is performed on the desktop using scanners designed for the desktop. In order to scan expertly, a significant amount of experience and knowledge is required on the part of the operator. This chapter introduces you to the elements of scanning using desktop scanners and provides you with the information you need to do your own scanning.

SCANNERS

The four basic types of scanners in use today:

- ◆ Flatbed: Most commonly used by designers, artists, and photographers due to their relative affordability and ease of use (see Figure 3.1).

- ◆ Slide: Are able to scan 35mm color slides and negative film only.

- ◆ Transparency: Capable of scanning color transparencies up to 4×5 inches, generally.

- ◆ Drum: There are a variety of drum scanners designed for the desktop that bring the user closer to the high quality capabilities of color prepress houses and service bureaus.

Figure 3.1

Flatbed scanners are the most popular amongst designers, photographers, and graphic artists.

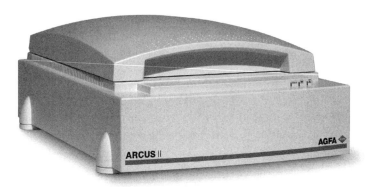

Technical Differences

The technical differences between flatbed, transparency, slide, and drum scanners are many. The most important differences, however, have to do with maximum attainable resolution and dynamic range. The dynamic range (amount of detail captured in the highlight and shadow areas) on flatbed scanners is significantly lower than that of a high-end drum scanner. For this reason, it is often difficult to scan all of the data necessary to produce a full range of detail with flatbed scanners. Flatbed scanners offer a scanning resolution of between 300 and 600 pixels per inch, whereas the high-end drum scanner can produce resolutions upwards of 3,000 pixels per inch.

Selecting a Good Scanner

Aside from the technical limitations of flatbed scanners, the overall capability of individual scanners varies considerably. The particular technology used by desktop scanners varies greatly. The method the scanner uses to capture the required data is not necessarily as important as the final result. The only way to realistically judge whether a scanner meets your quality standards is by comparing them using the same grayscale and color originals in a test scan. When shopping for a desktop scanner, bring some test images of good quality and base your buying decision on the following criteria:

- ◆ **Dynamic Range**—A good scanner captures a wide dynamic range from shadow to highlight. When scanning color, the flatbed scanner should be capable of capturing a full range of color as well as acute differences within this range.

- ◆ **Productivity**—How productive you are with your scanner depends in part on how easy the scanner is to use. Look for a scanner that requires a minimum of manual preparation and operation. When scanning your test images, calculate the total scan time—you'll likely be surprised by the variance between scanners. Compare the "preview" scan time as well, in both color and grayscale if available. Total the scan and preview scan time to get a good picture of productivity potential.

N o t e

Flatbed and slide scanners use a technology developed for television and satellite imaging called charge-coupled devices (CCDs). CCD chips capture image data by converting light to electrical charges that are converted to digital RGB (red, green, and blue) data. Flatbed scanners scan a stationary original in either a single pass—where the red, green, and blue values are captured in a single pass—or in three passes where the scanner reads in the red, green, and blue values for the entire image one color at a time. Even though a single pass scanner has to scan three times as much data at one time than the three pass scanner, the cumulative time is relatively the same. The three pass scanner's total scanning time can, however, be affected by how fast the scan head returns for each pass.

◆ **Consistency**—Scan the test image two or three times to compare the consistency of the results. If you can, scan three different photos that are similar in quality and composition.

◆ **Sharpness**—All scanners soften the image to some extent. Compare the sharpness of the scanned image to the original without setting any sharpening functions within the scanner software.

◆ **Photoshop Plug-In**—Inquire whether a Photoshop plug-in module is available for the latest version of Photoshop on your particular computer. Scanning into Photoshop saves time and facilitates adjusting each image before saving the file.

While drum scanners produce the highest quality scans, they also require a significantly higher operator skill level than flatbed technology. In general, flatbed scanners produce low to medium quality scans compared to drum scanners. Recent improvements in the transparency units of flatbed scanners make medium to high quality quite attainable. Compare the quality of scans you produce using your flatbed scanner to those you purchase from a prepress service bureau using a drum scanner. This helps determine the level of quality you can expect from your scanner.

In any case, regardless of the type of scanner you are using, the process involved in scanning your originals into Photoshop is the same. Always consider the type of project you are working on to determine if the capabilities of your desktop scanner are sufficient to provide the expected quality of reproduction.

Photoshop In the Real World

Removable Media for Those Large Files

Scanning can certainly produce very large files, especially in the case of RGB and CMYK color files. You definitely want to consider purchasing some sort of removable media device to transport those scans to service bureaus and printers. Here are some of the popular drives available as of this writing:

Iomega Removable Drives—Known for their Bernoulli drives, Iomega is also the maker of the popular Jaz and Zip drives. All of Iomega's drives are available as internal or external devices. Internal drives tend to be about $100 less expensive than external. Iomega drives are SCSI (Small Computer System Interface) devices available for both Macintosh and PC.

```
http://www.iomega.com/corporate/company/newsjaz/
prices.html
```

Drive	Capacity	Cartridges
Iomega Jaz	1.0G	3.5"
Iomega Zip	100M	3.5"
Iomega Bernoulli	90M, 150M, 230M	5.25"

SyQuest Drives—SyQuest is just one of the companies manufacturing removable cartridge drives that have come to be referred to as "SyQuests." Rivaling Iomega's offerings since removable cartridge drives first came on the desktop publishing market, the most popular sizes are 44MB, 88MB, and 200MB 5.25-inch cartridges and 105MB and 270MB 3.5-inch cartridges.

Magneto Optical Drives—Introduced by Sony in 1988, the Magneto Optical Disk (MO) is a dependable compact removable cartridge format. Marketed by most of the major manufacturers of peripheral devices, the most popular cartridge sizes are 128MB, 230MB, and 460MB 3.5-inch cartridges and 650MB, 1.3G, and 2.6G 5.25-inch cartridges.

Rewritable Optical Drives—Unlike the above removable cartridges, rewritable optical cartridges have two sides; each side's capacity equals one half the cartridge's capacity. The most popular sizes are 595MB (512 bytes per sector), 650B (1,024 bytes per sector), 1.2G (512 bytes per sector), and 1.3G (1,024 bytes per sector); 5.25-inch cartridges only.

continues

CD-R (Rewritable CD) Drives—These devices, although still relatively expensive for most consumers, enable you to master your own CD-ROM discs. A 74 minute CD-ROM can hold 650MB of data, and the media price is rather low comparatively (about $8 per CD at this writing). The CD's created with a CD-R device are read-only discs. This means that once your write data to a CD-ROM disc, it is permanent and cannot be erased or written over like other removable media, so this may not be the best choice for saving work-in-progress scans.

Tape Backups and Archives—The 4mm DAT (Digital Audio Tape) backup and archive system is rather popular these days with personal computer users because the tapes can store up to 2.3G of compressed data. There are a variety of tape sizes and recording technologies out there for tape backup on both the Macintosh and PC (not usually cross-platform). A tape backup records data linearly (in a stream). In order to retrieve the data at a later time a catalog has to be accessed to locate the requested data on the tape. This is a good method for backing up your hard drive and archiving files but not a very good choice for transporting your files to service bureaus and printers.

The removable media market is constantly changing, so by the time you read this there will likely be a faster, cheaper, and smaller alternative on the market. I recommend browsing the Web pages of manufacturers such as Sony, Maxell, and Iomega to get a good idea of what's available. The street price for drives tends to be rather stable and close, but great deals can be found for the media, so shop around before buying.

Scanner Resolution

Scanners have their own resolution independent of the scanned image's ultimate resolution. Desktop scanners are generally marketed based on their resolution, indicated in dots per inch (dpi). The scanner's resolution has a direct affect on the optimum resolution of the scanned image. In order for a scanner to capture image data, it must do so by breaking the image down via an invisible grid with a cell size determined by the scanner's resolution. If, for instance, you have a 600 dpi scanner, each cell represents 1/600 of an inch of the original photograph. A scanner that has a 600 dpi resolution is sufficient for grayscale and color scans enlarged to no more than 200% because a 200% enlargement on a 600 dpi scanner results in a maximum resolution of 300 pixels per inch for the scanned image. A scanner that has a 1200 dpi resolution is sufficient for grayscale and color scans enlarged to no more than 400% because a 400% enlargement on a 1200 dpi scanner results in a maximum resolution of 300 pixels per inch for the scanned image. Line art should be scanned at a minimum of 600 dpi, so a 600 dpi scanner would support line art scans of 100% and a 1200 dpi scanner would support line art scans up to 200% enlargement. See the section on Image Resolution in this chapter for an explanation of the correlation between the scanner's dpi and the image's ppi.

ORIGINAL QUALITY

To produce a high-quality electronic image, start with a high-quality original. Choose photographs based on their overall tonal quality and range of tones. Be sure the original is free of dust, fingerprints, and smudges before placing it on the scanning bed.

Transparent versus Reflective

The dynamic range in color transparencies and slides is much wider than that of a reflective original (photographic print). For this reason, along with the fact that scanners capture color more accurately when the light is transmitted rather than reflected, a transparency original is most desirable for high quality color scanning. Flatbed scanners are often outfitted with an overhead unit that provides a means to scan 35mm slides and transparency originals.

Identifying the Type of Original

Photographs are categorized by type based on the overall tonal range. The area of the photograph where the detail is concentrated determines the images *key* type. When detail in an image is concentrated in the highlight area of the photo, it is referred to as a high-key image. When detail in the image is concentrated in the shadow area, the photo is referred to as a low-key image. The key word here is *detail*. Examine the originals you plan to scan and identify whether the image is a low-key or high-key image. The ideal photograph contains detail throughout the image; an average-key image. Identifying the type of original aids in making tonal corrections in Photoshop. See the section on setting the white and black points at the end of this chapter.

Evaluating the Original

Examine the original photograph for possible trouble spots, such as heavy shadow areas or very bright highlight areas. Evaluate your original photographs using the following criteria.

◆ Poor **contrast** is a condition that can sometimes be improved or corrected entirely in Photoshop. Images with poor contrast often lack definition and appear flat.

◆ **Color Balance**—Color cast problems can often be compensated for using the scanning software and are usually correctable using Photoshop (see Chapter 11, "Color Correction").

◆ **Damaged Originals**—Damaged originals include photographs with torn or worn edges, faded spots, dirt specks, scratches and the like. Damaged originals can almost always be repaired in Photoshop utilizing the retouching tools such as the Rubber Stamp Tool (see Chapter 7, "Editing Images")

◆ **Poor Sharpness**—Photoshop offers a variety of sharpening techniques. An image that has poor sharpness lacks detail in the shadow area usually, and appears flat looking; lacking contrast overall (see Figure 3.2 and Figure 3.3). Try not to confuse lack of sharpness with out of focus originals.

◆ **Dull or Weak Colors**—The saturation level of colors in Photoshop imagery can be increased or decreased with exacting control. (See Chapter 11.)

Figure 3.2

This image has poor sharpness overall (left side of image), but can be sharpened in Photoshop (right side of image).

Figure 3.3

The image photographed out of focus lacks the detail to sharpen the image adequately.

- ◆ **Local Color Problems**—There are many variables such as lighting conditions, film type, exposure time, film processing, and the scanning process that can produce color problems for particular colors in the photograph. In product photography where a number of products (such as shirts for a catalog, for example) are photographed in a single session, it is likely that some of the subject's (shirt's) colors are correct, while others are not because color photography uses RGB negative film and the products may be a color that is not within the dynamic range of the RGB film used. In Photoshop, you can isolate an area of an image (see Chapter 5, "Selections, Paths, and Masks"), and make color adjustments to that portion.

◆ **Poor Focus**—Unfortunately, a poorly focused original does not lend well to repair in Photoshop.

◆ **Grainy Originals**—The problem with grainy originals is that the grain's pattern will more than likely be picked up by the scanner. This causes problems when modifying the image because any sharpening or color correction applied only accentuates the grain (see Figure 3.4 and Figure 3.5). All photographic media has a grain that often becomes apparent when enlarging the image too much, so be aware that the grain may not be visible to the naked eye when viewing the original.

Figure 3.4

A grainy original appears speckled or broken-down into a fine mesh pattern.

Figure 3.5

When we try to sharpen a grainy original in Photoshop, the grain is accentuated.

◆ **Blown Out Areas**—Blown out areas contain little or no tonal value. Even though these areas can be darkened in Photoshop, the result is often not realistic looking and can cause the highlight detail to flatten. Some blown out areas, such as the reflection of the sun off a chrome bumper, are desirable and often intentional on the part of the photographer. These are called specular highlights and should not be used to specify the absolute white point when scanning (see Figure 3.6).

◆ **Subject Moirés**—A moiré pattern is a secondary pattern that appears as a result of overlapping patterns or dots. Although the typical moiré is caused by a high density of CMYK halftone dots, the subject moiré is caused by a pattern in the photograph when it is converted to halftone dots (see Figure 3.8). Tweeds, herringbones, nylon, and mesh materials such as veils are often the culprits here.

Figure 3.6

Photograph with blown out highlight areas. Note the lack of detail in the sky and the white areas of the photograph.

Figure 3.7

This photo contains specular highlights created by reflection (on the wall next to subjects head) and by lens flare from the camera flash (on the can to the right of the subject).

Figure 3.8

A moiré pattern appears when halftone dots conflict with a pattern in the image. Note the swirling pattern and checkerboard board pattern in the table cloth.

◆ **Printed Images**—Avoid scanning previously printed originals whenever possible. The halftone dots used to print the original conflict with those generated at output time and cause a moiré pattern to be apparent. Most current scanning software includes a "descreen" checkbox. Checking this box causes the scanning software to blur or diffuse the image followed by some level of sharpening while scanning. Although this works to disperse the halftone pattern, the image quality suffers from the blurring and sharpening. If you have to use a printed original, scan it in normally and apply a combination of blur and sharpening filters from in Photoshop for more control.

LIGHTING CONDITIONS

The lighting conditions that you view the original under can greatly affect the appearance of the color composition. Professional prepress companies and printers view all color work under a 5,000 degrees Kelvin white light source (often referred to as a 5,000k light source). The fluorescent lamps that produce this type of light are manufactured precisely to simulate daylight white light. This standardization of viewing conditions ensures consistency from one time to the next, as well as in different locations. Natural daylight is too variable because time of day and weather conditions alter the light source. Standard white fluorescent light contains too much yellow and red and incandescent light increases the red and orange tones. If you do not have access to a 5,000k light source, viewing originals in bright daylight is best.

MONITOR RESOLUTION

The default resolution of the Macintosh monitor is 72 pixels per inch (ppi); the default resolution for PC monitors is 96 ppi. The 13-inch monitor is the most common monitor size with an image area of 640×480 pixels. Therefore, if you want to scan an image to be displayed on a computer screen only, the size of the image in inches can be found by dividing the pixel width and height by the screen resolution (72 ppi for Macintosh, 96 ppi for PC). For a 640×480 pixel image, for example, the size would be 8.89-inch×6.67-inch for Macintosh and 6.67-inch×5-inch for PC. Luckily, most scanning software enables you to specify image size in pixels as well as inches, picas, and points, so doing the math is unnecessary. It is also important to note that scanned imagery is usually placed into some sort of page layout or presentation graphics application capable of working in inches, so scanning the required imagery at 72 or 96 ppi at the desired width and height is sufficient.

Monitor Size

Monitor size plays a role in how the scanned image is displayed on the screen. In Photoshop, image pixels are translated into monitor pixels, so when the resolution of an image is higher than the monitor's resolution, it appears larger in the image window onscreen (see Figure 3.9). In previous versions of Photoshop, the ratio of image size to monitor size was reflected next to the filename at the top of the image window. The view percentage is now indicated next to the filename at the top of the image window (see Figure 3.10).

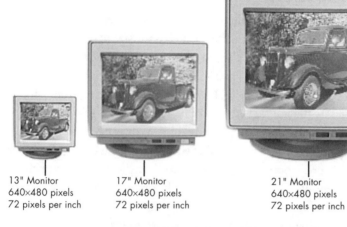

13" Monitor
640×480 pixels
72 pixels per inch

17" Monitor
640×480 pixels
72 pixels per inch

21" Monitor
640×480 pixels
72 pixels per inch

Figure 3.9

Different-sized monitors can be set to have the same pixel dimensions. In this example all three monitors are set to 640×480 pixels. The pixel size changes to accommodate the overall screen dimensions.

Figure 3.10

Photoshop displays the view percentage next to the filename in the image window.

Tip

Double click the Hand tool to jump to the "fit in window" percentage. Double click the Zoom tool to display the image at 100% or a 1:1 ratio.

SCREEN FREQUENCY

The most significant factor in determining the target resolution for an image that will ultimately be offset printed is the size of the halftone dot. Halftone dots break down the gray levels of your image into dots of varying sizes, so the printing press can print the grayscale using a single solid ink color (see Figure 3.11). The size of the halftone dot is determined by the number of lines of halftone dots in an inch (lpi); the screen frequency. The specific line screen or screen frequency is determined by the printer, the folks with the printing press. The paper being used, pressroom conditions, as well as the particular printing press are some of the factors that decide the optimum screen frequency. There is no magic number that applies to all printing projects, so communication with the printer is necessary to properly generate the prepress work.

Figure 3.11

Continuous tone images are broken down into halftone dots to be printed with solid inks.

PRINTER RESOLUTION

The printer resolution is the resolution of the output device, such as a laser printer or high resolution imagesetter. The laser printer or imagesetter is able to print your pages by using an array of dots whose size is determined by its resolution. Halftone dots are also created using these dots, so the roundness of the halftone dot depends on the size of the laser printer or imagesetter dots used to create it (see Figure 3.12). Most desktop laser printers are either 300 or 600 dpi, whereas an imagesetter can print at 1,200 dpi, 2,400 dpi, and higher. Because the size of the output device's dot affects the roundness of the halftone dot, high screen rulings, 85 lpi and higher, reproduce better on higher resolution printers.

Note

Some 600 dpi laser printers and color output devices such as the Iris Inkjet printer use screening methods other than halftoning. Talk to your service bureau or printer before scanning images for use on these devices—most require relatively a low ppi ratio compared to offset printing requirements.

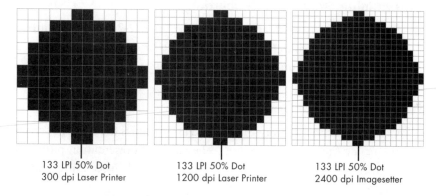

133 LPI 50% Dot   133 LPI 50% Dot   133 LPI 50% Dot
300 dpi Laser Printer   1200 dpi Laser Printer   2400 dpi Imagesetter

Figure 3.12

The halftone dots are created by the laser printer or imagesetter using spot sizes determined by the laser printer's or imagesetter's resolution.

IMAGE RESOLUTION

Image resolution is specified as ppi. Even though we're in the habit of calling image resolution dpi, the correct terminology is ppi because the electronic image is made up of square pixels. Getting the terminology right also helps in understanding how all three elements, dpi, lpi, and ppi, work together.

Determining Line Art Resolution

Line art is original artwork containing only solid black and solid white areas (no grays). A high resolution is required for line art because curved areas appear jagged without gray pixels to help smooth it out. Line art can be colorized after it is scanned in and placed in a page layout application such as QuarkXPress or PageMaker. Placing the art in one of these applications is desirable because the white areas can be made transparent or colorized separately. The file size of a line art image is significantly smaller than that of a grayscale image and line art images can be compressed to a remarkably small size using compression software like Stuffit on the Macintosh or PKZip on PCs. When scanning line art or type, a resolution of 600 ppi or higher is recommended. The best resolution would actually be the same as the printer resolution; When scanning line art to print on a 1,200 dpi imagesetter, a resolution of 1,200 ppi produces optimal quality. Scanning at the printer resolution can produce very large file sizes, though, and 600 ppi is sufficient for most artwork.

Determining Grayscale Resolution

Scan grayscale artwork and photography at 1 1/2-2 times the halftone screen frequency (lpi). A photograph scanned for a project to be printed at 133 lpi, for example, returns good results at 200 ppi resolution.

Determining Color Resolution

Color scans should always be scanned at two times the halftone screen frequency (lpi), unless they are to be used for presentation purposes only. Expect to get some pretty large file sizes when scanning color.

BEFORE YOU SCAN

There are three things you need to know before you can perform the scanning operation:

- Target Size (usually in inches)
- LPI (Halftone Screen Frequency)
- PPI (Target Image Resolution: 2×LPI)

Scanning for the Screen and Web Pages

In the case of scanning for presentation programs such as PowerPoint, Persuasion, or Director, as well as Web pages, a resolution equal to the monitor's screen resolution is sufficient. Macintosh monitors are usually 72 ppi while PC monitors are 96 ppi. When scanning for Internet web pages, shoot for the lowest settings used by your target audience; typically 72 ppi for a maximum pixel dimension of 640×480 pixels.

Scanning for Position Only

If you're not sure what the final sizes of your scans will be, consider working with For Position Only (FPO) scans. To expedite the creative process, scan the artwork and photographs at 72 ppi for Macintosh or 96 ppi for PC. Place these in your page layout application and scale and rotate them to your heart's content. After you settle on the final sizes and rotation, re-scan the originals at high resolution.

THE SCANNING INTERFACE

Adobe Photoshop supports most desktop scanners using a specific plug-in module designed explicitly for Photoshop by the scanner manufacturer. The Adobe Photoshop CD-ROM has a number of scanner plug-in modules in the Scanner Support folder. If you do not find the plug-in module for your scanner, contact the scanner manufacturer. If you are having problems scanning with the plug-in you are currently using, make sure you have the latest version. The scanner plug-in modules appear in the File➡Import submenu (see Figure 3.13).

Figure 3.13

The scanner plug-in modules are available in the Import submenu of the File menu.

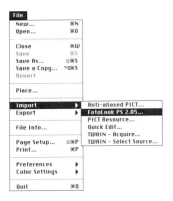

Installing Plug-In Modules

On the Macintosh: Drag the plug-in module into the Plug-ins folder in the Adobe Photoshop folder. On the PC in Windows: Copy the plug-in module into the "plugins" sub-directory in the "photoshp" directory.

The Plug-ins folder on the Macintosh and "plugins" directory in Windows are created when you install Adobe Photoshop. If you chose to install plug-ins during installation there are other plug-ins already resident in this directory (see Chapter 1 "Setting Photoshop Preferences" and Appendix C, "Online Resources").

Note

If a plug-in module is not available for your particular scanner, you can use the software provided by the scanner manufacturer to scan your images and then save them as TIFF, EPS, PICT, or BMP files to later open in Photoshop. Check with your scanner vendor or manufacturer to see if there is a Photoshop plug-in available for your scanner or if there is one in the works.

Scanning with TWAIN

Adobe Photoshop supports the TWAIN, TWAIN32, and TWAIN_32 standards for scanning. TWAIN is a cross-platform interface supported by an increasingly larger number of scanners and frame grabbers.

TWAIN is used instead of scanner plug-in software to input a scanned image and is only available for scanning devices that require or support it. With the TWAIN interface you can scan from different scanners on your network, for example, without the necessity of installing individual device drivers for each scanner (cross-platform). The device manufacturer must provide you with both a "Source Manager" and "TWAIN Data Source" for your device to work using the TWAIN interface.

If you have been using TWAIN source modules with Windows 3.1 and upgrade to Windows 95 or Windows NT, you have to update to 32-bit TWAIN source modules available from the scanner manufacturer. Photoshop is a 32-bit application, so older 16-bit TWAIN source modules probably won't work with Photoshop under Windows 95.

Tip

To use older versions of the TWAIN 32 source module in Windows, copy the "twain32.8ba" file to the "photoshp\plugins" directory and copy the "twain32.dll" file to the "windows" directory. If you are using Windows 3.1, load the "share.exe" file before starting Windows.

1. If this is the first time you're accessing a TWAIN device, choose File➡Import and then choose the correct "TWAIN Select... " command from the submenu. Select the device you are using. You only need to do this step once to define the Select Source device. If you have more than one TWAIN device installed, use the "TWAIN Select..." command to choose the desired device.

2. Choose File➡Import and select "TWAIN Acquire" from the submenu for Macintosh or select the appropriate TWAIN command from the submenu in Windows.

SCANNING

Regardless of the bells and whistles offered, all scanning software provides a method to choose Color Mode, Scale, and Resolution as well as a method for previewing and cropping (see Figure 3.14). The following are typical options available for desktop scanners, though they may be named or arranged differently.

Figure 3.14

Typical of many scanner plug-in modules and software, this is Agfa's FotoLook dialog box.

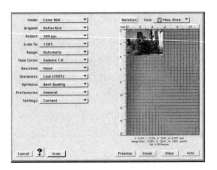

Preview

Place the original in the scanner and click the Preview button to preview the contents of the scanner bed. Some software enables you to specify the size of the preview scan, as well as whether to preview in color or grayscale. A grayscale preview displays significantly faster than a color preview.

Color Mode

Select Line Art (black and white with no grays), Color, or Grayscale. The Color choice may be broken down into RGB Color and CMYK Color. In this case the CMYK colors are generated using the scanner's built in color computer or Color Lookup Table (CLUT) in the scanner software. All scanners scan in RGB, so the CMYK process color generation is performed based on the pre-defined settings in the scanner software or hardware. I recommend scanning in RGB and performing the conversion to CMYK from within Photoshop because you have much more control over the color plate generation (See Chapter 10, "Working with Color Images").

Resolution

Choose a resolution that is two times the screen frequency for color, 1-1/2 times the screen frequency for grayscale and at least 600 ppi for line art. (See the section on resolution in this chapter).

Cropping

Adjust the cropping area by dragging the handles on the cropping rectangle in the preview screen. It's sometimes difficult to discern the edges in the preview window, so err on the side of a larger selection and re-crop in Photoshop. Note that you can crop and rotate at the same time in Photoshop if the original is not perfectly squared on the scanner bed. Try to get the originals placed as squarely as possible, though, because Photoshop has to use some interpolation (explained earlier in this chapter) to rotate the image.

Scale

Choose a scale percentage here. Some scanning software also provides a method for typing in the target size based on the cropped area. The resolution of your scanner determines the maximum enlargement possible at the desired ppi resolution. It is important to note that some scanners claiming to scan at resolutions above 600 dpi may use interpolation to achieve this resolution. Check your scanners manual to see if this is the case. See the section "Scaling Scanned Images" later in this chapter for important information about scaling the image at scan time.

Scan

Click the scan button after you select all of the settings. If you are using a Photoshop plug-in module, the image is displayed in the image window. If you are using separate scanning software, you are more than likely be prompted to save the file and choose a location and file format for your scan.

Sharpening

Sharpening may be a choice in your scanning software offering a few selections for amount of sharpening to apply. If the original appears relatively sharp to begin with, perform the sharpening in Photoshop using the Unsharp Mask filter (see Chapter 14, "Using Photoshop's Filters").

Descreen

The "descreen" checkbox in many scanner software packages and plug-in modules facilitates scanning of previously printed materials. The descreening process first diffuses the halftone dots, blurring the image, and then applies some degree of sharpening to re-sharpen the image. Although it's always a good idea to scan from original photographic prints, sometimes the only available artwork has a halftone dot. Use the descreen option only for these instances or use the Gaussian Blur in Photoshop followed by the Unsharp Mask filter to achieve the same results.

Black Point and White Point

The Black Point and White Point values are set to control the boundaries of the image's grayscale. The White Point indicates the brightest highlight value, whereas the Black Point indicates the darkest shadow value. The default setting for most scanning software is 0% for the White Point and 100% for the Black Point. When scanning for offset printing you should avoid setting the Black and White Point values to these extremes. It's always a good idea to find out from the printer what the highlight and shadow dot percentages should be. Things such as the ink, paper stock, printing press, and expected dot gain affect the size of the halftone dot and only the printer knows these specifics. If you are not sure of the print specifications when scanning, set the White Point to 5% and the Black Point to 95%. This gives you some leverage if you later have to make further adjustments.

Setting Black/White Point for Scanning

The majority of scanning software provides a method to indicate the black point and white point of the original. In this case there is likely a menu choice for Range (see Figure 3.15) or a Black Point/White Point button, usually indicated by an icon filled with half black and half white. If your scanning software enables you to set the black/white point, there should also be a way to input the desired values; either by double clicking the eyedropper tools in the scanning software or via a menu choice. Find the whitest highlight and click with the white point eyedropper to select it. When selecting the highlight, be sure to avoid selecting spectral whites caused by reflection. Spectral highlights should always be clipped to 0% (white paper). Find the darkest shadow area and click with the black point eyedropper to select it. Setting up the beginning and end points of the tonal range in this way results in a scanned image with a full tonal range.

Figure 3.15

Setting the White Point and Black Point defines the high and low end for the overall tonal range of the image.

FILE FORMATS

After you scan your image, save it in one of the formats supported by your page layout application (QuarkXPress or PageMaker or example). See Chapter 16, "Saving and Exporting," for detailed information on Photoshop's available file formats. Aside from the customary file formats used to save scanned imagery, such as TIFF, EPS, BMP and PICT; OPI and DCS are formats also available for color and grayscale scans.

Open Prepress Interface (OPI)

If you are having your high resolution scans done by a service bureau or color prepress house, they may be using the OPI method of providing you with low resolution images to place in your document to later be linked to the high resolution files on output. Not to be confused with FPO scans, these low resolution TIFF files act as placeholders for the high resolution images. In other words, they don't need to be physically replaced in the page layout application like an FPO scan before output. OPI servers generate a low resolution (usually 72 ppi) TIFF file from the high resolution file. These low resolution files are named the same as the high resolution files, so when you send your completed pages to the service bureau for output, the high resolution automatically replaces the low resolution. If you have to rotate or significantly scale the images, you should notify the service bureau/prepress house so they can take the proper action on the high resolution files because rotating or scaling the low resolution file does not change the rotation or scaling of the high resolution data.

Desktop Color Separation (DCS)

DCS files are EPS files separated into 5 parts; a controlling low resolution EPS file and one file for each of the process color plates (see Figure 3.16). You can generate these files yourself from Photoshop when saving in EPS format. In order to edit the DCS format files, all five parts must be located in the same directory. Although this is an effective way to facilitate the use of low resolution files for transporting using disks, file management can become tedious, especially on the PC with DOS naming conventions.

Figure 3.16

The DCS format creates five files; a low resolution controlling EPS file and one high resolution file for each of the process color plates (cyan, magenta, yellow, and black).

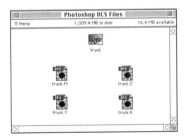

Note

Under no circumstances should you make changes to the low resolution files generated using OPI or DCS from within Photoshop. Color correction and image retouching must be performed on the high resolution files.

SCALING SCANNED IMAGES

A general rule of thumb to use when scaling scanned imagery is to limit the scaling to plus or minus 10 percent. Quality is always adversely affected by scaling, regardless of whether you're enlarging or reducing the scanned image.

Enlarging at Scan Time

It is important that the scanned image is rendered at the proper resolution and size to get the best possible output quality (see Figure 3.17). A noticeable loss of quality results when color transparencies are enlarged too much. With reflective originals (photographic prints) the limits of enlargement are rather widely dependent on the type of photographic paper used because the main concern is the grain of the paper becoming visible. Transparency originals have a film grain as well, so the size of the original determines the maximum amount of enlargement recommended (see Table 3.1).

TABLE 3.1

MAXIMUM RECOMMENDED ENLARGEMENTS FOR COLOR TRANSPARENCY ORIGINALS

Original	Enlargement
35mm	9×12 inches
4×5	12×15 inches
8×10	24×30 inches

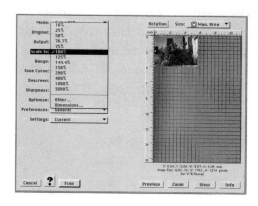

Figure 3.17

Current scanning software always provides a method to scale while scanning.

Enlarging in a Page Layout Application

When an image is enlarged in a page layout application the pixels in the image are distributed to accommodate the enlargement. A 3×2-inch image, for example, scanned at 300 ppi to be printed with a 150 lpi halftone screen enlarged in QuarkXPress or PageMaker to 6×4-inches results in a resolution of 150 ppi. The finite number of pixels in the image are redistributed over twice the distance to result in half the resolution (see Figure 3.18). The resulting image output more than likely appears pixelated because there isn't enough resolution to render the halftone dots at 150 lpi.

Figure 3.18

Enlarging a scanned image in a page layout application results in a reduction in resolution affecting the quality of the final output.

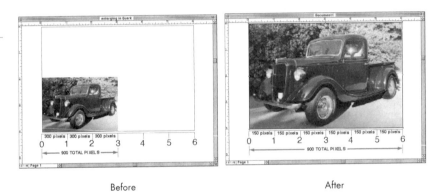

Before   After

Reducing in a Page Layout Application

When an image is reduced in a page layout application the pixels in the image are compressed into a smaller area. Because the target line screen of 150 lpi only requires twice the lpi for resolution, the extra pixels cause longer processing time and may adversely affect the quality of the image. If we use the above example, our 3×2-inch image reduced in our layout application to 1.5×1-inch results in an image with a resolution of 600 ppi—twice as many total pixels than is necessary (see Figure 3.19).

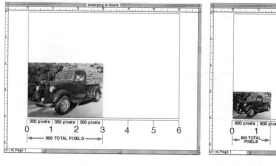

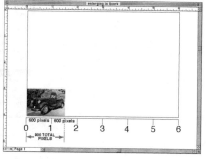

Before   After

Figure 3.19

Scaling the scanned image down in the page layout application results in unduly long output time and may affect the quality of the output.

Enlarging in Photoshop

Enlarging the scanned image in Photoshop, while preferable to enlarging in the page layout application, has its limitations as well. In Photoshop the image size can be modified as well as the resolution. Called resampling, Photoshop creates the needed pixels to increase the resolution based on the existing scanned pixels. The method Photoshop uses to enlarge an image while retaining it's resolution is called *interpolation*. There are three quality levels of interpolation that can be specified as the default method in the General Preferences; *Nearest Neighbor*, *Bilinear*, and *Bicubic*.

The Image Size dialog box contains a drop down menu to select the method of interpolation for a single instance. To resize the image and maintain the resolution, select Image Size from the Image menu (see Figure 3.20). Check the Constrain Proportions checkbox to maintain the aspect ratio of the image. Check the Resample Image checkbox to maintain the resolution while resizing (see Figure 3.21).

See Chapter 1, "Setting Photoshop Preferences," for more information on interpolation methods.

Figure 3.20

Select Image Size... from the Image menu.

Figure 3.21

You can set the interpolation method in the Image Size dialog box independent of the default settings.

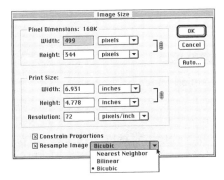

Note

Resampling an image up results in some blurring of the image (see Figure 3.22). Applying the Unsharp Mask filter after resampling an image may help to improve overall sharpness. For more information on how to use the Unsharp Mask filter refer to Chapter 14.

Resampling Down in Photoshop

Down-sampling in Photoshop is achieved by discarding the proper number pixels to arrive at a target size and resolution. There is no interpolation involved here because Photoshop has to decide which pixels to throw away. To resize the image and maintain the resolution, select Image Size on the Image menu. Check the Constrain Proportions checkbox to maintain the aspect ratio of the image. Check the Resample Image checkbox to maintain the resolution while resizing. The quality of the resulting image is largely dependent on how high the resolution is to begin with. A 6×6-inch, 300 ppi image, for example, resampled

down to 3×3-inch at 300 ppi only subtly affects the image quality,
whereas a 6×6-inch, 72 ppi image resampled down to 3×3-inch at 72
ppi displays a more apparent loss of quality. It's important to remember
that Photoshop uses logic-based algorithms to determine which pixels
to throw away, so sampling down too much can cause undesired
results. The Unsharp Mask filter can help improve quality after
resampling, though I suggest examining the pixel structure before and
after to observe the effect resampling has on the image (see Figure 3.23).

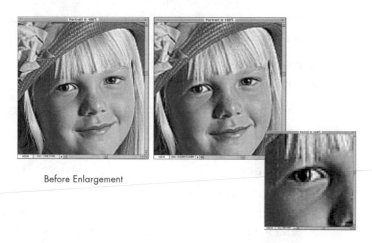

Before Enlargement

After Enlargement

Figure 3.22

*The interpolation of pixels
often results in a somewhat
blurred resulting image.*

Before Unsharp Mask

After Unsharp Mask

Figure 3.23

*Applying the Unsharp Mask
filter after resampling often
improves the adverse affects of
resampling.*

FIXING COLOR CASTS

1. Use a gray step wedge, available from most photography stores, to check color balance and gray tonal range.

2. Do not trust your monitor. Color perception is highly subjective and there are just too many variables to trust what you see on your monitor. This doesn't mean you shouldn't calibrate your monitor (See Chapter 2, "Calibrating Your System"), however, color casts are difficult to detect under the best circumstances. See the following section, "Identifying Color Cast," for help in determining if a color cast exists.

3. Check color and gray values using the Info palette in Photoshop.

4. Write down what works best for the types of media you are using to save time in the future.

Identifying Color Cast

The simplest method to check for color casts generated by the scanner is to use a photographic gray wedge. You can create your own in Photoshop, print it, then scan it in, but the printing process creates the gray levels using halftone dots. I recommend using an 11-step gray wedge available from most photography stores because this type of gray scale is photographically created and does not contain dots. Perform the following steps to determine if your scanner is generating a color cast:

1. Place the gray wedge in your scanner bed and scan it in RGB. Scan at 100% at a resolution of 72 ppi or higher.

2. From the Window menu choose Palettes➡Show Info.

3. Set one of the Info palette's color models to RGB by clicking the tiny arrow next to the eye dropper icon in the Info palette.

4. Position the cursor over one of the gray steps in the gray wedge and observe the RGB values in the Info palette (see Figure 3.24).

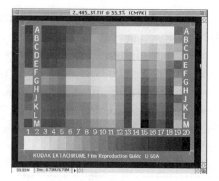

Figure 3.24

Use a gray wedge or a film reproduction guide that contains a gray wedge to check for color cast. This is the KODAK EKTACHROME Q-60A.

TIP

Select the Marquee tool so the cursor displays as a crosshair or press the Caps Lock key to make all tools use the crosshair.

5. When the Red, Green, and Blue values you read in the Info palette are all the same, the color of the pixel is considered to be a neutral gray. If the value for one of the Red, Green, or Blue colors is different than the other two, then the color cast exists in the color with the different value. If, for example, the values for a particular pixel are RED 150, BLUE 151, GREEN 200, the image has a GREEN cast (the 151 for blue is not significant enough to create a cast). Use Levels or Curves from the Image➡Adjust submenu and correct the color cast (See Chapter 11, "Color Correction").

6. Save the adjustments by clicking the Save button in the Levels or Curves dialog box.

7. Load and apply the settings you saved in Step 6 to your scanned images.

Fixing Color Cast When Scanning

The scanning software you are using more than likely provides a method to adjust the gamma curve or levels for each of the RGB colors (see Figure 3.25). You can achieve the same results as detailed earlier by making adjustments, scanning the gray wedge, and checking the values in the Info palette. This process takes some time because you have to re-scan after each adjustment to check the results. The advantage to performing the color cast correction using the scanning software, even though it is time consuming, is that it eliminates the color cast when scanning and saves you time on the color correction side in Photoshop. Most current scanning software provides a method to save these settings in a scanner profile.

Figure 3.25

Current scanner software often provides a method to adjust for color cast using gamma curves or levels. This is Agfa's Fotolook plug-in module.

SETTING BLACK/WHITE POINT IN PHOTOSHOP

Photoshop provides some excellent tools to evaluate the tonal range of your scanned image. Chances are that putting forth your best efforts to scan an image with the proper tonal range using the scanning software or plug-in module still produces an image that could use some tonal adjustments. Evaluate the tonal range of your scanned image using the Info palette and histogram in Photoshop.

Evaluating the Histogram

The histogram provides a clear picture of the tonal range and distribution in your scanned image. Select Image➡Histogram to view it.

Note

If a portion of the image is selected with the selection tools, the histogram displays the distribution for that selection only.

The histogram (see Figure 3.26) represents the gray values from left to right along the x axis; Zero (0) on the far left represents the darkest pixels (shadow or black point) and 255 on the far right represents the brightest pixels (highlight or white point). The y axis (height) represents the total number of pixels in each of the tonal values represented in the x axis. Therefore, an image that is too dark is heavily weighted on the left side of the histogram, whereas a too light image is heavily weighted on the right.

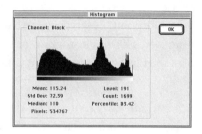

Figure 3.26

The histogram displays the distribution of gray levels for the entire image representing the total number of pixels at each of the 256 gray levels.

The seven fields under the histogram indicate the following:

♦ **Mean**—The mean represents the average brightness level of the entire image. This value is a good indicator of whether the image may be too bright or too dark.

♦ **Standard Deviation**—Standard deviation (Std Dev) indicates how widely the pixel values vary from the mean.

♦ **Median**—The median value is the middle value within the total range of values for the image or selected area.

♦ **Pixels**—The pixels field displays the total number of pixels in the entire image or selected area. The mean, standard deviation, and median statistics are derived from this value.

♦ **Level**—The level field displays the gray level of a specific point or range of values (0 to 255) in the histogram. To view the information for a specific point, position the cursor over a point in the histogram or click and drag to display a range of values.

◆ **Count**—When selecting a specific point or range of values in the histogram, the count field displays the total number of pixels with these values.

◆ **Percentile**—The percentile field displays the percentage of pixels below (darker than) the value displayed in the level field.

Setting the Black and White Point with Levels

Levels is one of a variety of methods that can be used in Photoshop to adjust the black and white point. Levels provides a method to adjust the tonal range of an image using the histogram paradigm. Perform the following steps to set the black and white point using the Levels dialog box.

1. Double click the Eyedropper tool and set the Sample Size to 3 by 3 Average (see Figure 3.27). This ensures that the Eyedropper selection is an average of a 3 by 3 pixel area rather than the value of a single pixel.

Figure 3.27

The Eyedropper tool options.

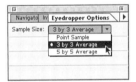

2. Display the Info Palette (Window➡Show Info). Drag the cursor around on the image and look for the darkest and brightest pixel values (see Figure 3.28). Because we're looking for a "printable" highlight, identify pixels with a highlight value lower than 255. A value of 255 indicates the absence of gray value. Specular whites such as those indicating an area of glare or flash reflection in the image should print with no dot (white paper), so ignore these areas when selecting a highlight area.

3. Select Levels from the Image➡Adjust submenu and double-click the white Eyedropper in the Levels dialog box (see Figure 3.29). The Photoshop color picker is displayed.

Figure 3.28

The RGB values in the Info palette represent the gray levels. A specular white represents white paper with no halftone dot.

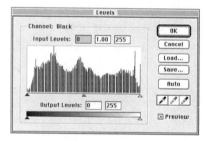

Figure 3.29

The Levels dialog box.

4. Enter the highlight value desired for the pixel area you identified using the Info palette (see Figure 3.30). If the image is going to print on white paper and is of average key, type in the following values:

   ◆ For CMYK color images: Cyan 5, Magenta 3, Yellow 3, and Black 0

   ◆ For RGB color images: Red 244, Green 244, and Blue 244

   ◆ For grayscale images set the Brightness (B) value in HSB color space to 96%. This represents a printable 4% dot.

Click OK in the color picker after you enter values for the highlight pixels.

Figure 3.30

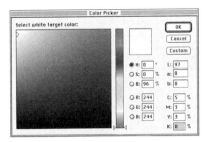

Enter highlight values in the Photoshop color picker.

5. With the Levels dialog box still open click the highlight area you identified in Step 2 with the white Eyedropper. The values of the pixels in the entire image are proportionately adjusted to accommodate this new highlight level. Any pixels with values greater than the pixels you clicked with the white Eyedropper tool become specular whites (no gray value). Observe that the RGB values in the Info palette display the before and after values if you position your cursor over pixels in the image while the Levels dialog box is open.

N o t e

If you make a mistake in selecting the pixels for the highlight value, you can reset the Levels dialog box by (Option-clicking)[Alt-clicking] the Reset button. This resetting method applies to all of Photoshop's dialog boxes.

6. Without closing the Levels dialog box, drag around in the image to find the shadow pixels. Take care not to click in the image area yet.

7. Double click the black Eyedropper tool in the Levels dialog box and enter the desired shadow value. If the image is going to print on white paper and is of average key, type in the following values:

   ◆ For CMYK color images: Cyan 65, Magenta 53, Yellow 51, and Black 95

- ◆ For RGB color images: Red 10, Green 10, and Blue 10

- ◆ For grayscale images set the Brightness (B) value in HSB color space to 4%. This represents a printable 96% dot.

Click OK in the color picker after you enter values for the shadow pixels.

8. With the Levels dialog box still open click the shadow area you identified in Step 6 with the black Eyedropper. The values of the pixels in the entire image are proportionately adjusted to accommodate this new shadow level. Any pixels with values lower than the pixels you clicked with the black Eyedropper tool now have a gray level of zero (0). The Info palette displays the before and after values for the pixels in the image while the Levels dialog box is open.

9. If you're happy with the new settings, click OK in the Levels dialog box.

View your image in the Histogram dialog box after these changes have been made and note the distribution of the pixel data (see Figure 3.31).

As stated earlier, this method is just one of many ways to adjust the highlights and shadows in your image. You can use the same steps to adjust for black and white points in the Curves dialog box as well. For more information on how to use the Levels and Curves dialog boxes, see Chapter 11. For a better understanding of gray levels (0 to 255), see Chapter 10, "Working with Color Images".

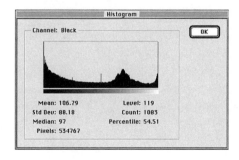

Figure 3.31

The histogram reflects the overall changes made in setting the highlight and shadow values

Using Auto Levels

Photoshop has an Auto Levels command available under the Image➡Adjust menu, as well as Auto buttons in both the Levels and Curves dialog boxes. Using this method to set the white and black points of your image sets the white point to 255 and the black point to zero (0). Although these methods redistribute the pixels in your image to achieve a well balanced tonal range, it is strongly recommended that you follow the steps outlined earlier to set the white and black points for images to be offset printed.

IMPORTING IMAGES

Besides being able to open documents saved in its own native format, Photoshop can read files saved in several other formats: BMP, GIF, EPS, Filmstrip, JPEG, Photo CD, PCX, PDF, PICT, PICT Resource, Pixar, PNG, Raw, Scitex CT, Targa, and TIFF. Import plug-ins that can be accessed through the Import command in the File menu enable you to acquire images in other ways. Combined with its capability to save files in most of these formats, these capabilities make Photoshop a handy (if somewhat large) graphics file translation utility as well as an image editor.

When Photoshop Forces a Format Change

When a file is open in Photoshop, it actually exists in two places: on the disk where it resides, and in the computer's RAM. The disk file retains the format the file was saved in, but the file in RAM technically doesn't have a format.

The first time you save a new image, you choose a name, a disk location, and a format. Every time you save the image after that, it's written to disk in its original format—unless you make changes not supported by that format. When Photoshop can't save a file in its previous format, it presents you with the Save dialog box, as though this were the first time you saved, and you must choose a new format. The only file format options available to you are the ones that support the Photoshop features you use. (You can also rename the file at this point if you want.)

This might occur when you open a TIFF image and then add layers. Converting an image to an unsupported color mode is another way to make this happen—opening a GIF image and converting it to CMYK mode, for example.

OPENING FILES

Opening and importing files into Photoshop is usually a matter of simply choosing the file in the Open dialog box (see Figure 4.1), double-clicking on the file's icon, or dragging the file onto Photoshop's application icon. Most file formats don't require that the user make any choices when opening the file—all the decisions have been made when the file was saved (see Chapter 16, "Saving and Exporting," for more information on saving files in different formats).

Although Photoshop can open files in a wide variety of formats, occasionally (very occasionally) it can't tell what format a file has been saved in. When this happens, it's usually because the filename has no extension, the wrong extension (PC files), or the file's header information (part of the file that contains information about its format) has been corrupted or damaged. If Photoshop doesn't recognize a file, you can specify a format for Photoshop to use when trying to open the image. On the Mac, follow these steps:

1. Choose Open from the File menu (see Figure 4.1).

2. Check the Show All Files checkbox to view all the files in a folder or disk, rather than just the ones in a specified format.

3. Click the name of the file you want to open, and then choose a format from the pop-up menu at the bottom of the dialog box.

4. Click Open to open the file.

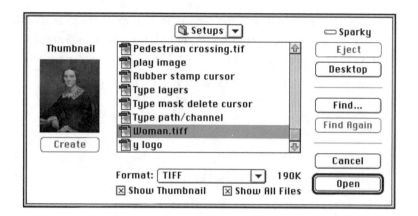

Figure 4.1

Photoshop's Open dialog box displays thumbnails and shows the format and size of selected files.

On a Windows system, follow these steps:

1. Choose Open As from the File menu.

2. Select the correct file format.

3. Choose the file you want to open.

4. Click Open to open the file.

If the file is damaged—or if you've chosen the wrong format—Photoshop won't be able to open the file. A dialog box appears telling you that the format you picked is not valid for that file (see Figure 4.2).

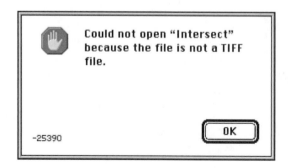

Figure 4.2

This Mac dialog box tells you that you chose the wrong format in which to open a file.

Most of the time, however, Photoshop can determine the format of the files it opens. The extensions for different file formats, which are almost always used on PCs and sometimes on Macs, are listed here.

Format	Extensions
Photoshop	PSD
Illustrator	AI
IFF	IFF
HAM	HAM
BMP	BMP, RLE
GIF	GIF
EPS	EPS
Filmstrip	FLM
JPEG	JPG
Photo CD	PCD
MacPaint	MAC, MPT
PCX	PCX
PICT	PICT
PICT resource	PICS
Pixar	PXR
PixelPaint	PXI
Raw	RAW
Scitex CT	SCT
TGA	ICB, TGA, VDA, VST
TIFF	TIF

Opening BMP files

Files saved in Microsoft's Windows Bitmap format use the BMP extension. Photoshop supports 24-bit BMP images. This format is used primarily in Windows applications development, and it can use a lossless compression method called RLE (see Chapter 18 for more information on image compression). There are no options when opening a BMP file, whether it's compressed or not—the file simply opens with no additional dialog boxes presented.

Opening GIF files

GIF (Graphics Interchange Format) files are most commonly found on the Internet, primarily displayed on the World Wide Web. The format, created by CompuServe, also is used to exchange graphics files via Usenet newsgroups. GIF files are usually found in one of two versions: GIF87 and GIF89a, named after the years in which the GIF format specification was revised to create these variations on the format. GIFs can be 8-bit color or grayscale images, and the format supports transparency (one color in the image can be specified to appear transparent), animation (several images can be stored in one file), and interlacing (the image can be displayed at a low resolution even before most of the image data is downloaded).

When you open a transparent GIF, you won't see the transparent color as transparent—it appears as a color (chosen by the creator of the image) that doesn't show up anywhere else in the image. This is the *transparency index* color, and when the image is displayed in a Web browser, this color is deleted, enabling the background color or pattern to show through. Unfortunately, Photoshop can't interpret the transparent color as being equivalent to its own layer transparency (maybe in the next version!), which enables image elements on underlying layers to show through. Don't worry about the transparency index color showing up in your image, though; as long as you continue to save the file in GIF format, the color you see in Photoshop is interpreted as transparent by Web browsers.

Note

Photoshop doesn't support GIF animations, so if you open an animated GIF in Photoshop, you only see one of the included images.

There are no options when opening a GIF file, in either version of the format.

Opening Raster EPS Files

Used mostly in prepress applications, the EPS (Encapsulated PostScript) format can contain either raster or vector information. Raster EPS files—the type Photoshop writes—often are used for scanned images, whereas vector EPS files are created by drawing programs such as Illustrator, FreeHand, Canvas, and CorelDRAW.

Each EPS file is made up of two parts: the PostScript description of the image, whether it's a raster or vector graphic, and a low-resolution bitmapped preview image that's displayed when the image is imported into another program. EPS previews can be TIFF, PICT, or JPEG. Some PC applications can't open or import EPS documents that have JPEG or PICT previews because they don't support QuickTime; Mac applications generally don't care what kind of preview is used.

Raster EPS files can be opened from Photoshop's Open dialog box, and there are no options to set when opening EPS files. They can be black-and-white, grayscale, or color (RGB, CMYK, or indexed), and they may include clipping paths that can be used to silhouette the images when they're imported into page layout programs. To view and use any paths in an EPS image, open the Paths palette. (For more information on clipping paths, see Chapter 5, "Selections, Paths, and Masks.")

Opening Vector (Illustrator) EPS files

Vector EPS files are a different story from raster EPS files. These files don't contain raster or bitmapped data, but PostScript vector artwork. Photoshop cannot open vector EPS files as vector files, so it has to do one of two things: open the screen-resolution preview image that's saved with the PostScript image, or rasterize the PostScript data, turning it into a bitmapped image. One reason you might want to do this is to convert Illustrator files to GIF files that can be used on the Web.

Warning

Keep in mind that after a vector illustration has been converted to raster artwork, it can't be converted back to vector artwork. Always save your original vector files in case you need to work on an illustration again in its originating program.

Photoshop can only rasterize Illustrator files, in any of Illustrator's formats (including Illustrator EPS and Illustrator 88). If you try to open a vector EPS image that's not an Illustrator EPS file, Photoshop opens only the 72-dpi screen preview. Fortunately, most other drawing programs, including CorelDRAW and FreeHand, can save files in Illustrator format. Once that's done, you can open them in Photoshop and rasterize to your heart's content. To rasterize an Illustrator drawing, follow these steps:

1. Choose Open from the File menu and select the file you want to open. Photoshop presents you with a dialog box containing several options (see Figure 4.3).

2. Choose the size you want the finished Photoshop file to be, in pixels, inches, points, or millimeters. Check Constrain Proportions if you want to make sure that the image's current proportions are maintained—if this option is on, then changing the image's size in one dimension results in an automatic change to the other dimension.

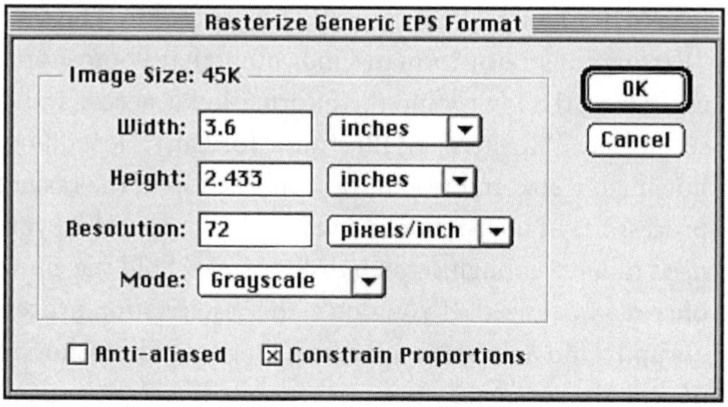

Figure 4.3

The Rasterize Generic EPS Format dialog box.

3. Choose a resolution. The default resolution is 72 dpi—screen resolution, but you can choose a resolution as high as 9999.99 pixels per inch or as low as 1 pixel per inch.

4. Select an image mode: Grayscale, RGB, CMYK, or Lab color.

   Choose grayscale if the image contains only shades of black and gray—or if it's color and you want to convert it to grayscale as you open it. Choose RGB for color images used for electronic display (Web graphics, for example) and CMYK for color images that will be reproduced in four-color process printing.

The Lab color mode lets you access all the colors the human eye can recognize, including all CMYK and RGB colors. Working in this mode allows you to change colors without affecting brightness and contrast, or vice versa. Because converting from RGB to CMYK (or converting in the other direction) changes colors, use this mode if you don't know yet whether the image will be reproduced electronically or in print, or if it will be used for both. Then create separate RGB and/or CMYK versions of the image when it's complete.

5. Turn on or off anti-aliasing.

   In general, you always want to use anti-aliasing; it smooths the edges of the image by adding medium-colored pixels between areas of different colors.

6. Click OK. You probably see two progress bars. The first says "Parsing Illustrator format," indicating that Photoshop is evaluating the file to find the information it needs, and the second says "Rasterizing Illustrator format." Depending on how high a size and resolution you've chosen, the rasterization process may take a while. As when opening any file, you also need to have enough scratch disk space to hold the entire image once it's rasterized. If you don't, the rasterization process stops abruptly and a message appears telling you Photoshop ran out of scratch disk space.

   If you don't see the progress bars before the image opens, don't panic—The progress bars only appear if the file takes more than a few seconds to open.

7. Once the rasterization process is complete, a window opens containing a raster version of the artwork at the size and resolution you specified. The image appears on a transparent layer named Layer 1; all areas that didn't contain any elements in the original artwork are transparent.

Placing Vector EPS Files in Photoshop Documents

If you want to insert an Illustrator file into an existing Photoshop file, use the Place command from the File menu. Unlike the Open command, this method doesn't require that you specify the image's size before importing it—you can resize it dynamically. Other than the sequence of steps, Photoshop rasterizes placed Illustrator files exactly the same as opened ones.

1. With the destination image open, choose the Place command from the File menu.

2. Choose the Illustrator file you want to place and click OK to import it.

3. Adjust the image to the size you want.

    The image appears on a new layer in a bounding box. You can move it by clicking on the box and dragging it. By dragging its corners, you can resize the placed image (see Figure 4.4). You can't, however, change the placed image's proportions.

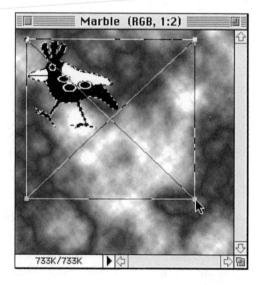

Figure 4.4

Placing an Illustrator file enables you to resize the image dynamically by dragging the corners of the bounding box.

4. When the image is sized and positioned the way you want it, click on it to begin the rasterization process. The bounding box

disappears, and a progress bar appears that reads "Placing image...." If you decide you don't want to place the image, click outside the bounding box to delete the image from your file.

Tip

If your drawing package doesn't save to Illustrator format—for example, if you're using a graphing package that only writes generic EPS files—you can use a Mac shareware utility called epsConverter from Art Age Software to translate your files to Illustrator format. You can find Art Age at `http:/ /users.aol.com/ArtAge/ArtAge.html`*; epsConverter is also available in the DTP areas of CompuServe and America Online, as well as major Mac shareware archives.*

Dragging and Dropping Vector EPS Files

Both FreeHand and Illustrator enable you to drag and drop images into Photoshop. Illustrator images also can be copied and pasted. To drag and drop images into Photoshop, follow these steps:

1. Open the Photoshop file into which you want to drag an Illustrator or FreeHand image.

2. In Illustrator or FreeHand, select the paths and objects you want to drag into Photoshop. Paths must be entirely selected; partially selected paths won't be transferred properly.

3. Using the Selection (pointer arrow) tool in Illustrator or FreeHand, drag the selected artwork from the Illustrator or FreeHand window into the Photoshop window.

4. When you release the mouse button, the artwork rasterizes and appears within the Photoshop window on a new layer. If the artwork is too large, part of it is hidden by the edges of the window. As long as the file is not flattened, however, the layer retains all the artwork because of Photoshop's new "big data" functionality in version 4.0.

Copying and Pasting from Illustrator into Photoshop

To copy and paste from Illustrator into Photoshop, follow these steps:

1. Open the Photoshop file into which you want to copy and paste an Illustrator or FreeHand image.

2. In Illustrator, select the paths and objects you want to copy and paste into Photoshop. Paths must be entirely selected; partially selected paths won't be transferred properly.

3. Copy the paths using the Copy command from the Edit menu or (Command-C)[Control-C].

4. Switch to Photoshop. As you do so, a box appears that reads "Changing clipboard to AICB format." The AICB format stands for Adobe Illustrator ClipBoard, a format Adobe uses to transfer vector-based artwork between applications.

5. Paste using the Paste Command from the Edit menu or (Command)[Control]-V. A dialog box appears (see Figure 4.5). Choose pixels to rasterize the image and make it part of the Photoshop image; choose paths to turn the Illustrator paths into Photoshop paths. If you choose pixels, then you should make them anti-aliased for a smooth edge.

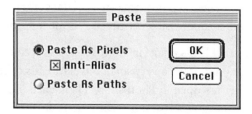

Figure 4.5

Pasting Illustrator objects into Photoshop brings up the Paste dialog box.

6. If you chose pixels in the last step, the artwork appears on a new layer within Photoshop. If you chose paths, the paths appear in the Paths palette and can be selected and used just like paths created in Photoshop.

Opening Filmstrip Files

You can edit Adobe Premiere video clips in Photoshop by exporting a Filmstrip file from Premiere and opening it in Photoshop. A Filmstrip file shows all the frames in the exported video, stacked vertically. Although you don't have to resave a Filmstrip file in Filmstrip format, if you don't, you won't be able to reimport it into Premiere.

When you open a Filmstrip file, you see a gray bar below each frame showing the time stamp for that frame in the video. You can move from one frame to the next quickly by pressing Shift-Page Down or Shift-Page Up.

Opening JPEG Files

JPEG (Joint Photographic Experts Group) is both a file format and a compression method that enables huge savings in file size. It's a *lossy* method, which means that using it reduces image quality—the higher the compression, the smaller the file, but the more loss in image quality. The level of compression is chosen by the creator of the file when it's saved.

These days, JPEG images are most often found on the Internet, particularly the World Wide Web. The format is best suited for use with photographic images without large areas of flat color (the compression damage, in the form of visible "artifacts," is most visible in flat areas).

When you open a JPEG image in Photoshop, it is decompressed so that you can work on it. If it's a very small file before it's opened, it may be very large after it's open in Photoshop. Then, each time you save and close the file, the compression is recalculated, further reducing image quality. It's best to use the JPEG format only for the final version of an image, keeping the file in a different format as it's worked on.

There are no options when opening a JPEG file.

Opening PhotoCD Files

PhotoCD is a format created by Kodak for storing scanned color images on CD-ROMs. It uses the YCC color model for defining the colors in the image. YCC is a variation on the CIE color space, the international standard for defining all the colors that the human eye can see (see Chapter 10, "Working with Color Images," for more information on color models). Both YCC and CIE can contain many more colors than RGB or CMYK, the color models used by computer monitors and printing devices, respectively.

Marketed as an alternative to high-end drum scans, PhotoCD images can be of very high quality, and it's inexpensive to have a roll of film scanned to a PhotoCD. The quality of the scans, however, depends on the type of film used (slide film can cause problems) and the skill of the scanner operator.

When you open a PhotoCD image, you're presented with several options (see Figure 4.6).

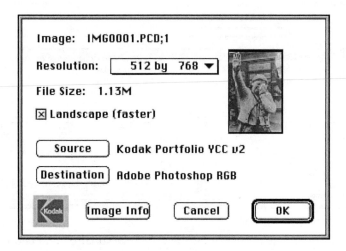

Figure 4.6

The PhotoCD dialog box enables you to choose an image resolution and source and destination device profiles for color management.

1. In the PhotoCD dialog box, choose a resolution.

    A PhotoCD file contains several versions of an image at different resolutions. Choose the resolution, in pixel dimensions, that you prefer. If you need a small thumbnail image at 300 dpi, for example, you might use the 512×768 pixel image size. It is 1.7 inches by 2.56 inches at 300 dpi.

2. If the image is in portrait format (it's taller than it is wide), you can open it in landscape mode instead by clicking the Landscape box.

It's faster to open a portrait image in landscape mode; if you need to rotate it after opening it, you can use the Rotate Canvas command in the Image menu.

3. Choose a Source profile. Click Source and choose a device from the pop-up menu (see Figure 4.7). Then choose a profile from the list below (there may be only one choice). This capability enables the KCMS color management software that comes with Photoshop to correct the image based on characteristics of the type of film from which the images were scanned.

Figure 4.7

Choosing a source profile allows Kodak's color management software to work its magic on a PhotoCD image.

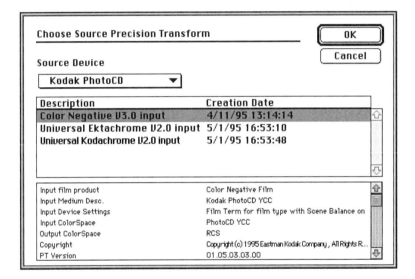

4. Choose a Destination profile. Click Destination and choose a device from the pop-up menu, and then choose a profile from the list (see Figure 4.8). Again, there may be only one choice. This allows KCMS to correct the image based on the characteristics of the device on which it is output (usually a color printer, a color monitor, or a printing press). If you don't have any device profiles installed, your only choices are Lab color or RGB.

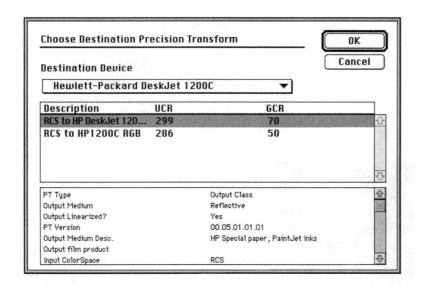

Figure 4.8

Destination profiles enable KCMS to adjust an image to output correctly on a particular printer or other device.

5. If you want to view information about the image, click Image Info.

   Information about the image can be added when it's scanned and saved in PhotoCD format, but doing this isn't required. If the information is available, it can include the following:

   ◆ Medium of the original image

   ◆ Product type of the original image

   ◆ Scanner vendor

   ◆ Scanner product

6. After all the options have been set, click OK to open the image.

7. Adjust the image to improve its color. Several standard adjustments can improve the quality of PhotoCD images. These changes can be made on an adjustment layer to preserve the original image, but before the file can be saved in a format that can be read by other programs, the layers need to be merged.

   Choose Image➡Adjust➡Levels (or press (Command-L)[Control-L]) (see Figure 4.9).

Select the white eyedropper and click on the lightest point you can find in the image. You can compare the lightest point to white by looking at the foreground/background paint swatches in the toolbox as you drag the eyedropper around the image. Select the black eyedropper and do the same, but this time look for the darkest part of the image. Click the OK button.

Figure 4.9

The Levels dialog box.

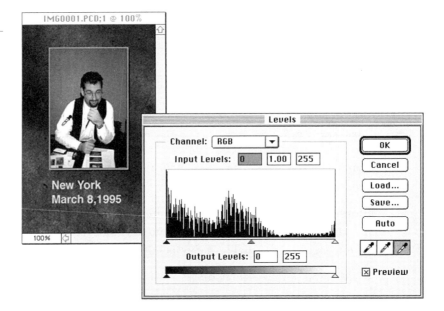

8. Save the image as a Photoshop file if you want to preserve layers. Otherwise, flatten the image and save it in another format.

   Flattening the image merges all the layers—irretrievably; choose Flatten Image from the Layers palette menu to flatten layers.

Note

Although Photoshop can open PhotoCD images and save them in other formats, it can't save files in PhotoCD format; Kodak hasn't licensed that technology.

Opening PCX Files

PCX is the native format used by the Windows paint program PC Paintbrush. Because of the widespread distribution of PC Paintbrush, there are many PCX images out there in the PC world, particularly clip art. PCX files can be bitmap (black-and-white), grayscale, or color (RGB, CMYK, or indexed). There are no options when opening a PCX file.

Opening PDF files

Although Photoshop 4.0 now can open and save PDF (Portable Document Format) files, the format used by Adobe Acrobat, don't be deceived; you can't open just any Acrobat file in Photoshop. Only PDF image files, which don't contain any text, can be opened by Photoshop, although you can create PDF files from your images that can be opened in Acrobat. There are no options when opening a PDF file.

Opening PICT Files and PICT Resources

PICT is primarily used on Macs, although Windows systems with QuickTime installed also can use it. This format isn't appropriate for printing (PICT files can cause nasty PostScript errors on PostScript printers), but it's often used for multimedia projects. It's also the format that Mac applications use for images displayed within the program, such as splash screens, and it's the format used by the Mac's Scrapbook. PICT files can contain both vector and raster information.

Photoshop can open both PICT files and PICT resources—the latter is the way PICT images are stored for applications to use them. To open a PICT file, select it in the Open dialog box and click Open.

The same procedure works for opening PICT resources, with a caveat. If the resource is stored in a file of its own, you can open it just like a PICT file. But most PICT resources are stored within applications. To open these, you have to specify the format.

1. In the Open dialog box, choose the application whose PICT resource you want to open.

2. Click Show All Files and then choose the PICT resource format.

3. Click Open to open the resource.

Note

There's a drawback to using this method to open PICT resources—you can only open the first resource Photoshop encounters. For a better way, see "Importing PICT Resources" later in this chapter.

Opening Pixar Files

High-end computer animation is done on Pixar workstations, which use a proprietary format called, amazingly enough, Pixar. Photoshop can open and edit RGB and grayscale Pixar images. There are no options when opening a Pixar file.

Opening PNG Files

Because of legal wrangling over rights to the compression method used in the GIF format, programmers created the PNG format as an alternative. Like GIF, PNG files use lossless compression to reduce file size, and they're likely to start popping up all over the Web in the near future as more software supports the format.

PNG images can be grayscale (bit depths up to 16) or color (up to 48 bits), or they can be up to 8-bit indexed color, for the smallest color files. A new, extremely fast interlacing scheme for PNG allows images to be displayed progressively, with a low-res preview showing as soon as 1/64th of the image's data is downloaded. Unlike GIF, PNG doesn't support animation.

There are no options when opening PNG images.

Opening Scitex CT Files

Photoshop can open and edit files created on the high-end prepress workstations made by Scitex, which are used for image editing and color separation. Scitex CT images always open in CMYK mode, and you want to keep them in that mode if they're destined to return to a Scitex system. There are no options when opening a Scitex CT file.

Opening Targa (TGA) Files

The correct name for this format is actually TGA; Targa is the name of the graphics display card that first used the format. It's a video format supported by high-end PC color applications, and it allows for chroma keying—overlaying computer animations onto video. In this format, alpha channels are used to indicate the area where the live video displays. Photoshop can be used to edit the images themselves or the alpha channels. TGA files can have bit depths up to 24 bits plus an 8-bit alpha channel; they can be indexed color, RGB, or grayscale. Although the TGA format supports several types of compression, Photoshop does not support compression in TGA files.

Opening TIFF Files

The most common format for scanned images in prepress, TIFF actually comes in several varieties, though it's unlikely that you'll ever encounter most of them. The most common everyday application for TIFF files other than prepress is faxing; the CCITT TIFF versions (Group 3 and Group 4) are the formats used in rasterizing fax images. Any professional-level paint program or image editor can write a TIFF file, and even drawing programs such as Illustrator now have the capability to rasterize their images and save them as TIFF files.

Like EPS files, TIFF files can contain clipping paths that page layout applications use to silhouette images. If you open a TIFF with a clipping path, the path appears in Photoshop's Paths palette and can be edited in Photoshop, along with the actual TIFF image.

TIFF files can use a lossless compression format called LZW. If you open a TIFF file that's been saved with LZW compression, the compression option remains on when you save the file, unless you specifically turn it off. There are no options when opening a TIFF image.

Tip

If you have a fax modem, you may be able to export faxes in a standard TIFF format that Photoshop can open. Look for an Export command under the File menu in your fax software. Two Mac fax packages that can do this are Faxcilitate and FaxSTF. Using this feature, you can edit faxes before printing them or refaxing them, or you can use OCR software to avoid retyping the text.

IMPORTING FILES

Plug-ins aren't just for filters. Photoshop also supports plug-ins that enable you to read and write different image formats, such as the Export GIF89a plug-in, which supports more of the GIF format's features than Photoshop's built-in CompuServe GIF format. Several import plug-ins come with Photoshop, and more are available from third-party vendors (see Chapter 20, "Third-Party Plug-Ins").

Importing Anti-Aliased PICTs

Although Photoshop can open raster PICT files directly, it can import vector PICT images (such as those created by MacDraw and Canvas) with anti-aliasing via the native Anti-aliased PICT plug-in. This involves a similar process to that used in opening and rasterizing vector EPS files. Incidentally, only Mac users of Photoshop can import anti-aliased vector PICTs; the plug-in isn't available for the PC.

1. Choose File➡Import➡Anti-aliased PICT.

2. The truncated dialog box that appears looks like the Open dialog, but it doesn't enable you to view a thumbnail or specify a format (see Figure 4.10). Choose the file you want to import and click Open.

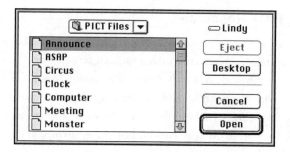

Figure 4.10

Import plug-ins have truncated dialog boxes that don't allow you to specify a format.

3. In the resulting Anti-Aliased PICT dialog box, enter the desired width and height of the image in pixels (see Figure 4.11).

   Because the image is a vector image, it can be scaled to any size with no loss of quality. Checking the Constrain Proportions box keeps the proportions of the image the same as they are in the original file; if you enter a width or height measurement, Photoshop automatically enters the correct measurement for the other dimension.

Figure 4.11

Just as with vector EPS images, you must specify a size for imported vector PICTs.

4. Choose a color mode for the image: grayscale or RGB color.

   The original image's mode does not matter; you can open the image in either mode. Open grayscale images in RGB mode if you plan to add color. Open RGB images in grayscale to eliminate color.

5. Click Open to open the file.

Importing PICT Resources

Although PICT resources in applications (images that users see as they're using the programs, such as splash screens) can be opened via the Open command, you only have access to the first PICT resource in each file with that method. A better way is to use the native PICT Resource plug-in, which enables you to view and import any PICT resource located in an application. For these purposes, the Scrapbook is considered an application.

1. Choose File➡Import➡PICT Resource.

2. In the Pict Resource dialog box (see Figure 4.12), select the resource you want to open.

    Using the left and right buttons, you can page through the different PICT resources in a file. A preview of each image is shown in the box in the lower righthand corner of the dialog box, and text to the left tells you how many PICT resources there are in the file.

Figure 4.12

You can extract PICT resources from Mac applications and from the Mac Scrapbook.

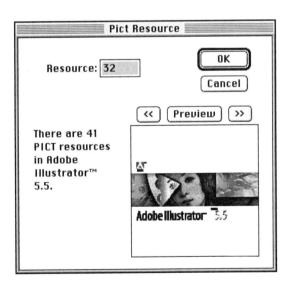

3. Click OK to open the resource you've chosen.

Note

PICT resources are always 72 dpi—that's enforced by the Mac system software.

Importing Images with ColorSync Profiles

Today's color management technology depends on the use of *device profiles*, data files that describe the quirks of different scanners, monitors, color printers, and printing presses in reproducing color. These profiles are at the heart of Apple's ColorSync color management system, which includes an acquire plug-in for applying ColorSync profiles to TIFF images as you open them.

The ColorSync plug-ins don't come with Photoshop, but they can be downloaded from Apple's Web site, and they're free. To use them, you also have to have the ColorSync system software installed. This also is available free from Apple's Web site (http://www.apple.com/). Device profiles are provided by the device manufacturers (for example, a dual-mode Seiko color printer might come with a profile for its dye-sublimation prints and one for its thermal wax prints). For the most accurate profiles, you need special software to create profiles customized to your own equipment.

To use the ColorSync acquire plug-in, after the software and plug-in are installed, follow these steps:

1. Choose Acquire TIFF with ColorSync Profile from the Import submenu of the File menu.

2. Select the file you want to acquire (it must be an uncompressed TIFF) and click Open.

3. In the ColorSync Import Module dialog box (see Figure 4.13), choose a quality level: Profile Default, Best, Normal, or Draft. The higher the quality level, the closer the onscreen results are to what you actually get when you print, but the longer the matching process takes before the file opens.

Figure 4.13

Apple's ColorSync plug-in lets you adjust colors when you open a TIFF file.

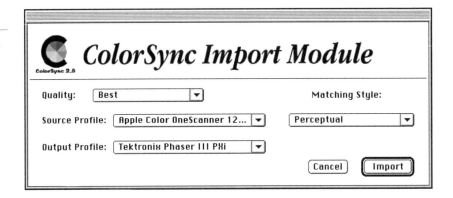

4. Choose a Source Profile. This should indicate where the image came from (usually, a scanner). If the image has already been color-corrected onscreen, then the source should be the monitor model used for the color adjustments.

5. Choose a Destination Profile. This should indicate where the image is output—it could be a color printer, a printing press, a color proofing system such as MatchPrint, or even a monitor, if the image is destined to be displayed only onscreen.

6. Choose a Matching Style. Your choices here are Profile Default, Perceptual, Absolute Colorimetric, Relative Colorimetric, and Saturation.

   Perceptual matching is intended to produce the best-looking results that the given devices can provide; it works best for photos. Colorimetric matching reproduces colors exactly as they are defined and clips (doesn't display) colors that can't be reproduced on a particular device. Relative colorimetric matching accounts for the change in perceived color when a color is seen next to a white area, and absolute colorimetric matching doesn't. This style usually is used for logos and other applications where colors must be exact. Saturation matching preserves the vividness of the image, without necessarily matching exact hues; it's suitable for display graphics where exact color isn't vital, such as charts and graphics.

7. After your settings are made, click the Import button to open the image.

Using the Quick Edit Plug-in

If you only need to edit part of an image, the native Quick Edit plug-in lets you open just that part, make your changes, and save the part back into the file. This is useful if you're low on RAM or if you're looking to save time. (The amount of time consumed opening, saving, and editing operations depends on the size of the file, so the smaller the file, the faster.)

Quick Edit only works with Photoshop 2.0, Scitex CT, or uncompressed TIFF files (watch out for that LZW compression!). To use Quick Edit, follow these steps:

1. Choose Quick Edit from the Import submenu of the File menu.

2. Select the file you want to edit and click Open.

3. In the Quick Edit dialog box (see Figure 4.14), select the portion of the image that you want to open by clicking and dragging the mouse.

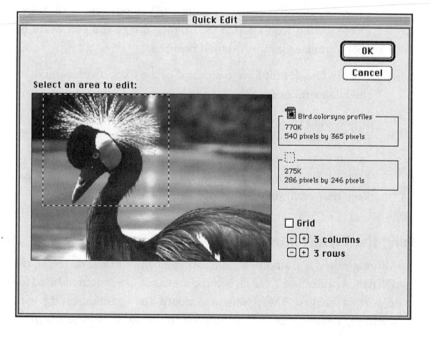

Figure 4.14

When OK is clicked, only the part of the image containing the bird's head opens.

To make precise selections, you can use these shortcuts.

- ◆ Use the arrow keys to move the selection marquee one pixel at a time.

- ◆ Press the = key to increase the selection marquee by one pixel. Press the – key to decrease the marquee's size by one pixel.

   As the size of the marquee changes, the file size and pixel dimensions of the selection are shown at the righthand side of the dialog box, below the file size and pixel dimensions of the whole image.

   Clicking the Grid box divides the image preview into a grid; you can specify how many columns and rows the grid has. Then just pick one of the grid's sections to open.

4. After you've selected the portion of the image you want, click OK to open the image.

5. Edit the file, but remember not to change its color mode, canvas size, or image size. If these attributes are changed, the image section won't match the original image and you won't be able to replace it in its original position.

6. Use the Quick Edit Save command in the Export submenu of the File menu to save the section back to the original file.

   If you want to save the area you're working on as a separate file, choose Save As or Save a Copy from the File menu and assign a new name and format. Photoshop automatically adds "[Quick Edit]" to the previous filename, but you don't need to keep that addition.

Using the TWAIN Interface

Although they're found in the Import submenu of the File menu, the TWAIN Acquire and TWAIN Select commands aren't actually used for importing images. TWAIN is a standard for communicating with scanners. These commands enable you to choose scanner software to be used from within Photoshop and then to activate it and acquire scanned images. See Chapter 3, "Scanning," for more information on scanning in Photoshop.

USING THE RAW FORMAT FOR MYSTERY FILES

Although most graphics files publishing professionals encounter are saved in a standard format, systems in other fields produce images that don't conform to standard file formats. Medical imaging systems and radar systems, for example, produce raster images in undocumented formats. To open images like these, the Raw format can be used to tell Photoshop how to interpret the data in the files.

1. In the Open dialog box, click the Show All Files box.

2. Select the image you want to open and select Raw from the file format pop-up menu, then click Open.

3. In the Raw Options dialog box (see Figure 4.15), Photoshop has filled in the information it can guess about the image. It's up to you to fill in the rest, to the best of your ability. If you don't know any of this information, just leave that field blank.

    Start by specifying the dimensions of the file in pixels if you know them—otherwise, click the Guess button. If the wrong dimensions are entered, the image opens, but it is (at best) distorted and (at worst) completely unrecognizable. In this case, try again with different dimensions.

    Clicking the Swap button switches the horizontal and vertical dimensions in the entry fields; clicking the Guess button makes Photoshop guess again and fill in what it thinks are the dimensions of the image.

Figure 4.15

The Raw format lets you specify file format options so that you can open image formats Photoshop doesn't otherwise support.

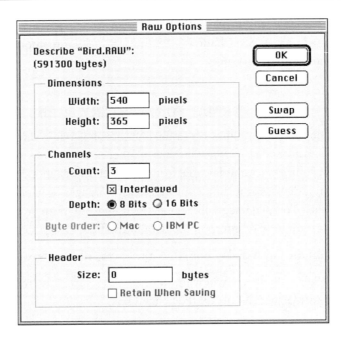

4. Enter the number of channels in the image if you know how many it has.

   RGB images use three channels; CMYK images use four channels. Specialized images may use more channels.

5. Check Interleaved if the image is interleaved. Interleaving saves the rows of pixels in the image out of order. If the image opens without any problems but looks completely incomprehensible, this may be the reason. Try it again setting Interleaved opposite of what you set it the first time.

6. Enter the image's bit depth if you know it—otherwise, skip it.

7. Enter the image's byte order if you know it—otherwise, skip it.

   This usually is easy to determine. Images from a Mac use Mac byte order, images from a PC use IBM PC byte order. Images from another computer system, however, are harder to determine, but it's likely that they use PC byte order.

8. Enter the size of the file's header if you know it. Not all files contain headers. In the files that do, the header contains information about the file's format. Because you know Photoshop can't read this format directly, you want Photoshop to ignore the header, so you need to tell it how many bytes of information to pass over before looking for image data in the file. Don't worry, Photoshop can take a good guess at this information. Click the Size field and then click the Guess button.

9. Decide whether you want to get rid of the header information when you save the resulting Photoshop file. If so, leave the Retain When Saving button unchecked. To keep the header information, check the box.

10. After all your settings are made, click Open to open the file.

The problem with the Raw format is that, although it offers you great power to open strange and mysterious files, it's not as smart as it thinks it is. Its guesses about image dimensions and header size aren't always correct, and without this information the file opens, but it won't be recognizable. If you need to open a file using this format, try to get as much information as possible about the file from its creator.

For information on saving files in the Raw format, see Chapter 16, "Saving and Exporting."

Chapter

5

SELECTIONS, PATHS, AND MASKS

One of the advantages of using Photoshop rather than traditional photographic or artistic techniques is that it's so easy to define different areas of your image and work on those areas alone, without affecting the work you've done in other areas. Selections, paths, and masks are all ways of doing just that.

◆ Selections are a way of temporarily choosing an area of the image that will be affected by subsequent actions, such as filters or color corrections. They're indicated by an animated dotted line (referred to as "marching ants"), and the area inside the line is the selected area. Clicking elsewhere in the image deactivates a selection.

◆ Paths work just like paths in FreeHand, Illustrator, and other drawing programs. They can be filled and stroked, and they can also be used to define a selection area. Complex selections are created by drawing a path with the Pen tool and then converting it to a selection.

◆ Masks are similar to selections in that they define an area to which changes can be made, but they can be used again and again, until they're purposely deleted. Photoshop offers several ways of implementing masks, including channels and layer masks.

SELECTIONS

Selections are essentially ephemeral. You use a selection tool to make a selection, you do something with the selection (copy it, paint within it, apply a filter to it), and then if you don't save the selection, you click somewhere else in the image and it's gone, although the pixels within it are still there.

Paths and mask channels provide two different ways of saving selections so that you can use them again, each with advantages and disadvantages. You can convert a selection into a path or save it in a channel as a mask. See "Paths" and "Masks," later, for more information on using these methods.

Selection Basics

Three basic commands at the top of the Select menu provide the easiest ways to make, alter, and drop selections. They are as follows:

◆ **All.** Choosing this command (or pressing (Command)[Control]-A) selects the entire image.

♦ **None.** This command deselects whatever is selected. The keyboard shortcut for this command is (Command)[Control]-D, short for "drop."

♦ **Inverse.** This command (Shift-(Command)[Control]-I) selects the portions of the image that weren't selected before and deselects whatever *was* selected before. Sometimes it's easier to select an area in an image by selecting everything else and then inverting the selection—for example, if you want to select the area around the Earth in a photo of our planet in space, you might make a circular selection around the planet and then invert it to select the starry background.

Note

Inverse often is confused with the Invert command in the Adjust submenu of the Image menu ((Command-I)[Control-I]). Invert changes the image (or the active layer or channel) to a black-and-white or color negative of itself. If you accidentally use Invert when you meant to use Inverse (or vice versa), just Undo ((Command-Z)[Control-Z]) right away to restore your image to its previous state.

Hiding Selection Borders

As you make and edit selections, you can temporarily hide the selection border to view your image without those distracting "marching ants." Choose Hide Edges under the View menu or press (Command-H)[Control-H]. Remember that the selection is still active until you drop it by clicking outside it or until you press (Command-D)[Control-D]. To show the selection's edges again, press (Command-H)[Control-H] again (or choose Show Edges from the View menu).

Saving a Selection

The Select menu's Save Selection command saves selections (not the selections' contents, but the actual selection outlines) in channels or as new documents. To save a selection, follow these steps:

1. Make a selection.

2. Choose Save Selection from the Select menu to bring up the Save Selection dialog box (see Figure 5.1).

Figure 5.1

The Save Selection dialog box lets you save a selection as a new document, as a new channel, or as part of an existing channel box.

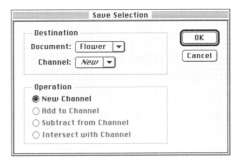

3. Choose a destination document and channel for the selection: a channel in the current document, a channel in any other open document, or a new document.

    Channels are grayscale representations of selections: black areas in a channel represent unselected areas, white areas represent selected areas, and gray areas represent partially selected areas (feathering) (see Figure 5.2). If you save a selection to a new document, it will be saved in the same way as it would be to a channel—a black, white, and gray outline of the selection area.

Figure 5.2

The feathered selection shown in the left window produces the channel shown in the right window.

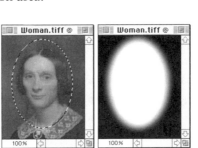

4. Choose an operation: New Channel, Replace Channel, Add to Channel, Subtract from Channel, or Intersect with Channel.

   New Channel creates a new channel using the selection outline. If you don't have any alpha channels (channels other than the RGB or CMYK color channels) in your document, this will be the only option available.

   If you do have other channels in your document, then you can choose one from the Channel pop-up menu and then apply the selection as a modification to that channel rather than as a new channel. If another channel is selected in the Channel pop-up menu, **Replace Channel** is the first choice in the Operations section of the dialog box, rather than New Channel. This command replaces the contents of the channel you choose with a channel made from the new selection. **Add to Channel** adds the currently selected areas of the image to the existing channel, while **Subtract from Channel** deletes the currently selected areas of the image from the existing channel. **Intersect with Channel** changes the existing channel to reflect only the areas that it and the new selection have in common—their intersection. See Figure 5.3 for an illustration of these options. The Add channel contains the area in both selections; the Subtract channel contains only the area in the flower channel that wasn't included in the rectangle; and the Intersect channel contains only the area that was included in both selections.

   Be careful with the Add to Channel, Subtract from Channel, and Intersect with Channel commands—they permanently replace the contents of the original channel with the results of your addition, subtraction, or intersection. To preserve a copy of the original channel, duplicate it before executing one of these commands.

5. Click OK to save the selection.

Figure 5.3

Combining a rectangular selection in the flower image with an existing channel of the flower's outline results in these three new channels.

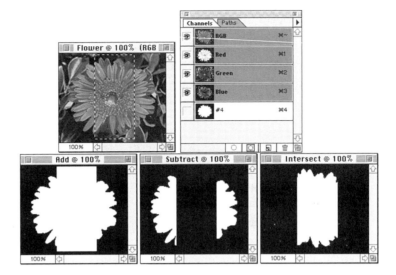

Tip

You can quickly save a selection to a new channel by clicking on the Save Selection as Channel button at the bottom of the Channels palette (see Figure 5.4). Doing this will use the settings from the last time you used the Save Selection command.

Figure 5.4

The Channels palette.

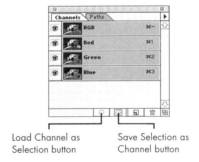

Load Channel as
Selection button

Save Selection as
Channel button

Loading a Selection

After you save a selection by creating a channel from it, you can reload the selection with the Load Selection command. To do so, follow these steps:

1. Choose the Load Selection command from the Select menu to bring up the Load Selection dialog box (see Figure 5.5).

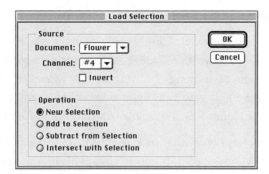

Figure 5.5

The Load Selection dialog box.

2. Choose a source document and channel. You can load selections from channels in any currently open document.

3. Check the Invert box if you want to load an inverted version of the selection. In other words, the new selection will include only the area that *wasn't* included in the selection you're loading.

4. Choose an operation: New Selection, Add to Selection, Subtract from Selection, or Intersect with Selection.

   Choosing **New Selection** makes a new selection. **Add to Selection** adds the area in the saved selection to an active selection, whereas **Subtract to Selection** removes the area in the saved selection from an active selection. **Intersect with Selection** leaves you with only the area selected that was common to both the current selection and the saved selection.

5. Click OK to load the selection.

Tip

You can save time by loading selections in other ways. First, click the name of the channel in the Channels palette and then click the Load Channel as Selection button at the bottom of the Channels palette. Second, and even faster, (Command-click)[Control-click] on the name of the channel in the Channels palette. Both of these methods will use the last settings you made in the Load Selection dialog box. You also can try dragging the channel name onto the Load Channel as Selection button. Finally, you can bring up the Load Selection dialog box by holding down the (Option)[Alt] key as you drag the channel onto the Load Channel as Selection button.

Making Marquee Selections

Photoshop provides several sets of tools for making selections. The first and most obvious is the Marquee selection tool, which is actually a group of tools containing the Rectangular Marquee, the Elliptical Marquee, the single row and single column Marquees, and the Cropping tool (see Figure 5.6). To use the Marquee tools, follow these steps:

1. If you're using another tool, press M to change the current tool to the Marquee tool. If you're already using the Marquee tool, press M to switch back and forth between the Rectangular and Elliptical Marquee tools. You also can switch Marquee tools in two other ways:

   ◆ Click the Marquee in the toolbox, holding down the mouse button, and slide the cursor over the tool you want before letting go.

   ◆ Double-click the Marquee tool in the toolbox to bring up the Marquee options panel of the Options palette (see Figure 5.7). Choose the tool you want from the Shape pop-up menu.

Figure 5.6

The Marquee tools.

Figure 5.7

The Marquee Options panel.

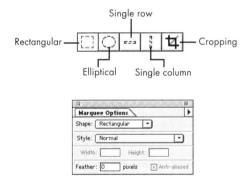

Note

You cannot select the Cropping tool from the pop-up menu in the Marquee Options panel. The only way you can reach this tool (which used to have its own position in the toolbox) is by clicking on the Marquee in the toolbox and choosing it from the tools that appear.

2. Choose a style from the pop-up menu (these styles are only available with the Rectangular and Elliptical Marquees). Your choices are Normal, Constrained Aspect Ratio, and Fixed Size.

- **Normal** lets you make any size and shape.

- **Constrained Aspect Ratio** lets you determine the proportions of your selections. Enter 1 in the Width field and 2.5 in the Height field, for example, to ensure that all your selections with the Marquee tool will be two and a half times as tall as they are wide.

- **Fixed Size** restricts you to making selections a certain number of pixels wide and high. Enter the pixel dimensions you want to use in the Width and Height fields. This is useful when you're making several selections that must all be the same size, such as copying people's heads from a group photo to use as head shots.

3. Choose a feathering value if you want your selections to be feathered as you make them.

Enter a number in pixels to "fade" the edges of your selections. The feathering will be visible if you apply a filter or adjustment to the selection—the effect will gradually fade out at the edges by the number of pixels you enter. If you copy and paste a feathered selection, the pasted image will have a soft edge defined by the feathering value. Feathering is particularly useful when you're creating a composite image by cutting and pasting because it smooths the transition between the pasted selection and the existing image, making for a more natural appearance.

When determining how much to feather a selection, keep in mind that feathering extends in both directions from the selection boundary. If, for example, you make a selection around a beach ball and set a feather of 10 pixels, the soft edge will extend five pixels out from the edge of the ball and five pixels in from the edge of the ball.

You can feather a selection after it's made by choosing Feather from the Select menu and entering a value in the Feather dialog box.

What is anti-aliasing?

Anti-aliasing smooths the edges of selections by reducing the opacity of pixels at the selection's edge (see Figure 5.8). This feature is helpful when you're copying and pasting selections, such as when you're creating a photomontage. The selection tools that can use anti-aliasing are the Lasso, the Polygon Lasso, the Elliptical Marquee, and the Magic Wand. Anti-aliasing also can be used when you're creating type and when you're rasterizing vector EPS elements, such as Illustrator images.

4. If you're using the Elliptical Marquee, you can anti-alias your selections to give them a smooth edge. Click the Anti-aliased box to turn off or on anti-aliasing. You can't anti-alias a selection after it's made, so make sure anti-aliasing is turned on before you make a selection if you want to use it. Of the Marquee tools, only the Elliptical Marquee enables you to use anti-aliasing.

5. After your options are set, click-and-drag in the image to make a selection.

The Rectangular Marquee will select a rectangular area of the image. The Elliptical Marquee will select an elliptical (oval) area of the image. Hold down the shift key as you drag to constrain the selection to a square or circle, with equal height and width. Ordinarily, the upper left-hand corner of the selection will be the point at which you started dragging. If you hold down the (Option)[Alt] key as you drag, that point will be the center of the selection.

Figure 5.8

Each of these circles was made by filling a circular selection with white, but anti-aliasing was used only on the right-hand circle. It has gray pixels around its edges that create the illusion of a smoother edge.

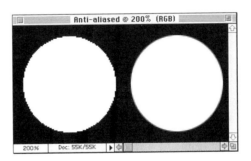

These modifier keys have the same effect on the Cropping tool. Hold down shift to constrain the selection to a square, and hold down (Option)[Alt] to make the point at which you started dragging the center of the selection. See "Cropping Documents" later for more on the Cropping tool.

The single row and single column Marquee tools, as their names imply, only select one column or one row of pixels at a time. The shift and (Option)[Alt] keys have no effect on selections made with these tools, and you don't actually have to drag to make the selection; you can drag it to its correct position after you've clicked to make it.

Making Selections with the Lasso Tool

Freehand selections in any shape, using curves and straight segments, can be made with the Lasso tool and its sibling, the Polygon Lasso tool (see Figure 5.9). To choose the Lasso tool, press L or click the Lasso in the toolbox. To choose the Polygon Lasso, click the Lasso, hold down the mouse button and move the cursor over the Polygon Lasso, then release the mouse button.

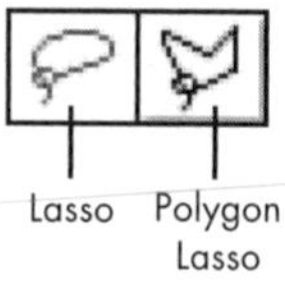

Lasso   Polygon
Lasso

Figure 5.9

The Lasso and Polygon Lasso tools.

Like the focus tools (Blur and Sharpen) and the toning tools (Dodge and Burn), you can switch between these tools by holding down the (Option)[Alt] key as you use either. In other words, if you're using the Lasso tool, you can make it act like the Polygon Lasso by holding down the (Option)[Alt] key and vice versa.

To set options for the Lasso tools, follow these steps:

1. Double-click the Lasso or Polygon Lasso tool in the toolbox to open its panel in the Options palette (see Figure 5.10). Both Lasso tools have the same options.

2. Set a feathering value in pixels if you want your selections to be feathered, giving them a soft edge. This will only apply to selections you make after setting the value.

3. Check the Anti-aliased box to make future selections anti-aliased, giving them a clean edge and avoiding the jaggies. By default, anti-aliasing is turned on.

Figure 5.10

The Lasso Options panel.

4. Make a selection. If you're using the regular Lasso, click and drag to make a selection. When you release the mouse button, the beginning and end of the line you've drawn will be connected to complete the selection. To make straight lines while using the Lasso, drag and hold the (Option)[Alt] key, release the mouse button at the point where you want the straight segment to begin, and click where you want the straight segment to end.

If you're using the Polygon Lasso, click to begin a selection, and then click at every point where you want a corner. To make freehand segments, hold the (Option)[Alt] key and drag. Release the mouse button and the (Option)[Alt] key to go back to making straight line segments. When you're done creating the selection outline, double-click or (Command-click)[Control-click] to have Photoshop connect the start and end points, or move your mouse over the starting point until the cursor has a circle next to it (see Figure 5.11) and click.

Figure 5.11

The small circle next to the Polygon Lasso cursor indicates that clicking will close (complete) the selection.

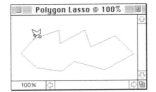

Tip

Sometimes you change your mind halfway through making a Polygon Lasso selection, but you can't select another tool while using the Polygon Lasso. If you have a Polygon Lasso selection gone wild, you can escape from it by pressing the Escape key. If the last thing you did before starting the Lasso

*selection was make another selection, with any selection tool, then that
selection will be restored. If your previous action was anything other than
making a selection, pressing Escape simply gets rid of the haywire selection
and lets you start fresh.*

Making Selections with the Magic Wand

Photoshop's Magic Wand tool really does seem magical the first time
you use it. It selects an area of the image by analyzing the color of the
pixel it's clicked on and selecting that pixel along with all the adjacent
pixels that are a similar color. To use the Magic Wand, first make sure
your image is not in bitmap mode, since it works only with color or
grayscale images.

1. Double-click the Magic Wand, shown below, in the toolbox to
   bring up the Magic Wand panel of the Options palette (see
   Figure 5.12).

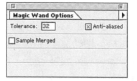

Figure 5.12

*The Magic Wand Options
panel.*

2. Enter a Tolerance setting from 0 to 255. This determines how
   picky the Magic Wand is about what colors to include in its
   selection. With a tolerance setting of 0, only pixels that are the
   exact color of the original pixel will be selected. With higher
   tolerance settings, pixels of slightly different colors will be
   included (see Figure 5.13).

3. Turn on or off Anti-aliased. If the box is checked, selections
   made with the Magic Wand will be anti-aliased, giving them
   the appearance of a smoother edge.

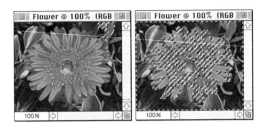

Figure 5.13

The Magic Wand selection on the left was made with a tolerance setting of 10; the selection on the right was made with a tolerance setting of 255.

4. Turn on or off Sample Merged. If the box is checked, the Magic Wand will base its selection on the colors in all the visible layers; if it's not, then only colors in the current layer will be used to determine the selection area. When you're using Sample Merged, keep in mind that you're not actually selecting pixels on more than one layer; your selection will only include the pixels on the current layer. To use the selection on another layer, choose the layer from the Layers palette—the selected area will stay selected.

5. Click a color in the image to select all adjacent pixels with that color.

Tip

Because selections stay active when you move from working on one layer or channel to another, you can make a selection in a color channel and then use it on the entire image (or on selected channels or layers). If you want to outline an apple in an image, for example, you may find it easier to select the apple with the Magic Wand if you make the selection on the Red or Magenta channel, then move back to the composite channel to work.

Making Selections with Quick Mask

Wouldn't it be great if you could just paint a selection using the same tools you use to paint or draw your image? Guess what? You can. This feature is called Quick Mask, and you can access it by pressing Q or clicking the Quick Mask button on the toolbox (see Figure 5.14). Probably the biggest advantage of using the Quick Mask mode, besides its ease of use, is that you can make soft edges by using soft brushes.

Standard selection mode 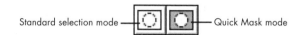 Quick Mask mode

Figure 5.14

The Quick Mask button is on the right; when you're in Quick Mask mode, clicking the button on the left returns you to the Standard selection mode.

If you want to start with a regular selection and modify it using Quick Mask, make the selection and then press Q or click the Quick Mask button. If you want to create the entire selection using Quick Mask, enter Quick Mask mode without making a selection first.

When you enable Quick Mask, a transparent red mask appears over your image. Old-fashioned print production types will notice that it looks like a piece of rubylith, which is reasonable because it works pretty much the same way. If you started with a selection, the area inside that selection will be clear and the area outside the selection will be red (see Figure 5.15).

Figure 5.15

The upper left-hand window shows the image before entering Quick Mask mode. The right-hand window shows the truck masked using Quick Mask. When Q is pressed to return the image to Standard selection mode, the background surrounding the truck will be selected.

Note

Rubylith is a colored film that is cut manually with an X-Acto knife to make masks that are used when shooting film for printing plates.

Paint on the mask with white paint (or use the eraser) to remove areas of the mask; apply black paint to add to the mask. Press X to switch the foreground and background colors and quickly go from white to black paint and back again. You also can paint with shades of gray to produce partially selected areas.

You also can use the regular selection tools, such as the Marquee tool, to edit a Quick Mask. Just make a selection and fill it or press Delete to remove the red mask color from that area. You also can apply transformations (rotate, scale, skew, and so on) to Quick Masks. Use a regular selection tool to select all or part of the mask, then choose a transformation from the Transform submenu of the Layer menu.

Press Q or click the Standard selection button on the toolbox to leave Quick Mask mode. The clear area in the mask will be selected when you return to Standard selection mode.

You can change the color and opacity of the Quick Mask from the default 50% red. To do so, follow these steps:

1. Double-click the Quick Mask button to bring up the Quick Mask Options dialog box (see Figure 5.16).

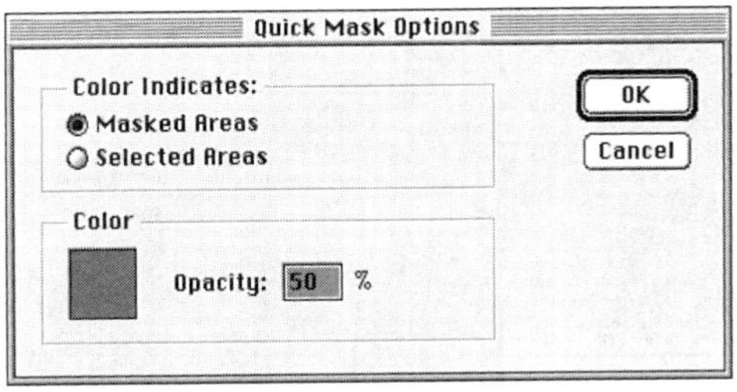

Figure 5.16

The *Quick Mask Options dialog box lets you choose a different color for the Quick Mask.*

2. Enter an opacity percentage between 1 and 100.

3. Click the red square and use the Color Picker to choose another color for the Quick Mask.

4. You also can determine whether the Quick Mask color indicates the masked area or the selected area. The default is Masked Areas, but you might prefer to have the color indicate the area that will be selected when you return to Standard selection mode.

Using the Color Range Command

The Color Range command enables you to select similarly colored pixels, with much more control than the Magic Wand offers; it's kind of like the Magic Wand on steroids. Color Range will select similarly colored pixels from all over the image rather than just those adjacent to where you click. It also has a menu of built-in selection criteria so that you can quickly select only the image's reds, yellows, blues, cyans, greens, or magentas, as well as its highlights, midtones, or shadows.

To make a selection using the Color Range command:

1. Choose Color Range from the Select menu to bring up the Color Range dialog box (see Figure 5.17).

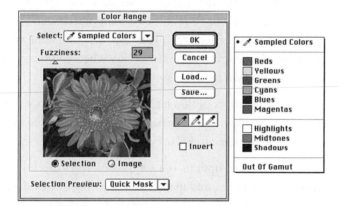

Figure 5.17

The Color Range dialog box.

2. Set the options for the dialog box's preview.

   Click a radio button to choose whether you want the dialog box's preview window to display the image itself (Image) or a view of the selection as a mask (Selection). As you work, you can toggle the dialog box preview between showing a preview of the mask and showing the image itself by pressing the (Command)[Control] key. In the dialog box's preview window, selected parts of the image will be black and unselected portions will be white.

147

You also can choose to preview the effects of your selection settings in the image in several different ways:

◆ A Quick Mask

◆ A grayscale image (this will look like black-and-white film)

◆ A black or white matte

The effect is temporary; it's only visible while you're in the Color Range dialog box. The black matte preview is particularly useful if you zoom in on your image before choosing the Color Mask command so that you can spot stray pixels in the mask.

3. In the Color Range dialog box, decide how you want Photoshop to make the selection. No matter which option you use, the selection will be visible as a temporary mask that's converted to a selection when you click OK, the same way a Quick Mask is converted to a selection when you return to Standard selection mode.

The Sampled Colors option lets you use an Eyedropper tool to select a color and use a Fuzziness slider to expand the range and enlarge the selection. This is the default setting.

The next group of options is a set of colors: reds, yellows, greens, cyans, blues, and magentas. Choosing one of these automatically selects only the color you've chosen.

You also can choose highlights, midtones, or shadows. Like the color options, choosing one of these selects only those tones.

Finally, you can choose Out of Gamut to select colors that can't be reproduced in the color mode of the image. Certain bright blues, for example, can't be printed using the CMYK process colors.

4. Choose a Fuzziness setting by entering a number or moving the slider. The Fuzziness setting operates like the Magic Wand's Tolerance setting; it determines the range of colors similar to the one you've chosen that will be selected. Choosing 0 restricts the selection to the exact colors you choose, while choosing 200 (the highest setting) selects all colors in the image.

5. Click the Invert box to invert the temporary mask you're creating.

6. Click Save if you want to save your color range settings for use on similar images. Click Load and choose a previously saved color range settings file to restore settings.

7. Use the Eyedropper tools to expand and contract your selection.

8. When your selection is complete, click OK to exit the Color Range dialog box. Figure 5.18 shows a completed selection just before exiting the Color Range dialog.

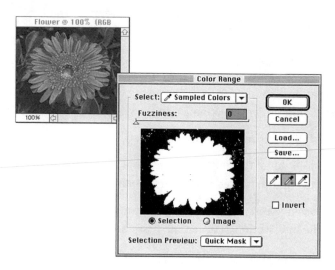

Figure 5.18

This selection is the result of using the addition eyedropper repeatedly to select the different shades in the flower's petals.

Tip

You can select color ranges within an already existing selection. To see what you're doing, set the Selection Preview to Grayscale or Quick Mask. When you select a color range within a selection, you are left with a new selection that is the intersection between the previous two.

Editing Selections

After you've made a selection, if it's not perfect, you don't have to start over again. There are several ways of editing selections to get them just right.

Adding to and Subtracting from Selections

When you're using the selection tools, you can add to a selection by holding down the Shift key and dragging to select another area of the image. The added selection doesn't have to touch the original selection; it can be in a completely different area of the image. Subtract from a selection by holding down the (Option)[Alt] key and dragging to define the area you don't want included in your selection.

Warning

If you've been using Photoshop for a while, watch out! Earlier versions of Photoshop used the (Command)[Control] key to subtract from a selection; if you try that now, you'll move your entire layer.

A variation on adding to and subtracting from selections is to select the intersection of two selection areas. To do so, follow these steps:

1. Make your first selection.

2. Hold down the Shift and (Option)[Alt] keys, and make another selection that overlaps the first one.

   When you release the mouse button, the selected area will be the intersection between the first and second selections.

The Grow and Similar commands in the Select menu act like the Magic Wand tool, adding to a selection based on the colors in it. Grow adds adjacent pixels to the selection if they're within the range of color currently specified in the Magic Wand Options palette's tolerance setting; if you have two or more areas of the image selected, both grow. Similar does the same thing as Grow, but it adds pixels from the entire image rather than just those adjacent to the original selection. You can apply these commands as many times as you want to keep enlarging the selection.

Using the Modify Commands on Selections

The Modify commands from the Select menu include Border, Smooth, Expand, and Contract.

◆ **Border.** This command selects an area around the original selection, based on the number of pixels you specify (see Figure 5.19).

Figure 5.19

Entering 12 in the Border dialog box results in this 12-pixel wide selection; the original selection included only the inner rectangle.

- **Smooth.** This command cleans up selections by checking for stray selections outside the main body of a selection and stray unselected areas inside the main body of a selection. When you invoke this command, Photoshop looks at the area around each pixel to find out how many nearby pixels are selected or unselected. If most of the neighboring pixels are selected, any unselected pixels are added to the selection; if most of the neighboring pixels aren't selected, then any selected pixels are deselected. How large an area around each pixel is determined by the number you enter in the Smooth dialog box, from 1 to 16 pixels.

This is a great tool for cleaning selections after using the Color Range command or Magic Wand tool. Figure 5.20 shows a selection before and after using the Smooth command.

Figure 5.20

Using the Smooth command on a Color Range selection (left window) eliminates unselected areas within a large selected area and deselected tiny selected areas within a large unselected area (right window).

- Expand makes a selection larger by adding the specified number of pixels all the way around.

- Contract decreases the size of the selection by the number of pixels you specify.

151

Moving and Floating Selections

Selections often are used to allow you to move the selected portion of the image to another location; you do this with the Move tool, shown below. However, you also can move just the selection outline to position it over another area of the image by choosing a selection tool from the toolbox and dragging the selection.

Tip

To avoid the long trip to the toolbox to select the Move tool, hold down (Command)[Control] while using the Marquee tool to temporarily transform it into a Move tool.

If you use the Move tool to move selected pixels, the selection turns into a floating selection. This is hazardous because when you click outside the selected area the pixels inside it drop into the current layer, covering up what was there before. To play it safe, turn the floating selection into a layer by pressing (Command-J)[Control-J]. The selected portion of the image is moved to a new transparent layer, but it's deselected. To reselect all non-transparent areas of the new layer (which amounts to your original selection), (Command)[Control]-click the layer's name in the Layer's palette.

Copying and Pasting Selections

Many times when you make a selection, all you want to do with it is copy the pixels inside it and paste them somewhere else. To copy the contents of a selection, make a selection and then press (Command-C)[Control-C]. To paste, press (Command-V)[Control-V].

To paste into a specified area, select the area into which you want to paste, then press Shift-(Command-V) Shift-[Control-V]. You could always do this, but the keyboard command is new to Photoshop 4.0.

Note

The Paste Into command in Photoshop 4.0 creates a new layer, containing the copied and pasted pixels, and a layer mask, defined by the area of the selection you made to paste the copied pixels into. For more information on layers and layer masks, see Chapter 9, "Layers."

◆ To empty a selected area of its contents, choose Clear from the Edit menu.

Cropping Documents

Photoshop users of days past were used to the Cropping tool, which appeared in the toolbox next to the Marquee tool and was used to reduce the size of an image to encompass only the area selected. You can still use the Cropping tool, but Adobe (in its infinite wisdom) has seen fit to hide it.

To use the Cropping tool, follow these steps:

1. Choose the Cropping tool by clicking on the Marquee tool in the toolbox and holding down the mouse button. At the tail end of the Marquee tools that appear will be the Cropping tool; slide your cursor over it and release the mouse button.

2. Click and drag to select the portion of your image you want to keep.

3. Adjust the selected area by clicking and dragging on the handles at its corners (see Figure 5.21).

4. When you have the selection the way you want it, move the cursor over the selected area and double-click.

It's harder to crop without using the Cropping tool, but it can be done. Using the Rectangular Marquee, select the portion of your image that you want to keep, add to or subtract from the selection if necessary, and choose the Crop command from the Image menu. This won't work with any other selection tool because you must have a rectangular selection to be able to crop your image using it.

Figure 5.21

To adjust the size and shape of the cropping marquee, move the corner handles.

Filling Selections

Like picture boxes in page layout programs, Photoshop selections can be filled with colors or patterns.

To fill a selection, follow these steps:

1. Make a selection.

2. Choose Fill from the Edit menu to bring up the Fill dialog box (see Figure 5.22).

Figure 5.22

The Fill dialog box lets you choose from a variety of sources and methods to fill a selection.

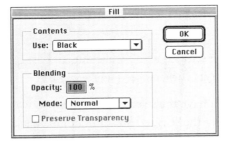

3. From the Contents pop-up menu, choose what you want to fill the selection with.

    You can fill the selection with a color by choosing:

    ◆ Foreground Color

    ◆ Background Color

- Black

- 50% Gray

- White

The selection also can be filled with a Pattern, the most recently saved version of the selected area, or a Snapshot of the image or another image. See "Filling with a Pattern" and "Filling with a Snapshot," later in this chapter, for more information.

4. Choose an opacity percentage, from 1 to 100.

5. Choose a blending mode to determine exactly how the new color you're applying will affect the color that already exists within the selected area. You have the following choices:

- **Normal.** This eliminates underlying colors completely, filling the entire selection with the color or pattern you choose.

- **Dissolve.** This blends the new color with the existing color in different amounts depending on the opacity of each pixel in the selection.

- **Behind.** This adds the new color only to transparent pixels and doesn't affect colored pixels.

- **Clear.** This makes the entire selected area transparent (only works on a layer, not on the background).

- **Multiply.** This multiplies the two colors to produce a darker color.

- **Screen.** This multiplies the inverse of each color to produce a lighter color.

- **Overlay.** This multiplies or screens each pixel depending on its original color; it retains the highlights and shadows of the selected area and mixes the original color with the new color.

- **Soft Light.** This darkens the colors if the new color is darker than 50% gray and lightens the colors if the new color is lighter than 50% gray.

- **Hard Light.** This is similar to Soft Light, but much harsher.

- **Color Dodge.** This brightens the original color to make it more like the new color.

- **Color Burn.** This darkens the original color to make it more like the new color.

- **Darken.** This replaces only pixels lighter than the new color.

- **Lighten.** This replaces only pixels darker than the new color.

- **Difference.** This subtracts the new color from the original color or vice versa, depending on which is brighter.

- **Exclusion.** This is similar to Difference, but softer.

- **Hue.** This uses the hue of the new color but retains the saturation and brightness of the original color.

- **Saturation.** This uses the saturation of the new color but retains the hue and brightness of the original color.

- **Color.** This uses the hue and saturation of the new color but retains the brightness of the original color.

- **Luminosity.** This uses the brightness of the new color but retains the hue and saturation of the original color.

6. Turn on Preserve Transparency if the selection is on a layer and you want to fill only pixels that are already colored. Transparent areas in the selection will remain transparent. If Preserve Transparency is turned off, the entire selected area will be filled.

7. Click OK to fill the selection.

You can use the following keyboard shortcuts to fill selections:

- To fill a selection with the background color, press (Command-Delete)[Control-Delete] or [Control-Backspace].

◆ To fill only colored areas with the background color (and ignore transparent areas), press (Shift-Command-Delete)[Shift-Control-Delete] or [Shift-Control-Backspace]. This is the same as turning on the Preserve Transparency option in the Fill dialog box.

◆ To fill a selection with the foreground color, press (Option-Delete)[Alt-Delete] or [Alt-Backspace].

◆ To fill only colored areas with the foreground color (and ignore transparent areas), press (Shift-Option-Delete)[Shift-Alt-Backspace]. This is the same as turning on the Preserve Transparency option in the Fill dialog box.

Filling with a Pattern

You can define an image or part of an image as a pattern and use it to fill a selected area; the pattern will be repeated as many times as will fit in the area. To define a pattern, follow these steps:

1. Open the image you want to use.

2. Select the part of the image you want to use as a pattern.

   You must have a rectangular selection to define a pattern, so if your selection isn't rectangular, press (Command-J)[Control-J] to make a new transparent layer with a copy of the selected area. Then use the rectangular Marquee to make a rectangular selection of your pattern element that includes a transparent area around it.

3. Choose Define Pattern from the Edit menu.

Tip

You can only have one pattern defined at a time, and Photoshop forgets about your pattern as soon as you quit the program. If you plan on using a pattern more than once, it's wise to copy the pattern selection before using it as a pattern, create a new document, and paste the pattern selection into the new document. Then you can retrieve the pattern by opening that document, pressing (Command-A)[Control-A] to select all, and choosing Define Pattern again.

Filling with a Snapshot

In addition to colors and patterns, you can fill a selection with a Snapshot of that same area of the image in a previous incarnation. To take a Snapshot, choose Take Snapshot from the Edit menu. If there's an active selection, only that portion of the image will be included in the Snapshot; otherwise, the whole image will be included.

When you fill a selection with a Snapshot of a partial image, the Snapshot will take up its original position in the image; so if the area selected to create the Snapshot only included part of the currently selected area, the rest of the selected area won't be affected.

You can only store one Snapshot at a time, and Photoshop forgets Snapshots when it quits. Snapshots are useful for restoring part of an image to a previous version—say, after you blurred the image and want to "un-blur" certain details in it.

Applying a Stroke to Selections

You also can apply a stroke to a selection to give the selected area a border. To do so, follow these steps:

1. Set the brush style and foreground color to the style and color you want to stroke the selection with.

2. Make a selection. It can be any shape; it doesn't have to be rectangular.

3. Choose Stroke from the Edit menu to bring up the Stroke dialog box (see Figure 5.23).

Figure 5.23

The Stroke dialog box lets you determine the width, location, opacity, and blending mode of a stroke.

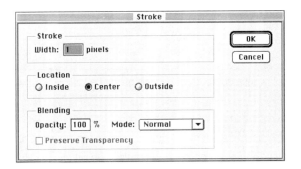

4. In the Stroke dialog box, enter a width in pixels for the stroke.

5. Choose a location for the stroke:

    ◆ Completely inside the selection

    ◆ Centered on the selection border

    ◆ Outside the selection

6. Enter an opacity percentage.

7. Choose a Blending Mode (see "Filling Selections," earlier in this chapter for a list of your choices).

8. Turn on or off Preserve Transparency. If it's on, transparent pixels that would otherwise be covered by the stroke won't be affected, they'll stay transparent.

9. Click OK to apply the stroke (see Figure 5.24).

Figure 5.24

A stroke applied to a circular selection.

Don't forget to plan ahead and choose your brush stroke and size before choosing the Stroke command because you can't choose a color in the Stroke dialog box; it will always be the foreground color. The current brush style will be used, including custom styles; this feature can be used for applying pictorial borders (such as snowflakes) around a selection.

PATHS

Because selection outlines disappear when you click outside them, you need a way to save selections for further use. That's one of the functions of paths; they are saved with an image and can be converted to selections so that you can revisit a particular portion of that image. Paths can be created freehand or from selections. Either way, if you're used to working with Bézier curves, you're going to love using Photoshop's paths. Bézier curves are defined in terms of groups of three points: one on the curve, and two outside it at the ends of control handles that you use to alter the direction and angle of the curve (see Figure 5.25).

Figure 5.25

Moving the control handles of the selected point adjusts the curves on either side of the point.

Note

When you draw a path, it may look as though you're actually drawing in your image, but you're not. Paths are used purely for defining areas within an image, and they won't show up in a finished image unless you specifically apply a stroke to them.

Making Paths

The quickest way to make a complex path is to convert a selection to a path.

Note

Calling it "a" path is rather misleading because a path actually can contain several subpaths that may or may not intersect. When you activate a path in the Paths palette, all the included subpaths are activated.

To convert a selection to a path, follow these steps:

1. Create a selection.

2. Choose Make Work Path from the Paths palette menu to bring up the Make Work Path dialog box (see Figure 5.26).

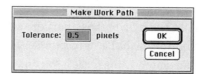

Figure 5.26

The only option in the Make Work Path dialog box is the tolerance setting, which determines how closely Photoshop follows the selection outline in creating the path.

3. Enter a Tolerance setting in pixels. This determines how exactly the path will follow the outline of the selection. Higher settings make smoother paths with fewer points, but detail may be lost. Lower settings make paths that follow the outlines of the selection more exactly, but these paths have more points and are more complex. Overly complex paths can be time-consuming to manipulate and can cause printing problems.

4. Click OK to create the path. It will appear in the Paths palette with the title "Work Path" (see Figure 5.27).

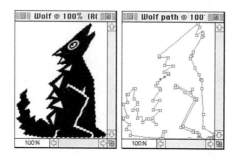

Figure 5.27

This path was created from a Magic Wand selection.

5. Double-click on Work Path in the Paths palette to bring up the Save Path dialog box and give the path a name of your choice (see Figure 5.28). If you don't rename the path, the next subpath you create will replace it in the palette, although both paths will still be in the document. You can save the original work path later by selecting it and choosing Save Path from the Paths palette menu.

Figure 5.28

The Save Path dialog box enables you to assign names to your paths.

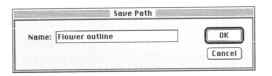

Another method of creating a path is to make a selection and click the Make Work Path button on the Paths palette (see Figure 5.29). The path will be created immediately using the last tolerance setting you entered. Then choose Save Path from the Paths palette menu to give the new path a name.

Figure 5.29

Click the Make Work Path button on the Paths palette to create a new path from a selection.

Making paths from selections lets Photoshop figure out where the path should go, and sometimes it guesses wrong. You'll almost always have to edit paths made this way to delete extra points and smooth out the curves. To get paths right the first time, you can make them from scratch with the Pen tool. Photoshop's Pen tool works essentially the same way Illustrator's does; you click to create points, and Photoshop draws a path segment between each pair of points. To draw a path, follow these steps:

1. Choose the Pen tool, shown below, from the toolbox.

2. Click in your image at the point where you want the path to begin. There are three types of points, each created a different way:

   ◆ **Corner point.** Just click. A corner point joins two straight line segments.

- ◆ **Smooth point.** Click and drag. A smooth point joins two curved line segments with a smooth curve, and it has two control handles pointing in opposite directions.

- ◆ **Sharp curve.** Click and drag, then (Option-click)[Alt-click] and drag the point again to change the angle of the forward control handle; a sharp curve joins two curved line segments with a curve that may not be smooth.

The path shown in Figure 5.30, created from left to right, contains all three types of points. The first two points (corner points) were created by simply clicking. The third point was created by dragging straight down, and the fourth and fifth points were created by dragging straight up (smooth points). The sixth point was created by dragging straight down and then clicking on the point again and dragging straight left (sharp curve). The final point was created by dragging straight up (smooth point).

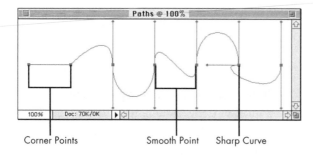

Corner Points   Smooth Point   Sharp Curve

Figure 5.30

This path contains corner points, smooth points, and a sharp curve.

When you're creating straight line segments, you don't need to do any click-dragging, just click to place each corner point. To constrain the line segments to multiples of 45 degrees, hold down the shift key as you click.

To preview a line segment before you click to place the second point that will define it, you can turn on the Rubber Band feature in the Pen Tool Options palette (see Figure 5.31). As you move the mouse, the path segment will constantly be redrawn to reflect the position of the point you're creating.

Figure 5.31

The Pen Tool Options palette only has one option, the Rubber Band feature, which previews the path segment you're in the process of creating.

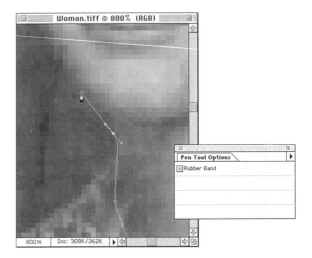

Tip

If you're new to Bézier curves, it can be difficult to decide which way to drag to create a smooth point. Remember this: When you drag to create control handles, the curve you create always follows behind the mouse cursor. So if you drag down to create a smooth point, the resulting path segment will curve up, away from the direction the mouse is going.

3. Click again to create a point along the outline you're defining with the path. Continue clicking to define different types of points until you get back to the first point.

4. As you move the Pen tool cursor near the first point you created, a small circle appears at the side of the Pen cursor. Clicking at this point closes the path.

5. When the path is complete, choose Save Path from the Paths palette menu to give it a name. You also can drag the Work Path in the Paths palette to the palette's New Path button, which looks like a pad of paper. If you don't save the path, it will still exist in the document, but you won't be able to access it via the Paths palette. You can go back later and change it from a Work Path to a saved path with a name by selecting it

before choosing Save Path from the Paths palette menu. You should save a Work Path before creating a new Work Path, or the new one will replace the original one.

Exchanging Paths with Illustrator

Adobe tries to ensure that its programs are completely compatible with each other. One of the big advantages of this policy for Photoshop users is the capability to trade paths with Illustrator, which is convenient whether or not you're working with an image that originated in Illustrator.

If you've imported an image from Illustrator into Photoshop to edit it, the paths you need to use to make Photoshop selections already exist in the Illustrator document. You can bring them into the Photoshop document by copying them in Illustrator, switching to Photoshop, and pasting them. You'll see a dialog box asking you whether you want to paste the Illustrator elements as pixels or paths. Choose paths, and click OK (see Figure 5.32).

Figure 5.32

You can paste Illustrator elements as Photoshop paths or rasterize them (paste as pixels).

Paths created in Photoshop also can be exported as an Illustrator document. You might want to do this for the following two reasons:

◆ If there's a lot of editing to be done to your paths, Illustrator's more extensive path editing features can help you. After you're done editing the paths you can paste them back into Photoshop.

◆ Photoshop's capability to convert selections to paths can produce more accurate results than Illustrator's autotracing feature; you can create paths in Photoshop that will form the basis of an Illustrator image such as a logo.

To export paths, follow these steps:

1. Create and select the paths you want to export.

2. Choose Paths to Illustrator from the Export submenu of the File menu (see Figure 5.33).

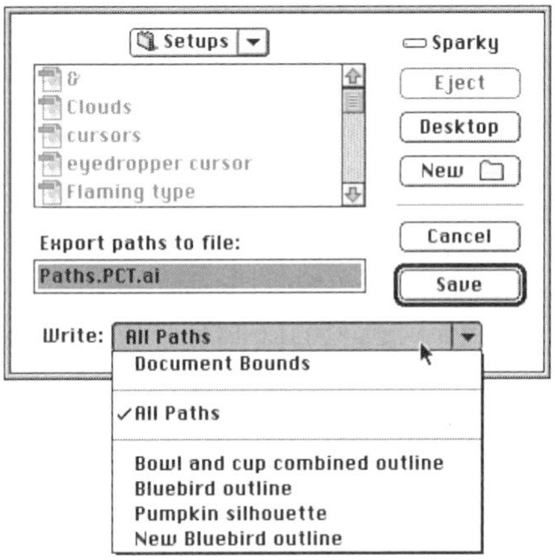

Figure 5.33

You can export Photoshop paths to an Illustrator document.

3. Assign a name to the Illustrator file that you're creating.

4. From the Write pop-up menu, choose an option:

- **All Paths.** Choose this option to include all your document's paths in the Illustrator file.

- **Document Bounds.** Choose this option to create a document containing one path that simply defines the size and shape of your Photoshop document.

- **A path listed in the menu.** Choose this option to save just one of your paths in the Illustrator document. All the named paths in your document will appear in this menu. Paths that you haven't saved yet won't show up.

Editing Paths

Once you've created a path, you can fiddle with it until it's just right. Photoshop has a full set of path tools, including the Pen tool (see Figure 5.34). The others, used for editing paths once you've created them, are as follows:

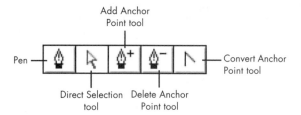

Figure 5.34

The path tools: Pen, Direct Selection tool, Add Anchor Point tool, Delete Anchor Point tool, Convert Anchor Point tool.

- **Direct Selection tool:** This is the main path-editing tool; you use it for selecting and moving points and control handles. You can temporarily access this tool while another path tool is selected by holding down the (Command)[Control] key.

- **Add Anchor Point tool:** This tool is used for adding points to a path.

- **Delete Anchor Point tool:** This tool is used for deleting points from a path.

- **Convert Anchor Point tool:** This tool changes points' type; you can convert smooth points into sharp curves or corner points, sharp curves into smooth or corner points, and corner points into smooth or sharp curves.

When you're editing paths, don't worry about accidentally editing your image instead. As long as there's an active path, any applicable command you invoke will be applied to the path and not to the pixels in your image. You can use the Undo command ((Command-Z)[Control-Z]) if you change your mind about a change you make to a path. There are a number of ways you can edit paths.

Adjusting Existing Curves

To modify a curve, you can use the Direct Selection tool to move its control handles, changing their angle and moving them closer or farther away from the point (see Figure 5.35); the two control handles for each point don't have to be the same length. If the control handles for a point aren't visible, click on the point to activate them.

You also can modify a curve by clicking on the path between points and dragging the curve. It can be difficult, however, to make fine adjustments this way.

Figure 5.35

Clicking and dragging the control handle adjusts the curve.

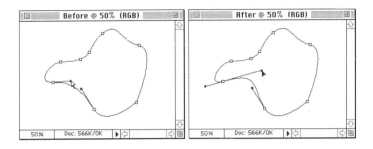

Moving Points on a Path

Use the Direct Selection tool to select one or more points and drag them to a new position (see Figure 5.36). To select more than one point at a time, hold down the Shift key as you click on the points, or drag a marquee around the points you want to select.

Figure 5.36

Moving a control point affects the curves on either side of the point.

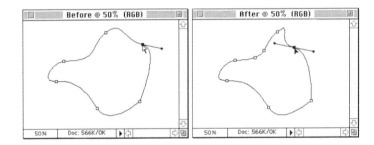

Adding Points to a Path

Choose the Add Anchor Point tool and click or click-drag on the path where you want to add a point: click to make a corner point and click-drag to make a smooth point. You can't make a sharp curve. You'll have to make a smooth point and convert it to a sharp curve as detailed below. To temporarily activate the Add Anchor Point tool while using the Direct Selection tool, hold down the (Command-Option)[Control-Alt] keys (see Figure 5.37).

Deleting Unnecessary Points

Choose the Delete Anchor Point tool and click on the points you want to delete. Click and drag to reshape the line segment at the same time as you delete a point (see Figure 5.38).

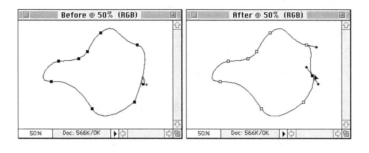

Figure 5.37

Clicking the curve with the Add Anchor Point tool adds a new point.

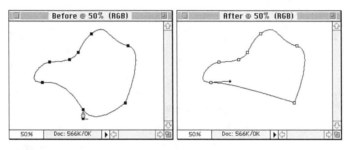

Figure 5.38

Clicking a point with the Delete Anchor Point tool removes the point and redraws the path accordingly.

Changing the Type of Existing Points

Choose the Convert Anchor Point tool from the path tools in the toolbox. To convert a smooth or sharp curve to a corner point (which has no control handles), just click on it. To convert a sharp curve or corner point to a smooth point, click-and-drag to create control handles. To convert a smooth point to a sharp curve, choose the Convert Anchor Point tool and move one of the point's control handles (see Figure 5.39).

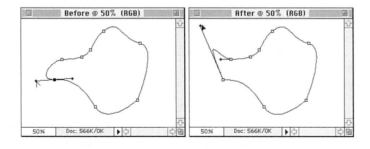

Figure 5.39

Moving a control handle with the Convert Anchor Point tool changes the curve from a smooth one to a sharp one.

Mac users can temporarily access the Convert Anchor Point tool while the Pen tool is active by holding down the Control and Command keys and clicking or click-dragging.

Deleting Line Segments

Using the Direct Selection tool, click a line segment between the points and press the (Delete)[Backspace] key. Shift-click to select more than one segment to delete (see Figure 5.40).

Figure 5.40

Delete a line segment by clicking it and pressing the (Delete)[Backspace] key.

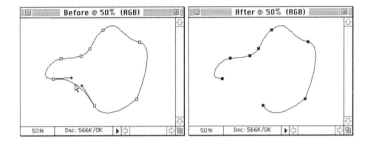

Adding to or Redrawing Sections of a Path

You can extend a path by clicking on one of its endpoints with the Pen tool and drawing more segments. After you click on a path endpoint, it's just as though you'd never stopped drawing that path; you can click and click-drag to create more points along the same path (see Figure 5.41). If you want to redraw existing segments, delete them, click on one of the newly created endpoints, and start drawing.

Figure 5.41

Click an endpoint with the Pen tool to continue drawing the path.

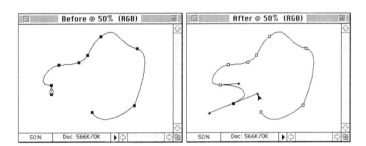

Moving a Path

(Option-click)[Alt-click] (you can do this with any tool) to select the entire path, then move it using the Direct Selection tool (see Figure 5.42). If the path extends beyond the border of the image, it won't be cropped. The whole path still exists, and you can later move it back within the image if you like.

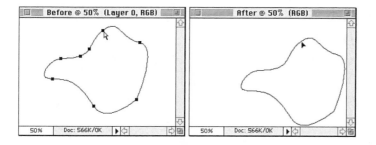

Figure 5.42

To move a path, (Option-click)[Alt-click] the path to select all of it first.

Duplicating a Path or Path Segment

To add another subpath to the current working path, click to select a segment of the path. Shift-click to select additional segments. Then copy and paste the line segments. To duplicate the entire subpath and add the copy to the working path, (Option-click)[Alt-click] to select the entire path and (Option-drag)[Alt-drag] to clone it. Don't forget to select all the lines you want to be included when you save your path to give it a name (see Figure 5.43).

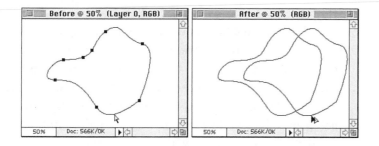

Figure 5.43

(Option-dragging)[Alt-dragging] a selected path clones it.

To make a separate path in the Paths palette that duplicates the selected path or part of a path, use the Direct Selection tool to select the path or part of a path you want to copy and choose Duplicate from the Paths palette menu. This will automatically bring up the Save Path dialog box; assign the new path a name and click OK to save it.

Deleting a Path

To delete an entire saved path from the Paths palette, drag the path's name to the Trash Can icon on the palette. To delete a subpath without deleting the saved path (it's possible to have a path in the palette with no subpaths in it), (Option-click)[Alt-click] on the subpath and press (Delete)[Backspace].

Tip

Although it's been said before, it's worth saying again. Holding down the (Command)[Control] key while using any path tool temporarily turns it into the Direct Selection tool.

Using Paths

Besides creating, duplicating, and deleting paths, the Paths palette is used for several other functions, including the following:

◆ To turn paths off and on, click the name of a path in the Paths palette to view it, and click each subpath in the image window to make it active. To turn off a path—or hide it—choose Turn Off Path from the Paths palette menu.

◆ To create a selection from a path, use one of three methods. First activate the path you want to use, then either choose Make Selection from the Paths palette menu or click on the Make Selection button at the bottom of the palette (see Figure 5.44). The first method will bring up the Tolerance dialog box, allowing you to determine how closely the selection follows the outlines of the path. The second method uses the last tolerance setting you made. The third method is the best—just (Command-click)[Control-click] the name of the path in the Paths palette to load the path as a selection without activating it first.

Figure 5.44

Click the Load Path as Selection button to create a selection from a path.

Load Path as Selection button

◆ To fill a path, just as you'd fill a selection, choose Fill Path from the Paths palette menu. The options are exactly like those in the Fill dialog box that you see when you fill a selection.

You can choose a color, a pattern, or a Snapshot to fill the path with; you can select a blending mode and enter an opacity percentage; you can elect to preserve transparency; and you can add feathering and anti-aliasing to the path. After you've made your preferred settings, click OK to apply the fill to the path.

- To stroke a path, choose Stroke Path from the Paths palette menu. The current foreground color and brush style will be used, just as when you apply a stroke to a selection, and the settings in the dialog box are the same. You can choose a width for the stroke (in pixels), a location (inside, outside, or centered on the path), an opacity percentage, and a blending mode, and you can elect to preserve transparency.

- You can specify a path to be used as a clipping path when the image is imported into another program. Clipping paths enable you to silhouette an image. If the program you're using supports clipping paths, then everything outside the path will appear transparent. (See "Silhouetting an Image for use in Another Program," later in this chapter for more information on creating clipping paths.)

- The final choice in the Paths palette menu is Palette Options (see Figure 5.45). The only option available to you is the size of the preview icon next to each path name in the Paths palette. You can choose from three different icon sizes, or you can choose to have no previews at all.

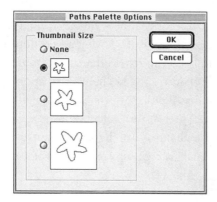

Figure 5.45

You can choose the size of the preview icons in the Paths Palette Options dialog box.

MASKS

In a sense, any selection is a mask, whether you create it with Quick Mask, the Magic Wand tool, the selection tools, or any other method. If there's an active selection, any painting, editing, or image adjustments you make to an image will only take effect within the selection outline, and you also can delete the pixels within the selection, in effect masking them permanently. But selections are temporary; if you want to use a particular area of an image more than once, you'll need to make a more permanent mask.

Understanding Different Types of Masks

Mask can be a confusing term because it doesn't refer to just one Photoshop feature. Layer masks, mask channels, transparency masks, clipping paths, clipping groups all are masks. Although you create them in different ways, they can all be used to accomplish the same basic functions: preserve and manipulate selections for later use, hide portions of an image while you're working on it and in the final image, and isolate areas to which you want to apply filters and image adjustments.

◆ Mask channels are what most people mean when they refer to Photoshop masks. Every Photoshop image has channels; you can view them in the Channels palette. Black-and-white and grayscale images have one channel, whereas color images have one channel for each color component. RGB images, for example, have three channels: one containing the image's red components, and one each for the green and blue components.

In addition to color channels, images can have alpha channels, also called *mask channels*. Saving a selection creates an alpha channel, and you can reload that selection from the channel at any time. You also can use channels to apply special effects to images, such as lighting effects (see Chapter 14, "Using Photoshop's Filters") and calculations (see Chapter 8, "Channels"). Mask channels are the key to many special effects used with type, such as creating embossed type (see Chapter 12, "Working with Type").

Channels can be thought of as invisible images, within an image. They're grayscale images that can be edited with the painting tools, the selection tools, and any of the rest of Photoshop's features, including filters.

♦ Layer masks affect only the image elements on the layer with which they're associated. Each layer can have one layer mask, which lets you hide and reveal portions of that layer without deleting pixels on the layer.

♦ Clipping groups are another type of mask associated with layers. Clipping groups enable you to group two or more layers together so that the bottom layer determines what area of the layers above it in the group will show.

♦ Transparency masks are default masks that are hiding in any document with transparent areas. To load the transparency mask for a layer, which selects all non-transparent areas on the layer, (Command-click)[Control-click] the name of the layer in the Layers palette.

♦ Clipping paths are a type of mask, too, although their effect isn't seen until an image leaves Photoshop. You can define one clipping path in an EPS or TIFF image that will outline the image, making all areas outside the path appear transparent when the image is imported into another program (such as a page layout or illustration package). This is most helpful because Photoshop's transparency feature is meaningless to any other program. You may have an image with transparent areas all around it, but they'll only stay transparent until you flatten the image, which you must do to save it in any format other than Photoshop's native format.

Using Masks

What type of mask you create depends on what you want to accomplish in any given situation. The first thing to take into account is whether you'll want to use the mask more than once; if not, you can usually just make a selection. If you do plan to go back to the mask, you'll need to make it more permanent by converting the selection to another type of mask.

Selecting Transparent or Non-transparent Areas on a Layer

Use a transparency mask to select non-transparent areas of a layer. To load a transparency mask, (Command-click)[Control-click] on the layer's name in the Layers palette (see Figure 5.46). If you invert the selection (Shift-Command-I)[Shift-Control-I], only the layer's transparent areas will be selected.

Figure 5.46

Figure 5.46

(Command-clicking)[Control-clicking] the monkey's layer selects only the monkey because the rest of the layer is transparent. The layer below, with the background pattern, is ignored when the selection is made.

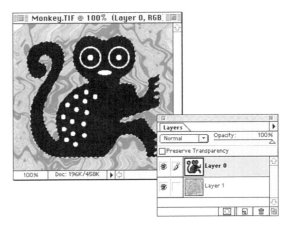

This is a quick way of creating a selection outline to be used elsewhere. If, for example, you had an image of a flower on a transparent background, you could load the transparency mask, save the selection to a channel, and then load that channel as a selection in any other open file.

Saving a Selection for Later Use

To preserve selection areas so that you can go back to them later, use paths or mask channels. Make a path by choosing the Make Work Path command from the Paths palette menu or clicking on the Make Work Paths button on the Paths palette. Make a mask channel by choosing the Save Selection command from the Select menu or clicking on the Save Selection as Channel button on the Channels palette.

Edit a Selection with Painting Tools

Photoshop's Quick Mask feature is designed for doing just this, but you also can edit channels as well as filters and image adjustments (such as Levels) with painting tools. Editing a channel can be easier on the eyes as well because you're working in black-and-white.

When you're working in a mask channel, you have the option of viewing only the mask or viewing the mask as an overlay, similar to a Quick Mask. The advantage is that channels are saved with an image, so you can go back and make more edits to a selection at any time, whereas Quick Masks are based only on the current selection, so they go away when you close the image or drop the selection.

Editing mask channels with painting tools offers you the most control over a selection. It's a good way to clean up a selection made with Color Range, for example (see Figure 5.47). To do this, use the following steps.

 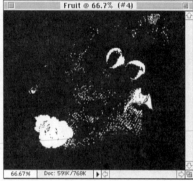

Figure 5.47

Attempting to select the rose at left with the Color Range command results in selected areas throughout the image that can be eliminated by painting over them once the selection is saved as a channel.

1. Use the color range tool or the Magic Wand to make a selection. Don't worry about selecting areas you don't want included in the selection—just make sure the areas you *do* want are selected.

2. Save the selection as a channel by choosing the Save Selection command from the Select menu or clicking the Save Selection as Channel button on the Channels palette.

3. View the new channel by clicking its name in the Channels palette. The foreground and background colors change to black-and-white at this point because you can't use color in channels.

4. Using the Paintbrush tool, paint over unwanted white areas with black in the mask channel to remove them from the selection; only white areas are selected when you load the channel as a selection. Press X to switch the foreground and

background colors, and paint with white over any black areas in the area you want selected.

In Figure 5.48 I wanted to select the rose in the lower-left corner of the image, so I painted over the white areas elsewhere in the image, leaving only the rose white.

5. Click the composite channel to return to editing the image. To load the mask channel as a selection, click the Load Channel as Selection button on the Channels palette.

Combining a Selection with Another Selection

To combine selections, you can use mask channels. When you create a new channel from a selection by choosing the Save Selection command from the Select menu, you're given the option of combining the selection with an existing channel in three ways: add, subtract, or intersect (see the section on "Selection Basics," earlier in this chapter). You can use these capabilities to create complex selections that can then be used to apply filters, make layer masks, or create clipping paths.

Hiding Part of a Layer

To mask part of a layer without affecting the other layers in an image, use a layer mask. Like channels, layer masks appear as grayscale images that you can edit. Layers with layer masks have an extra icon next to the layer icon preview in the Layers palette; you view the mask to edit it by clicking on the Layer Mask icon, and you return to viewing and editing the layer itself by clicking on the Layer Preview icon (see Figure 5.48).

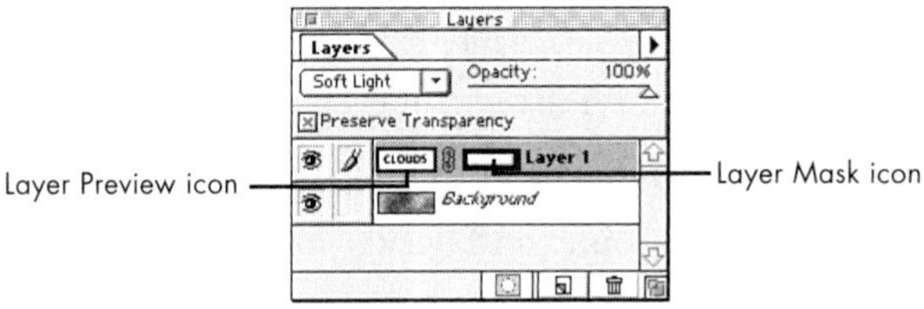

Figure 5.48

Click the Layer Mask icon to view and edit a layer mask, and the Layer Preview icon to return to viewing and editing the layer itself.

Layer Preview icon ——— Layer Mask icon

Black areas in the layer mask show the areas of the layer that are hidden by the mask, white areas indicate areas of the layer that will show through the layer mask. Gray areas will be partially visible. Where the layer mask hides portions of its own layer, it substitutes transparency so that the layers below can show through. After you've edited a layer mask to your liking, you can apply it to make the changes permanent or delete the mask without affecting the layer. Like layers, layer masks can only be saved in Photoshop's native format; they won't be preserved if you save your file in another format.

You can create a layer mask by clicking on the Add Layer Mask button at the bottom of the Layers palette, with an active selection or without one (see Figure 5.49). If there's no active selection, the entire layer mask will be white, letting the layer show through it. With a selection active, the area inside the selection will be white and the area outside it will be black. See Chapter 9, "Layers," for more information about layer masks.

Add Layer Mask button

Figure 5.49

Clicking the Add Layer Mask button creates a layer mask for the active layer.

Masking a Group of Layers

Clipping groups enable you to group several layers together and mask the upper ones based on the elements on the bottom layer of the group. The bottom layer in a clipping group masks the layers above it in the group; any transparent area in the bottom layer will act like a black area in a layer mask, preventing items in the layers above from showing through in that location. The bottom layer in a clipping group also determines what opacity and blending mode will be applied to all the layers in the group (see Figure 5.50).

All layers in the group have to be next to each other in the Layers palette; they're separated by dotted lines instead of the solid black lines that usually separate layers in the palette, and the preview icons of all the layers above the base layer of the group are indented. To create a clipping group, (Option-click)[Alt-click] on the black line separating layers in the Layers palette.

179

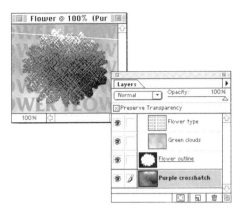

Figure 5.50

The Flower outline, Green clouds, and Flower type layers are part of a clipping group that only allows areas that are black in the bottom layer to show through. The area inside the flower outline in the bottom layer of the clipping group is transparent to allow the crosshatching layer below it to show through.

Blocking Off an Area of an Image while Editing

Use a selection to limit your edits to the part of an image you *want* to edit and keep from accidentally making changes elsewhere in an image. Create a selection by dragging with one of the standard selection tools, clicking with the Magic Wand, using paint tools in Quick Mask mode, or choosing the Color Range command from the Select menu.

This is an important editing technique. When you're doing fine retouching, it's important to make sure your edits don't overlap the section you're working on and spill over into other areas of the image (see Figure 5.51). If you were retouching a face to remove wrinkles, for example, you might use Quick Mask to select only the parts of the face that are wrinkled. That way you could avoid accidentally painting over the face's lips, nostrils, or eyes.

Figure 5.51

While editing this image to eliminate the man's black eye, the rest of the image was masked to keep from accidentally painting over it.

Applying Filters and Image Adjustments to Part of an Image

Just as you can select the area you want to edit with the paint tools, you also can select an area to which you want to apply filters or image adjustments. If there isn't an active selection when the results of filters and adjustments will be applied to the entire area of the active layer; if there is a selection active, then the effects of filters and adjustments will be confined to the area of the selection. Make selections by dragging with one of the standard selection tools, clicking with the Magic Wand, or choosing the Color Range command from the Select menu.

Creating Special Effects with Masks

Use mask channels to create special effects such as drop shadows and embossed text. To create a mask channel, make a selection and choose the Save Selection command from the Select menu or click on the Save Selection as Channel button on the Channels palette.

Many special effects used with type depend on channels, and the quickest way to make a channel for type is to create a type mask and make a channel from it. A type mask is simply a selection outline of a line of type, without any fill, so it's perfect for creating channels. See Chapter 12, "Working with Type," for examples of special type effects created with channels.

Figure 5.52 shows an effect applied with the Lighting Effects filter and a channel.

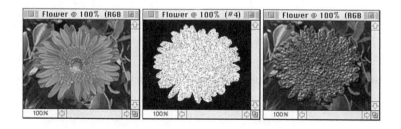

Figure 5.52

The Lighting Effects filter was applied to the image on the left using the channel shown in the center. The result was the image on the right.

Silhouetting an Image for use in Another Program

Use a clipping path to indicate transparent parts of your image to other programs. Even if there are pixels outside the clipping path in the Photoshop image, they won't show when the image is imported into another program with a clipping path.

To specify a clipping path:

1. Choose Clipping Path from the Paths palette menu to bring up the Clipping Path dialog box (see Figure 5.53).

Figure 5.53

The Clipping Path dialog box.

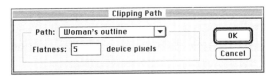

2. In the Clipping Path dialog box, select a path from the pop-up menu.

3. Enter a flatness value in pixels.

    This value determines how exactly the path will be followed when the image is printed; lower values force a printer to match the outline of the path more exactly, but very low values can cause printing problems and increase the amount of time it takes to print the file.

Note

Only the TIFF and EPS formats will retain clipping paths when you save an image, and not all software supports TIFF images with clipping paths, so EPS is the preferred format for saving images with clipping paths.

If you're saving a document in EPS format, you also can specify a clipping path at the time you first save the document. If you specify a clipping path and then save an image in EPS format, that path will already be selected in the clipping path pop-up menu of the EPS Options dialog; you can use that path or choose another one. Then enter a flatness value (see Figure 5.54). For high-resolution printing (1,200–2,400 dpi), use a value of 8–10. For low-resolution printing (300–600 dpi), use a value of 1–3. If you don't enter a value, the output device's default setting is used.

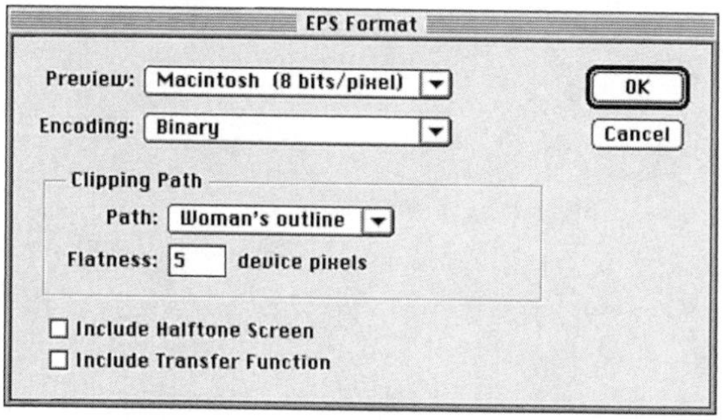

EPS Format

Preview: [Macintosh (8 bits/pixel) ▼]   (OK)

Encoding: [Binary ▼]   (Cancel)

Clipping Path

Path: [Woman's outline ▼]

Flatness: [5] device pixels

☐ Include Halftone Screen
☐ Include Transfer Function

Figure 5.54

You can choose a clipping path when you save an EPS file.

If the areas you want to block out are already transparent in the Photoshop image, you can load a transparency mask and convert it into a path (choose the Make Work Path command from the Paths palette) to create the clipping path. Paths created from selections may not be as accurate as you need them to be, so you'll probably need to edit a path you create this way.

Chapter

PAINTING

Photoshop offers a variety of tools and methods for painting the pixels in the image bitmap. This chapter describes the various painting tools and how to use them, how to fill and stroke selected pixels, and how to select foreground and background colors for painting. The powerful options of the painting tools enable you to paint subtle changes to an existing image, create original artwork on a blank canvas, or any of the possibilities in between.

SETTING FOREGROUND AND BACKGROUND COLOR

Photoshop uses the foreground color (see Figure 6.1) to paint, fill, and stroke selections. The background color is used to create gradient fills and is the color used when erasing or deleting a selected area (on the background layer only). When you launch Photoshop for the first time, the default foreground and background colors are displayed. The default foreground color is black and the default background color is white.

Figure 6.1

The Foreground and Background colors.

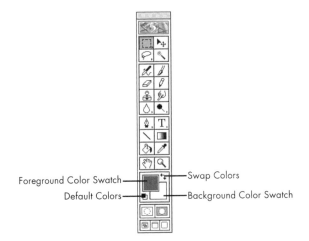

Foreground Color Swatch
Default Colors
Swap Colors
Background Color Swatch

Changing the Foreground and Background Colors

To change the foreground or background color:

1. Click the foreground or background swatch in the toolbox pictured in Figure 6.1.

2. The color picker displayed is determined by which color picker you selected in the Display & Cursors preferences dialog box: Photoshop, Apple, or Windows. If you have not changed this preference since you installed Photoshop, the default color picker is the Photoshop Color Picker that is used in this example (see Figure 6.2). See Chapter 1, "Setting Photoshop Preferences," for instructions on setting the Photoshop preferences.

3. Mix a color using one of the available color spaces and click the OK button.

4. The selected color is depicted in the toolbox's color swatch. Refer to Chapter 10, "Working with Color Images," for detailed information about the color models supported by Photoshop and how to specify color using the Photoshop Color Picker. When the Color Picker dialog box is displayed, you can also click the Custom button to select a color from the available color books (Figure 6.3). The color books supported by Photoshop are also detailed in Chapter 11, "Color Correction."

Tip

You can reset the foreground and background to their default values by clicking the Default Colors Icon pictured in Figure 6.1 or by simply typing the letter "d." To swap the foreground and background colors click the Swap Colors Icon pictured in Figure 6.1 or type the letter "x."

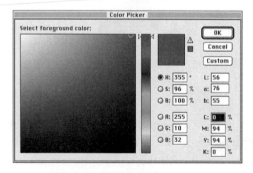

Figure 6.2

The Color Picker dialog box.

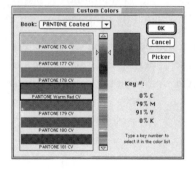

Figure 6.3

The Custom Colors dialog box.

Figure 6.4

You can select the custom color book to use by clicking on the Book drop-down menu.

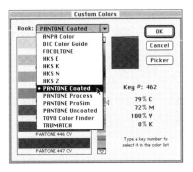

Using the Color Palette

To change the foreground and background colors using the Color palette:

1. Choose Window➡Show Color to display the Color palette (Figure 6.5).

Figure 6.5

The Window menu.

2. The Color palette is another way to set the foreground and background colors and contains foreground and background swatches. If you click the active color swatch (outlined in black), the color picker dialog box is displayed. Click the inactive color swatch (not outlined in black) to make it active.

3. Select the color model for the Color palette by clicking on the triangle in the upper right corner of the Color palette and making a selection from the palette menu (Figure 6.6).

4. The color bar at the bottom of the Color palette enables you to select a color from the color model's spectrum. Click the triangle in the upper-right corner of the Color palette to display the palette menu choices and select Color Bar to choose which color ramp is displayed at the bottom of the Color palette (Figure 6.7).

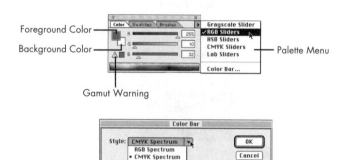

Figure 6.6

The Color palette and Color palette Menu.

Figure 6.7

The Color Bar choices for the Color palette.

5. Drag the triangle sliders to mix a color (Figure 6.6).

Using the Swatches Palette

The Swatches palette enables you to save the foreground or background color into a palette of colors for later use. The colors in the Swatches palette can be selected as the foreground or background color. You can create a color palette from scratch, add to the palette displayed, save the color palette, and load previously saved color palettes. The default swatches contain the current palette. See the section on Indexed Color in Chapter 10, "Working with Color Images," for detailed information about Photoshop's color palettes. To use the Swatches palette:

1. Choose Window➡Show Swatches (Figure 6.8) to display the Swatches palette (Figure 6.9).

Figure 6.8

The Window menu.

Figure 6.8

The Window menu.

Figure 6.9

The Swatches palette.

2. Position your cursor over one of the color swatches in the Swatches palette. The cursor changes to an eyedropper cursor.

3. Click a swatch to load that color as the foreground Color.

4. Hold down the (Option key)[Alt key] and click a color swatch to load that color as the background Color.

   To **add** a color, position your cursor over an empty space in the Swatches palette. If there are no empty spaces available, click and drag in the lower-right corner of the Swatches palette to change the height and reveal empty spaces. The cursor changes to a paint bucket. Click in the empty space to add the foreground color to the palette.

   To **replace** a color in the Swatches palette, hold down the Shift key and click the swatch to change the swatch color to the foreground color.

   To **insert** a color swatch, position the cursor over the color swatch in the palette that you want to insert the new swatch before. Hold down (Shift-Option)[Shift-Alt] and click the swatch to insert a new swatch in the foreground color.

To **delete** a color swatch in the Swatches palette hold down (Command)[Control]. When the cursor changes to the scissors icon, click a swatch to delete it.

To **reset the swatches palette** to the default swatch colors (current color palette), click the triangle in the upper right corner of the Swatches palette to display the palette menu (Figure 6.10). Choose Reset Swatches from the palette menu. A dialog box is displayed so you can choose whether to replace all the current swatches with the default color swatches or append the default color swatches to the current swatches (Figure 6.11).

To **save** a custom set of color swatches, click the triangle in the upper right corner of the Swatches palette and choose Save Swatches from the palette menu (Figure 6.10). Navigate to the folder or directory you want to save the swatches in and click the Save button. Save your swatches if you want to use them on another image at a later date. Opening an indexed color image or converting an image to indexed color replaces the custom color palette with the indexed colors.

To **replace** the current swatches with swatches previously saved, click the triangle in the upper right corner of the Swatches palette and select Replace Swatches from the palette menu (Figure 6.10). Navigate to the folder or directory containing the saved swatches and click the Open button. The current swatches are replaced with this new set.

To **append** swatches previously saved, click the triangle in the upper right corner of the Swatches palette and select Load Swatches from the palette menu (Figure 6.10). Navigate to the folder or directory containing the saved swatches and click the Open button. The loaded swatches are appended to the current set.

To **sample** colors from your image to add to the swatches palette, use the Eyedropper tool and click on the image to load the image colors as the foreground color. Click in an empty space in the Swatches palette to add them. See the following section on Sampling Colors for more details.

Figure 6.10

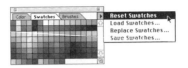

The Swatches palette menu choices.

Figure 6.11

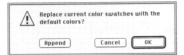

You can choose whether to replace the swatches with the default swatches or append them to the current set.

Sampling Colors from an Image

The Eyedropper tool is used to sample colors from an image and load them as the foreground or background color. You can sample the color of a specific pixel in the image or the average color of a square-pixel area. To sample colors from an image:

1. Double-click the Eyedropper tool in the toolbox to display the Eyedropper Options palette and select a Sample Size from the drop down menu in the Eyedropper Options palette (Figure 6.12).

   ◆ Choose **Point Sample** to set the Eyedropper tool to select the color of a single pixel.

   ◆ Choose **3 by 3 Average** to set the Eyedropper tool to load a color that is the average of the color values in each color channel of a 3 pixel by 3 pixel area.

   ◆ Choose **5 by 5 Average** to set the Eyedropper tool to load a color that is the average of the color values in each color channel of a 5 pixel by 5 pixel area.

Tip

Type the letter "i" to select the Eyedropper tool in the toolbox. If you are zoomed in close to sample a color, hold down the Spacebar to display the Hand tool. Click and drag with the Hand tool to move the canvas area around in the window.

Figure 6.12

The Sample Size pull-down
menu in the Eyedropper
Options palette.

2. To **define a Foreground color,** select the Eyedropper tool from
    the toolbox and position the Eyedropper cursor over the part
    of the image that contains the color you want to sample and
    click. If you hold down the mouse button and drag around the
    image with the Eyedropper tool selected, you can view the
    sampled colors in the color swatch in the toolbox.

3. To **define a Background color,** select the Eyedropper tool from
    the toolbox and position the Eyedropper cursor over the part
    of the image that contains the color you want to sample.
    (Option-click) [Alt-Click] to load the color as the background
    color. If you hold down the mouse button and drag around the
    image with the Eyedropper tool selected, you can view the
    sampled colors in the color swatch in the toolbox.

THE BRUSHES PALETTE

All of the painting tools in Adobe Photoshop use brushes whose size and
style are defined and chosen from the Brushes palette. The default
brushes are round brushes with hard and soft edges. The brush shape
and size is entirely user-definable, however, enabling you to be as
creative as you like when applying color to the image.

Choosing a Brush

Choose Show Brushes from the Window menu to display the Brushes
palette. The Brushes palette contains options available from the palette
menu to Reset, Load, Replace and Save brushes (Figure 6.13). The
brushes in the Brushes palette are displayed in their actual size unless
the brush is larger than the palette's cell size. In this case, the diameter
of the brush in pixels in indicated below the brush, as is the case with
the four brushes along the bottom row of the Brushes palette pictured
in Figure 6.13. Click on a brush to select it. The brush you select is used
for the particular tool that is selected, which means you must select a
brush type for each tool you use.

Figure 6.13

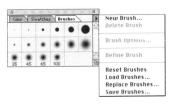

The Brush Options Palette.

Modifying Brush Options

You can modify the options for any of the brushes currently displayed in the Brushes palette, and specify the Diameter, Hardness, Spacing, Angle and Roundness of the brush. To modify an existing brush:

1. Double-click the brush in the Brushes palette or choose Brush Options from the palette menu. The Brush Options dialog box is displayed, enabling you to specify the Diameter, Hardness, Spacing, Angle and Roundness of the brush (Figure 6.14).

Figure 6.14

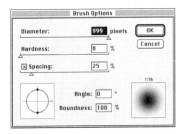

The Brush Options dialog box.

2. Set the brush **diameter**. The diameter of the brush is specified in pixels and ranges from 1 pixel to 999 pixels (Figure 6.15). The preview box in the lower-right corner of the Brush Options dialog box displays an actual size representation up to the size of the box. When the brush diameter is larger than the box, a ratio is displayed above the box to indicate the ratio of the size displayed to the actual size of the brush.

3. Set the brush **hardness**. The hardness of the brush edges is specified as a percentage with 0% the softest edge and 100% the hardest edge. The percentage indicated is actually the size of the solid brush with the fuzziness extending out to the brushes diameter (Figure 6.16).

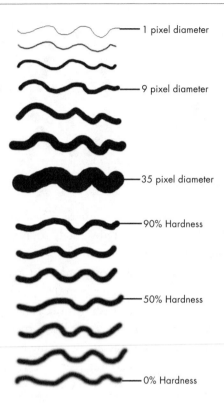

1 pixel diameter

9 pixel diameter

35 pixel diameter

Figure 6.15

The brush diameter determines the thickness of the brush in pixels.

90% Hardness

50% Hardness

0% Hardness

Figure 6.16

The hardness percentage determines the size of the solid area of the brush.

4. Set the brush **spacing.** The Spacing option controls the distance between the brush marks as a percentage of the brush size. The values range from 1% to 999%. When this value is set to 100%, for example, the brush paints side by side. When the spacing value is set to something larger than 100%, the brush mark is spaced out. The spacing for the default brushes is set to 25% so that the brushes overlap by 75% to ensure there are no humps in the painted line (see Figure 6.17). When a spacing percentage is selected, it does not matter how fast you paint with the selected tool because the spacing is always the spacing indicated. If you uncheck the checkbox for Spacing, the distance of the brush marks varies depending on how fast you drag with the painting tool.

Figure 6.17

A Spacing value of 100% sets the brush marks side by side; a percentage larger than 100 spaces the brush marks out.

100% spacing   150% spacing   70% spacing

5. Set the **Angle** and **Roundness.** The Angle of the brush applies to brushes that are not absolutely round. To set the Roundness of the brush, type a value from 0% to 100% to specify the ratio between the brush's long and short axes (an ellipse when less than 100% and greater than 0%). You can visually specify the Roundness of the brush by dragging the points on the vertical axis in the box in the lower left corner of the Brush Options dialog box. Click the arrow on the horizontal axis in the same box to set the brush Angle or type a value in. Use the Angle and Roundness options to create a chiseled effect (Figure 6.18).

Figure 6.18

Angle and Roundness effects with a 20 pixel diameter brush, 100% hardness and 25% spacing.

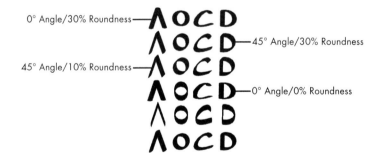

0° Angle/30% Roundness
45° Angle/30% Roundness
45° Angle/10% Roundness
0° Angle/0% Roundness

Creating and Deleting Brushes

Aside from modifying the default brushes, you can create your own and add them to the Brushes palette in the empty spaces. To create a new brush:

1. Click in any of the empty spaces in the Brushes palette to display the New Brush dialog box or click the triangle in the upper-right corner of the Brushes palette to display the palette

menu and choose New Brush. If you don't see any empty spaces, click and drag the lower right corner of the Brushes palette to change the height and reveal the empty spaces. The Brush Options dialog box is displayed, enabling you to specify the Diameter, Hardness, Spacing, Angle and Roundness of the brush.

2. Set the brush **diameter**. The diameter of the brush is specified in pixels and ranges from 1 pixel to 999 pixels. The preview box in the lower right corner of the Brush Options dialog box displays an actual size representation up to the size of the box. When the brush diameter is larger than the box, a ratio is displayed above the box to indicate the ratio of the size displayed to the actual size of the brush.

3. Set the brush **hardness**. The hardness of the brush edges is specified as a percentage with 0% the softest edge and 100% the hardest edge. The percentage indicated is actually the size of the solid brush with the fuzziness extending out to the brushes diameter.

4. Set the brush **spacing.** The Spacing option controls the distance between the brush marks as a percentage of the brush size. The values range from 1% to 999%. When this value is set to 100%, for example the brush paints side by side. When the spacing value is set to something larger than 100%, the brush mark is spaced out. The spacing for the default brushes is set to 25% so that the brushes overlap by 75% to ensure there are no humps in the painted line. See Figure 6.18. When a spacing percentage is selected, it does not matter how fast you paint with the selected tool because the spacing is always the spacing indicated. If you uncheck the checkbox for Spacing, the distance of the brush marks varies depending on how fast you drag with the painting tool.

To **delete brushes** from the Brushes palette:

1. Hold down the (Command)[Control] key and position the cursor over the brush you want to delete to display the scissors cursor.

2. Click the brush to delete it. You can also select the brush you want to delete and choose Delete Brush from the palette menu.

Creating Custom Brushes

You can define a brush in the shape of part of an image. If you create a custom brush from a portion of a color image, keep in mind that the brush is the grayscale equivalent and use areas of high contrast. To create a custom brush:

1. Use the rectangular Marquee tool to select a portion of an image (Figure 6.19). You can select an area up to 1,000 by 1,000 pixels in size.

Figure 6.19

Select the area in the image that you want to define as a brush.

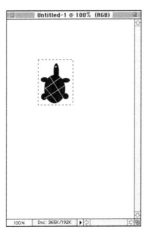

Tip

To see the size of a selected area in your image when making a selection, choose Show Info from the Window menu to display the Info palette. Choose Palette Options... from the Info palette menu and set the Mouse Coordinates to Pixels.

2. Choose Define Brush from the palette menu of the Brushes palette (Figure 6.20). The new brush is displayed in the palette.

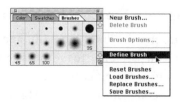

Figure 6.20

The Brushes palette menu.

3. Double-click the new brush to display the Brush Options dialog box. Custom brushes have only two options: Spacing and Anti-aliased (see Figure 6.21). Anti-aliased is not available as an option for large brushes. If Anti-aliased is available, click the checkbox to turn it on if you want your brush to blend with the background image. Select a spacing percentage. A percentage of 100 makes the brush marks abut. A spacing percentage of less than 100 overlaps the brush marks. A spacing percentage larger than 100% spaces the brush marks out.

Figure 6.21

Custom brushes have only two options in the Brush Options dialog box.

Importing and Exporting Brushes

Export your custom brushes to a file to import them at a later date. You can import saved brush sets as replacements for the current set of brushes or in addition to the current set. Resetting the Brushes palette replaces the current brush set with the default brushes. There are a number of other options at your disposal.

◆ Choose Save Brushes from the palette menu of the Brushes palette to save the current set of brushes.

◆ Choose Replace Brushes from the palette menu to replace the current set of brushes with a previously saved set.

◆ Choose Load Brushes from the palette menu to append a saved set of brushes to the current set of brushes.

◆ Choose Reset Brushes from the palette menu to set the brushes to Photoshop's default brush set.

Selecting Brushes with the Context Menu

Context menus are new in Photoshop 4.0, and enable you to see a context sensitive menu pertaining to the tool selected or the options for palette items. This new option gives you a quick way to work with commonly selected commands. On the Macintosh, hold down the Control key and click with the mouse to display the context menu choices. Windows users simply click the Right Mouse Button. See Figure 6.22 and Figure 6.23.

Figure 6.22

The Paintbrush Context menu.

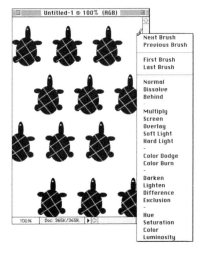

Figure 6.23

The Context menu in the Brushes palette.

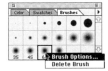

USING THE PAINTBRUSH TOOL

To use the Paintbrush tool, select the Paintbrush from the toolbox or type the letter "b" for brush and click and drag in the canvas area. Use the Paintbrush tool as you would an ordinary paint brush.

Tip

To paint in a straight line, click with the paintbrush on the canvas area, then Shift-Click somewhere else in the canvas area to create a straight brush stroke from the first point. If you hold down the Shift key while painting with the Paintbrush tool, you can constrain painting to either a vertical or horizontal plane.

Note

The Paintbrush tool always paints with an anti-aliased edge to blend the painted colors with the background, even if the brush selected has a hardness of 100% specified.

Setting the Paintbrush Options

The Paintbrush tool has options that can be set to define the way the paintbrush paints on the canvas area. The settings in the Paintbrush Options palette stay in effect for the Paintbrush tool, even if you choose another brush type from the Brushes palette. To set the Paintbrush options:

1. Double-click the Paintbrush tool in the toolbox to display the Paintbrush Options palette (Figure 6.24).

Figure 6.24

The Paintbrush Options palette.

2. The **blending** modes for the Paintbrush tool are available under a drop-down menu in the upper left corner of the Paintbrush palette (Figure 6.25). The blending modes affect the way the color you are painting with interacts with the underlying image. The available choices are as follows:

Figure 6.25

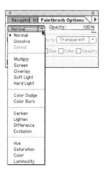

The Blending modes available for the Paintbrush tool.

◆ **Normal**—The Normal blending mode is the default mode when you first use Photoshop. Normal mode replaces the values of the painted pixels with foreground color. The Normal mode is called Threshold when you are working in Bitmap mode.

◆ **Dissolve**—The Dissolve blending mode replaces the values of the pixels *randomly,* based on the Opacity setting in the Paintbrush Options palette. Choose a large brush size and set the opacity to something less than 100% to view the effect of this mode.

◆ **Behind**—The Behind blending mode only works on transparent layers (see Chapter 9, "Layers"). The transparent pixels are exclusively affected with this blending option. Using the analogy of an image pasted on a piece of clear acetate to represent a transparent layer in Photoshop, the Behind blending mode is like painting the back side of the acetate or painting behind the non-transparent pixels.

◆ **Clear**—The Clear blending mode is only available when you are using the Line tool, Paint Bucket tool, the Fill or Stroke command, and working on a transparent layer. This option replaces the values of the pixels with the transparent value.

◆ **Multiply**—The Multiply blending mode multiplies the color values of the image and the color you are painting with to arrive at a darker complementary color. Painting over the same area multiple times creates successively darker colors;

whereas multiplying with white yields no results, and multiplying with black results in black. Try this mode with a 50% or 60% gray color and a soft brush to produce realistic looking shadows.

◆ **Screen**—The Screen blending mode produces a bleaching effect, making the painted area lighter depending on the color selected and the underlying color in the image. Painting with light colors has a stronger effect than painting with dark colors; therefore, darker colors create a more subtle effect.

◆ **Overlay**—The Overlay blending mode combines the color value of the foreground color with the colors of the image pixels while preserving the highlight and shadow values of the image. This mode is effective when colorizing a color image with the painting tools.

◆ **Soft Light**—The Soft Light blending mode darkens or lightens the image based on the color being used. A lighter color with a gray value less than 50% lightens the image, creating a dodged effect with the foreground color. A darker color with a gray value greater than 50% darkens the image, creating a burn effect.

◆ **Hard Light**—The Hard Light blending mode combines the effects of the Screen mode and the Multiply mode. When you paint with a color that has gray value less than 50%, the effect is like that described for the Screen mode above, and the image is lightened. When you paint with a color that has a gray value greater than 50%, the effect is like that described for the Multiply mode above and the result is a darkened image.

◆ **Color Dodge**—The Color Dodge blending mode lightens the color of the image pixels to reflect the lightness value of the selected color. Painting with dark colors produces a more subtle change than painting with light, bright colors. Painting with black yields no effect, while painting with white results in a blown-out effect.

- **Color Burn**—The Color Burn blending mode darkens the color of the image pixels based on the selected painting color. Painting with light, bright colors produces a more subtle effect than painting with dark color. Painting with white yields no effect, and painting with black yields black.

- **Darken**—The Darken blending mode changes the color of the pixels that contain values that are lighter than those of the foreground color. Pixels darker than the painting color are left unchanged.

- **Lighten**—The Lighten blending mode changes the color of the pixels that contain values that are darker than those of the foreground color. Pixels lighter than the painting color are left unchanged.

- **Difference**—The Difference blending mode evaluates the brightness values of the colors in each channel and compares these values with the comparable values in the selected color. The color with the lightest brightness value is subtracted from the color with the highest brightness value, resulting in the value for the image pixel. Painting with dark colors produces a more subtle effect than painting with light, bright colors. Painting with white results in an inverse image, much like a color negative.

- **Exclusion**—The Exclusion blending mode produces an effect similar to the Difference mode, but with a softer effect.

- **Hue**—The Hue blending mode replaces only the hue value of the image pixels, leaving the saturation and luminance values in tact.

- **Saturation**—The Saturation blending mode replaces the saturation value of the image pixels with the saturation value of the foreground color.

- **Color**—The Color blending mode replaces both the hue and saturation values of the image pixels with the hue and saturation values of the foreground color. Use this mode to paint in local color changes without affecting the grayscale portion of the image.

◆ **Luminosity**—The Luminosity blending mode maintains the hue and saturation of the image pixels, but changes the luminance value to that of the foreground color.

Note

The Blending Mode options are available under the context menu of the Paintbrush tool. Hold down the Control key and click anywhere in the canvas area to display the context menu.

Tip

When using the Paintbrush tool, hold down the (Option)[Alt] key and click the image to sample a color from the image with the Eyedropper tool.

3. The **opacity** level of the Paintbrush tool can be set to a value from 1% to 100% by dragging the triangle slider in the upper right corner of the Paintbrush Options palette or by typing a number on the keyboard. Simply type a single digit number from 0 through 9 to specify the opacity in 10% increments. For example: typing "5" changes the opacity setting to 50%; typing a "7" changes the opacity to 70% and typing "0" changes the opacity to 100%. If you type the numbers quickly, you can type an exact percentage like 43%.

4. To specify the **fade** for the Paintbrush tool, click the checkbox in the Paintbrush Options palette next to the word "Fade" and type in the number of steps in the fade. You can type a value from 1 to 9,999 for the fade steps, each step representing a single brush mark. Keep in mind that this value is affected by the brushes *spacing* value explained in the section on the Brushes palette in this chapter. Choose whether the brush stroke is to fade to transparency or the background color from the drop-down menu.

5. Set the Stylus Pressure Options. Photoshop supports the use of a variety of pressure-sensitive digitizing tablets. The three

checkbox items in the Paintbrush Options palette offer three methods to describe how applying pressure with the stylus affects the Paintbrush tool.

- ◆ **Size** increases the size of the Paintbrush when pressure from the stylus is increased.

- ◆ When the **Color** checkbox is selected, applying light pressure to the stylus paints with the background color; applying heavy pressure paints with the foreground color. Painting with medium pressure on the stylus results in a color between the foreground and background color.

- ◆ Click the **Opacity** checkbox if you want the stylus pressure to affect the opacity of the color you are painting with. Light pressure results in a lower opacity and high pressure results in a more opaque color.

6. Click the **Wet Edges** checkbox in the Paintbrush Options palette to create watercolor effects. The painting color is lighter in the middle with the solid color built up on the edges.

USING THE AIRBRUSH TOOL

To use the Airbrush tool, select the Airbrush from the toolbox or type the letter "a" for airbrush and click and drag in the canvas area. Think of the airbrush as spraying droplets of paint onto the canvas. If you stay on one spot, the paint accumulates in a spray pattern that matches the brush type selected.

Tip

To paint in a straight line, click with the Airbrush on the canvas area, then Shift-Click somewhere else in the canvas area to create a straight brush stroke from the first point. If you hold down the Shift key while painting with the Airbrush tool, you can constrain painting to either a vertical or horizontal plane.

Note

The Airbrush tool always paints with an anti-aliased edge to blend with the background, even if the brush selected has a hardness of 100% specified.

Setting the Airbrush Options

The Airbrush tool has options that can be set to define the way the airbrush paints on the canvas area. The settings in the Airbrush Options palette stay in effect for the Airbrush tool, even if you choose another brush type from the Brushes palette. To set the options for the Airbrush tool:

1. Double-click the Airbrush tool in the toolbox to display the Airbrush Options palette (Figure 6.26).

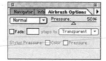

Figure 6.26

The Airbrush Options palette.

2. **Select a Blending Mode.** The blending options for the Airbrush tool are available under a drop-down menu in the upper left corner of the Airbrush palette. The blending options affect the way the color you are painting with interacts with the underlying image. The available choices are detailed in the section on the Paintbrush tool in this chapter.

Note

The Blending Mode options are available under the context menu of the Airbrush tool. On the Macintosh, hold down the Control key and click anywhere in the canvas area to display the context menu. Windows users must simply click on the canvas area with the right mouse button to access the context menu.

Tip

When using the Airbrush tool, (Option-click)[Alt-click] the image to sample a color from the image with the Eyedropper tool.

3. **Set the Airbrush Pressure.** The pressure setting for the Airbrush tool controls how fast the paint builds up on the canvas and can be set to a value from 1% to 100% by dragging the triangle slider in the upper right corner of the Airbrush Options palette or by typing a number on the keyboard. Typing a single digit number sets the Airbrush pressure in 10% increments. Typing "2," for example, changes the pressure setting to 20%. Typing "0" sets the airbrush pressure to 100%. Type the numbers quickly using the numeric keypad to enter exact percentages such as 83%.

4. **Set the Fade Rate.** To specify the fade-out rate for the Airbrush tool, click the Fade checkbox in the Airbrush Options palette and type in the number of steps in the fade. You can type a value from 1 to 9999 for the fade steps, each step representing a single brush mark. Keep in mind that this value is affected by the brushes *spacing* value explained in the section on the Brushes palette in this chapter. Choose whether the brush stroke is to fade to transparency or the background color from the drop-down menu.

5. **Set the Stylus Pressure.** Photoshop supports the use of a variety of pressure-sensitive digitizing tablets. The three check-box items in the Airbrush Options palette offer two methods to describe how applying pressure with the stylus affects the Airbrush tool:

    ◆ **Color**—When the Color checkbox is selected, applying light pressure to the stylus paints with the background color; applying heavy pressure paints with the foreground color. Painting with medium pressure on the stylus results in a color between the foreground and background color.

◆ **Pressure**—Click the Pressure checkbox if you want to control the pressure setting with the stylus. Set the low pressure setting in the Airbrush palette by dragging the triangle sliders for Pressure. Applying pressure with the stylus increases the pressure from this starting point up to 100%.

USING THE LINE TOOL

The Line tool enables you to draw straight lines by clicking on a starting point and dragging to an ending point on your image. To use the Line tool:

1. Select the Line tool from the toolbox or type the letter "n" for line and click and drag in the canvas area.

2. Select where you want to end the line and let go of the mouse button.

Tip

To constrain the line along the horizontal or vertical plane and to draw lines at 45° angles, hold down the Shift key while dragging.

Setting the Line Tool Options

With the Line tool you have options for including arrow heads, specifying opacity, applying blending modes and applying anti-aliased edges. To set the options for the Line tool:

1. Double-click the Line tool in the toolbox to display the Line Tool Options palette (Figure 6.27). The Line tool is not affected by the brush size selected.

2. **Select a Blending Mode.** The blending modes for the Line tool are available under a drop-down menu in the upper left corner of the Line toolbox. The blending modes affect the way the color of the line you are drawing interacts with the underlying image. The available choices are detailed in the section on the Paintbrush tool in this chapter.

Figure 6.27

The Line Tool Options palette.

Tip

When using the Line tool, (Option-click)[Alt-click] the image to sample a color from the image with the Eyedropper tool.

3. **Set the Opacity.** The opacity level of the Line tool can be set to a value from 1% to 100% by dragging the triangle slider in the upper right corner of the Line Tool Options palette or by typing a number on the keyboard. Type a number from 0 to 9 to specify the opacity in 10% increments. Typing "0," for example, sets the opacity to 100%, and typing "4" sets the opacity to 40%. Quickly type a two-digit number on the numeric keypad to set the opacity to an exact percentage like 12%.

4. **Set the Line Width.** The line width is always specified in pixels, so the thickness of the line varies depending on the resolution of your image. If, for example, your image is 300 pixels per inch, setting the line width to 1 pixel results in a line one three-hundredths of an inch (1/300") wide. To specify the line width for the Line tool in pixels, type a number between 0 and 1000. Because the Line tool can be set to a width as high as 1000 pixels, you may want to consider using the line tool to draw filled rectangles in some cases.

5. **Anti-aliased.** Click the Anti-aliased checkbox in the Line Tool Options palette to blend lines with the background image. Keep in mind, however, that a thin line may look fuzzy or out of focus with an Anti-aliased edge.

6. **Arrowheads.** The Line tool can draw lines with arrowheads on one or both sides of a line. Click the Start checkbox to put the arrowhead where you start drawing. Click the End checkbox to

put an arrowhead where you stop drawing. To edit the shape of the arrowhead, click the Shape button in the lower right corner of the Line Tool Palette to display the Arrowhead Shape dialog box (Figure 6.28). The following settings control the shape and size of the arrowheads:

◆ **Width**—The width value can range from 10 to 1,000 and represents a percentage of the line width. For example: If you specify an arrowhead width of 500%, the arrowhead will be five times larger than the width of the line.

◆ **Length**—The length value can range from 10 to 5,000 and represents a percentage of the line width. For example: If you specify an arrowhead length of 1000%, the arrowhead will be equal to ten times the width of the line.

◆ **Concavity**—The concavity value can range from -50% to +50% and determines where the line and the arrowhead meet. Think of the line as pushing or pulling the wall of the arrowhead to which it connects. When you set a positive value like 50%, the wall of the arrowhead is pushed toward the center of the arrowhead. When you set a negative value such as -50%, the wall of the arrow is pulled out from the center and look more like a diamond shape.

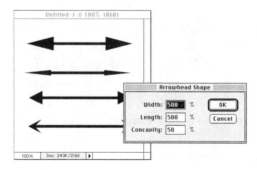

Figure 6.28

The Arrowhead Shape dialog box.

USING THE PENCIL TOOL

To use the Pencil tool, select the Pencil tool from the toolbox or type the letter "y," then click and drag in the canvas area. The Pencil tool is a freehand drawing tool that draws hard-edged lines. Only hard-edged

211

brushes are available for the Pencil tool. The Pencil tool changes the color of pixels as you drag through them, rather than painting color onto the image. Because the Pencil tool does not paint with an anti-aliased edge like the Paintbrush and Airbrush tools, it is ideal for changing the color of the image one pixel at a time or to simply paint without an anti-aliased edge.

Tip

To paint in a straight line with the Pencil tool, hold down the Shift key while dragging.

Setting the Pencil Options

The Pencil tool options affect the way the Pencil tool interacts with the pixels on the canvas. To set the Pencil options:

1. Double-click the Pencil tool in the toolbox to display the Pencil Options palette (Figure 6.29).

Figure 6.29

The Pencil Options palette.

2. **Select a Blending Mode.** The blending modes for the Pencil tool are available under a drop-down menu in the upper left corner of the Pencil palette. The blending modes affect the way the color of the area you are painting interacts with the underlying image. The available choices are detailed in the section on the Paintbrush tool in this chapter.

Note

The Blending Mode options are available under the context menu of the Pencil tool. On the Macintosh, hold down the Control key and click anywhere in the canvas area to display the context menu. In Windows, click in the canvas area with the right mouse button.

Tip

When using the Pencil tool, hold down the (Option)[Alt] key and click the image to sample a color from the image with the Eyedropper tool.

3. **Set the Opacity.** The opacity level of the Pencil tool can be set to a value from 1% to 100% by dragging the triangle slider in the upper right corner of the Pencil Options palette or by typing a number on the keyboard. Type a number from 0 through 9 to specify the opacity in 10% increments. Typing "1," for example, changes the opacity setting to 10%; typing a "0" changes the opacity to 100%. If you type the numbers quickly, you can type an exact percentage such as 33%.

4. **Set the Fade Rate.** To specify the fade-out rate for the Pencil tool, click the checkbox in the Pencil Options palette next to the word "Fade" and type in the number of steps in the fade. You can type a value from 1 to 9,999 for the fade steps, each step representing a single brush mark. Choose whether the line is to fade to transparency or the background color from the drop-down menu.

5. **Set the Stylus Pressure Options.** Photoshop supports the use of a variety of pressure-sensitive digitizing tablets. The three check-box items in the Pencil Options palette offer three methods to describe how applying pressure with the stylus affects the Pencil tool:

   ♦ **Size**—Click the Size checkbox if you want the size of the Pencil to increase when pressure is increased.

   ♦ **Color**—When the Color checkbox is selected, applying light pressure to the stylus paints with the background color; applying heavy pressure paints with the foreground color. Painting with medium pressure on the stylus results in a color between the foreground and background color.

   ♦ **Opacity**—Click the Opacity checkbox if you want the stylus pressure to affect the opacity of the color you are painting with. Light pressure results in a lower opacity, and high pressure results in a more opaque color.

6. **Auto Erase.** Click the Auto Erase checkbox in the Pencil Options palette to turn on Auto Erase. When you paint over a part of your image painted with the foreground color, the Pencil paints with the background color. When working on transparent layers, the Auto Erase function makes the pixels transparent instead of the background color.

USING THE ERASER TOOL

To use the Eraser tool, select the Eraser tool from the toolbox or type the letter "e" for eraser and click and drag in the canvas area. The Eraser tool changes the color of pixels as you drag over them, filling them with the background color on the background layer. When working on transparent layers, the Eraser tool erases to transparency. You can also set the Eraser tool to erase to the last saved version of a file.

Tip

To paint in a straight line with the Eraser tool, hold down the Shift key while dragging.

Setting the Eraser Options

One of the options for the Eraser tool is a tool drop-down menu where you choose the tool that will be used as the eraser tool. Each of the four tools available here (Paintbrush, Airbrush, Pencil and Block), have options in the Eraser Options palette that pertain specifically to the selected tool. To set the Eraser tool options:

1. Double-click the Eraser tool in the toolbox to display the Eraser Options palette (see Figure 6.30).

Figure 6.30

The Eraser Options palette.

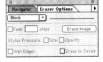

2. **Select a Tool**. There are four tools that can be used as Eraser tools available under a drop-down menu in the upper left corner of the Eraser palette (see Figure 6.31).

   ◆ **Paintbrush**—When using the Paintbrush, the Eraser tool works the same way as the Paintbrush tool with one exception: Blending modes are not available when using the Eraser tool because the Eraser tool cannot paint in the foreground color. See the section on the Paintbrush tool earlier in this chapter.

   ◆ **Airbrush**—When using the Airbrush as the Eraser tool, the available options for the Airbrush are displayed and it works like the Airbrush tool, with the exception of the blending modes. See the section on the Airbrush earlier in this chapter.

   ◆ **Pencil**—The Pencil Eraser tool works like the Pencil tool, except that the blending options are not available when it is used as the Eraser tool. See the section on the Pencil tool earlier in this chapter for further information.

   ◆ **Block**—The Block Eraser tool works like the Pencil tool with the following exception: The Block Eraser is always the same size, regardless of resolution. All of the other painting tool sizes are determined by pixel size, so the actual size of the brush is dependent on the resolution of the image. The Block Eraser is always the size of the cursor icon that represents it. If, for example, you zoom in to 1600% (Photoshop's maximum) and click with the Block Eraser, a single pixel is erased; zoom back out to 100% and click with the Eraser tool and an area 16 times larger is erased. The size of the area erased varies depending on the resolution of the image, but the size of the block never changes.

Figure 6.31

The Eraser tool list.

Note

The Eraser tool options are available under the context menu of the Eraser tool. Hold down the Control key and click anywhere in the canvas area to display the context menu for Macintosh, or simply click with the right mouse button for Windows.

Tip

You can cycle through the available Eraser tools in the drop-down list by (Option-clicking)[Alt-clicking] the Eraser tool in the toolbox or by typing the letter "e" on the keyboard.

3. **Set the Opacity or Pressure.** The opacity settings are available when you are using the Paintbrush or Pencil tool as an eraser tool in the Eraser palette. The pressure setting is available when using the Airbrush as an eraser tool. The opacity and pressure settings can be set to a value from 1% to 100% by dragging the triangle slider in the upper right corner of the Eraser Options palette or by typing a number on the keyboard. Type a number from 0 through 9 to specify the opacity or pressure in 10% increments. Type "6," for example, to change the opacity or pressure setting to 60%. If you type the numbers quickly, you can type an exact percentage like 61%.

4. **Set the Fade Rate.** To specify the fade-out rate for the Eraser tool, select the Paintbrush, Pencil, or Airbrush from the pull-down menu in the Eraser Options palette and click the Fade checkbox. Type in the number of steps in the fade. You can type a value from 1 to 9,999 for the fade steps; each step representing a single brush mark. The Eraser tool always fades from the background color to transparency on the background Layer and from transparency to 100% opacity on transparent layers.

5. **Set the Stylus Pressure Options.** The Stylus Pressure Options for the Eraser tool depend on the tool used as the Eraser tool. Size and Opacity are available for the Paintbrush, Pencil and Block tool; Size and Pressure are available for the Airbrush tool. The two checkbox items in the Eraser Options palette offer these methods to describe how applying pressure with the stylus affects the Eraser tool:

   ◆ **Size**—Click the Size checkbox if you want the size of the Eraser to increase when pressure is increased.

   ◆ **Opacity**—Click the Opacity checkbox if you want the stylus pressure to affect the opacity of the color you are painting with. Light pressure results in a lower opacity and high pressure results in a more opaque color.

   ◆ **Pressure**—Click the Pressure checkbox if you want to control the pressure setting with the stylus. Set the low pressure setting in the Eraser Options palette by dragging the triangle sliders for Pressure. Applying pressure with the stylus increases the pressure from this starting point up to 100%.

6. **Erase Image** and **Erase Layer.** Click the Erase Image button in the Eraser Options palette to erase the entire image and replace it with the background color. If you have layers in your image, this button changes to "Erase Layer" and erases the entire layer to transparency.

7. **The Magic Eraser.** Before you can use the Magic Eraser, the file must be saved. Click the Erase to Saved checkbox in the Eraser Options palette to turn on the Magic Eraser. This option is only available after you have made changes to a saved file. Painting with the Eraser tool with the Magic Eraser turned on restores the image from the saved version. When the Paintbrush, Airbrush or Pencil Eraser tools are used with Erase to Saved turned on, all of the options such as opacity, pressure and wet edges can be applied while restoring the image (see Figure 6.32).

Figure 6.32

The original image saved before using the Magic Eraser; the Magic Eraser used with the Paintbrush options in the Eraser Options palette; the Magic Eraser used with the Airbrush options in the Eraser Options palette.

Tip

You can hold down the (Option)[Alt] key when you are painting with any of the Eraser tools to activate the Magic Eraser (Erase to Saved).

8. **Wet Edges.** Wet Edges is only available when you are using the Paintbrush as the Eraser tool. In this case the erased effect builds up on the edges. The effect is like running a paintbrush through wet paint: the inside part of the brush paints with a reduced opacity and the edges of the brush become more and more opaque towards the edges. When you overlap, while painting with wet edges, the wet edges effect intersects the brush strokes, creating the effect of criss-crossing through wet paint with a paintbrush (see see Figure 6.33).

Figure 6.33

The Eraser tool with Wet Edges turned on.

USING THE PAINT BUCKET TOOL

The Paint Bucket tool combines the effects of the Magic Wand tool (see Chapter 5, "Selections, Paths, and Masks") and the Fill command (discussed later in this chapter). The Paint Bucket fills the pixel you click and adjacent pixels based on a Tolerance setting with either the foreground color or a defined pattern. To use the Paint Bucket tool, select the Paint Bucket tool from the toolbox or type the letter "k" for bucket.

Setting the Paint Bucket Options

The Paint Bucket options define how the Paint Bucket tool selects, then fills areas of an image. The Blending modes available in the drop-down menu in the upper left corner of the Paint Bucket Options palette and the Opacity settings in the upper right corner are the same as all the other painting tools described in this chapter. Refer to the section on the Paintbrush tool earlier in this chapter for details on the Blending modes and Opacity setting.

1. Double-click the Paint Bucket tool in the toolbox to display the Paint Bucket Options palette (see Figure 6.34).

Figure 6.34

The Paint Bucket Options palette.

2. **Tolerance.** The Tolerance setting requires a number from 0 to 255 and determines how close in gray level or color the adjacent pixels must be to the pixel you click. A setting of 0 (zero) selects only the adjacent pixels that have the exact same color value as the one you click when Anti-aliased is not turned on. When Anti-aliased is turned on, extra pixels are selected to smooth the edges of the selection. If you set the tolerance to 255, every pixel in the image is affected regardless of the pixel you click.

Tip

When using the Paint Bucket tool, start off with a relatively low number like 32 and see if you get all the pixels you want. Increase or decrease the value depending on how much of the area you want to select is actually affected.

3. **Contents Options.** There are two options for Contents, Foreground, and Pattern (see Figure 6.35). Choose foreground to fill with the foreground color and Pattern to fill with a predefined pattern. To define a pattern, drag a rectangular marquee around a portion of an image to use as a pattern and choose Define Pattern from the Edit menu.

Figure 6.35

The Paint Bucket Contents modes.

USING THE GRADIENT TOOL

The Gradient tool enables you to create a smooth blend between two or more colors. You can create either a linear blend, which blends in a straight line from one point to another, or a radial blend, which blends from the center of a circle out to a point you specify in all directions. Note that the Gradient tool is not available for bitmapped or indexed-color images. To use the Gradient tool, select the Gradient tool from the toolbox or type the letter "g" for **gradient**.

Note

The Gradient tool now supports linear and radial gradients of multiple colors and varying opacities. You can specify precisely what colors to use in the blend and have as many transitions as you like. After you have created custom gradients, you can save them by clicking the Save button in the Gradient Editor dialog box and reopen them on either the Macintosh or Windows platform by clicking the Open button in the Gradient Editor dialog box.

Creating a Linear Blend

Linear Blends follow a straight path you determine. Linear blends can run horizontally, vertically, or at any angle. Linear blends are drawn by selecting a starting point for the blend and dragging to an ending point.

1. Select the part of your image you want to fill with a linear gradient. If you do not create a selection, the entire image area is filled.

2. Double-click the Gradient tool in the toolbox to display the Gradient Tool Options (see Figure 6.36).

Figure 6.36

The Gradient Tool Options palette.

3. Select the type of Gradient you want from the Gradient pull-down menu in the Gradient Tool Options palette (see Figure 6.37).

Figure 6.37

There are a number of Gradient fill options in the Gradient pull-down menu.

4. Select Linear from the Type pull-down menu in the Gradient Tool Options palette.

5. Click the Mask checkbox if you want to turn on the transparency mask for the gradient fill (see "Editing the Transparency Mask" later in this section for information on the transparency mask).

6. Click the Dither checkbox to create a smoother blend with less chance of apparent banding.

7. Point and click the image where you want to begin the blend and drag to the point where you want to end and let go of the mouse button (see Figure 6.38). If you hold down the Shift key while dragging you can constrain the blend to a straight line or 45° increments.

Figure 6.38

Click a starting point and drag to the ending point with the Gradient tool.

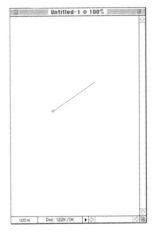 

Note

When you click and drag to create a gradient fill, the image area (or selected area) before the point you start dragging is filled with the first color, and the point after the point you stop is filled with the second color, depending on what option you choose from the Gradient drop-down menu. In other words, the blend only happens between the starting and ending points. If you have an image area that is 4 inches wide, for example, and you start a foreground to background blend at 1 inch and end the blend at 3 inches, the area between 0 (zero) and 1 inch is filled with the solid foreground color and the area between 3 inches and 4 inches is filled with the solid background color. Note the starting and ending points in Figure 6.38 and the resulting blend.

Creating a Radial Blend

A Radial blend radiates out from a center point you define. To create a radial blend, click the proposed center point and drag a straight line to define the radius.

1. Select the part of your image you want to fill with a radial gradient. If you do not create a selection, the entire image area will be filled.

2. Double-click the Gradient tool in the toolbox to display the Gradient Tool Options.

3. Select the type of Gradient you want from the Gradient drop-down menu in the Gradient Tool Options palette.

4. Select Radial from the Type pull-down menu in the Gradient Tool Options palette.

5. Click the Mask checkbox if you want to turn on the transparency mask for the gradient fill (See "Editing the Transparency Mask" later in this section).

6. Click the Dither checkbox to create a smoother blend with less chance of apparent banding.

7. Point and click the image where you want the center of your radial blend to begin and drag to the point you want to end and let go of the mouse button (Figure 6.39).

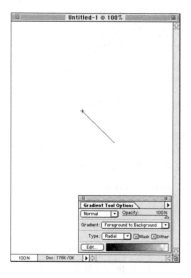 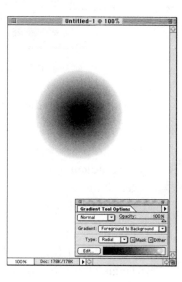

Figure 6.39

Click a starting point for the center of the radial fill and drag to the ending point (diameter) with the Gradient tool.

223

Note

When you click and drag to create a radial gradient fill, the image area after the point you stop is filled with the second color, depending on what option you choose from the Gradient drop-down menu.

Creating and Editing the Gradient Fill Type

You can edit a gradient fill type or create one of your own by clicking on the Edit button in the lower left corner of the Gradient Tool Options palette. To create or edit a gradient fill:

1. Click the Edit button in the Gradient Tool Options palette to display the Gradient Editor dialog box (see Figure 6.40).

Figure 6.40

The Gradient Editor dialog box.

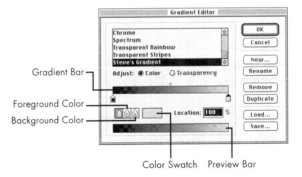

2. Select the Color radio button next to the word Adjust in the Gradient Editor dialog box.

3. To create a new gradient fill click the New button and give your gradient a name (Figure 6.41); to edit an existing gradient, select it in the scroll list. If you want to create a duplicate of an existing gradient and edit it, select it in the list and click Duplicate to give it a new name.

4. Click the far left box under the gradient bar. Notice that the triangle above the box turns black to indicate that this is the part of the gradient you are modifying (Figure 6.42).

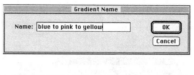

Figure 6.41

Give your new gradient a descriptive name.

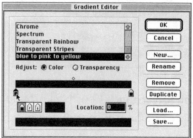

Figure 6.42

Click the left box under the gradient bar to define the start color of the gradient.

5. Select the starting color by doing one of the following:

◆ Click the Color Swatch in the Gradient Editor dialog box and select a color using the Photoshop Color Picker (Figure 6.43).

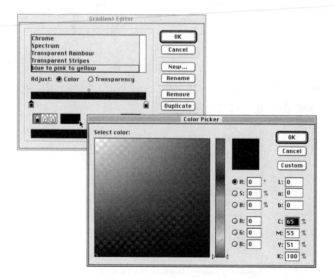

Figure 6.43

Click the Color Swatch to display the color picker.

◆ Position the cursor over the gradient bar and click with the eyedropper cursor to select a color in the gradient (Figure 6.44).

Figure 6.44

Click the gradient bar to choose a color.

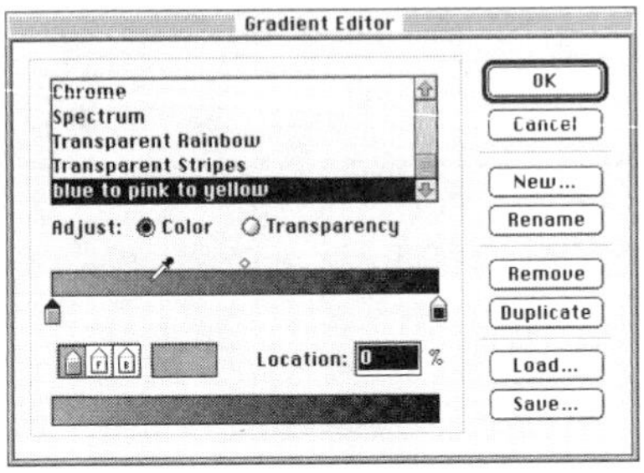

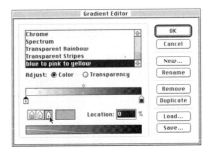

♦ Click the foreground (F) or background (B) color selection icon in the Gradient Editor dialog box (Figure 6.45).

Figure 6.45

Click the foreground or background icons to select a color.

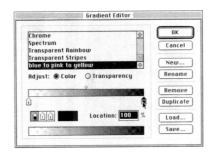

6. Define the ending color by clicking the far right square below the gradient bar (Figure 6.46) and choose from the options described in step 5.

Figure 6.46a

Click the right box under the gradient bar to define the end color of the gradient.

Figure 6.46b

A linear gradient from 0% to 100% with the midpoint of the gradient at 50% of the width of the gradient.

Figure 6.46c

A radial gradient from 0% to 100% with the midpoint of the gradient at 50% of the width of the gradient.

7. To adjust the starting point of the blend, click and drag the far left box under the gradient bar or type a location in the Location box that defines at what percent of the gradient length the color begins to blend (Figure 6.47).

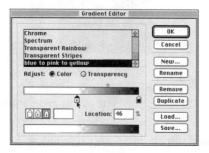

Figure 6.47

Change the starting point of the gradient.

8. To adjust the ending point of the blend, click and drag the far right box under the gradient bar or type a location in the Location box that defines at what percent of the gradient length the color stops blending (Figure 6.48).

Figure 6.48a

Change the ending point of the gradient.

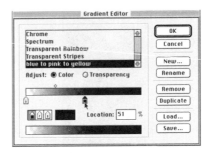

Figure 6.48b

A linear gradient from 100% to 0% that starts at 30% of the gradient width and ends at 70%. Note that the left 30% of the image area is filled with 100% black and the right 30% is filled with 0% black.

Figure 6.48c

A radial gradient from 100% to 0% that starts at 30% and ends at 70%. Note that the center of the blend starts at 30% and the radial bands end at 70%; 30% short of the outside edges of the image.

9. To adjust the midpoint of the gradient, click and drag the diamond above the gradient bar or type a percentage in the Location box that defines where the midpoint is in relation to the starting and ending points (see Figure 6.49a through Figure 6.49c). Note that when you change the starting and ending points, the midpoint stays constant relative to the start and end positions.

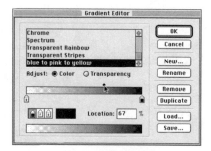

Figure 6.49a

Click and drag the diamond above the gradient bar to set the midpoint color.

Figure 6.49b

A linear gradient from 0% to 100% with the midpoint of the gradient at 75% of the width of the gradient.

Figure 6.49c

A radial gradient from 0% to 100% with the midpoint of the gradient at 75% of the width of the gradient.

10. To add intermediate colors between the starting and ending points, click in the space under the gradient bar and define the colors. Note that midpoint diamonds appear above the gradient bar between each set of defined points. See Figure 6.50a through 6.50c.

Figure 6.50a

Add intermediate colors that have their own midpoints.

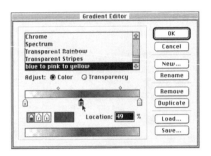

Figure 6.50b

A linear gradient that blends from 100% to 30% to 70% to 100%.

Figure 6.50c

A radial gradient that blends from 100% to 30% to 70% to 100%.

11. To remove any of the intermediate color points, click the box and drag it down and away from the gradient bar (Figure 6.51).

Figure 6.51

Drag away the intermediate color boxes under the gradient bar to remove them.

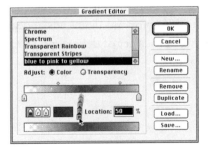

12. When you're happy with your new blend, click the OK button.

Editing the Transparency Mask

Gradient fills contain a transparency mask that determines the transparency of the fill at given points. The default transparency mask is set to 100% opacity, but you can change that by clicking on the Transparency radio button in the Gradient Editor dialog box (Figure 6.52). The transparency mask can be turned off in the Gradient Tool Options palette. Perform the following steps to adjust the transparency mask:

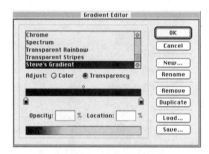

Figure 6.52

The Transparency options in the Gradient Editor dialog box.

1. Click the Transparency radio button for Adjust in the Gradient Editor dialog box.

2. Click the far left box under the gradient bar to adjust the starting opacity.

3. Type in an Opacity value and the starting Location percentage.

4. Click the far right box under the gradient bar to adjust the ending opacity.

5. Type in an Opacity value and the ending Location percentage.

6. To adjust the midpoint of the gradient, click the diamond above the gradient bar and set the midpoint Location.

7. Create intermediate transparency points by clicking under the gradient bar and setting the appropriate values.

8. You can preview the effect of the mask on the gradient bar at the bottom of the Gradient Editor dialog box. Click OK if you're done or select the Color radio button to perform further adjustments to the color values (see Figure 6.53a through 6.53c).

Tip

Save the gradient fills you define by clicking the Save button in the Gradient Editor dialog box. This is particularly important if you must delete the preferences files for Photoshop at some point because that's where the gradient fills are currently stored. Click the Load button to load saved gradient fills.

Figure 6.53a

The original image.

Figure 6.53b

Transparency to Foreground linear gradient drawn from the bottom of the image up using a foreground color of 50% black.

Figure 6.53c

Transparency to Foreground radial gradient drawn from the center out using a foreground color of 100% black.

FILLING SELECTIONS AND LAYERS

The Fill command enables you to fill selected areas or the entire image area with colors, patterns or from the saved image. Choose Fill from the Edit menu to display the Fill dialog box (Figure 6.54).

Figure 6.54

The Fill dialog box.

Select the type of fill to use from the Use drop-down menu in the Fill dialog box (Figure 6.55). The options for fill type are:

◆ **Foreground Color** fills with the foreground color.

◆ **Background Color** fills with the background color.

◆ **Pattern** fills with a pattern that you define. To define a pattern, simply drag a marquee around a rectangular portion of an image and choose Edit➡Define Pattern.

◆ **Saved** fills with the last saved version of the file. If you have a portion of the image selected, that portion will be filled from the saved file.

- **Snapshot** fills with a snapshot of the image that you previously captured. To capture a snapshot of the image, choose Edit➡Take Snapshot at any point while editing an image to enable you to return to that stage in the editing process.
- **Black** fills with 100% black.
- **50% Gray** fills with 50% black.
- **White** fills with white (0% black).

From the Blending Mode options in the Fill dialog box, select the opacity for the fill and choose a Blending mode from the Mode drop-down menu. The preserve transparency option is available when you are applying a fill to a transparent layer.

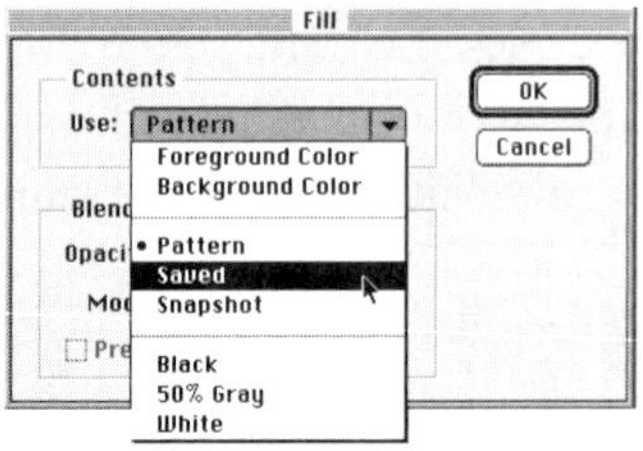

Figure 6.55

The Contents options in the Fill dialog box.

You can also fill with the foreground or background color using shortcut key combinations.

- To fill with the background color when on the background layer, select an area and press (Delete)[Backspace]. These keystrokes delete to transparency on a transparent layer.
- To fill with the background color when on a transparent layer, press (Command-Delete)[Control-Backspace].
- To fill with the foreground color, press (Option-Delete)[Alt-Backspace].
- To preserve the transparency and fill only the non-transparent pixels with the foreground color when on a transparent layer, press (Option-Shift-Delete)[Alt-Shift-Backspace].

◆ To preserve the transparency and fill only the non-transparent pixels with the background color when on a transparent layer, press (Command-Shift-Delete)[Control-Shift-Backspace].

◆ To display the Fill dialog box, press (Shift-Delete)[Shift-Backspace].

STROKING A SELECTION

You can specify a stroke with the foreground color to paint the border of a selection. To specify a stroke, perform the following steps:

1. Create a selection in your image to stroke.

2. Choose Stroke from the Edit menu to display the Stroke dialog box (Figure 6.56).

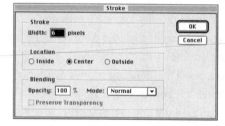

Figure 6.56

The Stroke dialog box.

3. Type in a width value from 1 to 16 pixels.

4. Select the Location of the stroke. Choose Inside to stroke inside the selection area, Center to center the stroke on the selection marquee, or Outside to stroke outside the selection area (Figure 6.57).

5. Enter an Opacity value in the Opacity box.

6. Choose a Blending Mode from the Mode drop-down menu in the Stroke dialog box. Preserve Transparency is available when you are on a transparent layer.

Figure 6.57

Stroke applied with the Inside option; Stroke applied with the Outside option; Stroke applied with the Center option.

USING THE SMUDGE TOOL

The Smudge tool (represented by the finger icon in the toolbox) simulates dragging your finger through wet paint. The point at which you start dragging smears the existing image pixels in the direction of the point you end up at. To use the Smudge tool, select the Smudge tool from the toolbox or type the letter "u" for smudge; click and drag an existing image to apply the smudge effect.

The Smudge Tool Options palette contains a limited number of blending modes and a triangel slider to control the pressure. The finger painting option enables you to paint with a color while applying the smudge tool effects. The Blending modes available in the drop-down menu in the upper left corner of the Smudge Tool Options palette and the Pressure settings in the upper right corner are the same as those used for the Airbrush tool described earlier in this chapter. To set the Smudge Tool options:

1. Double-click the Smudge tool in the toolbox to display the Smudge Tool Options palette (Figure 6.58).

Figure 6.58

There are a limited number of Blending modes available for the Smudge tool.

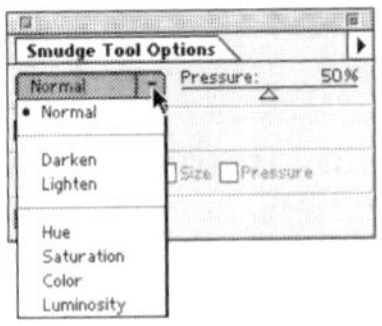

Note

The Blending Options for the Smudge tool are available under the context menu when using the Smudge tool. Hold down the Control key and click

anywhere in the canvas area on the Macintosh to display the context menu.
Click the canvas area with the right mouse button when using Windows to
display the context menu.

2. Click the image and drag in the direction you want to smear
   the image (Figure 6.59).

Figure 6.59

The Smudge tool effect with a
100 pixel soft brush.

3. **Finger Painting.** When you click the Finger Painting checkbox in
   the Smudge Tool Options palette, the point at which you begin
   dragging smudges using the foreground color (Figure 6.60).

Figure 6.60

The Smudge tool with a 100
pixel soft brush and Finger
Painting turned on.

Tip

Hold down the Option key (Macintosh); Alt key (Windows) as you drag with the Smudge tool to activate the Finger Painting option.

4. **Stylus Pressure.** Size and Pressure are the two options for Stylus Pressure in the Smudge Tool Options palette. The two checkbox items in the Smudge Tool Options palette offer these methods to describe how applying pressure with the stylus affects the way the Smudge tool works:

◆ **Size**—Click the Size checkbox if you want the size of the Smudge tool's brush to increase when pressure is increased.

◆ **Pressure**—Click the Pressure checkbox if you want to control the pressure setting with the stylus. Set the low pressure setting in the Smudge Tool Options palette by dragging the triangle sliders for Pressure. Applying pressure with the stylus increases the pressure from this starting point up to 100%.

5. **Sample Merged.** When you click the Sample Merged checkbox in the Smudge Tool Options palette, the Smudge tool affects the current layer and all layers (including the background layer) beneath it.

Note

The Smudge tool is not available in bitmapped or indexed-color images because a full range of gray levels must be available for the Smudge tool to work.

PAINTING INTO LINE ART

Painting into black and white line art is relatively simple because the white areas of the image can be isolated using the Darken blending mode. The Darken blending mode enables you to paint with a color and affect only the image areas that are lighter in gray value than the color you are painting with. In the case of line are, the black lines are always darker than the color you are painting with, unless you are painting with black. To paint color into line art:

1. Import, scan or create some black and white line art.

2. Choose a color mode (RGB or CMYK) from the Mode submenu under the Image menu. If you are starting off with a Bitmap image, you must convert to Grayscale mode before you specify a Color mode. See Chapter 10, "Working with Color Images," for information about switching color modes.

3. Click a color in the Swatches palette to load it as the foreground color.

4. Double-click the Paintbrush tool in the toolbox to display the Paintbrush Options palette.

5. Choose Show Brushes from the Window menu and choose a brush to paint with. If the Brushes palette is in the same palette group as the Swatches palette, click the palette tab and separate the brushes palette from the group.

6. Choose Darken from the Blending Mode options in the Paintbrush Options palette (Figure 6.61).

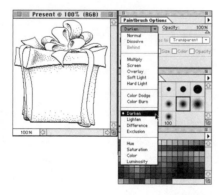

Figure 6.61

Select Darken from the Blending Mode options list.

7. Click the Wet Edges checkbox if you want to paint with a watercolor effect.

8. Paint on the image to apply color. You can paint right over the black lines if you want because the Darken mode only applies color to areas lighter than the color selected.

9. Try some of the other painting tools covered in this chapter. If your line art has connected lines you should get good results with the Paint Bucket tool with a low tolerance setting.

10. If you want to apply paint on different layers, turn on the Darken mode in the Layers palette drop-down menu. Be sure to click the Sample Merged button if you want to affect all the underlying layers with the painting tools.

Figure 6.62

Completed example of painting in line art.

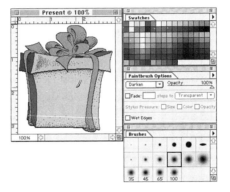

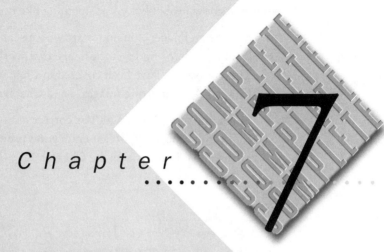

Chapter

EDITING IMAGES

Like Janus, the Roman god of doorways and gates, Photoshop has two faces. For artists, it's a powerful tool to create original artwork. For photographers and production types, it's an image editor used for editing and retouching existing artwork and scans. And many Photoshop users maintain that image editing is where the program truly shines.

Your workflow probably looks something like this:

◆ Acquire an image: You may start with a scan, create an image from scratch, or find a stock image that works for your project. These processes have been covered in Chapter 3, "Scanning"; Chapter 4, "Importing Images"; and Chapter 6, "Painting."

◆ Adjust the image's tones and/or correct its color: Hardware calibration, the ability to generate good proofs, and a good eye are essential in this stage; see Chapter 11, "Color Correction."

Tip

Extensis Corp.'s Intellihance plug-in can save you time if you do a lot of retouching. With Intellihance you can apply a Despeckle filter and adjust contrast, brightness, saturation, and sharpness, all in one dialog box. While the plug-in doesn't customize your settings for these operations, its convenience stems from the fact that all these operations—commonly needed with scanned photos—are available in one place and can be applied simultaneously.

◆ Remove defects and manipulate the image: That's what this chapter is about. Scanned and stock images have imperfections that need to be corrected before the images are suitable for reproduction—that's like the proofreading component of editing text—and the structure of the image can be altered in a number of ways. You can move and reshape portions of an image, combine it with parts of other images, remove or downplay elements you don't want, and highlight elements you like.

Photoshop offers several ways to push pixels around in the broad categories of tools, transformations, and filters. With so many functions, there's more than one way to accomplish any task, so you're able to pick the best technique to use in any situation. Removing dust, dirt, and scratches from a scan, for example, can be done with the Dust & Scratches filter, with the Rubber Stamp tool, or with the Airbrush. Each method has disadvantages: the Dust & Scratches filter can blur details; the Rubber Stamp can create a repetitive look; and the Airbrush only works well with a firm hand and in areas of smooth color. Which way you go depends on the image in question, your abilities, and the intended use of the image.

The important thing to remember is to be subtle—sure, you can edit out whole people or buildings with Photoshop, but is it appropriate to do so? Will the results look too fake? With care and a light touch, though, almost any image can be edited into something better than the original.

VIEWING IMAGES

Before you can edit an image, you need to be able to see all of it. Photoshop provides several ways to accomplish this.

Photoshop can display images at any percentage of their actual size between 0.54 and 1600 percent. To change view percentages, use one of these methods:

◆ Choose the Zoom In or Zoom Out command from the View menu to view the image at the next higher or lower percentage in this list of preset sizes: 0.54%, 0.7%, 1%, 1.5%, 2%, 3%, 4%, 5%, 6.25%, 8.33%, 12.5%, 16.67%, 25%, 33.33%, 50%, 66.67%, 100%, 200%, 300%, 400%, 500%, 600%, 700%, 800%, 1200%, and 1600%.

◆ Choose the Zoom tool (shown below) and click to move to the next higher zoom level in the earlier list, or (Option-click)[Alt-click] to switch to the next lower level in the list.

◆ Choose the Zoom tool, click, and drag in the image to define an area to be viewed. Photoshop zooms in or out to show the entire defined area in the window.

◆ Double-click in the view percentage field in the lower-left corner of the image window, type in a new percentage, and press Return.

◆ Double-click the Zoom tool in the toolbox to return to 100% view.

As in many graphics applications, Photoshop provides a Hand tool to let you move the image around in its window so that you can view different portions of it. To use the Hand tool (shown below), choose it from the toolbox or hold down the space bar while any other tool is active. Then click and drag to move the image. The Hand cursor changes to a closed fist as you drag, signifying that you're holding onto the image to move it.

While the Hand tool and the Zoom tool are useful, they're not always the best options for navigating images. A lot of editing work requires constant zooming in and out to view changes at different sizes, and moving all the way from one end of an image to the other using the Hand tool can be more than just tedious. Photoshop 4.0 provides an easy way to control your view of an image: the Navigator palette (see Figure 7.1).

Figure 7.1

The Navigator palette controls both view percentages and what area of an image appears in the image window.

Three of the Navigator palette's four controls affect zoom percentage.

◆ The zoom percentage field in the lower-left corner of the palette shows the current view. Double-click it to enter a new percentage: type in a number and press (Return)[Enter]—no need to add a percentage sign.

◆ The slider at the bottom of the palette also controls the view percentage; move it to the right or left to zoom in or out. The image changes magnification as you move the slider; release it when you reach the desired magnification.

◆ Click the Zoom In and Zoom out buttons on either side of the slider to zoom in and out based on Photoshop's preset percentages, listed earlier.

The main part of the Navigator palette contains a thumbnail view of the image, with a red rectangle (called a view box) representing the area of the image visible in the image window. To view a different area of the image, click and drag the view box to another area of the thumbnail. To change the magnification using the thumbnail, hold down the (Command)[Control] key as you click and drag in the thumbnail.

If the red color of the view box is difficult to see in your image, you can change the color by choosing Palette Options from the Navigator palette menu (see Figure 7.2). The Palette Options dialog box enables you to choose another color from a pop-up menu; if you want to define your own color, choose Custom from the pop-up menu to bring up the color picker.

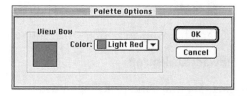

Figure 7.2

You can use any color for the Navigator palette's view box.

RETOUCHING IMAGES

There are many reasons to retouch an image in Photoshop: to eliminate distracting elements; to remove blemishes in the original photo; to focus attention on some elements and downplay others; and to improve image quality and make up for flaws introduced in the process of scanning the image. Some images don't need retouching, and it's always difficult to resist the temptation to mess around just because we can—Photoshop makes it so easy to tweak. But when there's a good reason to make judicious edits in an image, that's exactly what they should be—judicious. Keep your goal for an image in mind—if it's supposed to end up looking like a good photograph, then your edits shouldn't be detectable when you're done and the image is reproduced.

Tip

If you're the conservative type, you may want to do all your retouching on a separate layer from the original image, or even several layers. That way, you can always change your mind! This approach is made even easier by Photoshop 4.0's heavy use of layers. Every time you paste, for example, a new layer is created to hold the pasted selection.

There are two basic approaches to image processing, and which you use depends on your situation. In high-volume, limited-time situations, you'll be using batch techniques and won't have time to edit individual images much. When you do have the time, though, you can accomplish near-miracles in Photoshop using a wide variety of techniques. These include:

- Rubber stamp cloning

- Copying from undamaged or unobstructed areas and pasting over undesirable image elements

- Dodging and burning to lighten or darken details

- Sharpening and blurring areas of varying interest

- Erasing unwanted elements

- Airbrushing, painting, and penciling in details and tones

- Smudging

- Blending transitions (such as edges of pasted selections) with painting tools

Tip

When you're working on fine details of an image, it helps to have two windows displaying different views of the image: one at a high magnification to work on, and the other zoomed out so you can see the overall effects of your changes.

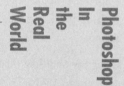

Working with Damaged Originals

Photos that are physically damaged—wrinkled or ripped—can cause shadows in the scanned image. The answer to this is to scan the photo twice, from different angles, and composite the two images to eliminate unwanted shadows.

1. Scan the photo.

2. Rotate it exactly 180 degrees and scan it again (it helps to attach it to a book or other heavy object with straight sides).

3. In Photoshop, open both images, rotate the upside-down one 180 degrees, and place it as a second layer in the same file as the right-side up image, with the layer's transparency set to 50%.

4. Move the second layer until it's perfectly aligned with the first, and flatten the image.

TURNING TO THE TOOLBOX

Photoshop tools are generally divided into two groups: painting tools and editing tools. This division can be useful, but there's some overlap. In particular, every tool can be used in some way when you're retouching an image.

Two tools that are nominally painting tools but come in quite handy when editing are the Eraser tool and the Rubber Stamp. Those tools actually considered as editing tools are the Smudge tool, the focus tools (Blur and Sharpen), and the toning tools (Dodge, Burn, and Sponge).

But I Can't Even Draw a Straight Line

Anyone can draw a straight line with any tool if you hold down the shift key as you drag—and that includes the editing tools covered in this chapter, such as the Eraser and the Rubber Stamp.

Using the Shift key results in vertical or horizontal lines. To draw a straight line between any two points, click and then shift-click where you want the line to end.

You can also use any tool along a curve or complex outline:

1. Create a path using the Pen tool, along the line where you want to apply the selected tool.

2. In the toolbox, select the tool you will be using when you stroke the path. (Choices are Pencil, Paintbrush, Airbrush, Eraser, Stamp, Smudge, Blur, Sharpen, Dodge, Burn, or Sponge.) Make sure its settings are specified as you want them.

3. Choose "Stroke Path" from the Paths palette menu or option- or alt-click the Stroke Path button at the bottom of the Paths palette.

Tip

When editing small areas of an image, you can use a frisket (a reversed mask) to keep your edits confined to the area you want to work on. Make friskets with the Marquee tool, the Lasso, the Pen, or QuickMask—whichever is best for the shape of the area you're working on. See Chapter 5 for more information on creating and editing selections.

Using the Eraser Tool

While at first it looks just like the plain square eraser found in any paint program, Photoshop's Eraser tool has hidden talents.

Its first function is to paint the background color over the existing image—not just white, but whatever color you've selected as the back-ground color in the toolbox. If you're working on a layer, using the Eraser creates areas of transparency (if you want the Eraser to reveal the background color on a layer, check "Preserve Trans-parency" on the Layers palette). And if you hold down (Option)[Alt] as you erase, the Eraser reveals the image as it looked the last time you saved—that's the "magic eraser."

Tip

In well-designed software, there's always a quicker way to choose a tool or change an option. In Photoshop, you can select the Eraser tool by pressing the "E" key, and hitting "E" again cycles through the different Eraser styles. You can also change Eraser styles by (Option-clicking)[Alt-clicking] the Eraser in the toolbox. The Eraser Options panel displays the Eraser style just as though you'd selected from the menu.

Whether you're using the regular Eraser or the magic one, you have a lot of control over how it works.

1. Double-clicking the Eraser tool, as with any tool, brings up a palette of options for that tool (see Figure 7.3). In this case, you can choose from four styles: block (16 screen pixels square), paintbrush, airbrush, or pencil. Each of these works just as you would expect, and you can use the Brushes panel of this palette to choose a brush size.

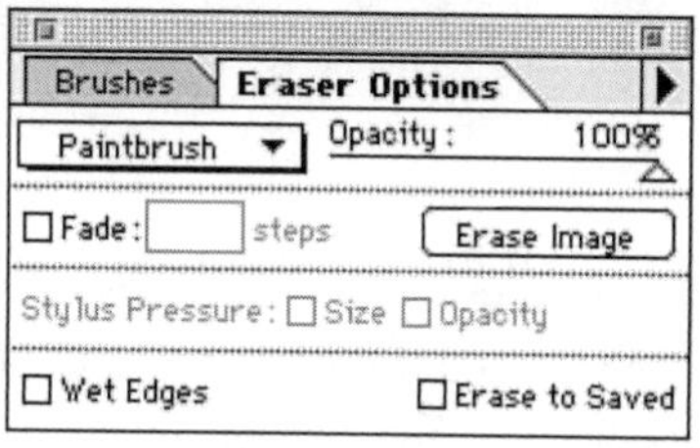

4. If you skipped Step 2, select a tool now from the pop-up menu in the Stroke Path dialog box (but you won't be able to change its settings).

5. Click OK.

Figure 7.3

The Eraser Options panel.

2. Select the opacity you want.

   The Opacity slider determines how strong the effects of the Eraser are; at 100%, you'll erase everything you drag over with the Eraser tool, while at lower percentages some of the image remains after you erase.

3. Turn Fade on or off.

   Checking the Fade box makes your strokes fade out after a certain number of steps, which you can specify.

4. Turn Wet Edges on or off.

   The Wet Edges option makes the eraser stroke more opaque at the edges than in the middle, just as it makes a paint stroke thicker at the edges (see Figure 7.4).

The left-hand stroke shows erasing with Wet Edges turned on; the right-hand stroke was made with Wet Edges turned off.

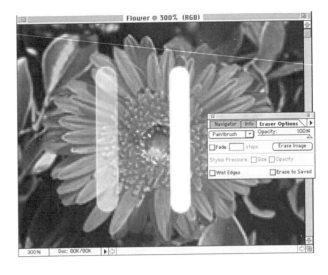

5. Select Erase to Saved to use the "magic eraser."

   If this option is checked, holding down the (Option)[Alt] key while you erase reveals the background color rather than the saved image (see Figure 7.5).

Figure 7.5

The eraser stroke through the top of the monkey's tail was made with 100% opacity, erasing all the way to the white background; the stroke through the base of the tail was made with 50% opacity, so the image is only half erased in this area. The stroke through the monkey's body was made with 100% opacity and a Fade setting of 20 steps, so it starts out erasing all the pixels and ends up erasing none.

Tip

It takes a minute for Photoshop to react the first time you use the magic eraser after saving because the saved image has to be loaded into memory.

To make sure the Eraser works in real-time—in other words, that you're not dragging it around and not seeing any results—(Option-click)[Alt-click] with the Eraser inside the image and wait for the saved image to load.

6. If you're using a graphics tablet with a pressure sensitive stylus, you can control what aspect of your Eraser strokes vary with pressure—the width of the stroke (Size), the opacity, or both.

7. The Erase Image button erases the entire image and reveals the background color.

8. Click once to erase a single spot—it is a square if the block option is selected and shaped like the selected brush shape if the paintbrush, airbrush, or pencil option is selected. Click and drag to erase larger areas.

Erasing on Layers

The Eraser tool works slightly differently if you're working on a layer. In that case, only the parts of the image that exist on that layer are erased. How this is handled depends on whether you've selected Preserve Transparency on the Layers palette. If Preserve Transparency is checked, the Eraser reveals the background color. If it's *not* checked, the Eraser reveals the image below—replacing the erased pixels with transparent ones (see Figure 7.6).

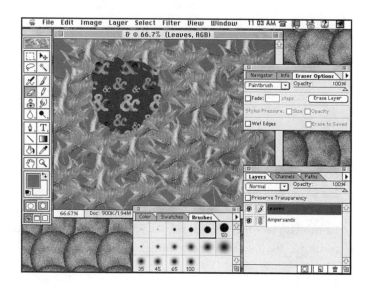

Figure 7.6

The ampersands are on one layer and the leaves are on another, so erasing the leaves allows the layer behind to show through.

If you're working in layers, notice another difference in how the Eraser works: The Erase Image button turns into an Erase Layer button and only erases the current layer.

Tip

Along with the painting tools, the Eraser can be applied around the perimeter of a path (like a stroke) by choosing the eraser from the toolbox while a path is selected and hitting (Return)[Enter] key. By doing this, you're stroking the path with the background color rather than the foreground color.

Using the Rubber Stamp Tool

Beloved of Photoshop novices, the Rubber Stamp is the tool that enables you to put an extra nose in the middle of someone's forehead. More technically called a cloning brush, this tool samples from a set point in an image (designated by (Option-clicking)[Alt-clicking]) and duplicates those pixels at another place in that image or in another one. You can choose the Rubber Stamp tool in the toolbox by hitting the "S" key.

1. Double-clicking the Rubber Stamp tool brings up an options palette (see Figure 7.7).

Figure 7.7

The Rubber Stamp Options panel.

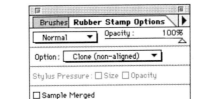

2. Select a paint mode.

Because the Rubber Stamp is considered a paint tool, unlike the Eraser, it can use brush modes such as Dissolve, Overlay, and Hue. These options work just as they would if you were using a Paintbrush or other tool to paint over the image; see Chapter 6 for more discussion of brush modes.

3. Set an opacity percentage.

4. Determine whether you want to sample from just the active layer or from all visible layers (Sample Merged). If you want to sample from more than one layer, but not all layers, hide the ones you don't want to use by clicking the eye icon in the Layers palette.

5. From the Option pull-down menu, choose one of several ways the Rubber Stamp tool can operate:

   ◆ Clone (aligned): After your reference point is selected, the Rubber Stamp creates a duplicate of the image anywhere else you start painting, expanding the duplicated portion of the image as you go. You can use as many "strokes" as you like, and even change brush size.

   ◆ Clone (non-aligned): After you choose a reference point and start to paint, the duplicate portion of the image is only expanded as long as you hold your mouse button down. If you let up and then start painting again, another duplicate appears starting over from your reference point.

   ◆ Pattern (aligned): If you define a pattern, you can apply it with the Rubber Stamp tool; it is tiled over the area as you paint. To define a pattern: Using the rectangular marquee, select an image or a portion of an image. Then choose Define Pattern from the Edit menu.

Note

Because Photoshop can only store one pattern at a time, and it only stores a pattern until you quit the program. Save patterns you want to use again as separate files.

   ◆ Pattern (non-aligned): This option works the same as Pattern (aligned), but the pattern starts over again each time you let up on the mouse button and then start painting again.

◆ From Snapshot: If you've taken a Snapshot of your image, choosing this option reveals the Snapshot as you paint. To take a Snapshot:

1. Display all the layers you want included in the Snapshot.

2. Make any changes to the image that you want to be reflected in the Snapshot. This isn't required to take a Snapshot—erasing to a Snapshot is just a handy way to apply changes selectively.

3. Choose Take Snapshot from the Edit menu.

4. If you want to apply the changes selectively, undo to restore the image to its previous state, and then use the Rubber Stamp to apply the changes where you want them.

◆ From Saved: This works just like the magic eraser—where you paint, the image reverts to the way it appeared the last time you saved.

◆ Impressionist: With this option, the last-saved version of the image is retrieved and repainted in a smeared, vaguely Impressionist fashion. The lower the spacing value (set individually for each brush), the more impressionistic the effect (see Figure 7.8).

6. If you have a graphic tablet installed, you can also select whether stylus pressure affects the size of the stamp, its opacity, or both. This option is grayed out if you don't have a graphics tablet installed.

7. Choose a brush shape and size from the Brushes palette.

8. Hold down the (Option)[Alt] key and click to choose the point from which Photoshop copies—the source point.

9. Click or click and drag at the point in the image where you want to insert the cloned pixels.

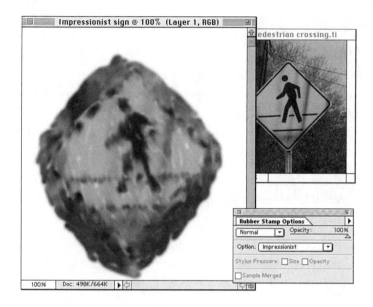

Figure 7.8

The Rubber Stamp tool's
Impressionist option makes for
some interesting effects, but it
would be more useful if you
could control the amount of
"impressionizing" that takes
place.

Figure 7.9

The Rubber Stamp cursor (left)
changes when you hold down
the (Option)[Alt] key to select
the area from which you want
to clone (right).

Retouching with the Rubber Stamp Tool

Not every Photoshop project involves creating a work of art; there are plenty of times when you're simply retouching a not-so-great scan. For this kind of work, the Rubber Stamp is just what you need.

Removing hickeys and blemishes from scanned photos is easy, though pretty tedious. While the Dust & Scratches filter can eliminate many blemishes, it works by blurring the pixels and can blur image details you want to keep, too. With the Rubber Stamp tool, if you're careful and go slowly, the edits can be undetectable.

Tip

Because the Rubber Stamp can use another window as a source point, you can clone pixels from another image or from another window showing the same image. If the area you're cloning from is too far away from your destination to fit on your monitor at the same time, open a new window to display the source area.

1. Choose an appropriate brush shape and size: hard-edged for small blemishes, soft-edged for larger or longer ones. Make the size just a bit larger than the biggest object you'll be removing.

2. Press the Caps Lock key to change the cursor to a crosshair that won't block out the pixels you're working on. (This step is optional, but it makes things a lot easier.)

3. (Option-click)[Alt-click] a portion of the image that matches the surroundings of a blemish, and then click the blemish. Don't click and drag—your changes blend in better this way. For larger blemishes, you may have to click several times. Notice that a crosshairs shows up at the point you sampled from and moves in concert with the mouse cursor to show where you're sampling from.

4. Make sure the edit doesn't show, then move on to the next blemish. If you don't like the results of your edit, undo and try again.

Note

Old photos degrade over time because they're made of paper and light-sensitive chemicals. Scan them and clean them up, and you get images that won't degrade and can end up looking better than the originals.

This technique can be expanded to cover removing other elements from photos, such as those obnoxious tourists who showed up in all your photos of Rome.

In this photo of a New England clam shack (Figure 7.7), for example, you might want to remove the dust specks in the upper quadrant—they're more visible because they're on the sky portion of the photo. If you were feeling more ambitious, you could take out some or all of the power lines, as well as the security lights on the roof of the right side of the building. It all depends on how confident you are in your ability to make the alterations invisibly, how "perfect" you want the image to look, and the purpose the image is serving. (See Real World section, "When Beauty Isn't Truthful," later in this chapter.)

If you want to try your hand at touching up this photo yourself, it's on the CD-ROM included with this book. The filename is CLAMSHAK.TIF (see Figure 7.10).

To make the changes mentioned to this image, you'd start by using a small Rubber Stamp brush to remove those dust specks, cloning an appropriately colored portion of sky over each one with a single click.

Then you'd move along the wires. The wires running through the trees are harder to deal with than those against the sky; pick your sample points carefully, being sure to match lines such as those along branch edges (see Figure 7.10). Then use the same technique to remove the security lights, matching the background that shows around each edge of the shape you're deleting. To be sure you don't alter the roof line of the building, lasso around the light carefully with a feather radius of 1. Your Rubber Stamp operations only affect the area inside the selection.

Figure 7.10

This photo needs some work. It has dust specks and intrusive elements that can easily be removed using the Rubber Stamp tool.

Figure 7.11

After removing the dust specks, go after the wires, periodically zooming out to check your work.

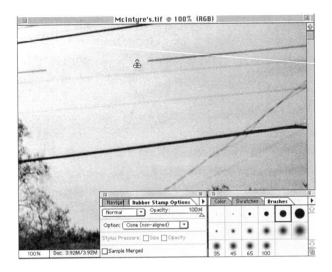

Examine the results of each clone click, and undo if they don't look realistic. Remember, you can vary the brush size as you go, and use soft- and hard-edged brushes to achieve the right effect for a particular section of the image. After the distracting image element has been covered up, you can fine-tune the appearance of that section of the image by more cloning.

Tip

If the area you're cloning from is very small, try creating a larger version of it by selecting it with the rectangular marquee, choosing Define Pattern from the Edit menu, creating a larger file, and filling the larger file with the pattern. Now you can use the new file as the source for your cloning.

If you're cloning a hard-edged shape, such as the edge of a building or a strip of windows, it may be hard to keep a smooth edge. After editing an area such as this with the Smudge and Paintbrush tools to smooth it out, clone again with a lower opacity (20–50%) to restore some structure to the area.

This kind of retouching has no hard and fast rules—experimentation is the key because every image is different.

Figure 7.12

Although you can't literally re-create the leaves behind the power lines, you can create a believable facsimile of the pattern they formed.

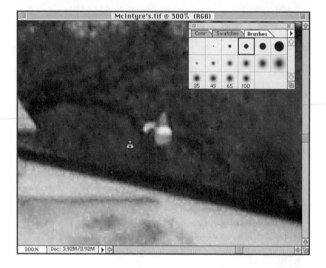

Figure 7.13

Removing the security lights is a matter of picking your sample points carefully.

Figure 7.14

The final image, sans wires, dust specks, and security lights.

When Beauty Isn't Truthful

Several years ago *National Geographic* caught all kinds of flak when it was revealed that the magazine's staff had digitally moved a pyramid in a cover photo to keep it from being cropped out of the image. More recently, *New York Newsday* ran a cover photo of Nancy Kerrigan and Tonya Harding skating side-by-side before they ever went to practice together. And a *Time* artist darkened O.J. Simpson's skin tones for a cover image.

While darkroom wizards have always been able to retouch photos, Photoshop and similar software, as well as high-end dedicated systems, offer much more scope, without leaving a shred of evidence that any change was made. When is it legitimate to alter an image? And how far is it ethical to go in making changes?

The answer to these ethical questions varies depending on the image and the circumstances. The photo I've used to demonstrate use of the Rubber Stamp tool here is one I took for use in a private newsletter distributed only to friends. As a matter of record, I didn't make any of the edits suggested here—I just removed the dust specks. But it wouldn't have made any real difference to anyone if I had changed the image—would it?

On the other hand, if the building were a murder site and the photo was published as part of the newspaper coverage of the crime, removing elements of the scene would misrepresent the truth.

One way to get around the question is to acknowledge in the image credits, as *New York Newsday* did with the Harding/Kerrigan image, that changes have been made. Ultimately, though, honesty only gets you so far.

Applying Patterns with the Rubber Stamp Tool

Although you can apply a pattern to a selected area by choosing Fill from the Edit menu and selecting Pattern from the Use pop-up menu, sometimes a project requires a more specialized application of a pattern. The Rubber Stamp tool enables you to essentially paint with a pattern, with all the options you usually have when painting—Opacity, Brush Size and Shape, and so on—as well as the choice of aligned cloning or nonaligned cloning.

To define a pattern:

1. Select a portion of the image or of another image using the rectangle marquee.

2. Choose Define Pattern from the Edit menu.

After a pattern is defined and the Rubber Stamp tool is selected, you can just start painting—no need to choose a sample point.

Tip

Photoshop stores only one pattern in its memory and flushes that pattern when you quit the program. If you want to use a pattern again in the future, copy the selection you've used to define the pattern, create a new file, and paste. To reuse that pattern, just select all and define the pattern. This file can also be used with the Render Texture Fill filter, as long as it's saved in the native Photoshop format and is a grayscale image.

Editing with the Smudge Tool

Welcome back to the world of finger painting—only with the power of the computer. The Smudge tool smears one color into another as you click and drag the mouse; you can select it in the toolbox by typing "S."

Taking the easy way: free patterns

Two collections of repeating patterns are bundled with Photoshop. Look in the Displacement Maps folder inside the Plug-Ins folder, and check out the PostScript patterns in the Brushes and Patterns folder within the Goodies folder (PC users: look in the Patterns directory within your Photoshop directory). These latter patterns are Illustrator artwork that can be rendered at any size when you open the files.

1. Double-clicking the Smudge tool in the toolbox brings up the Smudge Tool Options panel (see Figure 7.15).

2. Choose a brush mode.

Figure 7.15

The Smudge Tool Options panel.

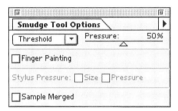

The Smudge tool can use some of the same brush modes as the paint tools: Darken, Lighten, Hue, Saturation, Color, and Luminosity.

3. Choose a pressure level.

Rather than an Opacity slider, as seen with painting tools, the Smudge Options panel has a Pressure slider that enables you to determine how hard you "press down" when smudging. Pressure determines how far the tool drags a color. Higher percentages drag colors farther, and a setting of 100% keeps the color dragging as long as you hold down the mouse button.

4. Choose whether you want to smudge one layer at a time (Sample Merged off) or all visible layers (Sample Merged on).

5. If you have a graphics tablet, you can choose whether the pressure of your stylus affects the brush size or the pressure setting, or both, as you smudge.

6. Turn Finger Painting on or off.

The Finger Painting option changes which color is dragged behind the smudging finger. If it's unchecked, the Smudge tool drags the color of the pixel you first clicked. If Finger Painting is selected, the tool first adds a blob of the foreground color and then smudges that as you drag into the surrounding pixels.

To use Finger Painting without going back to the Smudge Tools Options, hold down (Option)[Alt] as you smudge. If Finger Painting is on, then this key combination turns it off while you drag. The amount of color applied is determined by the pressure setting—100% gives you an effect just like that of the paintbrush.

7. Click and drag to smudge. Simply clicking doesn't accomplish much with this tool, for obvious reasons.

You can also vary the brush you use with the Smudge tool. Used with the Lighten or Darken option, you can smudge out dirt specks in flat, untextured areas, as an alternative to using the Rubber Stamp tool (see Figure 7.16).

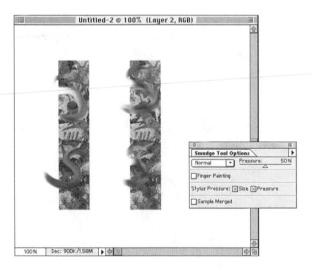

Figure 7.16

In these examples, the upper smudges were made with Finger Painting off and the lower ones with Finger Painting on. The left-hand smudges were made with 100% pressure, and the right-hand ones with 50% pressure.

Tip

If you just want to soften the line between areas of different colors, try using the Blur tool instead of the Smudge tool. That way you'll smooth the transition without altering the line.

Using the Focus Tools

The Focus tools, Blur and Sharpen, enable you to apply the Blur and Sharpen commands locally with the mouse, rather than from the Filter menu, where you would affect an entire image or selection. Doing this often requires a lot of wrist action, but if you need very specific areas of your image blurred or sharpened, the capability comes in handy. You can select the Focus tools and switch between Blur and Sharpen by pressing "R."

The Blur tool reduces the amount of color contrast between adjacent pixels, while the Sharpen tool increases contrast. Blurring sections of an image is a useful fix for oversharpening, and it can help blend the edges of a pasted element into the background. The Sharpen tool is handy for situations in which sharpening a whole image makes some parts stand out too much.

1. Double-clicking the Focus tools in the toolbox brings up the Focus Options panel (see Figure 7.17).

2. Choose a brush mode.

   The Focus tools can use the same group of brush modes as the Smudge tool: Darken, Lighten, Hue, Saturation, Color, and Luminosity.

Figure 7.17

The Focus Tools Options panel.

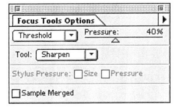

3. Choose a pressure level.

   As with the Smudge tool, the Focus tools have a Pressure slider instead of an Opacity slider because you're not applying color but adjusting the pixels that are already there. The Pressure setting determines how much effect each application of a Focus tool has, from 0% to 100%.

4. Choose whether you want to sharpen or blur one layer at a time (Sample Merged off) or all visible layers (Sample Merged on).

5. If you have a graphics tablet, you can choose whether the pressure of your stylus affects the brush size or the pressure setting, or both, as you sharpen or blur.

6. Choose a focus tool: Blur or Sharpen. You can also choose a tool by clicking the Focus tools in the toolbox and holding down the mouse button. A pop-up appears, showing both tools, and you can slide your cursor to the tool you want to use.

7. Click or click and drag to blur or sharpen. You may want to use a lower pressure setting and apply the tool repeatedly to fine-tune the effects. As with the Sharpen filters, be careful not to oversharpen portions of an image unless you're trying for a special effect.

You can also use different brush sizes and shapes for blurring and sharpening.

The Toning Tools

Three Toning tools occupy one place in the toolbox: the Dodge tool, the Burn tool, and the Sponge tool. They're used to selectively brighten, darken, saturate, and desaturate portions of an image. You can select the Toning tools and cycle through them by pressing "O."

1. Double-clicking the Toning tools in the toolbox displays the Toning Options panel (see Figure 7.18).

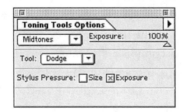

Figure 7.18

The Toning Tools Options panel.

2. Choose a Toning tool from the pop-up menu in the panel, or select a tool by clicking the Toning tools in the toolbox, holding the mouse button down, and sliding the cursor over the desired tool.

3. Choose what tones you want to affect in the image.

   Although you don't have access to all the painting brush modes when using the Toning tools, you can choose whether your dodging and burning strokes affect the image's highlights, shadows, or midtones.

   When you're using the Sponge tool, your choices are "Saturate" and "Desaturate" instead.

4. Using the slider, set the exposure or saturation level.

   When you're dodging or burning, you can choose an exposure level, which determines how much effect your strokes have. If you're using the Sponge, you choose how much each stroke saturates or desaturates the pixels touched by the sponge.

5. If you have a graphics tablet installed, you can choose to have stylus pressure affect brush size, exposure/saturation, or both. If you don't have a tablet installed, these checkboxes are grayed out.

6. After you set all these options, click and drag or just click to apply the Toning tools.

You can use different brush sizes and shapes with all three Toning tools.

Dodging and Burning

The Burn and Dodge tools are based on traditional photographers' techniques. While developing a print, masks can be placed between the light source and the paper to increase or decrease the amount of exposure each part of the image receives. Photoshop's equivalents of these techniques accomplish the same purpose, but they're much simpler and quicker to use, and you can be much more precise. Dodging and burning enables you to tone down overly bright lighting effects, brighten up overly dark areas, and enhance or disguise details in your images.

The Dodge tool lightens an image; in the darkroom, you would block light from the enlarger to keep it from striking the print and therefore lighten that portion of the print. Burning works the other way around—in the darkroom you would focus the light on just one part of the print, blocking light from reaching any other part of the paper. That part of the image would be darker—more deeply burned in—than the rest. If you were working in the darkroom, you'd be using pieces of cardboard or even your hand to dodge and burn (see Figure 7.19).

Figure 7.19

Burning and dodging are the solution to the strong sunlight and heavy shadows on the face in this photo. The left-hand image shows the results of using the Burn and Dodge tools to even out the tones on the face.

To create rays of sunlight in an image, use the Dodge tool; for shadows, use the Burn tool. Or use the tools on already existing areas of light and shadow to bring out or hide details.

Tip

People in scanned snapshots often have shadows on their faces. You can use the Dodge tool to remedy this problem quickly. To be sure you don't inadvertently affect other areas of the image, use the Lasso tool to select just the face you want to work on, choose Shadows in the Toning Options panel, and use a low exposure setting with multiple applications of the tool rather than one swipe with a high setting.

You can switch back and forth between the Dodge and Burn tools by choosing one of the two and then holding down (Option)[Alt] to temporarily switch to the other. And, as with all tools that can use different brushes, you can change brushes with the "[" and "]" keys.

What's happening technically when you use the Dodge and Burn tools? In the HSB color space model (hue/saturation/brightness), these two tools increase or decrease the brightness of the pixels to which they're applied. If you want to alter the saturation, you can use the Sponge tool, which increases (saturates) or decreases (desaturates) the intensity of colors or (in grayscale images) of contrast.

Using the Sponge Tool

Like the Burn and Dodge tools, the Sponge tool can be used for retouching scans—adjusting colors that didn't scan correctly, toning down the colors in elements you don't want to stand out, and punching up the colors in elements you *do* want to stand out.

Watch out that you don't make the colors *too* intense in images intended for CMYK reproduction. Because process printing inks have a smaller color gamut than color computer monitors, it's easy to end up with colors that won't print at anything approaching their intensity onscreen. Using the CMYK Preview (under the View menu or (Command-Y)[Control-Y]) lets you know what saturation adjustments can be reflected in the final CMYK image, even if you're editing in RGB mode.

If you have the opposite problem—your image already contains out-of-gamut colors—then you can use the Sponge tool to desaturate them to the point where they fall back within the CMYK gamut. Of course, you can convert all colors in an image at the same time by changing to CMYK mode, but converting from RGB to CMYK can cause flat areas in which several different RGB colors are all converted to the same CMYK color. Using the Sponge tool enables you to exercise more control over what CMYK color to which each RGB color is being converted (see Figure 7.20).

Tip

When editing colors in a RGB image destined for CMYK reproduction, watch for an exclamation point next to the CMYK color readout in the Info palette. It lets you know when a color won't reproduce properly in CMYK.

Figure 7.20

The blue handicapped parking sign in this photo (another New England clam shack) won't reproduce properly in CMYK—note the exclamation points after the CMYK values in the Info palette.

Note

To completely desaturate an image or selection, instead of using the Sponge tool, use the Desaturate command in the Adjust submenu of the Image menu. This command removes all color, essentially converting the image or selection to grayscale without changing the color mode of the file.

USING TRANSFORMATIONS

Transformations enable you to adjust the shape or size of portions of an image. There are several types of transformation accessible from the Layer menu:

- Scale: adjusts the size of a selection

- Rotate: enables free rotation of a selection

◆ Skew: enables a selection to be slanted

◆ Distort: enables a selection to be stretched in any direction

◆ Perspective: enables you to narrow or widen one side of a selection to give the illusion of perspective

◆ Numeric: enables you to perform several transformations at once by entering numerical parameters

◆ Arbitrary rotation: enables the image to be rotated 180° or 90° either clockwise or counterclockwise

◆ Flip: enables the layer or selection to be flipped horizontally or vertically

To transform all or part of a layer:

1. Either make the layer active with nothing selected or select part of the image on that layer.

2. Choose a transformation command from the Layers menu. Photoshop adds handles to the corners and sides of the selection.

3. Move the handles to alter the selection. You can apply one or several transformations by selecting different transformation commands from the menu as you go. Undo to remove the effects of a transformation.

4. When you're done making transformations, press Return (to accept the changes and move on) or Esc or Command (to leave transform mode without changing the selection). Not until you press Return does Photoshop calculate what the selection looks like, pixel by pixel, so you may see the watch or hourglass cursor for a second afterwards.

Note

In version 3.0 of Photoshop, holding down the (Option)[Alt] key while dragging transformation handles kept the selection from redrawing. In version 4.0 the (Option)[Alt] key changes the way the transformation works—read on for details.

Scaling

You can scale a selection by dragging either a corner handle or a side one. If you want to constrain the scaling so that the image keeps its present proportions, use a corner handle and hold down the Shift key as you drag (see Figure 7.21).

Figure 7.21

The upper-left window shows scaling in progress, whereas the lower-right window shows the results of the scaling operation.

Ordinarily, the selection's upper-left corner stays in place as you scale. To scale from the center instead, hold down the (Option)[Alt] key as you drag a handle.

To see the percentage and size of a selection as you scale it, display the Show Info palette before choosing the Scale command.

Note

Be aware that Photoshop interpolates pixels to scale an image or part of an image. Just as you can't expect good results from a tiny scan blown up several hundred percent, you may not like the results of using the Scale command to enlarge a selection. If you plan on doing lots of scaling, make sure your interpolation method is set to Bicubic (the default) in Photoshop's preferences for best results. Nearest Neighbor is a faster method that gives poorer results, and Bilinear falls between the other two in both quality and speed.

Rotating

To rotate a selection, drag on any handle, either clockwise or counter-clockwise. Holding down the Shift key as you drag constrains the rotation to 15-degree increments—15, 30, 45, and so on (see Figure 7.22).

Figure 7.22

The upper-left window shows rotation in progress, whereas the lower-right window shows the results of the rotation operation.

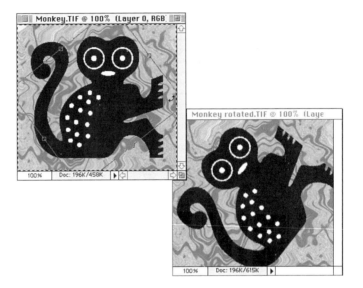

Tip

If you're importing Photoshop images into another program, such as Illustrator or QuarkXPress, be aware that images rotated in Photoshop print faster than those rotated after they're placed in another program.

Skewing

When you're changing the shape of a selection through skewing, the directions in which you can move each handle are restricted. Corner points can move left, right, up, or down. If you drag a side point, the two corner points it's closest to move with it, and the handle only moves along the line created by those two corner points.

If you hold down the (Option)[Alt] key as you drag a corner point, an adjacent corner point moves in tandem with the one you're clicking; which corner is determined by which direction you're moving the handle. If you're dragging a side handle, holding down the (Option) [Alt] key makes the handles on the other side of the selection move in the opposite direction to the way you drag (see Figure 7.23).

Figure 7.23

If the (Option)[Alt] key is held down as the point is dragged to the right, the upper-right handle moves with it. Dragging down instead would force the lower-left handle to move with the one selected.

Distorting

The Distort command works similarly to the Skew command, but it's less symmetrical—you can move corner points in any direction, not just the cardinal directions. Holding down the Shift key as you drag restricts movement to up, down, left, or right, the way the Skew command always works.

Holding down the (Option)[Alt] key as you drag a corner handle distorts the selection symmetrically around its center. The effect is that the opposite corner handle moves in the opposite direction. If you're dragging a side handle, the (Option)[Alt] key makes the opposite point move in the opposite direction, and (Shift-Option)[Shift-Alt] dragging gives the same effect as using the Perspective command (see next section).

Adding Perspective

Using this command to transform your selection brings back memories of high-school geometry because the command turns a rectangular selection into a trapezoid. Essentially, dragging a corner handle while using the Perspective transform makes one side of your selection shorter or longer, without affecting the opposite side. The adjacent sides adjust to match the new corner points, so that they end up angled instead of straight. This operation gives the optical effect of perspective (see Figure 7.24).

Using modifier keys with Perspective has no effect, and dragging a side handle gives the same effect as using Skew on a side handle.

Making Numeric Transformations

For precise numerical alterations to a selection, use Numeric Transformations. Using this feature, you can change the selection's position, scale the selection, rotate it, or skew it—or any combination of the four—by entering the numerical parameters you want used for each operation.

1. Choose Layer➡Transform➡Numeric. Then choose the transformations you want to apply. You can apply one, two, three, or all four at once (see Figure 7.25).

Figure 7.24

The upper-left window shows the perspective transformation in progress, whereas the lower-right window shows the results of the operation.

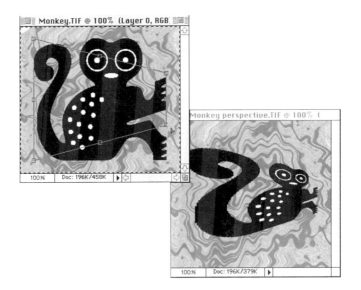

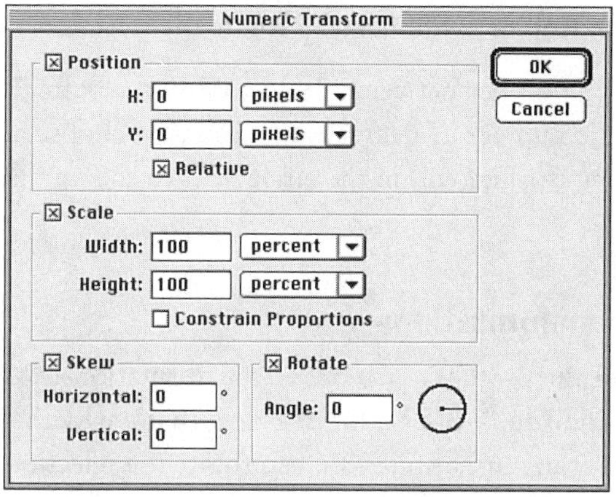

Figure 7.25

*The Numeric Transform
dialog box.*

2. Check Position if you want to move the selection within the
   image.

   Enter the position you want to move the selection to, in pixels,
   inches, cm, points or picas (the Units preferences don't affect
   this action). Alternatively, enter the numerical value you want
   to move the selection horizontally and vertically and check the
   Relative box.

3. Check Scale if you want to change the size of the selection.

   Enter the percentage by which you want to scale the selection
   in each dimension—from .01% to (believe it or not) 33,707.87
   percent. Checking Constrain Proportions forces the X and Y
   percentages to be the same, maintaining the original proportions of the selection.

4. Check Skew if you want to skew the selection.

   Enter the number of degrees you want to skew the selection
   horizontally and vertically, from 0 to 89.9. This number is used
   to rotate and scale the selection simultaneously. Entering
   negative numbers skews outward, making the selection larger
   in that dimension; entering positive numbers skews inward,
   making the selection smaller in that dimension.

5. Check Rotate if you want to rotate the selection.

Enter a number between -360 and 360 to rotate the selection a specific number of degrees. You can also choose an angle by turning the line within the circle next to the number entry fields.

Arbitrary Transformations

Quick and dirty—that's arbitrary transformations. Well, not really dirty, but they don't offer a lot of scope; that's why they're arbitrary. With these transformations, you can rotate the selection or image 90° clockwise, 90° counterclockwise, 180°, or flip it horizontally or vertically. Really, your only option with these commands occurs when you're rotating the entire image.

◆ To rotate the image and the canvas, so that no part of the image is cropped, just choose the appropriate command from the Transform submenu.

◆ To rotate the image without rotating the canvas, select All before choosing the Rotate command. If you've rotated the image 90°, unless it is perfectly square, you'll see that it's been cropped and that the shorter dimension is now flanked by areas of the background color (see Figure 7.26).

Figure 7.26

Rotating a rectangular image while it's selected results in cropping.

Caution

Watch out for text in flipped images!

Using the Free Transform Command

With the advent of Photoshop 4.0, transformations are, well, transformed. A new command called Free Transform enables you to make all your transformations in one operation, using the same set of handles. You can choose Free Transform from the Layer menu or press (Command-T)[Control-T].

What happens at each point of a Free Transform operation depends on where you click.

- ◆ To move the selection, click inside the border.

- ◆ To scale it, drag a handle, holding down the Shift key as you drag to constrain the selection's proportions.

- ◆ To rotate the selection, click outside the border, holding down the Shift key as you drag to constrain rotation to 15-degree increments.

- ◆ To skew the selection, press (Command)[Control] and Shift as you drag a side handle.

- ◆ To distort the selection, press (Command)[Control] as you drag a handle; adding (Option)[Alt] distorts symmetrically.

- ◆ To apply perspective, press (Command)[Control] and Shift as you drag a corner handle.

Note

Photoshop's new capability to apply more than one transformation at a time should result in higher image quality when more than one transformation is applied because all the transformations can be taken into account when the new positions of the image's pixels are calculated.

FILTERING REALITY

Most Photoshop filters are intended to help you achieve special effects—glowing type, planets on fire, or embossed just-about-anything. While splashy, glitzy filters are definitely more fun to use, Photoshop includes some more basic filters that can function as building blocks for complex special effects or as image editing tools. These basic filters include Blur, Noise, and Sharpen, as well as the new Fade command. For more information on all of Photoshop's native filters, see Chapter 14, "Using Photoshop's Filters."

Tip

MetaTools' KPT Convolver plug-in goes straight to the mathematical heart of many Photoshop filters, such as Gaussian Blur and Unsharp Mask (see Figure 7.27). By enabling you to directly edit the kernel, or value matrix, used in these effects, Convolver provides maximum control and enables you to customize each application for best results in a particular image. Just using it can teach a lot about how the filters actually work. It's really fast, too!

Figure 7.27

KPT Convolver, an omnibus plug-in from MetaTools, performs both creative and editing functions.

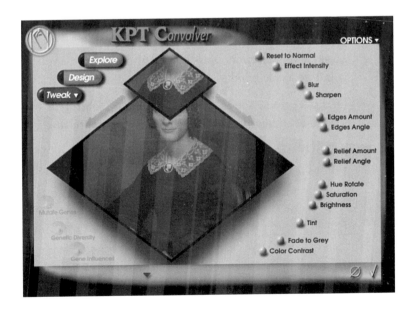

Using the Blur Filters

Photoshop offers two versions of the basic Blur filter: Blur and Blur More, which blurs three or four times as much as the plain Blur filter. Then there are Gaussian, Motion, Radial, and Smart Smooth filters. Here's a rundown on how each of these Blur variations works:

♦ Blur and Blur More: reduces contrast between adjacent pixels by lightening pixels next to well-defined edges and shadows, visually smoothing and softening an image.

♦ Gaussian Blur: uses a mathematical equation (a bell-shaped curve) to calculate the transitions between adjacent pixels, resulting in most of the blurred pixels ending up in the middle range between the two original colors, instead of on one end or the other (see Figure 7.28). Also, the Radius value lets you control the amount of blurring by choosing a value between 0.1 and 250; values between 0.1 and 1.0 are considered low, 1.0 to 5.0 are moderately blurry, and anything higher blurs all sense out of an image.

Figure 7.28

The Gaussian Blur dialog box.

♦ Motion Blur: gives the impression of motion in the image by adding directional and intensity controls for the blurring process. You can choose an angle from -90° to 90° and a distance from 1 to 999 pixels to control the effects of the Motion Blur filter (see Figure 7.29).

Figure 7.29

The Motion Blur dialog box.

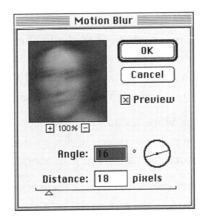

◆ Radial Blur: offers two choices. Spin creates a blur effect that looks as though the image is spinning around a center point. Zoom gives the effect of moving the camera away from or toward the image. You can set the amount (1 to 100) and the quality (Draft, Good, or Best) of the blur effect as well as choosing a center point (see Figure 7.30). The Spin version of the Radial Blur uses the amount setting to control the direction of rotation, and in both versions the amount of pixel movement increases the further away from the center point you go. The quality settings determine the interpolation method that's used: Good uses bilinear and Best uses bicubic, while Draft diffuses the image. As with all interpolation, the better the quality the longer the operation takes.

Figure 7.30

The Radial Blur dialog box.

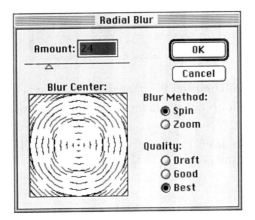

◆ Smart Blur: blurs the image, except for the edges. Smart Blur finds boundaries between different color regions and maintains those boundaries while blurring details in the rest of the image; most of the time you end up with an effect similar to blurring just the lightness channel. You can set the Radius and Threshold to determine how far the effect extends, the Quality to determine how the interpolation is accomplished, and the Mode (see Figure 7.31). The Normal mode shows the effects of the blurring; the Edge Only and Overlay Edge options show the edges that are maintained and thus help you make settings. Most of the time you'll change the mode back to Normal before hitting OK.

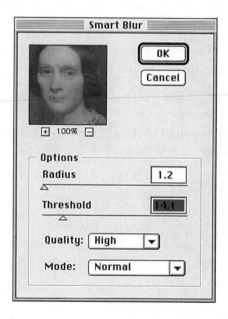

Figure 7.31

The Smart Blur dialog box.

In image editing, the Blur filters have several applications. You can blur backgrounds to emphasize the foreground subject rather than background detail. Blurring is also handy for adding motion effects. With poor quality scanned images, use blurring to soften and smooth spotty or grainy areas, especially in old photographs. And blurring provides the best method I've seen for retouching wrinkles in portraits:

1. Using the QuickMask feature in conjunction with the airbrush and paintbrush, mask only the areas of a face that you want to work on, convert the mask to a selection, and invert the selection. Now you've selected the wrinkled portions of the face (and perhaps the neck as well).

2. Copy the selection and paste it, creating a new layer on top of the original image.

3. Apply the Gaussian Blur to the new layer. The amount depends on the resolution of the image you're working on—use your eye to judge. You want to remove all traces of the wrinkles without eliminating facial details such as dimples and creases between the nose and the corners of the mouth that result naturally from smiling.

4. Add a small amount of noise to the new layer to restore grain and avoid an overly smooth "plastic" effect.

5. Now adjust the Opacity slider on the "dewrinkled" layer to apply the effect naturally. 1% won't affect the layer below; 100% has an extremely youthful effect. Most people should fall somewhere in the middle.

Tip

This technique of applying changes to a separate layer from the original image and then varying the opacity of the layer to apply the changes can be used with any filter, and it leaves you the option of taking out the changes altogether.

Using the Noise Filters

There are four filters grouped together under Photoshop's Noise filter submenu: Add Noise, Despeckle, Dust & Scratches, and Median. While Add Noise adds random pixels to an image, the other three filters are intended to be used in correcting badly scanned images or scans of poor originals.

◆ Add Noise: adds a grainy texture to an image, with the amount ranging from 1 to 999 (see Figure 7.32). That number determines how far from the original color Photoshop can change each pixel; values more than 255 enable colors to be chosen randomly from the entire spectrum, with white and black becoming more likely choices as you enter higher amounts. Uniform noise chooses colors randomly from the specified range, while Gaussian noise (calculated with the same bell curve used in the Gaussian Blur effect) is more chaotic because colors of noise pixels are likely to be either close to the original colors or very far away. Images treated with Gaussian noise may look lighter than if uniform noise were used. You can also choose to add monochromatic noise, which distributes noise equally in all color channels, resulting in grayscale noise.

Figure 7.32

The Add Noise dialog box.

◆ Despeckle: searches for edges in an image and then blurs everything *but* the edges, using the same value as the Blur More filter to smooth out changes in pixel color.

◆ Dust & Scratches: automates removal of image blemishes such as dust, hairs, and scratches. Its two options, Radius and Threshold, determine how big and how obtrusive an imperfection has to be to be affected (see Figure 7.33). Objects larger than the radius value or closer in color to the neighboring pixels than the threshold value won't be affected. Experiment with the settings, and don't expect the filter to remove all of an image's blemishes.

Figure 7.33

The Dust & Scratches dialog box.

Tip

With threshold values less than 40, the Dust & Scratches filter can help eliminate moiré patterns in scanned images. See Chapter 3, "Scanning," for more information.

◆ Median: averages the brightness of pixels within an image or selection to remove noise. This filter isn't too useful with grayscale images, unless you're looking for an overly smooth, plastic effect. But it does happen to be very helpful for simplifying an overly noisy bitmapped image, especially prior to autotracing (see Figure 7.34).

Figure 7.34

The Median dialog box.

Using the Sharpen Filters

The Sharpen filters start out by working the same way as the Blur filters—finding areas of contrasting color. The difference lies in what's done to those pixels; instead of blurring the image by decreasing contrast in those areas, the Sharpen filters increase contrast to seemingly bring the images into better focus (although they can't substitute for an image that's properly focused in the first place). There are four filters in the group:

◆ Sharpen and Sharpen More: increases contrast on a pixel level—the most primitive version of sharpening. Sharpen More sharpens about three times as much as the basic Sharpen filter.

◆ Sharpen Edges: works only on the areas in the image that contrast the most—the edges.

◆ Unsharp Mask: works the same way as the other Sharpen tools, but enables you much more control over the sharpening process. Named after a technique used with stat cameras, Unsharp Mask has three settings you must make. Amount, between 1% and 500%, specifies how much sharpening takes place (100% is equivalent to the Sharpen filter). Radius (0.1 to 250 pixels) determines how far from edge pixels the sharpening effect is extended. And Threshold (between 0 and 255 brightness levels) enables you to sharpen edges only, all pixels in the image, or any combination in between (see Figure 7.35).

Figure 7.35

The Unsharp Mask dialog box.

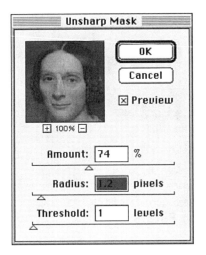

Note

The Unsharp Mask filter works just fine even if you don't understand exactly how it does its thing. But for those who just have to know, here's what happens: a negative copy of the image is blurred and then combined with the original, thus sharpening the edges only.

Because the Unsharp Mask filter accomplishes the same thing as the other Sharpen filters but enables you so much more control over what pixels get sharpened and how much, it's the only real choice for any serious image editing. Experimentation gets the best results with any particular image, but there are a few guidelines you can follow when making your settings.

♦ Amount: The higher the resolution of the image, the higher the amount needs to be. For 300-dpi images, start with a setting of about 150 and go from there. Too high an amount produces a grainy effect—useful as a special effect but unattractive (and a dead giveaway of computer manipulation) in regular photos (see Figure 7.36).

Figure 7.36

This photo has been drastically oversharpened (Sharpen More applied twice); notice how grainy it is and how the edges of shapes in the image (such as the building's eaves) have white highlights. See Figure 7.10 for the original version of this photo.

- ◆ Radius: Higher settings here also result in oversharpening, although you can offset that tendency by raising the amount along with the Radius value. A good starting point is 1 to 2 pixels.

- ◆ Threshold: This setting determines how much contrast there is between neighboring pixels for the sharpening to affect them, so a setting of 0 sharpens the entire image, while higher settings exclude more and more pixels. Use this value to restrict the sharpening effect to image details.

Tip

After sharpening, take one more look at your edits to make sure the sharpening process hasn't made them stand out too much.

Using the Fade Filter Command

Sometimes you need to mitigate the effect of a filter—it's just too much noise, for example. Photoshop 4.0's adjustment layers enable you to apply a filter or color adjustment to an empty layer and then determine how that layer affects those under it by using the layer opacity and blending mode controls. (For more information, see Chapter 9, "Layers.") An alternative to this technique is the Fade command under the

Filter menu, which eliminates the separate layer by enabling you to choose an opacity and blending mode to be applied to the filter effect.

1. After applying a filter or an image adjustment (such as a Levels operation), choose the Fade filter command from the Filter menu. If you applied the filter or adjustment to a selection, don't drop the selection before choosing the Fade command.

2. Turn Preview on or off, depending on whether you want the effects of your settings to be previewed in the image window as you change the settings.

3. To adjust the opacity of the filter or adjustment's effects, drag the slider—the minimum is 0% (eliminates the filter/adjustment effects) and the maximum is 100% (as though you hadn't used the Fade command).

4. Choose one of 17 blending modes—Normal, Dissolve, Multiply, Screen, Overlay, Soft Light, Hard Light, Color Dodge, Color Burn, Darken, Lighten, Difference, Exclusion, Hue, Saturation, Color, or Luminosity.

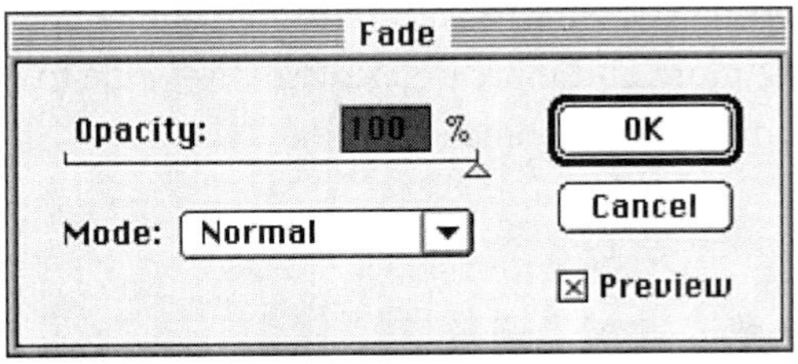

Figure 7.37

The Fade command enables you to vary the intensity of a filter effect on the image's pixels.

CHANNELS

Channels are one of the main elements of Photoshop. There are two types of channels, color channels and alpha channels, that accomplish some very important functions. First, the color information about the image is located in the color channels. Second, selections are saved and modified in the alpha channels.

How you manipulate an image in Photoshop directly affects the color channels. A color image is a product of the combined color channels. This defines the color mode. Red, Green, and Blue channels, for example, create an RGB composite that defines the document as being in RGB mode. Each of the color elements can be isolated and edited in the Channels palette. This permits image modification that is both subtle and complex.

The second function of channels is selections. Before you apply special effects, color corrections, or paint to an image, the area for modification must be selected. Channels supply the means for saving selections as alpha channels. They also enable sophisticated editing of those selections, including painting, cutting, and pasting. Selections can be combined using mathematical calculations. They also can be added to, subtracted from, or intersected with other selections.

The size of a file is equally divided among its color channels. Therefore, each of the three channels in a 12MB RGB file is 4MB. Every alpha channel that you include with this image accounts for an additional 4MB. There is an exception to this rule. If the alpha channel is simple, it can take up less space. Photoshop can do a lossless compression of the data when it saves the file. Nonetheless, many channels certainly add to a file's size, which slows down performance.

USING THE CHANNELS PALETTE

The channel functions are accessed from the Channels palette. Here you can create, duplicate, and delete channels. You can also split channels into separate images and merge independent channels into one composite image. To open the Channels palette, go to the Window menu and select Show Channels. The color composite is displayed first, followed by the individual color channels. Eye icons in the left column indicate the visible channels. To the right is a thumbnail image of the channel and a name bar. The black highlighted channels are the active or targeted ones. At the bottom of the palette are four buttons to perform shortcuts. They are load selection, save selection, new channel, and trash (see Figure 8.1).

Figure 8.1

The Channels palette.

The arrow in the upper-right corner of the Channels palette has a pull-down menu you use to create, duplicate, delete, and split or merge channels. You can also access channel and palette options from this menu (see Figure 8.2).

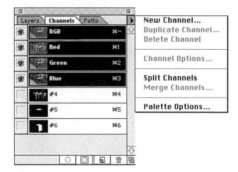

Figure 8.2

The Channels menu.

Viewing Channels

When a channel is visible, there is an eye icon in the box to the left of the channel name in the Channels palette. Click the eye and it disappears, as does the channel image in the active window. Click the empty box and the eye icon toggles back on. The image reappears in the active window. Dragging up or down through the eye column turns multiple eyes on or off. One eye icon must always be on. You cannot turn them all off.

Targeting Channels

Click the channel name or thumbnail in the Channels palette to make it the active or targeted channel. The name bar on an active channel is black. When it is not active it is white. A channel that is active becomes visible and at the same time, the other channels become hidden.

In order to edit a channel, it must be visible and active. Visible and active are independent features when dealing with channels. A channel can be visible but not active, and it can be active but not visible. A channel can also be both visible and active.

There are times when it is helpful to see one channel while you are editing another. You may, for instance, be editing an alpha channel and want to use a color channel for a tracing reference. This is a case where you would make a channel visible in addition to the active channel.

The name of the active channel is placed in parenthesis in the title bar at the top of the document window.

Channels can be made active with the following keyboard shortcuts:

- ◆ (Command-~)[Control-~] makes the color composite channel active.

- ◆ (Command-1)[Control-1] makes the first color channel active.

- ◆ (Command-2)[Control-2] makes the second color channel active.

This follows that the number 3, 4, 5, and so on are the keyboard commands for each successive color and alpha channel.

Note

Photoshop changed the colors for active channels and layers in version 4.0. Photoshop 3.05 for the Mac displayed active layers and active channels as gray and inactive ones as white. In the Windows version of 3.05, active layers and channels were white and inactive ones were gray. Now in version 4.0, both Mac and Windows designate active layers and channels as black and inactive as white.

Editing affects all active channels if more than one channel is made active at the same time. In this situation, all active channels do not have to be visible. The effects of editing are produced on all active channels but only one has to be visible.

- ◆ Add to an active channel by holding down the Shift key and clicking any inactive channel. Select the Red channel, for example. Now hold the Shift key down while you click the Blue channel. Both channels are active.

- When multiple channels are targeted, use the Shift key to deselect a channel. With the Red and Blue channel selected, hold down the Shift key and click Red. The Red channel is deselected, leaving only the Blue channel targeted.

Reordering Channels

You can change the order of channels by dragging them to a palette position above or below its present one. You cannot reorder color channels or move alpha channels above the color channels. Alpha channels must remain below.

Reordering channels is just for organization of the alpha channels. It does not change the way that a channel looks or performs in relation to other channels.

Do the following to reorder a channel (see Figure 8.3):

- Click the name or thumbnail of an alpha channel in the Channels palette and drag it on top of or beyond another alpha channel.

- When a channel is dragged over another, the border of the lower channel gets thicker. Let go of the drag at this point and the dragged channel moves into the new position.

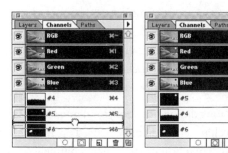

Figure 8.3

Reordering channels in the channels palette.

Setting Palette Options

The channel thumbnail is located between the eye icon and the channel name on the Channels palette. It is a useful visual aid because the correct channel can be selected quickly by looking at the thumbnails. Select one of three sizes for the thumbnail. Choosing none makes a smaller Channels palette. This may be a consideration if desktop space is a problem when working with a small monitor.

Choose Palette Options... from the Channels menu (see Figure 8.4). Select the thumbnail size you want to work with. Click OK.

Figure 8.4

The Channels Palette Options
dialog box.

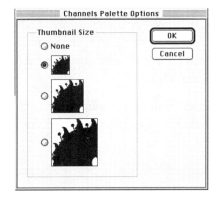

Creating a New Channel

Create a new channel in one of two ways. The first method is to choose New Channel from the Channels menu (see Figure 8.2). The Channel Options dialog box appears (see Figure 8.5). Fill in your options and click OK.

An alternate process for creating a new channel is to click the new channel button at the bottom of the Channels palette (the second button from the right). A new channel is created (see Figure 8.1). Hold down the (Option) [Alt] key while you click the new channel button and the Channel Options dialog box opens.

The Channel Options dialog box lets you name or rename and change the attributes of a channel. It can only be used on an alpha channel. You access the options when you create a new channel or by targeting an existing channel and choosing Channel Options... from the Channels menu. Double-clicking a channel name is a shortcut to the dialog box. Follow these steps to create a new channel:

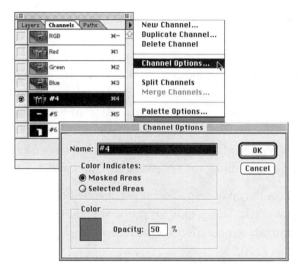

The Channel Options dialog box.

1. Choose New Channel from the Channels menu. The Channel Options dialog box opens.

2. Name the channel. By default, a new channel is created and given a number in the channel name bar of the Channels palette. The channel is numbered sequentially (#4, #5, #6), following the order in which it is created. You can use a more descriptive name if you want.

3. Specify whether color indicates masked areas or selected areas. Alpha channels are grayscale, but if more than one channel is visible, the alpha channels appear in the document window as a color. This is so the active alpha channel can be used as an overlay for editing. By default, the active mask appears in color, covering the other channels, and the selected areas are transparent, letting the channel images below show through. This is helpful when you want to use a color channel as a guide for editing an alpha channel.

4. Select the color that should overlay the other visible channels by double-clicking the square of color. The color picker comes onscreen and you can choose a new color. Red is the default color. The reason that you would change the color is to aid in separating the mask from the other visible channels. If you are using the mask to isolate a red apple from the background, the red color makes it difficult to determine which is the apple and which is the mask. Changing the color of the mask to blue makes the editing easier because the apple stands out.

5. Adjust the opacity to allow other channels to show through the color mask. This is only for previewing the channel while editing. It has no affect on the functioning opacity of the mask.

6. Click OK. The result is a blank channel that is all mask and no selection. The new channel becomes the active channel.

Tip

When you are making a complex image with a number of selections saved as channels, choose a different color for each alpha channel from the Channel Options dialog box. When you view all the channels for editing, the individual channels each appear as a different color overlay. This makes it easier to identify every channel and how they intersect.

Duplicating a Channel to the Same Document

There are a number of reasons for duplicating a channel. When you are experimenting, it is good to have a backup of the original channel to return to. You may want to make several duplicates so that you can create choices for yourself by experimenting in multiple directions. Also, a duplicate of a color channel can be a good place to start when you are making a mask to isolate a specific element. And finally, you may want to create a duplicate that you can apply filters to and use in conjunction with the original channel.

Use the Duplicate Channel command to make a copy of the active channel. Any channel can be duplicated except the color composite channel. When you duplicate a color channel, the copy becomes an alpha channel. There are several ways to accomplish the duplication process in the Channels palette.

◆ Drag the channel from the palette onto the image in its own document window. A copy of the channel appears below the other channels in the palette.

◆ Drag the channel to the new channel button at the bottom of the screen. This duplicates the channel and places it below the others.

◆ Select a channel and choose Duplicate Channel... from the Channels palette menu. The Duplicate Channel dialog box appears. It offers the following options (see Figure 8.6):

1. Duplicate As: Type in the new name of the channel.

2. Destination Document: Choose the original document name from the pull-down menu.

3. Check the Invert box if you want to reverse the mask and the selection in the new channel. Working in Photoshop, there are many times when it is useful to have an inverse mask. After working on a selection, you may want to adjust the masked area around the selection. Let's say you have an image of a building and a mask to select it, for instance. Make an inverse mask of the building and apply an effect to it such as Filter➡Render➡Clouds. You can use the new mask to put a cloud effect behind the building. You may also use the inverse mask to combine with other masks to create a new selection.

Tip

(Control-click) [right-click] any name in the Channels palette and a context menu appears with the choice to duplicate or delete the channel. This does not work with the color composite channel. If you choose duplicate, the Duplicate Channel dialog box opens. Choose delete and it trashes your channel.

Figure 8.6

*The Duplicate Channel
dialog box.*

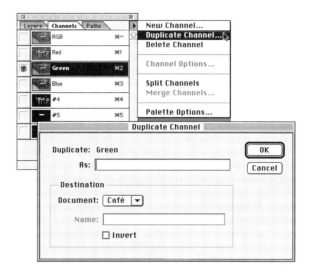

Duplicating a Channel to a Different Document

One reason to place a duplicate of a channel in another document is to create a library file to store alpha channels. A large number of channels increases the file size. Photoshop performance decreases as document size increases, causing operations to happen more slowly. Copy your mask channels to a new file serving as a library. Keep the library file closed. When you need a particular channel, open the library file and drag the channel back onto your original document.

You may also want to use the same selection in another image. Employ one of these methods to transfer channels to a different document:

◆ Drag the channel from the Channels palette onto the document window of another open document. A duplicate channel is created. The channel centers itself in a new mask if the file sizes of the two documents are different. The size of the new file must be the same size as the old file if you plan on returning the mask to the original document. This means that each file must have the same number of pixels in height and width. A different size file does not work correctly as a library file.

◆ Select, copy, and paste from one alpha channel to another.

1. Target the channel you want to copy.

2. Choose All from the Select menu or press (Command-A) [Control-A].

3. Select Copy from the Edit menu or press (Command-C) [Control-C].

4. Create a new channel in another document.

5. Choose Paste ((Command-V)[Control-V]) in the Edit menu, and the original channel is duplicated in the new mask.

◆ Use the Channels palette menu.

1. Target a channel and select Duplicate from the Channels palette menu. The Duplicate Channel dialog box appears (see Figure 8.6).

2. Select New from the pull-down menu in the Destination Document box. A new Multichannel mode document is created, the same size as the original. The file contains a single channel grayscale image that is a duplicate of the targeted channel. Instead of choosing a new document as your destination, you can select another listed file from the Destination Document pull-down menu. To be listed, the document must be open and the same size as the original file.

3. Click OK. A new file is created.

Note

There are a number of procedures for working with channels and multiple documents that require each document to be the same size. This occurs when it is necessary to do a pixel-to-pixel match between two documents. Imagine a situation where one file is placed on top of the other and each pixel from one file corresponds to a pixel in the other file. Each file has the same number of pixels in height and width. This is what is meant by referring to files of the same size.

Deleting a Channel

Delete a channel when you want it permanently removed from your image. The channel disappears from the Channels palette. You cannot delete the color composite channel. It only exists because of the color mode and the individual color channels. An RGB image, for example, has three channels. Each channel is assigned one color name; Red, Green or Blue. The individual channels are grayscale images with values representing one of the three colors. Together they make an RGB color composite. If you delete a color channel, the color composite disappears because it no longer has all the colors to make up the composite. As a result, the file mode changes to Multichannel. Take, for example, the RGB image with two alpha channels. Delete the green channel and the document mode is now Multichannel. The two remaining color channels and the two alpha channels are renamed #1 through #4. The channel information, however, has not changed. Each channel remains a grayscale image with the same 256 values from white to black. The difference is that the Red and Blue channels have been renamed and are no longer delineating the values of a color.

Channels may be deleted in a number of ways, but only one at a time:

◆ Select a channel and choose Delete Channel from the palette menu.

◆ Drag a channel to the Trashcan button at the bottom of the Channels palette.

◆ Select a channel and click the Trashcan button. To bypass the warning message that appears, hold down the (Option)[Alt] key when you click the Trashcan button.

Splitting Channels into Separate Images

If a file is too large to be saved or transported, the channels can be split, saved to separate files, and merged at a later date. When you split an RGB image with three alpha channels, you get six separate files. A 12MB CMYK document splits into four 3MB images.

1. Flatten the image if there are layers. A layered document cannot be split. Select Layer➡Flatten Image or choose Flatten Image from the Layers Palette menu.

2. Choose Split Channels from the Channels Palette menu to split a document (see Figure 8.2). All channels become separate files.

3. Each file is given a name that is a composite of the original file and individual channel before the split. An RGB file named Chair, for example, splits into a file named Chair.Red, Chair.Green, and Chair.Blue. The name can be found in the title bar at the top of the document window.

4. Each document as a result of the split is an 8-bit grayscale image saved in Grayscale mode.

Merging Channels into Composite Images

Merge Channels reconstructs a split document. This is a channels process and not to be confused with the layers merge operation. All images must be the same size, and each document to be merged must be open.

1. Select one grayscale image to be merged by making it the active document. This should be one of the color channels created with the Split Channels command.

2. Choose Merge Channels… from the Channels menu (see Figure 8.2).

3. The Merge Channels dialog box appears onscreen (see Figure 8.7). Pick the mode for the merged image: RGB color, CMYK color, Lab color, or Multichannel. You can only select a mode if the correct number of same size documents are open. A CMYK file, for example, is made up of four channels. If you do not have at least four same size documents open, CMYK color mode is grayed out in the Mode menu.

4. Select the number of channels for the merged image. The number of channels for a particular mode is listed in the channels box. It is limited to what the mode allows. The dialog box defaults to an appropriate number for the mode—RGB must be three; Lab three; CMYK four.

5. If you are using Multichannel mode, select your own number within the limits of same size open documents. Multichannel mode does not composite the channels.

6. Click OK.

7. A new Merge Channels dialog box comes up modified to the specific selected mode. If you choose RGB, for example, a Merge RGB Channels dialog box appears. Select the documents for the Red, Green, and Blue channels with the pull-down menus. All open, same-size documents are available, but the program defaults to a document with red in the name for the Red channel and the same with green and blue.

8. Click OK. The new merged file takes on a new name.

Figure 8.7

The Merge Channels dialog box.

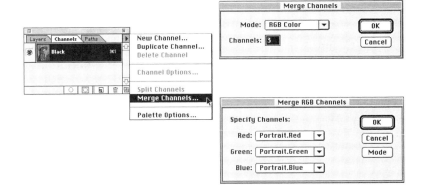

Tip

Alpha channels cannot be returned to a merged document unless the new document is a Multichannel file. A merged RGB image, for example, is limited to three channels. If your RGB file has two alpha channels, the image splits into five grayscale images. When you merge them, choosing RGB mode from the Merge Channels dialog box, you can only combine the three color channels to reconstruct your RGB image. Your two alpha channels are still separate grayscale files. After the merge, you can perform any duplicate method to reunite the alpha channels. That includes dragging the channels, copying and pasting, or using the Channels menu to duplicate.

WORKING WITH COLOR CHANNELS

Color channels are an essential part of the color documents you create or open in Photoshop. The color information is in the gray tones. Each RGB, Lab, or CMYK file is comprised of several 8-bit grayscale channels made up of 256 levels of gray from black (0) to white (255). The pattern of light and dark determines the position, density, and tonal qualities of the color portrayed. Every color channel adds its color element to the composite of the color channels. The blue channel in an RGB image, for example, combines blue or yellow (the inverse of blue) with the other color channels to create a color image. Editing a color channel affects the color balance of the total image.

How the grayscale values actually affect the color that you see varies with the different color modes. By way of example, RGB mode sees value 128 as a middle gray, and this is a neutral gray for any individual color channel (see the "Paint into Color Channels" sidebar). As you approach value 255 (white) the color of the channel becomes more intense. The Red RGB channel becomes more red. As you go down in value from 128 to 0 (black), the color of the Red channel becomes more cyan, which is the inverse of red.

The number of color channels that a document includes depends on the image mode.

- RGB and LAB mode images both contain three channels. The composite image for each mode is 24-bits per pixel (three 8-bit channels).

- CMYK images have four channels—one for each color—cyan, magenta, yellow, and black. The composite image contains 32-bits of information per pixel.

Saving Images with Alpha Channels

Alpha channels can only be saved in the following file formats. When you have a file with alpha channels you want to save, choose one of the formats from this list. When an alpha channel is included, the other formats in the Save dialog box are grayed out and can't be used.

- Native Photoshop: This is the default file format. It is the only format that works for saving a file that has layers as well as alpha channels. The Native Photoshop format supports all Photoshop image modes.

- TIFF: This is a widely used file format that works across platforms. TIFF supports LZW compression. Files with alpha channels can be saved in the TIFF format.

- Raw: This format does not work with compression and is often used in scientific applications where the formats are undocumented. Raw also works across platforms. This format can save files that include alpha channels.

PICT, PIXAR, PNG and Targa file formats are limited to four channels. They can save an RGB image and one alpha channel.

Paint into Color Channels

Do the following exercise to help you understand the relationship between the individual color channels.

1. Start with your foreground color in the default black setting.

2. Open an RGB image and look at the Channels palette (see Figure 8.1). The composite, labeled RGB, should be targeted. This means that the channel bar for the composite and RGB channels is black. The eye icon is on in the column to the left of the channel names.

3. Choose the Paintbrush from the toolbox. Use a wide brush and set the Opacity to 100%. Paint a stroke across the image. It makes a black mark.

4. Target the red channel by clicking the Red name bar in the Channel palette (see Figure 8.1). The Red channel is the only active channel. The other eye icons disappear and the image is grayscale.

5. Make the other color channels visible by clicking the box to the left of the composite channel. The eye icon appears next to each channel and the image is now full color. Only the red channel bar is black; the other channels are not active.

Each document is limited to a maximum of 24 channels. This does not include the color composite channel, which does not act like the other channels. The composite channel represents the interaction of the individual color channels. It functions as a shortcut. Clicking the composite makes all the color channels visible and active. Including the composite in the channel count would be redundant because each color channel is already included. The composite cannot be deleted. Deleting one of the color channels, however, makes the color composite disappear. The composite channel is named for the document mode. An RGB file has a composite named RGB. Likewise, a CMYK file has a CMYK composite.

Other color modes are Bitmapped, Grayscale, Duotone, and Indexed Color. Images with these modes each have one channel.

♦ Grayscale mode images have an 8-bit grayscale channel.

♦ Duotone mode also makes an 8-bit grayscale channel.

♦ Indexed Color images are made of a limited number of colors from a lookup table. Each pixel is one color from a palette of a maximum of 256 colors.

♦ Bitmapped images have 1-bit of color per pixel. All pixels are either black or white.

Viewing Channels in Color

The default settings show the individual color channels in grayscale. If more than one color channel is selected, they both display in color. When the Red channel, for example, is targeted in an RGB file, the screen shows a grayscale image, where the values from white to black determine how much red is added or taken away from the image. Make the Green layer active as well and the image is a combination of the red and green elements. To view a single channel in color, you can change the settings in Preferences (see Figure 8.8).

1. Select Preferences from the File menu and choose Display & Cursors from the submenu.

2. Put an X in the box for Color Channels in Color.

3. Click OK.

When you choose to view color channels in color, the channel keeps the light to dark values of the 8-bit grayscale image, but in addition, there is a color wash. It is as though a transparent acetate of pure color were overlaid on top of the grayscale image. The Red channel of an RGB image, for instance, appears red in the white areas and the dark parts go to black. Previewing channels in color might prove useful as a reminder as to which color channel you are editing. Or, it might subdue a channel by holding back the white, when you are editing an alpha channel and using one color channel as a visible guide. It is not, however, an accurate gauge of the color of a single color channel.

When you change the preferences to view color channels in color, a single color channel is seen as a grayscale image with a color wash that goes to black. This is a grayscale image and not what the color of that channel really looks like to the composite. The way that a single channel affects the color composite is as a saturated color that gets less saturated as the gray approaches a middle value and then becomes saturated as the inverse of the color.

6. Make a brush stroke next to the first one. Notice two things: The color is cyan, the complement of red, and the brushstroke is transparent.

7. Click the switch colors icon (double-headed arrow to the upper-right of your foreground and background colors on toolbox). White is now the foreground color.

8. Paint a brushstroke next to and through the cyan brushstroke. Observe that the color is red and that it completely replaced the cyan. They did not blend.

9. Make the Green channel active and repeat Steps 4-7. Note that when black is the foreground color, the paint is magenta, the complement of green. And when white is the foreground color, the paint is green. Also, the green or magenta brushstrokes add to the red or cyan paint.

10. Finally, repeat Steps 4-7 with the Blue channel selected. Paint over all the other brushstrokes. Observe that the paint is yellow with the black background and blue with the white background. Also, where the paint overlays with cyan,

continues

305

magenta, and yellow, the final color is black. Where the overlays are red, green, and blue, the final color is white.

11. Do this same exercise with a CMYK image.

When you view two color channels, the colors combine. That is what you are seeing. This means that if the Red channel is combining with the Green channel, red is being viewed with different saturations from red to cyan and this is combined with the Green channel, which is contibuting a color range of green to magenta (the inverse of green).

ALPHA CHANNELS

Alpha channels are masks that you create and store with your document. They are found in the Channels palette. The masks are grayscale images, often black and white. They are created when you select an area and save the selection (Select➡Save Selection). Alpha channels are edited with tools and effects, the same as any Photoshop image.

Making Masks

When you make a selection in an image, the area that is selected is active and can be altered. The area outside of the selection is the mask. It is the inverse of the selection and protects the image underneath the mask from change. This is like the stencils used by sign painters. You hold the stencil to a wall and paint across it. The stencil prevents the paint from getting outside of the selected area. In the same way, the graphics industry uses rubyliths and photographers use masks in the darkroom. In each of these situations the surface is divided, you have an area that selected and an area that is masked. When you make a selection in Photoshop, it can be saved as a channel for future use. The selection and its counterpart, the mask, are both saved.

Selections saved as a channels are called alpha channels and are located in the Channels palette below the color channels. They are used to store selections and are saved with the image. Alpha channels are the link between color channels and Photoshop's ability to manipulate images. The image is the color channels. The alpha channels determine what part of the image is affected by a particular operation.

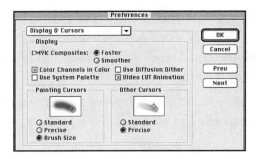

Figure 8.8

*Setting the Preferences to view
color channels in color.*

Each alpha channel is a combination of two elements: the selection and
the mask. The term mask is used interchangeably with alpha channel,
and selection usually refers to the selected area in the image. Alpha
channels are often seen as black and white; however, they are grayscale
images with 256 levels. They can have gradations and can be very
complex. You can only have three color channels, for example, in an
RGB file. If you duplicate the Red channel, the copy is an alpha channel.
When loaded into an image, it can be used as you would any other
selection.

Click the eye icon of an alpha channel to make it visible. If any other
channels are also visible, the alpha mask appears as a single color that
is semi-transparent. The default color is red with a 50% opacity. When
it is the only visible channel, the alpha channel produces an opaque
grayscale image in the image window. This is demonstrated by the
following exercise.

1. Make a rectangular selection in the center of an RGB image.

2. Paint a diagonal line from the upper-right to the lower-left
    corner. What you observe is that you can only apply paint
    where the brush passes through the selection.

3. Save the selection as an alpha channel by choosing Save
    Selection from the Select menu. Click OK. The alpha channel is
    placed below the RGB channels as #4 in the Channels palette.

4. Make the new channel, #4, visible by clicking in the left box of the channel to show the eye icon. All the eyes should now be on and you should observe the mask in the open document. It is a transparent red (see Figure 8.9).

5. Click the eye icon in the composite RGB channel to hide the color channels. The mask in the image changes to black and white.

Figure 8.9

A selection and mask channel.

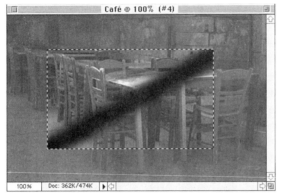
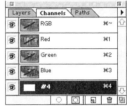

MAKING THE CONNECTION BETWEEN SELECTIONS AND CHANNELS

Use the Marquee tool, the Lasso tool, or the Magic Wand to make a selection. The selection appears as a border (see Chapter 5, "Selections, Paths, and Masks"). Selections are converted to alpha channels saved with the document. This makes selections available for future modification and use. When you save a selection as an alpha channel, your ability to edit the selection is greatly increased. In addition to painting, cutting, and pasting, you can combine channels by adding, subtracting or intersecting with other channels. You can create new channels with this procedure.

Tip

Using the Save Selection button—located at the bottom of the Channels palette—is a quick way to save a selection. Make a selection in your document, and click the Save Selection button to save it as a channel (see

Figure 8.1). Hold down the (Option)[Alt] key when you click the Save Selection button to bring up the Channel Options dialog box before you create the new channel.

Save Selection Command

After you create a selection, the Save Selection command enables you to convert the selection into an alpha channel. You do this with the following steps:

1. Make a selection in the active document. (see Chapter 5, "Selections, Paths, and Masks").

2. Choose Save Selection from the Select pull-down menu. The Save Selection dialog box appears onscreen. There are two parts to this dialog box: Destination and Operation (see Figure 8.10).

3. Destination tells Photoshop where to save the new channel. Select the Destination Document to which you want to save the selection from the Destination pull-down menu. The active document is the default. The selection must be saved into a file that is the same size as the active document. Additional names are listed if there are same-size files open on the desktop. You can also select New to create a new document the same size as the active window.

4. Next, choose an item from the Destination Channel pull-down menu. The default choice is New. It creates a new channel from the current selection.

5. Destination Channel also lists other alpha channels if any exist. This is an alternative to selecting New. Select an existing channel if you want to replace or combine the channel's selection with the selection you are saving.

6. If you select an existing channel, go to the Operation box. There is a bullet list offering four choices of how the current selection should interact with the selected channel.

   ◆ Replace Channel: This option replaces the existing channel selection with the current one.

♦ Add to Channel: Add to combines the current selection with the existing channel selection. The new channel selection includes the area of both selections.

♦ Subtract from Channel: This option creates a channel with the selected area of the existing channel minus the area of the current selection. If, for example, the existing channel selection is a large circle and the current selection is a small circle, the new channel selection looks like a donut.

♦ Intersect with Channel: The new channel selection includes only the area where the current selection and the existing channel selection intersect or overlap. Only that area is included in the new channel selection.

Figure 8.10

The Save Selection dialog box.

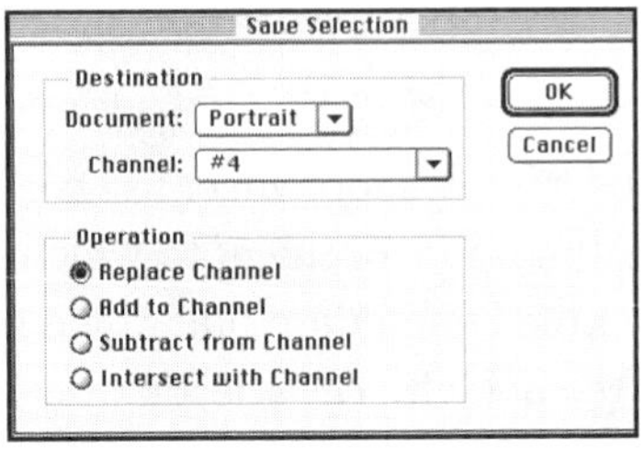

7. Click OK and you have created a new alpha channel.

Loading Selections from Channels

After a selection is saved in a channel, it can be retrieved at any time. Loading a selection converts an alpha channel into an active selection. Photoshop offers several methods for loading selections. A selection is loaded from the Select menu, the keyboard, or the Load Selection button in the Channels palette.

Load Selection from the Menu Bar

You can turn an alpha channel into a selection using the Select menu. This method has been around through many versions of Photoshop. It enalbes you to load a selection even if the Channels palette is hidden.

1. Choose Load Selection from the Select menu. The Load Selection dialog box comes onscreen (see Figure 8.11).

2. The Load Selection dialog box lets you choose the source document and channel to be used for the current selection. The Source box has a pull-down menu for Document. Here you can choose the current document or another open document. A file appears on the list only if it is the same size as the current document. The current document is the default.

3. After choosing the Source Document, select an alpha channel listed in the Source Channel drop-down menu. All alpha channels for the selected Source Document are in this list. This channel loads as the current selection.

4. Invert is the final choice from the Source box. Click invert if you want the selection to load with the mask area and selection area reversed.

5. If the document you are working with has no current selection, you are done. If there already is a current selection and you want the channel that you are loading to combine with it, go on to the next step.

6. Make a choice from the Operation box when there is a current selection. There are four options:

   ◆ New Selection: Replaces the existing selection with the channel you are loading.

   ◆ Add to Selection: The existing selection and the channel you are loading are combined to make one larger selection.

   ◆ Subtract from Selection: The result is the existing selection minus the area of the channel being loaded.

   ◆ Intersect with Selection: This creates a selection composed of the area common to both the existing selection and the channel being loaded.

7. Click OK.

Figure 8.11

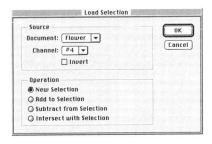

The Load Selection dialog box.

Load Selection Button

You can load a selection from the Channels palette. Click a channel to make it active and then click the Load Selection button located at the bottom of the Channels palette (see Figure 8.1). It is the last button on the left and looks like a dotted circle. The channel selection loads into the document as the current selection. Hold down the (Option)[Alt] key when you click the Load Selection button to bring up the Load Selection dialog box.

Tip

Save time when you load selections. You can also load a selection by dragging the channel that you want to load onto the Load Selection button. Hold down the (Option)[Alt] key when you do this and the Load Selection dialog box appears onscreen. Your alpha channel selection is loaded as the current selection in the document and the color channels remain active and visible. This saves time because you can do this in one step.

Load a Selection from the Keyboard

Using keyboard shortcuts speeds up production. It is often helpful to work in Photoshop with one hand on the keyboard and one hand on the mouse. After you get to know the commands, you can access them very quickly.

- ◆ Hold the (Command)[Control] key down and click the channel you want to load. (This was the (Option) [Alt] key in version 3.0.)

♦ A variation of this shortcut is to hold the (Command-Option) [Control-Alt] keys down while you press the keyboard number of the channel you want to load. (Command-Option-~) [Control-Alt-~] is the command for loading the color composite selection. After that, the channels follow in number order from 1-24. So for an RGB file, red is one, green is two, and blue is three.

♦ Add to a current selection by holding the (Command-Shift) [Control-Shift] keys while clicking an alpha channel. The resulting selection is a combination of the current selection and the alpha channel. (This was the (Option)[Alt] and Shift keys in version 3.0.)

♦ Subtract from a selection by holding the (Command-Option) [Control-Alt] keys while clicking a channel from the Channels palette. The resulting selection is the existing selection minus the area of the channel.

♦ Intersect with selection is accomplished by holding down the (Command-Option-Shift)[Control-Alt-Shift] keys while you click a channel in the Channels palette. The selected area includes only the area common to the existing selection and chosen channel.

EDITING AND COMPOSITING WITH CHANNELS

Editing a color channel at any time alters an image's appearance. Any visual change affects the grayscale values on one or all of the color channels, which causes the image to change. Alpha masks are stored selections, and any changes you make to the mask are seen in the selection. Editing an alpha mask can be as simple as painting a black and white shape. It can also be very sophisticated and complex, creatively employing many steps, numerous tools, color corrections, and effects. The end product of all your labor is a selection that does what you want it to.

Editing Color Information Channels

The approach to editing color channels is different from that of alpha channels. When you use the Image➥Adjust menu to change the hue, color balance, or levels of an image, you are editing the composite color channel, which means that you are altering all the individual color channels in that document. The same type of action can be performed on an individual color channel. A color cast can be corrected by selecting a color channel and using curves to change the grayscale values of that channel. If an RGB image has a red cast, it may mean that the grayscale values of the red channel need to be darker.

When the grayscale values of an RGB color channel get darker and approach a middle gray, the channel loses color saturation. As the channel goes beyond the middle gray and gets darker, it increases in saturation as the inverse of the color. So as the red channel becomes more cyan (the red inverse), the effect is similar to adding more green and blue. Together those colors make cyan.

Something else is happening here. As you make the grayscale values of the Red channel darker and move the color toward cyan, you are making the composite image darker. Likewise, if you make the Green and Blue channels lighter, you increase the cyan cast of the image and make the image as a whole lighter. So if you have a red cast to an image and you don't want to make the overall image lighter or darker, you may need to adjust all the channels. Make the Red channel darker and the Blue and Green channels lighter in equal proportions.

Do the following to change the color cast without altering the lightness or darkness of the image.

1. From the Channels palette, select the Red channel of an RGB image and make the composite RGB channel visible.

2. Select Curves from the Adjust menu. Notice that the at the top of the curves dialog box, it says Channel: Red. This confirms that you are only editing the red channel (see Figure 8.12).

3. Make sure that Preview is checked so that you can see the effects of the curves before you make them permanent.

4. Adjust the diagonal line on the curves graph to darken the grayscale values of the red channel. The image becomes less red, more cyan and darker overall. Make the adjustment half way. Do not completely adjust the color cast.

5. Click OK.

6. Select the Green channel and hold the Shift key down while you select the Blue channel. This should make both channels active.

7. Click the box to the left of the composite RGB thumbnail to make all the channels visible.

8. Go to the Curves menu again. At the top of the Curves dialog box it says Channel: GB to indicate that it will adjust only the green and the blue channels.

9. This time move the diagonal in the opposite direction to lighten the image. This increases the amount of cyan (blue and green) without changing the values of the Red channel. It also lightens the overall image.

10. Click OK.

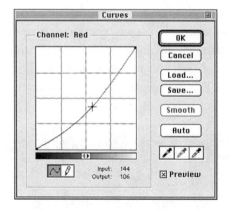

Figure 8.12

The Curves dialog box.

Tip

Sometimes a filter can be more effective or less obvious if it is applied to just one channel. A color gradation, for instance, shows some stepping. After inspecting each channel, you find that the problem is mostly with one channel. Select the problem channel and make the other color channels visible. Add some noise to the problem channel through the Filter menu and the gradation can improve.

Using a Color Channel to Create an Alpha Mask

At times it is easier to make a selection by duplicating and editing a color channel as opposed to using one of the other available methods. A color channel can be duplicated and the copy is an alpha channel. The grayscale image of each color channel usually differs. Often one channel is superior to the other channels or the composite for editing to make a selection.

1. Open the "Flower.psd" image from the CD-ROM. The goal is to make an alpha channel that selects the flower and masks the background.

2. First look at each color channel separately (see Figure 8.13). As individual channels, each is a grayscale image. Notice that in the red channel, the flower is almost white and the background is dark. Compare this to what you see in the blue and green channels. The contrast between the flower and the background in those channels is not as great.

Figure 8.13

Color Channels as grayscale images.

3. Create an alpha channel that is a copy of the Red channel. In the Channels palette, drag the Red channel onto the New Channel button. It is the second button from the right at the bottom of the palette (see Figure 8.1). The new alpha channel that appears is named #4. It is the active and only visible channel.

4. Select Image➥Adjust➥Threshold.

5. Check the preview box so you can see the effects as you make them.

6. Move the slider to 120. The image becomes very contrasty—all black and white.

7. Click OK. The mask is not perfect. The alpha channel has some black in the white area that selects the flower. It also has some white in the black mask area that holds back the background.

8. Use the Paintbrush to clean up the alpha channel that is still active and visible. Paint white into the selection and black into the mask in order to edit the alpha channel so that it only selects the flower (see Figure 8.14).

9. Make the composite channel visible so you can see the flower image under the red mask overlay.

10. Change the mask color to green in Channel Options to make a better contrast with the red flower.

11. Finish cleaning up the edges of the mask with the paintbrush.

12. Make the composite active and hide the alpha channel. It is now a mask that can be loaded to select the flower.

Figure 8.14

The alpha channel of the flower image before and after editing.

Using a Color Channel as a Template for a Selection

There are many situations where you want to make a small adjustment to part of an image. You may want to add a highlight because the image is too flat. Photoshop has many tools and filters to make these effects happen, but the first step is to create the correct selection. Color channels make a very good template for these kind of selections. Duplicate the color channel that best fits your needs. It copies as an alpha channel. Edit the alpha channel to create the subtle mask that you need. Then use the selection to adjust your image. Open the "Cafe.psd" photo in the CD, where the lighting is fairly even. To make it more interesting, you want to lighten the red chairs so they look as though they are being spotted by sunlight.

1. Drag the Red channel onto the New Channel button at the bottom of the Channels palette. The copy that this creates is the active and visible channel. The Red channel is chosen because of the three color channels; it has the lightest values in the red chairs. It is the red chairs that are being adjusted.

2. The next step is to use Levels to alter the new alpha channel. The goal is to create a mask that only selects the chair high-lights. Select Image➡Adjust➡Levels... and move the gray and white levels sliders to make a high contrast image. (The input numbers should be 0,17,196). This produces a mostly black image with blown out highlights (see Figure 8.15). Click OK.

3. Next, select Filters➡Gaussian Blur. Set the Radius to 2.7 pixels. The purpose of this step is to soften the edges of the selection so that the final effects blend with the chairs (see Figure 8.16).

Figure 8.15

Adjust the levels of the alpha channel.

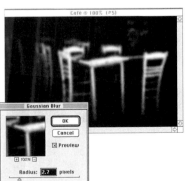

4. Click OK.

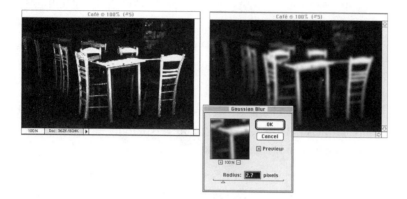

Figure 8.16

Apply a Gaussian blur to the image.

5. Make the composite colors the active channels by clicking the RGB name in the Channels palette.

6. Load the blurred alpha channel you just created and hide the selection for easier viewing.

7. Select Image➡Adjust➡Curves. Use the Curves command to lighten the current selection and create the sunlight effect. If preview is checked, you can see the effect on the chairs as you adjust the curve.

Creating Masks that Fade with Gradients

Gradient masks add interesting lighting and depth to an image. With a gradient mask you can make an object come out of a shadow or fade into the background. To illustrate, open the "Flower.psd" image from the CD. A shadow effect can be achieved by combining the overlapping areas of two masks to create a new mask (see Figure 8.17).

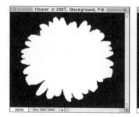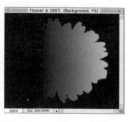

Figure 8.17

The flower selection, gradient mask, and flower gradient mask.

1. Make a selection and create an alpha mask for the flower. This separates the red flower from its background. By default it is named Channel #4.

2. Load the inverse of Channel #4. The background of the flower is selected. Select Filter➨Blur➨Gaussian.... Set the radius to 3.0 pixels. This puts the background out of focus.

3. Create a new channel by clicking the new channel button in the Channels palette. The new channel (Channel #5) is the active channel. The image is black.

4. Select the Gradient tool. Set the Gradient option to Foreground to Background (see Figure 8.18). Foreground and background colors are set to the default black and white. Using the Gradient tool, click in the image 1/3 from the left edge and drag the cursor horizontally to the right edge of the image. The image becomes a gradient from black on the left to white on the right. (This finished image is in the Flower.psd file on the CD. To see it, make the layer Finished Gradient visible.)

Figure 8.18

Gradient Tool Options palette.

5. Load Channel #4, the flower silhouette, via Load Selections on the Select menu.

6. Load Channel #5, the gradient mask, from Load Selections on the Select menu. Choose the Intersect operation in the Load Selection dialog box. Save this new selection (#6).

7. With Channel #6 loaded, use the Fill command to add a black gradation to the flower. Set the Opacity to 100%. Hide the selection edges so you can see the effect of the gradation. Fill a second time for a darker shadow.

WORKING WITH CALCULATION COMMANDS

Use Calculations… from the Image menu to create new channels. These channels are the products of blending modes that combine channels in unique ways. The effects range from subtle changes in color or lighting to graphic effects that alter hue, saturation and luminosity. Experimentation is key to working with Calculations because outside of some specific guidelines, many of the most interesting effects cannot be predicted. They need to be discovered instead.

With Calculations…commands, mathematical procedures are performed on the pixels from two source channels. One set of pixels is placed over another. Both files must be the same size—that is, the same number of pixels and the same proportion for each file. Each pixel interacts with its corresponding pixel in the other channel. The result is a new channel that is the product of the interaction of the two source pixels. The channels are grayscale images, and each pixel is allocated a value from 0 to 255. The value of each pixel is significant to how it interacts with its matching pixel. There are three Calculation commands: Duplicate, Apply Image, and Calculations.

Duplicating an Image

The Duplicate command makes a complete copy of the image, including all the channels, layers, and masks (see Figure 8.19). When you use Duplicate the copy exists in memory and appears onscreen next to the original image. Use the copy to experiment. If you don't like what you have, close the file without saving or use Save As to save the image. You can make many versions of your document and work on each in a distinct manner. With a duplicate copy, you can always return to the original image.

1. Select Duplicate on the Image menu bar. The Duplicate Image dialog box opens and asks you to name the duplicate image.

2. Click the Merged Layers Only box if you do not want any layers in the copy. The duplicate image comes out as a background only.

3. Click OK. Both the duplicate and the original file are now open.

Figure 8.19

*The Duplicate Image
dialog box.*

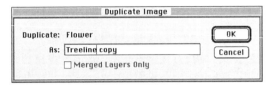

Creating Channels with the Apply Image Command

The Apply Image command carries out channel calculations on a document. Two images are blended together using mathematical operations on the corresponding pixels of each image. The data for these calculations can come from a source layer in the active document or from another image. The source document and the target document must have the same file size. The Blending menu in the Apply Image dialog box determines the type of calculation performed. The calculations can only be applied to an active channel in the target document. It is this channel that gets changed with Apply Image. You must choose the source document, layer and channel that you want to implement. Apply image works using any channels. This includes the color composite channel as the source or the target.

Follow these steps to use Apply Image. Both the source and the target documents must be open. The target document must be active. Target the channel and layer in the active document to which you want the calculations applied.

1. Select Apply Image from the Image menu. The Apply Image dialog box opens (see Figure 8.20). Click the preview to see the effects of the calculations in the dialog box.

Figure 8.20

The Apply Image dialog box.

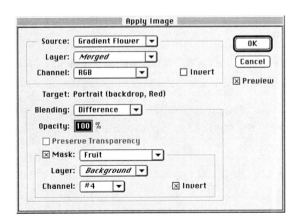

2. Choose the source document from the Source menu. This can be a different image from the target document, but it must be the same file size to appear on the list.

3. Select the layer for the source image. Choose merged if you want to use the composite of all the layers.

4. Pick the source channel from the Channel menu. You can check invert if you want to reverse the values of the source for the calculations.

5. The lower half of the dialog box lists the target. It tells you the document, layer, and channel selected. Below that is Blending. Select a mode from the Blending menu to determine the type of calculation performed (see the section that follows describing the blending modes). It is the different blending modes that determine the effects of Apply Image. Experimentation is the best way to understand what these calculations can do.

6. Fill in the opacity to set the intensity of the outcome.

7. If you want to apply the calculations through a mask, check the Mask box. You then have the choice of document, layer, and channel for the mask. Click the invert box if you want to transpose the values of the applied mask.

8. Click OK to execute the calculation.

Using Calculation Blending Options

The actual results from using the different modes can be difficult to describe. Experimentation is the key word here. Some modes such as Multiply, Hard Light, Darker, and Color Burn tend to darken the image. And Screen, Soft Light, Lighter, and Color Dodge lighten the image. But there are other things that going on as well that bring out parts of an image. This is where modes are particularly good. You may, for example, discover that one mode gives your image the right punch by changing the contrast of the edge pixels to make the image glow. The following list attempts to describe a little of what is happening technically when you use the different modes. The Blending modes are the calculations performed on two pixels. Each mode involves mathematical procedures on the grayscale value of each pixel in relation to the other. The base color is the original image and the blend color is the image that is applying the calculations. In a situation where the base is the changed image, it becomes the result color. Other times a new third image is created as the result color.

- Normal: This mode combines both pixels based on opacity. Essentially one pixel lays on top of the other and the opacity determines to what extent the two pixels blend.

- Multiply: The values of the two pixels are multiplied and then divided by 255. The effect is that of looking through two transparent images placed one on top of the other. The overall image is darker. When you multiply with black, the result is black. If you multiply with white, the color is unchanged.

- Screen: This style multiplies the inverse of the lightness or darkness of the two colors. The resulting image is lighter. The effect is similar to that of sandwiching two negatives together and making a photographic print through them.

- Overlay: Depending on the base color, this mode multiplies or screens the pixels. Overlay holds the highlight and shadow values and most of the blending is in the middle.

- Soft Light: The effect of a soft spotlight on the image is achieved through a combination of multiplying (darkening) and screening (lightening). Where the blend color lies in relation to a 50% gray determines whether it is multiplied or screened. Lighter colors are lightened and darker colors are darkened.

- Hard Light: This has the effect of a hard spotlight on the image. The calculations are similar to soft light. Here, too, there is a process of multiplying and screening.

- Color Dodge: With this mode, the base color is brightened in relation to the values of the blend color.

- Color burn: This is the opposite of color dodge. The base color is darkened in relation to the values of the blend color.

- Darker: This mode contrasts the brightness of the two pixels and shows the darker one.

- ◆ Lighter: This works opposite to the darker mode by comparing the values of both pixels and then displaying the lighter ones.

- ◆ Add: This mode adds the two pixels and divides them by a scale factor, a number you select between 1.00 and 2.00. Whites areas stay white and the black areas stay black where they intersect.

- ◆ Subtract: Here, the pixels of the source are subtracted from the target pixels. then divided by scale factor which can be any number between 1 and 2.

- ◆ Difference: This mode depends on which pixel has a greater brightness value. Either the blend color is subtracted from the base color or the base color is subtracted from the blend.

- ◆ Exclusion: This is similar to the difference mode, but the effects are softer. Black stays black. White inverts the base color values.

Calculations

Some of the most interesting image collages produced in Photoshop can be achieved using Calculations.... This Photoshop feature lets you combine two source channels by performing channel calculations on corresponding pixels from each document. You can select any two channels—color or alpha. The outcome of the mathematics is a new channel that can be placed in any same size document. As an option, the result can be a new document and a new channel.

The result channel can be used as a color channel. In this manner, it affects the appearance of the image. Use it to change the color information or combine other elements from other images with your document. The result channel can also be used as an alpha mask. In this form it works as a very specific mask that can be used to select areas for manipulation with any of the editing tools in Photoshop.

Apply Image and Calculations have a number of differences that help determine which gets used in different situations. Apply Image can utilize composite images for its source or target. With Calculations, only individual channels can be combined. This is an important difference. It means that you must use Apply Image when you want to affect the full color image. With Calculations, you can create a new document that does not have to be the targeted channel. Unlike Apply Image, the two source channels remain unchanged. Finally, Calculations offers a gray channel option for the source and the result channels. Gray gives the effect as if the document were converted to grayscale mode.

Follow these steps to perform Calculations.

1. Open any same size images that you want to use for the source and result documents.

2. Select Calculations... from the Image menu (see Figure 8.21).

Figure 8.21

The Apply Image dialog box.

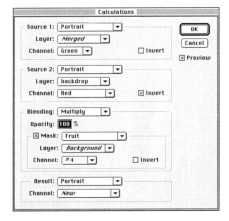

3. Click the Preview box to view the changes while in the Calculations dialog box.

4. Select the information in the Source 1 box from the pull-down menus. Choose the first source document for the calculations.

5. Choose the layer you want to use in the first source document. Select Merged if you want to use the composite of all the layers.

6. Select the source channel. Gray can be chosen if you want a grayscale mode effect from the selected channel.

7. Check Invert if you want to reverse the values in the calculations for this source channel.

8. Choose the document, layer, and channel information in Source 2 box.

9. Select a Blending option to create the type of effect you want to achieve (see the previous section describing the blending modes).

10. Fill in the opacity to determine the intensity of the calculations on the result channel.

11. Click the Mask box if you want to apply the calculations through a mask. This limits the effects of the calculations to the selected area defined by a channel. If chosen, Mask options appear in the dialog box. Enter the document, the layer, and the channel for the Mask. You may choose invert to reverse the values of the mask.

12. Select the result document and channel from the menus at the bottom of the dialog box. Choose existing or new items.

13. Click OK to execute the calculation.

Chapter · · · · · · · · · · · · · · · 9

LAYERS

Since its introduction in Photoshop 3.0, layers have been and remain one of the most important and powerful compositing tools that Photoshop has to offer. Layers have become the basic way of using Photoshop. With version 3.0, layers worked in conjunction with floating selections, the older method of compositing. With the improvements of version 4.0, layers management is expanded to its real potential. Floating selections are almost completely eliminated and keyboard additions, expanded features and button icons make using layers quicker, simpler and more intuitive. This makes layers a more productive tool for performing complex compositing.

The idea behind layers is very basic. You start with a background image and place another image on top. Then another image on top of that. Each image is a separate layer that can be moved and edited independent of the other layers. Editing a layer includes color corrections, filter effects, painting, and cropping. A layer can be opaque and cover what is below or it can be transparent. In this way, a layer acts like an image on a sheet of clear acetate. As one sheet of acetate is placed on top of another, you can see down through the layers in the clear areas. Layer opacity is variable and calculations can be done using modes to composite the pixels of one layer with the corresponding pixels underneath to create new pixels. The great thing about layers is that they enable nonlinear undos. When compositing images, you no longer have to permanently marry one element to another before you can approach the next component. Layers permit you to change the characteristics of any layer regardless of when it was added to the stack. This is an important feature of Photoshop because the need for revisions can be a reality at any stage of the production.

USING THE LAYERS PALETTE

Select Show Layers from the Window menu. The Layers palette appears (see Figure 9.1). The Layers palette lets you perform a number of creative and editing functions with layers.

Figure 9.1

The Layers palette.

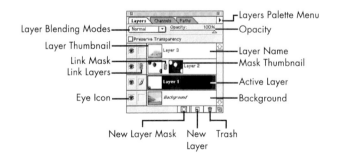

Note

There are two menus that list commands for creating and working with layers. It is easy to get confused as to which is being referred to because of the similarity of the names. One is the Layers menu. It is located in the menu bar at the top of the screen. The other is the Layers palette menu.

This pull-down menu is brought up by clicking the arrow in the upper-right corner of the layers palette (see Figure 9.2).

Figure 9.2

The Layer menu and the Layers palette menu.

Creating a New Layer

When you add a new layer to an image, it is active and located in front of the last active layer. The new layer is transparent.

To add a new layer:

1. Select New Layer... from the Layers palette pop-up menu, shown in Figure 9.3, or click the New Layer button. The New Layer button is the middle icon at the bottom of the Layers palette. Click the button and you create a new layer. If you (Option-click) [Alt-click] the New Layer button, the New Layer dialog box appears (see Figure 9.4).

Figure 9.3

Select New Layer... from the Layers palette pop-up menu.

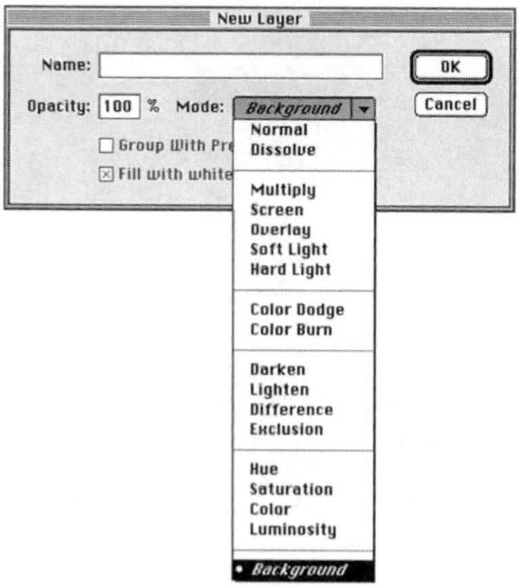

Figure 9.4

The New Layer dialog box.

2. Set the Opacity and the Mode. The Opacity slider determines how transparent the layer is when blending with the layers below. The Mode setting establishes how the pixels of this layer blend with the pixels below. (See the sections on blending modes and opacity in this chapter for more information.)

Making Layers Visible

The Eye icon establishes whether or not a layer is visible in the document window. The Eye is found in the leftmost column of the Layers palette (see Figure 9.5). Hide a layer by clicking its eye icon—both the eye in the Layers palette and the layer in the active window disappear. Click the now empty eye box and the Eye icon and layer image reappear.

Dragging up or down through the Eye column shows or hides a number of layers. Each layer that your cursor drags through changes to the same state as the first layer in your drag. All the layers in the drag end up visible or hidden.

Showing or hiding the Eye icon does not affect the active or inactive status of a layer. There is an important distinction between being a visible layer and an active layer. Active and visible are independent features. A layer can be active and hidden, only visible, both active and visible, or neither. A layer cannot be edited unless it is both active and visible.

Figure 9.5

Eye icons in the Layers palette.

Eye Icon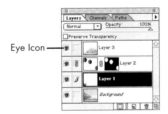

Tip

A shortcut for showing a single layer is (Option-clicking)[Alt-clicking] any Eye icon—the layer does not have to be active. Doing this hides all other layers and leaves only the selected layer visible. (Option-click)[Alt-click] that layer's Eye icon a second time and all the other layers are visible again. This can be very useful when editing. You can see the borders of an image that would normally blend into the background.

Activating a Layer

To make a layer active, click the name or the thumbnail. The layer is highlighted in black when it is selected. Inactive layers have a white bar. Only one layer at a time can be chosen. In order to edit a layer, it must be both visible and active (see Figure 9.6).

Figure 9.6

An active layer is highlighted in black.

When a layer is active, the box between the eye icon and the layer thumbnail shows a paintbrush or a gray rectangle with a white selection in the center. The latter image is a mask icon that signifies a layer mask is selected in this active layer. The paintbrush indicates that it is an active image layer. The image can be altered when the paintbrush is in view (see Figure 9.7).

This thumbnail represents the layer mask

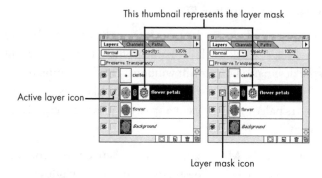

Active layer icon

Layer mask icon

Figure 9.7

The paintbrush indicates that the layer image or mask is active.

Duplicating a Layer

When duplicating a layer (creating a copy), you can select a destination other than your current file. This is useful if you want to create a library of layers or use the same layer in multiple documents related to the same project.

To duplicate a layer:

1. In the Layers palette, select Duplicate Layer from the pop-up menu or drag the layer you want to duplicate onto the New Layer button. The Duplicate Layer dialog box appears, as in Figure 9.8.

Figure 9.8

The Duplicate Layer dia-log box.

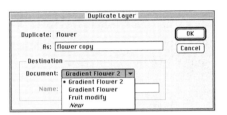

Note

To access the Duplicate Layer dialog box when using the New Layer button, hold down the (Option)[Alt] key while you drag.

2. Name your duplicated layer.

3. Select a destination for the new layer. You can copy the layer to any open file, or create a new document for the layer.

Dragging Layers from Another File

You can also duplicate a layer by dragging it from the Layers palette to the destination image. Click the layer name in the Layers palette and drag it onto the destination document window. The destination document window is now the active image. The duplicate layer is the active layer in the Layers palette, and it sits on top of the previous active layer in that document.

As an alternative, use the Move tool to drag an active layer from the current document window to the destination document window. This is another method for duplicating a layer. Place both windows side by side and then click and drag from the active image to the destination image and release the mouse button. The duplicate layer is now the active layer in the destination document.

Deleting Layers

There are several ways to delete a layer in Photoshop. If you drag a layer to the Trash button at the bottom of the Layers palette, it is deleted. Edit➡Undo gets the image back if it was a mistake. You can also delete a layer from any of several pull-down menus.

◆ Click the Layers palette menu and select Delete Layer to remove the active layer.

◆ Choose Delete Layer from Layer menu to delete the active layer.

◆ Use one of the context menus to select Delete. (Control-click) [right-click] the image to bring up the menu.

Tip

New to Photoshop 4.0 is the ability to delete a layer by clicking the Trash button. When you do, you get a warning that the active layer will be deleted. Click OK and the layer is gone. If you (Option-click)[Alt-click] the Trash button, the warning does not appear.

Naming Layers

When you create a new layer, you have the option of naming it in the New Layer dialog box. You can also rename an existing layer in the Layer Options dialog box (see Figure 9.9).

1. Open the Layer Options dialog box by double-clicking the layer name of an existing layer in the Layers palette. If you are creating a new layer, the New Layer dialog box opens.

2. Type in the name and click OK. You can always rename the layer by performing these steps at a later date.

Figure 9.9

The Layer Options dialog box.

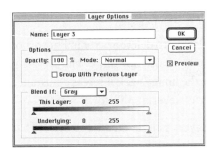

Setting the Opacity of a Layer

The Opacity slider is located at the top of the Layers palette. You can also find the Opacity slider in the Layer Options dialog box (see Figure 9.9). It is a matter of convenience which one you use; they perform the same function. Use the slider to adjust the opacity of the active layer. This determines how the pixels on top hide or blend with the pixels of the layer below. As you move the slider down the scale, the image becomes more transparent and the pixels of the image below become more visible.

Tip

As a shortcut, use the keypad numbers to set the opacity. Press the number 9 and opacity changes to 90%. The number 1 makes a 10% opacity, 2 sets opacity to 20%, and so on. The number 0 sets opacity to 100%.

Open "Graygirl.psd" on the *Photoshop Complete* CD-ROM. The document contains a background and one layer of the same image. The colors of the layer and the background are inverse—exact opposites. Each color pixel is the compliment of the corresponding pixel on the other image. When they are blended at 50% opacity the colors neutralize each other and the effect is that of a grayscale image.

1. Open the file "Graygirl.psd" from the *Photoshop Complete* CD-ROM.

2. Make Layer 1 active and move the Opacity slider to 10%, then 20%, then 30%.

3. Press numbers 6, 7, 8, and 0, one at a time. Notice how opacity effects the way that the two colors blend.

Selecting Layer Blending Modes

Use layer blending modes to establish how a layer, the color blend, combines with the images below, the base. The layer blending mode pull-down menu is located at the top of the Layers palette (see Figure 9.10) in the Layer Options dialog box, or in the New Layer dialog box (see Figure 9.4). Each mode uses different mathematical calculations to determine the interaction between the pixels of the active layer and those underneath. Those calculations take into account the value of each pixel, and a new pixel is formed as a result of a mathematical procedure. The resulting effects are combinations that use elements of both layers in unique ways. The special effects created with these modes can be blatant or subtle.

Figure 9.10

The Layer blending modes.

The results of the different modes can be difficult to describe. Experimentation is the key word here. Some modes such as Multiply, Hard Light, Darken, and Color Burn tend to darken the image. And Screen, Soft Light, Lighten, and Color Dodge lighten the image. But other things are going on as well that bring out selective parts of an image. This is because blending modes do more that just lighten or darken images. It can be the complete range of the hue, luminance, or saturation that is altered. This is where modes are particularly good. You may discover, for example, that one mode gives your image the right punch by changing the contrast of the edge pixels to make the image glow. You also may want to try painting with these modes. The textures created when painting in modes often build upon the last stroke. Each stroke can add to the last the way magic markers do, or they can build on themselves and create distortions that keep distorting with each additional stroke.

Do the following steps to explore some of the effects of the blending modes.

1. Open the file "Colorgirl.psd" from the *Photoshop Complete* CD-ROM. This is an RGB file with three layers.

2. Make the background layer visible, a grayscale image of a girl, and hide the other two layers.

3. The next layer above the background is named colorize. It makes the girl look like a color image. Click the name to make this layer active and visible. Notice that the blending mode is set to Color.

4. Hide the Background. This lets you see that the color layer is just painted color. It is the color mode that defines the way that it blends with the background to make it look like a color image.

5. Make the background visible again. Change the blending mode on the colorize layer to each mode in the list and notice the changes that take place. When you have tried all the modes, choose the Color mode again.

6. Explore the screen layer in the same way as the colorize layer. Notice the effects you get by combining several layers with different modes.

The following list attempts to describe a little of what is happening technically when you use the different modes.

◆ Normal: Combines both pixels based on opacity. Essentially one pixel lays on top of the other, and the opacity determines to what extent the two pixels blend.

◆ Dissolve: Arrives at the final color by editing or painting each pixel. Depending on the opacity of the pixels, either the base or blend color pixels are replaced. The effect is sometimes grainy or there are rough edges to lines.

◆ Multiply: Images combine and get darker overall. The effect is that of looking through two transparent images placed one on top of the other. When black is either the base or color blend, the result is black. If white is one of the colors, the other color is unchanged. When you paint into the same place each stroke builds on the next to get darker. The values of both pixels are multiplied and then divided by 255.

◆ Screen: The combination of images creates a lighter image, similar to sandwiching two negatives together and making a photographic print through them. If white is either the base or blend color, the result is white. Black does not change the other color. This mode multiplies the inverse of the lightness or darkness of the two colors.

◆ Overlay: Depending on the base color, this mode multiplies or screens the pixels. The effect can be lighter or darker. Most of the blending is in the middle. Highlight and shadow values remain the same.

◆ Soft Light: This mode creates the effect of a soft spotlight. Some values are multiplied and some screened. It is the values of the blend color in relation to a middle gray that determine whether the colors are lightened or darkened. The image can result in a high contrast because lighter colors are lightened and darker colors darkened.

◆ Hard Light: This creates the effect of a hard spotlight on the image with calculations similar to soft light. Here, too, there is a process of multiplying and screening. When black is applied as one of the colors, the result is black. And when white is applied, the result is white.

◆ Color Dodge: With this mode, the base color is brightened in relation to the values of the blend color.

◆ Color Burn: The opposite of color dodge, with color burn the base color is darkened in relation to the values of the blend color.

◆ Darken: The darker pixels dominate. The value of the pixels are compared and the darker one is displayed. Both Darken and Lighten work particularly well if you have a dark or a light pattern and want to combine it with a color or image.

- Lighten: Works opposite to the Darken mode. The pixel values are compared and the lighter one shows.

- Difference: This mode depends on which pixel has higher (lighter) value. Either the blend color is subtracted from the base color or the base color is subtracted from the blend.

- Exclusion: The brightness value determines whether the blend or base color is subtracted from the other. The effects are softer than the Difference mode. Using black results in black. White in the blend color results in an inversion of the base color values. Therefore, if you paint on a blue base color with white, the brushstroke is yellow (the opposite of blue).

- Hue: Hue refers to the actual color. This mode combines the hue of the blend color and luminance and saturation of the base.

- Saturation: Saturation is the intensity of the color. This mode combines the saturation of the blend color with the hue and luminance of the base color.

- Color: Combines the hue and saturation of the blend color with the luminance of the base color and the hue and saturation of the blend color. This mode is great for colorizing monochrome images. The color is applied, but the grayscale tonality of the image below remains. As a result, the color blends with the image instead of sitting on the surface.

- Luminosity: Luminosity is the brightness of the color. This mode combines the luminance of the blend color with the hue and saturation of the base color. It is the inverse of the Color mode.

Note

Layers are created transparent and you cannot use some of the mode effects with a transparent layer. They need a color that is neutral for the effect. For this reason, there is an option at the bottom of the New Layer dialog box to Fill with a Neutral Color. If the effect does not need a neutral color the box is grayed out. The color that is neutral for a particular mode varies. If you choose the neutral color and do not use the effect, the color is of no consequence to the image.

Blend If Box

Controlling the blend of two layers by including or excluding specific grayscale values in the blend is done as follows.

1. Open the Layer Options dialog box by double-clicking on the layer name in the Layers palette (see Figure 9.11). The Blend If box is located in the lower half of the dialog box. It is used to determine which value range of pixels from the current layer and the layer below blend or are excluded. All 8- or 24-bit images in Photoshop are comprised of single or multiple channels. Each channel image is limited to 256 grayscale values from black (0) to white (255). The Blend If sliders have values from 0 to 255.

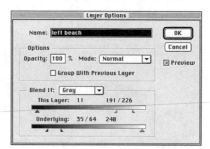

Figure 9.11

The Blend If box is located in the lower half of the Layer Options dialog box.

2. Check the Preview box to see the effects of the actions while in the dialog box. This is important because it is difficult to predict the exact effects by the numbers alone.

3. Choose which channel you want to blend.

   The pull-down menu at the top of the Blend If box lets you choose. With an RGB file there is a choice of Gray, Red, Green, or Blue. Gray is a single grayscale composite of the Red, Green, and Blue channels. With the color selections, only the individual color channel is affected.

4. Move the sliders for this layer. Any pixel values outside of the sliders won't blend. They are transparent and the pixels of the layer below show through.

5. Move the sliders for Underlying. Any values outside of the sliders won't blend. The underlying pixels show through the current layer and appear in the final image.

341

In its simplest use, Blend If is a useful technique for turning an image into a line drawing.

1. Open "Portrait.psd" from the *Photoshop Complete* CD-ROM (the finished file is saved on the CD-ROM as Graphic.psd).

2. Make a new layer and fill it with a light blue color. (Option-Delete)[Alt-Delete] is a shortcut to fill with the foreground color.

3. Double-click on the blue layer to open Layer Options.

4. Drag the left triangle in the Blend If: Underlying to 41.

5. Click OK. The fruit shows through the blue layer as a line drawing. (see Figure 9.12)

Figure 9.12

The Portrait graphic using Blend If.

Tip

With a blend cutoff point at a specific value, images tend to have harsh transitions. Make the blends softer when you use Blend If by splitting the sliders. Each slider can be split by holding down the (Option)[Alt] key as you click the left or right side of the slider and drag (see Figure 9.11). Two numbers appear over the split triangle. The cutoff edge acts like a gradient between the two numbers. This gives a soft edge that blends less sharply.

Creating Semi-transparence with Blend If

Combine Blend If with opacity to create more sophisticated effects. This example makes a leaf look semi-transparent while still having substance. It is accomplished by using Blend If to make only parts of the leaf transparent. A second leaf is placed underneath it to keep the transparency only partial. The completed file for this example is on the CD as "Sandleaf.psd."

1. Open "Sand.PSD" on the CD-ROM and "Leaf" from the Photoshop Samples folder (a finished version of this example is saved on the CD-ROM as "Sandleaf.PSD").

2. In Sand make the outline layer active.

4. Using the Move tool, drag the leaf image into the Sand document. The leaf is the active layer, located at the top of the layer stack (see Figure 9.13).

Figure 9.13

The Sand image with the leaf.

6. Using the Move tool, drag the leaf so that it lines up with the outline.

7. Hide the outline layer by clicking the eye icon. This layer was only for placement of the leaf.

8. Double-click the leaf name in the Layers palette to open the Layer Options dialog box. Rename the layer "leaf."

9. Move the Opacity slider to 34%.

10. Click OK.

11. Make a duplicate copy of the leaf layer from the Layers palette by dragging the leaf layer to the New Layer button. The layer is called leaf copy.

12. With the leaf copy active, select Layer Options from the Layer menu.

13. Make sure that Preview is checked so that you can see the effects before you make them permanent.

14. The opacity of the leaf copy layer is 34%, the same as the leaf layer. Change the opacity of leaf copy to 100%.

15. Set the Blend If sliders for this layer. Split the left triangle by holding down the (Option)[Alt] key while you drag. Make the two numbers over the left side read 108 / 128.

16. Drag the right slider so the number reads 215.

17. Split the triangle while dragging the left Underlying slider so that the numbers read 76 / 91.

18. Split and drag the right Underlying slider so that the numbers read 162 / 184 (see Figure 9.14).

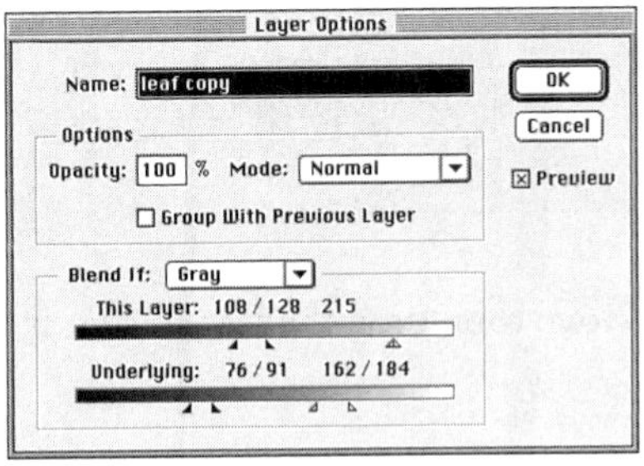

Figure 9.14

Set the Underlying slider in the Layer Options dialog box.

19. Click OK (see Figure 9.15).

Figure 9.15

The final image of leaf and beach.

Reset

When you are in the Layer Options dialog box, if you hold down the (Option)[Alt] key, the Cancel button changes to a Reset button. Click the Reset button and the options go back to what they were when you first opened the dialog box. You can preview various combinations of the Layer Options, such as the Blend If settings, and then choose Reset if you want to use start over.

Linking Layers

One or more layers can be linked to an active layer. When you link layers, multiple layers can be moved simultaneously. Only one layer at a time can be active. The link is made from an inactive layer and defines a relationship to an active layer. When that active layer is moved, the linked layers move with it in tandem.

1. Select a layer to be active.

2. The link layer box is located in the Layers palette between the Eye icon and the layer thumbnail. It is only empty in an inactive layer. Active layers have either a layer icon or a mask icon in that box. Click in the link box of an inactive layer in order to link it to the active layer. The layer remains inactive and the link icon toggles on (see Figure 9.16). If you click the box again, the link toggles off. The Link icon looks like links in a vertical chain.

Figure 9.16

Linked layers.

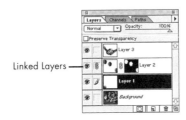

Linked Layers ——

3. Click on the link box of another inactive layer. The layer link icon appears in that layer as well. There is no limit to the number of layers that can be linked in a document at one time. The link icon shows in each linked layer.

4. Select the Move tool and drag a layer in your image window to move it. If the active layer is linked to another layer, both layers move. The spatial relationship between the contents of the linked layers remains unaltered when they move. For example, you have three layers, each with an image of a square button located at the bottom of the document window. The buttons are in a horizontal row—each is placed one inch from the next. When you link these three layers and move the active layer to the top of the document, they all move as a group. The buttons remain in a horizontal row, still one inch from the next.

5. Make another layer that is part of the active linking group. The previous active layer now has a link icon in the link box, and any other layers that were linked remain linked.

6. Starting with a group of linked layers, make a layer outside that group active. The links of the grouped layers disappear. This is only temporary because the links reappear when you make any of the layers in the linked group active.

7. Create links to the active layer and include layers that are part of the other linking group.

8. Make a layer in the previous linking group active. Any layers that were added to the second linking group are no longer part of the first group. You can have more than one group of linked layers in a document, but an individual layer can only be part of one linking group.

Preserving Transparency

Preserve Transparency is located at the top of the Layers palette. When checked, Preserve Transparency limits all editing of the layer solely to the opaque areas. This prevents you from adding pixels to the transparent areas of the layer. This is helpful if, for instance, you want to add color to some black type. Select Preserve Transparency and use the Fill command. Only the type has the new color, whereas the transparency remains empty. The keyboard shortcut for Preserve Transparency toggles it on and off. Press the forward slash key (/) to turn Preserve Transparency on and again to turn it off.

Adjusting the Image Thumbnail

A layer thumbnail, to the left of the layer name in the Layers palette, displays a small version of the layer image. As your work changes the image, the thumbnail changes.

1. Select Palette Options from the Layers palette menu (see Figure 9.17). The Layers Palette Options dialog box appears, which lets you select the size of the thumbnail.

2. Choose one of three image sizes or none. The default setting of the smallest size thumbnail is usually adequate.

3. If you are using a small monitor and need the space for your document, choosing none makes a smaller size Layers palette. You will not have a thumbnail but you can then identify the layers by the names you give them.

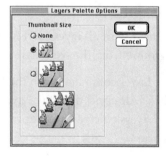

Figure 9.17

The Layers Palette Options dialog box.

Working with Backgrounds

In the Layers palette, an image is either a background or a layer (see Figure 9.1). The background, labeled Background in the Layers palette, is found at the bottom of the layer stack. By default, as long as it remains a background, it cannot be moved from this position in the stack, nor can it be renamed. The background sits below the layers and shows through the transparent sections of the layers. A background cannot contain transparency. When a background image is cut, that area is filled with the background color.

When you flatten the layers of an image, all the layers merge into a background.

It is not necessary to have a background. You can have a document that only contains layers. A background image can be turned into a layer by double-clicking the Background name bar. The Make Layer dialog box appears (see Figure 9.18). Fill in a name for the layer or accept the default Layer 0. The dialog box has an opacity option and a mode option. These can also be accessed from the Layers palette. Any choices you make for mode or opacity in the Make Layer dialog box can be undone in the Layers palette. Clicking OK makes the background into a layer. It is now capable of transparency and can be moved in the layer stack.

Figure 9.18

The Make Layer dialog box.

Creating a New Background

If you have a document with all layers and no background, you can create a new background from the New Layer dialog box.

1. Select the New Layer command from the Layers palette menu or (Option-click)[Alt-click] the New Layer button at the bottom of the Layers palette. In either case, the New Layer dialog box appears.

2. Select Background from bottom of the Mode pull-down menu and click OK.(This option is available only when there is no other layer named Background in the Layers palette.) The new background is filled with the background color(see Figure 9.4).

3. If you want to turn an existing layer into a background, make a new layer into a background as previously explained. Then merge the layer to be background with the new background.

Tip

Moving a background with the Move tool turns it into a layer. Backgrounds cannot be moved, but layers can be. By moving a background in the active image, you convert it into a layer. Select the Move tool and drag the active background image in the document window. The area that is no longer occupied by the background is now transparent and the background is a layer. All the layer options are now available and the background is renamed Layer 0.

Layer Options Dialog Box

The Layer Options dialog box lets you rename a layer. It also offers Opacity, Mode, Group with, and Blending options. If you check Preview, you can see the effects of the options before you select them. There are a number of ways to access the Layer Options dialog box (see Figure 9.9).

◆ Select Layer Options from the Layer menu.

◆ Select Layer Options from the Layers palette menu.

◆ The easiest way to access Layer Options is to double-click the layer thumbnail or name in the Layers palette.

There are several context menus as well that make Layer Options available. The thumbnail and name in the Layers palette are among them.

Using Context-Sensitive Menus

Photoshop has introduced context sensitive menus with version 4.0. These are different task-specific menus that pop-up for various palettes, screens, and tools. (Control-click)[right-click] a palette item or the document window to get a pull-down menu for layer, mask, tool, or selection commands (see Figure 9.19 and Figure 9.20). The menus are context sensitive, so each selected element produces a menu specific to its functions. Select an item on the menu and release the mouse button to apply the command. Using these menus is quite a time saver because you do not need to leave the area you are working in to perform commands.

Figure 9.19

Context-sensitive palette menus.

Figure 9.20

Some context-sensitive image menus.

SELECTING AND ARRANGING LAYERS

Layers stack one in front of the next. The opaque areas of the layer on top cover and hide the pixels of the layers below. You can select any layer by clicking it, which makes it active. You can also rearrange the layers by moving a layer's position up or down in the stack.

Reordering Layers by Dragging

Layers can be reordered by dragging one layer on top of another. A layer cannot be moved below a background and the position of the background in the Layers palette cannot be moved.

1. Drag a layer up onto the layer that you want it to be above or down to the layer that you want it to be below.

2. When the layer you are dragging is on top of or beyond the layer that you are supplanting, the border between the layers gets thicker, as in the left-hand image in Figure 9.21. This indicates that you have dragged far enough to successfully move the layer. Release the mouse button.

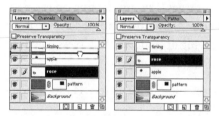

Figure 9.21

Rearrange layers by dragging them up or down.

Arranging Layers from the Menu

The Arrange command, on the Layer menu, is new to Photoshop 4.0. Using this command, the active layer can be moved forward or backward in relation to the other layers (see Figure 9.22). The following choices are available:

- Bring to Front (Command-Shift-])[Control-Shift-]]: Moves a targeted layer to the top of the stack.

- Bring Forward (Command-])[Control-]]: The selected layer is moved up one level in the Layers palette.

- Send Backward (Command-[)[Control-[]: The active layer is moved down one level in the Layers palette.

◆ Send to Back (Command-Shift-[)[Control-[]: The selected layer is placed at the bottom of the series of layers. This is a position above the background if there is one.

Figure 9.22

The Arrange command from the Layers menu.

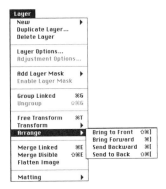

Using the Keyboard to Make a Layer Active

You can select a target layer by clicking on the name or thumbnail in the Layers palette. As an alternative, keyboard commands work as shortcuts for moving up or down the Layers palette to change the active layer. Start with an active layer:

◆ (Shift-Option-])[Shift-Alt-]] selects the layer at the top of stack.

◆ (Option-])[Alt-]] selects the next layer up.

◆ (Option-[)[Alt-[] selects the next layer down.

◆ (Shift-Option-[)[Shift-Alt-[] selects the layer at the bottom of stack.

Selecting a Layer from the Document Window

With the Move tool selected, hold down the (Control)[right mouse button] and click the document. The Move cursor does not change. A context menu appears listing the image layers stacked in order below the cursor (see Figure 9.23). This list does not include layers that are transparent at this point—the pointer only recognizes opaque areas. The layer you select from the drop-down menu becomes the active layer.

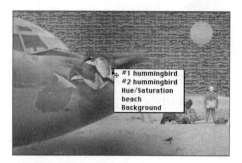

Figure 9.23

The Context menu for selecting the active layer.

Removing Halos With Matting

Matting is used to remove the background edge or halo from a selection after it is turned into a layer. An unwanted color fringe may surround an image when you select and paste it into a new layer. This halo is often caused by anti-aliasing, which makes an image blend with a softer edge and shows smoother curves by merging the edge pixels with the background color. When you copy an image and paste it to a background with a different color, a color fringe may follow.

1. Select Layer➡Matting➡Defringe..., Remove Black Matte, or Remove White Matte.

    Remove Black Matte removes black pixels from the edge of an image. **Remove White Matte** does the same for a white fringe. **Defringe...** substitutes the color of the edge pixels with a nearby color. Selecting this command brings up a Defringe dialog box asking for the number of pixels to defringe (see Figure 9.24).

Figure 9.24

The Defringe dialog box.

COMPOSITING WITH LAYERS

Compositing with layers, by adding layers and using the options for blending from one layer to the next, is very flexible in Photoshop 4.0. Photoshop 4.0 has made some changes and added commands that make it easier to get images into layers.

Cutting and Pasting into Layers

Photoshop 4.0's emphasis on layers makes cutting and pasting simpler, more direct, and there are more options. All the layers and layer masks work alike. Any layer or mask can be made active in the current document window. Then they can each be edited in the same way using standard cut and paste techniques. All layers and masks are independent, and, as long as the document maintains layers, the composite is not permanent.

1. Make a selection.

2. Cut or copy the selection to the clipboard.

3. Paste the image from the clipboard into the document.

The cut, paste, and copy commands are found in the Edit menu. Keyboard shortcuts are as follows:

- ◆ (Command-X)[Control-X]: Cut.

- ◆ (Command-C)[Control-C]: Copy.

- ◆ (Command-Shift-C)[Control-Shift-C] copies a merged visible selection to the clipboard. That is, the selection copied is a merged image of all the visible layers. This command does not actually merge the individual layers. They remain separate.

- ◆ (Command-V)[Control-V] is the keyboard shortcut for Paste. When you paste in Photoshop 4.0 a new layer is created.

New to Photoshop 4.0 are commands that perform cut and paste or copy and paste in one command. The selection is cut or cloned and made into a new layer in one step. The clipboard is not used to store the selection data. This makes Photoshop work quicker because it frees the RAM used to store the clipboard data and the procedure is performed with half the steps.

- ◆ (Command-J)[Control-J] clones a selection and turns it into a new layer.

- ◆ (Command-Option-J)[Control-Alt-J] brings up the Make Layer dialog box before it makes a cloned selection into a new layer.

◆ (Command-Shift-J)[Control-Shift-J] cuts a selection from the active image and turns it into a new layer.

◆ (Command-Shift-Option-J)[Control-Shift-Alt-J] brings up the Make Layer dialog box before making a new layer from a cut selection.

These same commands can be accessed from the Layer menu under New.

◆ Layer Via Copy creates a new layer from a selection.

◆ Layer Via Cut makes a new layer by cutting the selection from an active image.

Using the Paste Into Command

Paste Into, on the Edit menu, enables you to paste an image into the boundaries of a selection. The image is not visible outside of the selection walls. Although the end result is still the same, Photoshop 4.0 has changed the way that this works. Paste Into has moved from a selection to a layer function. That is, in version 3.0, Paste Into comes in as a floating selection. You can either defloat the floating selection or make it into a layer. In version 4.0, Paste Into creates a new layer along with a layer mask that corresponds to the outline of the selection.

The layer mask Photoshop creates for Paste Into is hidden. This is because with Paste Into you want to move the image behind the window of the mask. The mask should remain stationary while the image moves.

(Command-Shift-V)[Control-Shift-V] is the keyboard shortcut for pasting into a layer from the clipboard. You cannot select Paste Into unless a selection is made in the document. Here is an example of Paste Into.

1. Open "Reflect.psd" and "Beach.psd" from the CD-ROM.

2. In "Beach.psd," select all and copy the selection to the clipboard.

3. Make the Reflect.psd image the current document.

4. Go to Select➥Load Selection and choose reflection as the selection to load (see Figure 9.25).

Figure 9.25

The Reflect.psd image.

5. Select Edit➥Paste Into. The beach scene creates a new layer with a layer mask for the selection.

6. Use the Move tool to drag the image so that the red beach umbrella is on the side of the plane in the bottom third.

7. Select Filter➥Distort➥Ripple. In the Ripple dialog box, set the amount to 135% and the size to medium. Click OK (see Figure 9.26).

Figure 9.26

The Ripple filter dialog box.

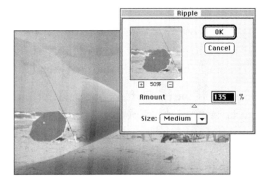

8. Move the Opacity slider at the top of the Layers palette to 25%. This makes the distorted beach image blend with the side of the plane like a reflection (see Figure 9.27).

Figure 9.27

The final image of the beach reflecting in the plane.

Converting a Floating Selection into a Layer

Cloning a selection by dragging is the only place that version 4.0 still uses floating selections. Hold down (Command-Option)[Control-Alt] while dragging to clone a selection. The cursor turns into a black arrow on top of a white arrow. A layer appears in the Layers palette named Floating Selection.

Once you have a floating selection, choose whether to make it into a layer or defloat. If you are going to make it into a layer, do one of the following:

◆ Double-click the floating selection in the Layers palette. The Make Layer dialog box opens. Select the options and click OK.

◆ In the Layers palette, drag the floating selection onto the New Layer button. The Make Layer dialog box opens. Click OK.

◆ With the floating selection active, click the New Layer Button. The floating selection turns into a new layer. If you hold down the (Option)[Alt] key while you click the New Layer button, the Make Layer dialog box appears.

◆ (Command-J)[Control-J] is the keyboard shortcut for making the floating selection into a new layer. (Command-Option-J) [Control-Option-J] brings up the Make Layer dialog box before creating the new layer.

Big Data

One welcome change from Photoshop 3.0 to 4.0 is how layers handle images larger than the active window. Photoshop no longer clips data outside the edges of the canvas. Images can now bleed off the edges, and you can paint, reposition, apply filters, and more but you don't have to worry about the image getting clipped.

If you are going to defloat the selection, make sure it's where you want it. The selection cannot be moved after it is defloated. Do any necessary editing and then select one of the following procedures to defloat.

◆ Select Defloat from the Layer menu.

◆ Choose Defloat from the Layers palette menu.

◆ (Command-E)[Control-E] is the keyboard command for defloating a selection.

Applying Fade with Color Adjustments and Filters

Use the Fade command to control the way a filter or color adjustment affects your image. The Fade command modifies the intensity of the effect that the operation has on the original image. Fade is found under Filters and it can only be accessed after you apply a filter or a color adjustment (see Figure 9.28). When you select Fade, a dialog box appears. This enables you to set the opacity and blending mode of the effect of the filter or color adjustment that was just applied. Fade works as though the filter or color adjustment is applied to a duplicate layer that sits above the original unchanged layer. You then use opacity and mode to determine how the changed copy blends with the original image. The keyboard shortcut for Fade is (Shift-Command-F)[Shift-Control-F]. You can Edit➡Undo the filter or color adjustment after you use Fade. That removes the effect and the fade. Do the following to apply Fade:

1. Choose and apply a filter or color adjustment from Image➡Adjust menu.

2. Go to Filter➡Fade and open the Fade dialog box.

3. Make sure the Preview checkbox is checked so you can see the Fade effect on the document.

4. Adjust the Opacity slider to achieve the blend that you want.

5. Select a blending mode.

6. Click OK. The opacity and blend is applied to the image.

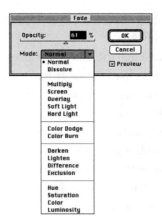

Figure 9.28

Applying the Fade command.

Selecting Layer Transparency

Selecting layer transparency is equivalent to masking the transparent areas of a layer and making a selection of the layer image. If you have a layer image of just a round ball, it is automatically surrounded by transparency. When you select layer transparency, you are selecting all the pixels that contain color information. The selection of the ball is a circle. Layer transparency saves time because you do not have to use the Magic Wand tool or some other means of selection. And layer transparency saves disk space because you do not need to save it as an alpha channel. Photoshop creates it on the fly.

You can load layer transparency from the Select menu.

1. Choose Select➥Load Selection to bring up the Load Selection dialog box.

2. In the Source Channel pull-down menu select the layer transparency; the channel with the name of the layer and ending in the word Transparency. This channel, unlike the alpha channels, is written in italics.

3. If there is an existing selection, you can choose whether the layer mask should replace, add, subtract, or intersect with that selection.

4. Click OK to make the selection.

Using the Keyboard to Load the Layer Transparency Selection from the Layers Palette

Click the layer thumbnail or name while executing the following keyboard commands to load the layer transparency and its accompanying operations. The cursor turns into a hand with a pointing index finger. There is a selection box on the back of the hand. For operations such as add, subtract, and multiply, the cursor incorporates a +, - or × in the back of the hand. If you have a layer mask, click the layer mask thumbnail while you perform these same commands. The layer mask loads its layer transparency, which is its mask. This also works with an adjustment layer. Click its thumbnail with the same procedure. You load it's layer transparency.

Figure 9.29

Add the layer transparency selection by clicking the Layer thumbnail in the Layers palette.

- ◆ Click a layer thumbnail in the Layers palette while holding down the (Command)[Control] key to load the transparency selection for that layer. The chosen layer does not have to be active.

- ◆ (Command-Shift)[Control-Shift] when you click the layer thumbnail to add the transparency selection to an existing selection.

- ◆ (Command-Option-click)[Control-Alt-click] the thumbnail to subtract the transparency selection from the existing selection.

- ◆ Press (Command-Shift-Option)[Control-Shift-Alt] when you click the layer thumbnail to create a new selection from the intersection of the layer transparency selection and the current selection.

Layer transparency can be loaded from a context menu in the Layers palette. (Control-click)[right-click] the layer thumbnail to bring up a context menu with a Select Layer Transparency option (see Figure 9.19).

If there is an existing selection, the add, subtract, and intersect operation options are available. If there is a layer mask, (Control-click) [right-click] the layer mask thumbnail to bring up a context menu. The context menu enables you to load the layer transparency of the layer mask. Follow the same steps with the thumbnail of an adjustment layer. It also has a context menu that enables you to load its layer transparency.

CREATING CLIPPING GROUPS

A clipping group is a technique that creates a common mask for a number of layers in an image. In a layer group the transparency mask of the bottom layer defines a mask that limits the layers grouped above. The first group layer is called the base. As an example of a clipping group, start with a square as the base layer. The transparent area surrounding the square defines a mask and the square is the selection. The layers grouped above are confined to the square selection. Add the next two layers above the square to the group. The image in each layer is a single flower. You cannot see the flowers where they go beyond the border of the square (see Figure 9.30).

Figure 9.30

Clipping groups affects which areas of the layers in the group are visible.

The base in a clipping group determines the opacity setting and the mode selection of the group as well. Any adjustments you make to the opacity of the lowest layer affects the other group layers in an identical fashion. You can, however, adjust the opacity of any of the upper group images without affecting the other elements. This process works the same with mode. The base layer controls the mode for the other group layers. Likewise, any mode changes to layers in the upper group only affect the image in that layer.

The layers in a clipping group must follow in succession. If you ungroup one layer, all layers above that point are ungrouped. This is not the case for Photoshop 3.0. In that version ungrouping a layer turns it into the base layer for any grouped layers above.

When you create a clipping group the solid divider line between two layers turns into a dotted line. The name of the base layer is underlined and the thumbnails of the grouped layers above indent.

Use one of these three options to create a clipping group:

- ◆ (Option-click)[Alt-click] the solid line that divides two layers. The cursor turns into two overlapping circles with an arrow pointing to the left.

- ◆ Go to the Layer Options dialog box and click the Group With Previous Layer checkbox. Click OK.

- ◆ Press (Command-G)[Control-G] to make a clipping group from the active layer and the layer below.

To ungroup a layer do one of the following:

- ◆ (Option-click)[Alt-click] the dotted divider line between two group layers. The line reverts to solid and the layers are ungrouped.

- ◆ Uncheck the Group With Previous Layer checkbox in the Layers Options dialog box. Click OK.

- ◆ Press (Command-Shift-G)[Control-Shift-G] from the keyboard to break up the clipping group.

MERGING LAYERS

Merging layers combines any number of layers into one. There are a variety of reasons to do this. When you are done working with some layers, you may want to merge them to keep the file size manageable. Each layer could feasibly add the size of the original background image to the document. The larger the document you are working on, the more you might need to contain its size. Also, you may want to merge some layers so that you can duplicate the new layer to another document. When you merge layers, the new layer that replaces the merged layers takes the name of the active layer before the merge.

You can find the merge layers commands in the Layer menu (see Figure 9.31) and in the Layers palette menu (see Figure 9.3). Select the merge command that you want and the selected layers merge.

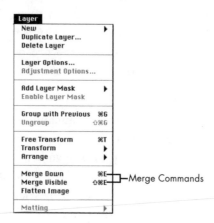

Figure 9.31

The merge layers commands in the Layer menu.

♦ **Merge Visible** lets you merge all visible layers. That is, all layers in the Layers palette with the eye icon showing in the left column. If you hide a layer by turning off the eye, it does not merge. Use (Command-Shift-E)[Control-Shift-E] as a shortcut to Merge Visible.

♦ Use the **Merge Down** command to merge the active layer with the layer directly below. Both layers must be visible for this command to work. (Command-E)[Control-E] is the keyboard shortcut for Merge Down.

Hold down the (Option)[Alt] key while selecting Merge Down from either the Layers palette menu or Layer menu to leave the active layer intact after merging down. This leaves you with two layers—the original active layer and a composite below. (Command-Option-E)[Control-Alt-E] is the keyboard equivalent to merge down and keep the active layer untouched.

If the active layer is linked to any other layers, Merge Down does not appear in either of the merge menus. In place of Merge Down is Merge Linked.

Note

The Merge Down command is new to Photoshop 4.0. With this version, floating selections have been mostly eliminated. People who are used to using floating selections and defloat will find that they can use Merge Down in much the same way. Now that images and type come in as layers, you can paste a layer and merge down the same way you used to paste a floating selection and defloat it.

◆ Use the **Merge Linked** command to merge layers that are linked to the active layer. This can save production time. If you have many layers, some hidden, and you want to merge a few, it is much easier to link those layers than it is to go through the stack hiding and then showing selected layers. In this case it is quicker to use Merge Linked than Merge Visible. The keyboard shortcut for Merge Linked is (Command-E)[Control-E].

◆ To merge a clipping group, all the layers in the group must be visible. Any hidden layers are discarded. Make the base layer active. When this is done, a **Merge Group** command is in the Layer menu or Layers palette menu. Choose Merge Group to merge the layers into one. After merging, the individual group layers no longer exist and in their place is one composite layer. Use (Command-E)[Control-E] as a keyboard shortcut.

Clone Merge: Retain the Layers in Addition to a Merge

Merging layers takes selected layers and combines them into one layer. The separate layers no longer exist after a merge. There are often times, however, when you need a merged version and you want to retain the individual layers. This is where the Clone Merge comes in. The Clone Merge commands let you create a new merged layer in addition to the original layers. It is accomplished by adding a keyboard command to the other merge commands.

Hold down the (Option)[Alt] key when you choose Merge Linked, Merge Group, or Merge Visible. The linked or visible layers merge into the active layer. All layers other than the active layer remain intact, but you lose the active layer to the merge. This can also be accomplished by holding down (Command-Option-Shift-E)[Control-Alt-Shift-E] to Merge Visible. And (Command-Option-E)[Control-Alt-E] is the keyboard shortcut for Merge Linked or Merge Group.

The one exception to this rule is if you perform an (Option)[Alt] Merge Link from an active layer and the background is part of the link. In this situation, the layers merge into the background instead of the active layer. It leaves the background merged and the other layers intact.

Tip

If you need a merged version of your document but want to keep all of the layers intact, using a Clone Merge presents a potential problem. You lose the active layer with this type of merge because the new merged composite replaces the active layer. The solution is to duplicate the active layer before you merge. You also must make sure that the original active layer (now just below the duplicate active) is not part of the merge. This is to avoid oversaturating the effect of that layer. If you did not remove the original active layer from the merge, you would be merging two copies of the same layer. This would increase the effect of that layer, making it out of proportion with the other layers in the merged composite.

Using the Copy Merged Command

Copy Merged is a new command in Photoshop 4.0. It copies the Merge Visible of a selection to the clipboard. Although no layers get merged, the result is as if you merged the visible layers and then copied the selection of the merged layer into the clipboard. The keyboard shortcut is (Command-Shift-C)[Control-Shift-C].

Tip

Use these keyboard commands with the Actions palette to create an action that gives you a new merged layer with one click. This action leaves all of

continues

your layers intact and creates a new layer at the top of the stack that is a merge of the visible layers.

1. *Create a new action in the Actions palette using the following commands (see Chapter 19, "Automating Photoshop with Actions").*

2. *Press (Shift-Option-])[Shift-Alt-]] to make the top layer active. The new layer is created above the active layer. Doing this step ensures that the new merged layer is created at the top of the stack.*

3. *Press (Command-A)[Control-A] to Select All. You need a selection in order to make a copy.*

4. *Press (Command-Shift-C)[Control-Shift-C] to perform a Copy Merged. The merged image is copied to the clipboard.*

5. *Press (Command-V)[Control-V] to paste a new layer with the visible merged image at the top of the layer stack.*

Sample Merged Option

When using the Rubber Stamp tool, the Focus tools, the Smudge tool, or the Paint Bucket with layers, you can choose the Sample Merged option from the Options palette. This enables the tool to act as though the layers are merged and use parts from all visible layers for the effect. Only the active layer is affected by these tools. If, for instance, you use the Rubber Stamp tool with Sample Merged selected, you can clone a visible image from another layer onto the active layer.

Merging an Adjustment Layer

You can use Merge Down, Merge Link, Merge Group, and Merge Visible with an adjustment layer. Several adjustment layers can be included in the merge, however, an adjustment layer cannot be merged to only another adjustment layer; an image layer must be involved in the merge. (See the section on adjustment layers in this chapter.) The adjustments become permanent as a result of merging. Any effects of the adjustment layer are only seen in layers that were merged with it. This is something to be aware of because until it is merged, the effects of the adjustment layer, unless masked, are seen on every visible layer.

FLATTENING LAYERS

When you are finished creating your document, flatten the image by selecting Flatten Image from the Layer menu (see Figure 9.31) or the Layers palette menu (see Figure 9.3). Only visible layers merge when you flatten a document. The hidden layers are discarded. A flattened image no longer contain layers. It is a background. Depending on the number of layers the document contained, the file size of a flattened document can be greatly reduced.

Only the native Photoshop format supports layers. The image must be flattened if it is to be saved in another format. If you want to import the image into another program, it needs to be in another file format.

If you plan to go back and edit your composite, save the layered version and make a flattened copy to use for exporting. Use the Save a Copy command to save a second file that is flattened.

WORKING WITH LAYER MASKS

Creating a layer mask enables you to edit a layer image in the following ways:

- Removing parts of an image and reveal transparency

- Taking away whole sections or just removing a color fringe around an object

- Making gradations that make an image fade into the background

One layer mask can be added to each image layer. While in the layer mask mode, painting with black hides the image and painting with white reveals it. Painting with gray gives you partial opacity. You can think of a layer mask as a selection that shows the image in the selected areas and hides the image by making it transparent in the masked areas. The thumbnail updates as you paint into the layer mask. The layer mask is an 8-bit Grayscale channel that is edited in the same way that you would any alpha channel. You can make that channel active and paint, paste, or add filters to alter the mask.

In a layer with a mask, the mask and the image take turns being active. In Photoshop 4.0, the Layers palette has changed the way that a layer mask is shown to be active. Instead of the black frame surrounding the active image or mask thumbnail, version 4.0 has introduced an active image or mask icon. If the image is active, the icon is a paintbrush. When the layer mask is active, the icon is the mask icon, a gray rectangle with a dashed circle in the center (see Figure 9.7). Either the paintbrush or the mask icon is located in a box between the eye icon and the image thumbnail. If the layer is not active, neither the paintbrush nor the mask icon shows. This is a great improvement because in version 3.0 it is often difficult to know which thumbnail has the black frame.

Tip

The keyboard shortcut for switching from a layer image to a layer mask in an active layer is (Command-\)[Control-\]. This shortcut does not take you back to the layer image when you are in the layer mask.

Adding Layer Masks

Adding a layer mask has been completely changed in 4.0. Layer masks are now added from the Layer menu in the menu bar (see Figure 9.32) or from the New Layer Mask button at the bottom of the Layers palette (see Figure 9.1). When you create a layer mask, options are available that lets you choose a mask revealing or hiding all. There are also options that are only applicable when the document has a selection.

Figure 9.32

The Add Layer Mask command from the Layer menu.

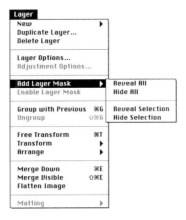

- Reveal All: In a layer mask, white is the selection that lets the image show through. A mask that reveals all comes in all white. In this mode, all is selected so you can see the layer image.

- Hide All: Black masks the image in a layer mask. Painting with black hides the image and leaves transparency on the layer. When a mask comes in as Hide All, it is completely black and the layer image is hidden.

- Reveal Selection: This option is only available when there is a current selection in the document. It creates a layer mask of the current selection. The selected area is white in the mask, revealing the image. The area outside of the selection is black, which makes the image in that area transparent.

- Hide Selection: This option is also only available when there is a current selection in the document. It is the inverse of Reveal Selection. The selection area is black in the mask and the area outside the selection is white. Therefore, the selected area appears transparent in the image and the masked area outside the current selection is visible.

To create a layer mask:

1. Select Add Layer Mask on the Layer menu.

2. A pull-down menu displays four choices: Reveal All, Hide All, Reveal Selection, and Hide Selection (see Figure 9.32). Select one to add a layer mask to the active layer.

The New Layer Mask button, at the bottom of the Layers palette, looks like a gray rectangle with a dashed circle in the center (see Figure 9.33).

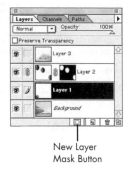

New Layer
Mask Button

Figure 9.33

The New Layer Mask button.

You have the following choices when using the New Layer Mask button to add a mask:

◆ Click the New Layer Mask button. A layer mask that reveals all is added to the active layer.

◆ Hold down the (Option)[Alt] key and click the Layer Mask button, creating a layer mask that hides all.

If the document has a selection, there are two other options available for creating a layer mask.

◆ Click the New Layer Mask button to get a layer mask that reveals the selection.

◆ Hold down the (Option-click)[Alt-click] the New Layer Mask button to get a layer mask that hides the selection.

Removing Layer Masks

Layer masks are saved with your document, but they do take up space. When you are done working with a layer mask you can permanently apply it to the layer image or discard it.

1. Make sure the layer mask is active.

2. Choose Remove Layer Mask from the Layer menu.

3. A dialog box comes onscreen asking if you want to apply the mask to the layer before removing. There are three choices: discard, cancel, and apply (see Figure 9.34).

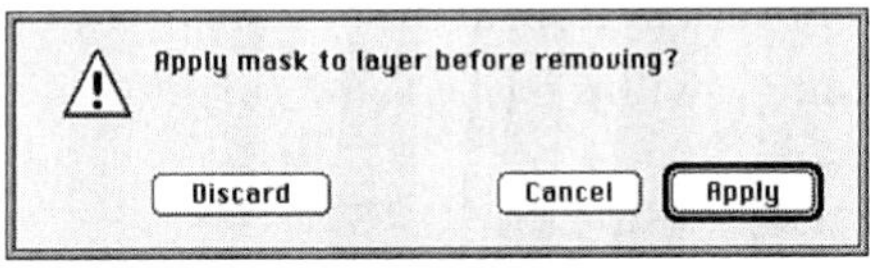

Figure 9.34

The dialog box for removing a layer mask.

An alternate method for removing the mask employs a context menu. Open the context menu you get by (Control-clicking)[right-clicking] the layer mask thumbnail (see Figure 9.35). Select Remove Layer Mask and a dialog box asks whether you want to discard, cancel, or apply the mask to the layer before removing. Make your selection.

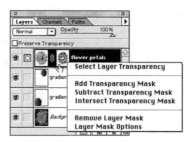

Figure 9.35

The layer mask context menu.

A third and probably simplest way to remove a layer mask is to use the Trash button at the bottom of the Layers palette. With the layer mask you want removed active, click the Trash button and the Remove Layer Mask dialog box comes onto the screen (see Figure 9.34). Choose whether to apply or discard the mask. You can also drag the layer down to the Trash button and as long as it is active, you get the remove layer mask dialog box. Be careful when you use the Trash button to remove the layer mask. If the layer image is active instead of the layer mask, you delete the layer.

Linking Layer Masks to the Image

The layer mask is linked to the image by default. The link icon is found between the image and layer mask thumbnails. It looks like a few links in a vertical chain (see Figure 9. 36). The link is added when you create a layer mask. Click the link to toggle between turning it off and on. If you move the image, the mask moves in conjunction and remains aligned. When you turn off the link, either the mask or the image can be moved independent of the other.

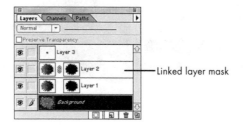

Figure 9.36

A layer mask linked to a layer image.

371

Turning a Mask On and Off

You can turn the layer mask off to see your full image without the effects of the mask and then go back to the masked version. Hold down the Shift key while you click the layer mask thumbnail in the Layers palette to turn the layer mask off. A red X covers the layer mask (see Figure 9.37). Clicking the layer mask thumbnail makes the layer mask active again.

Figure 9.37

The red X indicates that the layer mask has been turned off.

Editing the Layer Mask

When you select the layer mask and paint into your image, your editing is based on what you see of the image and what is transparent. There are times when it is helpful to see the mask as its own image and edit with brush tools, cutting and pasting, and filters. Whether you are painting in small holes or adding complex gradients in selected areas, a mask responds like any grayscale image (see Figure 9.38).

Figure 9.38

You can edit a layer mask when it appears in the document window as a grayscale image.

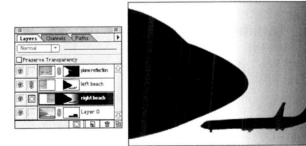

To edit a layer mask:

1. (Option-click)[Alt-click) the layer mask thumbnail in the Layers palette. The layer mask grayscale image replaces the layer image in the document window.

2. Use the Paintbrush or another brush tool to paint black, white, or gray directly on the mask. The painting effects the area selected by the mask.

3. When you are done, (Option-click)[Alt-click] to toggle back to the layer image instead of the mask.

To have the best of both worlds, you can edit the visible layer mask while showing the image. This is great when you want to mask an image and you need an outline to follow. The mask layer is visible as a color overlay that works exactly like the overlay in channel editing or quick mask mode.

To create an overlay layer mask:

1. Use (Shift-Option)[Shift-Alt] as you click the layer mask thumbnail. The image remains visible and a red transparent mask is the editable layer mask.

2. Although red in color, the mask is a Grayscale image and can be edited with black and white brush tools. Painting with black puts red on the canvas.

3. Click the layer mask thumbnail again while pressing (Shift-Option) [Shift-Alt] and the mask overlay is no longer visible.

Note

When you create a layer mask, it gets placed in the Channels palette as an alpha channel. It is only there when the layer is active. The mask is placed above the other alpha channels and named *"(image name) mask."* You can access the mask for editing from the Channels palette, and the same overlay and solid mask editing modes can be used.

Editing an Image Using Layer Masks

I have an image I want to adjust by editing the layer mask of one of the layers. Figure 9.39 is a beach scene with the nose of a plane and two small planes in the foreground (Open "Maskedit.PSD" on the CD-ROM). The composite image is made up of three layers. There is a background image containing the three planes. The background is followed by a beach scene layer. The beach layer has a layer mask that enables the planes to show through. There is a third layer on the top of the stack that makes a beach reflection in the nose of the plane. This layer also has a layer mask. The mask limits the reflection to the nose of the plane.

Figure 9.39

The "Maskedit.psd" image.

I don't like the way the two small planes look, so I want to remove them from the scene. The two small planes are in the scene because of the layer mask for the beach layer. The mask silhouettes the two small planes in black. This makes the beach image transparent in that area. If it weren't for the mask, the beach would completely cover all of the planes.

The solution to this problem is to edit the beach layer mask so that it no longer masks the beach in the area of the two planes. I (Option-click)[Alt-click] the beach layer mask thumbnail in the Layers palette so I can see the layer mask in the document window (see Figure 9.40). The mask can be edited in this state. I select the black silhouette of the two planes with the Lasso tool and fill the selection with white (see Figure 9.41). Then I make the beach image visible again by (Option-clicking)[Alt-clicking] the layer mask thumbnail. When the beach image returns, the two planes are gone (see Figure 9.42).

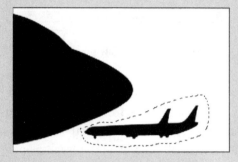

Figure 9.40

The layer mask grayscale image.

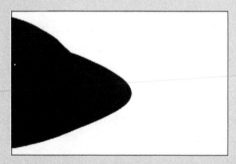

Figure 9.41

The layer mask after removing the two planes.

Figure 9.42

The final image after removing the planes.

Setting the Layer Mask Display Options

The Layer Mask Options let you select the color and opacity of the overlay layer mask (see Figure 9.43). This is useful when you want to edit the layer mask while it overlays the image. If you are editing the mask around a red apple, a red overlay makes it difficult to discern the apple from the mask. Changing the overlay to green solves this problem. Likewise, making the mask more transparent or more opaque might make your task easier.

Figure 9.43

The Layer Mask Display Options dialog box.

1. Select Layer Mask Options from the layer mask context menu (see Figure 9.35). In the Layers palette, (Control-click)[right-click] the layer mask thumbnail to reveal the pull-down context menu.

2. The Layer Mask Display Options dialog box lets you select the overlay color. Clicking the color square brings up the Color Picker.

3. Select a new color from the Color Picker and click OK.

4. Set the opacity to determine how the mask overlay appears on the layer image.

5. Click OK.

Using Gradient Masks within Layers Masks

Gradients are a very effective way of making images blend when creating a composite. Gradients add depth by giving the feel of fading into the background. They also add curves to round surfaces. When you edit a layer mask, you can select areas and build gradients inside the selections.

Figure 9.44, for instance, is the image of a plane on a beach, and you want to create some depth between the plane and the beach scene. Notice that the plane image is surrounded by a blue that is the color of the beach sky. Using a gradient to make the beach fade back in space helps create depth.

1. Open the image "Gradient.psd" from the CD-ROM accompanying this book (see Figure 9.44).

Figure 9.44

The image "Gradient.psd."

2. (Command-click)[Control-click] the beach layer mask thumbnail to load the layer transparency of the mask.

3. (Option-click)[Alt-click] the beach layer mask thumbnail. This brings up the layer mask grayscale image (see Figure 9.45).

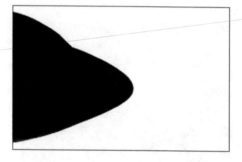

Figure 9.45

The layer mask grayscale image.

4. Set your colors on the toolbar to the mask default with a white foreground and black background.

5. Select the Gradient tool and in the Gradient Tool Options palette select Foreground to Background (see Figure 9.46)

Figure 9.46

The Gradient Tool Options palette.

6. Drag the Gradient tool horizontally across the grayscale image edge to edge from right to left. The nose of the plane remains black and the gradient goes from left to right, black to white (see Figure 9.47).

Figure **9.47**

The image with gradient addition.

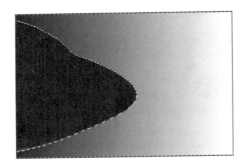

7. (Option-click)[Alt-click] the beach layer mask thumbnail to bring the layer image back. The image has a gradient effect around the plane (see Figure 9.48).

Figure **9.48**

The final image, with a gradient effect around the plane.

Copying a Layer Mask to Other Layers

There are many uses for copying layer masks to other layers. If you want an image to be seen through a number of successive layers that are sitting above, copy the same layer mask into each of the layers. You could cut and paste the mask from one layer to another, but Photoshop 4.0 simplifies this task.

1. (Command-click)[Control-click] the layer mask that you want to copy. This loads the selection in the document window.

2. Click the layer that is to receive the selection in order to make it active.

3. Choose Layer➡Add Layer Mask➡Reveal Selection (see Figure 9.32). A new layer mask is created with the current selection. It is a copy of the original layer mask.

USING ADJUSTMENT LAYERS

Adjustment layers put color adjustment features into the Layers palette. The same corrections accessed from the Image➡Adjust menu are found in adjustment layers. This makes color correction a more flexible tool. Image➡Adjust menu items make permanent adjustments to the pixel values in an image. Adjustment layers apply these same adjustments, but do not change the image data. The corrections could be removed at any time because the information for the adjustment exists as a separate layer. By using an adjustment layer, Photoshop 4.0 adds the nonlinear undo feature of layers to making color adjustments.

An adjustment layer works like any other layer. It can be moved, edited, or deleted. In addition, the adjustment layer affects all the layers below as though they were merged into one layer. Any visible image, no matter how many levels below the adjustment layer, can be affected. If you use the commands on the Image➡Adjust submenu to get the equivalent outcome, you have to perform the same correction to each layer or wait until they are merged.

Adjustment layers use masks that work exactly like layer masks. Use the adjustment layer mask to limit the effect of the correction to a selection. If, for instance, you only want to apply curves to one layer, load the layer transparency. Layer transparency excludes the transparent areas from the selection, so the effect stays confined to that layer. After you make a selection, create the adjustment layer. The selection translates into the adjustment layer mask. When you perform the color adjustment, it is confined to the individual layer.

Creating Adjustment Layers

Do the following to create a new adjustment layer. Make the layer to be adjusted the active layer. When you create a new adjustment layer, it appears in the Layers palette above the active layer.

1. Choose one of the following methods to create a new adjustment layer.

   ◆ Select Layer➥New➥Adjustment Layer…. (see Figure 9.49).

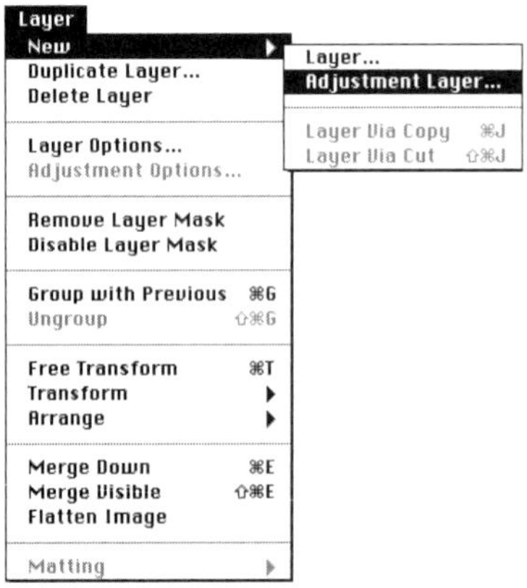

Figure 9.49

The New Adjustment Layer
command in the Layer menu.

◆ Select New Adjustment Layer from the Layers palette menu (see Figure 9.3).

◆ (Command-click)[Control-click] the New Layer button at the bottom of the Layers palette.

With any of these procedures, a New Adjustment Layer dialog box appears onscreen with the layer options shown in Figure 9.50.

Figure 9.50

The New Adjustment Layer
dialog box.

2. The first option in the New Adjustment Layer dialog box is the name. Fill in a name.

3. Select the type of adjustment you want to perform from the Type pull-down menu.

   ◆ **Levels** adjusts the tonal range of an image. Using sliders, you can set the highlights, midtones, and shadows on an individual or composite channel.

   ◆ **Curves** modifies the tonal range of an image from any value in the scale. This correction tool is very precise for working on the color composite or individual channels.

   ◆ **Brightness/Contrast** is the simplest method of adjusting the tonal range, but it also offers the least control. The highlights, midtones, and shadows are adjusted all at once. There is one slider for Brightness and one for Contrast.

   ◆ **Color Balance** adjusts the color range in the highlights, shadows, and midtones. It is a general tool and not capable of the precision of Curves. Color correct for red, cyan, green, magenta, blue, and yellow in the composite color channel.

   ◆ **Hue/Saturation** adjusts the hue, saturation, and lightness of an image. You can also colorize a grayscale image or create a monotone from a color image.

   ◆ **Selective Color** adjusts a color imbalance in the process colors (CMYK). With selective color you can shift the color balance in a particular color.

   ◆ **Invert** makes your image a negative, or if you have a negative, it can make it a positive. Pixels are mapped to their inverse value. Yellow becomes blue and red turns into cyan.

   ◆ **Threshold** converts color or grayscale images to black and white. You can select the threshold point by dragging a slider in the dialog box. Any values on one side are black and on the other white.

◆ **Posterize** is used to set a certain number of tonal levels. Pixels change value to the nearest match. You can use this to give a photograph a graphic look.

4. Select the Opacity for the adjustment.

5. Select the Mode to determine how the pixels blend (see Chapter 5, "Selections, Paths, and Masks," for a discussion of blending modes).

6. Check Group With Previous Layer if you want to make this layer part of a group.

7. Click OK. This brings up the dialog box for the chosen adjustment.

Note

The adjustment layer acts like a color-corrected copy of a visible merge of the layers below. It is as though there were only two layers and the adjusted copy sits on top of the unadjusted original. When you select an opacity and mode in the New Adjustment Layer dialog box, you determine how the pixels of the top adjusted copy blends with the original. In this way you control the intensity of the effect.

Changing the Adjustment Settings

Adjustment layers are very flexible. You can always go back to the particular adjustment dialog box for the adjustment layer and change the settings. Choose Layer➡Adjustment Options (see Figure 9.31) or double-click the name in the adjustment layer and the dialog box of the particular adjustment, with your original settings, appears onscreen. Adjust them to what you want and click OK.

Modifying the Layer Options

Bring up the Layer Options dialog box to change various options for the adjustment layer (see Figure 9.9). You can do this several ways.

1. Choose one of the following methods to open the Layer Options dialog box:

♦ Select Layer➡Layer Options….

♦ Select Layer Options on the Layers palette menu.

♦ (Control-click)[right-click] the adjustment layer mask thumbnail or the adjustment layer name. Choose Layer Options from the drop-down menu.

2. The Layer Options dialog box opens. Choose one of the options to change. You can adjust the Name, Opacity, Mode, Blend If, and Group With settings for the adjustment layer (see the sections in this chapter on the Layer Options dialog box, Blend If, and Grouping Layers)

3. Click OK.

Editing an Adjustment Layer Mask

Edit the adjustment layer mask to change the selected area (see the section on editing layer masks in this chapter).

1. Click the adjustment layer in the Layers palette to make it the target layer.

2. Choose one of the painting tools.

3. Paint on the canvas. Black hides or masks the effect and white adds to the selections, which lets the effect show through. Painting with any shade of gray adjusts the opacity of the effect. The closer the gray is to black, the more that it removes the effect of the adjustment.

Using filters, selections or other editing tools affects the mask as a grayscale image and changes the area of adjustment accordingly.

Also, as with layer masks, you can edit the grayscale image of the adjustment layer. You access the mask image in exactly the same way.

♦ (Option-click)[Alt-click] the adjustment mask thumbnail in the Layers palette to show the mask on the canvas. You can use painting or editing tools, cut and paste, or use filters to alter the grayscale image.

◆ (Option-click)[Alt-click] the mask thumbnail to return to the layer image in the canvas.

Turn on and off the mask.

◆ Shift-click the adjustment mask's thumbnail to turn off the effect of the mask. The adjustment covers the full canvas. A red X appears across the adjustment mask thumbnail.

◆ Click the adjustment layer thumbnail to turn the mask back on again.

Edit the mask as an image overlay.

◆ (Option-Shift-click)[Alt-Shift-click] the adjustment layer thumbnail to bring up the layer mask as a transparent overlay on the image. Edit the mask with black, white, and gray.

◆ (Option-Shift-click)[Alt-Shift-click] the adjustment layer thumbnail to turn off the overlay and leave only the image on the canvas.

C h a p t e r **10**

WORKING WITH COLOR IMAGES

Photoshop generates color images based on specific color models. The color models represented in Photoshop are red, green and blue (RGB), cyan, magenta, yellow and black (CMYK), hue, saturation and brightness (HSB), and CIE L*a*b. In addition to these color models, Photoshop also has modes for other color output, such as bitmap, indexed color, and duotone. A good understanding of color theory and the various color spaces will certainly help you comprehend what is going on in Photoshop when working with color images. This chapter covers some basic color theory along with further elaboration on the way Photoshop deals with color.

Because color perception is highly subjective and can vary greatly from one person to the next, an organized method of representing color using **Color Models** exists. Color models are a way to represent colors using numbers and to facilitate the use of computers to work with color. Using color models, color information can be communicated efficiently, ensuring consistency between computers, software applications such as PageMaker and Illustrator, and peripheral devices such as scanners and printers. Photoshop supports the color models necessary to produce color imagery on the computer screen as well as those needed to produce various forms of color output, most notably process color separations. The color modes in Photoshop enable you to work within the color spaces of particular color models to produce accurate and expected color results.

Photoshop supports the most common color models with a number of **color modes** for displaying, storing, and printing images. The available color modes are under the Image menu in the Mode submenu. Photoshop uses built-in algorithms (formulas) to convert colors from one mode to another and supports industry standards for color reproduction and generation. At first glance, it may appear that Photoshop handles all the variables involved in producing accurate color from scanning to color correction to color output. This is true to some extent, but an understanding of why a particular color mode lends itself to a particular process is absolutely necessary to produce professional quality color images for production, as well as for onscreen presentation purposes.

All Photoshop images are made up of one or more **channels**, depending on the color mode. Bitmap, Grayscale, Indexed Color, and Duotone images are contained in one channel. RGB is represented in three channels, (one for red, one for green, and one for blue), as well as a composite channel that displays the results of the RGB color combination. CMYK images are represented by four channels (one for cyan, one for magenta, one for yellow, and one for black), as well as a composite CMYK channel. The CMYK channels display the information that will be contained on the printing plates when the image is color separated. Lab mode contains a channel for lightness (L) and a channel for both the "a" and "b" values. Additional channels, called *alpha channels* or mask channels, can be added in all the color modes except Bitmap mode. Photoshop images can contain up to 24 channels. For more information on alpha channels, refer to Chapter 9, "Channels."

BITMAP IMAGES

Bitmap images, also called 1-bit images, are made up of pixels that contain one of two color values: black or white. Because the pixel depth is only 1 bit, bitmap images require the least amount of memory and disk space. See "Pixel Depth" later in this chapter for more information on pixel depth. Line art is often scanned as a bitmap to preserve the sharpness of the lines. Because page layout applications such as PageMaker and QuarkXPress can make the white pixels of a bitmap image transparent, grayscale images are sometimes converted to bitmap images with a halftone screen or dithered pattern applied. Many of the image editing options are disabled in bitmap mode, making it necessary to edit these images in grayscale mode, and then convert them back to bitmap mode.

In order to **convert to Bitmap mode,** the image mode must first be set to Grayscale. After you convert color images to Grayscale mode, the Bitmap mode option is available under the Mode menu (see Figure 10.1).

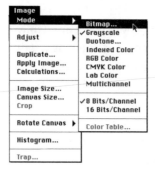

Figure 10.1

Only Grayscale images can be converted to Bitmap mode.

1. Choose Bitmap from the Mode menu. The Bitmap dialog box appears (see Figure 10.2).

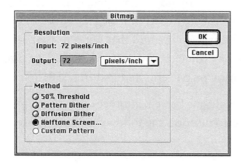

Figure 10.2

The Bitmap dialog box.

2. Select the units of measure from the pull-down menu.

3. Enter the output resolution. This will be the resolution of the resulting bitmap image. The current resolution is displayed automatically for output resolution.

4. Select one of the five options for bitmap conversion method.

   50% Threshold converts all gray pixels at or above 128 (50% black) to white and all gray values below 128 to black. **Pattern Dither** generates a dithered pattern of black and white pixels to represent the grayscale image. Bitmap images created using this method often print better than they appear onscreen. Some computer programs, such as email programs, only accept 1-bit per pixel bitmap images. **Diffusion Dither** is the best choice for generating grayscale images at 1 bit per pixel for display on computer screens. The diffused pattern creates the illusion of gray values using only black and white pixels. **Halftone Screen** emulates the process of applying a halftone screen to a gray-scale image. The resulting image is broken up into dots of various sizes to represent the grayscale. **Custom Pattern** enables you to apply another image as the pattern to create the bitmap image. You can create special screens (wood grain, mezzotint, or stipple pattern, for example) and apply them to the bitmap image. The pattern should be the same size as or larger than the image because smaller patterns are tiled to create the screen. Custom patterns capture more of the detail in the grayscale image when they contain gray areas. If you want to apply a pattern that is already bitmapped, convert it to grayscale first and apply the Gaussian Blur or Blur More filter to create some gray values. Keep in mind that patterns that are too tight may not print as you expect due to ink spread on press. For more information on patterns and textures, see Chapter 6, "Painting."

If you select Halftone Screen, another dialog box opens (Figure 10.3), and you need to perform the following steps:

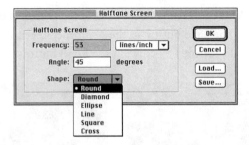

Figure 10.3

The Halftone Screen dialog box.

1. Select the units of measure from the pull-down menu.

2. Enter a Screen Frequency value. The screen frequency is the "line screen" and ranges from 1 to 999 lines per inch or 0.400 to 400 lines per centimeter (lines per inch is the U.S. standard). Decimal values are allowed here to accommodate matching advanced screening methods. Screen frequency for newspapers and circulars is usually between 65 and 85 lines per inch; magazines are usually between 120 and 150 lines per inch, but check with your printer before indicating a screen frequency because only the printer can tell you what the best line screen for your project is.

3. Enter the screen angle. The screen angle can range from -180° to +180°. The printer or service bureau can also tell you what to use here, though images that are going to print in black ink or one color are generally at a 45° angle.

4. Choose a dot shape from the Shape pull-down menu. Most halftone screens are created using either eliptical or diamond shapes. Refer to Chapter 15, "Printing," for further information on dot shape.

5. Click OK to accept these settings and generate the bitmap image. Converting grayscale images to bitmap images using the Halftone Screen option enables you to override the halftone screen that is applied when the film is generated. The three images in Figure 10.4 were created through halftone screening to facilitate the use of multiple screen frequencies on the same

page. You can save your halftone screen settings to a file by clicking the Save button in the Halftone Screen dialog box and reload the settings by clicking the Load button.

Figure 10.4

The Halftone Screen breaks the grayscale image up into dots. Examine the dots with a loupe to see the dot structure.

53 LPI

85 LPI

133 LPI

GRAYSCALE IMAGES

Grayscale images are represented by up to 256 shades or levels of gray. Each pixel in a grayscale image contains 8 bits of data to describe the pixel's brightness value. Gray levels range from 0 (black) to 255 (white). The pixels in a grayscale image are also represented as percent of black where 0% is white and 100% is black. Most scanners are able to scan directly into grayscale mode when the scanner software supports grayscale scanning. Bitmap and color images (RGB or CMYK) can be converted to Grayscale mode. When converting from color to grayscale, Photoshop discards all color information and generates the grayscale image from the luminosity values of the color image. You can also convert grayscale images to RGB or CMYK; the gray pixel values are converted to their comparable values in the respective color space. In RGB, for example, grays are represented by combining equal parts of red, green and blue such as 230 red, 230 green, and 230 blue to represent 10% grayscale. In CMYK the gray values are created using varied combinations of cyan, magenta, yellow and black; 12% cyan, 7% magenta, and 7% yellow to create 10% grayscale or 45% cyan, 32% magenta, 32% yellow, and 10% black to create 50% grayscale for example.

Grayscale Image

50%Threshold

Pattern Dither

Figure 10.5

The six basic image types available when converting to Bitmap mode.

Diffusion Dither

Halftone Screen

Custom Pattern

Converting Bitmap to Grayscale

Bitmap images are usually converted to grayscale to facilitate editing the image because many of the editing tools are not available in Bitmap mode. The resulting grayscale image contains just two gray levels; black (0) and white (255).

1. Choose Image➡Mode➡Grayscale to display the Grayscale dialog box (see Figure 10.6).

Figure 10.6

The Grayscale dialog box

2. Enter a size ratio for the conversion. A ratio of 1 creates a grayscale image of the same size. A number higher than 1 creates a smaller sized image. A ratio of 2, for example, generates a grayscale image at 50% of the size; Photoshop averages two pixels to create 1 pixel in the grayscale image in this case. Choosing a ratio value less than 1 may cause the image to fall apart because Photoshop has to invent the needed data based on the existing bitmap.

Converting Color to Grayscale

When converting from RGB, CMYK, Lab, or Multichannel to Grayscale mode, Photoshop uses the luminance values of the pixels to generate the grayscale image. Photoshop asks if you really want to discard all colors before completing the conversion to grayscale. To convert a color image to grayscale mode:

1. Open any RGB, CMYK, Lab, or Multichannel image.

2. Choose Image➡Mode➡Grayscale (see Figure 10.7).

3. A dialog box appears asking if you want to discard the colors. Click OK (see Figure 10.8). Note that after you discard the color information, converting back to RGB from grayscale does not restore the color information.

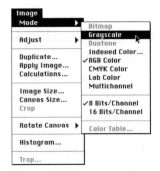

Figure 10.7

Choose Grayscale on the Mode sub-menu.

Figure 10.8

Converting to grayscale discards the color information.

Converting Grayscale to Color

You can convert a grayscale image into any of the available color modes, enabling you to add color or colorize a grayscale image. You can also create a "4-color halftone" or Quadtone by converting grayscale directly to CMYK mode. See Chapter 14, "Custom Colorization," for instruction on how to colorize grayscale images. To convert a grayscale image into RGB mode:

1. Open any grayscale image.

2. Choose Image➳Mode➳RGB (see Figure 10.9). You can select CMYK or Lab as color modes, as well.

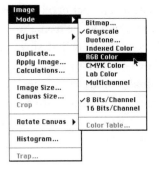

Figure 10.9

The Image menu.

RGB IMAGES

The RGB (red, green, blue) Color Model is representative of colors created using light. Televisions, scanners, and color monitors are examples of devices that must use RGB light to create color. The red, green, and blue levels are specified by integers between 0 and 255, indicating the amount of light used to create a pixel's color. The RGB colors are referred to as the additive or light primaries because when red, green, and blue light are generated at full and equal intensity on the same spot, white light is created. Necessity dictates the use of the RGB color model for color monitors, though RGB is restricted by the limitations of the particular device. Because the use of the RGB color model to produce color is *device-dependent*, colors can vary significantly between different monitors and even between two monitors of the same make and model. Things such as voltage, proximity to other electronic devices, and age of the monitor have an effect on how RGB color is displayed.

RGB color is also the color model used by all scanners, even if the scanner is capable of generating color in other color spaces. Color pixel data is captured by the scanner when it records the light reflected off an original (in the case of a photographic print), or transmitted through an original (in the case of transparency originals), converting this captured data to RGB values.

The **RGB mode** in Photoshop uses the RGB color model and represents color by using varying degrees of light intensity in each of the red, green, and blue channels (see Figure 10.10). The values for each color channel are created using 8 bits of data per pixel per color; therefore, each pixel in the RGB image contains a value from 0 to 255 for red, 0 to 255 for green, and 0 to 255 for blue. When all three color values are 255, the pixel displays as white. When all three color values are zero (0), the pixel displays as black. Equal proportions of the three colors result in a shade of gray. Because computer monitors are essentially RGB devices, you should become familiar with and work in the RGB mode to edit color images.

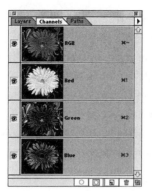

Figure 10.10

The RGB Channels.

CMYK IMAGES

CMYK images are used to produce the four process color plates used in four-color printing. Some scanning software can scan directly into CMYK mode. Scanners do this by converting the RGB data the scanner reads to CMYK data using built-in color lookup tables in the software or color computers in the hardware. For the most part, CMYK images are generated by Photoshop and programs like it from RGB images. To understand how CMYK plates are generated and why, start off by reading the following sections on the CMY and CMYK Color models.

The CMY Color Model

The CMY (cyan, magenta, yellow) color model is used to produce color using solid materials such as ink and toners. Traditional color separation techniques involved using red, green, and blue filters to capture the cyan, magenta and yellow components of color originals. When a color image, for instance, was photomechanically captured using a red filter, the resulting film would be the cyan color plate. Combining any two of the RGB colors (additive primaries) produces one of the CMY colors (subtractive primaries). Combining 100% of any two of the subtractive primaries (CMY) produces one of the additive primaries (RGB). In the CMY color model, color is perceived by the amount of color reflected off a substrate (white paper). In theory, combining 100% of cyan, magenta, and yellow produces black. That's why they are called the subtractive primaries; absence of all three produces white. In the perfect world, the white substrate would be 100% reflective and the combination of CMY at 100% would absorb all color. Because paper always absorbs and transmits some of the light, as well as unavoidable impurities in the process color inks (CMY), the color produced by combining CMY at 100% is more of a muddy brown color. For this reason, black was added as the fourth color to create the CMYK color model.

The CMYK Color Model

Four-color process printing is achieved by combining cyan, magenta, yellow and black to produce a full range of colors. Black is indicated by the letter K to avoid confusion with the color blue (B). The black plate contains much of the shadow and detail information in a four-color image. Depending on the method of black generation used, the black plate may contain more or less of the image data. Black generation is explained fully in the section on converting RGB to CMYK later in this chapter.

CMYK Mode

In CMYK mode, each pixel of the color image is assigned a value that represents percentages of cyan, magenta, yellow, and black ink. Light colors have low percentages of color; dark colors contain high percentages of ink. In CMYK mode, the lack of ink percentage is equivalent to the paper color (white for proofing). Black is often represented by a high percentage of black combined with some percentage of the other three process colors. When RGB images are converted to CMYK mode, the resulting color separation is generated using parameters in Photoshop's separation table. The separation table is generated to the specific settings in the Monitor Setup, Printing Inks Setup, and Separation setup dialog boxes. (See "Converting RGB to CMYK" in this chapter for further information.) When the original image starts out in RGB mode, make color and retouching adjustments in RGB before converting to CMYK. You can use the CMYK Preview command available under the

Image menu to view the image in CMYK while working in RGB. If the images are already in CMYK mode when you receive them (from a service bureau, for example), edit the color images in CMYK mode. Converting to RGB from CMYK and then back again can cause some undesirable color shifts. CMYK mode contains four color channels for each of the four process colors and one composite channel (see Figure 10.11).

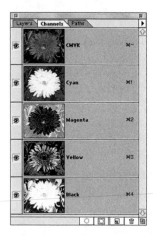

Figure 10.11

The CMYK Channels.

Converting to CMYK

A lot of preliminary work must be done in Photoshop before converting images to CMYK mode. Photoshop takes many factors into account when creating the separation table necessary to generate a CMYK image. When Photoshop converts a RGB image to CMYK, it first converts the image to Lab mode; internally, you don't see this. Photoshop uses the settings in the Monitor Setup to perform this interim conversion, so calibrating the monitor and entering the Monitor Setup information is necessary. See Chapter 2, "Calibrating Your System," for information on how to calibrate your monitor. The image is then converted from Lab mode to CMYK mode. During this step, Photoshop uses the settings in Printing Inks Setup and Separation Setup to generate the separation table. Refer to Chapter 2 for information on Monitor Setup, Separation Setup, and Printing Inks Setup. To convert to CMYK mode:

1. Open any Grayscale, RGB color, or Lab color image.

2. Choose Image➥Mode➥CMYK (see Figure 10.12).

Figure 10.12

The Image menu.

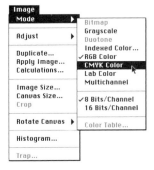

LAB COLOR

Lab color is a representation of the L*a*b color model and has continued to gain popularity among the Color Prepress initiated. You may never use Lab color in Photoshop, but the Photoshop application uses Lab transparently to perform color conversions. Lab color images print as four color process separations from Postscript Level 2 printers, and it is the best format for sending files to proprietary platforms such as Scitex or Silicon Graphics because it is a device and platform independent format.

The L*a*b Color Model

The L*a*b color model encompasses all the colors within the RGB and CMY color models and is used internally by Photoshop to convert between RGB and CMYK. Based on the CIE XYZ color model, developed in 1931 by the Commission Internationale de l'Eclairage (the International Committee on Illumination), the L*a*b color model has recently gained wide acceptance because it is a device *in*dependent color model. Color management systems developed by companies such as Kodak, Apple and Agfa are built around the L*a*b color model. A telling indicator of the widespread support of this color model is evidenced by its support in Adobe's PostScript Level 2. The three components used in the L*a*b color model are Luminance (lightness) and two color components: component "a" ranges from green to red, and component "b" ranges from blue to yellow.

Lab Mode

Lab mode uses the L*a*b color model to represent the color of pixels. Each of the three color channels in Lab mode contains 8 bits of data for each pixel, for a total of 24 bits (see Figure 10.13). "L" is the lightness component of the image; each pixel having a value in the range of zero (0) to 100. The "a" value (green to red) and the "b" value (blue to yellow) range from +120 to -120. Because the color specifications in the L*a*b color model are device independent, Lab mode is the best mode to use when transferring images from one system to another. Adobe recommends using Lab color to print to PostScript Level 2 devices, but check with your service bureau if they are doing the output. The Lab mode is the hardest to understand until you experiment with editing the lightness and color values separately.

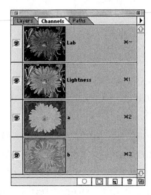

Figure 10.13

The LAB Channels.

Converting to Lab Mode

RGB and Indexed color images can be converted to Lab mode. You can adjust the "L" (lightness) value in lab mode to adjust the brightness of the image or parts of the image without affecting the color. The image can then be converted back to RGB or Indexed color without affecting the color values. Lab images can also be converted to CMYK for process color printing. Converting between Lab mode and other color modes or vice versa does not affect the original colors of the image in any way unless you adjust the "a" or "b" values in Lab mode. To convert to Lab mode:

1. Open any Grayscale, RGB, CMYK, Duotone, or Multichannel image. Bitmap images cannot be converted to Lab mode because Lab mode requires at least 8 bits of information per pixel; convert the bitmap image to grayscale first.

2. Choose Image➥Mode➥Lab (see Figure 10.14).

Figure 10.14

Choose Lab from the Mode sub-menu.

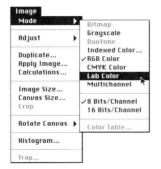

HSB COLOR

The HSB color mode represents the HSB color model. In the HSB color model colors are described by the three attributes humans use to describe color: Hue, Saturation, and Brightness. Hues are usually called by a common color name (orange, purple or tan, to name a few). The HSB color model is graphically depicted as a cylinder. Hue is specified by degrees, indicating a position around the circumference of the cylinder; hues follow a progression of red, orange, yellow green, blue, indigo, violet, and back to red again (see Figure 10.15). The saturation values are depicted from the center out. A saturation value at the center or core of the cylinder is at 0% saturation, a neutral gray. The cylinder is sliced horizontally into sections representing the brightness value, with the darkest values at the bottom (100%) and the brightest at the top (0%). Each slice of this cylinder represents a color wheel at a particular brightness percentage. The Apple color picker is shown in Figure 10.16 to illustrate the HSB color wheel. In the Apple color picker the Hue is represented by degrees around the wheel, Saturation is the value from the center of the wheel out, and Brightness is controlled by the slider under the color wheel. In the Photoshop Color Picker, HSB is the color model used to graphically depict color selections, though not with the usual color wheel (see Figure 10.17).

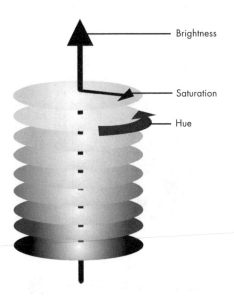

Figure 10.15

The HSB color model is usually represented as a cylinder.

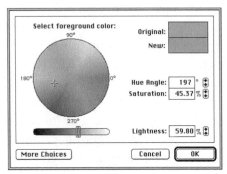

Figure 10.16

The Apple color picker.

HSB in the Photoshop Color Picker

The Photoshop Color Picker graphically depicts specified colors in the HSB color space. The large square (see Figure 10.17) contains brightness and saturation values for a particular hue, represented by the "rainbow" color slider to its right. Saturation percentage runs from left to right, 0% to 100% saturation of the selected hue. Brightness percentage runs from top to bottom in the color square, from 100% to 0% brightness. You click and drag horizontally to change the saturation, vertically to affect the brightness. The HSB color space is used only to specify and adjust color within Photoshop and does not have a corresponding color mode.

Figure 10.17

The Photoshop Color Picker.

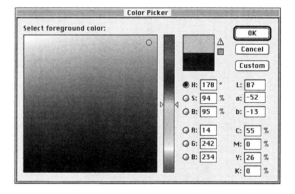

DUOTONES

When you choose Duotone from the Mode menu, the Duotone Options dialog box appears. A pull-down menu in this dialog box displays four available modes: Monotone, Duotone, Tritone, or Quadtone. Monotones are 8 bit per pixel, grayscale images printed with a non-black ink. Duotones are grayscale images printed with two colors, usually black and a spot color. Tritones and Quadtones are grayscale images printed with three and four colors respectively. Printing presses are generally capable of printing up to 50 levels of gray for one color, a lot less than the 256 gray levels generated by Photoshop. Duotones, Tritones, and Quadtones are often used to extend the gray levels of the printing process. When creating a Duotone, Tritone, or Quadtone, the gray values of the grayscale image are actually designated to the colors chosen, so the image is still an 8 bit per pixel image with the gray values mapped to two, three or four colors. Unlike the RGB, CMYK, and Lab modes; the colors used in Duotones, Tritones, and Quadtones are contained in a single 8 bit channel and are only adjustable using the curves in the Duotone Options dialog box.

Creating a Duotone

To create a duotone, start with a grayscale image. If you are using a color image, you have to convert it to Grayscale mode before continuing.

1. Open any Grayscale image and choose Image➡Mode➡ Duotone to display the Duotone Options dialog box (see Figure 10.18).

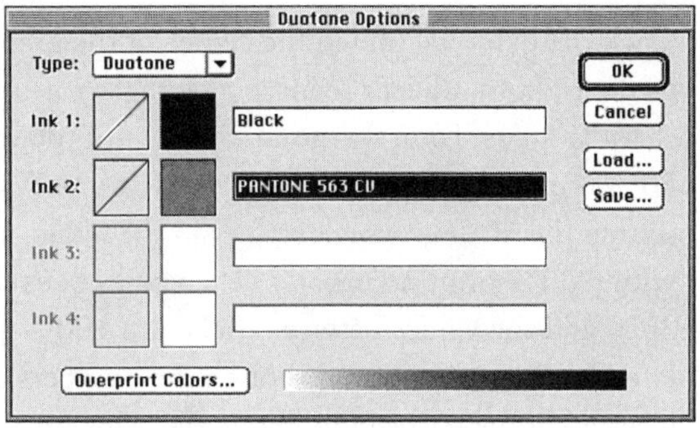

Figure 10.18

The Duotone Options dialog box.

2. Select Duotone from the Type pull-down menu.

3. Select the colors for your duotone by clicking the color box to the left of the color name. When the Photoshop Custom Color Picker is displayed, you can use any of the Custom Color models to select a color for your duotone, or click the Picker button to specify a color mix in one of Photoshop's color spaces. See Selecting Custom Colors later in this chapter for more information on specifying spot colors. If you choose a Custom spot color, be sure the color is named exactly as the color name in your page layout application (upper- and lowercase count as well).

4. To modify the duotone curve, click the curve box to the left of the ink swatch in the Duotone Options dialog box to display the Duotone Curve dialog box (see Figure 10.19). The default duotone curve is a straight diagonal line across the entire grid. The default duotone curve maps the printing ink percentages exactly to the grayscale values in the image; a 10% highlight

pixel in the image prints with a 10% dot of the ink color and a 60% midtone value prints with a 60% dot of the ink color, for example.

5. You can adjust the duotone curve for each of the ink colors by dragging points on the graph or by entering values for the printing ink percentages to correspond with the grayscale values in the image.

◆ Click the diagonal line in the center of the graph and drag to the right to adjust the ink percentages towards the shadow areas. Drag the point down until the value in the 50% box becomes 30% (see Figure 10.19). With this setting the 50% grayscale values in the image are printed with a 30% printing ink dot. The values between 0% and 30% and the values between 30% and 100% are recalculated by Photoshop, even though the numbers are not inserted in the corresponding boxes. This ink color maps the grayscale values in the image between 0% and 50% to print with the color ink between 0% and 30%, so the ink coverage is light in these areas. The ink coverage is highest for the midtone, 3/4 tone, and shadow areas because the largest proportion of ink percentage is distributed between the 50% and 100 grayscale values in the image.

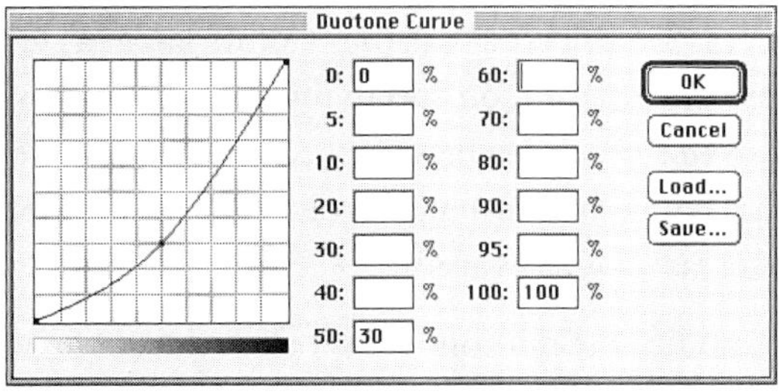

Figure 10.19

The Duotone Curve dialog box with the 50% grayscale pixel mapped to a 30% printing dot.

◆ Click the diagonal line in the center of the graph and drag to the left to adjust the ink percentages towards the highlight areas. Drag the point up until the value in the 50%

box becomes 70% (see Figure 10.20). With this setting the 50% grayscale values in the image are printed with a 70% printing ink dot. The values between 0% and 70% and the values between 70% and 100% are recalculated by Photoshop, even though the numbers are not inserted in the corresponding boxes. This ink color maps the grayscale values in the image that are between 0% and 50% to print with the color ink between 0% and 70%, so the ink coverage is heavy in the highlight and 1/4 tones. The ink coverage is lowest for the midtone, 3/4 tone, and shadow areas because the smallest proportion of ink percentage is distributed between the 50% and 100% grayscale values in the image.

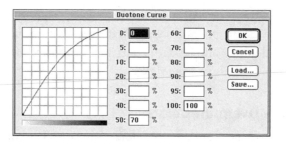

Figure 10.20

The Duotone Curve dialog box with the 50% grayscale pixel mapped to a 70% printing dot.

◆ You can click the diagonal line in the graph and add up to 13 points to set the values for the 13 boxes (see Figure 10.21). Note that the end points of the diagonal line can also be adjusted to set the 0% and 100% values. Photoshop calculates any intermediate ink percentages automatically.

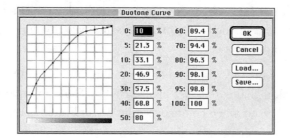

Figure 10.21

The Duotone Curve dialog box with all 13 values mapped on the diagonal line.

◆ Click and drag the points off the grid to remove them.

◆ Click the Save button in the Duotone Curve dialog box to save a particular curve setting.

◆ Click the Load button in the Duotone Curve dialog box to load a previously saved curve setting.

5. After you have adjusted the duotone curves, click OK in the Duotone Options dialog box. Duotones created with both colors having the same curve produce a duotone that prints one ink entirely over the other, so make sure you change the curve for at least one of the colors. If you want to readjust the color settings for your duotone, type Control-Z (Windows) or Command-Z (Macintosh) to undo the conversion and try again.

6. Save the file in Photoshop EPS format if you want to import the duotone into a page layout application such as QuarkXPress or PageMaker.

Setting the Overprint Colors

When two or more unscreened colors overlap in a Duotone, Tritone, or Quadtone, the overlapping colors create a new color (for example, red and yellow produce orange). You can adjust how these colors display on the screen only, which is helpful if you want to calibrate your screen display to accurately display the colors that will print in Duotone mode. Adjusting the colors for overprint does not affect the overall monitor calibration setup and only applies to the specific image you're working with. To set the overprint colors:

1. Choose Image➡Mode➡Duotone to display the Duotone Options dialog box. You can do this even if you're already in Duotone mode.

2. Click the Overprint Colors button to display the Overprint Colors dialog box (see Figure 10.22). The combinations that will result when colors overprint are indicated here.

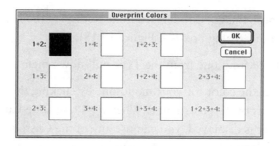

Figure 10.22

The possible color combinations are highlighted in the Overprint Colors dialog box.

3. Click the color swatch over the combination you'd like to adjust to display the Photoshop Color Picker.

4. Select the color you want for this combination and then click the OK button.

Perform steps 3 and 4 for all the color combinations you want to change before clicking OK in the Overprint Colors dialog box.

Loading and Saving Duotone Curves

You can save the duotone curve information in a file for later retrieval. Click on the Save button in the Duotone Options dialog box and give the file a name that reflects the colors used. To load saved duotone presets, click on the Load button in the Duotone Options dialog box. Photoshop comes with some presets for Duotones, Tritones and Quadtones located in the goodies directory (Windows) or the Goodies folder (Macintosh).

Creating a Monotone

Creating a Monotone is a simple process. Monotone images are grayscale images that have a color specification assigned to them. If you specify a Custom Color (PANTONE 186, for example) and save the file in EPS format, the file can be imported into a page layout application such as QuarkXPress and separates out to a color plate called PANTONE 186. To create a Monotone image, start out with a grayscale image and do the following:

1. Choose Image➡Mode➡Duotone to display the Duotone Options dialog box (see Figure 10.18).

2. Select Monotone from the Type pull-down menu.

3. Select the color for your monotone by clicking the color box to the left of the color name. When the Photoshop Custom Color Picker is displayed, you can use any of the Custom Color models to select a color for your monotone or click the Picker button to specify a color mix in one of Photoshop's color spaces. If you choose a Custom spot color, be sure the color is named exactly as the color name in your page layout application (upper and lowercase count as well). See "Selecting Custom Colors" later in this section for more information on specifying spot colors.

4. Click the Duotone Curve diagram to display the Monotone Curve dialog box. If you want to end up with a monotone image that represents the grayscale with a color, leave the duotone curve linear (a straight line from the bottom left to the top right).

5. Click OK. If you want to readjust the color settings for your monotone, type (Command-Z)[Control-Z] to undo the conversion and try again.

6. Save the file in Photoshop EPS format if you want to import the monotone into a page layout application such as QuarkXPress or PageMaker.

Creating a Tritone or Quadtone

Follow the steps outlined above for Creating a Duotone, but specify three colors to create a Tritone or four colors for a Quadtone image. Custom presets for Tritones and Quadtones are contained in the goodies directory (Windows) or the Goodies folder (Macintosh) in the Photoshop applications directory. The best way to get a feel for what settings to use for Duotones, Tritones, and Quadtones is to experiment and examine some of the presets provided with Photoshop.

Setting Screen Angles for Duotones

A Duotone, Tritone, or Quadtone creates overlapping areas of the grayscale image when it is created. In order for the halftone screens to print properly, the halftone screen angles for the color plates should be at least 30° apart. For four-color process separations, black is usually set to a 45° angle with magenta and cyan 30° away from that on either side (15° and 75°). Setting the angles 30° apart ensures that an overlapping of the halftone dots does not create a moiré pattern. For CMYK printing the yellow plate is printed at 90° (only 15° away from the nearest color). Yellow is chosen as the color that must overlap because it is the least dominant of the four colors. Use this same setup for Duotones, Tritones, and Quadtones. For Quadtones, keep in mind that with four inks, one of them has to overlap in the halftone dot area. Choose the lightest of the four colors to be set at the "yellow" angle.

Before you set the screen angles for your Duotone, Tritone, or Quadtone images in Photoshop, consult your printer or service bureau. Many screening algorithms are in use today, such as Agfa's Balanced Screening and Linotype Hell's Diamond Screening, not to mention advanced screening technologies for Stochastic Screening, sometimes called FM (frequency modulation) screening. It may cause more harm than good to set the screen angles independently for the image in Photoshop because service bureaus and printers may be using an improved screening technique that they can set up for your file during output. To set up the screen frequencies and angles yourself:

1. Open a Duotone image and choose Page Setup from the File menu to display the Page Setup dialog box (see Figure 10.23).

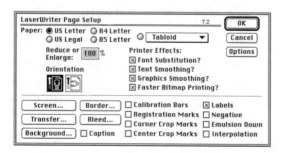

Figure 10.23

The Page Setup dialog box.

2. Click on the Screen button to display the Halftone Screen dialog box (see Figure 10.24).

3. Check the Use Printer's Default Screens checkbox and select the ink color from the pull-down list (see Figure 10.24). Note that the ink color list is composed of the colors used in your Duotone, Tritone, or Quadtone.

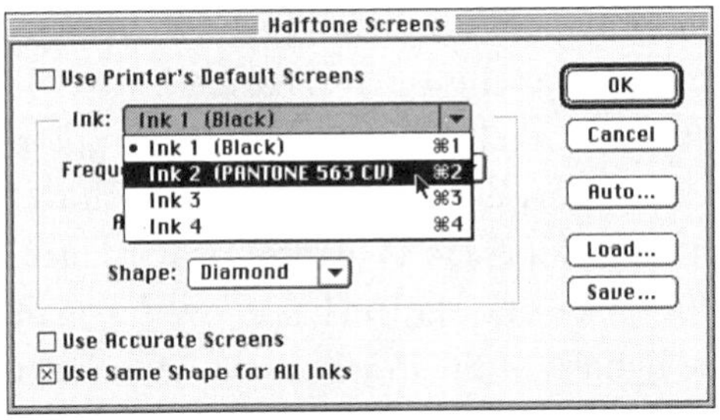

Figure 10.24

The Halftone Screens dialog box.

4. Enter a Screen Frequency and Angle for the color. Black should be at 45° with other colors 30° apart at either 15° or 75°. Talk to your printer for suggested angles.

5. Choose a dot shape from the drop-down list. For standard halftone screens, use a diamond dot here. If you want all plates to have the same dot shape, check the Use Same Shape for All Inks checkbox.

6. Check the Use Accurate Screens checkbox if your file will be printed to an output device using PostScript Level 2 or an Emerald controller or Emerald RIP (Raster Image Processor). If you check this box and do not print to one of the above devices, the accurate screens setting has no affect.

7. Specify the screen information for each color in your image.

8. You can save your settings to reload for subsequent images by clicking the Save button in the Halftone Screens dialog box. Click on the load button to reload the settings in the future. Click OK if you're done.

9. In order for the screens you just set up to be used for the image when it is saved as a Photoshop EPS file, you must check the

Include Halftone Screens checkbox when saving the file in Photoshop EPS format (see Figure 10.25). Photoshop detects your screen settings and checks this box for you.

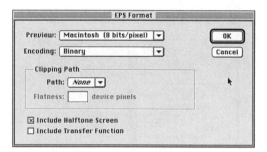

Figure 10.25

The EPS Format dialog box.

CUSTOM COLOR CHOICES

Aside from the capability to specify color in all the available Photoshop color spaces, you can also specify color using a variety of Custom Color choices. Photoshop does not provide a method to save spot colors in addition to the four process color plates to print correctly when placed in a page layout application. If you are in RGB mode and choose a Custom spot color, the color is converted into its RGB equivalent based on its CMYK breakdown. Conversely, when you are in CMYK mode, the spot color you choose is converted to the process color match based on built-in tables that conform with the color system's standard formulae. There are three ways to specify custom colors in Photoshop: from the Color Picker, from the Color Palette and when converting to Duotone mode, which uses the color picker (see Figures 10.26 and 10.27). Photoshop supports the PANTONE MATCHING SYSTEM, the TRUMATCH SWATCHING SYSTEM, the FOCOLTONE COLOUR SYSTEM, the TOYO 88 ColorFinder 1050 System, the ANPA-COLOR System and the DIC Color Guide.

Note

The supported Custom color options support printed color swatch books for the particular color system. You should always select spot colors from a printed swatch book. In other words, do not, under any circumstances, trust your monitor display blindly. Replace your printed color guides every year or so to avoid making selections of colors that have faded.

The following descriptions of the various color systems contain contact information to acquire further information from the company or to order a color guide.

Figure 10.26

Custom colors in the Photoshop Color Picker.

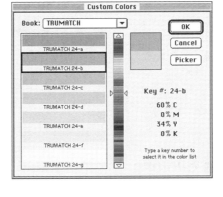

Figure 10.27

Custom colors in the Colors Palette.

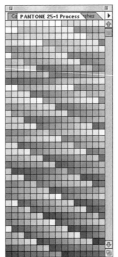

Specifying Custom Color

You can specify custom colors from the Color Picker as well as from the Color Palette's menu. To select a Custom color from the Color Picker:

1. Open the Adobe Photoshop Color Picker by clicking either the foreground or background color swatches in the toolbox or Color Palette.

2. Click the Custom button to display the Custom Colors dialog box (see Figure 10.28). The color shown is the closest match for the color selected. The color system displayed is the last one used.

3. Choose the color system from the drop-down list to the right of the word Book.

4. Locate the color by entering the ink number or scrolling through the list by dragging the triangles in the color bar. Click the top and bottom arrows of the color bar to move forward and backward one color at a time. Note that there is no field for typing in the code number for the color you want; you only have to type the number part of the color description.

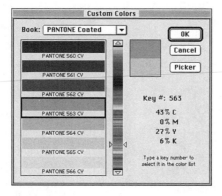

Figure 10.28

The Custom Colors dialog box.

5. Click the Picker button to see what the color equivalents are. Remember that Photoshop converts all spot colors to CMYK, except in the case of Duotone mode.

Selecting a Color System

The following descriptions contain contact information to acquire the color swatch books and color guides necessary to use the given color system.

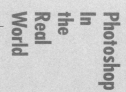

continues

PANTONE Matching System

PANTONE is the most popular system for selecting spot color inks in the United States. PANTONE color guides come in a variety of formats, each geared to a particular use. Some of the PANTONE color guides display CMYK equivalents to facilitate choosing matches for PANTONE colors with confidence. The PANTONE color gamut is significantly larger than that of CMYK, so many Pantone colors cannot be simulated accurately using CMYK inks. In Photoshop, you can choose from PANTONE Coated, PANTONE Uncoated, PANTONE Process, and PANTONE ProSim, which represent particular color guides or books you can acquire from PANTONE.

PANTONE, Inc.
590 Commerce Blvd.
Carlstadt, NJ 07072
(201) 935-5500
http://www.pantone.com

TRUMATCH SWATCHING SYSTEM

The TRUMATCH system covers the colors in the visible spectrum that reproduce well in CMYK. There are approximately 2000 color choices created as 40 variations of each hue, including four-color grays. Contact TRUMATCH for information and selection guide information.

TRUMATCH, Inc.
25 West 43rd Street
8th Floor
New York, NY 10036
(212) 302-9100
http://www.trumatch.com

FOCOLTONE COLOUR SYSTEM

The FOCOLTONE system contains 763 CMYK colors selected for their ability to blend well with other CMYK colors, hence avoiding trapping problems with process color plates. Color guides and charts are available from FOCOLTONE at the following address:

FOCOLTONE INTERNATIONAL, Ltd.
Churchview House
Penkridge
Acton Trussell, Stafford
ST170RJ
United Kingdom
(44) 0785-712667

TOYO 88 ColorFinder 1050

The TOYO 88 system contains more than 1000 colors based on the standard printing inks used in Japan. The TOYO Color Finder 1050 Book is available in the United States at many art supply stores. For further information about the TOYO 88 color system contact TOYO at:

Toyo Ink Manufacturing Co., Ltd.
3-13-2-chome Kyobashi
Chuo-ku, Tokyo 104
(011) 81-3-3272-0781

ANPA-COLOR

The ANPA-COLOR ROP Newspaper Color Ink Book contains the colors that print well on newsprint. To find out more about ANPA-COLOR, contact ANPA at:

Newspaper Association of America
Order Entry
11600 Sunrise Valley Drive
Reston, VA 22091
(703) 648-1367
http://www.naa.org

DIC Color

The DIC Color Guide is used primarily for printing projects in Japan. To acquire the color guides and more information contact DIC at:

continues

Dainippon Ink and Chemicals, Inc.
3-7-20 Nihonbashi
Chuo-ku, Tokyo 103, Japan
(011) 81-3-3272-4511
http://www.dic.co.jp

Photoshop In the Real World

INDEXED COLOR

Indexed color images are images that contain a specific color palette of up to 256 colors. An indexed color image can contain just the colors used in the image (if 256 or less), facilitating smaller file sizes and faster display in multimedia applications and Web pages. When you convert a color image from one of the other color modes to indexed color, Photoshop creates a color lookup table (CLUT) to store the color values for the image. If the image contains more than 256 distinct colors, Photoshop finds the closest matches and builds an *indexed* color table with 256 colors. The color table generated for indexed color images can also be edited to reduce the number of colors used.

Converting to Indexed Color

Choose Image➡Mode➡Indexed Color to display the Indexed Color dialog box (see Figure 10.29). These are the available options for generating an indexed color image:

Figure 10.29

The Indexed Color dialog box.

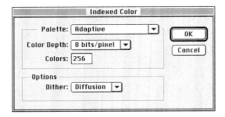

1. Open an RGB image and choose Image➡Mode➡Indexed Color.

2. Choose a **palette**. There are five palette choices to convert to indexed color in the Palette drop-down menu. You can view

the color table that is generated by choosing Image➥Mode➥ Color Table (see Figure 10.30) or by displaying the Swatches palette (see Figure 10.31).

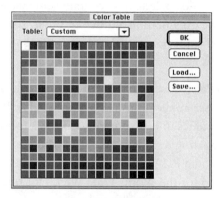

Figure 10.30

The Color Table dialog box.

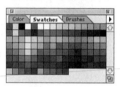

Figure 10.31

When in Indexed Color mode, the Swatches palette reflects the colors in the Color Lookup Table.

The **Exact Palette** is created with the exact same colors used in the RGB file, assuming the RGB file contains 256 colors or less. If the RGB contains more than 256 distinct colors, the Exact option will be grayed out.

The **System (Macintosh) palette** uses the Macintosh default color palette (see Figure 10.32). This palette contains an even sampling of the colors in the RGB color space. Note that the Macintosh color palette and Windows color palette may contain some of the same colors, but they are organized in a different order, so choose a System (Macintosh) color palette only when you're sure the image is used on a Macintosh only.

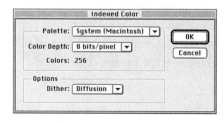

Figure 10.32

The System (Macintosh) palette option.

417

The **System (Windows) palette** uses the Windows default color palette. This palette contains an even sampling of the colors in the RGB color space. Note that the Windows color palette and Macintosh color palette may contain some of the same colors, but they are organized in a different order, so choose a System (Windows) color palette only when you're sure the image is used on a Windows computer only.

The **Web Palette** uses a palette of the 216 colors recognized by Web browser applications (see Figure 10.33). If you have created graphics to be exported to GIF89a format, choose Web when converting to Indexed color for the best results on both Macintosh and PC-Windows platforms. See Chapter 17, "Photoshop for the World Wide Web," for further explanation on the Web-ready 216 color palette.

Figure 10.33

The Web palette option.

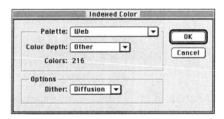

The **Uniform Palette** uses a uniform sampling of the colors in the RGB image's gamut of colors. The Uniform color palette's colors are generated based on the Color Depth specified. Specify dithering for Uniform indexed colors less than 8 bits per pixel color depth.

The **Adaptive Palette** samples the colors used in the image and builds a color table based on the most common occurrences, which can be really helpful for images weighted in specific color areas. You can also base the color table on a selected portion of the image. Select the portion of the image you want to base the indexed color table on before converting to Indexed mode. Photoshop uses the selected area of the image to weigh the color choices made for the color palette.

The **Custom Palette** is used to build your own color table of up to 256 colors. When you choose this option, the Color Table dialog box will be displayed. See the section "Editing the Indexed Color Table" later on in this chapter for information on how to enter the colors for the color table.

The **Previous** choice is only available if you chose the Custom or Adaptive options the last time you converted to Indexed Color. The Previous option uses the color palette from the previously generated "Custom" or "Adaptive" color palette, even if you didn't save the palette (see "Saving and Loading Color Tables" in this section).

3. Select a **Color Depth**. The Color Depth option is only available when you choose Uniform or Adaptive from the Palette drop-down list in the Indexed Color dialog box (see Figure 10.34). Photoshop uses the Color Depth information to generate the Indexed Color file. The maximum setting is 8 bits per pixel here because 8 bits per pixel generates 256 colors. Choosing a number less than 8 bits per pixel results in fewer colors, though the Indexed color image is still going to be an 8 bit per pixel image. When you choose Other as the Color Depth option, you can specify the exact number of colors desired. For more information on pixel depth and gray levels, see "Pixel Depth" later in this chapter.

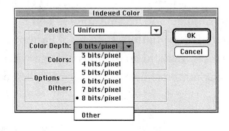

Figure 10.34

The Color Depth option is only available when choosing Uniform or Adaptive.

TABLE 1.2

THE COLOR DEPTH CHOICES IN THE INDEXED COLOR DIALOG BOX.

Pixel Depth	Adaptive Palette	Uniform Palette
3 bits/pixel	8 colors/grays	8 colors/grays
4 bits/pixel	16 colors/grays	8 colors/grays
5 bits/pixel	32 colors/grays	27 colors/grays
6 bits/pixel	64 colors/grays	64 colors/grays
7 bits/pixel	128 colors/grays	125 colors/grays
8 bits/pixel	256 colors/grays	216 colors/grays

4. Select a **Dithering Option** (see Figure 10.35). When the color table generated by converting to Indexed Color mode does not contain the exact 256 colors used in the RGB image, the resulting image appears posterized to some extent, unless some form of dithering is applied to the image. When dithering is used, the missing colors in the image are simulated by the application of a pattern. If you use the Exact Palette, the Dithering options will be grayed out (unavailable) because the image contains all the color values needed.

When **None** is selected and the RGB image contains more than 256 colors, posterization may become apparent because Photoshop fills in the blanks with the closest color in the palette. The **Pattern** method of dithering creates patterns of pixels to simulate the missing colors. You must be using one of the System Palette options to apply a Pattern dither. **Diffusion** offsets pixels to avoid an obvious pattern when dithering and is the most common choice for dithering, when dithering is necessary.

Figure 10.35

The Dithering options.

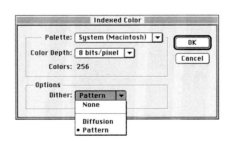

Making Color Table Choices

There are six predefined color tables available at the top of the Color Table dialog box (see Figure 10.36). You can apply any of these color table to the indexed color image.

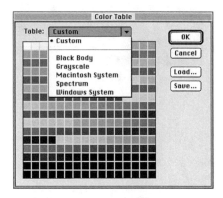

Figure 10.36

Display the Color Table dialog box by choosing Image➡Mode➡Color Table.

- ◆ **Custom** represents any color table that is not a Photoshop built-in color table.

- ◆ **Black Body** is based on the colors a black body radiator radiates when heating up. The colors range from black to red, orange, yellow, then white.

- ◆ If you select **Grayscale,** the image is rebuilt using 256 levels of gray.

- ◆ The **Macintosh System** color table displays the Macintosh 256 color palette.

- ◆ The **Spectrum** palette contains transitions between the primary hues: violet, blue, green, yellow, orange and red.

- ◆ The **Windows System** color table displays the Windows 256 color palette.

Saving and Loading Color Tables

You can save the displayed color table by clicking the Save button in the Color Table dialog box. To load a previously saved color table, click on the Load button in the Color Table dialog box. You can also load the saved color tables into the Swatches Palette. To load a color table into the Swatches Palette, choose Load Swatches or Replace Swatches from the Swatches Palette menu (see Figure 10.37). Locate a previously saved Swatch file or CLUT file and click the Open button.

Figure 10.37

Save and Load color swatches from the Swatches palette menu.

Tip

When you have converted an RGB image to Indexed Color mode, display the Swatches Palette to see the colors in the Color Table. From the Swatches Palette menu choose Save Swatches to save the colors from the table in a file to be used later. This method can be helpful when designing for multimedia presentations to maintain a uniform color palette for created graphics or added text.

Modifying the Color Table

The color table contains all of the colors (up to 256 of them) in your indexed color image. You may want to modify the colors that make up your indexed color image to combine similar colors into one flat color or to change the values of individual colors for effect. To modify the colors contained in the color table of an Indexed color image, do the following:

1. Choose Image➡Mode➡Color Table to display the Color Table dialog box.

2. Click a color to modify an individual color *or* click and drag through a range of colors.

3. The Photoshop Color Picker appears. If you clicked just one color tag, choose a new color and click OK. If you selected a range of colors, choose the first new color for the range and

click OK. The Color Picker reappears so you can select the last color in the range. The first color you pick also appears in the color picker the second time it is displayed, so simply clicking OK without entering a color changes the whole range of colors to the one color.

4. Click OK in the Color Table dialog box to apply the changes. If you click on the Cancel button the color palette is restored.

CONVERTING TO MULTICHANNEL MODE

When color images are converted to Multichannel Mode, the color plates are recreated as 8 bit per pixel grayscale channels numbered from 1 (see Figure 10.38). Converting an RGB image to Multichannel Mode, for example, would result in three channels numbered 1, 2 and 3 representing the red, green and blue channels of the RGB file. Converting a CMYK image to Multichannel Mode would create four channels numbered 1, 2, 3, and 4 to represent the cyan, magenta, yellow, and black plates respectively. Multichannel mode is not an option for Grayscale, Bitmap, and Indexed Color images because these contain only one channel to begin with. After you have converted to Multichannel mode, you can convert back to the original color mode or LAB mode. Multichannel mode lends itself well to breaking out particular color channels to create specialized printing effects such as bump plates where a fifth color is included to enhance a particular color value in the printed piece.

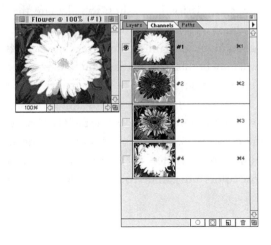

Figure 10.38

The Multichannel mode creates numbered grayscale channels.

COLOR GAMUT

The range of colors available in a specific color model is that model's color gamut. The visible spectrum (colors you can see with your eyes) is significantly larger than any of the available color model's color gamut. In Photoshop, Lab mode encompasses the largest color gamut, including all the colors in the RGB and CMYK gamut. The RGB gamut contains all the colors that can be generated on the computer monitor, as well as on television screens. The CMYK gamut, the smallest of all the color gamut's in Photoshop, contains all the colors that can be printed using the cyan, magenta, yellow and black process color inks. Because the RGB gamut is quite a bit larger than the CMYK gamut, it stands to reason that there are colors that can be displayed on the monitor that cannot be represented by process color inks. When colors displayed on the monitor are outside the range (gamut) of colors that can be produced using process color inks, these colors are considered to be *out-of-gamut*. In Photoshop, the colors that are indicated as out-of-gamut reflect the settings in the Printing Inks and Separation Setup preferences (explained in this chapter). Before using any of Photoshop's methods to bring colors into gamut, be sure these preferences are set correctly.

Identifying Out-of-Gamut Colors

Photoshop has a few methods to help you identify the colors outside the printable CMYK gamut. When working in RGB or HSB mode, choose Gamut Warning from the View menu (see Figure 10.39). You may have to wait a few seconds for Photoshop to calculate the out-of-gamut colors. A gray mask appears over your image indicating the areas of the image that contain out-of-gamut colors (see Figure 10.40). Activating the gamut warning in this way enables you to make specific modifications to the colors in your image to bring them into gamut (See Chapter 11, "Color Correction.") You can usually adjust the saturation of the color to bring it into gamut. If you convert a RGB image that contains out-of-gamut colors to CMYK, Photoshop adjusts the display of those colors to more closely match the colors that are printed; in effect bringing those colors into gamut. After you select Gamut Warning from the View menu, it remains active until you select it again to deactivate it. The performance of Photoshop is not affected when you have Gamut Warning turned on.

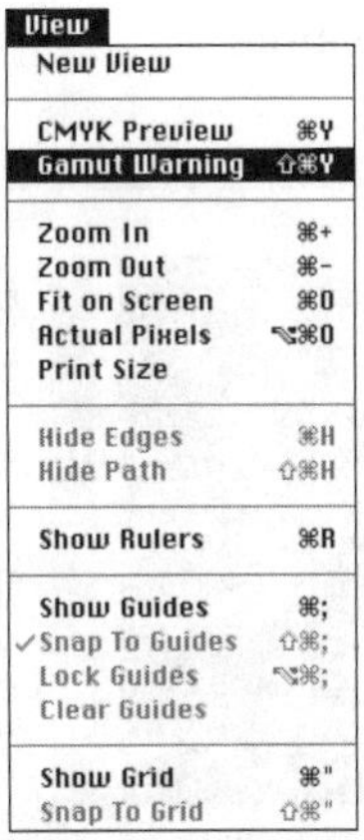

Figure 10.39

Choose Gamut Warning from the View menu.

Figure 10.40

Photoshop displays a mask over your image to indicate out-of-gamut colors.

Photoshop displays an exclamation point (!) inside a triangle to indicate out-of-gamut colors in the Photoshop Color Picker (see Figure 10.41), as well as the Picker palette (see Figure 10.42). When in RGB or HSB mode, drag the cursor over the image pixels with the Picker palette on the screen. When the cursor is over an out-of-gamut color, the gamut warning symbol is displayed next to a color swatch that shows the closest color within the CMYK gamut in the lower left corner of the Picker palette. Clicking the gamut warning symbol in either the Color Picker or Color palette adjusts the out-of-gamut color to the closest color within the CMYK gamut.

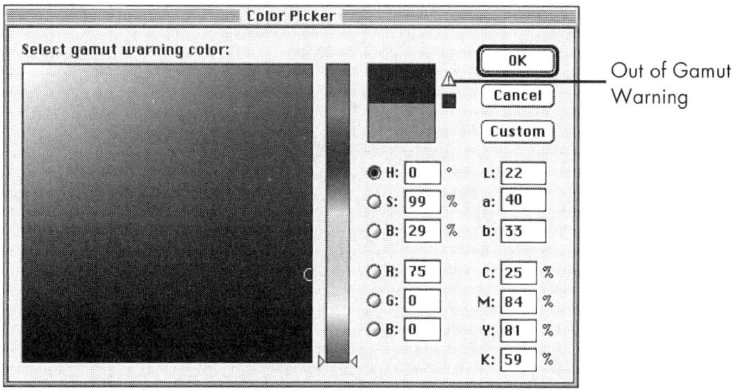

Figure 10.41

The Photoshop Color Picker displays the out-of-gamut warning under a color swatch representing the closest match within the CMYK gamut.

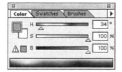

Out of Gamut
Warning

Figure 10.42

The out-of-gamut warning symbol is displayed in the lower left corner of the Color palette, next to a swatch to indicate the closest CMYK color.

Choose CMYK Preview from the View menu to display an RGB image the way it is converted to CMYK using the current separation table. Choosing CMYK Preview reflects the settings in the Printing Inks and Separation Setup dialog boxes. The CMYK Preview command gives you a picture of what the RGB image looks like in CMYK.

Tip

The best way to utilize the CMYK Preview command is to create a new window for your image by choosing New View from the View menu. Turn on CMYK Preview for one of the windows and work in the other window with Gamut Warning on. When you make color adjustments to the image, the changes are also reflected in the second window with CMYK Preview turned on.

PIXEL DEPTH

Photoshop is an application used to create, edit and export bitmapped images. All Photoshop images are made up of pixels (picture elements). The properties of these individual pixels are determined primarily by their size and pixel depth. The pixel size is determined by the image resolution. The pixel depth is determined by the number of binary bits of information each pixel can contain. Binary data is a number system of 1's and 0's understood by computers as alphanumeric characters (numbers and letters). In the case of bitmapped images, the color values of pixels are also described by binary digits, 1's and 0's. Think of the bits as the placeholders for the 1's and 0's. The pixels are created on the computer monitor using light of varying intensities directed at each individual pixel in the image. Pixel depth for computer images ranges from 1 bit per pixel to 24 bits per pixel. If you think of the binary digits used to describe pixels as actually describing the amount of light directed at the pixel, the following descriptions will be easier to understand.

1 Bit per Pixel

One bit per pixel images contain pixels that can only contain one bit of information (see Figure 10.43). In other words: to describe the pixel's color value, there is only one place holder for either a one (1) or a zero (0). In one bit per pixel images, each pixel can be one of two values: black (1) or lack of light, or white (0) or full intensity of light. In one bit per pixel images, the white value can be set to transparent.

Figure 10.43

When the bit is set to 1, the color is black; when the bit is set to 0, the color is white.

8 Bits per Pixel

A grayscale image that contains 8 bits of binary data per pixel can create the illusion of continuous tone because each pixel can be one of 256 levels of gray (see Figure 10.44). This pixel depth describes each pixel in a grayscale image in Photoshop with each pixel representing a distinct gray level on a scale of 0 to 255. A pixel with a value of 0 is displayed as black on the monitor because it contains no light. Conversely, a pixel that has a gray level of 255 is displayed as white or full intensity light.

Figure 10.44

In order to create the illusion of continuous tone, 256 levels of gray (8 bits of binary data) are required for each pixel.

24 Bits per Pixel

To describe the pixels in a grayscale image, 256 levels of gray are all that is required, 8 bits per pixel. To describe the pixels in a RGB color image, 256 levels of gray (8 bits of binary data) are required for each of the RGB colors (Red, Green, and Blue). (See Figure 10.45.) A pixel's red value, for example, is described by a value in the range of 0 to 255. The same is true for the pixel's green and blue values. Each of the RGB colors requires 8 bits of binary data , so each pixel contains 24 bits of binary data.

Red   Green   Blue

Figure 10.45

The RGB values in the image contain 8 bits of binary data to describe each color.

32 Bits per Pixel

In order to describe the image pixels in a CMYK image, 8 bits of binary data are required for each of the process colors (8 bits for Cyan, 8 bits for Magenta, 8 bits for Yellow, and 8 bits for Black). Each of the process colors contains pixels that are made up of 256 levels of gray for each of the process colors. All color computer monitors display color in the RGB color space, describing each pixel on the screen with 24 bits of binary information. Because CMYK color requires 32 bits of information in order to display each pixel correctly, viewing CMYK images on your computer monitor with 100% accuracy is impossible. Calibrating your color monitor can provide a close approximation, but can never take the place of a color proof to check for color accuracy.

Chapter 11

COLOR CORRECTION

Photoshop is a wonderful tool that takes much of the work out of image composition and manipulation, but when it comes to color correction, the burden still falls upon the user to achieve near-perfect results. Fortunately, Photoshop provides an immense suite of tools that dramatically assist in making your images as color-correct as possible. Not only can you match the color of original images, you can adjust the colors in images to achieve special effects—or even alter the appearance of reality, such as giving yourself the bright blue eyes you always wanted.

Two important issues for Photoshop's color correction tools are calibration and scanning. If your system isn't calibrated properly, all your color corrections are for naught. Likewise, if you're using a cheap-o scanner that you found for next to nothing at Rob's House of Cheezy Hardware, your results are degraded to the quality of your scan.

Of all the issues discussed within Chapter 2, "Calibrating Your System," the most important one to focus on (and the one you have the most control over) is your monitor. If your monitor is properly calibrated for your room lighting conditions, your color correction efforts are much more successful.

Scanning is discussed in Chapter 3. In a perfect world, you'd have a half-million dollar Scitex or Crosfield system at your disposal. But, because your last name probably isn't Gates, you might be using a less-than-perfect scanning device. Lower-priced scanners can introduce artifacts, or visible flaws, into an image (such as darker "stripes" overlaying the image), and they scan at lower resolutions. Older scanners can't recognize as large a color range as newer ones, so color reproduction might not be perfect. You can compensate for some of the flaws in a scanner, but the better your initial scan, the less work needed to make the image look good.

COLOR CORRECTION THEORY

Technically, colors can be measured scientifically, and absolute values can be assigned to them. Unfortunately, combinations of colors and textures are more difficult to evaluate this way. To that end, color correction becomes a very subjective procedure. How blue should a blue sky be? How green should a lawn be? Is there a spot of white in a flame or just a very bright yellow? If you ask five different people, you get five different answers. What looks good to you may look terrible to someone else.

Photoshop's color correction tools are based on numerical values (such as brightness levels and the proportions of different colors in an area of the image) that change as you manipulate sliders and controls. The feedback you gain from these adjustments, however, is strictly subject to your own interpretation of the colors you see onscreen.

More bad news: Not only is color correction subjective, but changes you make to an image with a fairly full range of colors result in improvements to certain areas and damage to other areas. Color correction isn't free; it comes at a price. The simpler methods of Brightness/Contrast or Hue and Saturation do the most damage, causing irretrievable loss to certain areas of an image—for example, brightening an image to reduce the effect of shadows also brightens light areas of the image, causing a loss of detail. Levels and Curves can also destroy image information, but the damage is much easier to control.

Color correction is traditionally aimed at the print professional. After all, does it really matter what the image looks like onscreen as long as it prints perfectly? Well, in 1997 the answer is a resounding yes. With the proliferation of multimedia, Web documents, and associated images, getting images to look good onscreen is almost (if not more) important than having them look good in print.

Note

Color correction, like most other Photoshop features, can be applied to either an entire document, certain layers, or to a specific selection. This provides a level of control that otherwise would be impossible to achieve.

COLOR CORRECTION THE EASY WAY

Whoever said that the easy way isn't the best way? Well, anyone who depends on getting accurate color representation from Photoshop. There are many upsides to each of these methods: Immediate visual feedback, a logical and understandable approach, and reliance on common sense. Still, using the controls discussed in this section without care and some experience can often do irreparable damage to your image.

After you master these methods, you probably want to move on to the more complex tools Photoshop provides for color correction: the Levels and Curves controls. Those are covered in the following section(s).

For RGB color correction, most of these methods are safe, as you can view the effects and judge for yourself if the benefits outweigh any visible damage. For CMYK, however, you might not be able to notice loss

RGB and CMYK Duke It Out

As discussed in Chapter 2, Calibration, RGB, and CMYK are two formats that are constantly at odds with one another. Not only are they opposites, but they're inaccurate opposites.

Cyan, magenta, and yellow are technically the respective opposites of red, green, and blue, so combining them should result in black, just as combining red, green, and blue light results in white light. But because ink pigments aren't perfect, this combination actually yields a muddy brown, so black ink is added in the printing process. As a result, what you see on a computer monitor *never* matches what you're printing until someone does what is currently impossible: create a CMYK monitor. Actually, it would be better if someone could create RGB "inks" on a back-lit surface paper.

All color correction done for images printed on paper (or another similar surface) should be adjusted and modified in CMYK mode (choose Image➡Mode➡CMYK). If the image is being viewed onscreen, work with it in RGB mode.

in detail onscreen; detail in shadows is very difficult to see onscreen, but can be quite apparent when printed.

The following sections discuss the features of each of the "simple" color correction tools in Photoshop, as well as pros and cons for their usage.

Using the Brightness/Contrast Control

The first time I used Photoshop, I scanned in a grayscale image that looked muddy. After goofing around with the plethora of options to choose from, I *knew* that Brightness/Contrast was the correct option for me. I wanted to make the image brighter and to give it more contrast. I cranked up both of the sliders and watched my image get (whadda ya know) brighter with more contrast. I twiddled for a while until it looked acceptable. The final image wasn't perfect, but it seemed better than the original.

The Brightness/Contrast dialog box couldn't be much simpler (see Figure 11.1). Brightness slider; dragging it to the right brightens the image, whereas dragging it to the left darkens the image. Contrast slider; dragging it to the right enhances the differences between light and dark areas, whereas dragging it to the left "muddies" the image, eventually turning it into a 50 percent gray.

Figure 11.1

The Brightness/Contrast dialog box.

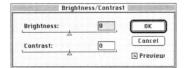

You can apply brightness and contrast adjustments to an entire image, just one layer, or the selected area of an image or layer. Start with an image that needs to be adjusted, then use the following procedure.

1. Using the Lasso tool, drag a marquee around an object you want to highlight.

2. Feather the selection (choose Select➡Feather) by 10 pixels.

3. Choose Select➡Inverse. Now everything but the object is selected.

4. Choose Image➥Adjust➥Brightness/Contrast.

5. Drag the Brightness slider to the left. This darkens the "background" of the image (see Figure 11.2).

Figure 11.2

The original image (left) and after applying Brightness/Contrast to darken the background (right).

Unfortunately, no amount of twiddling with these two controls comes even close to the effects that can be achieved by monkeying around with the Levels or Curves controls. Brightness/Contrast provides a quick, barely adequate method for enhancing your image. Use it a few times to get it out of your system. Now jump down to the section on Levels to see what adjusting brightness and contrast is really all about.

Note

Even Adobe knows that Brightness/Contrast is a terrible option. They kept the option in version 4.0, but they removed its key command (present for versions 1 through 3).

Adjusting the Color Balance

The Color Balance command enables colors to be "shifted" around the color wheel. Every color has an "opposite" on the color wheel. Color Balance lets you change colors in an image or selection so that they're closer to one of six colors (red, green, blue, cyan, magenta, and yellow). As you shift colors toward one color, the amount of its opposite in the image is decreased. Increasing cyan, for instance, reduces the amount of red in an image or selection. Color Balance is intended to be used for general color correction in an image, such as removing a yellow cast in an image scanned from an old photo whose paper has yellowed with age; it's also useful for things such as removing color casts from shadows caused by unusual lighting or poor photography.

Note

Don't be misled by the fact that the Color Balance command shows cyan, magenta, and yellow controls even when you're working in an RGB image. The file is still in RGB mode, but that doesn't mean it can't contain CMYK colors—it's just that those colors are represented (approximated, really) by various mixes of red, green, and blue pixels.

To use the Color Balance command:

1. Select the portion of the target layer that you want to adjust, or leave the layer unselected to adjust all of it. You can only adjust one layer at a time.

2. Choose Image➡Adjust➡Color Balance or press (Command-U) [Control-U] to bring up the Color Balance dialog box (see Figure 11.3).

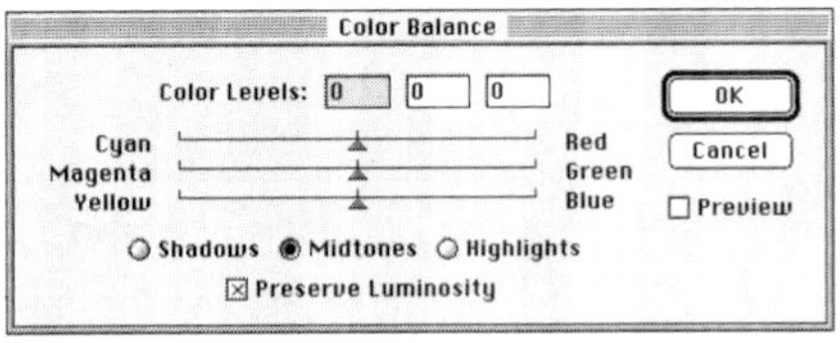

Figure 11.3

The Color Balance dialog box.

3. Choose Shadows, Midtones, or Highlights.

   You can modify the color balance of the midtones (90 percent of the image), the highlights (the lightest areas of the image), or the shadows (the darkest areas of the image). The changes you make in each of these are preserved throughout your stint in the Color Balance dialog box, so you can adjust each in turn to affect all the tones in the image.

4. Check Preserve Luminosity to prevent the brightness of the image from being altered as the colors are shifted. If you don't want to maintain the image's present brightness, leave this option unchecked.

5. Check the Preview box to see how your changes affect the current image or selection.

Note

As with other slider-based dialog boxes, checking the Preview box makes your adjustments affect only the current selection, and the change shows up only when you release the mouse button after moving a slider. If the Preview box is unchecked, the changes you make affect the entire screen—including visible areas that aren't part of Photoshop, such as your desktop. This is a handy way to see how a specific change affects several images at once. Keep the Preview box checked if you want to see how a color change affects only the selected portion of the image.

6. Adjust the image's colors by moving the sliders.

    As you do this, the numbers above the sliders change, indicating how much of a change you're making; they vary from 0 (your starting point) to –100 (toward cyan, magenta, or yellow) and +100 (toward red, green, and blue). If you want to make the same change to more than one image, you can note the numbers used in the first image and then type them in to the number fields for the rest of the images. Of course, if you're working with a large number of images, you'll probably want to use Photoshop's new Actions command to record the procedure and then apply it quickly to each image by pressing a function key.

7. After adjusting one part of the image's tones (its shadows, for instance), switch to another part (highlights or midtones) and adjust those tones. Repeat this process until the image looks the way you want it to.

8. Click OK to apply the Color Balance changes.

Unfortunately, although the concept behind this dialog box is a good one, the execution is poor. A shift in color always seems to hurt more than it fixes. Variations, Color Balance's powerful cousin, is much more useful than Color Balance; see "Using the Variations Command" later in this chapter, for more information.

Using Hue/Saturation to Adjust Color

Finally, a simplistic control with a lot of usefulness—although its name isn't entirely accurate. The Hue/Saturation actually lets you adjust hue (the colors in the image), saturation (the intensity of those colors), and brightness.

Hue/Saturation is useful for a variety of enhancement chores, such as increasing the intensity of computer-generated illustrations created by Adobe Illustrator or Macromedia FreeHand. Hue/Saturation is also used for colorizing images or parts of images—if, for example, you decide that blue type you created yesterday shouldn't be blue any more, just select its layer, turn on the Colorize option, and adjust the Hue slider until the type is a color more to your liking.

1. Select the portion of the target layer that you want to adjust, or leave the layer unselected to adjust all of it. You can only adjust one layer at a time.

2. Choose Master or one of the six colors shown to determine what colors in the image will be affected by your adjustments.

   To adjust all the colors in the image or selection, choose Master. To make adjustments to just one color range at a time, such as the red or cyan tones in an image, click that color. Changes made to one color are kept when you choose another color to edit, so you can adjust several colors successively with one trip to the Hue/Saturation dialog box.

   Remember that the color swatches next to the radio buttons are intended to indicate ranges of similar colors, not specific colors, so if you choose red, you won't be adjusting only that specific red you see in the dialog box, but all tones in the image that are in the red "family."

3. Click in the Preview box to preview the results of your adjustments in the image window.

4. Click in the Colorize box to colorize the image or selection.

   Checking the Colorize button instantly changes the image to a
   one-color representation of the image. You can modify the
   color by dragging the Hue slider. The Saturation slider affects
   the intensity of just that particular color, and Lightness serves
   the same brighten/darken function as before.

5. Adjust Hue by dragging the slider right or left or entering
   numbers in the entry field next to the slider.

   The hue control rotates colors around the color wheel. When
   Master is selected, you can adjust it from –180° to +180°, all
   the way around the color wheel. Moving the slider all the way
   to either end changes the hues in the image to their exact
   opposites (red to cyan, green to magenta, blue to yellow).
   When an individual color is selected, so you're adjusting only
   image colors that fall in that range, you can adjust the slider
   from –60° to +60°, meaning that you can change colors to their
   nearest neighbors on either side in the color wheel (red can
   move toward yellow or magenta).

6. Adjust Saturation by dragging the slider right or left or entering
   numbers in the entry field next to the slider.

   Increasing the Saturation slider (dragging it to the right)
   increases the intensity or amount of color in the selected area
   of the image. Moving the slider to the left makes the image's
   colors grayer, and dragging the saturation slider all the way to
   the left results in a grayscale image. Moving the slider to the
   right makes the image's colors more intense—it's like adding
   more dye when you're making Easter eggs.

7. Adjust Lightness by dragging the slider right or left or entering
   numbers in the entry field next to the slider.

   The Lightness control is similar to Brightness/Contrast's
   Brightness control, but it works in HSL (Hue, Saturation,

Lightness) color space, using different mathematical formulae to make its changes. Using the Brightness command and the Lightness slider with the same numbers won't result in the same changes because the equations are different, but the two work exactly the same way, and you can achieve the same results using either method.

8. Watch the color swatches in the dialog box to see how your changes affect specific colors.

   When the Master button is selected, all the swatches next to the radio buttons change to indicate the way the image's colors are moving along the color wheel. When an individual color is selected, only that swatch changes.

   If you want to track the changes to a specific color in the image, move the cursor out of the dialog box and over the image area, where it changes into an eyedropper. Click the color you're concerned about; this color replaces the previous color in the Sample box at the bottom of the Hue/Saturation dialog box, and the adjustments you make to the sliders are previewed there as well as in the swatches and in the image.

9. Repeat these adjustments for each color range you want to affect. The changes are cumulative, so you can keep tweaking the image until you're happy.

10. If you want to make the same adjustments to a series of images, you can save your settings by clicking the Save button (you are prompted to give the settings file a name). Reload saved settings by clicking the Load button—the sliders automatically move to the positions they had when you saved the settings. Using Photoshop's Actions feature is another way to apply the same settings to multiple images.

Tip

If you often receive images from the same source that need the same kind of adjustments (for example, Photo CD images or prints from a photo studio that habitually prints everything too dark for your purposes), use the

Save button to preserve the settings you use on each of these images. You can also copy saved Settings files from your computer to others—so after you determine the correct settings, everyone in your department can use them. You can save settings for many of Photoshop's commands, including Hue/Saturation, Levels, and Curves.

11. Click OK to exit the Hue/Saturation dialog box and apply the changes you made.

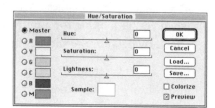

Figure 11.4

The Hue/Saturation dialog box.

Note

As in most of the Color Correction dialog boxes, pressing (Option)[Alt] changes the Cancel button to Reset. Clicking the Reset button resets the original values.

Using the Variations Command

What would happen if you took Brightness/Contrast, Color Balance, and Hue/Saturation and combined them with a full preview? The Variations command (found in the Image➔Adjust menu alongside the commands we just discussed) would happen. It still has the inherent limitations of each of the individual components, but Variations *does* have a unique previewing method that makes it much more useful.

Variations is designed to be easy to use. Instead of sliders and numeric values, images are adjusted by clicking the image that looks better than the current pick. The current pick is shown alongside the original so you can compare the two. To adjust your image using the Variations command:

Wash Out the Color Across an Image

Use this technique to go from grayscale on one side of an image to color on the opposite side—it gives the effect of the image "springing to life" and entering the modern age. It's particularly effective if one person or object is shown moving from one side to the other—stepping or driving from the grayscale side to the color side.

1. Open any full-color image in RGB mode.

2. Create a new channel.

continues

3. In the new channel, use the Blend tool to create a black to white gradient across the image, with black on the left and white on the right.

4. Return to the composite RGB channel.

5. Choose Load Selection on the Select menu.

6. Open the Hue/Saturation dialog box.

7. Drag the Saturation slider to the far left.

8. Click the OK button. The image is full-color on the left edge, and the right edge is grayscale. In between, the color appears to have been slowly washed out.

You can use this technique with a smaller portion of the image, as well—such as a small color "spotlight" on an element in an otherwise grayscale image.

1. Select the portion of the target layer that you want to adjust, or leave the layer unselected to adjust all of it. You can only adjust one layer at a time.

2. Choose Image➡Adjust➡Variations.

3. Move the slider to the left (Fine) or right (Coarse) to determine how much effect each change has on the image. The finest changes are almost undetectable; the coarsest changes are appropriate only when you're looking for a purposely exaggerated effect. By default, the slider is in the middle.

4. Click Show Clipping to determine whether Photoshop indicates areas of the image that are lightened, darkened, or intensified too much as you make adjustments. If this box is checked, a neon color (Photoshop decides which colors to use; you can't change them) is shown in the thumbnails to indicate that the maximum saturation for that color has been reached (see Figure 11.6).

5. If you're adjusting a color image, click the radio button for Saturation, Midtones, Highlights, or Shadows. If you're adjusting a grayscale image, these choices aren't available.

As with the Color Balance command, your changes can affect only one set of tones within the image at a time. When you're done adjusting the midtones (for instance), you can switch to adjusting highlights or shadows without losing the changes you made to the midtones. Choosing Saturation enables you to affect only the saturation of the image's colors, as you would with the Hue/Saturation command's Saturation slider.

6. If you clicked the Shadows, Midtones, or Highlights radio button, click the left-hand six thumbnail images to adjust the image's hue.

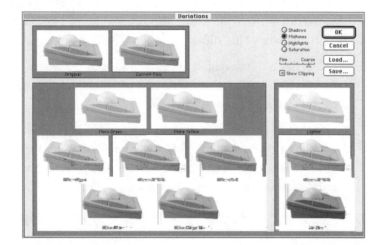

Figure 11.5

The Variations dialog box.

Figure 11.6

The white areas produced by Show Clipping indicate where values have reached their maximum.

In the lower left of the dialog box are six thumbnails surrounding a thumbnail showing the current pick, or state of your adjustments. Each of the six outer images shows your image as it would look if you increased the amount of one of the six major colors on the color wheel. As with the Color Balance command, increasing one color decreases another color; increasing green decreases magenta, and so on. Clicking these thumbnails approximates the effect of moving the Hue/Saturation dialog box's Hue slider.

As you click a thumbnail, it appears to slide to the center position (Current Pick), and all the outer thumbnails change to reflect the adjustment you just made.

7. If you clicked the Saturation radio button, the six thumbnails are replaced by three, marked Less Saturated, Current Pick, and More Saturated. Click the Less Saturated or More Saturated thumbnail to adjust the image's saturation.

   As you click a thumbnail, it appears to slide to the center position (Current Pick), and the outer thumbnails change to reflect the adjustment you just made.

8. Click the right-hand two thumbnail images to adjust the image's brightness.

   To the right side of the dialog are three more thumbnails; the top and bottom images show the current pick as it would look if you made it lighter or darker, whereas the middle image shows the current pick. Clicking these thumbnails approximates the effect of moving the Hue/Saturation dialog's Lightness slider.

   As you click a thumbnail, it appears to slide to the center position (Current Pick), and the Lighter and Darker thumbnails change to reflect the adjustment you just made.

9. If you want to make the same adjustments to a series of images, save your settings by clicking the Save button. Reload saved settings by clicking the Load button.

10. After you're done adjusting one portion of the image's tones, you can switch to another (for instance, fix the midtones, then click Shadows and adjust the shadows).

You can also change the Fine/Coarse setting at any time while you're working in the Variations dialog box. You may want to start with coarser adjustments and then move the slider toward Fine to make the final adjustments.

11. Click OK to exit the Variations dialog box and apply the adjustments you made.

Tip

All of the Image➡Adjust dialog boxes share a cool feature. When you return to a dialog box, have you noticed the settings automatically reset to their defaults? Well, if you press (Option)[Alt] while selecting the menu command (or while pressing the key command), the settings appear the same as they were the last time you were in that dialog box!

Variations is a useful tool for making quick fixes on images, and it is particularly good for adjusting images used primarily onscreen (mainly because you can see the previews of each image one step ahead of the current image).

CORRECTING IMAGES WITH LEVELS

Of all the tools available for color correction, Levels contains the most options, even more than its subtle sister Curves, which I cover in the next section. Using Levels can be as simple as clicking a few times with the Levels-based eyedroppers, or it can be an exercise in patience, as settings can be adjusted for each and every individual channel in the image.

The term levels refers to the brightness levels of the image's pixels; they're adjusted by moving sliders in the Levels dialog box. To adjust an image using Levels:

1. Select the portion of the target layer that you want to adjust, or leave the layer unselected to adjust all of it. You can only adjust one layer at a time.

2. Choose Image➡Adjust➡Levels. The Levels dialog box opens (see Figure 11.7).

Figure 11.7

The Levels dialog box.

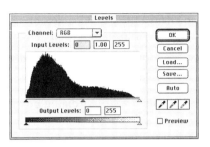

3. Click the Preview box to preview your changes in the image window as you move the sliders. Leaving this box unchecked previews your changes on your entire monitor screen, including your desktop.

4. If you're adjusting a color image, choose a channel from the Channel pop-up menu. If you're adjusting a grayscale image, there's no Channel menu.

   In a color image, you can view and adjust the histogram for the composite (RGB or CMYK) channel or individual color channels. When making corrections to a color image, it's generally best to adjust each channel individually, rather than working on the composite channel (which makes the same adjustments to all the channels at once).

5. To set the black and white points in the image, move the black and white sliders on the Input Levels graph (which is called a histogram—more on that later).

   In general, you want to move these two sliders toward the center of the graph, placing each at the point where the lines indicating dark and light pixels begin to rise. A more detailed explanation of how these adjustments should be made is later in this chapter, in "Reading a Levels Histogram."

6. To reduce the contrast in an image, move the sliders on the Output Levels bar at the bottom of the dialog box to limit the range of brightness levels in the image.

   The black slider controls the darkest tones in the image; moving it toward the middle of the slider bar lightens the image. Likewise, the white slider controls the lightest tones in the image, and moving it inward darkens the image. Dragging the black slider to the right brightens the darkest pixels in the image; no pixel in the image can be darker than the value shown in the left-hand Output Levels field. Similarly, moving the white slider darkens the brightest pixels in the image by restricting them to being no brighter than the value in the righthand Output Levels field. Moving these sliders closer together decreases the contrast in the image.

Note

You can "swap" the light and dark Output Levels sliders by dragging each past the other to the opposite end of the bar. This results in an inverted image.

7. To increase the contrast in the image, move the gray slider under the Levels histogram.

    The gray slider in the middle indicates the image's midtones, which you can darken by moving the slider right and lighten by moving the slider left.

    You can also change the black point, white point, and midtone settings by entering numbers in the Input Levels fields above the histogram. The left-hand field corresponds to the black slider, the right-hand one to the white slider, and the middle one to the gray slider. It's easier to use the sliders, though, because you can adjust them continuously until the image looks right. The numbers in the fields change as you move the sliders.

8. Alternatively, use the Eyedropper to adjust the sliders automatically based on your assessment of what should be the lightest, darkest, and median points in the image.

    Select the white-tipped Eyedropper and click the lightest part of your image. Using the black-tipped Eyedropper and click the darkest part of your image. Finally, if you have an area that you think is representative of 50 percent gray, use the gray-tipped Eyedropper to click that particular area.

Tip

The Eyedropper tools in the Levels dialog box are probably the quickest way to color-correct an image with reasonable accuracy. Include swatches of black, white, and 50% gray next to the color image when you scan it, and click these to instantly set the levels.

9. To have Photoshop adjust the levels based on its own assessment of the image, click Auto.

    Because this adjustment usually produces a high-contrast image, its results are seldom suitable for print reproduction, which generally can't handle very contrasty images. However, using the Auto button provides a good starting point. After using it, you probably need to use Curves to lighten the image and flatten its contrast a bit. For more on using Curves, see "Correcting Images with Curves" later in this chapter.

Tip

(Option-click)[Alt-click] the Auto button to bring up the Auto Range Options dialog box. To make sure it affects enough pixels, Photoshop actually makes the shadows a bit darker and the highlights a bit lighter than you specify. The default setting for this adjustment is 0.50%, but you can change it in this dialog box; raising the number results in more absolutely black and white pixels, and therefore a higher-contrast image. Lowering it results in fewer black and white pixels for a image with less contrast. Experiment with different settings until you like the results.

10. If you want to make the same adjustments to a series of images, save your settings by clicking the Save button. Reload saved settings by clicking the Load button.

11. Click OK to exit the Levels dialog box and apply your changes.

Reading a Levels Histogram

Before you can make adjustments to an image via the Levels dialog box, you have to understand what it's showing. It's simpler than it may seem at first. The Levels dialog box was never intended to intimidate, but it certainly can do so.

The histogram (that's what all those lines are) that appears when you open the dialog box looks menacing. Actually, it's a fairly simple visual representation—a bar graph, really—of the number of pixels at each of the 256 possible brightness levels in a Photoshop document. The left side of the histogram shows darker pixels (from black on the far end to 50% in the middle). The right side goes from 50% in the middle to 0% (white) on the end. Just as with a bar graph, higher lines mean that more pixels in the image are at that brightness level. In Figure 11.7, there are large dark areas of the image from which the histogram is drawn, resulting in longer lines at the left-hand side of the histogram.

A completely black document would have only one line at the far left of the histogram and reaching all the way to the top of the histogram area. A completely white document would have a similar line at the far right of the histogram, and a 50% gray document would have only one line right in the middle of the histogram, reaching all the way up.

To help understand what Levels is showing, take a look at Figures 11.8a through 11.8c. They are all the same image with variations only in brightness, but look at the differences in their Levels histograms.

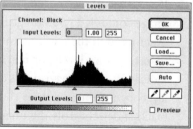

Figure 11.8a

The original image and its Levels histogram.

Figure 11.8b

The image adjusted to a lighter setting.

Figure 11.8c

The image adjusted to a darker setting.

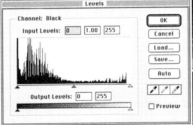

Notice that the histogram for the lighter image (refer to Figure 11.8b) has the majority of its pixels to the right of the 50% mark, and the darker image has most of its pixels to the left of the 50% mark. This indicates that the majority of the pixels in the lighter image are lighter than a 50% gray tone would be, and the majority of the pixels in the darker image are darker than a 50% gray tone.

If the levels along the length of the histogram are fairly even, then the image contains a good range of dark, light, and medium tones. On the other hand, if the levels at any part of the histogram are much higher than the other levels, or much lower (or even nonexistent), this may indicate that the image needs adjustments. Changes are made to image levels by moving the three sliders at the bottom of the histogram; the black slider controls the image's darkest areas (shadows), the white slider controls the image's lightest areas (highlights), and the gray slider controls the image's midtones (everything in between shadows and highlights).

By seeing what the histogram looks like, you can usually tell exactly what needs to be done to "fix" the image. The basic strategy here is twofold:

◆ Distribute the histogram bars evenly across the width of the graph by dragging the black slider to the point on the graph where the darker level bars start to rise and dragging the white slider to the point where the lighter levels start to rise. For color images, you get the best results if you perform this operation on each individual color channel rather than the composite channel.

Warning

In most cases redistributing the histogram levels is appropriate—but watch out for purposely light or dark images, such as a photo of a white flower on a white linen tablecloth, whose levels are bunched up at one end of the graph or the other. Don't destroy the brightness or shadowy effect of these high-key (light) or low-key (dark) images by distributing the levels across too great a range.

◆ Increase contrast (if necessary) in important detail areas of the image by adjusting the midtones with the gray slider. Move the slider to the right to darken the image, increasing contrast in highlight areas and reducing contrast in shadow areas. Move it to the left to lighten the image, reducing contrast in highlights and increasing it in shadows.

To fix the lighter image (shown in Figure 11.9), for instance, the midtone slider (the gray triangle in the middle of the top bar) can be dragged to the right, darkening the midtones in the image by placing more of the image's pixels (represented by the histogram's lines) between the darkest level in the image and the midtones. The left-hand image in Figure 11.9 shows the difference as the slider is dragged to the right.

The image shown in Figure 11.10 would benefit from having the white point slider moved to the left, to the point where the pixels start to form more of a clump. This distributes the pixels more evenly along the possible range of brightness levels, lightening the image overall by lightening the midtones and highlights.

Figure 11.9

The original image (left) and the corrected image (right).

Figure 11.10

To fix this image, the white point slider could be dragged to the left just slightly.

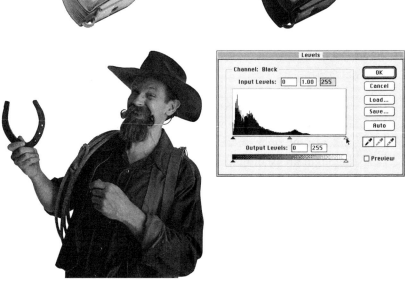

Creating a Watermark with Levels

Levels can also be used to create a "watermark" type of effect that can be placed behind text or other illustrations. The name of this effect comes from a papermaking technique that leaves a faint image in a piece of paper that's only visible when you hold the paper up to light. You won't have to hold the paper up to the light to view this image, though. You might use this technique to drop a company logo behind the text in an annual report, or to place your design firm's logo behind a customer's approval proof of an illustration so it can't be appropriated without your permission.

1. Choose Image➡Adjust➡Levels. The Levels dialog box appears.

2. Drag the left slider (dark) on the bottom bar to the right (about 200).

3. Click OK.

Figure 11.11

The original image (left) and the watermark created with the levels adjustment.

CORRECTING IMAGES WITH CURVES

The Curves dialog box is the single most powerful tool in the Photoshop arsenal. With it you can drastically modify the way your images appear, from touching up the colors slightly to creating Predator Vision from an ordinary image. Curves adjust the image the same way Levels do—only instead of being restricted to making changes at three arbitrary points in the image's brightness (shadows, highlights, and midtones), you can adjust the levels at any point by dragging the curve.

For everyday image processing, you can make the same adjustments using Curves as you can using Levels, but Curves can be most useful to adjust an image's overall "look" after Levels is used to place the tones in the image approximately where they should be.

1. Select the portion of the target layer that you want to adjust, or leave the layer unselected to adjust all of it. You can only adjust one layer at a time.

2. Choose Image➡Adjust➡Curves. The Curves dialog box opens (see Figure 11.12).

Figure 11.12

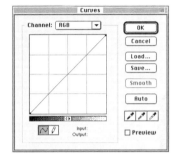

The Curves dialog box.

3. Click the Preview box on to preview your changes in the image window as you adjust the curve. Leaving this box unchecked previews your changes on your entire monitor screen, including your desktop.

4. If you're adjusting a color image, choose a channel from the Channel pop-up menu. If you're adjusting a grayscale image, there's no Channel menu.

   In a color image, you can view and adjust the curve for the composite (RGB or CMYK) channel or individual color channels. When making corrections to a color image, it's generally best to adjust each channel individually, rather than working on the composite channel (which makes the same adjustments to all the channels at once).

5. To determine what area of the curve you want to adjust, click in the image window and hold down the mouse button as you move the cursor over the image. A circle appears on the curve at the point representing each pixel you scroll over.

6. If necessary, adjust the brightness bar at the bottom of the Curves graph to edit brightness values (the gradation should

move from black on the left to white on the right) by clicking the double triangle button in the middle of the bar.

If the gradation goes from white to black, adjustments to the curve affect ink coverage, which is effectively the same thing, only you pull the curve the opposite direction as you would if you're editing brightness values. Either way, you're doing the same thing, but the examples in the rest of this section assume you're editing brightness values.

The numbers in the lower-right corner of the image are percentages if you're adjusting ink density and brightness levels (between 0 and 255) if you're adjusting brightness.

7. Click the curve to add points where you don't want the curve to move, then drag the curve on either side of those points to adjust the image. You can add up to 15 points to the curve.

Drag the curve up to lighten tones in the image and down to darken them.

8. You can also draw your own curve using the Pencil tool. Click the Pencil button and draw lines or curves on the grid.

If your curve has sharp angles or disconnected points (this can happen with the Pencil tool), click Smooth to connect them and turn them into a smooth curve, creating a smooth transition between these changes so that there isn't a serious jump from one brightness level to the next.

9. Alternatively, use the Eyedropper to adjust the curve automatically based on your assessment of what should be the lightest, darkest, and median points in the image.

Select the white-tipped Eyedropper and click the lightest part of your image. Using the black-tipped Eyedropper and click the darkest part of your image. Finally, if you have an area that you think is representative of 50 percent gray, use the gray-tipped Eyedropper to click that particular area.

10. To have Photoshop adjust the curve based on its own assessment of the image, click Auto.

Unfortunately, this button adjusts the image but doesn't reflect its changes in the curve graph.

11. If you want to make the same adjustments to a series of images, save your settings by clicking the Save button. Reload saved settings by clicking the Load button.

12. Click OK to exit the Curves dialog box and apply your changes.

The downside of using Curves is that it's anything but intuitive. The idea behind Curves is fairly straightforward: it enables you to change the pixels at each brightness level into any other brightness level. All the pixels that are 10 percent light, for instance, can be modified to be 20 percent light. The pixels at 5 percent light can be set to 2 percent light.

And, like Levels, the brightness controls in the Curves dialog box can affect not only the entire image, but also individual channels. This provides precision control for the brightness of the image that is unavailable elsewhere.

The graph works like this: the horizontal axis represents brightness as it is input (the original pixels before you start adjusting them), and the vertical axis represents output levels (how the pixels look after you apply the changes you're making). A value of zero (the lower-left corner) corresponds to black (or the darkest possible brightness). The upper-right corner represents the brightest input and output levels (see Figure 11.13).

Figure 11.13

The curve controls tones within the image's highlights, quarter-tones, midtones, three-quarter-tones, and shadows. The circle at the lower-left corner of the graph indicates the brightness level of the image pixel under the cursor (it's very dark, but not quite black).

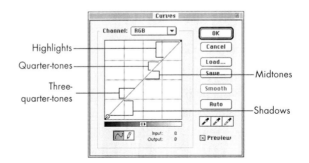

The curve is a diagonal line going from the lower-left to upper-right corner by default. This orientation of the curve enables input and output values to match exactly. The curve can be adjusted by clicking and dragging any point along the line. Clicking at the center point and dragging down, for instance, would darken the midtones of the image, as the 50 percent brightness input would be dragged below 50 percent. You can add new points by clicking and dragging anywhere on the line. Delete a point by dragging it outside of the graph. Existing points can be moved by clicking and dragging them.

The following examples show several curves and their effects on the same image. A slight S curve is often useful for increasing image clarity.

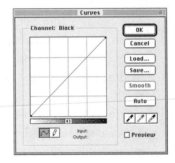

Figure 11.14a

The original image and its curve.

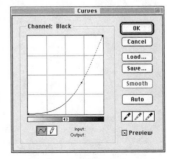

Figure 11.14b

A lighter version of the image and its curve.

Figure 11.14c

A darker version of the image and its curve.

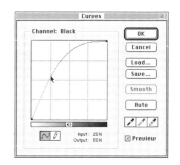

You can also adjust curves by using the Pencil tool in the brightness graph. Instead of actually adjusting a curve, you can click and set individual brightness input/output levels one at a time or small sections by dragging. Using the Pencil tool to draw these arbitrary curves can result in dramatic effects, including the aforementioned Predator Vision. There are no rules when you're drawing your own curves—this is a case where experimentation is the only way to go. The following examples show different curves settings created with the Pencil tool.

Figure 11.15a

The original image (left) and its curve.

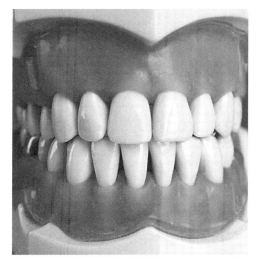

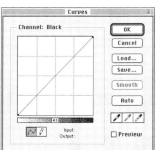

Tip

Draw straight lines with the Pencil by Shift-clicking.

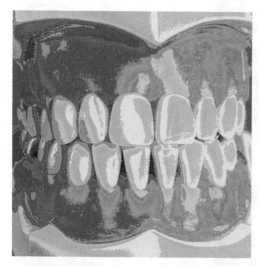

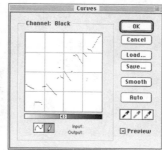

Figure 11.15b

Another version of the image and its arbitrary curve.

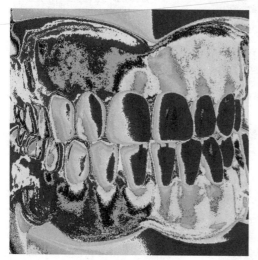

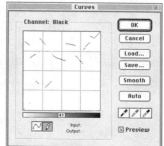

Figure 11.15c

Yet another version of the image and its even more arbitrary curve.

Because the Pencil tool can be used to draw broken sections of curves, a Smooth button is available to connect the broken sections and to reduce intense curves. Figure 11.16 shows the effects of repeated smoothing.

Figure 11.16a

The original pencil-curved image with its curve.

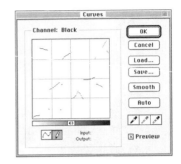

Figure 11.16b

The image after the curve has been smoothed.

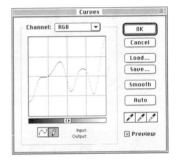

Figure 11.16c

The image after more curve-smoothing—it's almost back to normal now.

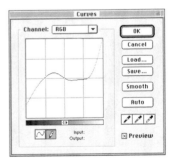

Creating a Watermark with Curves

To create a watermark using curves:

1. Choose Image➡Adjust➡Curves. The Curves dialog box opens.

2. Drag the point in the lower left up until it is just above the first graph marking (25 percent down from the top edge of the graph).

3. Click the OK button.

This effect is also useful for screening back a selected portion of a busy image so you can lay type over it; it looks as though you painted the selection with translucent white paint.

MAKING COLOR CORRECTIONS VIA ADJUSTMENT LAYERS

All of the color correction tools are useful, but their power increases tenfold when used in adjustment layers instead of through the dialog box. In fact, I can't think of any reason *not* to use adjustment layers in favor of the straight commands.

An adjustment layer is a special layer that doesn't contain any pixels; instead, it contains an image adjustment or effect (such as Curves) that affects the layers below it (see Figure 11.17). The intensity of the effect is determined by the adjustment layer's opacity and blending mode. Like normal layers, adjustment layers can be reordered within the document, and they can be duplicated and deleted.

Adjustment layers have important advantages over using straight adjustment commands:

♦ Can be undone at any time, even during a later Photoshop session.

♦ Editable. The values that the adjustment layers were last set to reappear the next time you open the adjustment layer so that you can make minor adjustments or corrections to the current settings.

◆ No loss of data. The original image is still there, so even if you adjust the image using Brightness/Contrast, you don't blow away any detail.

Figure 11.17

An adjustment layer in the Layers palette is indicated with a half-black, half-white circle.

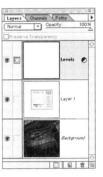

Another nice thing about adjustment layers is that they act like masks, so you can apply your adjustments to specific areas of the image. To make use of adjustment layers, follow the following steps.

1. On the Layers palette, select New Adjustment Layer… or (Command-click)[Control-click] the New Layer button on the Layers palette. If you want to apply the adjustment to only part of the image, select that part first.

2. Choose the type of Adjustment (Levels, Curves, and so on) from the pop-up menu. Click OK.

3. The dialog box for the adjustment you selected appears. If you selected the Curves adjustment, for instance, the Curves dialog box appears.

4. Edit the curves as you would normally.

5. Click OK. The image reflects the changes you make, and a new adjustment layer appears above the active layer.

6. To view the adjustment layer, (Option-click)[Alt-click] its Layer Preview icon on the Layers palette and use the painting tools to edit it.

   If you had an active selection when you created the adjustment layer, the selected area is white in the layer and the area outside the selection is black. Otherwise, the whole layer is white. To adjust the strength of the adjustment's effect, you can paint on the layer just as you would any image layer, except in grayscale only (just like layer masks and alpha, or mask, channels). Black areas on the adjustment layer keep the effect from showing up on the layers below, whereas white layers let the effect show through at full strength. Gray areas let the effect partially show through.

7. Click an image layer to return to viewing the image itself.

Normally, adjustment layers affect all the layers beneath them. New layers placed above an adjustment layer are not affected. To edit the settings for an adjustment layer, double-click its name in the Layers palette.

Don't overlook gradients, feathered selections, and patterns as ways to edit adjustment layers. To overlay an image with a faint pattern using an adjustment layer:

1. Make a rectangular selection in the source image or another image.

2. Choose Edit➡Define Pattern to use the selection as a pattern.

3. If the pattern selection is part of another image, return to your original image. If it's part of the original image, then drop the selection by pressing (Command-D)[Control-D].

4. Create a new adjustment layer by (Command-clicking) [Control-clicking] the New Layer button on the Layers palette. Choose Curves for the layer type.

5. In the resulting Curves dialog box, pull the curve down to lighten the image somewhat (as much or as little as you like) and click OK to exit the Curves dialog box and apply the effects of the adjustment layer.

6. (Option-click)[Alt-click] the adjustment layer's Layer Preview icon to view the adjustment layer.

7. Select all ((Command-A)[Control-A]) and choose Edit➭Fill. In the Fill dialog box, choose Pattern from the Use pop-up menu and enter 100% in the Opacity field.

8. Click an image layer to view the image itself. The pattern you used shows faintly (or not-so-faintly, depending on your Curves settings for the adjustment layer) throughout the image itself.

COLOR CORRECTING GRAYSCALE IMAGES

Yeah, I know, there's no color in black and white images (unless Ted Turner gets his hands on them, of course—see Chapter 13 for more details). All of the color correction tools discussed in this chapter, however, can also be applied to grayscale images.

Oddly enough, you've seen the results of this black and white manipulation throughout this chapter, as this book is unfortunately limited to black-and-white photos (what we Photoshop users know as grayscale images).

Start by scanning a black-and-white photo and opening it in Photoshop (if you use a Photoshop plug-in for scanning, the image is already open in an untitled Photoshop document). Then take the following steps:

1. Choose Image➭Adjust➭Levels to bring up the Levels dialog box.

2. Click the Auto button to give Photoshop a try at adjusting the image's levels.

3. After Photoshop applies its changes, drag the gray (midtones) slider to the left to lighten the image a bit. Watch the midtones value change; you probably need to move it from 1.00 to somewhere between 1.25 and 1.50.

4. Click OK to exit the Levels dialog box and apply your changes.

5. Choose Window➭Show Info to bring up the Info palette.

   As you move your cursor over the image, the Info palette displays the percentage of black ink that is used to reproduce each pixel in the image when it's printed, ranging from 0% (white) to 100% (black). Because paper absorbs ink, halftone dots tend to spread, making gray areas (composed of black dots with white space between them) appear darker. This is called dot gain, and if your image is destined for print reproduction, you need to account for it.

The key here is to have no pixels in the image that are completely white or completely black. You need to adjust the image so that white areas are really 3% to 5% black, and black areas are really between 80% and about 95% black.

6. Choose Image➡Adjust➡Curves to bring up the Curves dialog box.

7. Make sure the curve is set to show ink coverage, not brightness values, by clicking the "double triangle" button in the middle of the brightness bar at the bottom of the dialog box until the white end of the gradation is at the left and the numbers in the lower-right corner of the dialog box are percentages.

   Remember, this only affects which way you drag the curve to make your changes, not what the Curves command actually does.

8. Drag the top right point of the curve down a bit so that the Output Level shown at the bottom right of the dialog box changes to a number between 80% and 95%, then move your cursor over the darkest areas of the image (notice that it changes to an eyedropper). The Info palette should show levels no higher than the Output Level you chose.

   What output levels should you be going for in the image shadows? That depends on how absorbent the paper is that you're using. For newsprint, try for about 80–85%; for coated paper (magazines, posters, brochures), try 90–95%. These are general guidelines, and you have to work with your printer to discover the right settings for your particular circumstances.

9. Drag the bottom left point of the curve up a bit so that the Output Level changes to a number between 3% and 5%. Confirm the levels by moving your cursor over the highlights in the image and watching the Info palette.

10. Click OK to exit the Curves dialog box and apply your changes.

11. Choose Filter➡Sharpen➡Unsharp Mask to bring up the Unsharp Mask dialog box.

    Although it's not technically a tone correction (which is what you call color corrections when you make them to a grayscale image), one of the most important steps in correcting any scanned image is sharpening. Start with the following settings: Amount 100, Radius 1.5, and Threshold 20. Experiment with different settings, but above all don't oversharpen!

Tip

Here's a quick-and-dirty (but remarkably effective) way to increase the tonal range of faded scans: Drag the image onto the New Layer button on the Layers palette and give the new layer a blending mode of Multiply. Repeat as necessary. This combines the density of the new layers and the original layer, darkening the image. Then choose Image➡Adjust➡Levels and move the black slider to the right to bring the black point back to normal.

CORRECTING IMAGES WITH EXTENSIS INTELLIHANCE

Alas, Photoshop is not the end-all when it comes to color correction. Extensis Corp. has created a Photoshop plug-in called Intellihance 2.0, which is used for *automatically* color correcting an image. The idea behind Intellihance is that it intelligently enhances your images (Intellihance, get it?). And that it does.

On the surface, Intellihance's feature set is pretty limited. Its dialog box initially offers thumbnails of the image as it looks before and after the adjustments, densitometer readings (showing the gray, CMYK, or RGB levels), OK and Cancel buttons, Load and Save buttons, and a Fine Tune button (see Figure 11.18). The Preferences panel of this dialog box (behind the Original thumbnail) is really where you control exactly how the filter enhances your image (see Figure 11.19). Here is where you can indicate any particular areas for Intellihance to focus on. Settings can be saved and reused on other images.

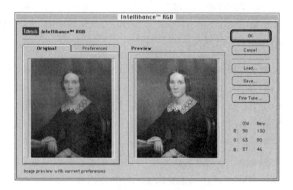

Figure 11.18

The business-like approach of Extensis Intellihance.

Figure 11.19

Intellihance's Preferences dialog box lets you specify how you want images corrected.

Using artificial intelligence algorithms, Intellihance analyzes each image independently and adjusts it so that the result matches the preferences you set for contrast, brightness, saturation, sharpness, and despeckling. Rather than instructing the plug-in to lighten all images' midtones, the preference settings are results-oriented. The Brightness pop-up menu, for example, has the following choices: Off, Deeper Shadows, Shadow Emphasis, Balanced Tone, Midtone Emphasis, and Highlight Emphasis. Because each image is adjusted according to its particular needs, the amount of adjustment Intellihance does each time it's used varies.

It takes a little bit of practice to get used to what results Intellihance yields with specific preferences, but once you've got it down, the plug-in can save a lot of time. It's pretty smart about making adjustments—it can, for example, adjust various tones in the image without affecting other tones or the color balance, so you can bring up the midtones without lightening the shadows. And when you can't get the results you want for a particular image, the Fine Tune option lets you make specific adjustments using similar tools to the ones you'd ordinarily use in Photoshop, such as Curves.

Intellihance can be useful for both Photoshop novices and experienced users. For novices, it offers an easy way around the mysteries of Levels, Curves, and the other tools discussed in this chapter. Photoshop pros, on the other hand, are able to use it to speed processing of multiple images because Intellihance uses the same tools they'd normally use, albeit in the background. Here's an idea of what you see and what you get with Intellihance's preferences:

◆ Contrast: makes the contrast adjustments you'd normally make with the Levels or Curves command.

◆ Brightness: makes the contrast adjustments you'd normally make with the Levels or Curves command or the Hue/Saturation command.

◆ Saturation: makes the saturation adjustments you'd normally make with the Hue/Saturation command.

◆ Sharpness: parallels the Unsharp Mask filter.

◆ Despeckling: parallels the Despeckle filter.

The one thing to keep in mind when using Intellihance is that it isn't really intelligent (not like a human being, anyway), and it isn't magic. Don't take it for granted, and always realize that you may get better results on your own. Above all, correcting images is a subjective art, so "better" results are the results that look better to you.

Note

Extensis PhotoTools, an excellent set of filters for Photoshop, contains a limited version of Intellihance that only works on RGB images.

Chapter 12

WORKING WITH TYPE

A picture may be worth a thousand words, but that doesn't mean you never use words in making your pictures. Type in Photoshop has both similarities to and differences from other image elements, and there are a couple of special tools for creating and working with type. Although Photoshop wasn't intended to be used for working with type, more and more designs (such as World Wide Web graphics) need to include both text and graphics in the same file because the software used to display them doesn't enable text and graphics from different sources to be layered in a document. Photoshop's text tools lack many of the features to be found in other types of graphics software, but you can accomplish a lot with them.

CREATING TYPE

Rather than being typed into the image, as with other programs, text in Photoshop is entered in a separate dialog box. This gives you as much time as you need to edit the type and choose style options before you hit OK and drop the type into your image. Take your time because after the text is dropped into the image, you won't be able to change those settings. The only way to change its text properties is to delete it and start over.

1. First, make sure the foreground color is set to the color you want the type to be.

2. Then choose the Type tool from the toolbox (or press T) and click your document where you want the text to appear.

   This brings up the Type Tool dialog box (see Figure 12.1). Set text formatting options at the top of the dialog and enter your text at the bottom.

Figure 12.1

The Type Tool dialog box.

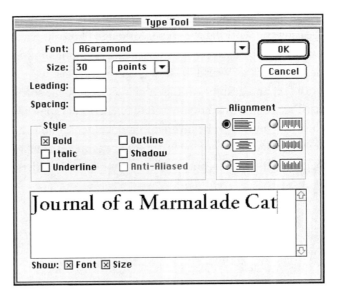

3. Check the Show: Font and Show: Size boxes to show the font and size of the final type in this dialog box; if the typeface you're using is hard to read, or if you're using very small or large type, you probably want to leave these options off.

4. Enter your text in the field at the bottom of the dialog box.

Entering and editing your text at this point works just as you'd expect—you can select words or characters you type with the cursor (double-click to select a whole word) as well as delete, cut, copy, and paste. Both the standard commands in the Edit menu and their keyboard equivalents (such as (Command-C) [Control-C] for copy) work here.

Although text automatically wraps to fit the boundaries of the Type Tool dialog box's text entry field, Photoshop places everything you type on one line unless you hit the Return key between lines. For that reason, you must use the Enter key to exit the dialog box (unless you're the old-fashioned type who still clicks the OK button). If you type more text than the text entry field shows, it's all there, but you have to use the mouse or arrow keys to see it all.

Tip

If your text already exists in another document, such as a word processor file, you can copy and paste it from that document into the text entry field in the Type Tool dialog box. Remember that any "local" formatting, such as italicized words or letters, is lost in the process.

Note

The first time you use the Type tool in a Photoshop session, you see the message, "Building the font menu. This may take a minute or so..." This is the result of Adobe's efforts to shorten Photoshop's startup time; the program doesn't bother to load the font menu type if it is not used during a session. Loading the fonts shouldn't take too long; if the wait starts to drive you crazy, consider using a program such as Suitcase (Mac only) or Adobe Type Manager Deluxe (Mac and Windows) to create a smaller font set you can use with Photoshop.

5. Choose a font from the pop-up menu by clicking either the font name displayed or the triangle to the right of the menu.

Tip

I couldn't live without Adobe Type Reunion, which organizes fonts into their various families, so you don't spend half your life scrolling up and down the font menu looking for CB Futura Condensed Bold. Instead, you find it in a neat submenu with all the other members of the Futura heading. Sorry, Windows users, it's for Mac only.

6. Choose a size for the type.

You can choose any point size between 4 and 1000, or you can measure your type in pixels. The latter comes in handy when type must fit a particular space within an image; because point size varies from typeface to typeface, you can't always accurately predict what size characters turn out to be if you measure type in points. Pixel-based point sizes must also be between 4 and 1000, and you must use whole numbers with both points and pixels. Create the type in the size you want it, rather than making it smaller and then scaling it, to avoid jagged, blocky edges.

Warning

The text entry field of the Type Tool dialog box previews your type at 72 dpi, so the size you see won't match the size you get unless your document resolution is also 72 dpi.

Figure 12.2

Like every other field, typography has its own terminology.

7. Choose a leading value.

    Measured from baseline to baseline, the vertical space between lines of text is called leading, and it's usually stated in points, just like type size. Photoshop uses the same unit of measure you specify for the type size to calculate the leading. If you don't enter a leading value, the default leading is 125 percent of the type size. Leading can be any whole number value between 1 and 1000—entering 0 is the same as not entering a value at all.

8. Choose a spacing value.

    Spacing refers to the space between letters—what's called letterspacing in typesetting. As with the leading value, Photoshop uses the same unit of measurement you choose for the point size—points or pixels—but unlike leading, spacing can be negative. You can enter values in tenths between –99.9 and 999.9. Negative values move letters closer to each other, and positive values space letters out.

9. Choose an alignment setting.

    There are six alignment options indicated by tiny diagrams. Three are pretty standard: left-justified, centered, and right-justified. The other three are more unusual, making the type run vertically: top-aligned, vertically centered, or bottom-aligned (see Figure 12.3). The point of alignment is wherever you click the Type tool in the image.

Type Terminology

Ascender: Part of a character that ascends above the x-height.

Baseline: The imaginary line running horizontally across the bottom of the characters in a line of type.

Descender: Part of a character that extends below the baseline.

Kerning: Adjusting the space between pairs of letters to give optically pleasing spacing. Given the letter pair "To," for example, the "o" should be slightly tucked under the top of the T—otherwise the space between the two letters appears to be too great.

Leading: Vertical spacing between lines of type in the same paragraph, measured from baseline to baseline.

Point: A unit of measure in typesetting; there are 72 points in an inch (in modern usage; formerly, there were 72.27 points to an inch) and 12 points in a pica. Type is measured in points, but nominal 72-point type isn't really 72 points tall; when metal type was

continues

used, the size of the metal block the type was molded on was used as the type size.

Sans serif: Without serifs; Helvetica, for example.

Serif: Small cross-stroke at the end of the main stroke in a letter form. Also used to describe typefaces: *Garamond is a serif typeface.*

X-height: the imaginary line running horizontally across the top of a line of lower-case type.

10. Choose text formats to be applied to the type.

As you might expect, Photoshop doesn't offer as many text formatting options as other programs. That's because it doesn't have to. Most special effects in Photoshop involving type don't depend on text formats, but rather on graphic treatments of type after it's created. Keep in mind that text formatting settings apply to all the type created; you can't select one word while in the Type Tool dialog box and apply a different font, style, spacing, or leading to it.

Figure 12.3

Photoshop offers three alignment options that most graphics programs don't: top-aligned, vertically centered, and bottom-aligned.

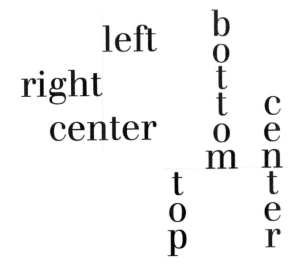

As it was in the beginning, is now, and ever shall be, you can choose Bold, Italic, Underline, Outline, and Shadow styles for your type. There's rarely a good reason to use the Underline, Outline, and Shadow styles in Photoshop because there are much more attractive ways of achieving similar effects. Use the Stroke command to make much nicer type outlines than the

Outline style can produce, and draw your own underlines with the Pencil or Paintbrush. Drop shadows for type are discussed later in this chapter.

One thing Photoshop does that other programs don't is enable you to pile extra styles on top of each other (see Figure 12.4). Because Photoshop rasterizes type right away (instead of waiting until a document's printed), you can, for example, use the bold style on a bold font and get *double* bold. The same thing goes for italics. With most other programs, you may be able to apply the extra styles, but they won't show up when you print the document.

Palatino
Palatino
Palatino

Figure 12.4

Photoshop enables you to apply styles to the style variations built into fonts, thus doubling the effect.

Tip

Don't make the mistake of thinking that using a typeface with the bold style option is always the same as choosing the bold version of the typeface from the Font menu. Sometimes it is; other times it isn't. Take a look at both options, and pick whichever fits your desired look.

11. Turn anti-aliasing on or off.

    Anti-aliased or not? The answer to this question is, without a doubt, "Yes." Anti-aliasing blurs the edges of a selection to give a smoother appearance (see Figure 12.5), and it's even more vital with type than with most other selections. Unless you're purposely going for a jagged-edge effect, use anti-aliasing to improve the appearance of your type. There are three exceptions: if you're working in such a high resolution that the jagged edges won't be noticeable; if you're working at exactly the same resolution your output device produces; or if you're setting very small type that is too blurry to read with anti-aliasing.

Figure 12.5

Anti-aliasing is a must for smooth edges on type characters.

alias

alias

Tip

For smooth, recognizable type, you need to use one of the following: TrueType fonts or PostScript fonts with Adobe Type Manager. Each PostScript font has two components: a set of screen fonts and a printer font; without ATM, your computer displays type onscreen using the screen fonts, which are only supplied to you in certain sizes. So if you don't happen to be using those sizes, type looks rough and blocky. ATM uses the printer font, which contains a vector description of each character, to display type smoothly onscreen at any size. TrueType fonts always use the outline font for screen display.

EDITING AND MANIPULATING TYPE

It's easy to see that sophisticated typesetting hasn't exactly been a priority for Photoshop's designers. That's OK—that's not what Photoshop is for. If you want to do things to type that you can't accomplish in Photoshop, maybe integrating another program into your workflow can help matters. There's a lot you can do, however, to work around Photoshop's type limitations.

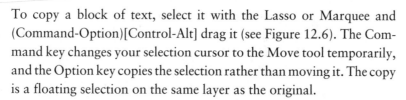

Note

Unlike page layout, word processing, and drawing programs, Photoshop treats type as graphics that happen to spell words. As with all elements in Photoshop, type is made up of pixels, so you can't edit it after you create it. One advantage of using type this way is that you don't have to worry about including fonts with your documents; another is that you can edit type the same way you would graphics: paint it, smear it, filter it, and more.

Moving, Cloning, and Deleting Type

After you enter your type, make your style choices, and click OK in the Type Tool dialog box, the type you've created appears, colored with the current foreground color, on a new layer (in earlier versions of Photoshop, new type appeared as a floating selection). You can move the type around the image as a block by holding down the (Command) [Control] key (or by switching to the Move tool) to move the whole layer.

To copy a block of text, select it with the Lasso or Marquee and (Command-Option)[Control-Alt] drag it (see Figure 12.6). The Command key changes your selection cursor to the Move tool temporarily, and the Option key copies the selection rather than moving it. The copy is a floating selection on the same layer as the original.

Deleting type works just the same as deleting any other element in Photoshop—select it and press the Delete key. To make sure you can delete type without affecting the rest of your image, don't merge the new type layer with other layers—leave it as it's created; transparent with nothing but type on it. If you've already merged the layers when you decide to delete the type, better hope you haven't saved the file since then—if you haven't, then you can use the Eraser tool's "Erase to saved" option to restore the image as it looked before you added the type. (For more information on the Eraser tool, see Chapter 7, "Editing Images.")

Figure 12.6

Clone blocks of text by holding down the (Command-Option) [Control-Alt] keys.

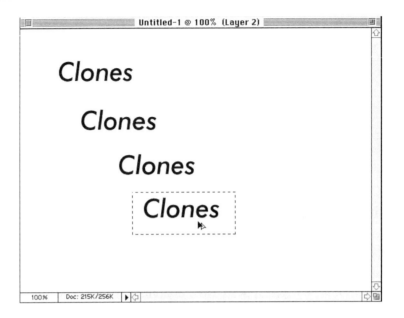

Kerning Type

Kerning refers to the spacing between pairs of letters. Generally, kerning means bringing letters closer together to improve optical spacing. Although Photoshop doesn't have a built-in method of kerning, you can move individual letters by selecting them, holding down the (Command)[Control] key, and using the arrow keys to move the letters closer together or further apart. Hide the "marching ants" that delineate the selection by pressing (Command-H)[Control-H], which makes it easier to see what you're doing.

Warning

In Photoshop 3.0, because type was created as a floating selection, kerning worked a bit differently. Holding down the (Command)[Control] key while the Type tool was selected produced the Lasso tool, which could be used to add to and subtract from the selection. That method doesn't work in 4.0—holding down the (Command)[Control] key brings up the Move tool.

If the active selection is a type mask (see "Creating Type Masks," later in this chapter) when the (Command)[Control] key is held down, the cursor alternates between the move cursor and a delete cursor—clicking with the latter removes the selection without changing the image (see Figure 12.7).

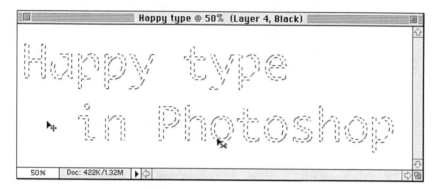

Figure 12.7

Hold down the (Command) [Control] key while a type mask is active, and one of two things happens: If your cursor is outside the mask, it becomes a move cursor; if it's inside the text, it becomes a delete cursor.

Editing Character Shapes

Sometimes you need more individuality than a commercial typeface can supply, such as when you're creating logos or type treatments for ads or magazine feature layouts. To easily adjust individual letters to suit your tastes, you can select them and convert the selection to a path—an outline of the shape that can be edited by moving its points and adjusting its curves.

1. Use the Magic Wand to select one letter, or load a transparency mask on the layer where the type has been placed.

2. To load a transparency mask (a selection of all non-transparent areas on a layer), (Command-click)[Control-click] the layer's name in the Layers palette.

3. Click the Make Work Path button on the Paths palette (see Figure 12.8). This uses the current tolerance setting to create the path; if you want to change the tolerance setting, (Option-click) [Alt-click] the Make Work Path button or choose Make Work Path from the palette's menu. Then enter a tolerance value between 0.5 and 10 pixels and click OK.

Figure 12.8

Clicking the Make Work Paths button at the bottom of the Paths palette, as shown here, is the quickest way to convert a selection to a path.

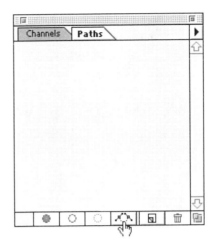

4. Edit the path, using the direct-selection tool from the Paths palette (or hold down the (Command)[Control] key to use the tool temporarily). Use the same Bézier-curve editing techniques you would use in FreeHand or Illustrator. You can apply transformations, as well, such as rotating or skewing the characters (see Figure 12.9).

Figure 12.9

You can edit character outlines using standard Bézier editing curves by converting a type mask selection to a path.

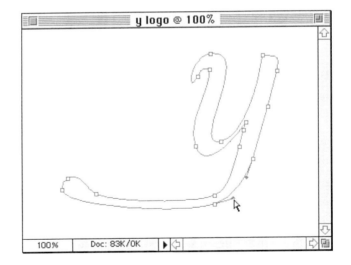

5. If you want to use this path again, double-click the Work Path button in the Paths palette and assign the path a name. Otherwise, it is replaced by the next Work Path you create.

6. When you're done altering the characters, click the Make Selection button on the Paths palette to change the path back to a marching ants selection.

7. Fill the selection with the color or pattern of your choice, or use it as a mask.

Tip

If you notice that long ascenders and descenders are clipped when you create type, check the settings in the Adobe Type Manager control panel. By default, ATM is set to "Preserve line spacing," which is fine for working in page layout software but can sometimes cause clipping in extraordinarily tall fonts. To solve this problem, change the ATM setting to "Preserve character shapes" and restart your computer. Don't forget to change the setting back again when you're done using the problem font in Photoshop.

Creating Type in Other Programs

Much of the time it's easier to create type in another program and bypass Photoshop's type capabilities altogether. There are two basic approaches to this:

◆ Create the type in Illustrator, FreeHand, or another drawing package, then import it into Photoshop.

◆ Create your Photoshop image without the type, import it into another package, and add the type there.

Each method has good and bad points. Drawing packages these days have pretty sophisticated type controls: automatic kerning, letterspacing, horizontal and vertical scaling, paragraph and character formats complete with tabs and indents—all kinds of features previously found only in page layout software (see Figure 12.10). Text editing options have also expanded—both FreeHand and Illustrator, for example, can now import text files, search and replace, and spellcheck. Plug-ins and filters enable special effects to be applied within these programs, and you can fill character outlines with any color, pattern, gradient, or combination of these you desire. Of course you can edit the actual character shapes—that's what this class of software is designed to do.

Figure 12.10

Illustrator's type controls are more comprehensive than Photoshop's.

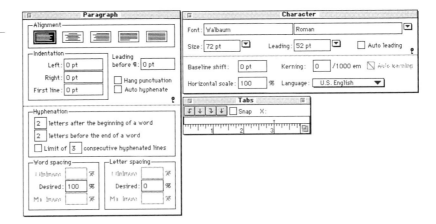

Page layout software, on the other hand, is better designed for handling large amounts of text. Text editing options and type controls are generally simpler to use, and their architecture is set up to keep them from slowing to a crawl when you add a lot of text to a file—a common problem with drawing packages. Features such as text wrap and multiple columns are likely to be more sophisticated than in drawing programs, but you can't edit character outlines or apply patterns, gradients, or other more exotic fills to the type.

The upshot is this: If you have a lot of type to deal with, use a page layout package. If you have a small amount of type that must be heavily modified, use a drawing package. Both kinds of software let you import an image from Photoshop and lay type over it, although there are a few issues to take into account when doing this.

First of all, be aware that trapping features generally don't deal correctly with imported images. And second, watch out for PostScript errors and other printing problems created by laying elements over imported images. Theoretically, you should be able to do this with no problems, but it's not a perfect world, and the PostScript gremlins sometimes object to this situation and respond with errors such as "limitcheck." Finally, though this isn't as much of an issue as it once was, if you import a Photoshop image into another application, you may have to go back to Photoshop to make changes to the image. Although Illustrator and PageMaker now support Photoshop plug-ins so that you can make some changes to Photoshop images within those programs, you're still pretty limited. Although it's not disastrous to be forced to keep moving back and forth between Photoshop and another application, it can be a pain—something you might rather avoid if you can.

Your other option is to create the type in another program and then import it into Photoshop (see Figure 12.11). This enables you to use the superior text-formatting and editing controls of other programs, but you still end up with type whose text attributes you can't edit after it is brought into Photoshop. Of course, you can always go back to the original application, edit the type there, and then re-import it. Whatever your approach, it's best to keep the type on its own layer, so you are able to change it if need be.

Trapping Imported Images in Page Layout Programs

Imported bitmap images (such as Photoshop TIFFs) can be set to knock out colored backgrounds or overprint them using QuarkXPress's Trap Information palette, and XPress elements such as lines, boxes, and text can overprint, knock out, or trap to background pictures. According to Quark tech support, though, there are a couple of limitations.

XPress text can't choke to multicolored backgrounds, for one thing. Also, if you import a grayscale image into a picture box with a background color other than white or none and leave the picture's color set to black, you get a negative of the image on the plate for the background color. To get around this, redefine the picture's color by adding 100% of the background color to it.

According to Adobe's tech support personnel, PageMaker doesn't trap to imported graphics. The program can, however, trap an object in front of imported graphics to a PageMaker object behind that graphic if "Traps over imported objects" is selected in

continues

the Trapping Options dialog box. So you can force text in front of an imported image to trap by placing an appropriately colored PageMaker object behind the imported image. The new object doesn't show, but it does force the text in front to trap to it.

As for Adobe FrameMaker, it doesn't trap at all in version 5; that may or may not change with the release of version 6.

Tip

This whole discussion may be moot before too long, if Extensis Corporation's PhotoText plug-in catches on—and it certainly deserves to do so. Part of Extensis PhotoTools, PhotoText is intended to replace Photoshop's standard Type tool and dialog box with one of its own that shows a preview of the document. By clicking in the preview window, you create a text block that can be moved and resized as much as you want. Meanwhile, you can apply a number of type styles (including some Photoshop doesn't offer, such as small caps) to your text, as well as adjust the text's leading, spacing, horizontal scaling, and other attributes. All styling is applied on a character level, which means different words or letters in your text can have different styles, and you can use multiple text blocks. Once you're satisfied, click the Apply button and your text is placed in the Photoshop document, at which point it becomes non-editable, just like normal Photoshop type. This is definitely a step forward for anyone who uses type in Photoshop. For more information on PhotoText, see Chapter 20, "Third-Party Plug-Ins."

Figure 12.11

The text in this image was created in Illustrator—which can create the small caps and kern the type—and imported into Photoshop, where the glow effect was applied.

MORE THAN WORDS: TYPE AS OUTLINES

In Photoshop, type is more than just words; it's an integral part of the image that can affect the rest of the image. One of the most useful ways of working with type is as a mask, and Adobe recognized that with the addition of the Type Mask tool to version 4.0. The two options for the Type tool—Type and Type Mask—are accessible from the toolbox (click the Type tool and hold down to see both options) or by pressing T to select the Type tool and to toggle between it and the Type Mask tool.

Type masks are used like any other masks—to mask portions of an image or to apply special effects only to part of an image. To fill type with a pattern, for example, you'd create a type mask and fill the selection with the pattern using the Fill command in the Edit menu (see Chapter 7, "Editing Images," for more on patterns). Many of the special type effects shown in this chapter use type masks as a starting point.

Creating Type Masks

There are two big differences between the Type tool and the Type Mask tool. The first and most obvious is that the Type Mask tool creates a selection outline of the type but doesn't fill it, while the Type tool fills an outline but doesn't retain the selection (see Figure 12.12). This is unlike earlier versions of Photoshop, where newly created type was a floating selection. The other big difference is that using the Type Mask tool does *not* create a new layer or a floating selection. It makes a movable selection on the layer you were editing before you created the type mask.

Warning

Make sure you choose the Marquee tool before moving a type mask selection; using the Move tool cuts a portion out of your image and moves it with the selection border.

Figure 12.12

The Type Mask tool creates
an empty selection.

To move individual type mask characters, switch to the Quick Mask mode. Select the characters you want to move with a marquee and hold down the (Command)[Control] key as you move the selection. When you're done, deselect the characters and go back to "marching ants" mode.

A common use for type masks is to use them to hold an image in the shape of text. Creating this effect got a lot easier with Photoshop 4.0:

1. Place the image you want to show through the type outlines in your Photoshop file.

2. Create a type mask, using the type formatting options you prefer. A heavy typeface works best for this.

3. Click the New Layer Mask button on the Layers palette.

That's it (see Figure 12.13)! After you make the layer mask, you can edit it as much as you want—delete type, add more type, or add other shapes. You can also apply special effects to the mask to view their effect on the layer without actually changing the layer. The white parts of a layer mask let the layer show through unaffected; black parts hide the layer; and gray parts make the layer partially visible. See Chapter 9, "Layers," for more information on working with layer masks.

Figure 12.13

The layer mask created from a type mask selection enables the flower image to show through.

Making Type Channels

The problem with selections, including type masks, is that you lose them as soon as you click elsewhere in the image. One way to save selections for future use is to use channels, which you can edit and then reconvert back into selections from the Channels palette. In channels, white areas are included in the selection, and black areas are not; gray areas are partially selected areas. To create an alpha channel from type:

1. Choose the Type Mask tool and click in the document to create a type mask for the type you want to use as a channel.

2. Make your preferred text formatting settings, enter the text, and click OK (or press Enter).

3. Click the Save selection as channel button on the Channels palette. Your selection remains active, and a new channel is created, white on black. Now you can drop the selection (Command-D)[Control-D] and get it back any time you want to use it.

4. To use the channel to recall the selection, click the Load channel as selection button on the Channels palette.

Making Type Outline Paths

Using paths to store type outlines has two advantages over using channels. First, although they're generally less accurate in reproducing a selection, paths take up a lot less space in your file than channels—file sizes really balloon as you add channels, but as with EPS vector graphics, paths are compact. Second, editing paths with Bézier curves is a much more sophisticated method of altering character outlines than editing alpha channels with painting tools. The results can potentially be the same either way, but it's a lot easier to make straight lines and smooth curves with the path tools.

On the other hand, especially at lower resolutions, paths aren't perfect. Converting a Type Mask selection into a path and back to a selection again can distort the character shapes and produce jagged edges (see Figure 12.14).

Figure 12.14

This path created from a type mask selection is jagged and imprecise.

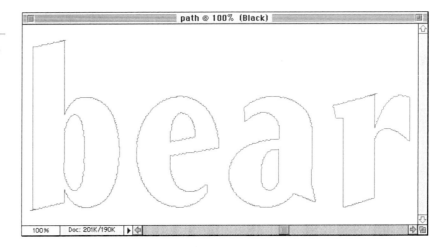

One thing alpha channels cannot do that paths can is act as clipping paths. Convert a selection, including a Type Mask selection, into a clipping path by choosing Clipping Path from the Paths palette menu. When imported into another program, only the portion of the image inside the path shows, with everything else remaining transparent (see Figure 12.15). See Chapter 5, "Selections, Paths, and Masks," for more information on clipping paths.

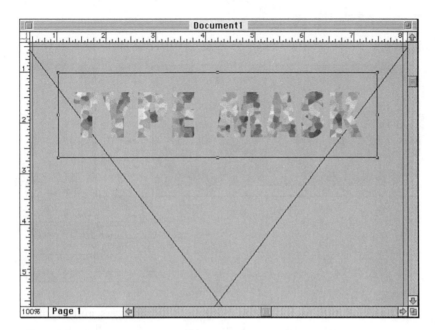

Figure 12.15

The clipping path around the text in this Photoshop EPS file enables the type to be silhouetted when it's imported into QuarkXPress.

Note

Page layout users, beware: Both Photoshop's TIFF and EPS file formats can include clipping paths, but QuarkXPress doesn't support TIFF clipping paths; it just ignores them.

To convert a Type Mask selection to a path, see the steps in the "Editing Character Shapes" section earlier in this chapter.

Manipulating Type with Layers

Because Photoshop 4.0 places type on a new layer when it's created, the full range of layer options is available to experiment without any intermediate steps (see Figure 12.16). The first and most obvious adjustment to make is to the opacity of type, adjusted using the Opacity slider in the Layers palette. In addition, all the usual layer modes are available: Normal, Dissolve, Multiply, Screen, Overlay, Soft Light, Hard Light, Color Dodge, Color Burn, Darken, Lighten, Difference, Exclusion, Hue, Saturation, Color, and Luminosity.

Figure 12.16

Using different layer modes is the easiest—and often a very effective—way to integrate type into an image.

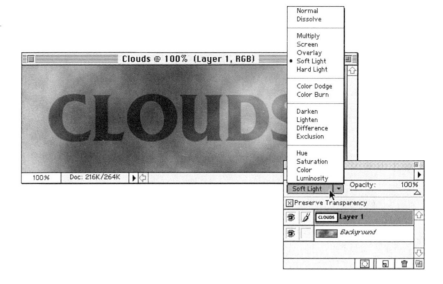

Layers are most useful in combination with other layers, and they make experimentation with special effects much less painful. The easiest way to try out new effects is to use new layers at each step, experimenting as you go with different filters, opacity settings, and layer modes. If your experiment is on a layer, you can always get rid of it or easily duplicate it. And layer modes and opacity settings don't permanently change layer contents, so you can always go back and try different settings.

TYPE SPECIAL EFFECTS

Here's where type gets fun. In Photoshop text is infinitely malleable— you can do anything from giving it an eerie radioactive glow to actually painting with it. Any special effect, including those used with type, can be arrived at in more than one way, so don't take these instructions as a rule book. They're intended to get you started and provide a reference for the easiest way to achieve commonly used effects. For more ideas on special type effects, take a look at *Photoshop Type Magic 1* and *Photoshop Type Magic 2*, and check out the dozens of Web sites devoted to Photoshop, where users can trade ideas and techniques. (See the appendices for a list of related Web sites.)

Tip

For a more casual or free-flowing effect than you can achieve with type, try writing text with Photoshop's painting tools rather than using type. Although you can use a mouse (or even a trackball) for this, it's easier (and you get better results) if you use a graphics tablet with a pen-shaped stylus. Try using the Eraser or the Rubber Stamp, too, rather than the Pencil or Paintbrush.

Making Glowing Type

Probably the easiest way to vary the appearance of your type is to use different feathering settings for Type Mask selections. For a nice, friendly (or not-so-friendly, depending on how you use it) glow around your type, try the following.

1. Create an image with a colored background. Darker colors tend to make the effect more scary; lighter ones are more cheerful. Try different color combinations for different effects.

2. Choose the Type Mask tool and create a line of type (see Figure 12.17). A heavy sans serif typeface works better with this effect, but don't let that keep you from trying different typefaces.

Figure 12.17

The Type Mask tool creates a selection with no fill.

3. Press (Command-C)[Control-C] to copy the selection (you're copying the background color here). Don't drop the selection—you're not done with it yet.

4. From the Select menu, choose Feather and enter a value that's about $1/20$ of your resolution. The image shown here was created at 72 dpi because it is only used onscreen and not printed, so I used a feathering radius of 4. Try different values for different amounts of glow; higher numbers give more glow. Amounts that are too high, though, tend to make an intended glow effect start looking like overspray from a spray paint can or airbrush. Of course, that can be an interesting effect in itself.

5. Switch the background and foreground colors so that white or a light color is the background color; this color provides the glow.

6. Press the Delete key to delete the dark color from the selection and show the lighter color. The feathering makes the effect of the deletion fade out toward the edges (see Figure 12.18).

Figure 12.18

The feathering around the edges of the selection makes the white fill fade out, creating a glow.

7. Press (Command-V)[Control-V] to paste the original selection back on top of the feathered one. Using the Move tool, position the new layer that's created by pasting to show the feathered edges of the deleted section around the edges of the sharp-edged one. See Figure 12.19 for the final image.

Figure 12.19

A glow around the edges of your type is a remarkably simple effect to achieve.

Making Drop Shadows

A quick-and-dirty way to add dimension to flat images, drop shadows make parts of an image appear to stand in front of the rest, thereby making a shadow. Drop shadows are so familiar to our eyes that we don't need to see the object creating the shadow to know what it looks like. They can be hard- or soft-edged; the latter look more realistic, but the former have their place as well.

Making hard-edged drop shadows is incredibly easy.

1. With the Type tool, set the type you want to use (see Figure 12.20). A new layer is created when you click OK in the Type Tool dialog box.

Figure 12.20

A new layer is created to contain the type.

2. Duplicate the layer by dragging its name on the Layers palette onto the New Layer button.

3. Drag the new layer below the original one on the Layers palette to place it behind the object casting the shadow.

4. If your original object is in color and you want a gray shadow, select the shadow layer and use the Desaturate command from the Adjust submenu on the Image menu to remove the color from the shadow.

5. Adjust the Opacity slider on the shadow's layer to lighten the shadow and distinguish it from the original object.

6. Holding down the (Command)[Control] key, click-drag to move the entire shadow layer up or down and to one side in your image, to offset the shadow slightly from the original object (see Figure 12.21).

Figure 12.21

Hard-edged drop shadows add dimension to an image without softening its impact.

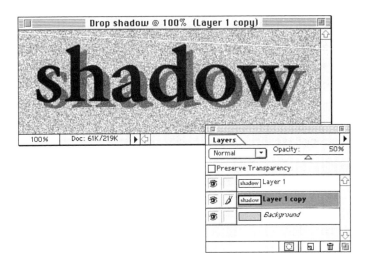

Making soft-edged drop shadows is a little more complex than creating hard-edged ones. The procedure is very similar to that used for creating glowing type effects, but you use lighter colors to make type glow and darker ones to give it shadows.

1. Using the selection tools or a transparency mask, select the type to which you want to add a shadow. (Command-click)[Control-click] its layer in the Layers palette to load a transparency mask for that layer.

2. Create a new layer by clicking the New Layer button on the Layers palette, and click the name of the new layer to make it active (see Figure 12.22). Don't drop the selection.

3. Choose Feather from the Select menu and enter a feathering value about $\frac{1}{20}$ of your image resolution (just like the glowing text effect). Higher feathering values give a blurrier, more diffused effect, as though there's more than one light focused on the object creating the shadow.

4. Choose Fill from the Edit menu and fill the selection with black at 100% opacity to create the shadow.

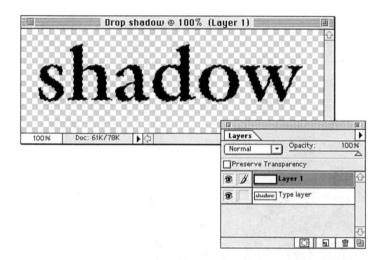

Figure 12.22

Maintain the selection after creating a new layer to hold the shadow.

5. Drag the shadow layer below the shadowing object's layer in the Layers palette so that it's behind the object creating the shadow (see Figure 12.23).

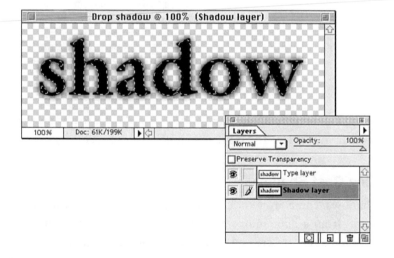

Figure 12.23

The blurred edges of the shadow can just be seen behind the type layer.

6. Adjust the opacity of the shadow layer to your taste. Hiding the type layer by clicking its eyeball icon on the Layers palette helps you see what you're doing.

7. Holding down the (Command)[Control] key, click-and-drag to move the entire shadow layer up or down and to one side in your image, to offset the shadow slightly from the original object.

8. Consider adding a textured background behind the shadow. This enhances the realism of the shadow effect by emphasizing that the shadow is actually transparent, rather than just light gray. See Figure 12.24 for the final image.

Figure 12.24

Varying the opacity and blurriness of the shadow enables quite a range of effects.

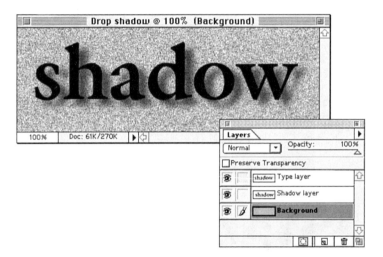

You can skip the feathering and add a Gaussian blur to just the shadow layer if you prefer. The results are much the same.

Making Cast Shadows

Shadows come in two varieties: drop and cast. Drop shadows result from a light source almost directly in front of a flat element. Cast shadows are created when light shines at an angle on a three-dimensional object, and these are actually more common in real life.

The procedure for making realistic cast shadows is pretty much the same as for making drop shadows, except that there's a Distort transform involved.

1. Using the selection tools or a transparency mask, select the type to which you want to add a shadow. (Command-click)[Control-click] its layer in the Layers palette to load a transparency mask for that layer.

2. Create a new layer by clicking the New Layer button on the Layers palette, and click the name of the new layer to make it active. Don't drop the selection (see Figure 12.25).

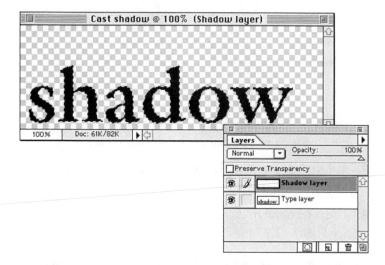

Figure 12.25

The new layer holds the cast shadow.

3. Choose Feather from the Select menu and enter a feathering value about $1/20$ of your image resolution—higher values for a diffused effect, lower ones for a sharper-edged shadow.

4. Choose Fill from the Edit menu and fill the selection with black at 100% opacity to create the shadow. Then Select All.

5. Select Layer➡Transform➡Distort and drag one of the middle handles away from the base of the type you're shadowing in a direction opposite the imaginary light. Hit the Return key when the transformation is to your liking (see Figure 12.26).

Figure 12.26

Distorting the shadow layer makes it appear that the imaginary light source is off to the side of the type.

6. Drag the shadow layer below the shadowing object's layer in the Layers palette so that it's behind the object.

7. Adjust the opacity of the shadow layer to make the shadow somewhat transparent.

8. Add a textured background behind the shadow if you want. See Figure 12.27 for the final image.

As with drop shadows, cast shadows can be achieved by skipping the feathering and blurring the shadow layer after it's properly distorted.

Figure 12.27

Cast shadows are the kind we see most of the time in real life, and they're easier than you'd think to create in Photoshop.

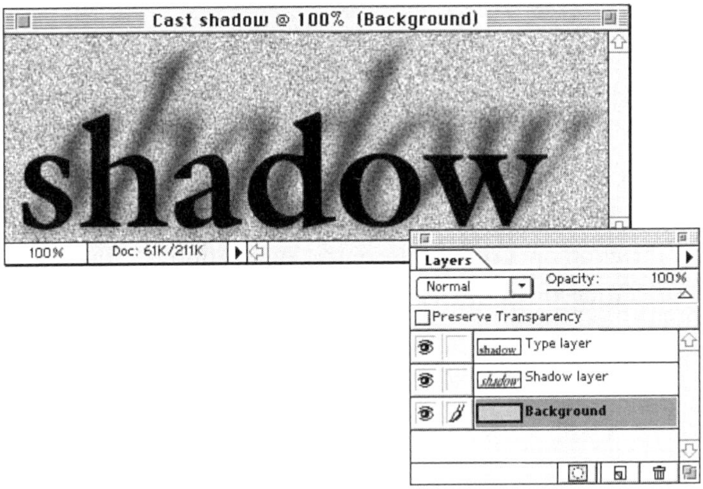

Making Embossed Type

Embossing is the process of stamping type or an image into paper to leave a three-dimensional imprint; in printing, blind embossing is embossing without using ink, so that the raised imprint is the only result. There are probably dozens of ways to emboss type in Photoshop, including the program's own built-in Emboss filter that changes all colors to shades of gray. For a true embossing effect that retains the image's colors, the following method is the simplest. Your image, however, must be in RGB mode for the Lighting Effects filter to work.

1. Choose or create a background. You can use anything at all, from a flat color to a complex photograph or abstract pattern.

2. Choose the Type Mask tool, enter the type you want to emboss in the Type Tool dialog box, and click OK (see Figure 12.28).

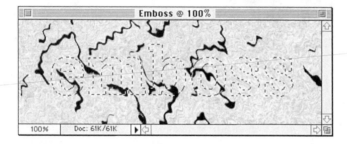

Figure 12.28

Use the Type Mask tool to create an outline of the type you're embossing.

3. Without dropping the selection, click the Save Selection as Channel button on the Channels palette to create a white-on-black alpha channel of the type. Drop the selection.

4. Select Filters➡Render➡Lighting Effects and adjust the settings to produce your desired effect—the preview window shows the results of your settings. The Light Type should be Omni, with a positive intensity. Under Properties, Gloss determines how reflective the embossed type is. Material ranges from plastic to metallic; the former reflects more light; the latter maintains the background texture better. The Exposure slider makes the whole image darker or lighter, and the Ambience controls determine how much ambient, or room, light appears to strike the image. See Figure 12.29 for the settings used to produce this example.

After you hit a combination of settings that works well, you can save that combination by clicking the Save button in the Lighting Effects dialog box and assigning that style a name. Then the settings appear in the Style menu, along with the default styles that come with Photoshop—selecting a style from the Styles menu restores all the Lighting Effects settings for that style in one step.

Figure 12.29

The Lighting Effects filter has several options to produce the effect of different kinds of light and different surfaces.

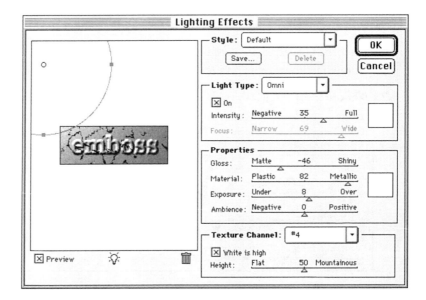

5. Position the lighting source in the preview window well away from the image, but position it so that the radius covers the corner of the image. Leave White is high checked. Choose the alpha channel containing the type from the Texture Channel pop-up menu, and adjust the Height slider (see Figure 12.30).

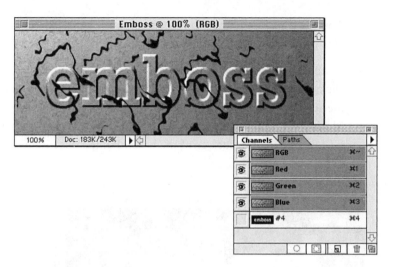

Figure 12.30

Photoshop's Emboss filter is fine—if you're working in a grayscale image. But you can fine-tune the effect and maintain color with this technique.

Making Beveled Type

Beveling type works similarly to embossing type, except that it always uses a sharp edge.

1. Create the type you want to bevel with the Type Mask tool.

2. Make the selection an alpha channel by clicking the Save Selection as Channel button on the Channels palette.

3. Duplicate that alpha channel by dragging its name onto the New Channel button on the Channels palette. Drop the selection (see Figure 12.31).

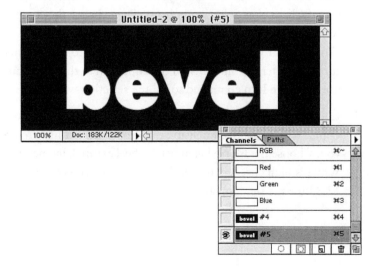

Figure 12.31

The second alpha channel provides the actual beveled edges of the type.

4. Apply a Gaussian blur to the second alpha channel. Make the blur radius about $1/20$ of the file's resolution.

5. Choose the first text channel, convert it to a selection by clicking the Load Channel as Selection button, and return to the second, blurred text channel. Choose Contract from the Modify submenu of the Select menu and shrink the selection a bit to make the top surface of the bevel. Fill the selection with white (see Figure 12.32).

Figure 12.32

Filling the selection with white gives the top surface of the beveled letters a hard edge.

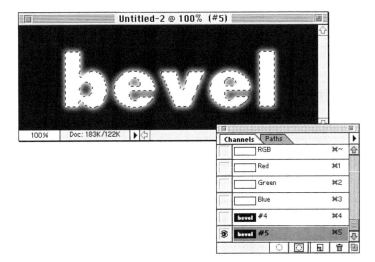

6. Choose the first text channel again and reload the selection (Load Channel as Selection button). Then choose the composite RGB channel and fill the selection with the color of your choice. Or, if you want to use a pattern or photo as a fill, make sure the pattern or image is on the clipboard at this point and use the Paste Into command to fill the selection with it.

7. Choose Filters➤Render➤Lighting Effects. Set Light Type to Omni, with a positive intensity; the Properties settings are up to you. Choose the blurred channel as the Texture Channel, with White is high checked and the height of your choice. See Figure 12.33 for the final image.

Figure 12.33

Beveled type can be filled with a color, texture, or pattern.

Making Distressed Type

"Distressed" is a catch-all term for type to which bad things have happened. To compensate for the computer's clean, precise perfection, you can make your type look as though it's been rubber-stamped, photocopied, crumpled, or typed on a very old Smith-Corona. The technique here produces the effect of a bad typewriter impression, but you can try different filter settings and combinations to come up with your own "distressed" effects in an infinite number of flavors. The key filters are Blur, Diffuse, and Add Noise.

1. Create a type mask for the type you want to distress and click the Save Selection as New Channel button on the Channels palette to make an alpha channel of the type mask selection (see Figure 12.34).

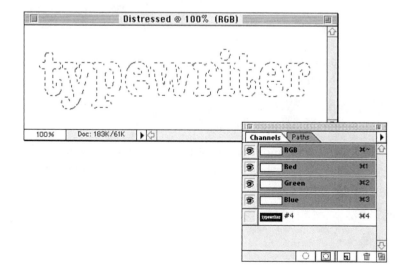

Figure 12.34

Distressing is applied to type in an alpha channel.

2. If you're experimenting, duplicate the channel (so you can go back and start over again later) by dragging the channel's name to the New Channel button on the Channels palette.

3. Working in the alpha channel, with the type mask selection still active, choose Add Noise from the Noise submenu of the Filters menu and add some Gaussian noise. The more you add, the worse off the typewriter is (see Figure 12.35).

Figure 12.35

Adding noise makes the type start looking a bit under the weather.

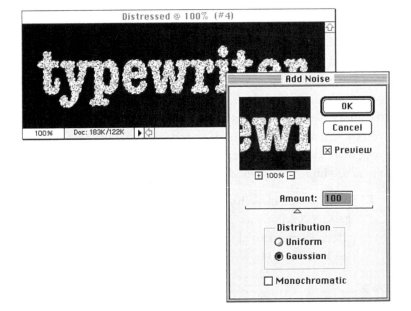

4. Keep the selection active and choose Filters > Stylize > Diffuse; use Normal mode.

5. Drop the selection and apply a Gaussian blur to the image to soften the edges of the type a bit.

6. Press (Command-L)[Control-L] to open the Levels dialog box and darken the image by dragging the middle triangle to the right (see Figure 12.36).

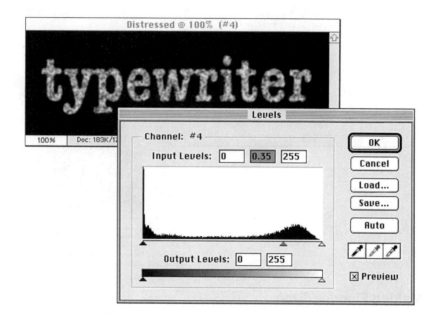

Figure 12.36

Darkening the alpha channel using the Levels dialog box restores some of the body of the distressed characters.

7. After leaving the Levels dialog box, you can make your distressed effect less fuzzy by choosing Image→Adjust→ Threshold, which converts the channel to black and white. Adjust the Threshold slider (you can click the Preview box to see the effect on your type) to determine the point above which a gray pixel is converted to black and below which it becomes white. For a more realistic impression, with varying ink amounts, skip this step.

8. Click the Load Channel as Selection button on the Channels palette and then switch to the main document channel. Fill the selection with the ink color of your choice. See Figure 12.37 for the final image.

Figure 12.37

Distressed type looks less than perfect in any number of ways. Here the effect is one of type from a really decrepit Smith Corona.

Making Flaming Type

This is a really spectacular (but easy) effect originated by Sal Giliberto. One of the interesting aspects of the technique is that it's all done in grayscale, then a flame-colored palette is loaded to provide the color.

1. Press D to change the foreground and background colors to their default values (black and white, respectively). Create a new file in grayscale mode, filled with black; if you create the file with a white background, press (Command-I)[Control-I] to invert the image to black. (Don't use Transparent as a Contents choice.)

2. Set the text you want to flame as a Type Mask and click the Save Selection as Channel button on the Channels palette to create an alpha channel of the type.

3. Keeping the type mask selection active, press Delete to fill the selection with white (see Figure 12.38).

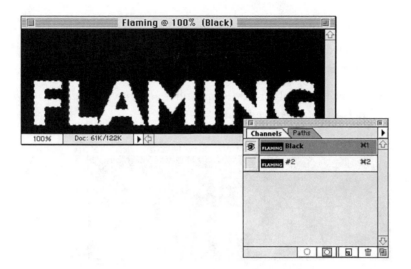

Figure 12.38

Flaming type starts with white letters on a black background.

4. Under the Image menu, select Rotate Canvas 90° counter-clockwise. Your type selection is no longer active.

5. Choose Filters➡Stylize➡Wind. Set the direction to left, and choose a method depending on your image—the idea is to end up with "flames" that are about half the height of your type. Then rotate the canvas back the other way so it's right-side-up again (see Figure 12.39).

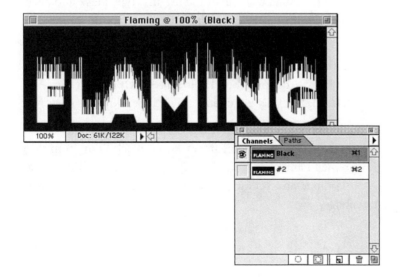

Figure 12.39

The Wind filter must be applied when the image is sideways; once the letters are suitably blown away, the canvas is rotated back to its former position.

6. Select Filters➡Stylize➡Diffuse, using Normal mode.

7. Apply a Gaussian blur with a radius about $^1/_{40}$ the resolution of your image. You should still be able to read the type.

8. Select Filters➡Distort➡Ripple filter and apply it with the default settings (see Figure 12.40).

Figure 12.40

The Ripple filter keeps the flames from being too straight.

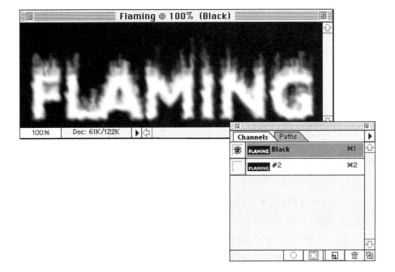

9. Select the alpha channel of the original type mask and click the Load Channel as Selection button; then click the original (black) channel in the Channels palette.

10. Feather the selection with a small radius and fill it with black (if black is the foreground color, press (Option-Delete)[Alt-Delete]). For fully engulfed flaming type, skip this step.

11. Convert the image to Indexed Color mode, then choose Image➡Mode➡Color Table. Choose Black Body from the pop-up menu and click OK. This remaps the grays in the image to an orange-and-yellow palette. See Figure 12.41 for the final image.

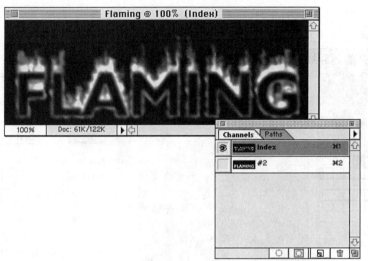

Figure 12.41

The final step in creating flaming type is to apply the orange and yellow colors of the flames.

Tip

To make your own custom color tables (such as a blur range for gas flames), choose Custom from the Color Table pop-up menu. To maintain black and white points in the image, select the top row of squares (by click-dragging over the entire row of squares) and choose black for both the first and last colors when prompted by the color picker dialog box; do the same to make the bottom row white. Then choose a range of colors for the rest of the palette, with the darkest distinguishable color for the first color and the lightest for the last color (see Figure 12.42). Click the Save button and give the color table a name to save it for future use.

Figure 12.42

As soon as you select a square or range of squares, the color picker comes up so that you can choose a color (or, for a range, a first and a last color) for that square or range.

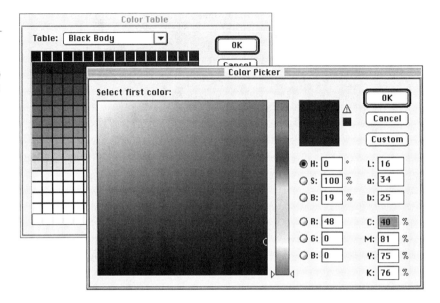

Painting with Type

For effects requiring multiple impressions of a word or letter, you can define a custom brush in the shape of a character or word. This is handy for logo treatments, as well as any image that calls for a "trail" of letters. You can also use a dingbat or picture font when creating custom brushes from type. Follow these steps:

1. Create the type you want to use as a brush, up to 1000 pixels across.

2. Make any adjustments to it, such as blurring it a bit to give it a soft edge.

3. Select the type and choose Define Brush from the Brushes palette menu.

4. Your new brush appears in the Brushes palette, just like the standard ones that come with Photoshop. You can adjust its spacing by double-clicking the brush and entering a new spacing value.

5. Save your brush for later use by choosing Save Brushes from the Brushes palette menu; you can load the brush with the Load Brushes command from the Brushes palette menu.

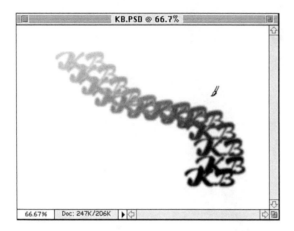

Figure 12.43

Adjust the spacing and fade options to create effects with type-shaped custom brushes.

Chapter 13

CUSTOM COLORIZATION

This chapter covers colorizing imagery in Photoshop to achieve special effects, as well as techniques to work around the limitations of Photoshop when it comes to working with and exporting spot colors. Using practical examples, we discover the methods necessary to add color to grayscale images, selectively desaturate parts of images, create spot color separations without using the Duotone modes, and selectively re-color CMYK and RGB images. The latest version of Photoshop provides you with new tools to isolate color modifications with multiple undos, not to mention the ability to apply a set of commands to multiple images with just a few keystrokes and mouse clicks.

MAKING SPOT COLOR PLATES

The procedures for creating Duotones, Tritones, and Quadtones are detailed in Chapter 10, "Working with Color Images." Photoshop does a nice job of creating Duotones, Tritones, and Quadtones, but it has limitations as far as specifying exactly what part of the image goes on which color plate. When creating Duotones, Tritones, or Quadtones, the colors are controlled by adjusting curves that determine which part of the image the color affects. In order to create a file where we can specify precisely which elements go on a color plate, the image must be separated into spot colors from Photoshop using the CMYK channels to emulate the spot color plates. In process color printing colors are created by combining percentages of the process color inks (cyan, magenta, yellow, and black). In order to reduce printing costs and access a wider gamut of colors, spot colors are used. These spot color inks either come pre-mixed or are mixed by the printer using a formula provided by the ink vendor. Pantone inks are the most commonly used spot color inks in the United States, though there are a variety of ink vendors to choose from. For more information on the available ink vendors and how spot colors are used in Photoshop, see Chapter 10.

Of course, the drawback to making spot separations this way is that you have to work on your image using colors (CMYK) different from those you plan to use to print the file. If I want to print a file that has a purple triangle, an orange circle, and a brown square using three spot color inks, for example, I would draw the triangle in the Cyan channel, the circle in the Magenta channel and the square in the Black channel; substituting cyan for purple, magenta for orange, and black for brown. When I have the file separated to negative film for printing, I tell the printer which colors to substitute, or better yet, scratch the spot color names on the plates and opaque out the process color names.

Alpha Channels

The alpha channels are commonly used to store selections and to achieve special effects like vignettes and fades. The alpha channels are also sometimes referred to as mask channels because they are grayscale channels that can be used as masks to affect a grayscale or color image. If you are familiar with traditional design techniques, you can think of the alpha channels as "frisket masks." When you display the Channels palette, you will notice that there is a channel for each of the colors in the particular color space you're working in. When in grayscale mode, one channel is all that is needed to represent the grayscale image; this channel is named Black. When in RGB mode the Channels palette contains a composite channel named RGB and one channel for each of the RGB components named Red, Green, and Blue respectively. Since an RGB image contains three color channels, alpha channels are

This method works fine for images similar to the one described, but what if we want to isolate parts of a grayscale image and colorize them to print on spot color plates. In the following example we take a grayscale image and copy it to two alpha channels (see sidebar) that we use to represent two spot color inks for viewing purposes. We use the Paintbrush tool to paint changes on these alpha channels, erasing parts of the image and changing the opacity of others, to generate a composite image that closely resembles the printing objective: using two spot color inks instead of four CMYK inks. Once we have an acceptable looking composite, we copy the information from the alpha channels onto two of the process color plates. We do this because color separations can only be generated using the process colors. In short, we use alpha channels to represent each spot color, modify our image, and then paste those spot color separations into two of the standard CMYK channels for output.

The following example makes a two-color file to be printed using spot color inks. We use the mask colors for alpha channels to facilitate seeing the actual colors we use to print onscreen.

Open the file "grandpa.ps4" in the Examples folder on the CD-ROM accompanying this book.

1. Start out with a grayscale file.

2. Choose All from the Select menu ((Command-A)[Control-A]).

3. Copy the entire image to the clipboard by choosing Copy from the Edit menu ((Command-C)[Control-C]).

4. Choose New from the File menu ((Command-N)[Control-N]) and accept the dimensions and resolution offered here, but change the

named beginning with "#4". When in CMYK mode the Channels palette contains a composite channel named CMYK and one channel for each of the CMYK components named Cyan, Magenta, Yellow, and Black respectively. Since a CMYK image contains four color channels, alpha channels are named beginning with "#5". You can change the name of the alpha channel to anything you like. The alpha channel will be automatically named when a spot color is assigned to it as a mask color. In order to distinguish alpha channels from each other when more than one alpha channel is present, Photoshop enables you to assign a color using the Photoshop Color Picker. When you make the alpha channels visible by clicking on the "eyeball" to the left of the channel in the Channels palette, the contents of the grayscale alpha channel will be displayed in the chosen mask color. The default mask color is Red with a 50% opacity so you can see the image underneath. Even though you can save the alpha channels with your file in many file formats including TIFF, they cannot be separated onto their own plates when printing color separated film. Alpha channels are covered in depth in Chapter 9, "Layers."

mode to CMYK and be sure the Contents is set to White. This creates a new file of the exact dimensions and resolution of the image on the clipboard.

5. Display the Channels palette by choosing Show Channels from the Window menu and create a new alpha channel by choosing New Channel from the palette's menu or by clicking the new channel icon (just to the left of the trash can icon at the bottom of the Channels palette). To create a new channel without displaying the Channel Options dialog box, (Command-click) [Control-click] the new channel icon. This creates a new channel named #5 (see Figure 13.1).

Figure 13.1

New alpha (mask) channels are numbered beginning with #5 for CMYK images.

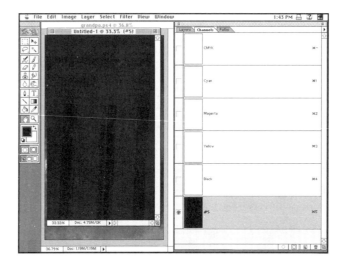

6. Double-click the name of the new channel in the Channels palette to display the Channel Options dialog box (see Figure 13.2).

7. Click the color swatch to display the Photoshop Color Picker and click the Custom button. Choose PANTONE (Coated) from the Book menu at the top of the Custom Color dialog box.

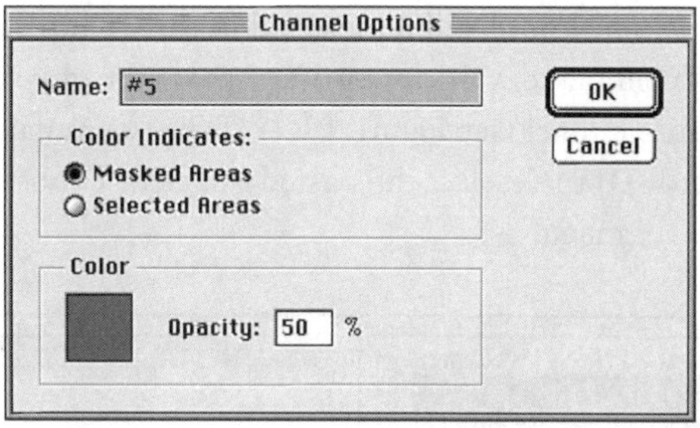

Figure 13.2

The Channel Options dialog box.

8. Type the number of the PANTONE color desired. In this case we're going to use 1595 (see Figure 13.3). Click OK and note that the name of the alpha channel changes to the PANTONE color name. We still refer to this channel as Channel #5 for this exercise.

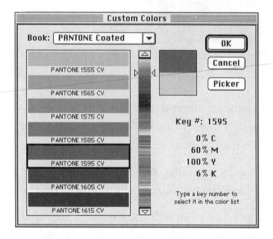

Figure 13.3

Choose PANTONE (Coated) from the Book pull-down menu and type the key number of the PANTONE color.

9. Set the opacity for this color to 80%. Most offset printing inks are not wholly opaque, so we're setting the opacity for this color to emulate the opacity of the ink when it prints on top of our second ink color. If you want to be exact, talk to your printer for specific information about estimated opacity. For most light colors, 80–85% works well. Click OK.

10. Channel #5 should still be selected in the Channels palette. Press (Command-V)[Control-V] to paste the grayscale image into this channel (see Figure 13.4). Type (Command-D) [Control-D] to deselect the pasted image or choose None from the Select menu.

Figure 13.4

Paste the grayscale image into the alpha channel.

11. Create another alpha channel by choosing New Channel from the palette's menu or by clicking the new channel icon. This creates a new channel named #6.

12. Double-click the name of the new channel in the Channels palette to display the Channel Options dialog box.

13. Click the color swatch. If the Custom Color dialog box is not displayed, click the Custom button in the Photoshop Color Picker and click the Custom button. The PANTONE (Coated) book should still be displayed.

14. Type the number of the PANTONE color desired. We're going to use 3298. Click OK and note that the alpha channel name changes to the Pantone color name. We still refer to this channel as Channel #6 for this exercise, however.

15. Set the opacity for this color to 100% because this is going to represent the first color printed. Click OK.

16. Channel #6 should still be selected in the Channels palette. Press (Command-V)[Control-V] to paste the grayscale image into this channel. Press (Command-D)[Control-D] to deselect the pasted image or choose None from the Select menu.

17. Make these two new alpha channels visible by first clicking the top CMYK Channel and then clicking in the "eyeball" column to the left of each alpha channel's picture icon, as shown in Figure 13.5.

Eye Icon

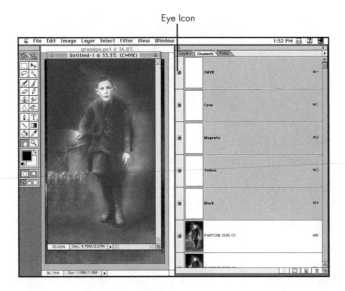

Figure 13.5

The Eye icon makes the channel visible and displays alpha channels in the mask color set for that channel.

Right now, we have two of the same images overlaying each other creating a single color that is the composite of the 80% PANTONE 1595 printing on top of PANTONE 3298. You can use any of the editing tools to modify the alpha channels; we use the Paintbrush tool for this example.

18. Double-click the Paintbrush tool. In the Paintbrush Options palette, set the opacity of the Paintbrush to 30% so we can make gradual changes to the alpha channels (see Figure 13.6).

Figure 13.6

The Paintbrush Options
palette.

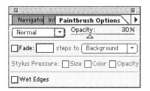

19. Select Show Brushes from the Window menu to display the Brushes palette and select a relatively large brush with a soft edge (see Figure 13.7).

Figure 13.7

Select a brush from the
Brushes palette.

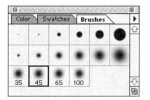

20. Select Channel #5 from the Channels palette ((Command-5) [Control-5]).

21. Make the foreground color white by typing the letter "d" to reset the default colors of black foreground/white background. Then press the letter "x" to swap the foreground and back-ground colors. You can also click the foreground color swatch in the Tool palette and set the color to 255 Red, 255 Green, and 255 Blue (0% Cyan, 0% Magenta, 0% Yellow, and 0% Black).

22. With both alpha channels visible, but Channel #5 selected in the Channels palette, paint over the clothing of the little boy in the image, revealing the second color (see Figure 13.8).

23. With both alpha channels visible, but Channel #6 selected, paint over the hands and face to remove the underlying color (see Figure 13.9). Note that you should still be using the Paintbrush tool with a 30% opacity to paint with white as the foreground color.

Go back and forth between these two channels and make changes by painting with white to remove the parts of the image on one channel to reveal the parts on the other channel. Painting with black, however, does not restore the picture data that has already been painted over with white. If you want to restore the image in a particular channel, select the channel in the Channels palette and choose Paste from the Edit menu. The clipboard still retains the original grayscale image unless you have copied or cut something else since the beginning of this exercise, in which case you must open the original grayscale image, copy it, and paste it back into the alpha channel of the work file.

Figure 13.9

Painting with white removes the image data on one alpha channel making the image data on the other visible.

24. Select Channel #5 from the Channels palette and choose All from the Select menu ((Command-A)[Control-A]). Press (Command-C)[Control-C] to copy the image.

25. Select Magenta from the Channels palette and paste ((Command-V)[Control-V]). It doesn't matter which color channel you use in this step, though I tend to choose the color channel closest to the spot color I am using. See Figure 13.10.

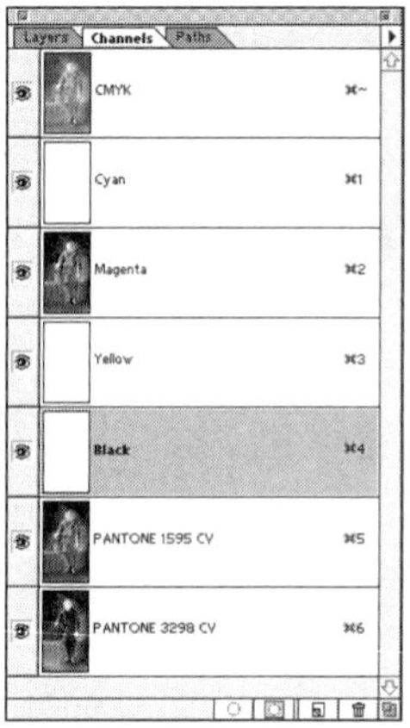

Figure 13.10

Paste the grayscale image copied from the alpha channel into a process color channel.

26. Select Channel #6 from the Channels palette and choose All from the Select menu. Press (Command-C)[Control-C] to copy the image.

27. Select Black from the Channels palette and choose Paste from the Edit menu.

28. Select CMYK in the Channels palette to preview the composite using the process inks (see Figure 13.11).

29. Save this file in Photoshop format in case you want to edit the color specification further, then save the file in a format that can be imported into your page layout application. You should find out what angles to print the halftone screens at for each color from your printer if you are bringing the file to a service bureau for output. Be sure to let the printer or service bureau know what you have done so they can output only the colors necessary. In a page layout application such as QuarkXPress or

Adobe PageMaker you have to color the page elements using the process color substitutions in place of the spot colors as well.

Figure 13.11

The process color plates represent the spot colors selected for printing.

Open "grandpa2.ps4" on the CD-ROM that accompanies this book to see the above example completed. Open "grandpa3.ps4" on the CD-ROM to see an example of the same file using three spot colors.

Emulating Duotones

You can use the preceding procedure to add color objects such as text to a Duotone file (see Figure 13.12). You can also make adjustments to selected areas of the alpha channels using the Curves or Levels dialog box. See Chapter 11, "Color Correction," for information on using the Curves and Levels dialog boxes.

Open "grandpa4.ps4" to see an example of a Duotone created using the alpha channels with text added in one of the colors (see Figure 13.12).

Figure 13.12

Adding text to one of the spot color plates is easy when using the process color substitution method.

Tip

There is a plug-in for Adobe Photoshop called PlateMaker by In Software that enables you to export files in the DCS 2 format. This format saves alpha channels to be used as spot color inks, varnish plates, and flash plates, along with the CMYK plates.

COLORIZING A GRAYSCALE IMAGE

There are a multitude of methods for colorizing a grayscale image, from colorizing the entire image for printing in a CMYK-specified image to painting color into the image using the Paintbrush and Airbrush tools. The trick to effectively colorizing grayscale images is to maintain the tonal balance (luminosity) of the image while making discrete color changes. You will see that there are buttons, checkboxes, and menu selections that affect the luminosity of the image or in many cases protect the luminosity values from change. In Chapter 10, "Working with Color Images," the Duotones section covers the method used to generate a monotone image to be printed using a single ink. The following examples look at methods used to create a single color image by adjusting the Hue and Saturation values of pixels as well as techniques for fully colorizing grayscale imagery.

The Hue value for each pixel is often referred to as that pixel's color; orange, purple, pink, and green are all hues. When a grayscale image is converted to RGB mode, the hues of the pixels are desaturated, meaning the color (hue) level is reduced until only grayscale data remains. Increasing the saturation levels makes the specific hues assigned to the pixels become more apparent. Adjusting the brightness (luminance) value of the pixels results in changes to the tonal (gray) balance of the image, an undesirable effect when colorizing grayscale imagery. In the following exercises we will be changing the Hue and Saturation values of the pixels in our image to change their color. Since we will be depending largely on our image for the brightness values, the colors we are able to specify are limited to those with the existing pixel's brightness value for the most part.

USING ADJUSTMENT LAYERS TO COLORIZE

You may want to take advantage of Photoshop's adjustment layers (new in version 4) to make changes to the image. Adjustment layers enable you to make adjustments to the image's grayscale, color balance, and brightness and contrast settings using a layer that can be turned on and off. Adjustment layers can also be stacked on top of each other to apply more than one adjustment to an image. Because you can combine, hide, or remove adjustments, you can undo any changes you make easily. To create adjustment layers, choose Show Layers from the Window menu and choose New Adjustment Layer... from the Layers palette menu. See Chapter 9, "Layers," for information on how to use the adjustment layers.

Open the file "grandpa.ps4" in the Examples folder on the CD-ROM that accompanies this book.

1. Choose Image➡Mode➡RGB Color to convert the grayscale image into RGB mode.

2. Display the Layers palette and choose New Adjustment Layer... from the Layers palette or (Command-click)[Control-click] the New Layer Icon (see Figure 13.13). When the New

Adjustment Layer dialog box is displayed, select Hue/Saturation for Type and click OK. The Hue/Saturation Layer dialog box is displayed (see Figure 13.14).

Figure 13.13

When you select New Adjustment Layer… the new layer is inserted above the selected layer.

Figure 13.14

The Hue/Saturation Layer dialog box.

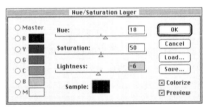

3. Click the Colorize and Preview checkboxes in the lower-right corner of the Hue/Saturation Layer dialog box. When the Colorize checkbox is selected, the Hue and Lightness value is set to zero (0) and the Saturation value set to 100. You can change the Hue and Saturation values by dragging the triangle sliders. For example: change the Hue to 18 and the Saturation to 27 to colorize the image with a warm light brown color or try a Hue of −180 and a Saturation of 10 to subtlely tint the image with light blue. Note that the black and white pixels do not change color because their lightness values are at the ends of the lightness scale.

4. If you want to make further changes, drag the triangle slider under Hue and Saturation until you're happy with the settings.

You end up with a "fake" duotone because the totally black and totally white pixels do not change color. This method of colorizing creates an image that appears like a duotone but is actually printed using the process color inks.

5. Save these settings for future use by clicking the Save button in the Hue/Saturation Layer dialog box. Clicking the Load button loads these or other saved settings.

6. Click OK and convert the image to CMYK mode before saving the file for input to a page layout application. See Chapter 10, "Working with Color Images," for information on converting from RGB to CMYK.

7. Using the adjustment layer created in Step 2, you can further adjust the Hue/Saturation effect by dragging the Opacity slider in the Layers palette. Drag the Opacity slider to the left (less than 100%) to decrease the saturation level specified in the Hue/Saturation adjustment layer. Note that if you drag the slider all the way to 0%, the image once again appears grayscale.

8. Choose a blending mode from the pull-down menu at the top of the Layers palette. The blending mode modifies the way the Hue/Saturation adjustment layer affects the image pixels. See Chapter 6, "Painting," for detailed information on each of the available blending modes.

Open the file "grandpa5.ps4" in the Examples folder on the CD-ROM that accompanies this book to see the previous exercise completed.

Using the Adjustment Layer to Isolate Changes

The adjustment layer created in the preceding section is actually a mask layer similar to the layer masks used for regular layers. The adjustment layer is a grayscale mask in which painting with white applies the full effect of the adjustment layer; in our example Hue/Saturation. Painting with black masks the painted areas, so the Hue/Saturation adjustment layer does not affect the image in these areas. When you first create an adjustment layer the mask color is set to white; that's why the thumbnail preview in the Layers palette is a white box. This means that the Hue/Saturation adjustment layer is applied to the entire image. If you set the foreground color to black and paint with the Paintbrush tool set to 100% opacity, you can mask the areas that you want to leave unaffected by the Hue/Saturation adjustment layer. If you change the foreground color to a percentage of black and paint with the Paintbrush, the Saturation value of the Hue/Saturation adjustment layer is modified (just like using the opacity slider in the Layers palette, but on the painted area only). To change the adjustment layer's mask:

1. Click the adjustment layer's name in the Layers palette.

2. Select the Paintbrush tool from the tool box and choose a medium sized brush with soft edges.

3. Use Black, White or a percentage of Black and paint on the image to affect the adjustment layer. The changes are displayed in the adjustment layer's thumbnail picture (see Figure 13.15).

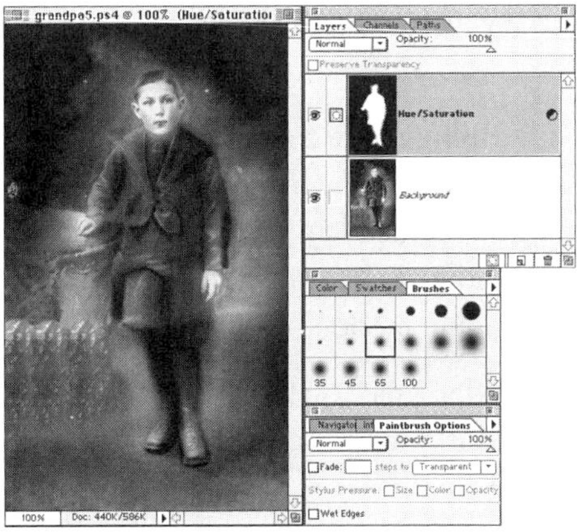

Figure 13.15

The thumbnail in the adjustment layer represents the changes made to the mask by painting with a level of gray.

4. When you are happy with your adjustments, choose Merge Down from the Layer menu or Layers palette menu or press (Command-E)[Control-E]. See Figure 13.16.

Figure 13.16

*Merge options are available from
the Layers palette menu.*

Open the file "grandpa6.ps4" in the Examples folder on the CD-ROM
that accompanies this book for an example of using Adjustment Layers
to colorize.

TINTING A GRAYSCALE IMAGE

Before color photography was widely available, hand-tinting photographs was a common occurrence. Using the painting and selection
tools available in Photoshop, we can create the popular effect of hand-
tinting photographs. We examine four methods of tinting a grayscale
image in this section: using the painting tools, using selections, using
layers, and using adjustment layers. The painting tools, like the
paintbrush and airbrush, are effective tools for tinting when you want
to achieve the look of hand-tinted photographs, especially since you can
intentionally create uneven coverage of the tints by repainting areas.
The selection tools such as the Marquee, Lasso, and path tools enable
you to make precise selections of the image area and tint them evenly.
Using layers, we can paint on top of our image without committing to
the changes right away. The adjustment layers enable us to make
specific changes to our image using adjustment dialog boxes for things
such as Hue/Saturation, Brightness/Contrast, and Posterization.

Open the file "grandpa.ps4" in the Examples folder on the CD-ROM
that accompanies this book.

Tinting with the Painting Tools

1. Select Image➡Mode➡RGB Color to convert the grayscale
    image to RGB mode.

2. Double-click the Paintbrush tool to display the Paintbrush Options palette.

3. Choose Color from the Blending mode pull-down menu (see Figure 13.17).

4. Set the Opacity slider to 20%.

5. Select a foreground color; choose a bright green color for this example.

6. Paint the boy's clothing in the image with the paintbrush. Keep the mouse button down and apply the color in one application. If you let go of the mouse button and begin painting again, avoid painting over the same area because this applies another 20% of the color to the image.

7. Perform the above steps with other colors on different parts of the image.

Open the file "grandpa7.ps4" in the Examples folder on the CD-ROM that accompanies this book to see a fully colorized version of the original grayscale file.

Tinting with the Selection Tools

1. Select Image➡Mode➡RGB Color to convert the image to RGB mode.

2. Use the Lasso tool or the Magic Wand tool to select the parts of the image you want to tint (see Figure 13.18). If you use the Lasso tool, double-click the tool to display the Lasso Options palette and type in a feather radius of 2 pixels to aid in blending the tints with the image. If you use the Magic Wand tool, display the Magic Wand Options palette by double-clicking the Magic Wand tool and check the Anti-aliased checkbox in the Magic Wand Options palette.

Figure 13.18

Use the selection tools to isolate a part of the image.

3. Select a foreground color and choose Fill from the Edit menu or (Shift-Delete) [Shift-Backspace] (see Figure 13.19).

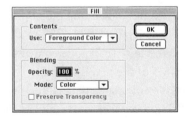

Figure 13.19

The Fill dialog box.

4. Select Foreground Color from the Use drop-down menu.

5. Select Color from the Blending Options drop-down menu in the Fill dialog box.

6. Choose an opacity percentage in the Fill dialog box and click OK.

7. Perform the preceding steps with other colors on different parts of the image.

Tinting with Layers

1. Choose New Layer from the Layers palette menu or click the New Layer Icon.

2. Use any of the preceding methods to paint this layer with 100% of the color you want to tint with (see Figure 13.20).

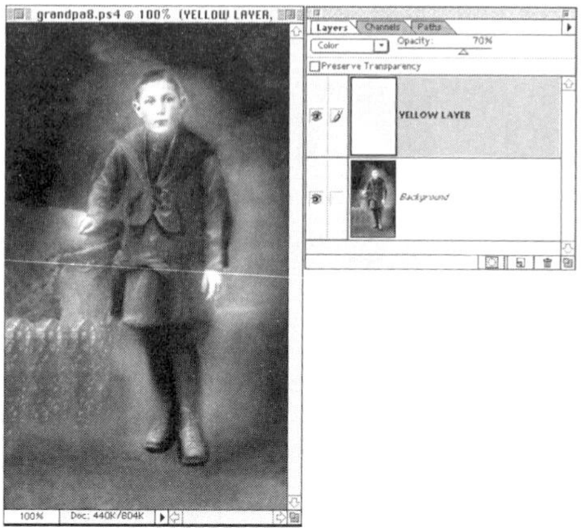

Figure 13.20

The thumbnail preview in the Layers palette displays the painting effect applied to the image.

3. Choose Color from the Blending mode pull-down menu in the Layers palette (see Figure 13.21). We're choosing the Color blending mode because this mode changes only the Hue and Saturation values of the pixels we paint to the Hue and Saturation values of the color specified as the foreground color, leaving the Brightness level (grayscale) of the image intact.

4. Set the Opacity slider at the top of the Layers palette to adjust the opacity. The opacity you choose here depends on the color you chose to paint with and how washed-out you want the color to appear.

Figure 13.21

The Blending mode pull-down menu in the Layers palette.

5. Create a new layer for each tint color.

6. Save this file in Photoshop format if you want to come back later and make adjustments or changes to the tint layers.

7. Choose Flatten Image from the Layers palette menu before saving the image in a format that can be used in a page layout application.

Tip

When you're working in a Photoshop format file containing layers, you can choose Save a Copy from the File menu and click the Flatten Image checkbox. This way you can continue to work on the image with the layers intact.

Figure 13.22

Choosing Save a Copy from the File menu enables you to flatten the image while saving.

Open the file "grandpa8.ps4" in the Examples folder on the CD-ROM that accompanies this book to see the above example completed.

Tinting with Adjustment Layers

1. Use any of the selection tools to make a selection within the image.

2. We are going to posterize the grayscale image in this exercise to 16 distinct gray levels and then color each of the levels to achieve a special effect. Display the Layers palette and create a new adjustment layer by choosing New Adjustment Layer… from the Layers palette menu or (Command-click)[Control-click] the New Layer Icon. Choose Posterize from the Type drop-down menu in the New Adjustment Layer dialog box (see Figure 13.23), click OK, then select 16 Levels. Click OK. Note that the adjustment layer's mask thumbnail represents the selection made (see Figure 13.24).

Figure 13.23

The New Adjustment Layer dialog box

Figure 13.24

When you have a selection made before creating an adjustment layer, the adjustments apply only to the selected area.

3. In addition to the change we made to the image using the adjustment layer, we also change the color of our image using the Variations dialog box. Select the Background layer in the Layers palette.

4. Make a selection in the image using any of the selection tools.

5. Choose Image➡Adjust➡Variations to display the Variations dialog box (see Figure 13.25).

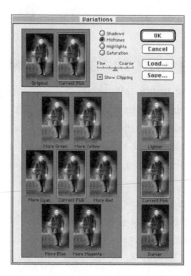

Figure 13.25

The Variations dialog box.

6. Click the Midtones radio button in the Variations dialog box. Changes made only to the midtone areas of the image keep the changes from looking too fake.

7. Select a setting between Coarse and Fine by dragging the slider at the top of the Variations dialog box. Coarse makes a greater color change than selecting Fine. Start off near Coarse to get closer to the color you're aiming for, then set the slider closer to Fine to fine-tune the color change.

8. Add hues to the image by clicking the picture thumbnails labeled "More." Choosing the Lighter or Darker options can cause the color change to look unreal, so use them sparingly with a Fine setting.

9. To further adjust the hue and saturation of the selection you just colorized with the Variations dialog box, keep the part of the image you want to change selected. Create a new Adjustment Layer and choose Hue/Saturation from the Adjust Layer Type dialog box.

10. Make further adjustments to the hue of the selected area by using the Hue and Saturation sliders in the Hue/Saturation Layer dialog box. Experiment with different settings using the adjustment layers and Hue/Saturation Layer dialog box.

APPLYING COLOR WITH THE BLENDING MODES

Using the blending modes available in Photoshop, we can selectively paint-in color changes in our images. Chapter 11, "Color Correction," deals specifically with making color adjustments to make the file match the original. The following examples look at a few methods to change the colors of parts of images. All of the blending options perform some type of calculation between the pixels of the image and the color used to paint these pixels. In some cases the pixels are lightened or darkened depending on the blending mode selected. Each blending mode illustrated below is described at the start of the section. Refer to Chapter 6, "Painting," and Chapter 8, "Channels" for more information about the Blending Options.

When you use the blending modes in the Layers palette, you can paint on layers with flat color and use the blending modes to apply the color to the image. In the following examples, we use the blending modes in the Layers palette rather than the blending modes in the Paintbrush palette to modify our image. A blending mode of Normal is equivalent to having no blending mode, so we keep the blending mode for the Paintbrush palette set to Normal because we want to affect the way the layers blend with the image. Using the file called "steve.ps4," follow these steps to sample some of the effects:

 Open the RGB file "steve.ps4" in the Examples folder on the CD-ROM that accompanies this book in the following section.

Open the RGB file "steve2.ps4" in the Examples folder of the CD-ROM that accompanies this book to open the completed image and follow along.

Blending with Hue

The Hue blending mode preserves the luminance and saturation of the image pixels and changes only the hue (color) of the pixels to the hue of the selected foreground color. Even though we're specifying colors in RGB because we're working in RGB mode, the color we specify has corresponding Hue, Saturation, and Brightness (luminance) values. When you choose an RGB color from the Photoshop Color Picker by typing in the Red, Green, and Blue values, the corresponding Hue, Saturation, and Brightness values are adjusted as well. In this section we are going to paint over the face with a light brown color and change only the Hue values of the image so the detail isn't lost.

1. Create a new layer by clicking the New Layer icon in the Layers palette (the turned up page icon in the lower-right corner of the Layers palette) or Choose New Layer from the Layers palette menu. Double-click the new layer you created and name the layer "Face" (see Figure 13.26). We are going to use this layer to make changes to the skin tone of the face.

Figure 13.26

The Face Layer in the Layers palette.

2. Double-click the Paintbrush tool to display the Paintbrush Options palette.

3. Choose Normal from the Blending modes pull-down menu in the Paintbrush palette and set the Opacity to 44% (see Figure 13.27).

Figure 13.27

The Paintbrush Options palette.

4. Select a medium-sized paintbrush with a soft edge from the Brushes palette. We'll be using this brush to paint the color change over the face, so choose a brush that is in the middle row somewhere (see Figure 13.28).

Figure 13.28

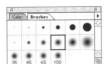

The Brushes palette.

5. Create a foreground color that is brown using the RGB values: 78 Red, 54 Green, and 12 Blue (see Figure 13.29).

Figure 13.29

Choose Show Color from the Window menu to display the Colors palette.

6. Make sure the Face layer is selected in the Layers palette.

7. Paint over the face of the subject in the photo, covering all the skin tones. Try not to paint the same sections again when you let go of the mouse button because this adds additional color to the image. See Figure 13.30.

8. Our objective here is to change the skin tone to a darker color (give this guy a tan). Choose Hue from the Blending modes drop-down menu in the Layers palette to change the hue values of the pixels in the face only (see Figure 13.31). Click the Eye icon next to the Face layer to toggle a before and after preview.

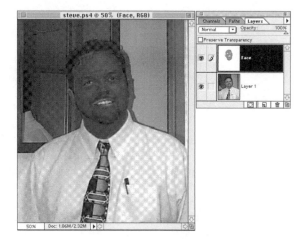

Figure 13.30

Paint on the Face layer with the brown color.

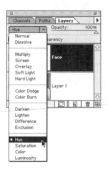

Figure 13.31

Choose Hue from the blending options drop-down menu in the Layers palette.

Blending with Color Burn

The Color Burn blending mode looks at the color information for each of the image's color channels (in this exercise, the Red, Green, and Blue channels) and darkens the pixels to reflect the color you are blending with. The Color Burn mode has no effect on white pixels.

1. Create a new layer by clicking the New Layer icon in the Layers palette (the turned up page icon in the lower-right corner of the Layers palette) or choose New Layer from the Layers palette menu. Double-click the new layer you created and name the layer "Shirt" (see Figure 13.32). We are going to use this layer to colorize the shirt of the subject in the photograph.

Figure 13.32

The Shirt layer in the Layers palette.

2. Double-click the Paintbrush tool to display the Paintbrush Options palette.

3. Choose Normal from the Blending modes pull-down menu and set the Opacity to 44%.

4. Select a medium-sized paintbrush with a soft edge from the Brushes palette.

5. We are going to paint the shirt blue, so create a foreground color that is: 0 Red, 110 Green, and 159 Blue (see Figure 13.33).

Figure 13.33

The Color palette.

6. Make sure the Shirt layer is selected in the Layers palette.

7. Paint over the shirt area of the subject in the photo (see Figure 13.34). Try not to paint the same sections again when you let go of the mouse button because this adds additional color to the image.

8. Choose Color Burn from the Blending modes pull-down menu in the Layers palette (see Figure 13.35). Note that this blending mode does not affect the white pixels and creates an effect similar to overexposing the painted areas. For a more realistic look, change the blending mode to Color in the Layers palette.

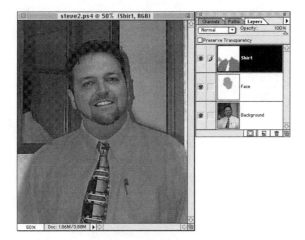

Figure 13.34

Paint on the Shirt layer with the Blue color.

Figure 13.35

Choose Color Burn as the Blending Mode from the pull-down menu.

Blending with Overlay

The Overlay blending mode multiplies the selected color with the image pixels to create a new color. The highlights and shadows are not affected by this blending mode, so the resulting image contains varying degrees of the painting color depending on the color of the image pixels.

1. Create a new layer by clicking the New Layer icon in the Layers palette and name it "Tie" (see Figure 13.36).

Figure 13.36

The Tie layer in the Layers palette

2. Double-click the Paintbrush tool to display the Paintbrush Options palette.

3. Choose Normal from the Blending modes pull-down menu and set the Opacity to 100%.

4. Select a smallish paintbrush with a soft edge from the Brushes palette (see Figure 13.37).

Figure 13.37

The Brushes palette.

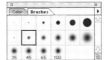

5. Create a foreground color that is dark blue by specifying these RGB values: 0 Red, 132 Green, and 188 Blue (see Figure 13.38).

Figure 13.38

The Color palette.

6. Make sure the Tie layer is selected in the Layers palette.

7. Paint over the tie of the subject in the photo, covering all the areas, even the white areas (see Figure 13.39). Try not to paint the same sections again when you let go of the mouse button because this adds additional color to the image.

Figure 13.39

Paint on the Tie layer with the blue color.

8. Choose Overlay from the Blending modes drop-down menu in the Layers palette (see Figure 13.40).

Figure 13.40

Choose the Overlay blending mode from the drop-down menu in the Layers palette.

Blending with Soft Light

The Soft Light blending mode darkens or lightens the image based on the color being used. A lighter color with a gray value less than 50% lightens the image, creating a dodged effect with the Foreground color. A darker color with a gray value greater than 50% darkens the image, creating a burn effect. In the following example, we change the color of the wall and woodwork on the right side of the photo. Because the wall has gray values less than 50% and the woodwork has gray values greater than 50%, the contrast between the two is accentuated with this option.

1. Create a new layer by clicking the New Layer icon in the Layers palette and name it "Walls" (see Figure 13.41).

Figure 13.41

The Walls layer in the Layers palette.

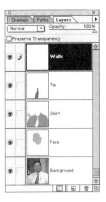

2. Double-click the Airbrush tool to display the Airbrush Options palette.

3. Choose Normal from the Blending modes drop-down menu and set Pressure to 40%.

4. Select a medium-sized brush with a soft edge from the Brushes palette.

5. Create a foreground color that is: 255 Red, 238 Green, and 129 Blue (see Figure 13.42).

Figure 13.42

The Color palette.

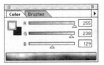

6. Make sure the Walls layer is selected in the Layers palette.

7. Paint the walls in the photograph (don't worry about the walls in the mirror's reflection unless you're feeling particularly ambitious) (see Figure 13.43).

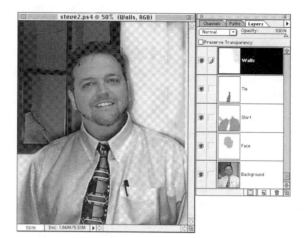

Figure 13.43

Paint the Walls layer with the yellow color.

8. Choose Soft Light from the Blending modes pull-down menu in the Layers palette (see Figure 13.44).

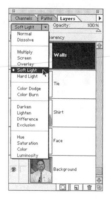

Figure 13.44

Choose the Soft Light blending mode from the drop-down menu in the Layers palette.

Blending with Multiply

The Multiply blending mode multiplies the color values of the image and the color you are painting with to arrive at a darker complementary color. Painting over the same area multiple times creates successively darker colors, whereas painting on white yields no results and painting on black results in black.

1. Create a new layer by clicking the New Layer icon in the Layers palette and name it "Window" (see Figure 13.45).

Figure 13.45

Figure 13.45

The Window layer in the Layers palette

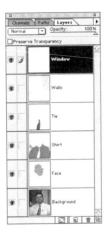

2. Double-click the Airbrush tool to display the Airbrush Options palette.

3. Choose Normal from the Blending modes pull-down menu and set Pressure to 100% (see Figure 13.46).

Figure 13.46

The Airbrush Options palette.

4. Select a small-sized brush with a soft edge from the Brushes palette.

5. Create a foreground color that is green by setting these RGB values: 50 Red, 125 Green, and 24 Blue (see Figure 13.47).

Figure 13.47

The Color palette.

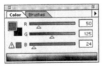

6. Make sure the Window layer is selected in the Layers palette.

7. Paint over the window frame in the photo (see Figure 13.48).

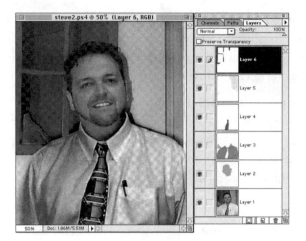

Figure 13.48

Paint on the Window layer with the green color.

8. Choose Multiply from the Blending modes pull-down menu in the Layers palette (see Figure 13.49).

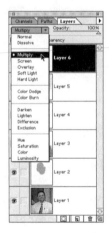

Figure 13.49

Choose Multiply from the blending modes drop-down menu in the Layers palette.

POSTERIZING IMAGES

With the Posterize command you can specify the number of gray levels contained in your image. Posterizing maps all of the grays in your image to the closest gray level depending on what number of grays (how many levels) you indicate. Posterizing works best in grayscale images, though you can come up with some pretty neat stuff in color modes as well. For this exercise, we are going to take a grayscale file, posterize it to 8 levels, and then colorize the individual levels. This technique is used by screen printers to generate multiple plates for screen printing (usually 10 or more colors), and you can use it to generate color plates for screen printing or to create a painting effect.

Open a grayscale image. I'm using the file called "Hands" included as one of the sample files with Photoshop. If you installed the sample files on your hard drive, the file should be located in the Samples folder in the Adobe Photoshop folder (Macintosh); in the samples directory within the Photoshp [sic] directory.

1. Open any grayscale image.

2. Choose Image➡Adjust➡Posterize to display the Posterize dialog box (see Figure 13.50).

3. Type 8 into the Levels box in the Posterize dialog box.

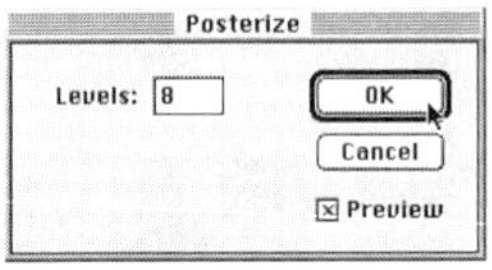

Figure 13.50

The Posterize dialog box.

4. Double-click the Magic Wand tool to display the Magic Wand Options palette.

5. Set the Tolerance to 0 and be sure that Anti-aliased is turned off (see Figure 13.51). We are setting the tolerance to zero because we want to limit the Magic Wand tool's selection to just one gray level. Anti-aliased is turned off because it expands the selection area to include near gray levels, and we want only a single gray level to be selected.

Figure 13.51

The Magic Wand Options palette.

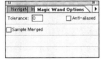

Note

The Eyedropper Options palette contains a setting that controls the area selected when clicking the image. Double-click the Eyedropper tool in the Tool palette and set the Sample Size to "Point Sample" for this exercise. When the Sample Size is set to "Point Sample," clicking the image samples only the data from the single pixel you click. In the case of the Eyedropper tool, the color of a single pixel is sampled. This setting also controls how other tools, such as the Magic Wand and Paintbucket, work. We are setting this option in the Eyedropper Options palette to control how the Magic Wand selects pixel data. If you leave the sample size set to 3×3 average, when you zoom in close and click a pixel that has surrounding pixels with different gray values, the Magic Wand creates a selection that is the average of a 3×3 pixel area. We want to be able to select one gray level at a time with the Magic Wand tool, so setting this value to Point Sample ensures this.

6. Choose Show Layers on the Window menu to bring up the Layers Options palette.

7. Find the darkest (blackest) area on your image and click it with the Magic Wand tool. You may have to zoom in close to see the gray level breakdown (see Figure 13.52).

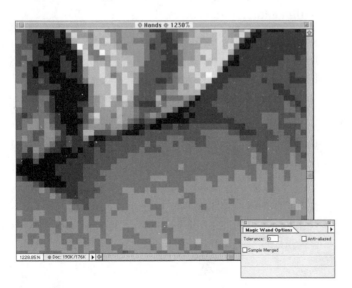

Figure 13.52

Zoom in close to see the individual gray levels.

8. Choose Similar on the Select menu; this selects all of the other pixels in the image with the same values as those selected with the Magic Wand tool.

9. Create a new Layer by clicking the new layer icon at the bottom of the Layers palette and name this layer "Gray 1."

10. Be sure the Gray 1 layer is selected in the Layers palette.

11. Type the letter "D" to set the foreground and background colors to the default black and white respectively.

12. Press (Option-Delete)[Alt-Backspace] to fill the selected area with the foreground color (black). The "Gray 1" layer now contains a solid black area that is representative of the darkest gray in the image.

13. Select the Background layer in the Layers palette. Click the next-darkest level in your image with the Magic Wand tool.

14. Choose Similar from the Select menu.

15. Create a new Layer by clicking the new layer icon at the bottom of the Layers palette and name this layer "Gray 2."

16. Be sure the Gray 2 layer is selected in the Layers palette.

17. Press (Option-Delete)[Alt-Backspace] to fill the selected area with the foreground color (black).

18. Perform Steps 12 through 16 until you have created separate layers for each of the 8 gray levels (see Figure 13.53). Remember to select the Background layer before using the Magic Wand to select similar pixels before making the new layers.

19. After you have 8 layers, plus the background layer, select the background layer in the Layers palette and choose All on the Select menu.

20. Press Delete to fill your selection with the background color (white). You may also opt to keep the background as is and simply make it invisible by clicking the Eye icon next to the layer name in the Layers palette.

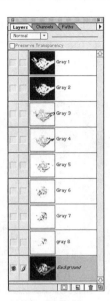

Figure 13.53

You should have eight new layers, plus the Background layer.

21. Convert the Grayscale image to a color mode such as RGB or CMYK. Note that when you convert from grayscale to RGB or CMYK, you are asked whether you want to flatten the image. Click the **Don't Flatten** button to preserve the layers we created in the previous steps. This would also be a good time to save your file in Photoshop format so you won't have to recreate all the layers due to a crash or mistake.

22. Choose the Gray 1 layer and check the Preserve Transparency checkbox at the top of the Layers palette.

23. Choose a new foreground color (your choice).

24. Make sure the Gray 1 layer is selected and press (Option-Delete)[Alt-Backspace] to fill the non-transparent areas with the foreground color.

25. Perform Steps 21 through 24 for each of the 8 new layers. Experiment with the blending modes in the Layers palette.

26. Be sure to save the file in Photoshop format so you can make changes in the future. Flatten the image when you have a version you want to use by choosing Flatten Image from the Layers palette menu.

Open the Photoshop file "hands2.ps4" in the Examples folder on the CD-ROM that accompanies this book to view the completed posterizing example detailed above (see Figure 13.54).

Figure 13.54

The posterized image after it is colorized using layers.

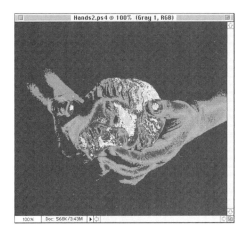

Printing the Individual Layers

You may want to print the individual layers to create separated films for screen printing or in some cases offset printing. It is somewhat of a time consuming task, but you can make it simpler by using the new Actions palette in Adobe Photoshop 4. Perform the following steps to save the layers into separate grayscale files:

1. Select each layer and fill the non-transparent areas with solid black before continuing. Follow the preceding steps for filling with a color to fill the color data in the layers with black. Remember, we're going to be printing each layer with a solid ink color on press.

2. Select the Gray1 layer in the Layers palette.

3. Choose Show Actions from the Window menu to display the Actions palette (see Figure 13.55).

Figure 13.55

The Actions Palette.

4. Click on the triangle in the upper-right corner of the Actions palette to display the Actions palette menu (see Figure 13.56) and choose New Action to display the New Action dialog box (see Figure 13.57).

Note

If the New Action option is not available in the Actions palette menu (grayed out), be sure that Button Mode is not selected in the Actions palette menu. If it is selected, choose it to deactivate button mode.

Figure 13.56

The Actions palette menu.

5. Type a name for your action such as "Layers to Grayscale" and assign a function key if you like.

Figure 13.57

The New Action dialog box.

6. Click on the Record button to begin recording the actions you want to assign to an action button.

7. Choose All from the Select menu or type ((Command-A) [Control-A]).

8. Choose Copy from the Edit menu or type ((Command-C) [Control-C]).

9. Choose New from the File menu to display the New dialog box

10. Type a name for the file that is representative of the color the file is to be printed in and change the Mode to Grayscale by selecting it from the Mode drop-down menu. Click OK.

11. Choose Paste from the Edit menu or type ((Command-V) [Control-V]).

12. Choose Stop Recording from the Actions palette menu.

13. Choose Save from the File menu to save the file in the desired format.

14. Close the new Grayscale image by choosing Close from the File menu or by typing ((Command-W)[Control-W]).

15. Select the next layer in the layers palette.

16. Choose Button Mode from the Actions palette menu to display the new action as a button in the palette.

17. Click on the Button in the Actions palette to save the layers in a grayscale file or type the Function key if you assigned one.

18. Perform steps 15 through 17 for each of the layers until all are saved to separate grayscale files. Remember to save each of the files with a new name before closing the grayscale file.

Now you know the basic techniques for colorizing imagery in Adobe Photoshop. As you learn more about Photoshop, you will encounter a multitude of ways to apply what you learned in this chapter. There are no hard and fast rules about which technique to use for a given circumstance because the task can probably be accomplished in a variety of ways. The best advice I can give you here is to think the project through before beginning so you can choose the shortest and most productive path.

Chapter 14

USING PHOTOSHOP'S FILTERS

Filters are one of Photoshop's most versatile tools, enabling the user to edit an image with an astounding range of effects, a range that goes from Accented Edges all the way to Zigzag. And they're all covered in this chapter. The filters in this chapter are organized by type: The Artistic filters are grouped together, the Blur filters are grouped together, etc. To make things easier, if you're not sure what category to look under for a filter you're interested in, the following page has a table of contents listing each filter and the page it is on. Enjoy!

USING FILTERS—A GENERAL APPROACH

Photoshop uses filters to change image data in a variety of ways. Instead of using the Blur tool, for example, on a large portion of your image, you can use one of the Blur filters and change all of the pixels in your selection at one time. You can alter the lighting in your image by using the Lighting Effects filter. You can add tiny bits of random color to your image using the Add Noise filter...You get the idea!

There are ninety-seven filters in Photoshop 4.0. While some are more useful than others, this chapter describes them all. You really need to work with them, however, to discover their full potential. Filters are one area where "playing by the rules" is not always the best idea. Although each filter has something it was designed to do "best," your most creative uses often occur when you use the filter "wrong."

Tip

Take the time to play and experiment with the filters. Then put comments about how you created the effect you like in the Caption field of the File➡File Info command. These comments stay with your image to help you remember what you did.

Principles of Filter Use

No one can give you "rules" for using filters. The "filter police" are not going to shut down your business if you violate one. Nevertheless, there are more effective—or less effective—ways to approach the use of filters. Here's a list of suggestions:

◆ **Know your filters.** Play with them enough to get a good sense of what they can do. You will find that you have a number of "favorites."

◆ **Master a new filter every week** (That will take you close to two years!). Experiment with a new filter first using the default settings. Next, try setting the controls to the lowest and then the highest settings. See what the middle settings will do. If there are multiple controls, drag one high and one low. Reverse the settings. See how the results change. Instead of using the Undo command, work on a relatively small image and keep copying the original. This lets you compare the results. Make note of any settings you really like.

◆ **Apply a Filter to a Layer**. Before you apply a filter, place your selection on a layer and apply the filter to that layer. This enables you to blend the filter into the image if you do not want it at full strength, or change the Blending mode. It also enables you to change your mind at any point in your design process.

◆ **Experiment with the Fade... command** (even if you have applied a filter to a Layer). The Filter➡Fade command is new in Photoshop 4.0. It enables you to keep only a percentage of the filter you applied and to change the Blending mode as well. This is a wonderful new feature! It does everything for you that filtering a layer does except that after you are done, you are done. You cannot change your mind past the original Undo.

◆ **Filter in a single channel for a special effect**. Some filters (any filter that works on a grayscale image) can be applied to a single channel at a time. You can get some very interesting effects by applying a filter to only the green channel, for example.

◆ **Filter an alpha channel and use that channel as a selection mask**. You can get some really exciting results by applying a filter to data in an alpha channel (a grayscale version of your image, perhaps). Then, use that channel as a selection and apply another filter to the whole image through that selection. The Crystallize filter is especially effective for this technique.

◆ **Misuse the filters**. See what happens when you break the rules. You can get wonderful special effects—sometimes—when you apply a filter using what might otherwise be inappropriate settings (a too large Unsharp Mask setting or a Dust & Scratches Setting that smoothes the image much too much for color correction).

◆ **Think "multiple applications."** Another good special effects technique is to reapply the same filter to the same selection a few times. This is particularly good with One-Step filters (see discussion on categories). It can, however, work with many of the filters. You can also try re-filtering the selection with the same filter, different settings, or a completely different filter.

◆ **Make the filter effect your own.** This one is just my Puritan work ethic showing! I almost feel as if using a single-effect filter, such as the Colored Pencil filter (or most of the old Gallery Effects filters) is cheating. To just filter an image and say "OK, now it's art," is not only inaccurate, it doesn't seem right. And if it is art, it isn't your art. You can make it your own by changing Blending modes, adding your own textures, and combining effects. Of course, if you are on a tight deadline and the canned effect is just what you want, use it. That's what it is there for. But you will grow artistically if you find a way to incorporate the filters into your own style rather than just letting the filter be the artistic statement for you.

◆ **Use a little restraint.** Some filters are very distinctive and a little goes a long way. Especially with filters that were part of the original Adobe Gallery Effects collection (Artistic, Brush Strokes, Sketch, Texture), you need to make sure that they do not fight with one another visually in the filtered image. An over-filtered image is like a sampler. Samplers were wonderful devices for teaching needlework, but they were rarely good art. Don't use "one-of-each" just because you can. Let the filter support the artistic purpose of the image.

FADING A FILTER

After you apply a filter, a new menu item is enabled near the top of the Filter menu: Fade... This item enables you to incrementally "un-apply" the last filter used to the image—or to change the blending mode. This is a very powerful command.

In Photoshop 3, you could duplicate your image into a new layer and then filter the new layer. If you were not happy with the results, you could either throw the whole layer away or cut its opacity to mix it with the unfiltered layer beneath. You could also change the blending mode for the layer to change the result of the filter. In 4.0 you still can. The Fade command, however, which is new to Photoshop 4.0, can do exactly the same thing without the added overhead in RAM and file size. The only thing you lose is the ability to change the image later in the design process.

Try it.

1. Open the image "FallFlwr.Psd."

2. Apply the Glowing Edges filter by selecting Filter➡Stylize ➡Glowing Edges using the settings in Figure 14.1.

Figure 14.1

The Glowing Edges dialog box.

3. Select the Fade... command (Filter➡Fade Glowing Edges). The dialog box shown in Figure 14.2 appears. Set the Opacity of the filter to 70% and change the Blending mode to Hard Light.

Figure 14.2

The Fade Glowing Edges dialog box.

4. Click OK. Figure 14.3 shows the final, faded image.

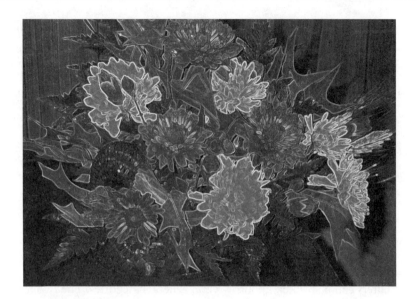

Figure 14.3

The faded Glowing Edges filtered image.

Interpreting the Chart

At the end of each filter description is a chart summarizing the main characteristics of that filter. Here's a brief explanation of each category.

Filter type	Category	Supported Color Modes	Preview type	Data Dependent	Color Dependent
Parameter	Stylizing Filter	RGB, Grayscale	Small Filter Preview	Yes. A blank image produces a blank filtered image.	Yes. Background colors is the "brightness" color.

Filter Type

There are three main types of filters.

- ◆ A **One-Step filter** applies the filter with no user control. The Blur filter, for example, softens the pixels in an image so that the color in each pixel becomes a little bit closer to the color of the pixels nearest to it. You cannot specify *how* soft you want the pixel to be. You select the filter name from the menu, the filter does whatever it does, and you are done. You can apply it multiple times, but you cannot change the amount by which it filters the image. These filters can be spotted in the Filter menu because they do not have ellipses (...) after their names.

♦ A **parameter filter** gives you choices. You need to set sliders or controls to specify what the filter will do. Most of the native filters that come with Photoshop are of this variety.

♦ A **mini-application filter** is a filter that enables you to save and recall settings and creates its own environment inside of Photoshop. Many third-party filters (ones not created by Adobe and which you need to purchase separately) are mini-apps; none of the Photoshop native filters are.

Category

Filters can be broken up into several general categories. The two most basic ones are Production and Special Effects. A production-oriented filter is used for color correction or focus correction to help prepare an image for print. A special effects filter changes the image in a non-realistic way. The categories are further broken down in this part of the chart as follows:

♦ Pre-Press—Filter is used to help prepare an image for printing.

♦ Special Effects—Purpose is to change the image for an artistic, rather than realistic, purpose.

♦ Color Change—Filter alters the color values in an image.

♦ Deformation—Filter alters the geometry of the image by bending, warping, stretching, or otherwise misshaping it.

♦ Displacement—Uses another image or a built-in algorithm as a map to control the distortion of the original image. Makes the image look as if it is being viewed through some type of other surface, such as water or glass.

♦ Destructive—Filter replaces the image with its own effect; original image does not affect the filter results.

♦ Distressed—original image alters the effect of the filter, but the filtered image is not readily recognizable.

- Focus—Filter alters the focus of the image, making it either sharper or softer in some manner.

- Stylizing—Filter creates a slightly abstract and stylized version of the original

- Texture—Filter creates surface interest

- 3D—Filter appears to create a third dimension in the image

A filter can belong to more than one category. The "Special Effects" and "Pre-press" categories are intentions (as in *why* you want to filter the image) rather than results. They are likely to be used in combination with other categories on the charts.

Supported Color Modes

A filter may work on RGB, Grayscale, CMYK, or Lab colors modes—or only in some of them. This place on the chart tells you which color modes work for a specific filter. Images in Bitmap or Indexed Color modes cannot be filtered at all.

Preview Type

It is always helpful to be able to see the effect of a filter before you add it to your image. This is particularly important when you are using a parameter filter, because it helps you to select the desired settings and shortens the time it takes to "get it right." Many of Photoshop's filters have preview—areas in the filter dialog itself that allow you to see what will happen when you apply the filter. None of the One-Step filters have previews. There are a few different types of filter previews:

- None: the filter has no preview.

- Small Filter Preview: There is a small area in the dialog box that shows a tiny section of your image with the filter applied.

- Full Image Preview: in addition to the small box, you can see the results on your original image. Both the small preview and your image are updated as you change the parameter settings.

- WireFrame Preview: a schematic shows the deformation path that will be used to filter the image. You do not see any image data or color at all.

Data Dependent

This is a "Yes/No" category on the chart. A filter that is data dependent ("Yes"), needs something other than a blank image in which to work. Filtering a blank (solid colored) image with a data dependent filter will cause no change to the image. A data-independent filter ("No") will produce a result of some kind even if the image is totally blank. Some of the data-independent filters only work if the image is not white; the Clouds filter is the only filter that will produce results on a totally transparent (empty) Layer. Every other filter must at least have pixels on which to work (and will give you an error if you try to apply it to a transparent Layer).

Color Dependent

This is another "Yes/No" category. A "No" means that it does not matter what colors you have selected in the Toolbox as your Foreground or Background colors. A "Yes" means that the filter uses either the Foreground or Background color or both as part of the effect. Changing the color changes the effect of the filter.

The Filter Menu

Photoshop's native filters appear on the Filters menu in thirteen categories. Let's discuss them in the order in which they appear:

- ◆ Artistic
- ◆ Blur
- ◆ Brush Strokes
- ◆ Distort
- ◆ Noise
- ◆ Pixelate
- ◆ Render
- ◆ Sharpen
- ◆ Sketch
- ◆ Stylize

- ◆ Texture
- ◆ Video
- ◆ Other

PHOTOSHOP'S NATIVE FILTERS—ARTISTIC

The fifteen filters in the Artistic category are new to Photoshop 4.0. They were part of the three Aldus (later—Adobe) Gallery Effects series of third-party plug-ins. They have been added to Photoshop's native filter list for the first time.

These filters are used to apply a specific "art style" to your image. While they can be used in conjunction with other filters or on a selection, they make strong enough statements individually that they are hard to combine. Use these filters on an entire image for the best "intended" results.

The filters in this category can filter images that are in RGB or Grayscale modes only. They do not work on images in CMYK or Lab colorspace. In addition, none of them will work on an empty Layer. They are all parameter filters—that is, they have specific parameters (controls) that you can set for different results. All of the filters in this category have small previews in the filter dialog box, but none of them use a full-image preview.

Colored Pencil

The Colored Pencil filter takes an image or selection and stylizes it to resemble, supposedly, colored pencils on neutral (black-to-white) paper stock. In reality, the filter uses the predominant colors in the image and removes areas that it changes to the "paper color" depending upon the parameter settings. This filter leaves a type of cross-hatching that is attractive but not especially reminiscent of Pencil strokes. If anything, it almost looks like oil paints applied with a palette knife and feathered at the edges.

Try it:

1. Open the image "Fallflwr.Psd." Duplicate the image
   (Image➡Duplicate➡OK).

2. Open the Colored Pencil dialog box (Filter➡Artistic➡Colored
   Pencil) (see Figure 14.4).

Figure 14.4

Colored Pencil dialog box.

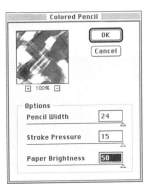

3. Drag the Pencil Width to 24.

   The Pencil Width setting varies from 1-24. This parameter
   controls the size of the background color that shows through
   the image. At 1 the image is almost solid, and scratches of the
   background color show through. At 24 the image is broken up
   into roughly equal areas of original image and background
   color. It is as if the Pencil color used is actually the "paper"
   color setting, and you specify *its* width using the Pencil Width
   setting. You can set the slider anywhere along the length,
   though your detail will reproduce better on a large image (one
   with a high dpi setting and large number of pixels) if you use a
   slightly higher Pencil Width setting (above 3 at least).

4. Set the Stroke Pressure to 15.

   The Stroke Pressure can vary from 0 to 15. This parameter
   controls the intensity of the color in the image. When Stroke
   Pressure is 0, no image is produced—regardless of the other
   settings. When it is at 15, the original brightness of the image is
   preserved. A Stroke Pressure of 1 shows some color in the

brightest areas of the original image and no color at all in the darkest areas of the original.

5. Finally, set the Paper Brightness to 50.

   The Paper Brightness varies from 0-50. A brightness of 0 makes the "paper color" black, and a brightness of 50 makes it whatever color is set in your Background color in the Toolbox. A Paper Brightness of 25 is a mixture between the two. If your Background color is white, my advice is to use a Brightness of either 0 or 50, as the in-between settings tend to muddy up the image.

6. Click OK. Figure 14.5 shows the result, which could be suitable for a Thanksgiving greeting card.

Figure 14.5

The Colored Pencil filter applied.

Filter type	Category	Supported Color Modes	Preview type	Data Dependent	Color Dependent
Parameter	Stylizing Filter	RGB, Grayscale	Small Filter Preview	Yes. A blank image produces a blank filtered image.	Yes. Background colors is the "brightness" color.

Cutout

The Cutout filter, an enhancement of the Posterize command, simplifies the colors of your image into the number of levels that you request. But the Cutout filter uses colors from the original image—rather than colorspace "primitives" (RGB or CMYK) as does the Posterize command. It is a "smart" filter in that it looks for shapes to simplify, and it creates anti-aliased edges where the colors meet. The Cutout filter is computationally intensive and the preview is very slow. The filter, however, delivers a look that ranges from so-abstract-that-you-can't-figure-out-what-it-is (at 2 Levels, Edge Simplicty of 0, Edge Fidelity of 1), to a paint-by-numbers look (at 8 Levels, Edge Simplicty of 0, and Edge Fidelity of 3). You get the most detailed results from this filter by using a high contrast image as your original. In certain limited situations, the Cutout filter could be helpful in trying to make a mask.

Try it:

1. Open the image "FallFlwr.Psd." Duplicate the image (Image➡Duplicate➡OK).

2. Open the Cutout dialog box (Filter➡Artistic➡Cutout) to see the dialog box shown in Figure 14.6.

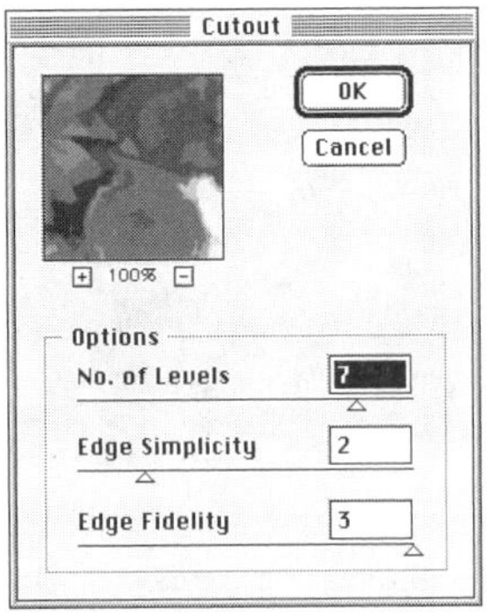

Figure 14.6

The Cutout dialog box.

3. Drag the Number of Levels to 7.

The Number of Levels setting varies from 2 to 8. This parameter controls the number of colors in the filtered image. At its lowest setting, the parameter finds two levels in the original image. This still translates into a significant number of colors, however, though it greatly simplifies the image.

4. Set the Edge Simplicity to 3.

   The Edge Simplicity varies from 0 to 10. At the higher settings, the edges are so "simple" that there are none; the filter produces a solid colored block. The best settings for this parameter seem to be from 0 (the highest detail in the edge) to about 5.

5. Finally, set the Edge Fidelity to 2.

   The Edge Fidelity can vary from 1 to 3. This parameter does not seem to affect the image if the Edge Simplicty is set to 0. If, however, the Edge Simplicty is set to 5, you see a big difference in the edges of the shapes by varying the Edge Fidelity slider. A setting of 1 produces the most abstract edge (similar to selecting a loose autotrace setting in a vector program). A setting of 3 tries to capture the actual edge of the area as best it can.

6. Click OK. Figure 14.7 shows the result.

Figure 14.7

An example of the Cutout filter applied.

Filter type	Category	Supported Color Modes	Preview type	Data Dependent	Color Dependent
Parameter	Stylizing Filter	RGB, Grayscale	Small Filter Preview	Yes. A blank image produces a blank filtered image.	No. The Foreground/ Background settings have no effect.

Dry Brush

This is one of the rare filters that seems to produce good results at every setting—although what you get varies widely. I like this filter a lot. It imitates the traditional dry brush technique of dragging a loaded Paintbrush until it runs out of paint. The edges then fracture and fray across the canvas. In this electronic version, that means the edges are aliased and hard, though the internal shading still retains the variations and soft shading.

There are no settings in this filter that produce a blank image. With the settings of Brush Size = 0, Image Detail = 0, and Texture = 1, you get an almost lace-like effect with aliasing at all of the edges in the image. Change the Image Detail to 10 and you get a softly abstracted oil painting that is close in detail to the original but different in "feeling," as it is no longer photographic. If the settings are Brush Size = 10, Image Detail = 10, and Texture = 3, you get a very chunky oil painting that looks like it was done by patting down various colors.

Try it:

1. Open the image "FallFlwr.Psd." Duplicate the image (Image➥Duplicate➥OK).

2. Open the Dry Brush dialog box shown in Figure 14.8 (Filter➥Artistic➥Dry Brush).

3. Drag the Brush Size to 2.

    The Brush Size varies from 0 to 10. It controls the size of the strokes, with 10 as the largest.

Figure 14.8

The Dry Brush dialog box.

4. Set the Brush Detail to 8.

   The Brush Detail can vary from 0 to 10. It determines how much detail will be captured from the original image. A setting of 10 captures the most detail.

5. Finally, set the Texture to 1. The Texture setting varies from 1 to 3. A setting of 1 produces a smooth image. A setting of 3 produces an image that contains bits of color that were not in that location in the original image. It adds flecks of pixels to the image.

6. Click OK. Figure 14.9 shows the result.

Figure 14.9

An example of the Dry Brush filter applied to an image.

Filter type	Category	Supported Color Modes	Preview type	Data Dependent	Color Dependent
Parameter	Stylizing Filter	RGB, Grayscale	Small Filter Preview	Yes. A blank image produces a blank filtered image.	No. The Foreground/ Background settings have no effect.

Film Grain

The Film Grain filter is a Noise filter combined with logic to lighten and intensify parts of the image. The Add Noise filter can obliterate an image with noise. This filter, even at its highest setting, does not. In addition, the Film Grain filter enables you to specify a highlight and intensity amount that adds more noise to the darker areas of the image than to the highlighted areas. This filter looks good when used on text, but I don't find this an especially attractive special effects filter. You might want to use it for pre-press where you would use the Add Noise filter.

At the lowest settings, the Film Grain filter does nothing. The filter seems to flatten the colors in the image—the higher the Grain setting, the flatter the colors get.

Try it:

1. Open the image "FallFlwr.Psd." Duplicate the image (Image➡Duplicate➡OK).

2. Open the Film Grain dialog box shown in Figure 14.10 (Filter➡Artistic➡Film Grain).

3. Drag the Grain to 20.

   Grain controls the amount of noise added and varies from 0 to 20.

4. Set the Highlight Area to 1.

   Highlight Area varies from 1 to 20 and controls the amount of the image that is lightened. The lightening occurs on the areas of the image that were lighter and more saturated in the original.

Figure 14.10

The Film Grain filter dialog box.

5. Finally, set the Intensity to 10.

   The Intensity varies from 0-10 and controls the amount of highlighting that occurs. If the Intensity is set to 0, it does not matter where you set the Highlight area. With the Intensity at a high setting, the film grain is noticeably less in the intense areas.

6. Click OK. Figure 14.11 shows the result.

Figure 14.11

An example of the Film Grain filter applied.

Filter type	Category	Supported Color Modes	Preview type	Data Dependent	Color Dependent
Parameter	Stylizing Filter	RGB, Grayscale	Small Filter Preview	No. If you filter a solid-colored image at high settings, you will see film grain.	No. The Foreground/ Background settings have no effect.

Fresco

This filter is very similar to the Dry Brush filter, but it intensifies the contrast in the image and makes the darks much bolder. The Fresco filter has exactly the same controls as the Dry Brush filter. All settings in this filter produce a usable image.

The Fresco filter is good for abstracting an image and sharpening the contrast. The colors become very intense.

Try it:

1. Open the image "FallFlwr.Psd." Duplicate the image (Image➡Duplicate➡OK).

2. Open the Fresco dialog box shown in Figure 14.12 (Filter➡Artistic➡Fresco).

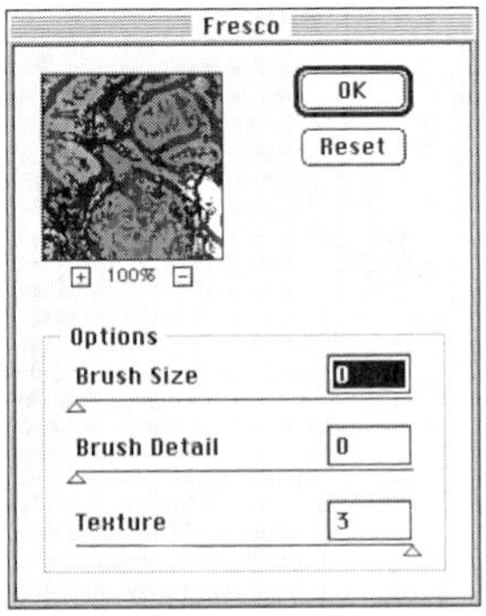

Figure 14.12

The Fresco filter dialog box.

3. Drag the Brush Size to 0.

The Brush Size varies from 0 to 10. It controls the size of the strokes, with 10 as the largest.

4. Set the Brush Detail to 0.

The Brush Detail determines how much detail will be captured from the original image. It varies from 0 to 10. A setting of 10 captures the most detail.

5. Finally, set the Texture to 3.

The Texture setting varies from 1 to 3. A setting of 1 produces a smooth image. A setting of 3 produces an image that contains bits of color that were not in that location in the original image. It adds flecks of pixels to the image.

6. Click OK. Figure 14.13 shows the result.

Figure 14.13

An example of the Fresco filter applied to an image.

Filter type	Category	Supported Color Modes	Preview type	Data Dependent	Color Dependent
Parameter	Stylizing Filter	RGB, Grayscale	Small Filter Preview	Yes. A blank image produces a blank filtered image.	No. The Foreground/ Background settings have no effect.

Neon Glow

The Neon Glow is a very odd filter. I'm not very fond of it at any setting. It makes a strange duo or tri-tone from your image, depending upon your color choices.

Unless you want a strange negative image or an odd-colored one, I'm not sure this has any major uses. It can give an other-worldly feel to an image given the right color choice, and could also be effective when used on a selection or on text. If black and white are your foreground/background colors you will get a grayscale image with the "Color" color as your glow. Make sure that the selection has some very bright values in it, however, if you are going to use positive values in the Size slider. This filter is extremely color dependent. It reacts to the settings of the Foreground and Background colors and to a third color selected in the filter itself. Pick contrasting colors for the most noticeable results.

Try it:

1. Open the image "FallFlwr.Psd." Duplicate the image (Image➡Duplicate➡OK).

2. Pick a deep orange from the image as your foreground color, and a light yellow as the background color.

3. Open the Neon Glow dialog box shown in Figure 14.14 (Filter➡Artistic➡Neon Glow).

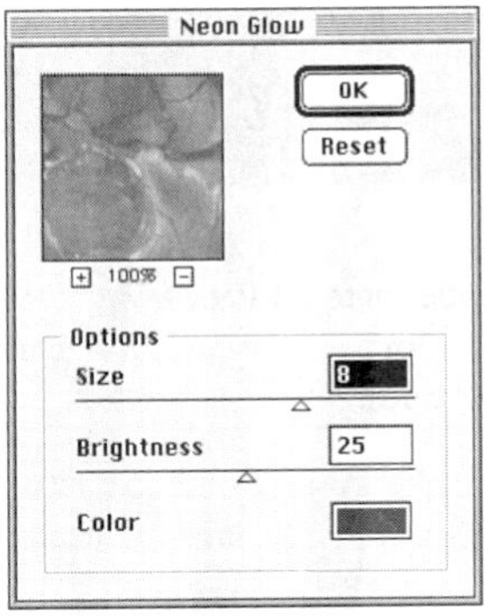

Figure 14.14

Neon Glow dialog box.

4. Drag the Size to +8.

The Size setting runs from -24 to +24.

5. Set the Brightness to 25.

   The Brightness goes from 0 to 50. With a Brightness of less than 7, you get no results regardless of the Size setting. When the Size is in the negative numbers, you get a negative image.

6. Click the color icon to select a bright blue as your Color setting.

   The Color setting interacts in an odd way with the Brightness and Size settings. When Brightness is 50 and Size is -24, the darkest areas show the Color, the highlights show the Foreground color, and the midtones shows the mixture of Foreground/Background. When Brightness is 50 and Size is +24, the lightest areas show the Background, the highlights show the Foreground color, and the midtones shows the mixture of Foreground/Background; the Color is not used. At a Size setting of 0, the lightest areas in the image show up in the Color setting.

7. Click OK. Figure 14.15 shows the result.

Figure 14.15

The Neon Glow filter applied.

Filter type	Category	Supported Color Modes	Preview type	Data Dependent	Color Dependent
Parameter	Stylizing Filter	RGB, Grayscale	Small Filter Preview	Yes. A blank image produces a blank filtered image.	Yes. Foreground/ Background settings have a profound effect.

Paint Daubs

This filter is supposed to look like spots of paint. It doesn't. There are, however, many settings here that give pleasing results—even if they don't match the filter name. The logic of this filter seems to be a cross between the Dust & Scratches filter with a Radius of 16 and a Threshold of 0 (that is, blurry areas of color) and the Unsharp Mask filter. It is as if you can select the amount of sharpening that you want after the image has been divided into color regions. The Paint Daubs filter can also select a brush that performs further mathemagic on the filter. This works nicely on an entire image to stylize and abstract it.

When the Brush Size and Sharpening are each about halfway, the Sparkle brush seems to give the same effect as if you had used the Gaussian Blur filter and the Find Edges filter and then sharpened these edges. It is an interesting look.

The middle ranges of the Brush Size and Sharpness settings seems most useful. If you set both Brush Size and Sharpness very low, you will see no change in your image.

Try it:

1. Open the image "FallFlwr.Psd." Duplicate the image (Image➡Duplicate➡OK).

2. Open the Paint Daubs dialog box shown in Figure 14.16 (Filter➡Artistic➡Paint Daubs).

3. Drag the Brush Size to 8.

   The Brush Size setting varies from 1-50. The Brush Size controls the size of the color-block regions.

Figure 14.16

The Paint Daubs dialog box.

4. Set the Sharpness to 7.

   The Sharpness can vary from 0-40. The Sharpness controls the amount of sharpening applied (surprise!).

5. Finally, set the Simple brush.

   There are a number of brushes: Simple, Light Rough, Dark Rough, Wide Sharp, Wide Blurry, and Sparkle. The Rough brushes are noisy.

6. Click OK. Figure 14.17 shows the result.

Figure 14.17

An example of the Paint Daubs filter applied.

Filter type	Category	Supported Color Modes	Preview type	Data Dependent	Color Dependent
Parameter	Stylizing Filter	RGB, Grayscale	Small Filter Preview	Yes. A blank image produces a blank filtered image.	No. The Foreground/Background settings have no effect.

Palette Knife

The Palette Knife filter can make your image look as if it had been painted using a palette knife—if you select the correct settings and *want* to use a palette knife that leaves paint perfectly flat on the canvas. The flatness is the only thing that I do not like about this filter. It is unnatural given the name of the filter.

The filter looks as if you are placing strokes of color on a canvas that was underpainted with black. The darkest shadow areas turn solid black, and the image seems to gain in saturation. The filter can help to enhance a simple line art graphic. The filter is good for an entire image or wherever you might wish to use the Crystallize filter. This could be a good filter for texture creation at large Stroke Sizes. It is also good combined with the Emboss filter.

Try it:

1. Open the image "FallFlwr.Psd." Duplicate the image (Image➧Duplicate➧OK).

2. Drag the Background Layer icon to the New Layer icon at the bottom of the Layers palette to duplicate it. Turn off the Eye icon so that you can see the Background layer.

3. Click on the Background Layer to make it the active Layer. Apply the Emboss filter (Filter➧Stylize➧Emboss) to it with any setting that you like.

4. Click on the top Layer and turn the Eye icon back on.

5. Open the Palette Knife box shown in Figure 14.18
(Filter➡Artistic➡Palette Knife).

Figure 14.18

The Palette Knife dialog box.

6. Drag the Stroke Size to 50.

   The Stroke Size ranges from 1-50, but at the larger sizes you
   lose all of the detail in your image and just have blobs of color.
   At the smallest Stroke Sizes, you see no change. A Stroke Size
   of 12 is a good choice to keep image detail.

7. Set the Stroke Detail to 3.

   The Stroke Detail controls the shape of the paint strokes. The
   control ranges from 1 to 3. At a setting of 1, the colors are
   applied almost as if you were using the Crystallize filter. At a
   setting of 3, you see almost a dry brush effect, which is more
   attractive.

8. Finally, set the Softness to 0.

   The Softness setting controls the amount of anti-aliasing on the
   edges of the strokes. The setting ranges from 0-10, with 0 being
   aliased and 10 being very soft.

9. Click OK. Change the Blending mode to Hard Light with an
   Opacity of 90%. Figure 14.19 shows the result.

Figure 14.19

The Palette Knife filter applied over embossing.

Filter type	Category	Supported Color Modes	Preview type	Data Dependent	Color Dependent
Parameter	Stylizing Filter	RGB, Grayscale	Small Filter Preview	Yes. A blank image produces a blank filtered image.	No. The Foreground/Background settings have no effect.

Plastic Wrap

Maxine Masterfield, in her book *Painting the Spirit of Nature* (Watson-Guptill, 1984), describes how she uses plastic wrap to create texture and shine in her abstract images. She often crumbles the plastic wrap into the wet paint and guides the paint into the paths that she wishes it to follow.

Unfortunately, you have no such control over the digital version. It follows the contours in your image rather than the reverse. However, it can still be used to give shine to portions of your image or to give you entire image an extremely dimensional look. The Plastic Wrap filter can also help to enhance a simple line art graphic. This filter looks good when used on text.

If you filter a solid-colored image at the highest settings, you get a star shape. Repeated filtering creates a very interesting plastic blob. If you take a portion of that blob and create a seamless pattern from it, you can get a bump map or a displacement map.

Try it:

1. Open the image "FallFlwr.Psd." Duplicate the image (Image➥Duplicate➥OK).

2. Open the Plastic Wrap dialog box shown in Figure 14.20 (Filter➥Artistic➥Plastic Wrap).

Figure 14.20

The Plastic Wrap dialog box.

3. Drag the Highlight Strength to 20.

   Highlight Strength, which goes from 0 to 20, must be greater than 0 in order to see some change in your image, regardless of the other settings. The highlight strength sets the amount of reflection that you get from the plastic wrap.

4. Set the Detail to 1.

   The Detail setting determines how closely the plastic wrap "clings" to the nooks and crannies in the image. A setting of 1 does not show much cling, whereas a setting of 15 (the maximum) follows every contour and causes many more (frequently too many) areas of reflectiveness.

5. Finally, set the Smoothness to 8.

The Smoothness setting seems to control the thickness of the film of plastic wrap. A setting of 1 gives only artifacting and is not useful at all. A setting of 15 buries the image in plastic.

6. Click OK. Figure 14.21 shows the result.

Figure 14.21

An example of the Plastic Wrap filter applied.

Filter type	Category	Supported Color Modes	Preview type	Data Dependent	Color Dependent
Parameter	Stylizing Filter	RGB, Grayscale	Small Filter Preview	No. A blank image produces a star shape.	No. The Foreground/Background settings have no effect.

Poster Edges

The Poster Edges filter posterizes the image in its own colors and adds black detail around the edges. All settings produce visible changes in the image. This can be good for a woodcut-type look. You can get similar results by using the High Pass filter at a setting of 1.6 and the Threshold command and placing this image over the original in Multiply mode.

Try it:

1. Open the image "FallFlwr.Psd." Duplicate the image (Image➡Duplicate➡OK).

2. Open the Poster Edges dialog box shown in Figure 14.22 (Filter➡Artistic➡Poster Edges).

Figure 14.22

Poster Edges dialog box.

3. Drag the Edge Thickness to 0.

   The Edge Thickness controls how much black is placed around the edges of the image ("edges" here is used as in the Find Edges filter). The controls go from 0 to 10. A setting of 0 produces almost no edge.

4. Set the Edge Intensity to 10.

   The Edge Intensity controls the number of edges found. A setting of 0 finds only the major dark areas and shapes and intensifies the shadows around them. A setting of 10 finds many more edges—if the Edge Thickness is set low enough for the edges to be seen separately.

5. Finally, set the Posterization to 6.

   The Posterization setting works backwards. A setting of 0 produces the most posterization (as in dropping out the most colors), and a setting of 6 produces the least. Think of the Posterization setting as controlling the number of Levels in the Posterization, and it will work properly.

6. Click OK. Figure 14.23 shows the result.

Figure 14.23

An example of the Poster
Edges filter applied.

Filter type	Category	Supported Color Modes	Preview type	Data Dependent	Color Dependent
Parameter	Stylizing Filter	RGB, Grayscale	Small Filter Preview	Yes. A blank image produces a blank filtered image.	No. The Foreground/Background settings have no effect.

Rough Pastels

The Rough Pastels filter reacts to textures built-in to the filter, or it can use another file as a texture file. For a novel effect, apply any filter to a copy of your image. Use this filtered copy as the texture when you are asked to choose a texture for this filter. The pastels "rub-off" on the high parts of the texture (the darks). The Rough Pastels filter can help to enhance a simple line art graphic and looks good when used on text. The Rough Pastels filter is good for generating textures on a blank image filled with light to medium noise.

This is a very complex filter with a large number of parameters you can vary. The most critical parameter is the texture itself, which makes an enormous difference to the final result. The Rough Pastels filter looks much different with a brick texture than it does with a burlap texture. You can change the texture by inverting it or by changing the Scaling, the Amount of Relief, or the Light Direction.

Try it:

1. Open the image "FallFlwr.Psd." Duplicate the image (Image➥Duplicate➥OK).

2. Open the Rough Pastels dialog box shown in Figure 14.24 (Filter➥Artistic➥Rough Pastels).

Figure 14.24

Rough Pastels filter dialog box.

3. Drag the Stroke Length to 24.

   The Stroke Length setting varies from 0-40. When the Stroke Length and Stroke Detail are set to their maximums (40 and 20, respectively), the image looks as if it were stroked back and forth diagonally across the canvas with multiple colors as the pastel was moved down diagonally. With the Stroke Length pulled back to 0, the long diagonal lines are broken, but the multiple colors remain.

4. Set the Stroke Detail to 15.

   The Stroke Detail can vary from 1-20 . When the Stroke Detail is reduced to 1, but the Stroke Length is left at 40, the pastels

589

seem to be darker values of the colors in the image and move across the image horizontally in lines but on a diagonal as well. Making the Stroke Length shorter cuts the horizontal lines.

5. There are a number of settings that concern the texture to be applied. Set the Texture to Brick.

   The Textures included are Brick, Burlap, Canvas, and Sandstone, but you can load your own texture from a Photoshop file.

6. Set the Scaling to 100%.

   Textures can be scaled from 50-200%. At 100%, you are using the original size of the texture-pattern.

7. Set the Relief to 20.

   You can set Relief to values of 0-50. This sets the elevation or "3D-ness" of the texture.

8. Select Top Right as the Light Direction. You can select from any 45 degree angle. You may also invert the texture if you wish to reverse the embossing (don't for now).

9. Click OK. Figure 14.25 shows the result.

Figure 14.25

An example of the Rough Pastels filter applied.

Filter type	Category	Supported Color Modes	Preview type	Data Dependent	Color Dependent
Parameter	Stylizing Filter	RGB, Grayscale	Small Filter Preview	No. A blank image still gets some texture but it can be very subtle.	No. The Fore-ground/Back-ground settings have no effect.

Smudge Stick

The Smudge Stick filter looks as if you took a towel and smudged a chalk or pastel drawing. With all of the settings at their minimum values, the image looks gently smudged and muddied. The colors are muted and rubbed into one another. The Smudge Stick filter is another good texture-generating filter when used on a blank image that has had noise added.

Try it:

1. Open the image "FallFlwr.Psd." Duplicate the image (Image➡Duplicate➡OK).

2. Open the Smudge Stick dialog box shown in Figure 14.26 (Filter➡Artistic➡Smudge Stick).

Figure 14.26

Smudge Stick dialog box.

3. Drag the Stroke Length to 2.

   The Stroke Length goes from 1-10 and determines how long you have "pushed the towel" before letting up on the pressure. A smaller Stroke Length seems to intensify the shadow areas of the image more.

4. Set the Highlight Area to 4.

   The Highlight Area can vary from 1-20 and is something that cannot be duplicated easily in the real world. This enables you to intensify the light areas in your image while muddying up the shadows.

5. Finally, set the Intensity to 4.

   The Intensity varies from 1-10, determining the degree to which the Highlight area is visible. A very high setting brightens the brights in the image, especially if a large Highlight Area setting is also selected. If a large Highlight Area is selected but the Intensity setting is low, you will not see it.

6. Click OK. Figure 14.27 shows the result.

Figure 14.27

An example of the Smudge Stick filter applied.

Filter type	Category	Supported Color Modes	Preview type	Data Dependent	Color Dependent
Parameter	Stylizing Filter	RGB, Grayscale	Small Filter Preview	Yes. A blank image produces a blank filtered image.	No. The Foreground/Background settings have no effect.

Sponge

The Sponge filter looks like someone is dabbing paint on the image. The amount of paint and the size of the sponge are controllable. This is one of the more successful stylizing filters.

The settings that use a small brush and a low Smoothness are very attractive—both with or without a high Definition. Larger brush sizes with high Smoothness settings look like the Median filter.

This makes a wonderful grained paper effect when applied repeatedly to a solid color image. Use the Sponge filter as is or make either a repeat texture or a texture in a channel to use as "paper," the way you would in Painter.

Try it:

1. Open the image "FallFlwr.Psd." Duplicate the image (Image➡Duplicate➡OK).

2. Open the Sponge dialog box shown in Figure 14.28 (Filter➡Artistic➡Sponge).

3. Drag the Brush Size to 0.

   The Brush Size setting varies from 1-10. The Brush Size controls the size of the sponge.

4. Set the Definition to 25.

   The Definition can vary from 1-25. The Definition controls the value difference of the sponge with the image behind it. A high definition causes the colors sponged on the image to take on a much darker value than the original.

5. Finally, set the Smoothness to 1.

Figure 14.28

The Sponge dialog box.

The Smoothness varies from 1-15. The Smoothness setting determines the amount of aliasing at the edges of the sponge. A small setting causes a lot of aliasing; a large setting is anti-aliased.

6. Click OK. Figure 14.29 shows the result.

Figure 14.29

The Sponge filter applied to an image.

Filter type	Category	Supported Color Modes	Preview type	Data Dependent	Color Dependent
Parameter	Stylizing Filter	RGB, Grayscale	Small Filter Preview	No. A blank image can be textured.	No. The Foreground/Background settings have no effect.

Underpainting

It is almost uncanny how good the Underpainting filter is. Using the Canvas texture and a small brush with the highest Texture Coverage setting, you get an image so real that you'd think the paint was still wet. The image looks just the way it would if you had sketched in the details with thin oils on a canvas. It can also help to enhance a simple line art graphic.

You can use this exactly as you would traditional underpainting and add back in the detail from the original image. Here's how:

Try it:

1. Open the image "FallFlwr.Psd." Duplicate the image (Image➡Duplicate➡OK).

2. Open the Underpainting dialog box shown in Figure 14.30 (Filter➡Artistic➡Underpainting).

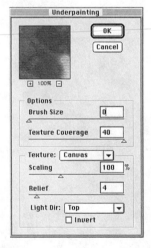

Figure 14.30

The Underpainting dialog box.

3. Drag the Brush Size to 0.

   The Brush Size setting varies from 0-40. If a large brush Size is used, the area covered by the brush does not show texture, so the coverage is very spotty.

4. Set the Texture Coverage to 40.

   The Texture Coverage can vary from 0-40. If both the Texture Coverage and the Brush Size settings are low, the texture appears chopped up.

595

5. A number of Texture settings exist. Set the Texture to Canvas.

   Textures included are Brick, Burlap, Canvas, and Sandstone, but you can load your own texture from a Photoshop file.

6. Set the Scaling to 100%.

   Textures can be scaled from 50-200%. At 100%, you are using the original size of the texture-pattern.

7. Set the Relief to 4.

   You can set Relief to values of 0-50.

8. Select Bottom as the Light Direction. You can select from any 45-degree angle. You may also invert the texture if you wish to reverse the embossing (don't for now). Click OK. Figure 14.31 shows the result.

Figure 14.31

The Underpainting filter applied to an image.

9. Press the Shift key (to make the images align) and with the Move tool, drag the original image on top of the filtered image as a new Layer.

10. Create a Layer Mask (Layer menu➡Add Layer Mask➡Hide All). This covers the entire original image so that none of it is visible.

11. Using white paint and a soft brush at low opacity, brush back in some of the original detail as desired. Figure 14.32 shows the result.

Filter type	Category	Supported Color Modes	Preview type	Data Dependent	Color Dependent
Parameter	Stylizing Filter	RGB, Grayscale	Small Filter Preview	Yes. A blank image produces a blank filtered image.	No. The Foreground/Background settings have no effect.

Watercolor

The Watercolor filter is supposed to make an image look as if it was painted with watercolors. It doesn't. The Watercolor filter's results are very similar to the Fresco filter, but the Fresco filter adds more outlining around the edges of the shapes it identifies. The Watercolor filter does the "right" things in terms of finding shapes and simplifying colors. It produces a very good range of values and shapes in the process of simplifying the colors from "photographic" to "painted." The hallmark of a watercolor, however, is usually its light, airy feel, and this filter is very heavy. The Watercolor filter intensifies the dark areas in the image far too much, and the final colors are extremely strong. This filter is popular, however, as it provides the easiest way to "sort-of" get something to look like a watercolor in Photoshop—but if you paint with the Wet Edges option on in the Brush palette, you will get an image that is much closer to a watercolor.

An interesting variation on the Watercolor filter is to filter the image with a setting of 1 for the texture and then filter another copy of the original at a setting of 3. With the Move tool, drag one copy on top of the other and set the Blending mode to Difference. Duplicate the image (Image➡Duplicate) as Merged. At this point, you can:

◆ Select Image➡Adjust➡Auto Levels to apply the Auto Levels command.

◆ Invert the image and select New Adjustment Layer...from the Layers palette. Set the Type to Levels and the mode to Multiply. Click OK.

◆ Drag a Watercolor-filtered copy onto this image in Screen mode.

◆ Experiment with other Blending modes in a Levels Adjustment Layer.

Look at the file "WaterFX.Psd" on the CD-ROM to see how this is done. Figure 14.33 shows the effect in grayscale—much lighter and softer than the usual method.

Figure 14.33

The "Soft" Watercolor Effect is one of the variations you can create with the Watercolor filter.

Try it the "normal" way:

1. Open the image "FallFlwr.Psd." Duplicate the image (Image➡Duplicate➡OK).

2. Open the Watercolor dialog box shown in Figure 14.34 (Filter➡Artistic➡Watercolor).

Figure 14.34

The Watercolor filter dialog box.

3. Drag the Brush Detail to 14.

   The Brush Detail setting varies from 1-14, determining whether the filter tries to duplicate the original image or just picks up the general color and feel of the photograph. A setting of 14 keeps the detail, but even a setting of 1 produces a recognizable image if your original is large enough. This lightest setting produces an almost lacy effect as the "paint" is spattered about.

4. Set the Shadow Intensity to 10.

   The Shadow Intensity can vary from 1-10 but should be left to 1 unless you really like black watercolors. The image is too dark on the lowest setting and almost completely black at the higher settings.

5. Finally, set the Texture to 3.

   The Texture varies from 1-3. The Texture setting is very subtle. There is not a huge difference between using a setting of 1 or 3, but there is some. Actually many of the pixels change between the two settings, but unless you compare two versions using Difference, the changes may be hard to see.

6. Click OK. Figure 14.35 shows the result.

Figure 14.35

The Watercolor filter applied.

Filter type	Category	Supported Color Modes	Preview type	Data Dependent	Color Dependent
Parameter	Stylizing Filter	RGB, Grayscale	Small Filter Preview	Yes. A blank image produces a blank filtered image.	No. The Foreground/Background settings have no effect.

PHOTOSHOP'S NATIVE FILTERS—BLUR

The Blur filters are used to reduce the difference in color between nearby pixels. Depending upon the specific filter, you can select a pixel radius to blur. The Blur filters can all be used for production or for special effects, though some, such as the Radial Blur, tend to be more useful for special effects work.

Blur

The Blur filter applies a very tiny—almost unnoticeable—blur to an image or selection. It is not useful for major corrections, though it can be applied multiple times.

The Blur filter is used to "take the edge off" an image that is too sharp or to very gently soften it. Use the Gaussian Blur filter instead for more control.

Try it:

1. Open the image "Amanda.Psd." Duplicate the image (Image➡Duplicate➡OK).

2. Select the Blur filter (Filter➡Blur➡Blur). There is no image because the difference is not visible in the printed image.

Filter type	Category	Supported Color Modes	Preview type	Data Dependent	Color Dependent
One-Step	Production/ Focus	RGB, Grayscale CMYK, Lab	None	Yes. A blank image produces a blank filtered image.	No. The Foreground/Background settings have no effect.

Blur More

The Blur More filter applies a little more blurring than the Blur filter. Use this filter to give an image a tiny blur. Use the Gaussian Blur filter for more control.

Try it:

1. Open the image "Amanda.Psd." Duplicate the image (Image➡Duplicate➡OK).

2. Select the Blur More filter (Filter➡Blur➡Blur More). Once again, the results are not visible in print.

Filter type	Category	Supported Color Modes	Preview type	Data Dependent	Color Dependent
One-Step	Production/ Focus	RGB, Grayscale CMYK, Lab	None	Yes. A blank image produces a blank filtered image.	No. The Foreground/Background settings have no effect.

Gaussian Blur

The Gaussian Blur filter is one of the most useful and basic filters. It is the one critical filter used when making a drop shadow and is also useful when you need to anti-alias edges where they meet. The Gaussian Blur filter is used to soften the differences between nearby pixels and to help remove grain. It is also used to blur shadow areas for creating drop shadows.

You can use the Gaussian Blur filter after applying the Add Noise filter to soften an image's noise. You can also use it under a copy of an original image to get the effect of painting on ivory.

Let's create an "ivory painting" effect and then place text with a drop shadow on top of it.:

1. Open the image "Amanda.Psd." Duplicate the image (Image➥Duplicate➥OK).

2. Drag the icon for the Background layer to the New Layer icon (the center icon at the bottom of the Layers palette) to duplicate the Layer.

3. Change the Blending mode of the top Layer to Darken.

4. Make the Background Layer active by clicking it in the Layers palette.

5. Open the Gaussian Blur dialog box shown in Figure 14.36 (Filter➥Blur➥Gaussian Blur).

Figure 14.36

The Gaussian Blur filter dialog box.

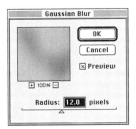

6. Drag the Radius to 12.

The Radius setting, where you can specify the pixel-radius, varies from 0.1-250. This is the only control. A larger image needs more blurring to achieve the same results as a smaller image, so this filter is resolution dependent. The detail in the image will fade out a bit and the image will begin to glow. It will look as if it were drawn on ivory. Click OK.

7. Make a new layer (click the New Layer icon at the bottom of the Layers Palette).

8. Load Channel #4 (Option-Command-4)[Alt-Control-4].

9. Pick a color from the icing as your Foreground color and fill the selected area (Option-Delete)[Alt-Delete].

10. Drag the icon for the text layer to the New Layer icon (the center icon at the bottom of the Layers palette). Name this new Layer "Shadow" and drag it below the text in the Layers palette.

11. Click the Preserve Transparency button to turn it on.

12. Press D to set the colors back to the default of black and white.

13. Fill the area (Option-Delete)[Alt-Delete].

14. Remove the Preserve Transparency button by clicking it.

15. Apply the Gaussian Blur filter to the Shadow channel with the same setting of 12 pixels.

16. Press the Modifier key (Command)[Control] and offset the shadow by moving it up and to the right.

17. Change the Layer opacity to 50%. Figure 14.37 shows the result.

Filter type	Category	Supported Color Modes	Preview type	Data Dependent	Color Dependent
Parameter	Production/ Focus/ Special Effects	RGB, Grayscale CMYK, Lab	Full Image	Yes. A blank image produces a blank filtered image.	No. The Fore-ground/Back-ground settings have no effect.

Figure 14.37

Here the Gaussian Blur filter helps create a drop shadow.

Motion Blur

The Motion Blur filter blurs your image so that it looks like either the camera or the subject moved as the picture was taken. It's interesting that we try to re-create digitally an image that we'd toss away if it came out of a camera!

The filter is used to add motion to an image. If you only want to add motion to part of the image or a portion of the main subject, control the Motion Blur filter using Layers.

Try it:

1. Open the image "Amanda.Psd." Duplicate the image (Image➡Duplicate➡OK).

2. Drag the icon for the Background layer to the New Layer icon (the center icon at the bottom of the Layers palette) to duplicate the Layer.

3. Open the Motion Blur dialog box shown in Figure 14.38 (Filter➡Blur➡Motion Blur).

Figure 14.38

The Motion Blur dialog box.

4. Drag the Angle to -25.

   The Angle setting varies from 0-360 degrees (or in negative degrees if you drag backwards). The Angle setting is a dial you can set visually or numerically, determining the direction of the blur.

5. Set the Distance to 47.

   The Distance control, varying from 1-999, sets the distance for the blur and determines the length of the motion "trail" that is left.

6. Click OK. Figure 14.39 shows the result.

Figure 14.39

The Motion Blur filter applied.

7. Add a Layer Mask (Layer➥Add Layer Mask➥Hide All). The "Hide All" setting makes the Layer mask remove the entire top Layer from view.

8. Using a soft brush and white "paint," paint back in the areas on the top Layer you wish to be blurred. Figure 14.40 shows the result.

Figure 14.40

Here the Motion Blur filter is controlled.

This technique gives you the maximum amount of control, as you are not destroying any data and can change your mind as many times as you need to. If you do not like your results, paint over them with black to remove the editing.

The Motion Blur filter is also very good for creating textures. Here is one of my favorite texture "recipes."

1. Create a new image 400×400 pixels. Choose either White or Background Color as the Content because Transparent does not work with this "recipe."

2. Apply the Add Noise filter with Gaussian Noise of 200, not monochromatic.

3. Apply the Motion Blur filter with a Distance of 800 (twice the image width) and whatever angle you want (so long as it is not horizontal or vertical).

4. Drag the icon for the Background layer to the New Layer icon (the center icon at the bottom of the Layers palette) to duplicate it.

5. Change the Blending mode for the top Layer to Color Burn or Exclusion. Multiply, Screen, Overlay, Hard Light, or Soft Light also give you good results.

This technique makes a cross-hatching that is good for backgrounds. With some effort, it can also be changed into a seamless repeat.

Filter type	Category	Supported Color Modes	Preview type	Data Dependent	Color Dependent
Parameter	Focus/ Special Effects	RGB, Grayscale CMYK, Lab	Full Image	Yes. A blank image produces a blank filtered image.	No. The Foreground/Background settings have no effect.

Radial Blur

The Radial Blur filter causes the image to blur either by spinning it or by taking it up to warp speed as if you were making a space jump. This is clearly a Special Effects filter.

Simulating the effect of a space warp is probably the most consistent use I can find for this filter. You, however, can use it anywhere you want spinning or zooming blurs.

Try using the Radial Blur on the texture you created with the Motion Blur filter. If you select a Spin Blur with a fairly high Amount and place the center of the spin (by click-dragging in the Blur box) at the lower right of the image, you get a very subtle effect that also makes a good background. You may want to apply a Gaussian Blur to it to smooth it out a bit first.

Try it:

1. Open the image "Amanda.Psd." Duplicate the image (Image➡Duplicate➡OK).

2. Open the Radial Blur dialog box shown in Figure 14.41 (Filter➡Blur➡Radial Blur).

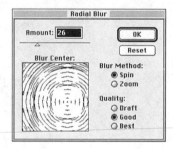

Figure 14.41

The Radial Blur dialog box.

3. Drag the Amount to 26.

    The Amount setting varies from 1-100. This parameter controls the intensity of the effect and specifies how much blurring occurs. The preview shows a motion trail of the settings that you select, but does not show any of your image (you have to guess what it will look like!).

4. Click the Spin button for Blur Method.

    The other option is Zoom.

5. Next, set the Blur Quality to Good. Draft or Good are usually sufficient; Best is exceptionally slow to compute.

6. Finally, drag the Blur center to the position shown in the dialog box (see Figure 14.41).

7. Click OK. Figure 14.42 shows the result.

Figure 14.42

An example of applying the
Radial Blur filter.

Filter type	Category	Supported Color Modes	Preview type	Data Dependent	Color Dependent
Parameter	Focus/ Special Effects	RGB, Grayscale CMYK, Lab	Wire Frame	Yes. A blank image produces a blank filtered image.	No. The Foreground/Background settings have no effect.

Smart Blur

The Smart Blur filter finds the edges in an image and blurs only within the area bordered by an "edge." The parameter settings determine where Photoshop "sees" the edge.

This is an excellent production filter to help you get rid of grain in fleshtones. Because the filter effects are localized, you don't get the muddying effects that you would from the Gaussian Blur filter. Keep the Threshold low and the Radius fairly low as well (though it can exceed the Threshold amount).

Mode options are Normal, Edge Only, and Overlay Edge. The Edge Only and Overlay Edge effects with high Thresholds will find only the major shapes in the image. This can be very helpful for turning your image into outlines or making masks. You can also get good Pencil sketches from this effect. In the Edge Only mode, The Smart Blur filter operates like an intelligent Find Edges filter.

Try it:

1. Open the image "Amanda.Psd." Duplicate the image (Image➡Duplicate➡OK).

2. Open the Smart Blur dialog box shown in Figure 14.43 (Filter➡Blur➡Smart Blur).

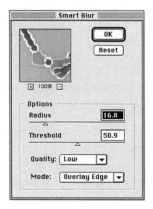

Figure 14.43

The Smart Blur dialog box.

3. Drag the Radius to 16.8.

The Radius setting varies from 0.1-100, determining how far from a given pixel the filter will blur the image. This setting works like the Radius in Pixels in the Gaussian Blur filter. However, the "edges" of the image become sharper and more pixelated as the radius amount increases.

4. Set the Threshold to 50.9.

The Threshold can vary from .1-100. The Threshold setting seems to work the way the same setting does in Unsharp Mask—to determine how much the filter will affect the image—but it is actually the opposite. A low Threshold setting "sees" many edges, so the overall effect will be slight. A larger Threshold setting sees many fewer edges, so there will be a larger number of pixels in the area to be blurred.

5. Set the Quality setting to Low.

The Quality setting determines the amount of processing needed to calculate the effect. Low or Medium are fine; High takes much longer—though not as long as the Best setting in the Motion Blur filter.

6. Select Overlay Edge as the Mode. The Mode is a very interesting setting as it totally changes the way in which the filter works and the results that the filter produces.

   ◆ Normal blurs the areas between the edges, but does not show the edges.

   ◆ Edge Only shows only the edges found by the filter (in white) on a black background. If you invert the image, you can almost see a Pencil sketch.

   ◆ Overlay Edge shows the white edges on top of the blurred image.

7. Click OK. Figure 14.44 shows the result.

Figure 14.44

An example of the Smart Blur filter applied.

Filter type	Category	Supported Color Modes	Preview type	Data Dependent	Color Dependent
Parameter	Focus/ Special Effects/ Production	RGB only	Small Image Preview	Yes. A blank image produces a blank filtered image.	No. The Fore-ground/Back-ground settings have no effect.

613

PHOTOSHOP'S NATIVE FILTERS—BRUSH STROKES

The Brush Strokes filters, new to Photoshop 4.0, are part of the Gallery Effects filter sets. None of them work in CMYK or Lab mode, and they all have small previews embedded in the filter dialog box. This class of filter is best used to stylize an image or to create texture. All of these filters work wonderfully on a blank image that has had the Add Noise filter run on it. Try this as the start of many exciting textures.

Accented Edges

The Accented Edges filter is another Edge filter that is similar to the Find Edges filter. But it can be used to give more texture to an image—hence it is in this Brush Strokes category. The Accented Edges filter looks best when the Edge Width is kept small—large edges destroy the image. With a tiny Edge Width and minimum Brightness and Smoothness, the image is dark but very textured, acquiring an almost woodcut look. At a small Edge Width, but maximum Brightness and Smoothness, you almost feel as if you are looking at liquid, colored chrome.

Try it:

1. Open the image "Deer.Psd." Duplicate the image (Image➡Duplicate➡OK).

2. Open the Accented Edges dialog box shown in Figure 14.45 (Filter➡Brush Strokes➡Accented Edges).

Figure 14.45

Accented Edges dialog box.

3. Drag the Edge Width to 4.

The Edge Width setting varies from 1-14, controlling the thickness of the edges that are found.

4. Set the Edge Brightness to 38.

The Edge Brightness can vary from 0-50. This controls the intensity or glow of the edges. At 50, the edges are highly saturated.

5. Finally, set the Smoothness to 5.

The Smoothness varies from 1-15, controlling the number of edges found and their Path. At 1, the filter will find many tiny edges. At 15, it finds fewer edges but they look longer and smoother.

6. Click OK. Figure 14.46 shows the result.

Figure 14.46

An example of the Accented Edges filter applied.

Filter type	Category	Supported Color Modes	Preview type	Data Dependent	Color Dependent
Parameter	Stylizing Filter	RGB, Grayscale	Small Filter Preview	Yes. A blank image produces a blank filtered image.	No. The Foreground/Background settings have no effect.

Angled Strokes

The Angled Strokes filter makes an image look as if diagonal brush strokes of oil paints have been applied to a canvas. The effect is really quite nice with a long, sharp stroke, though all settings in this filter produce results. This filter does a very good job of identifying main image areas.

Try it:

1. Open the image "Deer.Psd." Duplicate the image (Image➡Duplicate➡OK).

2. Open the Angled Strokes dialog box shown in Figure 14.47 (Filter➡Brush Strokes➡Angled Strokes).

Figure 14.47

The Angled Strokes dialog box.

3. Drag the Direction Balance to 50.

   The Direction Balance setting varies from 0-100, controlling the direction of the strokes. A setting of 0 makes the strokes appear from the upper left to lower right. A setting of 100 puts them in the opposite direction. A setting of 50 gets you half-and-half.

4. Set the Stroke Length to 50.

    The Stroke Length can vary from 3-50. A stroke of 3 has a minimal result other than to make a gentle texture.

5. Finally, set the Sharpness to 10.

    The Sharpness varies from 0-10. A sharpness of 10 enables the "paint" to look as if you can see where each bristle on the brush went over the canvas. A setting of 0 blurs the stroke.

6. Click OK. Figure 14.48 shows the result.

Figure 14.48

The Angled Strokes filter applied.

617

Filter type	Category	Supported Color Modes	Preview type	Data Dependent	Color Dependent
Parameter	Stylizing Filter	RGB, Grayscale	Small Filter Preview	Yes. A blank image produces a blank filtered image.	No. The Foreground/Background settings have no effect.

Crosshatch

The Crosshatch filter is one of my favorites. It can be attractive at most settings (especially the intermediate ones) and creates lovely textures. The Crosshatch filter can make an image look as if a brush were stroked at cross angles on a canvas. It can also give the impression of a random weave.

Try it:

1. Open the image "Deer.Psd." Duplicate the image (Image➡Duplicate➡OK).

2. Open the Crosshatch dialog box shown in Figure 14.49 (Filter➡Brush Strokes➡Crosshatch).

Figure 14.49

The Crosshatch dialog box.

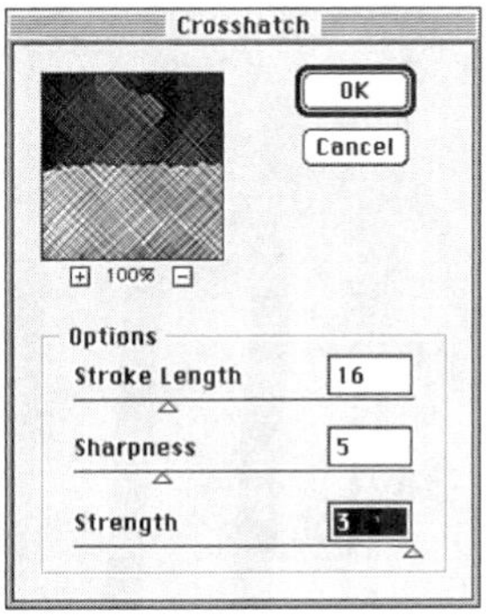

3. Drag the Stroke Length to 16,

The Stroke Length setting varies from 3-50, controlling the distance that the stroke travels. The stroke length should be above 6 for the characteristic "crosshatch" to appear. A setting of 3 with maximum sharpness and strength produces a wonderful "bramble and tangles" texture.

4. Set the Sharpness to 5.

   The Sharpness, varying from 0-20, controls the visibility of each stroke—how well you see it against all of the other strokes. At highest settings, this setting "fights" with the Strength control and adds spurious colors. It is best used high when Strength is low.

5. Finally, set the Strength to 3.

   The Strength varies from 1 to 3. This parameter controls the embossing that occurs on each stroke.

6. Click OK. Figure 14.50 shows the result.

Figure 14.50

The Crosshatch filter applied.

Filter type	Category	Supported Color Modes	Preview type	Data Dependent	Color Dependent
Parameter	Stylizing/ Texture Filter	RGB, Grayscale	Small Filter Preview	Yes. A blank image produces a blank filtered image.	No. The Fore-ground/Back-ground settings have no effect.

Dark Strokes

The Dark Strokes filter is similar to the Angled Strokes, but you cannot see the brush strokes clearly. The brush strokes are fairly soft and subtle (especially with a low White Intensity). The Dark Strokes filter gives more control over the colors in the finished effect. This is not one of my favorite filters as it is too similar to others in the set without adding any major benefit.

Try it:

1. Open the image "Deer.Psd." Duplicate the image (Image➡Duplicate➡OK).

2. Open the Dark Strokes dialog box shown in Figure 14.51 (Filter➡Brush Strokes➡Dark Strokes).

Figure 14.51

The Dark Strokes dialog box.

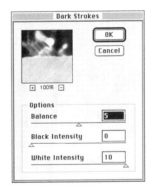

3. Drag the Balance to 5.

   The Balance setting varies from 0-10. This parameter controls the direction of the strokes. A setting of 0 makes all of the strokes appear from the upper left to lower right. A setting of 10 puts them in the opposite direction. A setting of 5 gets you half-and-half.

4. Set the Black Intensity to 0.

   The Black Intensity can vary from 0-10. When set higher than 0, it begins to remove all dark colors from the image and change them to black.

5. Finally, set the White Intensity to 10.

   The White Intensity varies from 0-10. A setting of 10 makes the light areas of the image bright and very saturated. A setting of 0 still shows up but it is, obviously, much darker.

6. Click OK. Figure 14.52 shows the result.

Figure 14.52

An example of the Dark Strokes filter applied to an image.

Filter type	Category	Supported Color Modes	Preview type	Data Dependent	Color Dependent
Parameter	Stylizing Filter	RGB, Grayscale	Small Filter Preview	Yes. A blank image produces a blank filtered image.	No. The Foreground/Background settings have no effect.

Ink Outlines

The Ink Outlines filter is very similar to the Dark Strokes filter, but it enables you to control the Stroke Length rather than the stroke direction. The Ink Outlines filter always strokes in a cross-hatched direction, but if the stroke length is short, that will not be apparent. It also performs a "sort-of" find edges that can be very attractive.

Try it:

1. Open the image "Deer.Psd." Duplicate the image (Image➡Duplicate➡OK).

2. Open the Ink Outlines dialog box shown in Figure 14.53 (Filter➡Brush Strokes➡Ink Outlines).

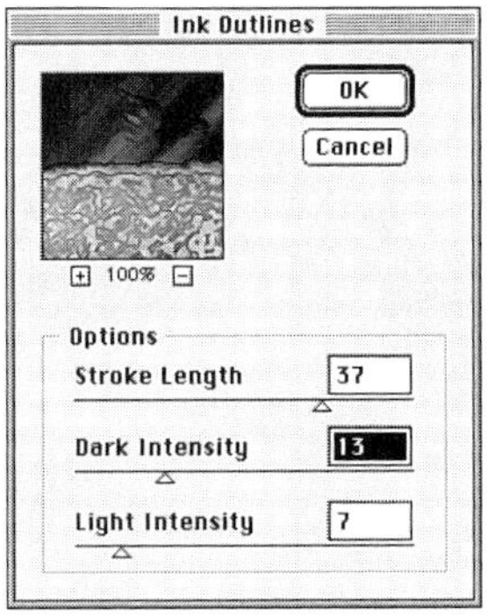

Figure 14.53

The Ink Outlines dialog box.

3. Drag the Stroke Length to 37.

   The Stroke Length setting varies from 1-50. This parameter controls the distance of the cross-hatch stroke. Both small and long strokes look good with this filter.

4. Set the Dark Intensity to 13.

The Dark Intensity can vary from 0-50. It looks best when kept low, so that it does not change all of the dark values to black.

5. Finally, set the Light Intensity to 7.

The Light Intensity varies from 0-50. This parameter builds up quickly, so it looks best at low settings unless you want it to take over the image with super-saturated color.

6. Click OK. Figure 14.54 shows the result.

Figure 14.54

An example of the Ink Outlines filter applied.

Filter type	Category	Supported Color Modes	Preview type	Data Dependent	Color Dependent
Parameter	Stylizing Filter	RGB, Grayscale	Small Filter Preview	Yes. A blank image produces a blank filtered image.	No. The Foreground/Background settings have no effect.

Spatter

The Spatter filter can help to enhance a simple line art graphic. This filter looks good when used on text. At low Smoothness settings the Spatter filter looks as if someone forced the image through an airbrush and it came out in little dots of paint. At higher Smoothness settings, it would be very good for making reflections in water.

Try it:

1. Open the image "Deer.Psd." Duplicate the image (Image➡Duplicate➡OK).

2. Open the Spatter dialog box shown in Figure 14.55 (Filter➡Brush Strokes➡Spatter).

Figure 14.55

The Spatter dialog box.

3. Drag the Spray Radius to 17.

   The Spray Radius setting varies from 0-25. This parameter controls the size of the spray. As this parameter increases, more of the image becomes the spray. The lighter image areas are first affected and the radius continues to increase over more of the image as the setting increases.

4. Set the Smoothness to 2.

   The Smoothness can vary from 1-15. When the Smoothness is 1, the filter sprays fine dots. As the Smoothness increases, the effect becomes more painterly—as if paint were dribbled and smudged, but the Spray Radius needs to increase as well. A high Smoothness on a low Radius shows almost no effect, where as a setting of 3 and 3 looks very good.

5. Click OK. Figure 14.56 shows the result.

Figure 14.56

The Spatter filter applied.

Filter type	Category	Supported Color Modes	Preview type	Data Dependent	Color Dependent
Parameter	Stylizing Filter	RGB, Grayscale	Small Filter Preview	Yes. A blank image produces a blank filtered image.	No. The Foreground/Background settings have no effect.

Sprayed Strokes

The Sprayed Strokes filter can help to enhance a simple line art graphic. This is one of the few "stroke" filters that enables you to stroke an image horizontally or vertically. The Sprayed Strokes filter works well at most settings as long as the Stroke Radius is kept towards the lower end of the scale. It is similar to the Dark Strokes, Spatter, and Ink Outlines filters.

Try it:

1. Open the image "Deer.Psd." Duplicate the image (Image➡Duplicate➡OK).

2. Open the Sprayed Strokes dialog box shown in Figure 14.54 (Filter➡Brush Strokes➡Sprayed Strokes).

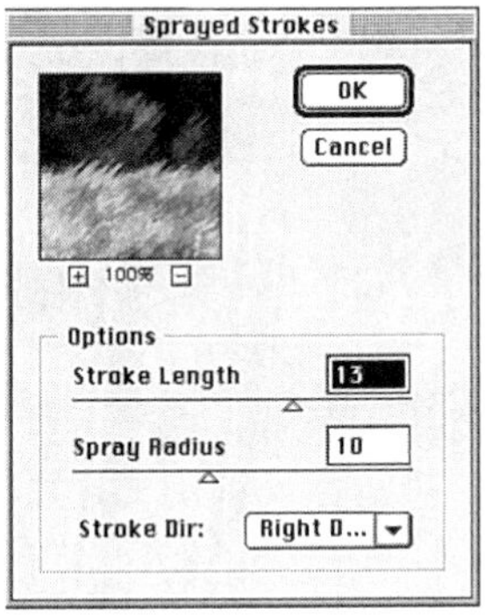

Figure 14.57

The Sprayed Strokes dialog box.

3. Drag the Stroke Length to 13.

The Stroke Width setting varies from 0-20, controlling the linearity of the stroke. It is good at all settings, though it begins to show up at settings above 3.

4. Set the Spray Radius to 10.

   The Spray Radius can vary from 0-25. Keep this fairly low so that you see more of your image and fewer random sprays.

5. Finally, set the Direction to Right Diagonal.

   The Direction can also be Horizontal, Left Diagonal, or Vertical.

6. Click OK. Figure 14.58 shows the result.

Figure 14.58

An example of the Sprayed Strokes filter applied to an image.

Filter type	Category	Supported Color Modes	Preview type	Data Dependent	Color Dependent
Parameter	Stylizing Filter	RGB, Grayscale	Small Filter Preview	Yes. A blank image produces a blank filtered image.	No. The Foreground/Background settings have no effect.

Sumi-e

The Sumi-e filter is a calligraphy filter that works very well in special effects and with text. The Stroke Pressure is the key control here. It makes the difference between the filter being unique and repeating much of what the other filters in the set do.

Try it:

1. Open the image "Deer.Psd." Duplicate the image (Image➥Duplicate➥OK).

2. Open the Sumi-e dialog box shown in Figure 14.59 (Filter➥Brush Strokes➥Sumi-e).

Figure 14.59

The Sumi-e dialog box.

3. Drag the Stroke Width to 10.

    The Stroke Width setting varies from 3-15. This parameter controls the width of the stroke (surprise!).

4. Set the Stroke Pressure to 12.

The Stroke Pressure can vary from 0-15, determining how much black appears carved out of the image. A high stroke pressure shows a lot of black, while a low stroke pressure results in a smooth appearance.

5. Finally, set the Contrast to 14.

The Contrast varies from 0-40. A low contrast maintains the original image lights and darks where as the higher settings intensify both the light and dark values. This parameter does better on the low side.

6. Click OK. Figure 14.60 shows the result.

Figure 14.60

An example of the Sumi-e filter applied to an image.

Filter type	Category	Supported Color Modes	Preview type	Data Dependent	Color Dependent
Parameter	Stylizing Filter	RGB, Grayscale	Small Filter Preview	Yes. A blank image produces a blank filtered image.	No. The Foreground/Background settings have no effect.

PHOTOSHOP'S NATIVE FILTERS—DISTORT

The Distort category of filters includes a number of filters that turn your image into a tangle of pixels. They wave, ZigZag, spherize, ripple, displace, and generally mangle the contents of the image for special effects.

Diffuse Glow

The Diffuse Glow filter adds a subtle—or not-so-subtle—glow to the highlight areas of your image. I have no idea what it is doing in the "Distort" category of filters as it really does not change the geometry of the image as most of the Distort filters do. The Diffuse Glow filter is one of the original Gallery Effects filters. When you set all three controls to their lowest settings, you have no image—it replaces the entire image with your Background color. Setting all three controls to their highest point can still give you a usable image. The Diffuse Glow filter can be applied both to the entire image or to selected areas with good results. It also looks good when used on text.

Try it:

1. Open the image "Seal.Psd." Duplicate the image (Image➤Duplicate➤OK).

2. Set the background color to a soft yellow.

3. Open the Diffuse Glow dialog box shown in Figure 14.61 (Filter➤Distort➤Diffuse Glow).

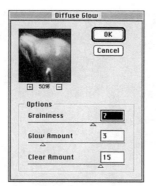

Figure 14.61

The Diffuse Glow dialog box.

4. Drag the Graininess slider to 7.

   The Graininess setting varies from 0-10. This parameter controls the amount of noise in the image. The noise is applied most heavily to the shadow areas in the image. If you move this control to 10 and set the other sliders to 0, you see the faint hint of your image in the pattern of graininess that emerges.

5. Set the Glow Amount to 3.

   The Glow Amount can vary from 0-20, controlling how much of the background color is visible in the image, but it is linked to the Clear Amount as well. A setting of 20 makes the glow overwhelm your image—regardless of the Clear Amount setting. But if you set the Clear Amount too low, all you see is the background color, even if the Glow amount is also set low. For most uses, you will probably want to keep the Glow Amount set below 10.

6. Finally, set the Clear Amount to 15.

   The Clear Amount varies from 0-20. The Clear Amount controls how much of the darker portions of the image are retained. At 0, none of the original image is seen. At 20, the amount of the visible image seen depends upon the Glow Amount setting. If the Glow Amount is also set to 20, only the deepest values in the original image appear.

7. Click OK. Figure 14.62 shows the result.

Figure 14.62

An example of the Diffuse Glow filter applied to an image.

Filter type	Category	Supported Color Modes	Preview type	Data Dependent	Color Dependent
Parameter	Stylizing and Color Change	RGB, Grayscale	Small Filter Preview	Not exactly. A blank image can pick up the background color and noise.	Yes. The Background setting is the "glow" color.

Displace

The Displace filter is a very complex one. Briefly, it reads a second image (a Displacement map) and moves each pixel in the filtered image according to the values in the displacement map. White and black pixels in the displacement map have the most effect. They cause the pixels to be moved the maximum amount in opposite directions. A middle gray value (128) in the Displacement Map causes no movement.

The Displace filter is used for special effects. You can create realistic results that mimic looking at an image through a sheet of glass or through water. You can also create wild effects using one of the pre-created Displacement maps that are stored inside of the Plug-Ins/Filters folder. You can use any grayscale or color image as your displacement map so long as it is saved in Photoshop format. You should not, however, use a layered image as the Displacement map because you can get some unexpected results. You can get very interesting results by using the image as its own Displacement map or by using an otherwise-filtered version of the image as its Displacement map.

Try it:

1. Open the image "Seal.Psd." Duplicate the image (Image➥Duplicate➥OK).

2. Open the Displace dialog box shown in Figure 14.63 (Filter➥Distort➥Displace).

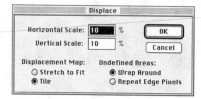

Figure 14.63

The Displace dialog box.

3. Set the Horizontal and Vertical scale boxes to 10%.

   The Horizontal and Vertical scale settings vary from -999 to 999. This parameter controls the direction and amount of the displacement. You may enter a different amount for each box.

4. Click the Tile button of the Displacement Map setting.

   You can elect to tile the Displacement map (use it as a repeat pattern if it is smaller than your original image) or have it Stretch to Fit (resized so that it is the same dimensions as your image).

5. Finally, set the Undefined Areas to Wrap Around.

The Undefined Areas are basically the outer the perimeters of your image (or the edges of the selection). These can wrap (the right edge moves to the left edge as it leaves the image) or the edges can repeat the pixels, which gives it almost the look of a motion blur.

6. Click OK. You will then see a standard "Open File" dialog box that asks you to select the Displacement map image. Select the Displace.Psd image (shown in Figure 14.64). Figure 14.65 shows the result.

Figure 14.64

The Dipslace.Psd Displacement Map.

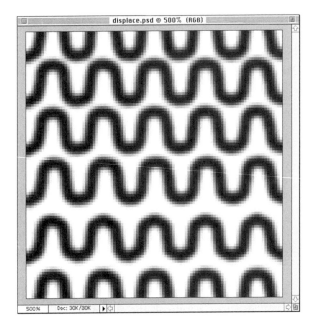

7. Either save this image and make another copy of the original or Undo the filter. See how much different a result you get by selecting Stretch to Fit. First, however, load Channel #4 (Option-Command-4)[Alt-Control-4]. This selects everything in the image *but* the seal.

8. Apply the filter again (Command-Option-F)[Alt-Control-F]. Click the Stretch to Fit button and click OK. Select the Displace.Psd image again. Figure 14.66 shows the result.

Figure 14.65

The Displace filter applied to an image.

Figure 14.66

An example of the Displace filter applied with Stretch to Fit.

Filter type	Category	Supported Color Modes	Preview type	Data Dependent	Color Dependent
Parameter	Special Effects— Displacement Filter	RGB, Grayscale CMYK, Lab	No Preview	Yes. A blank image produces a blank filtered image.	No. The Foreground/Background settings have no effect.

Glass

Another one of the original Gallery Effects filters, the Glass filter is similar in concept to the Displace filter. It performs an action that is very close to a Displacement mapping. The Glass filter was designed, however, to simulate the effect of viewing your image through a pane of glass. It can be used to enhance a simple line art graphic, though you need to add some noise or shading to it first. The Glass filter also looks good when used on patterned text.

Try it:

1. Open the image "Seal.Psd." Duplicate the image (Image➡Duplicate➡OK).

2. Open the Glass dialog box shown in Figure 14.67 (Filter➡Distort➡Glass).

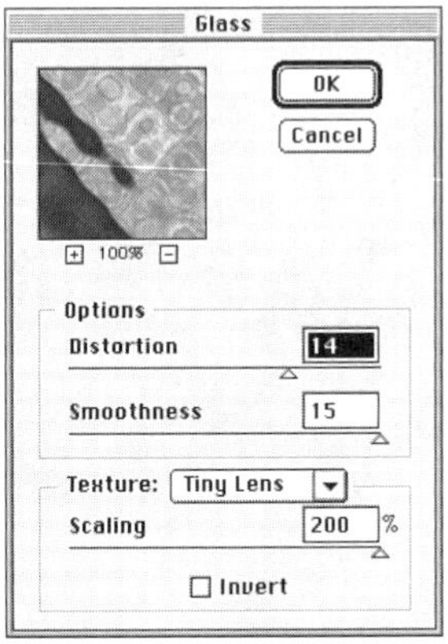

Figure 14.67

The Glass dialog box.

3. Drag the Distortion setting to 15.

   The Distortion setting varies from 0-20, controlling the amount of distortion applied. A setting of 0 produces almost no change. A setting of 20 represents a very thick pane of glass.

4. Set the Smoothness setting to 15.

   The Smoothness can vary from 1-15. A setting of 1 creates a distortion that is very noisy. As the smoothness increases, it is as if the waves in the pane of glass stretch and become more fluid.

5. Next, select the Texture.

Choose the Tiny Lens texture from the list that includes Blocks, Canvas, Frosted, Tiny Lens, or a file that you have selected to use as a texture. You can use the Displacement maps very successfully as textures here. You can even try this with the Displace.Psd image on the CD-ROM.

6. You can Scale the texture from 50% to 200%.

Select the 200% scaling. This makes the texture larger.

7. If you wish, you can Invert the texture. This makes the light areas of the texture pattern dark and vice versa, which inverts the filter effect. Do not select this option right now.

8. Click OK. Figure 14.68 shows the result.

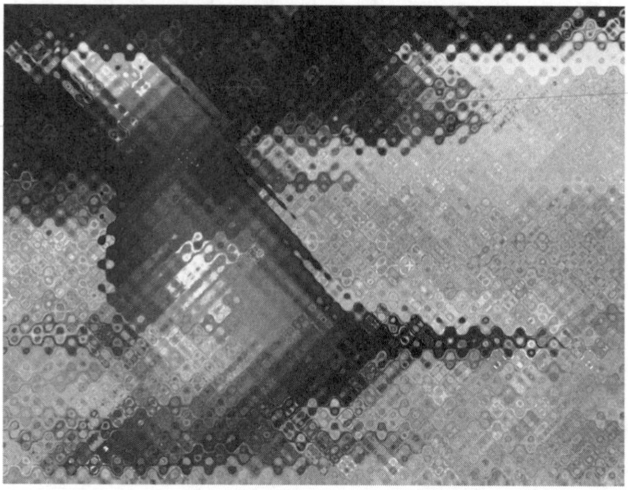

Figure 14.68

The Glass filter applied to an image.

Filter type	Category	Supported Color Modes	Preview type	Data Dependent	Color Dependent
Parameter	Special Effects— Displace- ment Filter	RGB, Grayscale	Small Filter Preview	Yes. A blank image pro- duces a blank filtered image.	No. The Fore- ground/Back- ground settings have no effect.

637

Ocean Ripple

The Ocean Ripple filter is another Gallery Effects that performs a displacement on the image. It is designed to make the image look as if it is under water. You can get much the same look with the Glass filter, but you have more control over the final Glass filter results. The Ocean Ripple filter is "hard-wired" and does not enable you to select the map used for the effect. It can help to enhance a simple line art graphic and looks good when used on text.

Try it:

1. Open the image "Seal.Psd." Duplicate the image (Image➥Duplicate➥OK).

2. Load Channel #4 (Option-Command-4)[Alt-Control-4]. This selects everything in the image *but* the seal.

3. Open the Ocean Ripple dialog box shown in Figure 14.69 (Filter➥Distort➥Ocean Ripples).

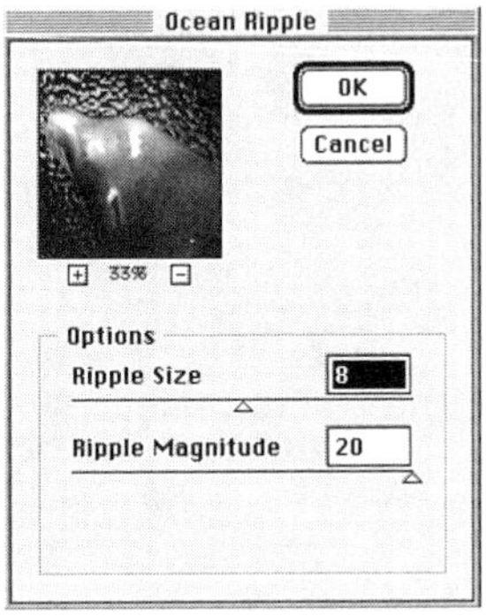

Figure 14.69

The Ocean Ripple dialog box.

4. Drag the Ripple Size to 8.

   The Ripple Size setting varies from 1-15, controlling the actual size of the wave that is used. A setting of 1 still produces a result.

5. Set the Ripple Magnitude to 15.

   The Ripple Magnitude can vary from 0-20. The Ripple Magnitude controls the pull the wave has on the image. A setting of 0 has no pull, therefore, no change occurs—regardless of the Ripple Size setting. By the time the setting is changed to 3, however, you can see an effect if you have a Ripple Size of more than 3. The setting of 15 gives a very noticeable effect— even if the Ripple Size is set to 1.

6. Click OK. Figure 14.70 shows the result.

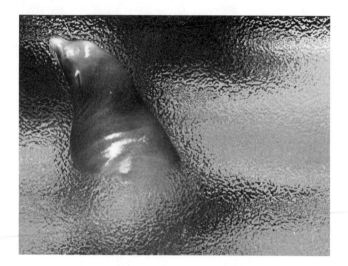

Figure 14.70

The Ocean Ripple filter applied.

Filter type	Category	Supported Color Modes	Preview type	Data Dependent	Color Dependent
Parameter	Special Effects—Displacement Filter	RGB, Grayscale	Small Filter Preview	Yes. A blank image produces a blank filtered image.	No. The Foreground/Background settings have no effect.

Pinch

A "bloat and pinch" filter, the Pinch filter can make the selected area smaller by squeezing in the center or can make it larger by inflating it through the center of the selection. This filter can be used for serious photo-correction if you have a careful hand and make a good selection. You can use the Pinch filter to reduce the size of a model's nose or lips, or to enhance the size of the model's eyes. It can also be used, of course, for special effects.

Try it:

1. Open the image "Seal.Psd." Duplicate the image
   (Image➡Duplicate➡OK).

2. Load Channel #4 (Option-Command-4)[Alt-Control-4}.
   Reverse the selection (Select➡Inverse). This selects only the
   seal.

3. Open the Pinch dialog box shown in Figure 14.71
   (Filter➡Distort➡Pinch).

Figure 14.71

The Pinch dialog box.

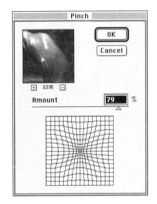

4. Drag the Amount to 79%.

   The Amount setting varies from -100 to +100%. A negative
   amount bloats the selection, a positive amount pinches it.

5. Click OK. Figure 14.69 shows the result.

Filter type	Category	Supported Color Modes	Preview type	Data Dependent	Color Dependent
Parameter	Special Effects or Production Filter	RGB, Grayscale CMYK, Lab	Small Filter/ Wire Frame Preview	Yes. A blank image produces a blank filtered image.	No. The Foreground/Background settings have no effect.

Figure 14.72

The Pinch filter applied to an image.

Polar Coordinates

The Polar Coordinates filter is a special effects filter that has a number of non-obvious uses. It remaps the pixels in an image is as they were going from Rectangular to Polar or Polar to Rectangular mapping (think of the difference between viewing the map of the world as a rectangle or as a flattened globe). You can use this filter to reshape images for wild special effects. You can also use it to create concentric circles from straight lines (Rectangular to Polar) or to make a pattern tile that is seamless on two sides (Polar to Rectangular). You can get very unique results if you work in one coordinate space, change the other, draw some more, and then change back.

Try it:

1. Open the image "Seal.Psd." Duplicate the image (Image➡Duplicate➡OK).

2. Make a new layer (press the modifier key (Option)[Alt] and click the New Layer icon at the bottom of the Layers Palette).

3. Press D to set the colors back to the default of black and white.

4. Select the Marquee tool (M) and choose the Elliptical shape. Draw a circle near the center of the new Layer (about 500 pixels in diameter). Press the Shift key to constrain the ellipse to a circle. Fill the circle with the foreground color, black.

5. Open the Polar Coordinates dialog box shown in Figure 14.73 (Filter➡Distort➡Polar Coordinates).

Figure 14.73

The Polar Coordinates dialog box.

6. Select the Rectangular to Polar setting. Click OK.

7. Using the Line tool (L) set to draw 8-pixel lines, draw three diagonal lines across the circle in each direction.

8. Select the Polar Coordinates filter again (Command-Option-F) [Alt-Control-F]. Choose the Polar to Rectangular setting.

9. Click OK. Figure 14.74 shows the result.

Figure 14.74

An example of the Polar Coordinates filter applied.

Filter type	Category	Supported Color Modes	Preview type	Data Dependent	Color Dependent
Parameter	Deformation Filter	RGB, Grayscale, CMYK, Lab	Small Filter Preview	Yes. A blank image produces a blank filtered image.	No. The Foreground/Background settings have no effect.

Ripple

The Ripple filter is very similar to the Ocean Ripple filter. It is, however, one of the original Photoshop filters, whereas the Ocean Ripple filter belonged to the Adobe Gallery Effects set. The uses are identical, but the results—though both wavy—are a bit different. The Ripple filter is good for simulating marbling.

Try it using a little different technique to localize the effect:

1. Open the image "Seal.Psd." Duplicate the image (Image➡Duplicate➡OK).

2. Drag the icon for the Background layer to the New Layer icon (the center icon at the bottom of the Layers palette).

3. Open the Ripple dialog box shown in Figure 14.75 (Filter➡Distort➡Ripple).

Figure 14.75

The Ripple dialog box.

4. Drag the Amount to 279.

   The Amount setting varies from -999 to 999. This parameter controls the height and direction of the wave. At the ends of the scale, the image begins to pixelate heavily. Your smoothest values are around the 100-300 (+ and -) settings.

5. Set the Size to Large.

   The Size is a drop-down menu of Small, Medium, or Large. The Small ripple is similar to a cross-hatching, the Medium to single waves, and the Large to a double wave.

6. Create a Layer Mask (click the Add Layer Mask icon—the left-most icon at the bottom of the Layers palette). Using black paint, paint over the details in the Seal's face and body until you have restored as much of the original image as you wish.

7. Click OK. Figure 14.76 shows the result.

Figure 14.76

The Ripple filter applied.

Filter type	Category	Supported Color Modes	Preview type	Data Dependent	Color Dependent
Parameter	Displacement/ Deformation Filter	RGB, Grayscale, CMYK, Lab	Small Filter Preview	Yes. A blank image produces a blank filtered image.	No. The Foreground/Background settings have no effect.

Shear

The Shear filter warps images vertically along a grid. The dialog box is a bit confusing, but you can create a variety of curves with it as well as creating straight line effects. The Shear filter is very useful for pattern work or for creating folds in garments. If you need to apply the filter horizontally, change the orientation of your image (Image➥Rotate Clockwise), apply the filter, then rotate back into its original position.

Try it by creating a pattern tile to composite with the main image:

1. Open the image "Seal.Psd." Duplicate the image twice (Image➥Duplicate➥OK).

2. Reduce one copy to 100 pixels wide (Image➥Image Size➥Pixel, Dimensions 100 pixels width, Constrain Proportions, Resample Image Bicubic).

3. Open the Shear dialog box shown in Figure 14.77 (Filter➥Distort➥Shear).

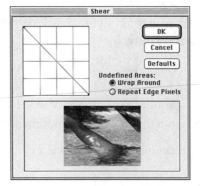

Figure 14.77

The Shear dialog box.

4. Drag the top point into the upper-left corner of the grid. Drag the bottom point into the lower-right corner of the grid.

   You can create additional points by clicking the black skew line to make a point and then moving the point somewhere along the grid. Leave the straight lines for this example. Click OK. Figure 14.78 shows the result.

5. Select the entire image (Command-A)[Control-A]. Define this as a pattern (Edit➥Define Pattern).

6. Click the other copy to make it active. Make a new layer (press the modifier key (Option)[Alt] and click on the New Layer icon at the bottom of the Layers Palette).

Figure 14.78

The Shear filter applied.

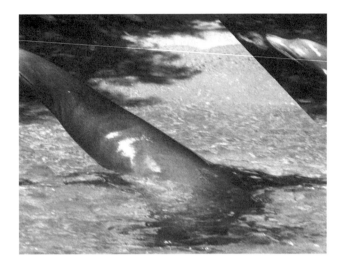

7. Fill the image with the pattern (Shift-Delete➡ Pattern, 100 percent opacity, Normal).

8. Load Channel #4 (Option-Command-4)[Alt-Control-4]. Create a Layer Mask (click the Add Layer Mask icon—the left-most icon at the bottom of the Layers palette). The seal is revealed and the pattern only shows up behind the seal.

9. Change the Blending mode to Screen. Figure 14.79 shows the result.

Figure 14.79

The Shear filter blended into an original image.

Filter type	Category	Supported Color Modes	Preview type	Data Dependent	Color Dependent
Parameter	Deformation Filter	RGB, Grayscale, CMYK, Lab	Small Filter Preview	Yes. A blank image produces a blank filtered image.	No. The Foreground/Background settings have no effect.

Spherize

The Spherize filter bloats a selection or creates a spherical form on an image. It works horizontally, vertically, or in both directions. The Spherize filter is only useful for special effects. It does not add lighting to the sphere as do the KPT Glass Lens filters. The Spherize filter is also useful for creating water drops.

Try this technique of filtering the image in only one channel:

1. Open the image "Seal.Psd." Duplicate the image (Image➡Duplicate➡OK).

2. In the Channels palette, click the Red channel so that it becomes the only one selected. Click the Eye next to the RGB channel to view the composite channel.

3. Open the Spherize dialog box shown in Figure 14.80 (Filter➡Distort➡Spherize).

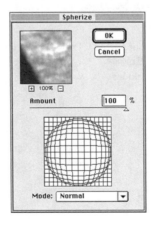

Figure 14.80

The Spherize dialog box.

4. Drag the Amount to 100%.

The Amount varies from -100 to +100. The negative numbers squish the image.

5. Set the Mode to Normal.

The Mode can be Normal, Horizontal Only, or Vertical Only.

6. Click OK. Figure 14.81 shows the result to the Red channel. This technique of spherizing in a channel creates a ghost image that shows up very well in color but does not reproduce in black and white.

Figure 14.81

An example of the Spherize filter applied to the Red channel only.

Filter type	Category	Supported Color Modes	Preview type	Data Dependent	Color Dependent
Parameter	Deforma-tion Filter	RGB, Grayscale, CMYK, Lab	Small Filter/ Wire Frame Preview	Yes. A blank image pro-duces a blank filtered image.	No. The Fore-ground/Back-ground settings have no effect.

Twirl

The Twirl filter can give an image a little twist, or it can place it in the center of a maelstrom. The Twirl filter takes the pixels in the image and stirs them as if they were liquid. The result, depending upon the settings selected, can look like you've just mixed chocolate into a bowl of vanilla cake batter by swirling it in a circular manner. This filter is very useful in creating seamless pattern effects when it is used to twirl the area where the tiles meet (you can see that technique in the Offset filter section).

Try it:

1. Open the image "Seal.Psd." Duplicate the image (Image➡Duplicate➡OK).

2. Load Channel #4 (Option-Command-4)[Alt-Control-4].

3. Open the Twirl dialog box shown in Figure 14.82 (Filter➡Distort➡Twirl).

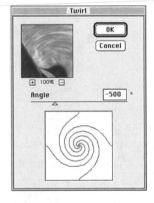

Figure 14.82

The Twirl dialog box.

4. Drag the Angle to -500.

   The Angle setting varies from -999 to +999, controlling the direction and angle of the twirl, which you can see in the wire frame preview. This setting rotates the center of the image more so than the outer edges, creating a twirl, or vortex, that is counter-clockwise (with negative settings) or clock-wise (with positive settings).

5. Click OK. Figure 14.83 shows the result.

Figure 14.83

The Twirl filter applied to an image.

Filter type	Category	Supported Color Modes	Preview type	Data Dependent	Color Dependent
Parameter	Deformation Filter	RGB, Grayscale,	Small Filter/ Wire Frame Preview	Yes. A blank image produces a blank filtered image.	No. The Foreground/Background settings have no effect.

Wave

The Wave filter is the most complex of the native Photoshop filters. It has more parameters than almost any other filter. The Wave filter is a very useful filter for texture creation, but it can totally obliterate the content of the image. Most settings destroy the image completely. It is also used to simulate marbling. This filter's settings have no real "logic;" you need to fiddle with them until you see a preview you like. This is tacitly implied by the "randomize" button built into the filter.

Try the Wave filter at settings that do not quite remove the entire image:

1. Open the image "Seal.Psd." Duplicate the image (Image➡Duplicate➡OK).

2. Open the Wave dialog box shown in Figure 14.84
   (Filter➧Distort➧Wave).

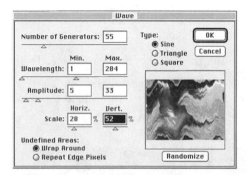

Figure 14.84

The Wave dialog box.

3. Drag the Number of Generators to 55.

   The Number of Generators setting varies from 1-999. This
   parameter controls the number of wave forms that the filter
   produces. The larger the number, the more complex the image.
   Good results, however, can be obtained with very few waves
   (3-5) as well.

4. Set the Wave Length minimum to 1 and the maximum to 284.

   The Wave Length, with settings ranging from 1-999, represents
   the distance horizontally between each up-and-down of the
   wave. A short wave length causes many more up-and-down
   spikes across the image, whereas the longest wave length is just
   a single curve.

5. Set the Wave Amplitude minimum to 5 and the maximum to 33.

   The Wave Amplitude varies from 1-999. It describes the height
   of the wave, with 1 being a shallow wave and 999 being very
   high.

6. Set the Horizontal Scale to 28% and the Vertical Scale to 52%.

   The Scale sets the size of the effect. At low numbers, depending
   upon the type of wave selected and the number of generators,
   you can create almost solid runs of colors. If both settings are
   0, however, the filter shows no change.

7. Set the Undefined areas to Wrap Around.

   These are the areas where the wave leaves the canvas. You can set these to wrap or to repeat the edge pixels.

8. Set the Type to Sine.

   This specifies the shape of the wave: Sine, Triangle, or Square. The shape of the wave has a major impact on the filter results—even with all other settings held the same. Click OK. Figure 14.85 shows the result.

Figure 14.85

The Wave filter applied to an image.

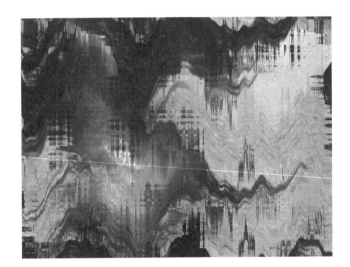

9. Drag the icon for the Background layer to the New Layer icon (the center icon at the bottom of the Layers palette). Re-open the filter dialog box (Command-Option-F)[Alt-Control-F].

10. Change the Type to Square. Leave all of the other settings alone. Click OK.

11. Change the Blending mode to Darken. Figure 14.86 shows the result.

Figure 14.86

An example of the Square Wave filter applied with the Blending mode changed.

Filter type	Category	Supported Color Modes	Preview type	Data Dependent	Color Dependent
Parameter	Deformation Filter	RGB, Grayscale, CMYK, Lab	Small Filter Preview	Yes. A blank image produces a blank filtered image.	No. The Foreground/Background settings have no effect.

ZigZag

The ZigZag filter is another way to add ripples, ridges, or wavelets to your image. It is similar to the other wavelet filters (Ocean Ripple, Ripple, Twirl), but it works on concentric circles of sorts. The ZigZag filter is the best filter for producing the ripples of a stone cast into a river.

Try it:

1. Open the image "Seal.Psd." Duplicate the image (Image➡Duplicate➡OK).

2. Load Channel #4 (Option-Command-4)[Alt-Control-4].

3. Open the ZigZag dialog box shown in Figure 14.87 (Filter➡Distort➡ZigZag).

Figure 14.87

The ZigZag dialog box.

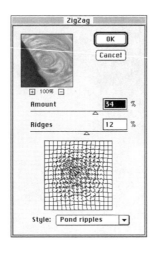

4. Drag the Amount to 34%.

The Amount setting varies from -100 to +100%, controlling the direction and elevation of the ridge. A negative number ridges in where a positive setting ridges out.

5. Set the Ridges to 12%.

The Ridges can vary from 1% to 20%. This controls the amount of rings in the final effect. The percent is not clear, but the effect does work differently depending upon the size of the area being filtered. A set of numbers that looks wonderful on a tiny image looks lost on a larger one.

6. Finally, set the Style to Pond ripples.

The other options are Around center, which looks like the Twirl filter with additional wavelets on each spoke, and Out from center, in which the pull of the effect is strongest along the four main "arms" right at the center of the filter.

7. Click OK. Figure 14.88 shows the result.

Figure 14.88

An example of the ZigZag filter applied.

Filter type	Category	Supported Color Modes	Preview type	Data Dependent	Color Dependent
Parameter	Deformation/ Displacement Filter	RGB, Grayscale, CMYK, Lab	Small Filter Preview	Yes. A blank image produces a blank filtered image.	No. The Foreground/Background settings have no effect.

PHOTOSHOP'S NATIVE FILTERS—NOISE

The Noise category of filters are used for pre-press as well as for special effects. They are among the most valuable and frequently used filters in Photoshop's native set. The filters both add and remove noise from images (Noise is defined as extraneous pixels that either are film grain or imperfections such as dust in the image).

Add Noise

The Add Noise filter is used to add some texture to an image by way of tiny pixel dustings. Add Noise is one of the only "something-for-nothing" filters. It gives you basically the same results regardless of the image content. The Add Noise filter and a blank image are frequently the starting ground for many interesting textures. Add Noise is used to conceal "touch-ups" of flat color on an image, on areas where an image needs to be re-grained, and, inside of individual channels to keep gradients from banding (by adding a tiny but different amount of noise to each channel).

Try it:

1. Open the image "Elf.Psd." Duplicate the image (Image➡Duplicate➡OK). This image is typical of a "bad-but-cute" photo that a photo lab might be asked to retouch. We need to remove the background and replace the door with a gradient.

2. Load Channel #4 (Option-Command-4)[Alt-Control-4].

3. Select the Gradient tool (G). In the Gradient Editor, select the NewBkg as the Gradient (Gradient Options➡Edit... button➡Load➡NewBkg). Drag the Gradient from the upper-left corner to the bottom-right corner. The Gradient is OK but too flat. It needs grain to match the image.

4. Open the Add Noise dialog box shown in Figure 14.89 (Filter➡Noise➡Add Noise).

5. Drag the Amount to 10.

   The Amount setting varies from 1-999, controlling the amount of noise added. A tiny bit of noise (10 and under) is all that is needed to match film grain. Amounts larger than that are for special effects or mezzotints and textures.

6. Set the Distribution to Gaussian.

   The Distribution can be Uniform or Gaussian. These are statistical concepts. A Uniform distribution has even coverage throughout, while a Gaussian distribution has some heavier clumps and some thinner spots (Have you ever noticed that a fast restaurant seems to be either very busy or empty? That people seem to enter a store in clumps rather than at a consistent rate? These are Gaussian distributions).

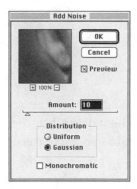

Figure 14.89

The Add Noise dialog box.

7. Finally, make sure Monochromatic is not checked.

When it is set, the Noise that is added is only grayscale rather than RGB or CMYK.

8. Click OK. Figure 14.90 shows the result.

Figure 14.90

The Add Noise filter applied to an image.

Filter type	Category	Supported Color Modes	Preview type	Data Dependent	Color Dependent
Parameter	Production and Special Effects Filter	RGB, Grayscale, CMYK, Lab	Full Image Preview	No. This is a "something-for-nothing: filter.	No. The Fore-ground/Back-ground settings have no effect.

Despeckle

The Despeckle filter is used to remove extraneous bits of noise from an image after it is scanned—and usually before it is color-corrected. This is a one-step filter that has no parameters. The Despeckle filter can, however, be applied multiple times. It smoothes out a damaged histogram and helps to restore missing (gapped) values.

Try it:

1. Open the image "Elf.Psd." Duplicate the image (Image➡Duplicate➡OK).

2. Select the Despeckle filter (Filter➡Noise➡Despeckle). Before and After Levels histograms are shown in Figure 14.91 and 14.92. Notice the After is a bit more smooth and that some of the spikes on the histogram are less pronounced. There is no point in showing a filtered image however, as the difference is not apparent to the naked eye.

Figure 14.91

The Levels Histogram before the Despeckle filter is applied.

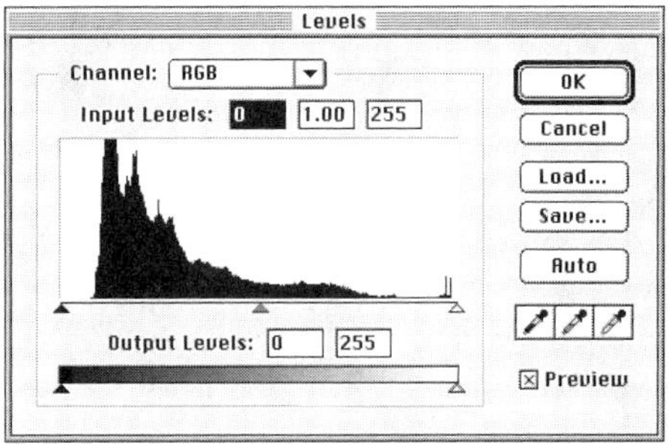

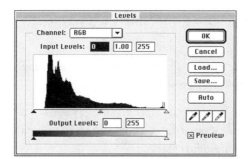

Figure 14.92

The Levels Histogram after the Despeckle filter is applied.

Filter type	Category	Supported Color Modes	Preview type	Data Dependent	Color Dependent
One-Step	PrePress Filter	RGB, Grayscale, CMYK, Lab	None	Yes. A blank image produces a blank filtered image.	No. The Foreground/Background settings have no effect.

Dust & Scratches

The Dust & Scratches filter helps remove imperfections from an image. It is best used in tiny selections, as it performs a blurring action within a selection and tries to make the colors in the selected area blend into one another. The Dust & Scratches filter can be used very successfully for special effects, however, by setting the Radius to 16 (the maximum) and the Threshold to 0 (the minimum). At these settings, the filter performs a full image blur that retains bright areas of the image without muddying them the way that the Gaussian Blur filter does. Figure 14.93 shows the dialog box and screen capture of the image with a tiny scratch selected.

Figure 14.93

The Dust & Scratches dialog box with a scratch selected.

659

Try this example for special effects as a way to salvage this cute-but-low-quality photo:

1. Open the image "Elf.Psd." Duplicate the image (Image➡Duplicate➡OK).

2. Drag the icon for the Background layer to the New Layer icon (the center icon at the bottom of the Layers palette). Set the Blending mode to Darken.

3. Click the Background Layer name in the Layers palette to make the Background Layer the active one.

4. Open the Dust & Scratches dialog box shown in Figure 14.94 (Filter➡Noise➡Dust & Scratches).

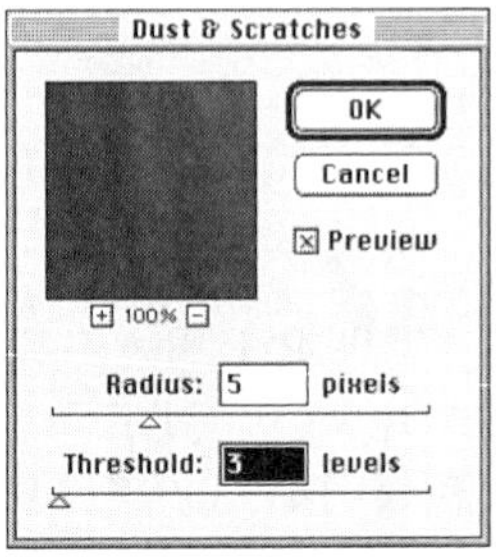

Figure 14.94

The Dust & Scratches dialog box.

5. Drag the Radius to 16.

   The Radius setting varies from 1-16. This parameter controls the distance from each pixel that the filter "looks" when calculating the result. A Radius of 16 blurs a very large area.

6. Set the Threshold to 0.

   The Threshold can vary from 0 to 255. This parameter controls how similar a value is needed before a pixel is considered in the calculation. A Threshold of 0 considers every pixel; as you increase the Threshold, you decrease the number of pixels to be filtered. By the time you reach a Threshold of 10, you have usually removed all of the nearby pixels and will see no change in your image.

7. Click OK. Figure 14.95 shows the result.

Figure 14.95

An example of the Dust & Scratches filter applied to a Background layer.

Filter type	Category	Supported Color Modes	Preview type	Data Dependent	Color Dependent
Parameter	PrePress and Special Effects/ Focus Filter	RGB, Grayscale, CMYK, Lab	Full Image Preview	Yes. A blank image produces a blank filtered image.	No. The Foreground/Background settings have no effect.

Median

One of the original Photoshop filters, the Median filter is the early prototype of the Watercolor filter. It selects the "average" or median color of a selection for the distance of the Radius. In that sense, the Median filter is very close to the Dust & Scratches filter (which made its debut in Photoshop 3.0), but it does not have as many controls, which is why Dust & Scratches is better for pre-press.

Try it:

1. Open the image "Elf.Psd." Duplicate the image (Image➡Duplicate➡OK).

2. Load Channel #5 (Option-Command-5)[Alt-Control-5]. This confines the filter to everywhere but the child's head.

Figure 14.96

The Median dialog box.

3. Open the Median dialog box shown in Figure 14.96 (Filter➡Noise➡Median).

4. Drag the Radius to 10.

   The Radius setting varies from 1-16. This parameter controls the distance the filter looks from each pixel in order to calculate the result. A larger radius results in a blurrier image.

5. Click OK. Figure 14.97 shows the result.

Filter type	Category	Supported Color Modes	Preview type	Data Dependent	Color Dependent
Parameter	Special Effects/ Focus Filter	RGB, Grayscale CMYK, Lab	Full Image Preview	Yes. A blank image produces a blank filtered image.	No. The Foreground/Background settings have no effect.

Figure 14.97

The Median filter applied to an image.

PHOTOSHOP'S NATIVE FILTERS—PIXELATE

The Pixelate filters work by breaking up the image into clumps of pixels—square blocks (Mosaic filter), irregular blocks (Crystallize), random dots (Mezzotint), and so on. They all stylize an image at low settings, and they can destroy the content of the image at higher settings.

Color Halftone

The Color Halftone filter changes your image into a poor quality newsprint color image. Why, you ask? This is basically a special effect. It has no value as a production tool. The Color Halftone filter makes images look like an old comic book strip, but you can select the size and angle of the halftone dots. My advice is to not change the default screen angles unless you really have a good reason to do so.

Try it:

1. Open the image "Cactus.Psd." Duplicate the image (Image➡Duplicate➡OK).

2. Open the Color Halftone dialog box shown in Figure 14.98 (Filter➡Pixilate➡Color Halftone).

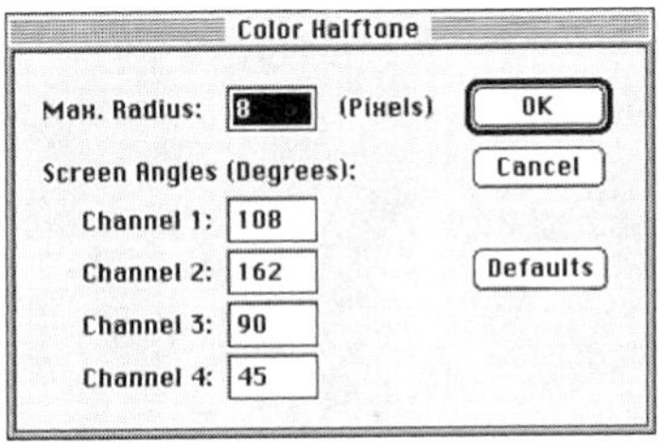

Figure 14.98

The Color Halftone dialog box.

3. Drag the Max Radius to 8.

   The Max Radius setting varies from 4-127. This parameter controls the size of the halftone dot. At 4, you get fine-grained poor quality newsprint; at 127, you obliterate your image totally.

4. Leave Channel #4's settings at their default. The values vary from 0 to 360 degrees. These represent the screen angles for each plate.

5. Click OK. Figure 14.99 shows the result.

Filter type	Category	Supported Color Modes	Preview type	Data Dependent	Color Dependent
Parameter	Sylizing/ special effects Filter	RGB, Grayscale CMYK, Lab	None	No. A blank image still produces a result.	No. The Fore-ground/Back-ground settings have no effect.

Figure 14.99

The Color Halftone filter applied.

Crystallize

The Crystallize filter changes your image into colored cells or honey-combs based on the image colors. This is a special effects filter that can leave your image looking very different. Crystallize is a very useful filter, however, for creating stylized versions of an image or for using in a channel and then using the channel as a mask for applying a different filter. The resulting shades of gray then vary the filter results in a seemingly random way.

Try it:

1. Open the image "Cactus.Psd." Duplicate the image
   (Image➡Duplicate➡OK).

2. Open the Crystallize dialog box shown in Figure 14.100
   (Filter➡Pixilate➡Crystallize).

3. Drag the Cell Size to 40.

Figure 14.100

The Crystallize dialog box.

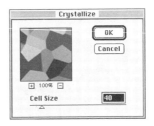

The Cell Size setting varies from 3-300, controlling the size of the crystal cells. If you want your image to be recognizable, you need to keep the size below about 10.

4. Click OK. Figure 14.101 shows the result.

Figure 14.101

An example of the Crystallize filter applied to an image.

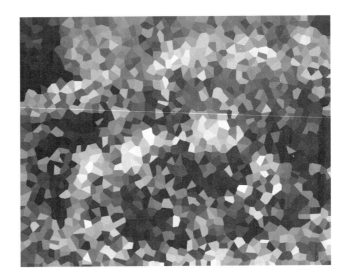

Filter type	Category	Supported Color Modes	Preview type	Data Dependent	Color Dependent
Parameter	Distressed Filter	RGB, Grayscale, CMYK, Lab	Small Filter Preview	Yes. A blank image produces a blank filtered image.	No. The Foreground/Background settings have no effect.

Facet

The Facet filter removes some of the anti-aliasing from the edges of an image. It is a One-Step filter that may need to be applied a number of times before you see a result. The Facet filter is a special effects filter.

Try it:

1. Open the image "Cactus.Psd." Duplicate the image (Image➥Duplicate➥OK).

2. Select the Facet filter (Filter➥Pixilate➥Facet). Figure 14.102 shows a close-up of the "before" image.

Figure 14.102

An image before the Facet filter is applied.

3. Figure 14.103 shows a close-up of the result.

Filter type	Category	Supported Color Modes	Preview type	Data Dependent	Color Dependent
One-Step	Stylizing Filter	RGB, Grayscale, CMYK, Lab	None	Yes. A blank image produces a blank filtered image.	No. The Foreground/Background settings have no effect.

667

Figure 14.103

The image after the Facet filter is applied.

Figure 14.103

The image after the Facet filter is applied.

Fragment

The Fragment filter is a One-Step filter that makes your image look as if it has been in a 4.2 earthquake (just enough to look shaken, but not enough to get broken).

Try it:

1. Open the image "Cactus.Psd." Duplicate the image (Image➡Duplicate➡OK).

2. Select the Fragment filter (Filter➡Pixilate➡Fragment).

3. Click OK. Figure 14.104 shows the result.

Filter type	Category	Supported Color Modes	Preview type	Data Dependent	Color Dependent
One-Step	Stylizing Filter	RGB, Grayscale, CMYK, Lab	None	Yes. A blank image produces a blank filtered image.	No. The Foreground/Background settings have no effect.

Figure 14.104

The Fragment filter applied.

Mezzotint

The Mezzotint filter is a very unsuccessful attempt to duplicate the traditional process of creating a mezzotint. I do not like this filter at any setting. It can be used for special effects work but produces much too coarse an image to use as a mezzotint. You get better results creating a grayscale mezzo by using the Diffusion Dither option on the Bitmap conversion. If you need a color mezzotint, break your file into the component channels (select Split Channels in the Channels palette—any layers will have to be merged or flattened first, if you wish to work with them). Change each channel to a bitmap and then back to grayscale mode, and re-combine them by selecting Merge Channels in the Channels palette.

Try it:

1. Open the image "Cactus.Psd." Duplicate the image (Image➥Duplicate➥OK).

2. Open the Mezzotint dialog box shown in Figure 14.105 (Filter➥Pixilate➥Mezzotint).

Figure 14.105

The Mezzotint dialog box.

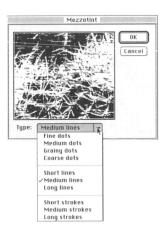

3. Drag the pull-down menu to Medium Lines.

This filter is really a One-Step filter with 10 filters combined. You can only control the method used. You can select from Dots: Fine, Medium, Grainy, or Coarse; Lines: Short, Medium, or Long; or Strokes: Short, Medium, or Long.

4. Click OK. Figure 14.106 shows the result.

Figure 14.106

The Mezzotint filter applied.

Filter type	Category	Supported Color Modes	Preview type	Data Dependent	Color Dependent
Parameter	Stylizing/ Distressed Filter	RGB, Grayscale, CMYK, Lab	Small Filter Preview	No. A blank image produces an interesting texture.	No. The Fore-ground/Back-ground settings have no effect.

Mosaic

The Mosaic filter changes your image into large pixels—solid blocks of color. It finds the average color in the size block that you select and uses that to create the blocks. The Mosaic filter produces a result that is an abstraction of the image. It is similar in action to the Crystallize filter, but it makes square blocks rather than polygonal cells. The Mosaic filter is very useful for simplifying an image or background.

Try it:

1. Open the image "Cactus.Psd." Duplicate the image (Image➡Duplicate➡OK).

2. Open the Mosaic dialog box shown in Figure 14.107 (Filter➡Pixilate➡Mosaic).

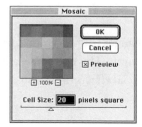

Figure 14.107

The Mosaic dialog box.

3. Drag the Cell Size to 24.

   The Cell Size setting varies from 2-64. This parameter controls the size of the blocks created.

4. Click OK. Figure 14.108 shows the result.

671

Figure 14.108

An example of the Mosaic
filter applied.

Filter type	Category	Supported Color Modes	Preview type	Data Dependent	Color Dependent
Parameter	Stylizing/ Distressed Filter	RGB, Grayscale, CMYK, Lab	Full Image Preview	Yes. A blank image produces a blank filtered image.	No. The Foreground/Background settings have no effect.

Pointillize

The Pointillize filter changes your image into tiny dots—like a pointillist painting by Georges Seurat. This can create a lovely stylized effect. The Pointillize filter is a special effects filter, and can also be used for texture creation.

Try it:

1. Open the image "Cactus.Psd." Duplicate the image (Image➡Duplicate➡OK).

2. Select a brownish tone from the image as your background color. This is the color that will appear between the dots as the background.

3. Open the Pointillize dialog box shown in Figure 14.109 (Filter➡Pixilate➡Pointillize).

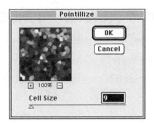

Figure 14.109

The Pointillize dialog box.

4. Drag the Cell Size to 9.

The Cell Size setting varies from 3-300, controlling the size of the dots created. Sizes over about 15 (depending upon your original image size) make the original unrecognizable.

5. Click OK. Figure 14.110 shows the result.

Figure 14.110

The Pointillize filter applied to an image.

Filter type	Category	Supported Color Modes	Preview type	Data Dependent	Color Dependent
Parameter	Stylizing/ Distressed Filter	RGB, Grayscale, CMYK, Lab	Full Image Preview	No. A blank image produces a very pretty dot pattern.	Yes. The Background color setting becomes the background color.

PHOTOSHOP'S NATIVE FILTERS—RENDER

The Render filters create special effects with light. They add clouds, lens flares, and lighting effects. The Render filters are the most computationally intensive filters in Photoshop.

Clouds

The Clouds filter is the only filter that works in a totally transparent, empty Layer. The filter replaces any image data that is present and does not take the image data into its calculations at all. You can use this filter to create cloudy environments such as skies, smoke, and haze. Your best technique is to apply the Clouds filter to an empty Layer and then composite it into the image.

Try it:

1. Open the image "Tulips.Psd." Duplicate the image (Image➡Duplicate➡OK).

2. Make a new layer (press the modifier key (Option)[Alt] and click the New Layer icon at the bottom of the Layers Palette).

3. Select white as your foreground color and pick a brown from the image as your background color.

4. Apply the Clouds filter (Filter➡Render➡Clouds).

5. Change the Blending mode to Darken. Figure 14.111 shows the result.

Figure 14.111

The Clouds filter applied.

Filter type	Category	Supported Color Modes	Preview type	Data Dependent	Color Dependent
One-Step	Destuctive Filter	RGB, Grayscale	None	No. You can use an empty layer.	Yes. The Fore-ground/Back-ground settings become the cloud colors.

Difference Clouds

The Difference Clouds filter takes the Clouds filter and uses the foreground and background colors to apply a Difference calculation to the existing image. As the filter creates the clouds, instead of seeing their color, you see the difference between the cloud color and pixel in the image. This can produce startlingly beautiful results, but the Difference Clouds filter is only a special effects filter.

Note

This filter does not work with Lab mode images.

Try it:

1. Open the image "Tulips.Psd." Duplicate the image (Image➡Duplicate➡OK).

2. Pick a yellow and purple from the image as your foreground and background colors.

3. Apply the Difference Clouds filter (Filter➡Render➡Difference Clouds). Figure 14.112 shows the result.

Filter type	Category	Supported Color Modes	Preview type	Data Dependent	Color Dependent
One-Step	Stylizing/ Special Effects Filter	RGB, Grayscale, CMYK	None	No. A Blank image still let the Difference calculations appear.	Yes. The Fore-ground/Back-ground settings have a major effect.

Figure 14.112

The Difference Clouds filter applied.

Lens Flare

The Lens Flare filter simulates the effect of the sun hitting a camera lens as the picture is taken. It is the kind of "real effect" that you'd probably toss out a negative for, but in the digital world, you actually create it deliberately. Truthfully, the Lens Flare filter is a neat effect. You can keep the effect fluid by applying in a Layer that is filled only with neutral gray and a Blending mode of Overlay, or Soft or Hard Light. That way you can control how it composites with the rest of your image.

Try it:

1. Open the image "Tulips.Psd." Duplicate the image (Image➡Duplicate➡OK).

2. Make a new layer: press the modifier key (Option)[Alt] and click the New Layer icon at the bottom of the Layers Palette. In the Options dialog box, select Hard Light mode and Fill with Hard Light—Neutral Color (50% Gray).

3. Open the Lens Flare dialog box shown in Figure 14.113 (Filter➡Render➡Lens Flare).

4. Drag the Brightness to 114.

   The Brightness setting varies from 0-300%. This parameter controls the intensity of the effect. If the setting gets too high, all you see is a flash of white light.

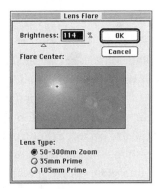

Figure 14.113

The Lens Flare dialog box.

5. Set the Style to 50-300mm Zoom.

   Your other choices are 35mm Prime and 105mm Prime.

6. Click OK. Figure 14.114 shows the result.

Figure 14.114

The Lens Flare filter applied to an image.

Filter type	Category	Supported Color Modes	Preview type	Data Dependent	Color Dependent
Parameter	Special Effects Filter	RGB only	Small Filter Preview	No	No. The Foreground/Background settings have no effect.

Lighting Effects

The Lighting Effects filter is, along with the Wave filter, the most complicated filter in Photoshop's native set. This filter enables you to change the lighting in the image and to add texture and embossing effects. The Lighting Effects filter can simulate the effects of a light source or multiple light sources on the colors in your image. It can be used as a production filter to correct lighting or to correct images being composed so that they fit together better. You can also use this filter to emboss text into your image. Of course, it is also useful for wild special effects. Photoshop comes with a large number of lighting styles built-in, and you can save and load your own as well. This is the closest native filter to a mini-application within the program.

Try it:

1. Open the image "Tulips.Psd." Duplicate the image (Image➡Duplicate➡OK).

2. Open the Lighting Effects dialog box shown in Figure 14.115 (Filter➡Render➡Lighting Effects).

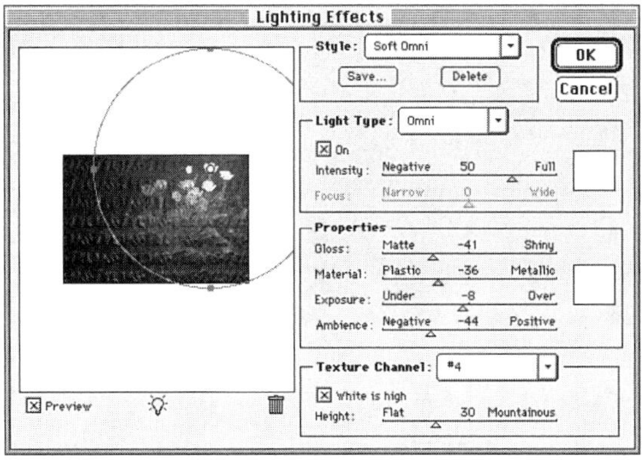

Figure 14.115

The Lighting Effects dialog box.

3. Set the Style to Soft Omni.

   There are many styles from which to choose. Preview a few before selecting the Soft Omni style.

4. Move the Omni light on the preview box so that the center of the light is on top of the middle yellow tulip in the top right.

You can move the light by clicking its center and dragging it. Stretch the light by clicking and dragging the small box on top of it until it touches the top of the preview area.

5. Finally, Select Channel #4 as your texture channel and check the "White is High" box. Move the Height slider to 30.

By checking "White is High," you tell the Lighting Effects filter to use the lightest values in Channel #4 as a bump map to give the image the optical illusion of height or embossing. The darkest areas of the channel become the "low points" in the filtered image.

6. Click OK. Figure 14.116 shows the result. Notice how the text was embossed into the image.

Figure 14.116

An example of the Lighting Effects filter applied.

Filter type	Category	Supported Color Modes	Preview type	Data Dependent	Color Dependent
Mini-app	Color Change/ 3D Filter	RGB only	Small Filter Preview	No. A blank image can still be lit.	No. The Foreground/Background settings have no effect.

Texture Fill

The Texture Fill filter is a "helper" filter for the Lighting Effects filter. It opens a grayscale image (and *only* grayscale) saved in Photoshop format, uses that file as a pattern, and fills your image with it. The Texture Fill filter is designed to be used on a channel, which then becomes a texture channel for the Lighting Effects filter.

Try it:

1. Open the image "Tulips.Psd." Duplicate the image (Image➡Duplicate➡OK).

2. Click the New Channel icon in the center of the Channels palette to create a new channel (Channel #5).

3. Select the Texture Fill filter (Filter➡Render➡Texture Fill) and choose the image Texure.Psd as the fill pattern. Figure 14.117 shows this image.

Figure 14.117

The Texture Fill "source" pattern.

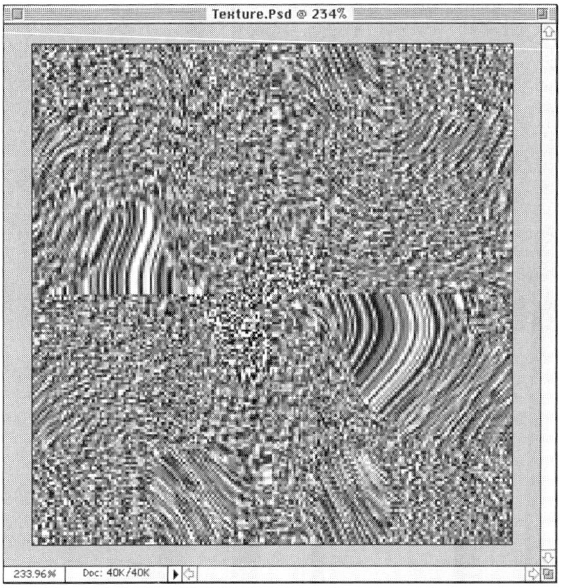

4. Apply the Lighting Effects filter to the RGB channel (Filter➡Render➡Lighting Effects). Select the Five Lights Down style.

5. Click OK. Figure 14.118 shows the result.

Figure 14.118

The Texture Fill filter applied.

Filter type	Category	Supported Color Modes	Preview type	Data Dependent	Color Dependent
Parameter	Destructive Filter	RGB, Grayscale, CMYK, Lab	None	No	No. The Foreground/Background settings have no effect.

PHOTOSHOP'S NATIVE FILTERS—SHARPEN

The Sharpen filters are production-oriented filters that help enhance the focus of the image to improve its quality and to help prepare it for the slight loss of focus (softening) that occurs when it is half-toned prior to printing. The only filter you really need to use is the Unsharp Mask filter, however.

Sharpen

The Sharpen filter is a One-Step filter that applies a tiny bit of sharpening. The amount is so slight that it is not always visible to the eye.

Try it:

1. Open the image "Tulip.Psd." Duplicate the image (Image➡Duplicate➡OK).

2. Apply the Sharpen filter. (Filter➡Sharpen➡Sharpen).

Filter type	Category	Supported Color Modes	Preview type	Data Dependent	Color Dependent
One-Step	Focus	RGB, Grayscale, CMYK, Lab	None	Yes. A blank image produces a blank filtered image.	No. The Foreground/Background settings have no effect.

Sharpen More

The Sharpen More filter is a little bit stronger than the Sharpen filter—but not much.

Try it:

1. Open the image "Tulip.Psd." Duplicate the image (Image➡Duplicate➡OK).

2. Apply the Sharpen More filter (Filter➡Sharpen➡Sharpen More).

Filter type	Category	Supported Color Modes	Preview type	Data Dependent	Color Dependent
One-Step	Focus Filter	RGB, Grayscale, CMYK, Lab	None	Yes. A blank image produces a blank filtered image.	No. The Foreground/Background settings have no effect.

Sharpen Edges

The Sharpen Edges filter is another basically useless filter in the Sharpen category. It, too, is a One-Step filter and is also almost invisible unless you home in on the individual pixels.

Try it:

1. Open the image "Tulip.Psd." Duplicate the image (Image➡Duplicate➡OK).

2. Apply the Sharpen Edges filter (Filter➡Sharpen➡Sharpen Edges).

Filter type	Category	Supported Color Modes	Preview type	Data Dependent	Color Dependent
One-Step	Focus Filter	RGB, Grayscale, CMYK, Lab	None	Yes. A blank image produces a blank filtered image.	No. The Foreground/Background settings have no effect.

Unsharp Mask

The Unsharp Mask filter is the most significant pre-press filter in the native filter set. This production filter is used to replace the focus that an image has lost when it is scanned and to sharpen the image prior to half-toning. Most images require two "rounds" of sharpening. One, just after the image is scanned (or during the scanning process) to restore lost focus, and the other, as the last step in the color-correction process prior to conversion to CMYK mode. The amount applied in this last sharpening step depends upon the final image use. An image that is going to be halftoned can stand significantly more sharpening than an image that is destined for a film recorder. Because blurring is *not* the inverse of sharpening, it is important not to over-sharpen an image because you cannot get it back to where it was. The correct use of the Unsharp Mask filter could almost occupy an entire chapter on its own. I will give you only some general guidelines here.

Try it:

1. Open the image "Tulip.Psd." Duplicate the image (Image➡Duplicate➡OK).

2. Open the Unsharp Mask dialog box shown in Figure 14.119 (Filter➡Sharpen➡Unsharp Mask).

3. Drag the Amount to 136.

   The Amount setting varies from 1-500. This parameter controls how much sharpening is applied. The Rule of thumb is to drag this parameter up to 500 and then cut back (generally a lot!). When you see a sharp halo on the screen, you are probably over-sharpening the image.

Figure 14.119

The Unsharp Mask dialog box.

4. Set the Radius to 1.5.

   The Radius can vary from .1 to 250. A good starting value is to divide your resolution by 200 (300 dpi /200 = 1.5). The Radius and Amount are seesaw controls: you can vary them, but to keep the same general degree of sharpening, as one goes up, you need to bring the other down. The Radius determine how far from each pixel the effect is applied.

5. Finally, set the Threshold to 9.

   The Threshold varies from 0-255, working with levels (values) of the pixels. Threshold determines how different a pixel can be from the pixel being filtered, in order to include it in the filtering process. At a Threshold of 0, everything is included. As the Threshold increases, a pixel has to be very similar in value in order to be sharpened. Because the sharpening works by emphasizing the *edges* found in an image (an edge is an area where the colors change) and making more of a color differ-ence at those edges, you will see much less sharpening on an image with a high Threshold. You should, generally, set the Threshold to at least 5 or so to keep from sharpening noise in the image.

6. Click OK. Figure 14.120 shows the result.

Figure 14.120

The Unsharp Mask filter applied.

Filter type	Category	Supported Color Modes	Preview type	Data Dependent	Color Dependent
Parameter	Production Filter	RGB, Grayscale, CMYK, Lab	Full Image Preview	Yes. A blank image has nothing to sharpen.	No. The Foreground/Background settings have no effect.

PHOTOSHOP'S NATIVE FILTERS—SKETCH

The Sketch filters are all taken from the Adobe Gallery Effects set of filters. They represent a variety of artistic styles resembling hand-drawing an image using limited color palettes. In most cases, the foreground and background colors you set in the Toolbox become the main colors in the image. These filters tend to simplify the shapes in the image, and, as such, are helpful in constructing gross masks for your image. The Sketch filters typically use the logic of either the Find Edges or the Threshold commands in order to work. They only are applicable to RGB or grayscale images.

Bas Relief

The Bas Relief filter helps simplify complex images and helps enhance a simple line art graphic. This filter looks good when used on text and is a lovely filter if you select the right colors for the image. The Bas Relief filter creates a relief of the image—almost as if it is embossing the shapes within it. It uses the Foreground color for the highlights and the Background color for the shadows. So picking colors too strong or of unnatural values for the lights and darks results in a confusing image. The Bas Relief filter can produce good results at either end of the scale, but the settings that I really like use the lowest values of smoothness. The settings in the example create an image that looks like it has been cast in sand. You should, however, also try changing the Detail control to the lowest value instead of the highest. There is a lot of artifacting, but the effect is wonderful.

Try it:

1. Open the image "Clown.Psd." Duplicate the image (Image➥Duplicate➥OK).

2. Pick a yellow from the image as a foreground color and red from the image as a background color.

3. Open the Bas Relief dialog box shown in Figure 14.121 (Filter➥Sketch➥Bas Relief).

Figure 14.121

The Bas Relief dialog box.

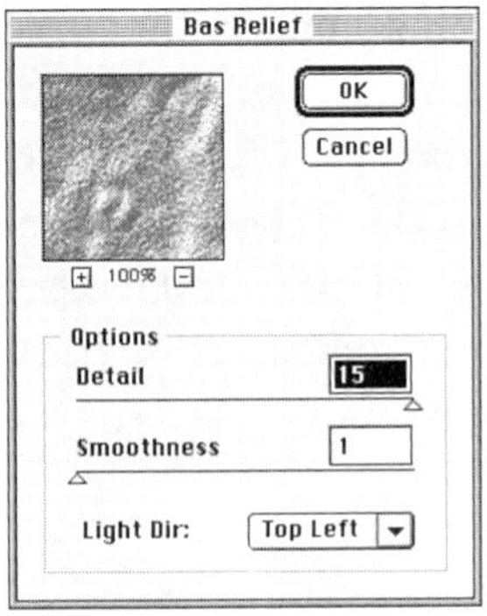

4. Drag the Detail to 15.

The Detail setting varies from 1-15. This parameter controls the amount of detail and works at just about any setting—especially at either end of the scale.

5. Set the Smoothness to 1.

The Smoothness can vary from 1-15. This setting looks best towards the lower end as it begins to remove too much detail—regardless of detail setting as it becomes very smooth.

6. Finally, set the Light Direction to Top Left.

The Light Direction can be set from the Bottom, Bottom Left, Left, Top Left, Top, Top Right, Right, or Bottom Right.

7. Click OK. Figure 14.122 shows the result.

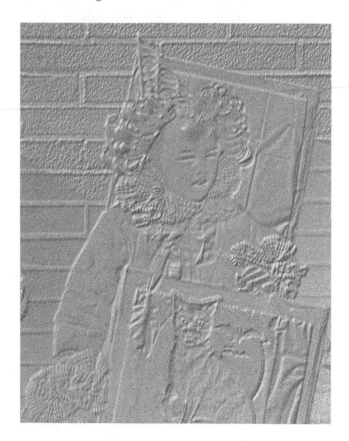

Figure 14.122

An example of the Bas Relief filter applied.

Filter type	Category	Supported Color Modes	Preview type	Data Dependent	Color Dependent
Parameter	Texture/ 3D Filter	RGB, Grayscale	Small Filter Preview	No. A blank image produces a gradient.	Yes. The Foreground/Background are the only colors used.

Charcoal

The Charcoal filter simulates the look of charcoal on paper. Using black and white, you can get a very convincing sketch at the right settings. This filter can help simplify complex images. It renders the areas of greatest contrast—unlike the "edge finding" filters in the Brush Strokes category. The Charcoal filter is one of the best of the stylizing/sketching filters.

Try it:

1. Open the image "Clown.Psd." Duplicate the image (Image➡Duplicate➡OK).

2. Press D to set the colors back to the default of black and white.

3. Open the Charcoal dialog box shown in Figure 14.123 (Filter➡Sketch➡Charcoal).

Figure 14.123

The Charcoal dialog box.

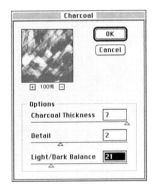

4. Set the Charcoal Thickness to 7.

The Charcoal Thickness can vary from 1-7. This setting works at all values along the scale. It varies from a light look at 1 to a bold statement at 7.

5. Set the Detail to 2.

The Detail varies from 0-5. A Detail of 0 is attractive with a Charcoal Thickness of 7, but if all three settings are dragged to the left, you get a solid background-colored image. Detail usually looks good at the higher settings.

6. Drag the Light/Dark Balance to 21.

The Light/Dark Balance setting varies from 0-100. This parameter controls the proportion of foreground to background color.

7. Click OK. Figure 14.124 shows the result.

Figure 14.124

The Charcoal filter applied to an image.

Filter type	Category	Supported Color Modes	Preview type	Data Dependent	Color Dependent
Parameter	Stylizing Filter	RGB, Grayscale	Small Filter Preview	Yes. A blank image produces a background-colored image.	Yes. The Foreground/Background settings are the only colors in the effect.

Chalk & Charcoal

The Chalk & Charcoal filter shows the effect of drawing with both chalk and charcoal. The Chalk uses the background color and the Charcoal uses the foreground color. This filter looks for areas of contrast in the image. You can set the chalk and the charcoal intensities separately. Once again, the choice of colors helps the success of the Chalk & Charcoal filter, black and white being two of the better colors.

Try it:

1. Open the image "Clown.Psd." Duplicate the image (Image➠Duplicate➠OK).

2. Select a Yellow for the Foreground color and a Red for the background (or whichever two colors from the image you prefer).

3. Open the Chalk & Charcoal dialog box shown in Figure 14.125 (Filter➠Sketch➠Chalk & Charcoal).

Figure 14.125

The Chalk & Charcoal dialog box.

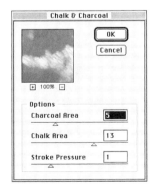

4. Drag the Charcoal Area to 5.

   The Charcoal Area setting varies from 0-20. This parameter controls the darkness of the chalk setting. Areas not colored appear in gray.

5. Set the Chalk Area to 13.

   The Chalk Area can vary from 0-20, controlling the darkness of the chalk setting. Areas not colored appear in gray. Even at the lowest settings, you see some chalk and charcoal.

6. Finally, set the Stroke Pressure to 1.

   The Stroke Pressure varies from 0-5. The intensity builds up very fast in this filter. You may find that settings above 1 produce a solid color.

7. Click OK. Figure 14.126 shows the result.

Figure 14.126

The Chalk & Charcoal filter applied to an image.

Filter type	Category	Supported Color Modes	Preview type	Data Dependent	Color Dependent
Parameter	Stylizing Filter	RGB, Grayscale,	Small Filter Preview	Yes. A blank image produces a gray filtered image.	Yes. The Foreground/Background settings produce the effect.

Chrome

The Chrome filter can help enhance a simple line art graphic and looks good when used on text. It changes the image into a grayscale image that looks as if it is reflecting light—as chrome does. The image, however, becomes almost unrecognizable at any setting. The best way to control this filter is to use it under an image (the original or another reflected image) that is placed in Color mode.

Try it:

1. Open the image "Clown.Psd." Duplicate the image (Image➡Duplicate➡OK).

2. Drag the icon for the Background layer to the New Layer icon (the center icon at the bottom of the Layers palette).

3. Turn the Eye icon off for Layer 1 and click the Background name in the Layers palette to select it.

4. Open the Chrome dialog box shown in Figure 14.127 (Filter➡Sketch➡Chrome).

Figure 14.127

The Chrome dialog box.

5. Drag the Detail to 9.

   The Detail setting varies from 0-10, controlling the number of reflective edges found.

6. Set the Smoothness to 10.

   The Smoothness can vary from 0-10. This controls the smoothness of the edges—a higher smoothness setting also sees fewer edges. Click OK.

7. Select Layer 1 in the Layers palette and change its Blending mode to Color. Drag the Opacity setting to around 80%. Figure 14.128 shows the result.

Figure 14.128

The Chrome filter applied.

Filter type	Category	Supported Color Modes	Preview type	Data Dependent	Color Dependent
Parameter	3D/ Distressed Filter	RGB, Grayscale,	Small Filter Preview	Yes. A blank image is changed to a solid gray.	No. The Foreground/Background settings have no effect.

Conté Crayon

The Conté Crayon filter can help simplify complex images when it is run with no texture. It looks best when done in black and white or with tones of gray because it always uses a mid-gray for the mixture of colors—regardless of the other two colors you select. In black and white, this is a very attractive filter. The Conté Crayon filter is a good choice for Web graphics as well, as the image easily reduces to about six colors. This filter works best on images that have areas of contrast—definite lights and darks. On a muddy image, it cannot locate enough "different" areas to give interest to the image.

Try it:

1. Open the image "Clown.Psd." Duplicate the image (Image➡Duplicate➡OK). Press D to set the colors back to the default of black and white.

2. Open the Conté Crayon dialog box shown in Figure 14.129 (Filter➡Sketch➡Conté Crayon).

3. Drag the Foreground Level to 8.

   The Foreground Level setting varies from 1-15. This parameter controls the intensity of the foreground color in the image. At low settings, you see gray and a fair amount of whatever texture you have selected. At the higher settings, you see almost no texture in the foreground color, but very little gray as well.

4. Set the Background Level to 8.

   The Background Level can vary from 1-15. The low setting produces a background-colored area with very little texture and a mixture of gray. At the highest setting, you see mostly background color with a lot of texture if the foreground setting is also high. You see somewhat less texture if the Foreground Level is set low.

Figure 14.129

The Conté Crayon dialog box.

5. There are a number of settings that concern the texture to be applied. Set the Texture to Canvas.

   The Textures included are Brick, Burlap, Canvas, and Sandstone, but you can load your own texture from a Photoshop file.

6. Set the Scaling to 100%.

   Textures can be scaled from 50-200%.

7. Set the Relief to 6.

   You can set Relief to values of 0-50. At settings well past 10, all you see is the texture—you have wiped away the image detail.

8. Click OK. Figure 14.130 shows the result.

Figure 14.130

An example of the Conté Crayon filter applied to an image.

Filter type	Category	Supported Color Modes	Preview type	Data Dependent	Color Dependent
Parameter	Stylizing/ Texture Filter	RGB, Grayscale	Small Filter Preview	No. This filter adds texture to a blank image.	Yes. The Foreground/Background settings are the colors used for this effect.

Graphic Pen

The Graphic Pen filter can help simplify complex images. This filter looks good when used on text. It does its best on an image that has a good range of lights and darks and is large enough to tolerate being "scratched over." The Graphic Pen filter renders a photograph as if it were a sketch drawn with ink in long strokes (or short dots, depending upon the setting). The filter uses only two colors with no in-between shades generated. If you like the look of Conté crayon but want to use colors other than black and white, this filter may be better for you than the Conté Crayon filter. It is not as suitable, however, for Web work, even though it uses fewer colors: unless your image is very simple and very contrasty, at small sizes, the filter loses all detail. On a large image destined for 150 lpi printing, the Graphic Pen filter is wonderful. The optical illusion of the lines will show up as a marvelous black and white bitmap. It does a very good job of preparing an image for bitmapped printing as either a type of mezzotint or as an alternative method of screening.

Try it:

1. Open the image "Clown.Psd." Duplicate the image (Image➧Duplicate➧OK).

2. Open the Graphic Pen dialog box shown in Figure 14.131 (Filter➧Sketch➧Graphic Pen).

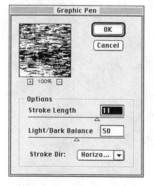

Figure 14.131

The Graphic Pen dialog box.

3. Drag the Stroke Length to 11.

   The Stroke Length setting varies from 1-15, controlling the length of the stroke. At tiny sizes, you see dots instead of lines.

4. Set the Light/Dark Balance to 50.

   The Light/Dark Balance can vary from 0-100. At either end of the scale, you get a blank image in either the foreground or

697

background color—not very useful. Keep the balance towards the mid-range. At 50%, you get the best all-over detail.

5. Finally, set the Stroke Direction to Horizontal.

The Stroke Direction can be Right Diagonal, Horizontal, Left Diagonal, or Vertical. This is one of the few filters that lets you stroke horizontally or vertically.

6. Click OK. Figure 14.132 shows the result.

Figure 14.132

The Graphic Pen filter applied to an image.

Filter type	Category	Supported Color Modes	Preview type	Data Dependent	Color Dependent
Parameter	Stylizing Filter	RGB, Grayscale	Small Filter Preview	No. This filter adds texture to a blank image.	No. The Foreground/Background settings are the effect colors.

Halftone Pattern

The Halftone Pattern filter is a wonderful use of halftoning that offers significant differences from the standard bitmap conversion halftoning. You can apply a halftone pattern *over* an image—without converting the image to bitmap. This lets you retain areas of gray and still get a definite pattern. The Circle Pattern type is completely different for other halftoning algorithms as it halftones by drawing a concentric circle over the image. At large pattern sizes, this filter makes a major graphic statement. It can tolerate being viewed at a distance (or at high resolution) where the optical illusion gets full room to be appreciated. The Halftone Pattern filter really does create a bi-level image if the contrast is set at the maximum. If you select colors other than black and white, make the darker color your foreground color unless you wish the halftone to look like a negative.

Try it:

1. Open the image "Clown.Psd." Duplicate the image (Image➡Duplicate➡OK).

2. Open the Halftone Pattern dialog box shown in Figure 14.133 (Filter➡Sketch➡Halftone Pattern).

Figure 14.133

The Halftone Pattern dialog box.

3. Drag the Size to 1.

   The Size setting varies from 1-12, controlling the size of the halftone pattern. You can get good results at all sizes, but the larger the size you select, the more graphic and abstract the results will be. Also, an image with many pixels can tolerate a higher setting without losing all detail.

699

4. Set the Contrast to 50.

The Contrast can vary from 0-50. At low settings, you get a pattern superimposed over a grayscale (or duotone) image. As you move the slider towards the higher contrast, however, you begin to lose the intermediate values. As you increase the contrast, you need to think about how the image will look when it is printed—when it needs to be halftoned again if it still contains gray values. You might want to skip directly to the highest contrast setting once you are in the top quarter of the range.

5. Finally, set the Type to Dot.

The Type can be a Circle, Dot, or Line. All effects look good, though the dot is the most traditional of them.

6. Click OK. Figure 14.134 shows the result.

Figure 14.134

The Halftone Pattern filter applied to an image.

Filter type	Category	Supported Color Modes	Preview type	Data Dependent	Color Dependent
Parameter	Stylizing Filter	RGB, Grayscale	Small Filter Preview	No. This filter adds texture to a blank image.	Yes. The Foreground/Background settings are the effect colors.

Note Paper

The Note Paper filter can help simplify complex images and can also help to enhance a simple line art graphic. This filter looks good when used on text.

Try it:

1. Open the image "Clown.Psd." Duplicate the image (Image➡Duplicate➡OK).

2. Open the Note Paper dialog box shown in Figure 14.135 (Filter➡Sketch➡Notepaper).

Figure 14.135

The Note Paper dialog box.

3. Drag the Image Balance to 14.

    The Image Balance setting varies from 0-50. This parameter controls the balance between light and dark areas of contrast. At the extreme settings, you get no detail at all. The Image Balance does best somewhere on one side or the other of the center—depending upon the image itself and the effect that you want. You can think of this setting as creating the Threshold for the image and use it as you would the Threshold command.

4. Set the Graininess to 10.

   The Graininess can vary from 0-20. At 0, the image is smooth. At 20, the grain is a bit too powerful, but still acceptable.

5. Finally, set the Relief to 10.

   The Relief varies from 0-25. At 0, there is no illusion of 3D. At 25, the illusion is destroyed because there is too much black in the grain. If the Graininess setting is low, the image can tolerate a higher Relief setting.

6. Click OK. Figure 14.136 shows the result.

Figure 14.136

The Note Paper filter applied to an image.

Filter type	Category	Supported Color Modes	Preview type	Data Dependent	Color Dependent
Parameter	Stylizing Filter	RGB, Grayscale	Small Filter Preview	No. This filter adds texture to a blank image.	Yes. The Foreground/Background settings are the effect colors.

Photocopy

The Photocopy filter finds the areas of greatest contrast in the image and creates a duotone from the major shapes that it finds. It can help simplify complex images and looks good when used on text. The Photocopy filter is suitable for Web output, as it reduces the colors in the image to about 6, but the filter still can retain enough detail on a small image to see the original subject. The Photocopy filter is a very attractive and useful filter for stylizing images.

Try it:

1. Open the image "Clown.Psd." Duplicate the image (Image⮕Duplicate⮕OK).

2. Open the Photocopy dialog box shown in Figure 14.137 (Filter⮕Sketch⮕Photocopy).

Figure 14.137

The Photocopy dialog box.

3. Drag the Detail to 22.

   The Detail setting varies from 1-24. This parameter controls the amount of detail that the filter finds. If Detail and Darkness are both 0, you are out of toner. Even if Detail and Darkness are at the maximum, however, you get a usable image.

4. Set the Darkness to 39.

   The Darkness can vary from 1-50. This controls the depth of the lines that the filter produces as it outlines each major shape.

5. Click OK. Figure 14.138 shows the result.

Figure 14.138

The Photocopy filter applied to an image.

Filter type	Category	Supported Color Modes	Preview type	Data Dependent	Color Dependent
Parameter	Stylizing Filter	RGB, Grayscale	Small Filter Preview	Yes. A blank image produces a blank—though colored— filtered image.	Yes. The Foreground/Background settings are the effect colors.

Plaster

The Plaster filter can help simplify complex images and looks good when used on text. It is not only sensitive to the Foreground and Background colors, but it considers their values into the effect. The Foreground color is used for the main image details (the areas that would show up as black if you applied the Threshold command). However, the filter then shades the elevation of the effect by blending dark and light. If your Foreground color is dark, the effect looks indented. If the Foreground color is light, the effect is raised (almost like an image negative).

Try it:

1. Open the image "Clown.Psd." Duplicate the image (Image➦Duplicate➦OK). Select two browns from the image as your Foreground and Background colors. Make the darker shade the Foreground color.

2. Open the Plaster dialog box shown in Figure 14.139 (Filter➦Sketch➦Plaster).

Figure 14.139

The Plaster dialog box.

3. Drag the Image Balance to 12.

   The Image Balance setting varies from 0-50. This parameter controls the Threshold level of the image. A good way to pre-set this control is to try the Threshold command on the image and find a good level. Threshold runs from 0-255, and this control runs from 0-50. To convert one to the other, divide 255 by the desired Threshold amount. Then divide 50 by that result. Use that number as the Image Balance. Remember, though, just as with Levels, at either end of the scale, you get a solid, blank, image.

4. Set the Smoothness to 1.

   The Smoothness can vary from 1-15. You can have rough plaster (1) to very smooth plaster (15).

5. Finally, set the Light Position to Top Left.

   The Light Position varies from Bottom, Bottom Left, Left, Top Left, Top, Top Right, Right, and Bottom Right.

6. Click OK. Figure 14.140 shows the result.

Figure 14.140

The Plaster filter applied to an image.

Filter type	Category	Supported Color Modes	Preview type	Data Dependent	Color Dependent
Parameter	Stylizing/ 3D Filter	RGB, Grayscale	Small Filter Preview	Yes. A blank image produces a blank filtered (but colored) image.	Yes. The Foreground/Background settings are the effect colors.

Reticulation

The Reticulation filter can help simplify complex images. It is essentially a graytone Mezzotinting filter that uses contour mapping to report the results. At extreme settings (no Density and maximum black and white), the Reticulation filter renders the image in black and gray (or whatever colors you have selected) with a tiny bit of elevation. It is not performing a Threshold, so you do get different areas than you would using the Plaster filter.

Try it:

1. Open the image "Clown.Psd." Duplicate the image (Image➡Duplicate➡OK). Press D to set the colors back to the default of black and white.

2. Open the Reticulation dialog box shown in Figure 14.141 (Filter➡Sketch➡Reticulation).

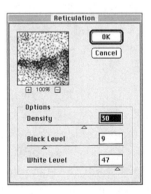

Figure 14.141

The Reticulation dialog box.

3. Drag the Density to 30.

The Density setting varies from 0-50. This parameter controls the contour mapping and dot density. At 0, the image looks like a series of grayscale contour maps on top of each other. At 50, the mapping is reversed and the background color is dominant and mottled. At 25, there is a balance and the image almost looks flat. In between, the image is dotted towards either foreground (1-24) or background (26-49).

4. Set the Black Level to 9.

The Black Level can vary from 0-50 and is controlled by the Foreground color. This carries the image detail. If the level is low, then there will be more detail in the image. As this number gets higher, the results become more abstract.

5. Finally, set the White Level to 47.

The White Level varies from 0-50. The White level is controlled by the Background color. As this number gets higher, the results become more solid in tone with fewer gray values.

6. Click OK. Figure 14.142 shows the result.

Filter type	Category	Supported Color Modes	Preview type	Data Dependent	Color Dependent
Parameter	Stylizing Filter	RGB, Grayscale	Small Filter Preview	Yes. A blank image produces a blank filtered, but colored, image	Yes. The Foreground/Background settings are the effect colors.

Stamp

The Stamp filter can help simplify complex images and looks good when used on text. It is a good choice for Web images as it can retain a lot of detail with few colors. The Stamp filter is very similar to the Photocopy filter, but it can produce a 2-color image where Photocopy cannot. It can be both sharper or softer than the Photocopy filter because of the Smoothness option that controls the edge detail and the number of edges found. A large Smoothness setting removes most of the detail from the image but leaves very soft, curved shapes.

Figure 14.142

The Reticulation filter applied to an image.

Try it:

1. Open the image "Clown.Psd." Duplicate the image (Image➡Duplicate➡OK).

2. Open the Stamp dialog box shown in Figure 14.143 (Filter➡Sketch➡Stamp).

3. Drag the Light/Dark Balance to 12.

   The Light/Dark Balance setting varies from 0-50, controlling the Threshold level of the image. A good way to pre-set this control is to try the Threshold command on the image and find a good level. Threshold runs from 0-255, and Light/Dark Balance runs from 0-50. To convert one to the other, divide 255 by the desired Threshold amount. Then divide 50 by that result. Use that number as the Light/Dark Balance.

Figure 14.143

The Stamp dialog box.

4. Set the Smoothness to 5.

The Smoothness can vary from 1-50. At 1, there are no anti-aliased edges in the image and as much detail as possible is saved. At 50, there are few shapes, as most of them have been smoothed away (as if you had blurred the sharp version of the image and then used the Levels command to find the smoothest setting).

5. Click OK. Figure 14.144 shows the result.

Filter type	Category	Supported Color Modes	Preview type	Data Dependent	Color Dependent
Parameter	Stylizing Filter	RGB, Grayscale	Small Filter Preview	Yes. A blank image produces a blank filtered image with a color change.	Yes. The Fore-ground/Back-ground settings are the effect color.

Figure 14.144

An example of the Stamp filter applied to an image.

Torn Edges

The Torn Edges filter can help simplify complex images and can help enhance a simple line art graphic. This filter looks good when used on text. The Torn Edges filter is a close relative to the Plaster filter except that instead of elevation, the filter produces fuzzy edges between the areas of light and dark.

Try it:

1. Open the image "Clown.Psd." Duplicate the image (Image➡Duplicate➡OK).

2. Open the Torn Edges dialog box shown in Figure 14.145 (Filter➡Sketch➡Torn Edges).

Figure 14.145

The Torn Edges dialog box.

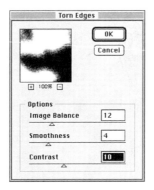

3. Drag the Image Balance to 12.

   The Image Balance setting varies from 0-50, controlling the Threshold level of the image. A good way to pre-set this control is to try the Threshold command on the image and find a good level. Threshold runs from 0-255, and Image Balance runs from 0-50. To convert one to the other, divide 255 by the desired Threshold amount. Then divide 50 by that result. Use that number as the Image Balance.

4. Set the Smoothness to 4.

   The Smoothness can vary from 1-15. At 1, the edges are an attractive, soft speckled blur. At 15, the edges are very crisp and sharp—though not especially smooth (except in the sense that smooth means aliased).

5. Finally, set the Contrast to 10.

   The Contrast varies from 1-25. At 1, the foreground and background colors mix softly in the area where the foreground color dominates (Black areas of the Threshold command). At 25, they speckle in sharp dots within the foreground color area. At 12, the foreground and background colors do not mix at all except at the edges.

6. Click OK. Figure 14.146 shows the result.

Figure 14.146

The Torn Edges filter applied to an image.

Filter type	Category	Supported Color Modes	Preview type	Data Dependent	Color Dependent
Parameter	Stylizing Filter	RGB, Grayscale	Small Filter Preview	Yes. A blank image produces a blank filtered—but colored—image.	Yes. The Foreground/Background settings are the effect colors.

Water Paper

The Water Paper filter can help to enhance a simple line art graphic. This filter looks good when used on text. Unlike many filters in this category, however, it does not simplify the colors of the image into two tones. The Water Paper filter makes the image look as if it were placed in a pail of water and the paper fibers absorbed the ink. The controls in this filter perform a balancing act. If the Contrast and Brightness are set to either extreme of the scale, the Fiber Length is the most critical determinant of the filter success. It needs to be kept towards the low end of the range or else the image is all water. If the Brightness and Contrast settings are set towards the middle, then the Fiber Length can increase with quite good results.

Try it:

1. Open the image "Clown.Psd." Duplicate the image (Image➡Duplicate➡OK).

2. Open the Water Paper dialog box shown in Figure 14.147 (Filter➡Sketch➡Water Paper).

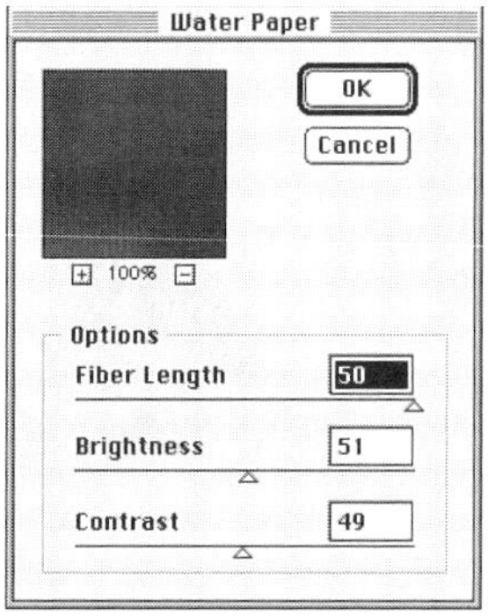

Figure 14.147

The Water Paper dialog box.

3. Drag the Fiber Length to 50.

   The Fiber Length setting varies from 3-50. This parameter controls the wetness of the effect as well as the length of the strokes. If the fiber length is long, unless the Brightness and Contrast are near the middle, the image will look very soft and blurred with no sharpness to it.

4. Set the Brightness to 51.

   The Brightness can vary from 0-100. At 0, if all of the other controls are low, the image looks as if the ink washed away.

5. Finally, set the Contrast to 49.

The Contrast varies from 0-100. When Contrast is lower than Brightness, the fibers are not well-defined. If Contrast is too much higher than Brightness, the image becomes too dark.

6. Click OK. Figure 14.148 shows the result.

Figure 14.148

The Water Paper filter applied to an image.

Filter type	Category	Supported Color Modes	Preview type	Data Dependent	Color Dependent
Parameter	Stylizing Filter	RGB, Grayscale	Small Filter Preview	No. A blank image produces a subtly textured image.	No. The Foreground/Background settings have no effect.

PHOTOSHOP'S NATIVE FILTERS—STYLIZE

The Stylize filters are among the most commonly used of the special effects filters. They abstract the image being filtered by changing colors, finding edges, or moving pixels around.

Diffuse

The Diffuse filter.

Try it:

1. Open the image "Cherry.Psd." Duplicate the image (Image➡Duplicate➡OK).

2. Open the Diffuse dialog box shown in Figure 14.149 (Filter➡Stylize➡Diffuse).

Figure 14.149

The Diffuse dialog box.

3. Select Normal as the Mode.

   In Normal mode, the pixels are diffused in all directions. In Lighten Only mode the scattered pixels only show up when they are lighter than the pixel on which they land. In Darken Only mode, it is the opposite.

4. Click OK. Figure 14.150 shows the result.

Filter type	Category	Supported Color Modes	Preview type	Data Dependent	Color Dependent
Parameter	Stylizing Filter	RGB, Grayscale, CMYK, Lab	Small Filter Preview	Yes. A blank image produces a blank filtered image.	No. The Foreground/Background settings have no effect.

Figure 14.150

The Diffuse filter applied to an image.

Emboss

The Emboss filter is used to give an image a 3D look—as if it is coming up out of the background (or was stamped into it). The Emboss filter turns the entire image gray, except to trace colors that occur if you use high settings. If you need to return color to the image, you can filter the background Layer and place a copy of the color image in the top Layer for compositing in Color mode (or one of a number of other modes that work). The Emboss filter is frequently the start of many texture and channel effects.

Try it:

1. Open the image "Cherry.Psd." Duplicate the image (Image➥Duplicate➥OK).

2. Open the Emboss box shown in Figure 14.151 (Filter➥Stylize➥Emboss).

3. Drag the Angle to 141 degrees or type in the number.

   The Angle setting varies from 0-360 (though it gives minus readings if you drag the pointer backwards). This parameter controls the direction of the light.

4. Set the Height to 3.

   The Height, varying from 1 to 10, sets the elevation of the effect.

Figure 14.151

Figure 14.151

The Emboss dialog box.

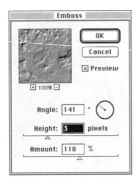

5. Finally, set the Amount to 118%.

   The Amount varies from 1-500 and controls how much detail the filter sees to emboss. At low settings, almost nothing is raised up. At high settings, the filter sees edges to emboss everywhere in the image. Your best results occur at the lower end of the scale (to about 300% maximum).

6. Click OK. Figure 14.152 shows the result.

Figure 14.152

An example of the Emboss filter applied to an image.

Filter type	Category	Supported Color Modes	Preview type	Data Dependent	Color Dependent
Parameter	Stylizing/ Special Effects/3D Filter	RGB, Grayscale, CMYK, Lab	Full Image Preview	Yes. A blank image produces a blank filtered image.	No. The Foreground/Background settings have no effect.

Extrude

Extrude is a bit of an odd filter. It can definitely destroy the content of your image, or it can minimally abstract it. The Extrude filter could make a good basis for charting a photograph for counted craft techniques such as knitting or needlepoint. It can also add cracks to the image. The Extrude filter can make your image look as if it was pulled up into the air as a series of blocks or pyramids.

Try it:

1. Open the image "Cherry.Psd." Duplicate the image (Image➡Duplicate➡OK).

2. Open the Extrude dialog box shown in Figure 14.153 (Filter➡Stylize➡Extrude).

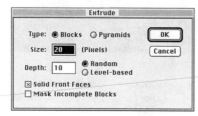

Figure 14.153

The Extrude dialog box.

3. Drag the Type to Blocks.

    The filter extrudes either Blocks or Pyramids.

4. Set the Size to 20.

    The Size of the extruded forms can vary from 2 to 255. Larger sizes contain only huge blocks—all image content is lost.

5. Next, set the Depth to 10.

    The Depth varies from 1-255. This controls the distance in space that the extrusion seems to travel.

6. Select the "Random" radio button. The other control, Level-Based, creates a more orderly extrusion.

7. Check "Solid Front Faces" to make each block a color based on the image. When not checked, you see the image itself with darker shades to show the intersections.

8. Do not check "Mask Incomplete Blocks." When checked, you see no blocks that extend beyond the edges of the image. If a block cannot be completed, it does not appear at all.

9. Click OK. Figure 14.154 shows the result.

Figure 14.154

The Extrude filter applied to an image.

Filter type	Category	Supported Color Modes	Preview type	Data Dependent	Color Dependent
Parameter	Stylizing Deforma- tion Filter	RGB, Grayscale, CMYK	None	No. A blank image can be filtered.	No. The Fore- ground/Back- ground settings have no effect.

Find Edges

The Find Edges filter is one of the most useful of the Photoshop filters even though it is a special effects filter. It is an active participant in many texture-creation "recipes" and can create edge interest in an image when applied in Multiply or Screen in a layer over the original image. As a One-Step filter, however, Find Edges gives you no control over the results. Your only way to influence the identification of "edges" is to run the High Pass filter on the image first. You can then desaturate the edges or use the Threshold command on them to selectively change the edges to black. In versions of Photoshop prior to 3.0, the Find Edges filter inverted the result. Seeing the edges in the image against black can be very attractive. To re-create the effect, you need to select the Invert command after the filter is applied.

Try it:

1. Open the image "Cherry.Psd." Duplicate the image (Image➡Duplicate➡OK).

2. Apply the Find Edges filter (Filter➡Stylize➡Find Edges) to see the image shown in Figure 14.155.

Figure 14.155

The *Find Edges* filter applied to an image.

3. Invert the image (Command-I)[Control-I]. Figure 14.156 shows the result.

Figure 14.156

The *Find Edges* filter inverted.

Filter type	Category	Supported Color Modes	Preview type	Data Dependent	Color Dependent
One-Step	Stylizing/ Distressing Filter	RGB, Grayscale, CMYK, Lab	None	Yes. A blank image produces a blank filtered image.	No. The Foreground/Background settings have no effect.

Glowing Edges

The Glowing Edges filter is a super-set of the Find Edges filter. It automatically does a "find edges and invert." In addition, you can select the size of the edge and the amount of edges found. The filter looks good when used on text.

Try it:

1. Open the image "Cherry.Psd." Duplicate the image (Image➡Duplicate➡OK).

2. Open the Glowing Edges dialog box shown in Figure 14.157 (Filter➡Stylize➡Glowing Edges).

Figure 14.157

The Glowing Edges dialog box.

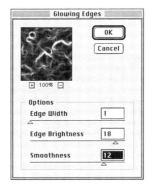

3. Drag the Edge Width to 1.

   The Edge Width setting varies from 1-14. This parameter controls the size of the line drawn around the edges.

4. Set the Edge Brightness to 18.

   The Edge Brightness can vary from 0-20. This controls the intensity of the edge color.

5. Finally, set the Smoothness to 12.

   The Smoothness varies from 1-15. The Smoothness determines how many edges the filter "sees." A high Smoothness setting sees many fewer edges than does a small setting. The edge is therefore longer and less jagged.

6. Click OK. Figure 14.158 shows the result.

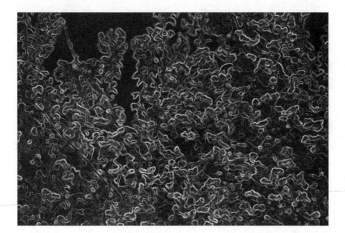

Figure 14.158

An example of the Glowing Edges filter applied to an image.

Filter type	Category	Supported Color Modes	Preview type	Data Dependent	Color Dependent
Parameter	Stylizing/ Distressed Filter	RGB, Grayscale	Small Filter Preview	Yes. A blank image produces a blank filtered image.	No. The Foreground/Background settings have no effect.

Solarize

The Solarize filter creates an other-worldly color change on an image by changing the Curves of the image so that values lighter than 50% are reversed to black. The effect is a digital re-creation of the photographic technique by the same name that blends a positive and a negative image.

Try it:

1. Open the image "Cherry.Psd." Duplicate the image (Image➡Duplicate➡OK).

2. Select the Solarize filter (Filter➡Stylize➡Solarize) to see the results shown in Figure 14.159.

Figure 14.159

The Solarize filter applied to an image.

3. Figure 14.160 shows the Curve that is actually being applied.

Figure 14.160

The Solarize filter Curve.

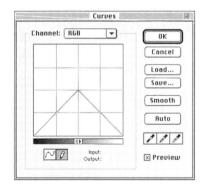

Filter type	Category	Supported Color Modes	Preview type	Data Dependent	Color Dependent
One-Step	Stylizing Filter	RGB, Grayscale, CMYK	None	No. It may invert the original color.	No. The Foreground/Background settings have no effect.

Tiles

The Tiles filter is a relative of the Extrude filter. Think of it as Extrude's 2D cousin. Tiles fractures your image into a user-specified number of blocks across. Each block contains a section of the original image, offset from its original position by a random, maximum amount. You can select how you want the image *between* the blocks to appear. If you select the unaltered image, then you see the filter only as pieces of the image moved from where they belong (almost like viewing it through a major hangover). Tiles is, obviously, a special effects filter.

Try it:

1. Open the image "Cherry.Psd." Duplicate the image (Image➡Duplicate➡OK).

2. Open the Tiles dialog box shown in Figure 14.161 (Filter➡Stylize➡Tiles).

Figure 14.161

The Tiles dialog box.

3. Drag the Number of Tiles to 25.

   The Number of Tiles setting varies from 1-99. This parameter controls the number of tiles created in each row.

4. Set the Maximum Offset (%) to 50%.

   The Maximum Offset (%) can vary from 1-99%. This indicates the maximum amount that each piece of the image can be moved from its original location.

5. Finally, set the Fill Empty Areas With to "Inverse Image."

   Your other options are Background Color, Foreground Color, and Unaltered Image. This sets the method for filling in the gaps between the offset blocks.

6. Click OK. Figure 14.162 shows the result.

Figure 14.162

The Tiles filter applied.

Filter type	Category	Supported Color Modes	Preview type	Data Dependent	Color Dependent
Parameter	Stylizing/ Displace- ment Filter	RGB, Grayscale, CMYK, Lab	None	No. Settings other than "Unaltered Image" pro- duce results.	No. The Fore- ground/Back- ground settings can have an effect if you wish.

Trace Contour

The Trace Contour filter can be used to find shapes in an image. It is similar in concept to Find Edges, but it finds areas of contrast and renders them to each channel. You can get interesting compositing effects by merging the contours with the original image. The contours are not usually all that useful by themselves. Good results are possible by offsetting the image slightly from the original. A simple image will use this technique better than a complex one (like our example image).

Try it:

1. Open the image "Cherry.Psd." Duplicate the image (Image➡Duplicate➡OK).

2. Open the Trace Contour dialog box shown in Figure 14.163 (Filter➡Stylize➡Trace Contour).

Figure 14.163

The Trace Contour dialog box.

3. Drag the Levels to 120.

   The Level setting varies from 0-255. This parameter controls the areas (values) in the image that will be seen by the Trace Contours filter.

4. Set the Edge to Lower.

   Edge, which can be Lower or Upper, controls the specific shape of the contour generated by the Level setting. Lower Edge indicates the color values that fall below the Level setting. Upper Edge indicates the color values that are above the Level setting.

5. Click OK. Figure 14.164 shows the result.

Figure 14.164

The Trace Contour filter applied to an image.

Filter type	Category	Supported Color Modes	Preview type	Data Dependent	Color Dependent
Parameter	Stylizing/ Distressed Filter	RGB, Grayscale, CMYK, Lab	Small Filter Preview	Yes. But blank image produces a white filtered image.	No. The Foreground/Background settings have no effect.

Wind

The Wind filter shoots a burst of air at the pixels in the image and sweeps them from their accustomed position in a horizontal manner (if you want the image filtered vertically, rotate the image before applying the filter). The Wind filter is a special effects filter but it is very useful for helping to create textures or when used on a shadow behind text. This is a good filter to apply multiple times because you cannot control the amount of the effect applied.

Try it:

1. Open the image "Cherry.Psd." Duplicate the image (Image➥Duplicate➥OK).

2. Open the Wind dialog box shown in Figure 14.165 (Filter➥Stylize➥Wind).

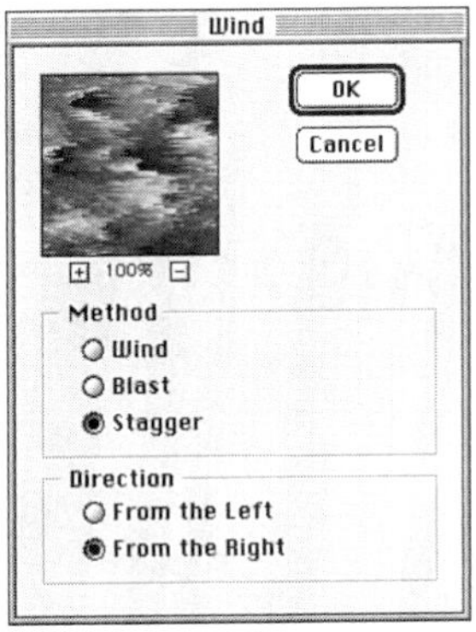

Figure 14.165

The Wind dialog box.

3. Set the Method to Stagger.

    The Method controls the technique used to filter the image. You can have Wind (sprinkles of pixels in a blast line), Blast (straight, long, horizontal lines), or Stagger (short and long lines).

4. Set the Direction to "From the Right."

You can make the wind blow from the Right or Left.

5. Click OK. Figure 14.166 shows the result.

Figure 14.166

The Wind filter applied.

Filter type	Category	Supported Color Modes	Preview type	Data Dependent	Color Dependent
Parameter	Stylizing/ Distressed Filter	RGB, Grayscale, CMYK, Lab	Small Filter Preview	Yes. A blank image produces a blank filtered image.	No. The Foreground/Background settings have no effect.

PHOTOSHOP'S NATIVE FILTERS—TEXTURE

The Texture filters are all taken from the Adobe Gallery Effects filter sets. They add some type of texture to your image—usually either a grain or an embossing—and all of them work in a blank document to create interesting textures. When applied to a photographic image, the Texture filters abstract and stylize it.

Craquelure

The Craquelure filter looks good when used on text or other simple objects and makes wonderful textures in blank images. A number of ways exist, however, to make this effect look awful—usually by setting the controls too near to either end of the sliders. This filter is designed to make an image look as if it is a very old watercolor that has cracked from age.

Try it:

1. Open the image "Roses.Psd." Duplicate the image (Image➥Duplicate➥OK).

2. Open the Craquelure dialog box shown in Figure 14.167 (Filter➥Texture➥Craquelure).

Figure 14.167

The Craquelure dialog box.

3. Drag the Crack Spacing to 20.

The Crack Spacing setting varies from 2-100. This parameter controls the distance between cracks. The cracks are fine but infrequent when the control is set to 100. A setting of 2 produces a blank, darkened image, however, because the cracks are so close together that there is no image.

4. Set the Crack Depth to 5.

The Crack Depth can vary from 0-10. At 0, the effect is subtle; at 10 it is too black to sustain the illusion. Keep it somewhere in-between.

5. Finally, set the Crack Brightness to 4.

The Crack Brightness varies from 0-10. Surprisingly, the higher settings are not really better because they are too bright to set off the cracks as well. At 0, the cracks are black—maybe not the best idea. Somewhere in-between is the best balance.

6. Click OK. Figure 14.168 shows the result.

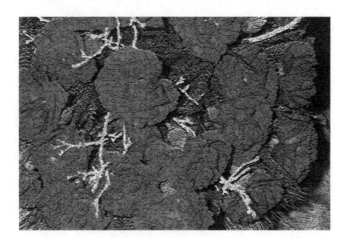

Figure 14.168

The Craquelure filter applied to an image.

Filter type	Category	Supported Color Modes	Preview type	Data Dependent	Color Dependent
Parameter	Texture Filter	RGB, Grayscale	Small Filter Preview	No. This filter adds texture to a blank image.	No. The Foreground/Background settings have no effect.

Grain

The Grain filter is a super-set of the Add Noise filter. It adds a variety of noise to your image and uses a variety of methods to do so. Settings that work with one type of noise (the example below uses Clumped noise) will not work well with other Grain types (such as Normal or Sprinkles). In addition, some of the methods use the Foreground and/ or Background color to create the grain. This filter can be used in texture "recipes" just as you would use the Add Noise filter. The Grain filter makes a wonderful start to a variety of effects. Check out the image file GrainGrd.Psd. The same settings were used in it as in this example, except that each grid square received a different Grain Type (in order from left to right, top to bottom) from the Grain Type menu. The Layer names explain the image color and the Foreground/Background colors as well.

Try it:

1. Open the image "Roses.Psd." Duplicate the image (Image➥Duplicate➥OK).

2. Open the Grain dialog box shown in Figure 14.169 (Filter➥Texture➥Grain).

3. Drag the Intensity to 100.

   The Intensity setting varies from 0-100. This parameter is a balance. With some types of grain, you will see no result at either ends of the scale.

4. Set the Contrast to 50.

   The Contrast can vary from 0-100. A setting of 50 keeps it in balance between the lights and darks.

5. Finally, set the Grain Type to Clumped.

   The Grain Type can be Regular, Soft, Sprinkles, Clumped, Contrasty, Enlarged, Stippled, Horizontal, Vertical, or Speckle.

6. Click OK. Figure 14.170 shows the result.

7. For the sake of trying something different...Select the Fade Grain filter command (Filter➥Fade). Change the Mode to Exclusion and the Opacity to 70%. Figure 14.171 shows the result.

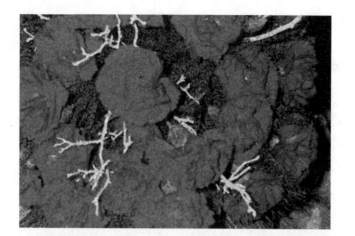

Figure 14.170

The Grain filter applied to an image.

Figure 14.171

The Grain filter faded in Exclusion Mode.

Filter type	Category	Supported Color Modes	Preview type	Data Dependent	Color Dependent
Parameter	Texture Filter	RGB, Grayscale	Small Filter Preview	No. This filter adds texture to a blank image.	Yes. The Foreground/Background settings do affect the Sprinkled and Stippled Grain Types.

Mosaic Tiles

The Mosaic Tiles filter is a close relative of the Craquelure filter. It produces, however, irregularly-contoured squares at regularly-spaced intervals. The Mosaic Tiles filter does not really resemble mosaic. However, it is an interesting-enough look for you to be able to find something to do with it. It could also make an interesting treatment for image-filled text.

Try it:

1. Open the image "Roses.Psd." Duplicate the image (Image➥Duplicate➥OK).

2. Open the Mosaic Tiles dialog box shown in Figure 14.172 (Filter➥Texture➥ Mosaic Tiles).

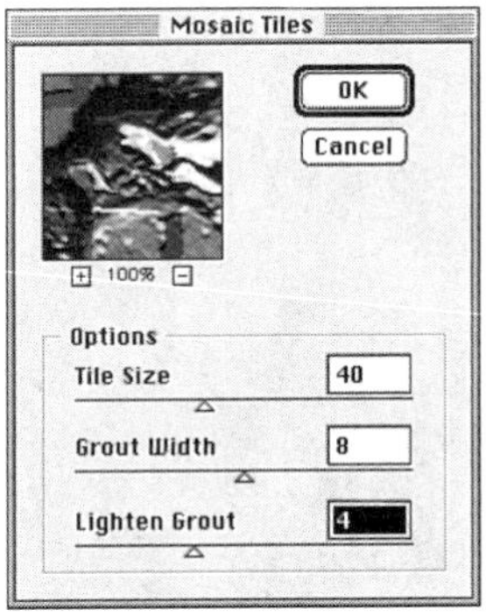

Figure 14.172

The Mosaic Tiles dialog box.

3. Drag the Tile Size to 40.

   The Tile Size setting varies from 2-100. Even when the tile size is small, it produces useful results. The small sizes are almost more interesting because when they overlap, no tile is produced. This creates an irregularity missing at larger sizes.

4. Set the Grout Width to 8.

   The Grout Width can vary from 1-15. It should, however, be smaller than the tile size.

5. Finally, set the Lighten Grout to 4.

The Lighten Grout varies from 0-10. When this setting is high, you do not see the effect very much. This setting does a fairly subtle embossing that highlights edges but no longer looks like grout at high settings. Keep this below 5.

6. Click OK. Figure 14.173 shows the result.

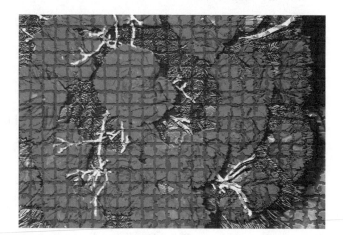

Figure 14.173

An example of the Mosaic Tiles filter applied to an image.

Filter type	Category	Supported Color Modes	Preview type	Data Dependent	Color Dependent
Parameter	Texture Filter	RGB, Grayscale	Small Filter Preview	No. This filter adds texture to a blank image.	No. The Foreground/Background settings have no effect.

Patchwork

The Patchwork filter is really what you might expect the Mosaic Tiles filter to be. It is basically the Mosaic filter (Filter➡Pixelate➡Mosaic) with elevation added. The Patchwork filter, however, adds a few twists at the end of the ranges that give totally different and unexpected results (try a Square Size of 0 with a Relief size of 0 or 25). It works best on images that have clearly defined color differences. The roses in the example image are too flat. A way to change that will be shown.

Try it:

1. Open the image "Roses.Psd." Duplicate the image (Image➡Duplicate➡OK).

2. Use the Select➡Color Range command to select just the red roses in the image (you do not need to be extremely precise).

3. Open the Patchwork dialog box shown in Figure 14.171 (Filter➡Texture➡Patchwork).

4. Drag the Square Size to 6.

5. Set the Relief to 10.

   The Relief can vary from 0-25. Even a Relief of 0 is visible, whereas a large Relief seems to shoot the tiles up in space a bit (somewhat like the Extrude filter).

6. Click OK. Notice that is image is very flat.

Let's try it again—with a few changes.

1. Open the image "Roses.Psd." Duplicate the image (Image➡Duplicate➡OK).

2. Drag the icon for the Background layer to the New Layer icon (the center icon at the bottom of the Layers palette) *twice*. Make the Background copy (the middle Layer) the active Layer and turn the Eye icon off the top layer.

3. Use the Select➡Color Range command to select just the red roses in the image (you do not need to be extremely precise).

4. Equalize the selection (Image➡Adjust➡Equalize➡Selection Only). Deselect (Command-D)[Control-D].

5. Open the Patchwork dialog box shown in Figure 14.174 (Filter➡Texture➡Patchwork).

6. Drag the Square Size to 6.

   The Square Size setting varies from 0-10. A tiny square size looks like large sprinkles.

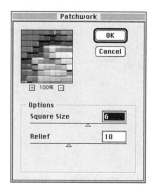

Figure 14.174

The Patchwork dialog box.

7. Set the Relief to 10.

   The Relief can vary from 0-25. Even a Relief of 0 is visible, while a large Relief seems to shoot the tiles up in space a bit (somewhat like the Extrude filter).

8. Equalizing the roses made them exhibit much more difference between the adjacent tiles, but it also turned them pink. Make the top Layer both visible and active. Apply the Patchwork filter to it at the same settings (Command-F)[Control-F].

9. Notice how flat the roses are. Change the Blending mode to Color, and you will get the red back into the roses but retain the altered values of the tiles. Figure 14.175 shows the result.

Figure 14.175

The Patchwork filter applied to an image.

Filter type	Category	Supported Color Modes	Preview type	Data Dependent	Color Dependent
Parameter	Texture Filter	RGB, Grayscale	Small Filter Preview	No. This filter adds texture to a blank image.	No. The Foreground/Background settings have no effect.

Stained Glass

The Stained Glass filter is another mosaic-tile wannabe. This may actually be the closest one to real mosaic tiles. It looks, however, nothing at all like stained glass. The Stained Glass filter is a crystallize filter with grout and more intensity.

Try it:

1. Open the image "Roses.Psd." Duplicate the image (Image➡Duplicate➡OK).

2. Open the Stained Glass dialog box shown in Figure 14.176 (Filter➡Texture➡Stained Glass).

Figure 14.176

The Stained Glass dialog box.

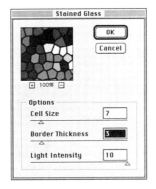

3. Drag the Cell Size to 7.

The Cell Size setting varies from 2-50. When this parameter is high, you create an image that has two colors—one on each diagonal half of the tile. The cell size is proportional to the image size, so you do not need to select a larger cell size when you are working on a large (in pixels) image. Keep the tile size fairly low to retain any detail in the image.

4. Set the Border Thickness to 3.

   The Border Thickness can vary from 1-20. It should be less than the Cell Size. This control uses the Foreground color setting.

5. Finally, set the Light Intensity to 10.

   The Light Intensity varies from 0-10. The light shines directly in the center of the image and radiates out. A setting of 0 does not shine anything; a setting of 10 causes the center of the image to white out.

6. Click OK. Figure 14.177 shows the result.

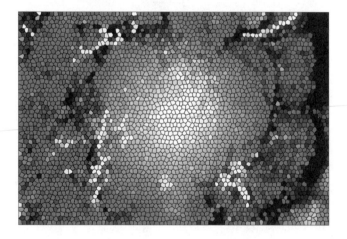

Figure 14.177

An example of the Stained Glass filter applied to an image.

Filter type	Category	Supported Color Modes	Preview type	Data Dependent	Color Dependent
Parameter	Texture Filter	RGB, Grayscale	Small Filter Preview	No. This filter adds texture to a blank image.	Yes. The Foreground color is the grout color.

Texturizer

The Texturizer filter looks good when used on text. This filter is actually the precursor of the Lighting Effects filter. Until the advent of that filter in Photoshop 3.0, using the Texturizer filter was the only way to easily add embossed textures and bump maps to images (other than to bring them into Painter). It is still an easier filter to use than the Lighting Effects filter, but it gives you less control. The Texturizer filter is similar to other filters in the Gallery Effects set that let you add texture as part of the filter. But in this case, the only thing that this filter does is add texture.

Try it:

1. Open the image "Roses.Psd." Duplicate the image (Image➡Duplicate➡OK).

2. Open the Texturizer dialog box shown in Figure 14.178 (Filter➡Texture➡Texturizer).

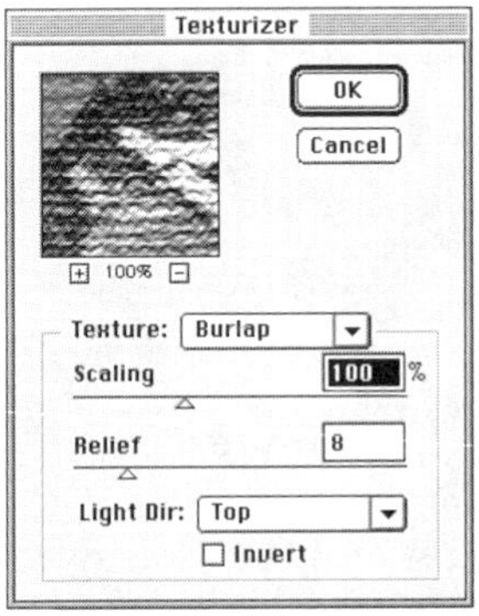

Figure 14.178

The Texturizer dialog box.

3. There are a number of settings that concern the texture to be applied. Set the Texture to Burlap.

   The Textures included are Brick, Burlap, Canvas, and Sandstone, but you can load your own texture from a Photoshop file.

4. Set the Scaling to 100%.

   Textures can be scaled from 50-200%. At 100%, you are using the original size of the texture-pattern.

5. Set the Relief to 8.

   You can set Relief to values of 0-50.

6. Select Top as the Light Direction. You can select from any 45-degree angle. You may also invert the texture if you wish to reverse the embossing (don't for now).

7. Click OK. Figure 14.179 shows the result.

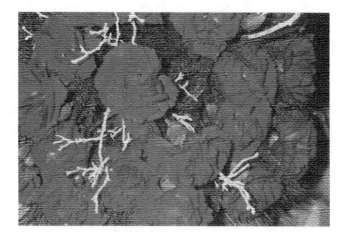

Figure 14.179

The Texturizer filter applied to an image.

Filter type	Category	Supported Color Modes	Preview type	Data Dependent	Color Dependent
Parameter	Texture Filter	RGB, Grayscale	Small Filter Preview	No. This filter adds texture to a blank image.	No. The Foreground/Background settings have no effect.

PHOTOSHOP'S NATIVE FILTERS—VIDEO

These two Video filters are used to prepare images for writing to a videotape and to help fix images imported from videotape.

De-Interlace

The De-Interlace filter is used to help remove the jitter and fuzziness from an image imported from a video source—either a tape, still, or motion video. Because most video images are created by interlacing—

showing the odd and then the even scan lines onscreen—they can be very noisy when brought into the computer. This filter helps to remove some of that jitter by either building new odd or even lines based on the image (interpolation) or by simply repeating the line above it. You can also use this as a special effects filter with a little extra work as shown below.

Try it:

1. Open the image "TuRed.Psd." Duplicate the image (Image➡Duplicate➡OK).

2. Drag the icon for the Background layer to the New Layer icon (the center icon at the bottom of the Layers palette).

3. Open the De-Interlace dialog box shown in Figure 14.180 (Filter➡Video➡De-interlace).

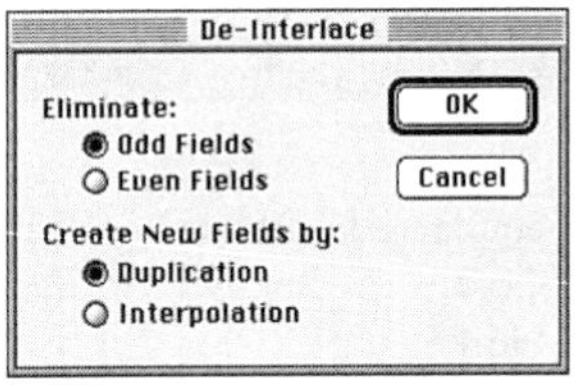

Figure 14.180

The De-interlace dialog box.

4. Set Eliminate to Odd Fields.

   You can eliminate either the odd or even scan lines.

5. Set the "Create New Fields by" setting to "Duplication."

   You can also interpolate between the odd or even lines that surround the line being removed.

6. Click OK.

7. Set the Blending mode to Difference and Flatten the image.

8. Use the Auto Levels command (Image➡Adjust➡Auto Levels). Figure 14.181 shows the result. This action actually shows the changes that the filter has made to the image.

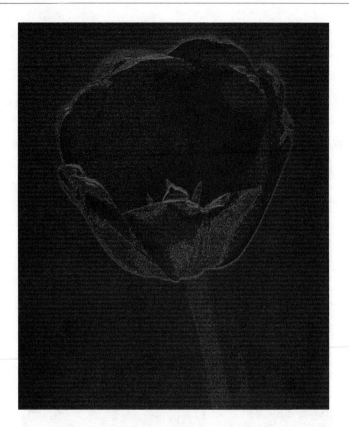

Figure 14.181

The De-Interlace filter applied to an image.

Filter type	Category	Supported Color Modes	Preview type	Data Dependent	Color Dependent
Parameter	Production (and Special Effects) Filter	RGB, Grayscale, CMYK,	None	Yes. A blank image produces a blank filtered image.	No. The Foreground/Background settings have no effect.

NTSC Colors

The NTSC Colors filter changes the colors in the image to colors that will display on a video screen without vibrating and bleeding into other scan lines. It does this by moving the "unsafe" color to the nearest legal color.

Try it:

1. Open the image "TuRed.Psd." Duplicate the image
   (Image➡Duplicate➡OK).

2. Apply the NTSC Colors filter (Filter➡Video➡NTSC Colors) to
   see the result shown in Figure 14.182

Figure 14.182

*The NTSC Colors filter applied
to an image.*

Filter type	Category	Supported Color Modes	Preview type	Data Dependent	Color Dependent
One-Step	Production (Color Change) Filter	RGB only	None	No. It will find a legal solid color.	No. The Foreground/Background settings have no effect.

PHOTOSHOP'S NATIVE FILTERS—OTHER

The "Other" category of filters contains a variety of workhorse filters that do not seem to fit under any other category.

Custom

The Custom filter is one of the more complex filters and a major time-consumer—once you know enough theory to "play" with it. This filter is really an engine that enables you to create a number of different effects numerically on an image. You can load different settings and save settings as well. The saved settings are called Convolution Kernels because the Custom filter performs a convoluted form of math on a matrix (Note: groan at my pun if you wish—but don't believe my reason for calling these Convolution Kernels!). The filter, however, *does* use a 5×5 grid matrix to obtain its results. For each pixel in the image, the filter multiplies the center matrix value with the brightness value of the current pixel and uses the other values to calculate the brightness values of nearby pixels. The filter divides the sum of the total brightness amounts by the scale value and adds in the offset amount. It then repeats this process for every other pixel in the image. Whew!

What can you do with the Custom filter? The basic effects that you can achieve are those of sharpening, blurring, edge detection, and embossing. In addition, you can perform certain types of color changes. If the complexity of this filter completely frustrates you, you can also purchase KPT Convolver from MetaTools, which does the same thing but in a much more user-friendly way!

There is a trick to this filter, however. You almost always get some type of usable result so long as the sum of the numbers in the matrix divided by the Scale amount is equal to 1.

Try it:

1. Open the image "TuRed.Psd." Duplicate the image (Image➧Duplicate➧OK).

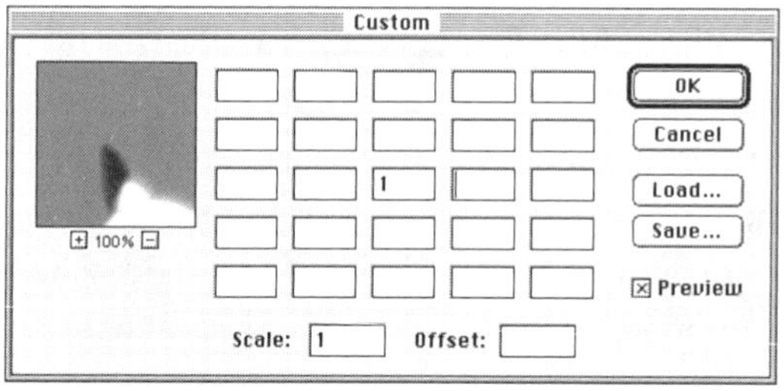

Figure 14.183

The Custom dialog box.

2. Apply the Custom filter (Filter➤Other➤Custom). Your dialog box may not look like Figure 14.183 when it appears. It contains either the default settings or last settings used. The numbers shown in this dialog box produce no change in the image at all.

3. Change the numbers in the Matrix so that they are the same as the values shown in Figure 14.184. Notice that when you add up all of the positive and negative numbers, they add up to 1. When divided by the Scale amount of 1, the result is still 1. These settings start to produce an embossing effect as you can see in Figure 14.185.

4. Now, add an offset amount of 128. This makes many of the values in the image a neutral gray and emphasizes the embossing effect. Figure 14.186 shows the finished image.

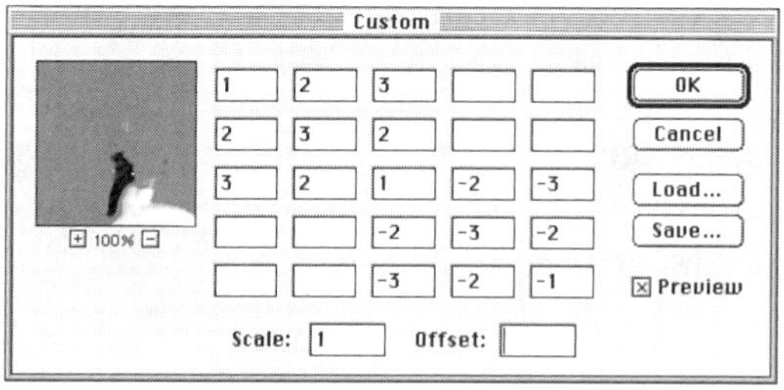

Figure 14.184

The Custom dialog box showing new settings.

You can get very creative with this filter. Just remember to try to make the numbers come out to 1. Sometimes it does not matter, but if you vary too far afield, you end up with an image that is all white or all black—an effect that is not especially useful. Try arranging the matrix symmetrically and non-symmetrically. See what different results you can get.

Figure 14.185

Filtered image with no offset amount.

Filter type	Category	Supported Color Modes	Preview type	Data Dependent	Color Dependent
mini-app	Special Effects	RGB, Grayscale, CMYK, Lab	Full Image Preview	Yes. A blank image produces a blank filtered image.	No. The Foreground/Background settings have no effect.

Figure 14.186

The filtered image with offset of 128.

High Pass

The High Pass filter reduces the contrast in an image. It is very useful for simplifying an image prior to finding edges or applying the Threshold command. The High Pass filter can also be a good starting point for developing a mask or selection. Though it is not especially attractive as its own filter (the High Pass filter in Painter is much prettier), it is very useful for creating woodcut effects.

Try it:

1. Open the image "TuRed.Psd." Duplicate the image (Image➡Duplicate➡OK).

2. Drag the icon for the Background layer to the New Layer icon (the center icon at the bottom of the Layers palette).

3. Open the High Pass dialog box shown in Figure 14.187 (Filter➡Other➡High Pass).

Figure 14.187

The High Pass dialog box.

4. Drag the Radius to 22.

   The Radius setting varies from 0.1-250. This parameter controls the distance in pixels that the filter looks as it applies the effect. A setting of 1.6 produces a very fine woodcut look. The setting of 22 gives a solid outline.

5. Click OK. Figure 14.188 shows the result.

Figure 14.188

The High Pass filter applied to an image.

6. Select the Threshold command (Image➥Adjust➥Threshold) and drag the slider to 121. This leaves only the strongest blacks in the image.

Figure 14.189

The Woodcut look achieved.

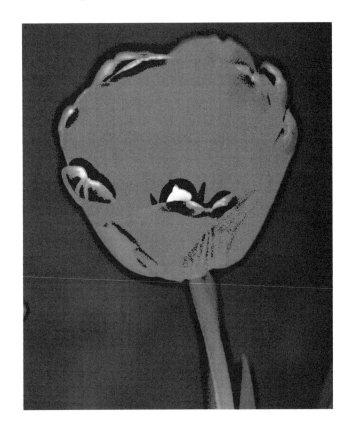

7. Set the Blending mode to Multiply. Figure 14.189 shows the result.

Filter type	Category	Supported Color Modes	Preview type	Data Dependent	Color Dependent
Parameter	Production/ helper filter	RGB, Grayscale, CMYK, Lab	Full Image Preview	Yes. A blank image produces a blank filtered image.	No. The Foreground/Background settings have no effect.

Minimum

The Minimum filter emphasizes the dark pixels in an image. This filter is most useful for working in channels where you want to reduce a selection. It can also be used to choke-trap areas of a channel if you are working in spot colors.

Try it:

1. Open the image "TuRed.Psd." Duplicate the image (Image➟Duplicate➟OK).

2. Open the Minimum dialog box shown in Figure 14.190 (Filter➟Other➟Minimum).

Figure 14.190

The Minimum dialog box.

3. Drag the Radius to 10.

   The Radius setting varies from 1-10. This parameter controls the distance from each pixel that the filter uses to see the darkest pixel value.

4. Click OK. Figure 14.191 shows the result.

Filter type	Category	Supported Color Modes	Preview type	Data Dependent	Color Dependent
Parameter	Production/ Helper Filter	RGB, Grayscale, CMYK, Lab	Full Image Preview	Yes. A blank image produces a blank filtered image.	No. The Foreground/Background settings have no effect.

Figure 14.191

The Minimum filter applied to an image.

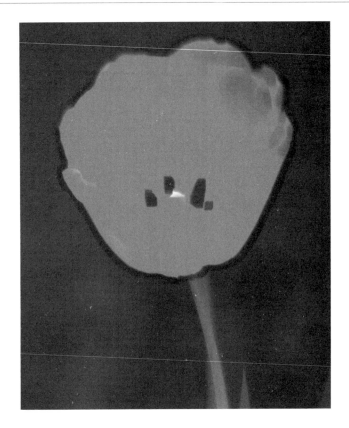

Maximum

The Maximum filter emphasizes the light pixels in an image. This filter is most useful for working in channels where you want to enlarge a selection. The Maximum filter can also be used to spread-trap areas of a channel if you are working in spot colors.

Try it:

1. Open the image "TuRed.Psd." Duplicate the image (Image➥Duplicate➥OK).

2. Open the Maximum dialog box shown in Figure 14.192 (Filter➥Other➥Maximum).

Figure 14.192

The Maximum dialog box.

3. Drag the Radius to 7.

   The Radius varies from 1-10. This parameter controls the distance from each pixel the filter uses to see the lightest pixel value.

4. Click OK. Figure 14.193 shows the result.

Figure 14.193

The Maximum filter applied to an image.

Filter type	Category	Supported Color Modes	Preview type	Data Dependent	Color Dependent
Parameter	Production/ Helper Filter	RGB, Grayscale, CMYK, Lab	Full Image Preview	Yes. A blank image produces a blank filtered image.	No. The Foreground/Background settings have no effect.

Offset

The Offset filter is incredibly useful for making patterns. It enables you to move part of an image from one location in the image to another and wrap the pixels that "fall off the edge" to the other side. Let's see how it can be used to create a seamless brick pattern repeat from the TuRed.Psd image.

Try it:

1. Open the image "TuRed.Psd." Duplicate the image (Image➡Duplicate➡OK).

2. Use the Image Size command (Image➡Image Size) to reduce the image to 100 pixels wide and 121 pixels high.

3. Drag the icon for the Background layer to the New Layer icon (the center icon at the bottom of the Layers palette).

4. Press D to set the colors back to the default of black and white.

5. Use the Canvas Size command (Image➡Canvas Size) to change the size of the image to 100 pixels wide by 242 pixels high (anchor in the top center box).

6. Open the Offset dialog box shown in Figure 14.194 (Filter➡Other➡Offset).

7. Type in 50 for the Horizontal (pixels) right.

   The Horizontal (pixels) setting varies from -30,000 to 30,000. A setting of 50 pixels in a 100-pixel wide image offsets the image by half.

8. Set the Vertical (pixels) to 121.

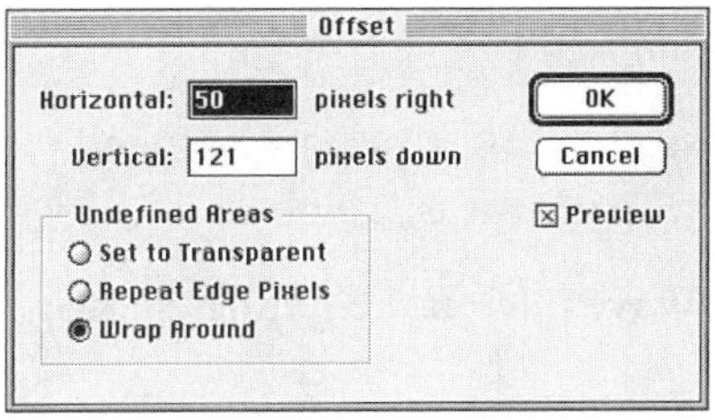

```
                  ▒▒▒▒▒ Offset ▒▒▒▒▒
    Horizontal: [50     ]  pixels right      ( OK )

    Vertical: [121    ]   pixels down      ( Cancel )

    ┌ Undefined Areas ─────┐      ☒ Preview
    │  ○ Set to Transparent │
    │  ○ Repeat Edge Pixels │
    │  ⦿ Wrap Around        │
    └────────────────────────┘
```

Figure 14.194

The Offset dialog box.

The Vertical (pixels) can vary from -30,000 to 30,000. This parameter controls the distance, in pixels, towards the bottom (positive number) or top (negative numbers) that the image will move.

9. Select Wrap Around to make the pixels move from one edge onto the other. Your other options are to repeat the edge pixels, or, if you are filtering in a Layer, set to transparency (or background color if not in a Layer).

10. Click OK. Figure 14.195 shows the result.

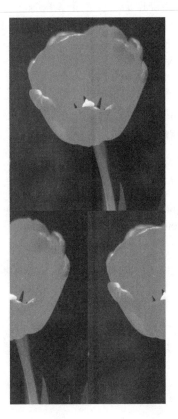

Figure 14.195

The Offset filter applied to an image.

11. Flatten the image.

12. Use the Lasso to draw a Marquee around the area where the seams meet. Feather it by 10 pixels.

13. Apply the Wave filter at the settings shown in Figure 14.196. Click OK.

Figure 14.196

The Wave filter settings.

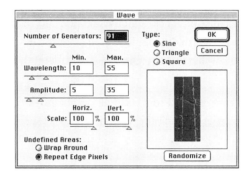

14. Apply the Offset filter again, at 50 pixels right, 121 pixels down, Wrap Around. This puts the image back to show the other set of seams. Select those as you did in Step 8. Feather this by 10 pixels.

15. Apply the Wave filter at the same settings. Click OK.

16. Select the entire image (Command-A)[Control-A]. Define this as a pattern (Edit➡Define Pattern).

17. Create a new document (Command-N)[Control-N] 1,000×1,000 pixels.

18. Fill the image with the pattern (Shift-Delete➡Pattern, 100 percent opacity, Normal). Figure 14.197 shows the result.

Filter type	Category	Supported Color Modes	Preview type	Data Dependent	Color Dependent
Parameter	Production/ Helper Filter	RGB, Grayscale, CMYK, Lab	Full Image Preview	Yes. A blank image produces a blank filtered image.	No. The Foreground/Background settings have no effect.

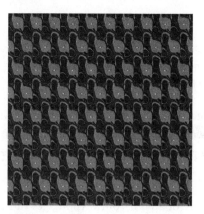

Figure 14.197

The Offset filter pattern applied to an image.

WATERMARKING IMAGES

Photoshop 4.0 also contains a filter set that helps you to protect and copyright your images. These filters, the Embed Watermark and Read Watermark filters, appear below all of the native Photoshop filters in the menu. These two filters were developed by Digimarc and are being included by Adobe as a way to help prevent unauthorized copying of images.

Watermarking is an old process. In traditional printing, a watermark was a stamp or logo applied to paper to identify the maker. It acts as both a certificate of authenticity and a means of identification. It is subtle enough not to detract from the printed page but visible if you know to look for it.

The electronic watermark is very similar—except that you need a specialized program to see if it is present because it should not be apparent to the naked eye. The Digimarc Embed Watermark filter works by adding a user-controllable amount of noise to an image. The noise is actually a pattern that contains the identifier of the artist who created the image; an identifier that must be "rented" from Digimarc for $150 per year.

The watermark is designed to survive rough handling. Even if the image is printed, the watermark is still there and can be recaptured by scanning the printed piece back into the computer. Blurring or sharpening the image does not remove the watermark, nor does cropping.

Warning

Once you have put a water mark on a file, you cannot remove it. Always save a copy of the original file before you water mark it in case you need to revert to that file.

You need to obtain a personal ID before you can embed anything other than a demo watermark in your images. You can obtain the ID by accessing the Digimarc Web site on the Web (http//www.digimarc.com).

Try it:

1. Open a copy of any of your own images (unless you have your own ID, you do *not* want to brand your only copy of an image with a demo ID).

2. Open the Embed Watermark dialog box (Filter➥Digimarc➥ Embed Watermark). The dialog box shown in Figure 14.198 appears.

Figure 14.198

The Embed Water mark dialog box.

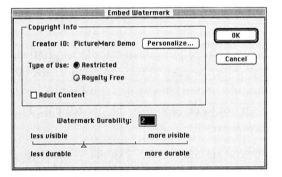

3. You may place your image in the public sector or make it available as a restricted-use image only only. You may also brand the image as "Adult Content."

4. Finally, select the strength of the watermark that you desire. Remember, the stronger and more durable the watermark, the more likely it is to detract from the original image.

5. Click OK.

Viewing a Watermark

If you'd like to see the watermark that you've embedded, follow these steps to make it visible.

1. Drag an unmarked copy on top of the watermarked copy (with the Shift key pressed to make the images align).

2. Change the Blending mode to Difference.

3. Duplicate the 2-layered image and flatten it.

4. Invert the result. You will see only the added noise that carries the watermark.

Reading a Watermark

Every time you open an image into Photoshop, if the Read Watermark filter is present, it scans the image to see if it can find a watermark. If it does, it displays the copyright symbol after the name of the image. If you wish to use this image, you need to check Digimarc's database to see who owns it and then contact the artist for permission to use the image.

To read a watermark that has been embedded in an image, choose Read Watermark from the Digimarc submenu of the Filters menu (see Figure 14.199).

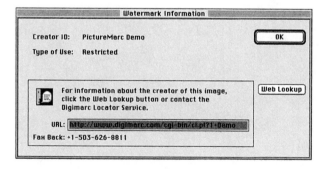

Figure 14.199

If this watermark had been embedded by someone with a Digimarc ID number, you could click on the Web lookup button to locate the artist's name and other information at the Digimarc Web site.

Chapter 15

PRINTING

You scanned, painted, or drew your initial images; you blurred, sharpened, lightened, and diffused the composite image; you duplicated, rotated, and cropped individual elements, adjusted hues and saturations, applied cool gradients and textures, and spent hours (or days) tweaking and nudging every conceivable aspect of your image until it was perfect. Now all you need to do is get what's onscreen onto paper, transparencies, film, or whatever other final media you want.

Theoretically, this should be as simple as choosing the Print command from the File menu or saving your image to disk to send to a service bureau. Unfortunately (as many of us have discovered), getting final printed output of a Photoshop image is rarely that easy. This is, I believe, the only time that Photoshop users are envious of Word users. The process of producing printed output of digital images (known as *imaging*, although this term also applies to creating purely digital output such as graphics for Web or multimedia use) requires a little knowledge, a lot of forethought, and plenty of patience.

Output Options

There are several options for producing hard copy of your work, each of which has its own advantages and disadvantages.

Inkjet: One of the most affordable paths to color output is the inkjet printer. Inkjet printers provide fair-to-good quality output for about half the price of a good laser printer. High-end inkjet printers, costing tens of thousands of dollars, provide truly excellent output. The Iris inkjet printer is a favorite of professional digital artists, providing outstanding, color-accurate output and able to handle a wide variety of papers.

Laser: Ideal for newsletters, catalogs, flyers, or other documents that feature black-and-white photographs, the 300 to 600 dpi resolution of laser printers produces great results for grayscale imaging. Many laser printers (most notably those from Apple and Hewlett-Packard) can also subtly alter the size of their dots, providing impressive detail and subtlety when printing grayscale photos. Laser printer output is convenient, inexpensive, and (relatively) fast.

Color laser printers combine some of the advantages of laser printers with the bonus of color. While still relatively expensive, color laser printers

This chapter focuses on five key areas:

- Preparing Photoshop for printing (including discussions of different printer types and some important printing concepts)

- Understanding and working with halftones

- Mastering Photoshop's Page Setup and Print commands

- Creating color separations

- Understanding miscellaneous printing issues such as calibration, trapping, proofs, cross-platform printing, and printing from other applications such as QuarkXPress or PageMaker

PREPARING PHOTOSHOP

When printing color images from Photoshop it is important to remember that in order to get good color output at the end of the editing process, you should configure Photoshop for an image's final printing destination (whether to a local inkjet or dye-sub printer, or to a commercial press for color separations) at the start of the image-editing process—*before* you start working with the image. This is especially important when working with high-end printers, but even a lowly desktop ink-jet printer can produce better, more accurate output if Photoshop has been properly configured. If you are only printing to a black and white or grayscale device such as a laser printer, this preparation is not as critical. (Keep in mind, however, that an image intended initially for grayscale printing may eventually be output on a color printer. As a general rule, always configure Photoshop for your most often used color output device.) This configuration deals primarily with three dialog boxes: Printing Inks Setup, Separation Setup, and Separation Tables, all of which can be accessed from the Color Settings submenu located in the File menu.

Setting Printing Inks

The Printing Inks dialog box is used to change Photoshop's built-in RGB to CMYK conversion tables (see Figure 15.1). These conversion tables are used whenever you convert an image from one color space (RGB or CMYK) to the other. Even if you are not converting an image from one color space to another, these conversion tables are sometimes used by Photoshop for subtle color manipulation tasks, often without you being aware that color conversions are taking place. A classic example of this is when you are working in an RGB image, but select a color in the color picker by entering or modifying CMYK values. This CMYK color then has to be converted to RGB before being applied to your image. For the average user, though, the main reason for configuring Photoshop's color settings is to match a proof from a new printer or press. Photoshop's default settings work well for most mid- to high-end printers, though, so we recommend not altering the values within this dialog box unless you are already familiar with color separations and conversion tables. As always, work closely with your print shop or service bureau to determine the best settings for a particular print job.

There are three primary parameters that can be adjusted within the Printing Inks Setup dialog box: Ink Colors, Dot Gain, and Gray Balance.

are becoming more of a viable option for the individual artist or small studio.

Dye-sublimation (dye-sub) printers are capable of output equal to that available photographically. Dye-sub printers are generally expensive and have a high price-per-page ratio because of the special ribbons and paper that they require, but their output is as good as it gets. Most service bureaus have dye-sub printers, so you can always get the quality of printing that they provide without having to buy one yourself.

Thermal Wax: Another affordable color printing option, thermal wax printers provide excellent color output at prices comparable to those of laser printers. As with dye-sub printers, thermal wax printers use special ribbons and paper, although thermal wax printers that accept regular bond paper are becoming more common. Because of the materials used, thermal wax printers excel at producing transparencies.

Imagesetters are large, expensive machines capable of producing exceptionally high-resolution output (1,200 to 2,400 dpi or better). The imagesetter "burns" the high-resolution image onto photographic film or paper, which is

continues

Figure 15.1

The Printing Inks Setup dialog box.

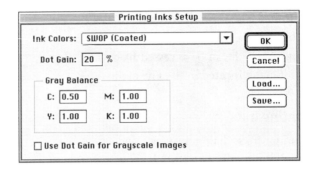

then developed and used to make printing plates for a commercial print run.

Imagesetters are monochrome printing devices. In order to produce truly high-resolution color, an imagesetter must create spot- or process-color separations used to make printing plates for a color print run.

Film Recorders: While not technically "printing," imaging your artwork with a film recorder is a popular way to create hard copy output. Film recorders use a cathode ray tube (CRT) or similar device attached to a camera back to record an onscreen image. The better the film recorder, the higher the resolution of the recorded image. (As with traditional printing, higher resolution means more detailed output.)

Film recorders always use the RGB color channels, which eliminates the need to do CMYK conversions. When using film recorders, it is important that your image resolution matches that of the film recorder or is an even

1. Select the target printer (or paper type) from the **Ink Colors** pop-up menu. Based on this information (and that in the Separation Setup dialog box, if you are doing color separations) Photoshop interprets what your colors will look like when printed. Selecting the wrong target printer or paper type can lead to less-than-perfect colors or poor detail and definition in your final output.

If you are not sure what to pick, select SWOP (Coated) (the default). SWOP (Specifications for Web Offset Publications) is the industry standard for color separation in the U.S. The most common ink color specifications are also available in this pull-down menu, and you should choose the one that best describes your printing environment. Also, be sure to choose the Coated (for glossy paper), Uncoated (for regular paper such as standard bond), or Newsprint variations depending on the type of paper being used. This color profile adjusts the onscreen color display of your file to best represent what the printed file would look like, based on the type of paper and printing ink set specified here. The default dot gain values can also be increased slightly, but try not to go more than 3-5 percent over the defaults.

2. Adjust the **Dot Gain** value as necessary to compensate for unwanted dot gain in a proof or at the request of your printer. Higher dot gain values increase the size of the printed dots, creating a darker image, while smaller dot gain values decrease the size of the print-ed dots, creating lighter images. See the "Dealing with Dot Gain" section, later in this chapter, for more information on dot gain.

> divisor thereof (that is, if you have a 4096 dpi film recorder, your image should be 4096 ppi, 2048 ppi, 1024 ppi, and so on).

3. The **Gray Balance** section can be used to compensate for gamma changes made to individual color channels or to compensate for a printer that tends toward one color or another. (If your inkjet or dye-sub printer tends to print too much blue, for example, you can reduce the Cyan value here to compensate.)

Note

"Gamma" can be a confusing term, especially if you are new to color theory. Basically, the gamma of a color determines how heavily the color is weighted toward light or dark. Adjusting the gamma is similar to adjusting the brightness, except that adjusting the brightness produces a linear change (all shades of a color are shifted by an equal amount toward light or dark), whereas adjusting the gamma produces a logarithmic, or curved, change (shades closer to light or dark are shifted more than midrange shades). This is a simplified explanation of a very complex topic, but it should provide at least a working understanding of what gamma does.

Normally, these settings only affect color images and so are ignored when printing in grayscale. Grayscale images, however, can have dot gain problems, too. Click the Use Dot Gain for Grayscale Images checkbox to have Photoshop use the Dot Gain values entered for color printing when printing grayscale images.

Setting Color Separations

Unlike the Printing Inks Setup dialog box, the Separation Setup dialog box has no effect on how your CMYK files look onscreen (see Figure 15.2). It does, however, have a lot to do with how those files look when printed.

Figure 15.2

The Separation Setup dialog box.

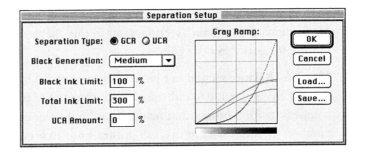

When Photoshop converts RGB files to CMYK files, it determines what percentages of cyan, magenta, yellow, and black ink are used to simulate the various shades of red, green, and blue contained in the original file. Different percentages of CMYK inks can theoretically be used to create the same composite color, but in actual practice, that never quite works out (due, in large part, to the seemingly infinite variations in ink quality, paper quality, paper type, absorption rate, and other factors).

GCR, UCR, and UCA

GCR, UCR, and UCA refer to different printing techniques for translating light-based colors (such as those on your monitor, created by combining red, green, and blue) into ink-based colors (such as those on a printed page, created by combining cyan, magenta, yellow, and black). Theoretically, black shouldn't be necessary, as pure cyan, magenta, and

Keep in mind that for the majority of print jobs, Photoshop's default settings work fine. But if you have a color-critical print job, you should talk to your print shop or service bureau and, *based on their recommendations*, make changes to the Separation Setup dialog box.

1. Within the Separation Setup dialog box, select whether you want to use GCR (gray component replacement) or UCR (undercolor removal) as the separation type. With GCR selected, all dialog box options are active. With UCR, only Black Ink Limit and Total Ink Limit are active.

2. Use the **Black Generation** pop-up menu to select the degree of black generation (Custom, None, Light, Medium, Heavy, or Maximum). The default setting is Medium, which works well for most images. Selecting None means no black plate is printed, and Custom lets you manually adjust the black generation curve.

3. You can enter any desired values for **Black Ink Limit** and **Total Ink Limit**. The Black Ink Limit determines the maximum percentage of black ink used by the printer to create the darkest parts of your image. Total Ink Limit is the maximum combined percentage of cyan, magenta, yellow, and black inks at that can be used anywhere in the image. The Total Ink Limit value should generally be set between 240 and 320 percent.

4. The **UCA** Amount (undercolor addition) can be increased from its default setting of 0 percent to add cyan, magenta, and yellow inks to darker areas of your image (after removing some black ink) for a richer black than black ink alone can create.

The Separation Setup dialog box doesn't affect any Photoshop operation other than converting RGB color information to CMYK mode (which includes printing an RGB file to a CMYK printer).

yellow inks should combine to form black. In practice, though, because there is no such thing as "pure" cyan, magenta, or yellow ink, they combine to create a dark brown. To compensate for this, printers add black ink in place of some of the cyan, magenta, and yellow. GCR (gray component replacement) and UCR (undercolor removal) are the two methods most often used to accomplish this. With GCR (Photoshop's default setting) black ink is added in varying amounts to a fairly broad spectrum of colors. For this reason, GCR separations tend toward darker, richer colors and better gray balance. With UCR, black ink is only added to shadow areas (for more depth) and to neutral colors. Because less ink is used with UCR separations, it can be better for certain materials (transparencies and certain paper types). UCA (undercolor addition) is used in conjunction with the GCR technique to produce richer, more detailed shadows by removing some black from these areas and replacing it with cyan, magenta, and yellow.

Using Separation Tables

The Separation Tables dialog box (see Figure 15.3) lets you save your Printing Inks Setup and Separation Setup settings as a separation table that can be loaded back into Photoshop through this dialog box. Each separation table contains the values entered into both the Printing Inks Setup *and* the Separation Setup dialog boxes and is simply a convenient way to retrieve those settings. After a table is saved and loaded, the Separation Tables dialog box enables you to switch between the current Printing Inks Setup and Separation Setup settings and those stored in the separation table. This is especially useful if you have access to more than one color printer or regularly work with different service bureaus. You can create one separation table for each printer or service bureau and load the appropriate table for the printer you're using.

Figure 15.3

The Separation Tables dialog box.

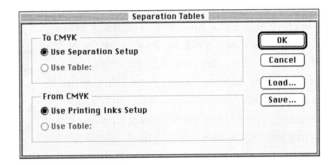

WORKING WITH HALFTONES

We perceive real-world images as smooth gradations of colors and shades. (We don't actually *see* them that way, but our brain fools us into *perceiving* them that way.) This type of imaging is referred to as continuous tone (or contone) imaging, wherein one color flows smoothly into the next with no discernible gaps or steps. A halftone is a way of reproducing an image with a collection of dots, rather than a continuous flow of ink, paint, light, and so on (see Figure 15.4). Traditionally, a photographic process is used to convert a continuous tone image (such as a photograph or painting) into a grid or screen of evenly spaced dots of equal intensity. This grid is referred to as a halftone screen. The dots in this screen, though evenly spaced and equally intense, can vary in size, creating the illusion of darker and lighter shades. (Larger dots on a fixed grid have less white space between them, resulting in a darker-looking image.) The term *halftone* refers to the fact that gray is created not by printing gray ink, but by only printing every other dot in the grid (resulting in a grid that is half black and half white, even though it appears gray). The defining characteristic of halftone printing is that the intensity (or tint) of the inks cannot be varied. Either a spot on the page has color (that is, ink) or it doesn't. Printing these dots with different-colored inks provides a way to create images of varying shades and tints. Most desktop printing and the vast majority of commercial printing is accomplished with halftones. All halftones consist of three basic parameters: screen frequency, screen angle, and dot shape (see Figure 15.5).

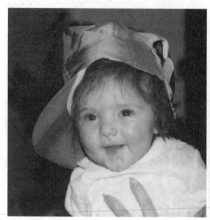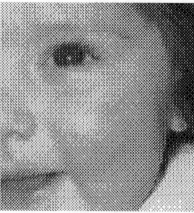

Figure 15.4

A sample image (left) and a close-up showing the halftone in detail.

If you do customize the halftone screens and are sending images to a service bureau or other commercial printer, be sure to discuss with your printer the optimal settings for your halftone screens.

If you create custom halftone settings be sure to save your image as an EPS file and click the Include Halftone Screen checkbox. This ensures that your custom halftone screen values are included with your image. These values override your printer or page layout application's halftone screen settings (but only for your image).

Setting Screen Frequency

Screen frequency refers to how tightly packed the dot grid is. A grid with 133 rows of dots per inch is referred to as having a screen of 133 lpi (lines per inch). The higher the screen frequency, the better the detail of the image but the fewer possible tints (or shades of gray). This is because tints are created by varying the size of the dots on the grid, and on a tighter grid, there is less room for variation in dot size.

Figure 15.5

A sample image printed with
five different halftone screens.

To change the halftone screen frequency settings, click the Screen button in the Page Setup dialog box and enter a new Frequency value. Frequencies can be entered in lines per inch or lines per centimeter.

Setting Screen Angle

Screen angle refers to the angle of the dot grid. 45° is the standard screen angle for monochrome (black and white) printing. Screen angle becomes extremely important when printing two or more colors, as the grid of dots, when superimposed on one another, can create distracting patterns (known as moiré patterns). In the majority of commercial printing, four different grids are used (for each of the four process colors: cyan, magenta, yellow, and black). To avoid as much moiré interference as possible, the screen angles of these four plates are set 30° apart, except for yellow, which is offset by 15° (see Figure 15.9).

To change the halftone screen angle, click the Screen button in the Page Setup dialog box and enter a new Angle value.

Selecting Dot Shape

Dot shape is exactly what it sounds like: the shape of the dots that compose the grid. Traditionally round, different dot shapes can produce different effects. A relatively new dot shape, diamond, works very well and is slowly replacing round as the default dot shape. (See Figure 15.9).

To change the shape of the dots used to create the halftone, click the Screen button in the Page Setup dialog box and select a new dot shape from the Shape pop-up menu. The Custom option lets you enter PostScript commands for creating custom spot functions.

When customizing the halftone screen parameters, I recommend using the Diamond dot shape because it produces much better results in the mid-range of halftones (medium-light to medium-dark grays or tints).

Compensating for Dot Gain

"Dot gain" refers to how much the ink spreads as it soaks into the paper (see Figure 15.6). High dot gain can cause halftone dots to run together, creating a dark, "muddy" image. Most commercial print shops prefer to do their own adjusting for dot gain (after all, they know their papers and inks better than anyone). Occasionally you may want or need to adjust the dot gain yourself, either at the request of your print shop or, when printing yourself, because of poor image quality caused by too much, or, less frequently, too little toner or ink being absorbed by the paper.

Figure 15.6

Detail of an image printed normally (left) and with too much dot gain.

You can compensate for unwanted dot gain by adjusting the Dot Gain value in the Printing Inks Setup dialog box (available in the Color Setting submenu of the File menu. Change this **Dot Gain** value to more accurately reflect the dot gain of a printed proof or to compensate for unwanted dot gain caused by paper quality or type. Lower values reduce dot size and make the image appear lighter, whereas higher values increase the dot size and make the image appear darker. Dot gain values should generally not be set below the low 20s.

The Transfer dialog box (accessed by clicking the Transfer button in the Page Setup dialog box) can occasionally be used to compensate for dot gain in special situations. We highly recommend using the Printing Inks command (found in the File menu, Color Settings submenu) to compensate for dot gain. The two major disadvantages to using this dialog box is that modifications made in this dialog box can only be saved in an EPS file, and that saving transfer functions can occasionally interfere with imagesetter calibration software.

Using Dithering

Another method for printing or displaying continuous tone images is based on repeated dot patterns, rather than a strictly-ordered grid. This method is called dithering and is often used on computer monitors and non-Postscript printers. There are two types of basic dithers: pattern dithers and diffusion dithers. Pattern dithers have an orderly appearance and are often used on computer displays. Diffusion dithers are based on random patterns and have a much smoother appearance.

A more sophisticated form of dithering called FM (frequency modulation) screening or stochastic screening can be used with PostScript-based imagesetters. FM screening uses clusters of extremely small dots to form the image. Because these microdot clusters aren't placed on a grid (as with traditional halftone screens), moiré and other interference patterns don't arise. The main drawback of FM screening is that, because each dot is smaller and closer together, the dots produce more relative dot gain (that is, they are more likely to spread near or into one another).

Photoshop itself does not contain any controls for selecting dithering parameters for printing. If you want to print using dithering, discuss this with your print shop or service bureau. Depending on the press, paper, and inks, they can provide guidance as to the advisability of dithering or stochastic screening for your print job.

Halftone vs. Continuous Tone Printing

Photographic reproduction and some digital printers (color copiers, dye-sub printers and high-end inkjet printers) can vary the *intensity* of the individual dots to create continuous tone or near-continuous tone images. This is significantly different from printing presses which cannot control the intensity of the ink dots. With continuous tone printing, a spot on the page can have varying intensities of color.

Continuous tone printing is a fairly straightforward process compared to halftone printing. With continuous tone printing, the biggest problem is making sure that the printer's ink colors match those of your onscreen image. You and your print shop or service bureau don't have to think about or deal with different color plates, halftone screens, dot gain, and so on. The big disadvantage of continuous tone printing is that it is slow and expensive to produce large quantities of prints, which is why halftone printing is used for most commercial print jobs, and continuous tone printing is reserved, for the most part, for fine art output.

PREPARING THE PAGE

Preparing your image only gets you halfway to printed output. Preparing the page gets you the rest of the way there. Most of the decisions you need to make regarding page setup can be found, strangely enough, in the Page Setup dialog box. The Page Setup dialog box is where you create custom halftone screens, select which printer marks you want to use, and decide whether or not to include plate labels, create negatives, and so on.

The Page Setup Command

The Page Setup dialog box (see Figures 15.7 and 15.8), accessed by selecting the Page Setup command on the File menu, contains options for selecting paper size, creating custom halftone screens, adding printer's marks, and so on. The following section explains all of the standard options within the Page Setup dialog box. Macintosh- and Windows-specific issues and options are discussed at the end of the section.

Figure 15.7

The Macintosh Page Setup dialog box.

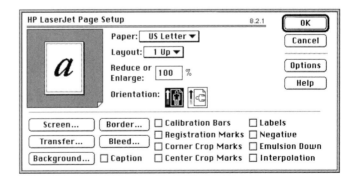

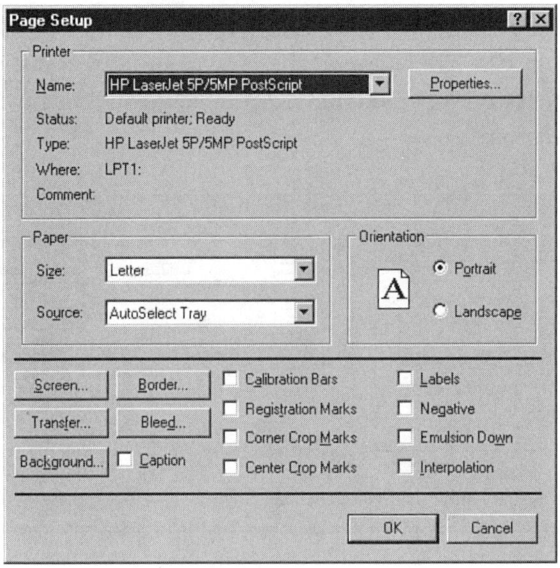

Figure 15.8

The Windows Page Setup dialog box.

1. To create custom halftone screens, click the Screen button and change the values in the resulting Halftone Screens dialog box (Figure 15.9). Creating custom halftone screens is discussed in detail in the "Working in Halftones" section of this chapter. You can also opt to use your printer's default halftone screen settings by clicking the Use Printer's Default Screens checkbox. If you are sending image data to an imagesetter that uses PostScript level 2 or an Emerald processor, click the Use Accurate Screens checkbox.

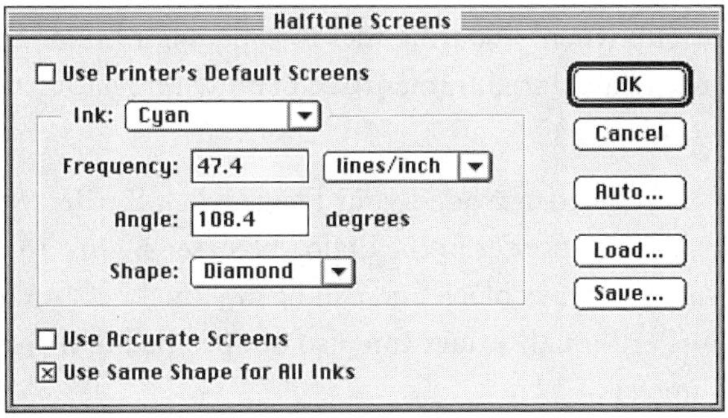

Figure 15.9

The Halftone Screens dialog box.

2. Click the Transfer button to bring up the Transfer Function dialog box (see Figure 15.10), where you can adjust the transfer curve, modifying the printed gray levels towards lighter or darker.

Figure 15.10

The Transfer functions dia-
log box.

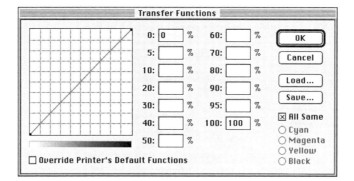

3. Click the **Background** button to bring up a color picker (see Figure 15.11), within which you can select a background color to be printed outside of your image area. (The background color selected here is for printing only. It does not affect the actual image data.) All parts of the printed page outside of your image are filled with this color, effectively framing your image. You could do this within your image by increasing the canvas size and filling the empty space with a color, but all of those unnecessary colored pixels take up space and slow printing. Obviously, this option has no effect if your image is as large or larger than the printed page. Selecting a background color can be useful when preparing files for imaging to film recorders, as it creates a colored, rather than plain white, background for your images.

4. To add a border around your image, click **Border**. Specify the width of the border in the dialog box (see Figure 15.12). The border is always black and can be any thickness up to 10 points (although values can also be specified in inches or millimeters).

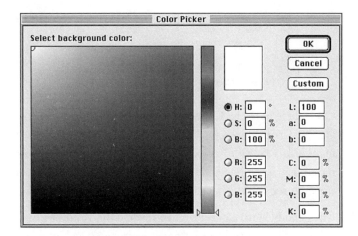

Figure 15.11

A Photoshop Color Picker dialog box.

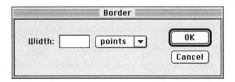

Figure 15.12

The Border dialog box.

5. Click the Bleed button to bring up a dialog box for specifying
   the bleed area of the image (see Figure 15.13). The bleed is the
   portion of the image that is cut off at the paper's edge. Bleed
   doesn't actually alter the image size, it just alters where the
   paper is cut. Increasing the bleed value moves the crop marks
   within the image boundaries, effectively cutting off part of the
   image for the final printed output. Values can be entered as
   points, millimeters, or inches, but the value entered cannot
   exceed one-eighth of an inch.

   The only way to preview a bleed on desktop printers (which
   cannot print all the way to the edge of the page) is to reduce
   the image size before printing, and then cut the paper along the
   crop marks.

6. Click the Labels checkbox if you want the filename to print
   next to the image. If you are printing color separations, the
   name of each color channel is also printed next to the image on
   each color plate.

Figure 15.13

The Bleed dialog box.

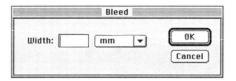

7. Click the Captions, Calibration Bars, Registration Marks, Corner Crop Marks, or Center Crop Marks checkboxes to include any or all of these printer's marks or image information on your printed page. These options are discussed in detail in the next sections.

8. Click the Negative checkbox to reverse the values of the printed image, producing a negative image (see Figure 15.14). With direct printing (that is, to a local printer such as a laser printer or color inkjet) positive printouts are desired, but images printed to film for commercial offset printing are usually printed as negatives. This checkbox specifies you want to print a negative.

9. Click the Emulsion Down checkbox to print a mirror image (mirrored horizontally) of your image. Emulsion down is often preferred for printing directly to a file (as with a commercial print run), but, as always, check with your printer.

10. Click the Interpolation checkbox to turn interpolation on. The idea behind interpolation is that a low-resolution image printed to a PostScript level 2 printer can benefit from on-the-fly re-sampling done by the printer as it processes the image data. If you are not printing a low-resolution file or if you don't have a PostScript level 2 printer, you probably won't see any difference. Even if you do have PostScript level 2 and a low-resolution file, the difference may not always be that noticeable.

Including Captions

Clicking the Caption checkbox causes the contents of the Caption field in the File Info dialog box to be printed next to the image. The File Info dialog box can be accessed via the File menu. This is a good place to include copyright or contact information for your images.

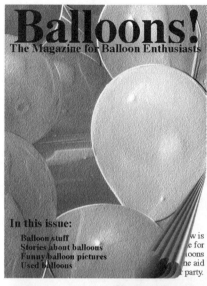
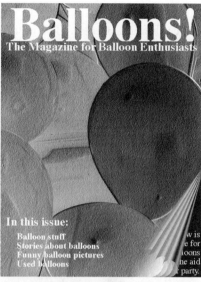

Figure

Figure 15.14

A normal image (upper left), a negative image (upper right), a normal image with emulsion down (lower left), and a negative image with emulsion down.

Printing Calibration Bars

If you want calibration and color bars printed with your image, click this checkbox. A calibration bar is a grayscale ramp divided into 11 discrete shades (or gray densities) from 0 to 100 percent (inclusive). Color bars are the colored equivalents of grayscale calibration bars, with 11 tints of color. The purpose of these bars is to aid in the calibration process. (The individual swatches can be easily measured with a densitometer and compared to equivalent onscreen values.) (See Figure 15.15 for examples of calibration bars and other printer's marks.)

Figure 15.15

A printed page showing all printer's marks.

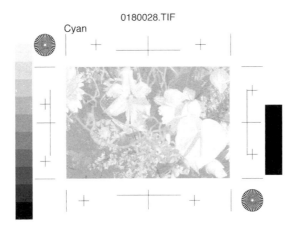

Printing Registration Marks

Clicking this checkbox produces 10 registration marks around your image (eight standard bull's-eye marks and two more precise pinpoint marks).

Printing Crop Marks

Clicking the corner crop marks or center crop marks checkboxes produce crop marks around the corners or sides of your image, telling a printer where the page should be trimmed or centered.

Similar to corner crop marks, center crop marks aid in the cropping process by pinpointing the center of the image.

Macintosh/Windows Issues

The Page Setup dialog box has subtle differences depending on whether you are using the Macintosh or Windows version of Photoshop. Fortunately, these differences are pretty basic, and anyone familiar with basic Macintosh or Windows printing issues should already know what the different platform-specific options do.

The top portion of the Macintosh Page Setup dialog box contains standard LaserWriter (or whatever other printer you have selected) options such as paper size, scaling, orientation, and so on.

The top portion of the Windows Page Setup dialog box contains standard Windows printing options such as which printer you want to print to and paper size, source, and orientation. The Windows Page Setup dialog box also contains a Properties button that gives you access to a four-part Properties dialog box for the current printer, within which you can set such parameters as paper size and layout, printer resolution and custom halftone settings, printer-specific device options, and Postscript output format.

Some cross-platform and platform-specific printing issues are discussed in the "Printing from Photoshop" section later in this chapter.

CREATING COLOR SEPARATIONS

All halftone printers are monochrome printers and, thus, can only print one color (or color plate) at a time. Halftone reproduction of color images is done by separating an image into several color images and then creating one plate for each color for use on a commercial printing press (see Figure 15.16). The paper is fed through the press several times, with the plate and ink color changing each time. The process of separating an image into its component colors is referred to as creating color separations.

Creating Process Color Separations

The most common type of color separation, process color separation, involves creating four different versions of an image: one that contains all of the cyan in the image; one that contains all of the magenta; one that contains all of the yellow; and one that contains all of the black. These four inks (CMYK, with K representing black), in the correct combinations, create all of the colors necessary for reproducing most images (see Figure 15.5).

Figure 15.16

*A CMYK image with the
individual cyan, magenta,
yellow, and black plates.*

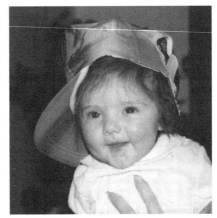

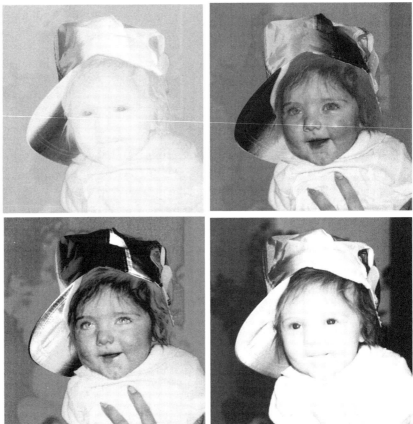

As mentioned earlier, virtually all commercial printing is accomplished by creating color separations of an image, printing each color onto an individual color plate, then running each plate on an offset press to create a composite color image.

There are two different kinds of color separations that can be done in Photoshop: process color separations and spot color separations.

Process color separations always use four channels: cyan, magenta, yellow, and black. Process color separations are used to create full color images on commercial printing presses.

If you want to print in process colors, the best advice WE can give you is to have your images scanned (or re-scanned, if necessary) in CMYK mode. This saves tremendous amounts of time, money, and frustration down the road, enabling you to concentrate on the actual image-manipulation part of Photoshop (which is a lot more fun than calibration and proofing).

If you must create your own process color separations within Photoshop, here's a step-by-step procedure for getting from RGB scan (or image) to CMYK printout.

1. Calibrate your system as described in Chapter 2, "Calibrating Your System." If you don't have your system properly calibrated, you can't reliably predict how your images will look when printed.

2. Pick a commercial printer or service bureau and ask them the following questions:

   ◆ What screen frequency should you use? (Have your image scanned at this resolution.)

   ◆ How much dot gain is there from *film* to press sheet? (Not from *proof* to press sheet.) (Adjust the Printing Inks Setup values accordingly.)

   ◆ What black ink limits and total ink limits should you use? (Adjust the Separation Setup values accordingly.)

   ◆ Should you generate the black plate with GCR or UCR? (Adjust the Separation Setup values accordingly.)

3. Convert your image from RGB to CMYK.

4. Perform any desired color correction (if you haven't already done so).

5. Sharpen your image. (Most people never sharpen their images enough.)

6. Create traps, if necessary. (It's probably not, unless you have hard edges separating plain, colored fills.)

7. To print only certain color plates, hide the unwanted channels in the Channels palette.

8. Print your image as color separations (that is, click the Print Separations checkbox in the Page Setup dialog box), including any desired printer's marks such as crop marks, registration marks, and so on. Which marks you want printed can be specified in the Page Setup dialog box.

9. Have a laminated proof made. Check this carefully against your onscreen image. If necessary, adjust your image's Printing Inks Setup, Separation Setup, or Halftone Screen values and re-print.

Creating Monotones, Duotones, Tritones, and Quadtones

A monotone is a grayscale image printed with one colored (that is, something other than black) ink. Duotones, tritones, and quadtones are grayscale images printed with two, three, or four different colored inks (one of which is often black). The main reason for creating duotones, tritones, and quadtones (other than adding color to grayscale images) is that single-ink print runs can only produce about fifty shades of a particular color, but by printing the image with different inks, much more detail and depth can be acheived.

To print monotones, duotones, tritones, or quadtones:

1. Calibrate your system as described in Chapter 2.

2. Pick a commercial printer or service bureau and ask them the following questions:

- ◆ What screen frequency should you use? (Have your image scanned at this resolution.)

- ◆ How much dot gain is there from *film* to press sheet? (Not from *proof* to press sheet.) (Adjust the Printing Inks Setup values accordingly.)

- ◆ What black ink limits and total ink limits should you use? (Adjust the Separation Setup values accordingly.)

- ◆ Should you generate the black plate with GCR or UCR? (Adjust the Separation Setup values accordingly.)

3. Convert your image from RGB or CMYK to Grayscale.

4. Select Image➡Mode➡Duotone.

5. Within the Duotone dialog box, select Monotone, Duotone, Tritone, or Quadtone for one-, two-, three-, or four-color separations. After selecting the desired number of colors, click a color swatch to pick a desired PANTONE spot color. The transfer control next to each color swatch can be used to set the transfer levels for each channel.

6. Set the screen angles and frequencies manually using the Screens button in the Page Setup dialog box. Screen angles should mimic those used in process colors. (45 degrees for the darkest color, then the other colors each offset by an additional 30 degrees. If you are printing a Quadtone, offset the lightest color by 15 degrees.)

7. Print your image as color separations, including any desired printer's marks such as crop marks, registration marks, and so on. The marks you want printed can be specified in the Page Setup dialog box.

8. Have a laminated proof made. Check this carefully against your onscreen image. If necessary, adjust your image's Printing Inks Setup, Separation Setup, or Halftone Screen values and re-print.

Creating Spot Color Separations

Spot color separations are similar in principle to process color separations, but they use as few as two or as many as four channels of any color the user desires. Spot color separations are often used for less expensive print jobs such as brochures and newsletters, where a single color or two can be used to accent a traditional black and white print run.

Photoshop does not directly support spot color separations, but there are two ways to get around this limitation and prepare an image for printing with spot colors.

If the spot color is used throughout the image, the easiest way to create the spot color separations is to treat the image as a duotone, with a different spot color used for each color plate. See the "Creating Monotones, Duotones, Tritones, and Quadtones" section earlier in this chapter.

If one or more spot colors are to appear on specific parts of the image (as text or a logo, for example), you can use the CMYK channels to prepare your image, but substitute your spot colors for the standard cyan, magenta, yellow, and black. The tricky part to this is that you have to create custom inks in the Printing Inks Setup dialog box. Before making any changes to this dialog box for spot color separations, be sure to save your current settings (by clicking the Save button in the Printing Inks Setup dialog box).

To create spot color separations:

1. Convert your image to grayscale.

2. Copy the entire image.

3. Convert your image to CMYK.

4. Select the black (K) channel and paste in the grayscale image information. All of the image data is now in the black channel.

5. One at a time, select the cyan, magenta, and yellow channels and delete the information stored there. These channels can now be used as "surrogate" spot color channels.

6. Create an empty grayscale document.

7. Convert the empty document to Duotone (select Image➡Mode ➡Duotone).

8. Click the color swatch and select a desired spot color. After you select a spot color, click the Picker button and note the Lab values for this color.

9. Exit the dialog boxes and switch to your real image.

10. Select File➡Color Settings➡Printing Inks Setup.

11. Select Custom from the Ink Colors pop-up menu.

12. Click the color swatch for C, M, or Y and enter the lab values for the desired spot color. Click the OK buttons to exit the dialog boxes.

13. Repeat this procedure for additional spot colors.

After you have substituted your spot colors for one or more of the CMY colors, you can work as you normally would on a CMTK image, adding all spot color art or text to the appropriate CMY channel.

ADJUSTING TRAPPING

When separate color plates are used to create a final, composite print, a slight misalignment or error in registration can cause slight gaps where two solid colors should meet, but don't quite. This gap between colors may be noticeable and can detract quite a bit from the overall quality of the printed image. To avoid this, a technique called trapping is often used. With trapping, adjacent solid colors are overlapped so that minor misalignment of the color plates won't leave noticeable gaps of white space (see Figure 15.17).

The Trap dialog box on the Image menu enables you to specify in pixels, points, or millimeters the amount of color overlap. This command is only available when working with a CMYK image because trapping is only an issue with color separations. Some things to keep in mind about trapping: First, it is only necessary when you have hard-edged transitions from one solid color to another (such as with single-color text on a single-color background). Second, enter trap values in points or millimeters rather than pixels because the size of pixels changes based on your image's resolution. Lastly, trapping should be the last step before printing color separations, as it has no effect on your onscreen image.

Figure 15.17

A sample, misregistered image with no trapping (left) and with trapping.

Photoshop does not support choking (that is, colors can only spread to overlap other colors— they never shrink). As a general rule, you should always trap with the lighter of two colors because size changes to lighter colored elements are less noticeable.

Keep in mind that unless you are doing *extremely* high-resolution line art in Photoshop (which almost never happens) you really don't need to worry about trapping. Most registration errors are smaller than most Photoshop image pixels, so trapping usually isn't necessary.

PROOFING YOUR WORK

Unless you like the image you're working on so much that you never want to leave it, get in the habit of having proofs made during different stages of your work. An early color proof can save you the frustration of having to redo hours (or even days) of color-critical work. (This is also why it's important to calibrate your monitor before you begin to work, as mentioned in Chapter 2.) Aside from color issues, the importance of getting proofs made of sample work should be immediately apparent to any artist or designer who has ever worked with a finicky customer. There are four different kinds of proofs: digital, overlay, laminated, and press.

Digital proofs are made on desktop color printers such as inkjet or thermal wax printers. While good for conceptual proofing, these printers cannot accurately show important offset printing issues such as color, dot gain, and trapping. Also, continuous tone (or pseudo-continuous tone) desktop printers cannot accurately reflect how a final halftone print run will look.

Overlay proofs (or color keys) are made on an imagesetter from color film separations. Each of the color plates is printed on a separate sheet of acetate and then placed on a white base sheet. One advantage of overlay proofs is that because they are printed on an imagesetter, the individual colors and halftones are print-run accurate. Another big advantage is that each color plate can be viewed individually. The primary disadvantage is that the composite color image is not accurate because it must be viewed through several acetate layers.

Because of their accurate color and dot gain, as well as their capability to reveal halftone-related problems and errors in registration, the industry standard for image proofing is **laminated proofs**. Laminated proofs are created with true CMYK color separations made on a high-end imagesetter and fused to a white (or specific paper color) base material. These proofs, because of their accuracy, are often used as a "contract" between the client and the printer.

The most expensive proofs, **press proofs**, are created on an actual press and give an absolutely true representation of how a printed image will look. Press proofs are expensive, but they are sometimes required for print jobs where the color (and everything else) has to be exactly right.

PRINTING DIRECTLY FROM PHOTOSHOP

Well, a chapter on printing certainly wouldn't be complete without the Print command. Here it is in all it's glory, although after all the preparation, the simplicity of the Print command itself may be anti-climactic.

The Print Command

The Print command, although fulfilling the same role on both the Macintosh and Windows platforms, has a different layout and contains different options depending on which version of Photoshop you are using (see Figures 15.18 and 15.19). These differences, as well as some general Macintosh/Windows issues, are discussed at the end of this section.

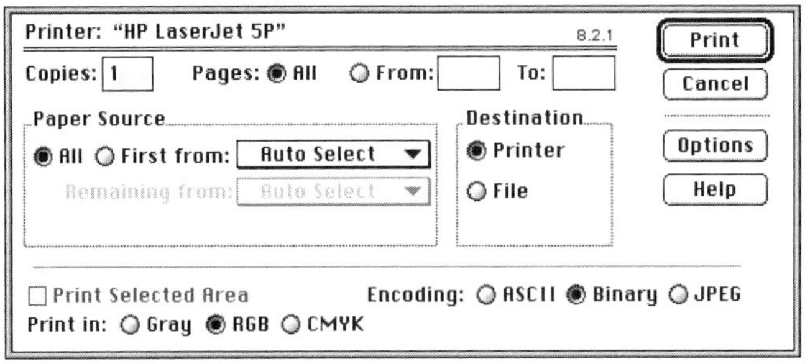

Figure 15.18

The Macintosh Print dialog box.

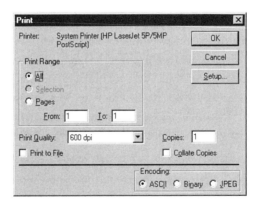

Figure 15.19

The Windows Print dialog box.

1. If your image is in either CMYK or Duotone mode *and* the composite color channel is active in the document window, clicking the **Print Separations** checkbox causes Photoshop to print each channel as a separate color plate.

Tip

By default, Photoshop prints all color channels as separate plates. Photoshop only prints, however, the channels visible in the document. So if you do not want to print certain channels, hide them in the Channels palette. (Click the eyeballs next the Cyan, Yellow, and Black channels, for example, to print only the Magenta channel.)

If your image is in either RGB or Indexed Color mode and the composite color channel is active in the document window, the Print Separations checkbox is replaced with three Print In option buttons: Gray, RGB, and CMYK. Click the desired color space to select the type of data you want Photoshop to send to the printer. For laser printers and other black and white printers, use Gray. For film recorders, use RGB. Despite what you might think, you should probably also use RGB for most desktop color printers, unless you have calibrated your system using the Monitor, Printing Inks, and Separation Setup dialog boxes. This is because Photoshop will use the existing Monitors, Printing Inks, and Separation Setup information to perform a color mode conversion from RGB or Indexed Color to CMYK as it sends the data to the printer, with often disappointing results. If you haven't already properly configured these dialog boxes, let your printer convert the image data from RGB to CMYK.

2. Use the ASCII, Binary, and JPEG option buttons to select the **encoding** method Photoshop uses when sending your image data to the printer. ASCII encoding is understood by all PostScript devices, making it a good choice, especially on DOS or Unix networks. Binary encoding takes only half the space of ASCII encoding, resulting in faster printing than ASCII encoding. Try Binary encoding first, but if it doesn't work, switch to ASCII encoding. JPEG encoding is faster than either ASCII or Binary encoding, but it does result in some data loss. This loss is fairly minimal and might be worth the speed gain, but print a

test page (or portion thereof) before sending your file(s) to the printer. Keep in mind that JPEG encoding only works with PostScript level 2 printers (PostScript level 1 can't decode JPEG data).

Note

Despite what you may be thinking, the encoding option has nothing to do with securing your data. Rather, it simply refers to how Photoshop "packs" your image data before sending it to the printer. The tighter the packing job, the faster your image prints. JPEG and Binary are very tight formats, but JPEG loses a little data on the way and not all PostScript printers understand Binary (or JPEG either, for that matter), which is why ASCII is a reliable fall-back format.

Macintosh/Windows Issues

The top portion of the Macintosh Print dialog box contains standard Macintosh printing options, as determined by the installed Macintosh printer driver. These options include:

◆ The number of copies to be printed

◆ The page range

◆ The paper source

◆ The destination (printer or file on disk)

The bottom portion contains three Photoshop-specific options:

◆ Print Selected Area

◆ Print Separations (or Print In)

◆ Encoding

Clicking the Print Selected Area checkbox lets you print—you guessed it—just the selected area of an image. This option is not available if you are using a feathered selection.

The top portion of the Windows Print dialog box contains standard Windows printing options, as determined by the installed printer driver. These options include:

- Print range (specific pages or just the selected area)

- Print quality

- Whether you want to print to a file on disk instead of to an actual printer

- Number of copies and whether those copies are collated

- Print Separations (or Print As)

- Encoding

In addition to just being aware of the differences in the two versions of the Print dialog box, there are some other, more important, things to keep in mind when printing across the Macintosh/Windows fence.

Always create a procedure for getting the files from start to finish, test the procedure, and *stick to the procedure*. If your client, for example, is on the Windows platform and wants you, a Macintosh graphic artist, to perform some image manipulation, have the client scan the image and send it across the fence to you (or you can scan it yourself). Make sure that the file formats used to scan the image provide all the information you need for your Macintosh-based image manipulation. Then send the revised image back to the client and have them check the file format and either print it on their printer or send it to their service bureau. Make sure that your procedure works every step of the way *before* you start doing all of the work, and be sure to follow the procedure for each piece that you work on.

Secondly (and this should be a part of the procedure mentioned earlier), stick to Photoshop's native file format whenever possible. This ensures that Photoshop has as much data as possible to work with and that the data is in an easily understood format. The Windows file extension for a Photoshop document is .PSD. If the Photoshop format can't be used on both sides of the fence, use either RGB or CMYK TIFF files (.TIF on Windows). Lastly, EPS files can also be used if neither Photoshop nor TIFF are viable file formats.

Warning

Do not use JPEG encoding with EPS files because Windows applications (for the most part) do not support JPEG-encoded EPS files.

Note

The Windows PostScript driver does not support Binary or JPEG encoding. You must use ASCII encoding when printing from Windows, unless you install the Adobe PostScript Driver for Windows. If you own a late-model PostScript laser printer from Hewlett-Packard (such as the 4, 4P, 5, 5P, 5MP, and so on), call Hewlett-Packard to receive a free copy of the Adobe PostScript Driver for Windows.

Printing Part of an Image

Far too many Photoshop users spend far too much time copying, pasting, and cropping an image in order to print just a desired portion of a larger image. This is a lot more work than it has to be, but the quickest way is all too easily overlooked.

To print part of an image select the area you want to print with a non-feathered, rectangluar selection and choose the Print command from the File menu. In the print dialog box, click the Selected Area checkbox under Print Range (for Windows) or the Print Selected Area checkbox (for Macintosh).

PRINTING FROM OTHER APPLICATIONS

The vast majority of Photoshop images are never printed directly from Photoshop. QuarkXPress, PageMaker, FrameMaker, and other page layout programs are the most common vehicles for bringing your images to their final, printed form. Some Photoshop images make their way into other image-editing applications (Painter springs to mind), and still others end up in Illustrator, FreeHand, or a similar vector-based drawing program (although usually it goes the other way; line art is brought into Photoshop).

Getting your images printed from within any of these other applications is a matter of making sure you save your image in a compatible format (as discussed in Chapter 16, "Saving and Exporting"), importing it from within the target application, manipulating, and printing. Any image-specific settings, such as halftone screens or custom colors, should transfer with the image and override the default settings of the printer or page layout application. For more information on Photoshop's file formats and their compatibility with other applicatons, see Chapter 16.

Chapter **16**

SAVING AND EXPORTING

Originally conceived as a file translation utility, Photoshop can read and write a wide variety of formats, and users have a lot of different options within those formats: EPS with JPEG encoding or binary encoding? Interlaced GIFs or not?

Because their data is organized in different ways, each of Photoshop's formats is suitable for a different use, and they're not all available at all times. You can't, for example, save a CMYK color file in BMP or PCX format; you have to convert it to RGB mode first. It's important to know what formats are best suited for your application, in terms of image quality, portability, file size, and compatibility with other software.

PREPARING IMAGES

Opening and working with Photoshop files in Photoshop is one thing, and taking those files into another application is something else entirely. How you set up and save your image may determine whether or not it prints or displays correctly.

Making Sure Print Images Print

◆ For print applications, stick to TIFF and EPS images unless you have a compelling reason to use another format.

◆ If you need to silhouette an image, use EPS with a clipping path, but avoid overly complex paths and monstrously high flatness values; these can cause printers to choke. Experiment with your output device to find a happy medium—good quality with no printing problems.

◆ Don't include halftone screens and transfer functions when saving EPS files unless you want those settings to override the settings made in the page layout application into which the file is imported.

◆ Don't use JPEG compression unless you're sure the output device supports it. Remember, Level 1 PostScript devices can't output EPS images with JPEG previews, so stick to TIFF (PCs) or PICT (Macs).

◆ In general, use TIFF LZW compression. It doesn't cause printing problems, doesn't degrade the image, and can reduce file size dramatically.

Making Sure Electronic Images Display Correctly

◆ Make sure you use the RGB color mode for electronic images to get accurate depiction onscreen of how they'll look and to be sure they open in multimedia applications. CMYK is intended to be used only with images printed on color printers or process printing presses.

◆ Use an appropriate bit depth for the image's destination. Eight-bit color is the highest bit depth. It's reasonable to use for most electronic images. If the colors in your image are vital, use indexed color mode to save a custom palette in the image file. Otherwise the colors may be dithered or approximated with a mix of other colors when the image is displayed on someone else's screen.

◆ For Web graphics, most browsers support interlaced GIFs and JPEGs, which display much faster than noninterlaced images. Avoid using interlacing on Web page backgrounds, though; interlaced images can actually be slower to display when they're used as backgrounds.

◆ The only way to be absolutely sure that your image looks right on different platforms is to view it on different platforms. Mac users can use the Gamma control panel that comes with Photoshop to approximate the brightness of PC monitors; this can be helpful in determining how images look on PCs.

Determining Resolution and File Size

Different images and different purposes demand different resolutions. To keep file sizes manageable, always use the lowest resolution appropriate for your purpose because file size is largely determined by resolution.

◆ Use screen resolution for most electronic images, including those destined for the Web: that's 72 dpi for Macs, whereas PC systems use resolutions ranging from 72 dpi to 120 dpi.

◆ Use at least 600 dpi for line art that will be printed to avoid jagged, stairstepped lines (1,200 dpi is even better). Use TIFF and don't worry too much about file sizes because LZW compression works wonders on images with large areas of one color, such as line art.

◆ For photos and grayscale art that will be printed, resolutions can be lower. The easiest way to determine the correct resolution is to double the line screen used when the image is printed. Most magazine printing, for example, is done at 133 lines per inch. So 266 dpi is an appropriate resolution for scanned photos. Higher resolutions won't generally hurt, although some experts warn that the interpolation that takes place when the image is sampled down for output can distort details.

SAVING FILES

The most important thing to know about Photoshop's Save command: Use it often! As you're working on an image in Photoshop, it's stored in your computer's RAM. If Photoshop quits or your computer unexpectedly shuts down, every change you've made to an image since the last time you saved is lost. If you haven't saved the image at all, such as with a scan acquired from the scanner by Photoshop, the whole thing is lost.

Saving also enables you to go back to previous stages of an image. Photoshop has only one level of undo, meaning that if you make two changes in a row, you can only undo the latest one. You can, however, use the Revert command in the File menu to return an image to its status the last time it was saved.

The first time you save an image, the Save dialog box appears. After that, you only see it if you use the Save As or Save a Copy commands.

Using the Right Save Command

Photoshop has three Save commands in the File menu: Save, Save As, and Save a Copy. Each of these commands writes the file in RAM to a disk, overwriting the previous version if the file has been saved before with the same name and in the same location. Save As and Save a Copy enable you to change the name and location of the file when Photoshop saves it; the difference is that after you Save As you're working in the new file, while after you Save a Copy you're still working in the old file. All three commands use the same dialog box (see Figure 16.1).

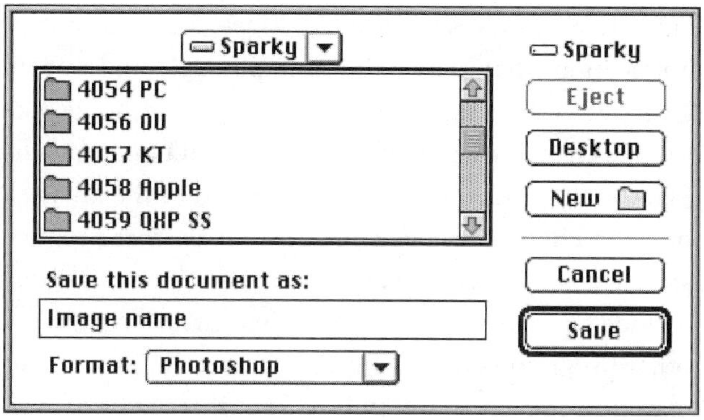

Figure 16.1

The Save, Save As, and Save a Copy dialog boxes in Photoshop 4.0 all look the same.

Save As and Save a Copy are useful for backing up files before performing major operations. If, for example, you're about to apply a glow effect to the text in your image and you're not sure you'll like the results, you can Save As with a different name (tack "glow" on the end of the filename, perhaps) to make changes only in the new file. You can also use the Save As and Save a Copy commands to save copies of your files in different formats.

Including Previews in Your Files

Previews enable you to see what a Photoshop image looks like from within other programs or when choosing a file to open from within Photoshop. There are three types of image previews, and whether or not you can use all three depends on whether you're using a Mac or a PC.

♦ Icon previews are supported by Macs and by PCs running Windows 95 or Windows NT; a file saved with this option has a desktop icon that is a tiny version of the image in the file. While icon previews are a handy way to keep track of what's what when you're not in Photoshop, they can slow down the display of desktop icons and make files larger.

♦ Thumbnail previews are supported by Macs and PCs; these are the previews that you see in Photoshop's Open dialog box when you click the name of a file.

◆ Full size previews, supported by Macs, are used by other applications that import Photoshop images and display only a 72 dpi preview image. Without this preview, some applications can make their own previews; others can't and only display a placeholder, such as a gray box, instead of the image. Whether or not a Photoshop image previews in another program, it should print correctly (barring other problems). If you don't include a preview in your image, and the Mac page layout or other program you're using can't create one, you see only a placeholder such as a gray box—but this won't happen too often because it's rare that professional-level software is unable to create its own preview.

Note

In general, it takes longer to save files with previews.

You can set preferences for the previews Photoshop adds to your images (see Chapter 1, "Setting Photoshop Preferences"). If you choose the "Ask When Saving" option, you can choose whether to include previews on a file-by-file basis in the Save dialog box (see Figure 16.2).

Figure 16.2

The Saving Files Preferences dialog box enables you to control filename extension, previews, and file compatibility.

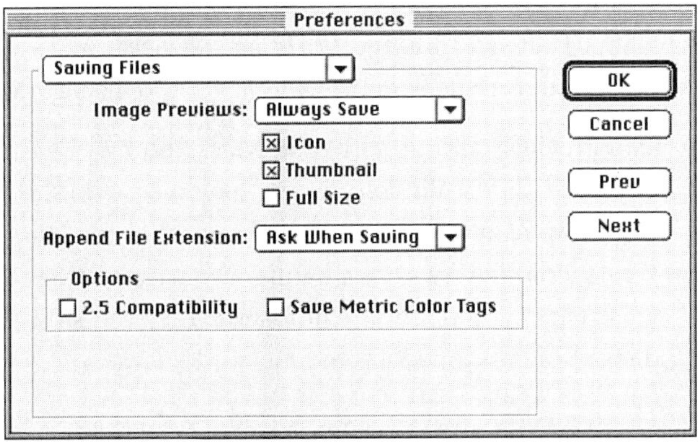

Mac users can include all three types, and PC users can include thumbnail previews. There's a somewhat convoluted procedure to add icon previews on PCs:

1. Save the file.

2. Choose Save As from the File menu.

3. In the dialog box, click the file's name with the right mouse button and choose Properties from the contextual menu.

4. Choose the Photoshop Image tab, select the preview icon, and click OK (see Figure 16.3).

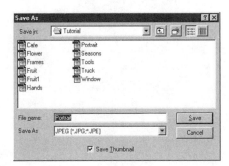

Figure 16.3

The Save As dialog box.

Compressing Images

It doesn't take much experience with Photoshop to realize that image files can get really big, really fast. You can make files smaller in a number of ways:

♦ Reduce the resolution

♦ Reduce the number of colors in the image palette

♦ Use a more compact file format

♦ Use compression

File formats are discussed later in this chapter; see Chapter 11 for information on resolution and color tables. As for compression, some file formats make use of mathematical parlor tricks to store data.

There are two kinds of image compression: lossy and lossless. These names refer to whether or not compression causes the loss of image data, thereby reducing image quality and detail. Lossy compression schemes cause image deterioration; the more you compress the image, the more data it loses. Lossless compression schemes don't "squeeze" images as much as lossy compression; they don't remove image data and therefore don't affect image quality. Figures 16.4 and 16.5 show the same image saved with lossless compression and with lossy compression.

Figure 16.4

This is an image saved in the TIFF format with lossless LZW compression. The image stays just the way it is whether it's compressed or not.

Figure 16.5

This is the same image as in Figure 16.4, saved in the lossy JPEG format with Maximum compression. There are haloes around the stone columns and the whole image looks as though it's made up of small tiles—these are created when pixel colors are averaged to make their data more compact.

There's no good reason not to use lossless compression if it's available and all your applications can read compressed images. On the other hand, using lossy image compression is optional when your images are stored on your own system and you have plenty of hard drive space (although it's impossible to ever really have enough!). Compression becomes a necessity when you're creating images for use on the World Wide Web, in multimedia presentations, or in other situations where time and storage space are limited. A good compromise—if you have the space—is to keep a copy of each image that's saved without compression, and save new copies using compression as needed for distribution. That way you'll always have the original image in its best possible condition—without compression.

Lossy compression schemes are best used with photographic images where "artifacts" (visually obvious blips or glitches in an image) are less noticeable. For images with large areas of one color, such as logos, use lossless compression; file sizes aren't much larger than with lossy compression, and the artifacts resulting from lossy compression are much more apparent.

File formats with their own compression schemes include TIFF (LZW, a lossless scheme), GIF (which also uses LZW), BMP (RLE, also lossless), EPS (Huffman, lossless), PICT (JPEG, lossy), and JPEG (JPEG, lossy).

- LZW (Lempel, Ziv, and Welch, the people who created the compression algorithm): LZW compression is lossless and supported by GIF, TIFF, PDF, and PostScript Level 2 formats. GIF always uses LZW, while the other formats may or may not, depending on user preferences. A similar format, LZ77, is used by file compression programs such as PKZIP for compressing text.

- RLE (Run-Length Encoding): Used by the Windows BMP format, it is a lossless method.

- Huffman: The ASCII encoding option for EPS files uses this compression algorithm; it's a lossless scheme that changes repeating values to a single value to save space.

- JPEG: Developed by the Joint Photographic Experts Group, the lossy compression method JPEG can produce smaller files than any other compression mode available from Photoshop. JPEG averages the values of blocks of adjacent pixels and changes them to the same value.

How Big is Big?

If you always use the same file formats, you're used to the size of your files and don't think too much about them—until your hard drive fills up. It's interesting to look at the difference using another file format can make in the size of your files.

Don't forget, though, that different formats might not be appropriate for your how you use your images. To use RLE compression when saving in BMP format, for example, you have to convert the image to 8-bit indexed color—not something you'd do with an image intended for high-quality color reproduction.

Figure 16.6, a 24-bit RGB image, was saved in all Photoshop's formats except the Filmstrip format, which can only be used for images exported from Adobe Premiere. The formats, options, and resulting file sizes are listed below.

Figure 16.6

This image can have different file sizes—depending on the format used.

Format	Options	File size
BMP	RLE compression	193K
BMP	No compression	593K
EPS	8-bit Mac preview; binary encoding; no paths, halftone screen, or transfer function included	833K

Format	Options	File size
GIF	8-bit indexed color	128K
GIF 89a export	8-bit indexed color	120K
JPEG	Maximum quality (10); baseline format; no paths included	190K
JPEG	Medium quality (5) ; baseline format; no paths included	48K
JPEG	Low quality (1) ; baseline format; no paths included	33K
PCX		628K
PDF		118K
Photoshop 2.0		593K
Photoshop 3.0/4.0		590K
PICT file	32 bits/pixel; no compression	588K
PICT resource	32 bits/pixel; no compression	583K
Pixar		595K
PNG	Paeth encoding	368K
Raw		593K
Scitex CT		595K
TGA (Targa)	24 bits/pixel	593K
TIFF	File contains two embedded ColorSync profiles (for the input device and the output device); LZW compression	958K
TIFF	LZW compression, Mac encoding	395K

CHOOSING FILE FORMATS FOR PREPRESS

The two main considerations when creating Photoshop files for prepress applications are quality and ease of output. Although no one wants image file sizes to be larger than they have to, most prepress professionals accept the fact that color image files are going to take up a lot of storage space no matter what. It's more important to ensure that images are sharp and clear, and that colors reproduce clearly. Also, it's important to make sure that output devices can handle the formats used—output problems cost time and money.

Saving TIFF Files

Specifically designed for use with scanned images, the TIFF (Tag Image File Format) format is the most widely used raster format in the print publishing world. It's generally very reliable, and its built-in compression scheme (LZW) can produce very small files, depending on the composition of the image. Even without compression, TIFF files can be much smaller than their EPS counterparts. They can be bitmap (black-and-white), grayscale, or color (RGB, CMYK, or indexed). Most page layout programs can color separate TIFF files.

Tip

When opening TIFF files created in programs other than Photoshop, you may encounter different varieties of the TIFF format. Fax images, for example, use the TIFF version CCITT Group 3. Photoshop sometimes encounters a TIFF version it can't read; utilities such as DeBabelizer and GraphicConverter can be used to translate these files into a format Photoshop can read.

When you save a TIFF file, you're presented with two choices, as shown in Figure 16.7. First, you must decide whether the file should be encoded for use on Macs or PCs; then you must decide whether or not to use LZW compression. If the application you plan to import the TIFF file into supports LZW, you should use it because it's lossless. Most professional-level publishing software, including QuarkXPress and PageMaker, supports LZW. Neither the encoding nor the compression affects how the TIFF image looks, just how the data in the file is organized. As for the Mac/PC encoding question, use Mac if you're using the file only on Macs, and use PC if you're using the file on PCs or on both systems.

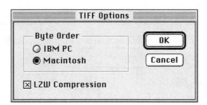

Figure 16.7

The TIFF Options dialog box is pretty much a no-brainer. Mac or PC? Compression? In general, always use LZW compression.

Saving EPS Files

The EPS (Encapsulated PostScript) format is widely used in prepress applications, which for the most part operate in a PostScript environment. Because EPS images are already translated into PostScript, they don't take as much time to print on PostScript output devices. If the application generating the images writes clean PostScript code, then the files tend to print with few PostScript errors, too. On the other hand, the EPS format isn't very compact—the same file saved as TIFF LZW and as EPS can be three or four times larger in EPS format. EPS files can be bitmap (black-and-white), grayscale, or color (RGB, CMYK, or indexed). Most page layout programs can color-separate EPS files.

Note

EPS images can be vector graphics or raster graphics, otherwise known as bitmap graphics (not to be confused with Photoshop's bitmap mode, which means black and white). FreeHand, Illustrator, and other PostScript drawing programs produce vector graphics, which are infinitely scaleable and very compact. Photoshop EPS files are not vector graphics; they're raster graphics and therefore can't be scaled any more than TIFF files—which is to say, not very much.

To save an EPS file:

1. Choose EPS from the format pop-up menu in the Save dialog box.

2. In the EPS Format dialog box, choose a preview type (see Figure 16.8).

809

Figure 16.8

This is the EPS Format dialog box you see when saving a bitmap image, grayscale image, or a color image in a mode other than CMYK. The options are slightly different for black-and-white images and for CMYK images.

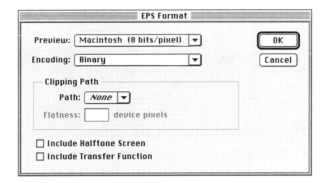

EPS documents have two parts: the actual PostScript description of the image and a low-resolution, bitmapped preview image that's displayed when the image is imported into another program. These previews can be in one of several formats: TIFF, PICT, or JPEG. PC applications require a TIFF preview in EPS documents, whereas Mac applications can use a PICT preview or a JPEG one. JPEG previews are smaller and look better onscreen, but EPS files with JPEG previews only print on Level 2 PostScript devices, so you can't use them for files output on many older printers and imagesetters. Also, files with JPEG previews open and place a bit slower than other types of EPS files because the preview has to be decompressed. Of the other two alternatives, PICT previews are slightly smaller than TIFF previews.

Note

Mac users must have QuickTime installed to use JPEG previews with EPS files.

3. If you're saving a CMYK file, you must choose whether to use the DCS feature, which saves your color image as five files: one for each color channel and one showing a low-resolution preview image. See "Saving DCS Files" later in this chapter for more information on using this option. This option isn't available in any other image mode, so you only see it in the dialog box when saving a CMYK image.

4. **Choose an encoding method.**

   Photoshop offers you a choice of how data in an EPS file is encoded: binary, ASCII, or JPEG. In general, use binary encoding; ASCII should be readable but takes much longer to print. If you need to optimize the file size and are printing to a Level 2 output device, you can use JPEG encoding with a choice of low, medium, high, and maximum quality. The higher the quality level you choose, the lower the amount of compression. Even with maximum quality selected, the image deteriorates somewhat, so this option should only be used for images that aren't critical.

Note

PCs must use the Adobe print driver to print images with JPEG encoding.

5. **Specify a clipping path, if you created one, and enter a flatness value.**

   EPS files can include clipping paths that enable images to be silhouetted. To specify a clipping path, select it from the Path pop-up menu in the Photoshop EPS Format dialog box and enter a flatness value. This value determines how accurately output devices render a clipping path—with lower values, the printer or imagesetter uses more short line segments to create the path and therefore is more accurate. For high-resolution printing (1,200–2,400 dpi), use a value of 8–10; for low-resolution printing (300–600 dpi), use a value of 1–3. If you don't enter a value, the output device's default setting is used.

   If an EPS image with a clipping path is imported into an application that recognizes clipping paths, the area outside the path is transparent when the file is printed. TIFF (PC) previews don't show transparent areas, so PC EPS images won't look right onscreen, but they should print correctly. PICT and JPEG (Mac) previews do support transparency, so Mac EPS images display and print correctly.

6. Turn Include Halftone Screen and Include Transfer Function on or off.

Don't check the "Include Halftone Screen" and "Include Transfer Function" boxes unless you have specified halftone screens and transfer functions in your images. If these boxes are not checked, this information isn't included with your file, and a page layout or other application uses the same screening and transfer function information it uses for the rest of the document into which the image is imported. If the boxes are checked, Photoshop's screening and transfer function information is used when printing the image from another application, regardless of the other application's settings. This option isn't available in bitmap mode, so you only see it in the dialog box when saving a grayscale or color image.

7. Turn Transparent Whites on or off.

If you're saving a raster image in EPS format, you can choose to have white areas of the image treated as transparent when the image is printed. This option isn't available in any other image mode, so you only see it in the dialog box when saving a black-and-white image.

Saving DCS Files

DCS is not really a separate format—it's a variation of the EPS format developed by Quark, Inc. DCS creates four color-separated files and one low-resolution color preview image, and it's only available as an option in the EPS dialog box when saving a CMYK file. DCS is widely used in prepress applications for pre-separating color images. Because the separation is done when the file is saved, output of the final separated film is much faster. DCS files can be used in applications other than QuarkXPress, including Corel Ventura and PageMaker.

If you're saving a CMYK file, the DCS option appears in the EPS Format dialog box. When using DCS, you can choose to include a 72-dpi composite version of the image in the preview file; this is used for proofing the color in the image by printing the composite to a color proofing device before outputting the final separated film. To include a color composite, choose On: 72 pixel/inch color; to include a grayscale composite, choose On: 72 pixel/inch grayscale. Including a composite image in the preview file makes it fairly large; for a smaller preview file, choose On: No composite PostScript.

Note

There are two versions of DCS, 1.0 and 2.0. The later revision, 2.0, enables you to create extra plates for use with spot colors, die cuts, and other printing needs. Photoshop's native support of DCS is limited to version 1.0, but plug-ins such as PlateMaker (Mac only, A Lowly Apprentice Production, Inc.) can export DCS 2.0 files.

Saving Scitex CT Files

High-end prepress work (image editing and color separation) is often done on Scitex workstations. Photoshop can save RGB, CMYK, and grayscale images (which can be read by those workstations) in the Scitex CT (continuous tone) format, and it can import Scitex CT images. Files created on a Scitex system always open in Photoshop in CMYK mode. Saving images in Scitex CT format isn't necessarily required to transfer them to a Scitex system, which can accept more common formats such as TIFF, too.

Saving PCX Files

PCX is the extension given by PC Paintbrush to images in its native format. The format has a built-in compression scheme, but it's not particularly efficient. Because of the widespread distribution of PC Paintbrush, there are an awful lot of PCX images out there in the PC world. PCX files can be bitmap (black-and-white), grayscale, or color (RGB, CMYK, or indexed).

CHOOSING FILE FORMATS FOR MULTIMEDIA

Multimedia projects contain some combination of sound, video, animation, and still images. Many multimedia projects are designed to be displayed onscreen, rather than printed, so they have different requirements.

Saving PICT Files

The native format for graphics on the Mac is PICT; these files can contain raster and vector data (in QuickDraw format). If you copy an image to the Scrapbook or just copy it and leave it on the Clipboard, the image is translated into a PICT file. In this form, you can paste it into applications, such as QuarkXPress, that ordinarily wouldn't enable you to embed graphics.

PICT files are notorious for causing printing problems with PostScript output devices, so they're best used for onscreen display rather than print applications.

To save a PICT file:

1. Choose PICT from the format pop-up menu in the Save dialog box.

2. In the PICT File Options dialog box, choose a resolution (see Figure 16.9). This setting affects the bit depth of the image—the number of colors in its palette—rather than the image resolution.

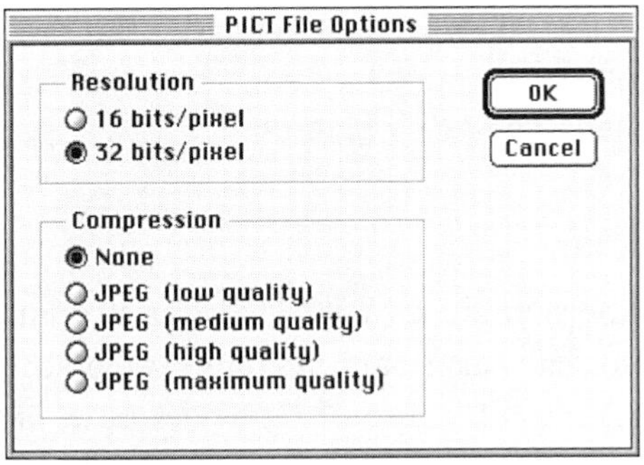

Figure 16.9

The PICT File Options enable you to choose a bit depth and compression level for the file. This is the RGB version of the dialog box; if you're saving a grayscale file, your bit depth choices are 2-bit, 4-bit, or 8-bit.

Grayscale or black-and-white PICT files can contain 2, 4, or 8 bits per pixel, while color images can be saved with 16 or 32 bits per pixel.

3. Choose a compression level.

You don't have to use compression, and you should leave this set at None if the image will be opened on a computer system that doesn't have QuickTime installed or if image quality is crucial.

If JPEG compression is used (only available if QuickTime is installed), there are four quality levels to choose from: low, medium, high, and maximum. The lower the quality level you use, the smaller the file is, but the quality of the image deteriorates the more it's compressed.

4. Click OK to save the file.

Macs also use the PICT format to store images used within applications, such as splash screens. Photoshop can acquire PICT resources directly from other applications (it won't let you acquire its own PICT resources), and it can save a file in this format. The PICT resource file format is really only useful for creating Mac startup screens, custom images to replace the "Welcome to Macintosh" screen that you see when a Mac boots up. To make your own startup screen:

1. Create the image of your choice. If it's not the same size as your screen, the image is surrounded by a gray border when displayed at startup.

2. Choose PICT Resource from the format pop-up menu in the Save dialog box, and name the file "StartupScreen" in the PICT Resource Options dialog box (see Figure 16.10). The name must be exactly that, with both "S"s capitalized and no space. Choose None from the compression options; because this image is loaded at startup before QuickTime is loaded, the Mac won't be able to display it if compression is used. Choose a bit depth.

3. Put the new file in your System Folder and restart.

Figure 16.10

*The PICT Resource Options
dialog box enables you to
specify a resource ID, a
filename, a bit depth, and a
compression level.*

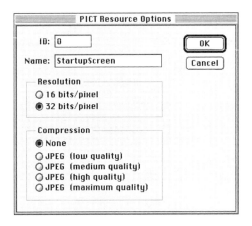

Saving BMP Files

Many PC applications support the BMP (Windows Bitmap) format developed by Microsoft, which has its own compression scheme called RLE. Photoshop supports 24-bit BMP images. This format is primarily used in Windows applications development.

To save a BMP file:

1. Choose BMP from the Format pop-up menu in the Save dialog box.

2. In the BMP Options dialog box, specify what operating system the file will be used on (see Figure 16.11).

Figure 16.11

The BMP Options dialog box.

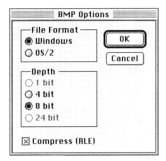

Your choices are Windows/DOS or OS/2.

3. Choose a bit depth from 1-bit (black-and-white) to 24-bit. This determines how many colors are used in the image's palette after it's saved as a BMP file.

816

4. Turn RLE compression on or off. If you use compression, the resulting file is smaller; this compression method is lossless, so the quality of the image won't be affected.

Saving Pixar Files

Pixar is the format used by Pixar workstations, where a lot of high-end computer animation is done; the movie *Toy Story* was done at Pixar and was the first completely computer-animated feature film. Photoshop supports RGB and grayscale Pixar images, and there are no options offered when saving Pixar files.

Note

Pixar was originally part of Lucasfilms and was bought and established as a separate company in 1986 by Steve Jobs, formerly of Apple Computer.

Using Video Formats

Although Photoshop isn't a video-editing application, it can be used to edit individual images that are part of a video stream.

Filmstrip

Adobe Premiere can export a file format called Filmstrip, and files in this format can be opened in Photoshop, edited, and resaved for transfer back to Premiere. A Filmstrip file shows all the frames in the exported video, stacked vertically. The only files you can save in Filmstrip format are ones exported from Premiere in the format. Be careful not to change the number of frames in the filmstrip or the size of the image when editing the file, or the image won't relink correctly to its Premiere source.

When you view a Filmstrip file, you see a gray bar below each frame showing the time stamp for that frame in the video. You can move from one frame to the next quickly by pressing Shift-Page Down or Shift-Page Up.

TGA (Targa)

The TGA format is often called Targa, but that's actually the name of the graphics display card that first used the format. TGA is a video format supported by high-end PC color applications, and it enables chroma keying—overlaying computer animations onto video. In this format alpha channels are used to indicate the area where the live video displays. TGA files can have bit depths up to 24 bits plus an 8-bit alpha channel; they can be indexed color, RGB, or grayscale (see Figure 16.12). Although the TGA format supports several types of compression, Photoshop does not use compression when saving TGA images.

Figure 16.12

The Targa Options dialog box enables you to determine only the file's bit depth.

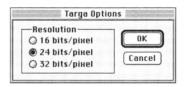

CHOOSING FILE FORMATS FOR THE WEB

The advent of the Web has increased use of the Internet unimaginably over the last few years. Why? Because the Web is graphical. Suddenly the Internet had a face, and that meant a whole new profession: Web designer.

Just as with print designers these days, Web designers have to be very aware of issues such as bandwidth. Not everyone has a high-speed connection to the Internet. Web graphic file sizes must be as small as possible so that users don't have to wait a long time for graphics to load into their browsers. The common graphics file formats used on the Web all have built-in compression. Other features of these formats include progressive rendering and transparency. Progressive rendering enables an image to display onscreen at a low resolution before it's completely downloaded. Transparency enables users to make a color in an image transparent; whatever's behind the color shows through when the image is displayed in a Web browser.

Most images on the Web today are JPEG or GIF files; JPEG is most useful for photographic images, and GIF is appropriate for images with flat areas. PNG is a new format that's starting to be supported by Web browsers and other programs, and PDF is Adobe's Acrobat format, which can be viewed live on the Web through the use of browser plug-ins. For more information on preparing images for use on the Web, see Chapter 17, "Photoshop for the World Wide Web."

Saving GIF Files

There are two ways to create GIF files in Photoshop. First, you can use the CompuServe GIF format option in the Save dialog box to save indexed color and grayscale images as GIF files. The only option when saving GIF files is whether they should be interlaced or not (see Figure 16.13). Interlaced GIFs display progressively when they're viewed in a Web browser.

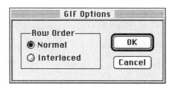

Figure 16.13

The GIF Options dialog box.

The GIF file's size is largely dependent on the palette options you make when switching to indexed color mode (see Chapter 10, "Working with Color Images"). The more colors the image uses, the larger the file. Reducing the number of colors forces the image to use dithering, in which other colors are combined to produce the illusion of a color that's not actually used. This is similar to the illusion of full color created by using cyan, magenta, yellow, and black inks when doing process printing. While dithered colors enable you to use a smaller palette to achieve a smaller file size, they don't look exactly like the colors in the original image.

The other way to create a GIF file is to use an export plug-in such as the GIF89a module that comes with Photoshop. This method enables you to save RGB or indexed color images to GIF format, and it supports transparency.

To save an RGB image as a GIF file:

1. If you want part of the image to be transparent, make a layer mask covering the part of

How Does Interlacing Work?

Interlacing is accomplished by saving the file out of order. An interlaced image, for example, may be displayed in three "passes," so the first part of the file consists of every third row of pixels, the second part consists of the rows immediately below those, and the third part consists of the remaining rows. When the first third of the file has been downloaded, every third row is displayed, with the colors extended down to fill up the empty space between rows. So the image is visible, but it looks blocky. When the image is two-thirds downloaded, more image data is added between the rows already visible. When the entire file is downloaded, the final pass shows the complete image.

the image that should be transparent by making a selection and
clicking the Make Layer Mask button on the Layers palette (see
Chapter 5, "Selections, Paths, and Masks," and Chapter 9,
"Layers," for more information on making layer masks).

2. Choose File➡Export➡GIF89a.

3. In the GIF89a Export dialog box, choose a palette option (see
Figure 16.14).

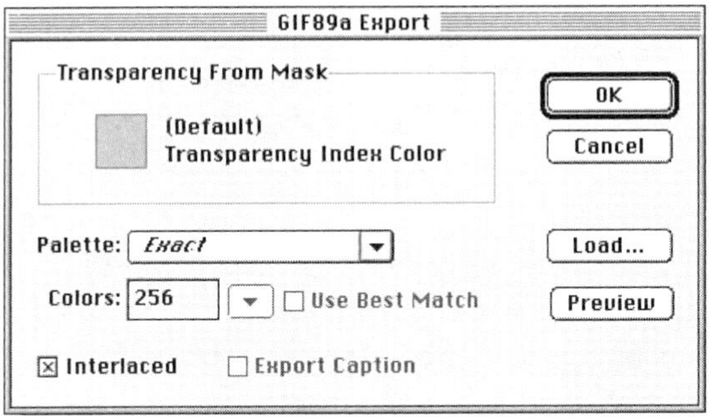

Figure 16.14

*If you export an RGB image to
GIF89a format, it is converted
to indexed color on the fly—
the dialog box asks you to
choose a method and a
palette size.*

Your options are Exact, which uses the colors used in your
image if there are 256 or fewer colors; Adaptive, which creates
a palette using a representative sample of the colors in the
image; or System, which uses only the colors in the default
palette of the platform you're using (Mac or Windows).

If you choose System palette, click Best Match to convert the
colors in your image to their closest system equivalents.

If you have a palette file to which you want to map the colors,
such as the 216-color Web-safe palette (this palette includes
only the colors common to both Windows and Macintosh
system palettes), click the Load button and select the palette file
(CLUT) you want to use.

4. Choose the number of colors you want to include in the file.

Photoshop inserts the number of colors used in the image, but
you can reduce this number. The more colors you allow to be
included, the larger the file is. If you enter a lower number,

then the missing colors are dithered—simulated by placing pixels of two or more other colors next to each other.

5. To see how the image looks click the Preview button. You'll see the colors used laid out in swatches, as well as your image (see Figure 16.15). The transparent areas of the image are gray. If you don't like what you see, return to the main dialog box by clicking OK and then hold down the (Option) [Alt] key and click the Reset button that appears to restore the original settings.

Figure 16.15

When you're exporting an RGB image to GIF89a format, you can see how the image looks in this Preview dialog box.

6. Click the Interlaced box to make the file an interlaced GIF that displays progressively.

7. If you've entered a caption for the image in the File Info dialog box (choose the File Info command in the File menu), you can check Export caption to attach the caption information to the file's header.

8. Click OK to export the image.

To save an indexed color image as a GIF file:

1. If you want to specify transparent areas of the image, you can use a mask channel.

To make a mask channel, select the portions of the image that should be transparent and click the Save Selection as Channel button on the Channels palette (see Chapter 5, "Selections, Paths, and Masks," and Chapter 8, "Channels," for more information on making mask channels). Mask channels are different from layer masks, which are used to specify transparent areas when exporting RGB images using the GIF89a Export plug-in.

You don't have to use a mask channel to specify transparent areas. If the colors used in the area to be made transparent are *not* used elsewhere in the image, you're able to specify the transparent area by choosing those colors in the GIF89a Export dialog box.

2. Choose File➥Export➥GIF89a.

3. In the GIF89a Export dialog box, turn interlacing on or off (see Figure 16.16). Interlacing makes the GIF image display progressively when it's displayed in a Web browser.

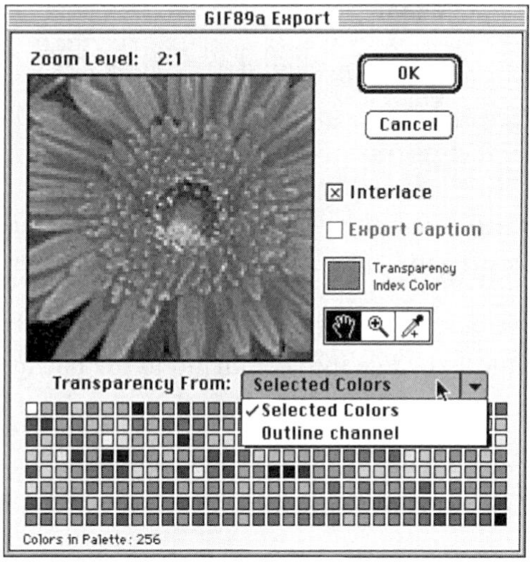

Figure 16.16

If you export an indexed color image to GIF89a format, you can choose a color to be designated as transparent or opt to use a mask to define a transparent area.

4. Click Export Caption if you want to save caption information in the File Info dialog box (choose File Info from the File menu) with the file.

5. Click the gray box labeled Transparency Index Color to change the color Photoshop uses to designate transparent colors. This color won't show when the image is displayed in a Web browser.

6. From the pop-up menu, choose a method for determining what areas are transparent in the image: selected colors or a mask channel. Any mask channels in the image show in the menu.

   If you choose Selected colors, use the Eyedropper tool in the dialog box to click an image color that should be transparent. You can choose colors from the image and from the palette swatches, and you can pick more than one color to be transparent. These colors will be transparent throughout the image, so be sure that they're ones you don't want displayed anywhere in the image. Photoshop indicates which colors are transparent by adding a thick black border to their boxes in the palette.

   This dialog box has a dynamic preview—the preview window shows the transparent areas using the color you specify as a transparency index color. You can move the image around in the box using the Move tool, and you can zoom in and out using the Zoom (magnifying glass) tool.

7. Click OK to export the image.

Saving JPEG Files

Though JPEG compression can be used by some other formats (such as EPS for its preview images), Photoshop can also save images in a JPEG format that takes full advantage of the JPEG compression algorithm.

JPEG compression enables you to trade image quality for a smaller file size, and you can specify exactly how much quality you're willing to give up. Photoshop restricts you to 10 levels between the highest and lowest quality, but third-party plug-ins enable finer control over the trade-off between compression ratios and quality. When you're using the JPEG format, remember that the image degrades more each time you compress it by saving, closing, and opening it again; it's usually best to work in another format and save your image in the JPEG format after it's complete.

To save a JPEG image:

1. Choose JPEG from the format pop-up menu in the Save dialog box.

2. In the JPEG Options dialog box, choose an image quality level by typing in a number from 1 to 10, choosing an option from the pop-up menu, or adjusting the slider (see Figure 16.17). Each method accomplishes the same thing. The higher the quality level, the larger the file; lower quality levels permit more compression and result in smaller files.

Figure 16.17

The JPEG Options dialog box enables you to choose a compression method and determine how much compression should be used.

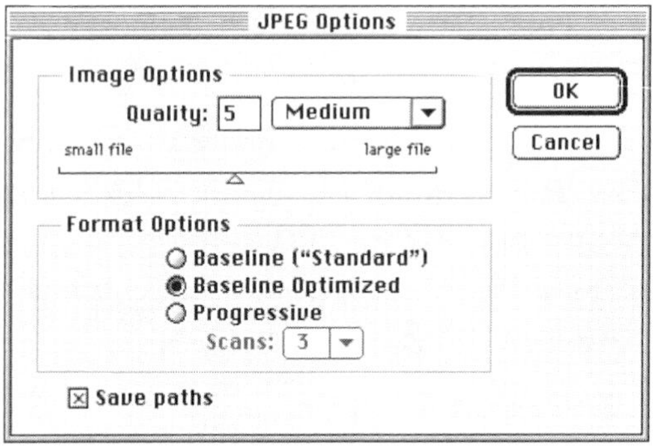

3. Choose a format option.

Your choices are Baseline ("Standard"), Baseline Optimized, and Progressive; choosing standard baseline will minimize the amount of data lost in compression; optimized baseline will optimize image quality, and progressive allows progressive rendering for images intended to be viewed via a Web browser.

(Not all Web browsers support progressive JPEG images.) You can choose the number of scans, or steps, used in the progressive rendering, from 3 to 5.

4. Click OK to save the file.

The JPEG format can also preserve paths used in the file.

Saving PNG files

PNG (Portable Network Graphic) files are now supported by programs such as HotMetal Pro, Office 97, FreeHand Graphics Studio, xRes, and, of course, Photoshop 4.0.

PNG was originated to replace the GIF format because of a legal battle over the compression technology used in GIF that will result in huge licensing fees being owed by any developer who releases a product that saves in the GIF format. As long as they were starting from scratch, the programmers who created the PNG format decided they might as well make a *better* format—so PNG has higher compression levels (but still lossless, meaning compression doesn't affect image quality) and displays faster when it's interlaced. Because it's a new format, PNG isn't yet supported by all major applications, but it looks as though it will be successful.

When you save an image in PNG format, you have two sets of options (see Figure 16.18). First, choose whether the file should be interlaced or not; for interlaced files, choose the Adam7 option—that's the method used for interlacing PNG files. Second, choose a filter option for the image's compression. All PNG images use the format's built-in lossless compression, but different filter options prepare the image for compression in different ways. Your choices are None, Sub, Up, Average, Paeth, and Adaptive. For indexed color images and those with bit depths less than 8, use None. For color or grayscale images with bit depths of 8 or more, try Paeth first; depending on the image, the other options may work better, but the Paeth option is likely to give the best all-around compression results.

Figure 16.18

The PNG Options dialog box enables you to specify a filtering method and choose whether the image is interlaced.

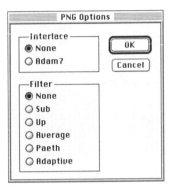

Saving PDF Files

Saving your image as a PDF (Portable Document Format) using an Adobe Acrobat file is one way to distribute it for viewing on Mac, PC, and Unix systems. PDF is based on PostScript Level 2 (not surprising because Adobe also invented PostScript) and can be used to represent vector and raster graphics as well as type; PDF uses standard compression algorithms such as LZW. When saving a Photoshop image as a PDF file, no options are presented.

USING OTHER FORMATS

It probably seems as though this chapter has covered more than enough formats by now, but there are more to come. The formats discussed so far are useful for prepress and multimedia applications; occasionally, one of the following formats is needed for another application.

Saving Files in Photoshop's Native Format

To preserve parts of your files native to Photoshop, those files must be saved in Photoshop's native format, which comes in two flavors: 2.0 and 4.0. Photoshop's native format is the only one that can handle all image modes, as well as features such as layers and alpha channels. The 4.0 native format is the only format that supports adjustment layers, guides, and grids. Opening and saving files saved in native format is faster than in any other format, and version 3.0 and later use a proprietary compression scheme that reduces file sizes somewhat.

Note

TIFF images can be saved with alpha channels intact.

To use Photoshop 4.0 files in earlier versions of Photoshop:

◆ 2.0—Save As using the Photoshop 2.0 format. 4.0-only features and layers are discarded. Make sure you're not in Lab mode because that color mode isn't supported in 2.0.

◆ 2.5—Turn on 2.5 Format Compatibility in preferences and save as Photoshop 4.0 format. 4.0-only features and layers remain in the file but won't be read; they're discarded if you save the file in Photoshop 2.5. Make sure the image has 16 or fewer channels.

◆ 3.0—Save as Photoshop 4.0 format. 4.0-only features remain in the file but won't be read; they're discarded if you save the file in Photoshop 2.5. Layers are not affected.

When discarding data it can't read, Photoshop doesn't affect how the image looks, just how you can edit it. If a layer mask, for example, is discarded when you open a file in Photoshop 2.0, the image looks the same as it did with the mask, but you won't be able to edit the mask or the layer because that version of the software doesn't support those features.

If you're not exchanging files with someone who needs to open them in Photoshop 2.5, you should leave 2.5 Format Compatibility turned off because it increases the size of your files. The increase is due to the fact that a flattened version of the file is stored along with the layered version, just in case the file is opened by Photoshop 2.5.

Tip

Use Save As or Save a Copy to preserve a copy of your file with the layers intact before you flatten them to save the file in another format, such as TIFF.

Attaching File Information

Photoshop's TIFF format supports the addition of text information to image files; this capability can be used to store captions, keywords, categories, credits, and other information about the file. Newspapers use this information to identify transmitted images, and it's also used by image cataloging programs such as Extensis Fetch that enable users to search the information. To enter file information, choose File Info from the File menu and use the pop-up menu or the Next and Previous buttons to move through the different sections (see Figure 16.19).

Figure 16.19

The File Info dialog box enables you to attach text to an image.

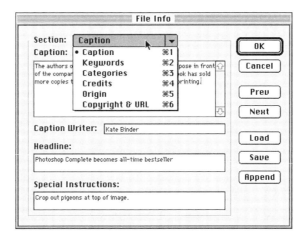

The Keywords section can be searched by image browser software; the other sections are used primarily by organizations such as the Associated Press, with its Associated Press Picture Desk system. If you choose Caption in Page Setup, the information in the caption field appears below the image when it's printed from Photoshop (but not when it's printed from other applications).

Saving in Other Formats

Of the formats covered in this section, MacPaint and PixelPaint are essentially obsolete—but they do come in handy for trading files with people who haven't yet *realized* they're obsolete. The Raw format can be used to exchange files with users of imaging systems in fields other than publishing, such as radar and medical imaging, where nonstandard formats are often used.

MacPaint

MacPaint is the format used by the MacPaint application, one of the programs that shipped with the original Macintosh computers. MacPaint is still available from Claris Corp., Apple's software subsidiary. The Photoshop format called MacPaint is restricted to 72 dpi black-and-white images, and no matter what the size of your actual drawing, the whole drawing area is saved—a size of 576 pixels by 720 pixels (8×10 inches). Although no options appear when you're saving a MacPaint image, you are able to choose to have the image at the top left or in the center of the file when you open a file saved in this format. While this format is almost obsolete, you can still find MacPaint clip art. The only reason you'd use this format would be to supply artwork to a MacPaint user—for example, some schools may still be using MacPaint.

Before you can save files to the MacPaint format, you must install the plug-in. The plug-in is on your Adobe Photoshop 4.0 Application CD-ROM, in Other Goodies➡Optional Plugins➡File Format. Drop the MacPaint icon into the File Format folder of your Adobe Photoshop plug-ins folder.

PixelPaint

A step up from MacPaint is PixelPaint, the first color paint program for the Mac. The current version is PixelPaint Pro, which uses a 24-bit native format and also reads TIFF and PICT files. Earlier versions (1.0 and 2.0) used an 8-bit native format to which Photoshop can save. When saving a PixelPaint file, you must decide whether the image appears in the upper-left corner of the canvas or in the center. PixelPaint images can be black-and-white, grayscale, or indexed color.

Before you can save files to the PixelPaint format, you must install the plug-in, which is on your Adobe Photoshop 4.0 Application CD-ROM, in Other Goodies➡Optional Plugins➡File Format. Drop the PixelPaint icon into the File Format folder of your Adobe Photoshop plug-ins folder.

Raw

The Raw format isn't really a format at all. It's a way to save Photoshop images in an almost naked form in which you can specify the file type and creator. This is handy when you need to supply files to someone whose computer system doesn't handle standard image formats. Medical and scientific imaging programs often use proprietary formats that can be opened in Photoshop using the Raw format, and Photoshop Raw images can often be opened on these proprietary systems.

Raw files are made up of binary data and preserve all channels and the full bit depth of the images. Besides the file type, creator, and header information, you can choose whether the image is saved in its natural order or interleaved order (see Figure 16.20). To use this format, you need to find out the settings the destination system expects and enter those when you save a file as Raw.

Figure 16.20

The Raw Options dialog box enables you to choose a file type and creator.

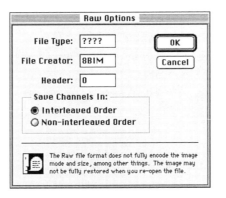

What Photoshop formats can popular programs import?

Here's a rundown of the Photoshop file formats that some major applications can import. Most of these programs support other formats as well.

Program	Mac	Windows
Canvas	BMP	BMP
	EPS	EPS
	GIF	GIF
	IFF	IFF
	JPEG	JPEG

Program	Mac	Windows
	MacPaint	MacPaint
	PCX	PCX
	PDF	PDF
	Photo CD	Photo CD
	Photoshop	Photoshop
	PICT	PICT
	TGA	TGA
	TIFF	TIFF
Director	BMP	BMP
	EPS	EPS
	GIF	GIF
	MacPaint	MacPaint
	PCX	PCX
	Photo CD	Photo CD
	PICT	PICT
	TIFF	TIFF
FrameMaker	EPS	EPS
	MacPaint	MacPaint
	PCX	PCX
	TIFF	TIFF
FreeHand	BMP	BMP
	EPS	EPS
	GIF	GIF
	JPEG	JPEG
	Photoshop	Photoshop
	TIFF	TIFF
Illustrator	BMP	BMP
	EPS	EPS

continues

Program	Mac	Windows
	Filmstrip	Filmstrip
	IFF	IFF
	MacPaint	MacPaint
	PCX	PCX
	Photo CD	Photo CD
	Photoshop	Photoshop
	PICT	PICT
	Pixar	Pixar
	PixelPaint	PixelPaint
	Targa	Targa
	TIFF	TIFF
PageMaker 6.5	BMP	
	DCS 1.0/2.0	
	EPS	
	GIF	
	MacPaint	
	PCX	
	Scitex CT	
	TIFF	
Persuasion	EPS	
	GIF	
	JPEG	
	Photo CD	
	Photoshop	
	PICT	
	TIFF	BMP
		EPS
		GIF
		JPEG

Program	Mac	Windows
		PCX
		Photo CD
		Photoshop
		PICT
		TIFF
Premiere	Filmstrip	
	Photo CD	
	Photoshop	
	PICT	
	TGA	BMP
		Filmstrip
		Photoshop
		PICT
		TGA
		TIFF
QuarkXPress	BMP	
	DCS 1.0/2.0	
	EPS	
	JPEG	
	MacPaint	
	PCX	
	Photo CD	
	PICT	
	Scitex CT	
	TIFF	BMP
		DCS 1.0/2.0
		EPS
		GIF
		PCX
		TIFF

CROSS-PLATFORM COMPATIBILITY

Trading files among different computer systems is a lot easier than it used to be. Windows PCs and Macs can read each others' disks and talk to each other over local networks—two capabilities that a few years ago seemed fantastic.

Exchanging Files between Macs and PCs

Macs and PCs both support the standard professional graphics formats—TIFF, EPS, GIF, and JPEG—and Photoshop 4.0 can open any Photoshop file, regardless of format, even if it was created on another platform. When saving an image that's destined to be used on a different platform, check the dialog box options and make sure you select the appropriate ones for the platform you intend. For the most part, no matter what platform-specific options you choose, you are still able to open Photoshop files on either platform. The exception is when you're using QuickTime JPEG compression for PICT images and JPEG encoding for EPS images—it's much less common for PCs to have QuickTime installed than for Macs, so files saved with these options might not translate properly to some systems on other platforms.

Cross-platform file transfers are not completely glitch-proof, however. In the process of being moved and opened on another computer system, files can lose preview and file type information. Both of these situations can be dealt with. Lost previews are easily replaced by resaving the image on the new platform, adding the preview at that point.

Lost file type information can be slightly more difficult to deal with. Macs store file type information in the resource fork of the file, which PCs can't read. PCs, on the other hand, depend on filename extensions. So if your file doesn't have an extension, or it doesn't have the right one, you may have to tell Photoshop yourself what file format it is.

The Windows version of Photoshop has an Open As command in the File menu. Choose the correct file format, select the file, and click the Open button. Macs enable you to specify a file format in the standard Open dialog box by clicking Show all files. If this option is selected, a file format pop-up menu appears, from which you can choose the format for the file you want to open.

Exchanging Files with Amigas

When saving files for use on Amiga computers, you want to use the IFF and HAM formats. IFF (Interchange File Format) is the basic Amiga graphics format. HAM (Hold and Modify) is a compressed version of IFF that can be used primarily for files in one of two standard sizes: 320×200 pixels or 320×400 pixels; HAM cuts the file size approximately in half. Photoshop supports 8-bit color HAM images and 24-bit color IFF images. The IFF format appears in the format listing in the Save dialog box, whereas HAM files are created by using the Export command.

Before you can save files to the Amiga IFF format, you must install the plug-in. The plug-in is on your Adobe Photoshop 4.0 Application CD-ROM, in Other Goodies➡Optional Plugins➡File Format. Drop the Amiga IFF icon into the File Format folder of your Adobe Photoshop plug-ins folder.

Tip

If your image is not one of the two standard sizes, it is displayed on the Amiga with rectangular pixels, rather than square ones. To compensate for this, resize the image 83% vertically and 120% horizontally (noninterlaced images) or 166% vertically and 60% horizontally (interlaced images) before exporting to the HAM format.

Naming Cross-Platform Files

Although many PCs now run Windows 95 or Windows NT, which support longer filenames, it's wise to use eight-letter filenames with three-letter extensions when transferring files between Macs and PCs. Photoshop can be set to add the correct extension for each file format when a file is saved, and if you're transferring files between platforms on a regular basis, it's a good idea to use this option.

1. Select File➡Preferences➡Saving Files.

2. Choose one of three options: Never add extensions, Always add extensions, or Ask When Saving (this adds a checkbox to the Save dialog box marked Append File Extension).

Never assume that a file format has to match the filename extension. Be careful if you're assigning your own extensions—use the right ones. Here's a list:

Photoshop	PSD
Illustrator	AI
IFF	IFF
HAM	HAM
BMP	BMP
	RLE
GIF	GIF
EPS	EPS
Filmstrip	FLM
JPEG	JPG
Photo CD	PCD
MacPaint	MAC
	MPT
PCX	PCX
PICT	PICT
PICT resource	PICS
Pixar	PXR
PixelPaint	PXI
Raw	RAW
Scitex CT	SCT
TGA	ICB
	TGA
	VDA
	VST
TIFF	TIF

Moving Files across Platforms

Depending on the software you have installed, you can move Photoshop files between different platforms in the same ways you would move them on the same platform.

Transferring Files Using Disks

Macs can read and write to PC floppies, Zip disks, SyQuest disks, and other media—that capability is built into the MacOS, as is the capability to format PC floppies. Windows doesn't offer this capability, but there are programs that do. On a Windows system, a Mac disk looks like a PC disk, with directories and files; there may be some files floating around that are normally invisible to Mac users, such as custom icons, but these can safely be ignored. To a Mac user, a PC disk looks like a Mac disk, with folders and icons, but all the files have generic document icons, and they won't open by double-clicking unless you've configured the PC Exchange control panel to recognize the filename extensions and open them in the correct application. Using the Open command from the File menu enables you to bypass this procedure.

Note

Mac-in-DOS Plus (Pacific Micro), MacDisk (Insignia Solutions), MacAccess (Hypro Technologies), Here & Now (Software Architects), and MacOpener (DataViz) all enable PC users to read, write, and format high-density Mac floppies. Some of these programs also enable access to CD-ROMs, SyQuest drives, Bernoulli drives, Zip drives, and other removable media.

Transferring Files Using Local Area Networks

Just as with disks, once you're able to access a different computer over a network, you can deal with the files just as you would files on your own computer. Neither Windows systems nor Macs, however, come with software for cross-platform communication over a local area network (LAN).

Note

With Personal MacLAN Connect (Miramar), a Windows PC can share Mac AppleShare volumes and PC directories with Macs; the program also lets both systems use all the printers on a network, Mac and PC alike. Personal MacLAN works with LocalTalk, Ethernet, and token-ring networks. After the software is installed on the PC, the Mac can use the PC's volumes without installing additional software. Timbuktu for Windows (Farallon) is a similar product.

Transferring Files Using the Internet

The Internet is the ultimate cross-platform network. It links Macs, PCs, Amigas, workstations, mainframes, and just about any other type of computer you can imagine. Because of this, information that flows through the Internet has to be reduced to the most generic format possible. This doesn't refer to Photoshop file formats but to compression and encoding options used by file transfer programs and email applications.

First of all, if bandwidth is limited (and when isn't it?) on one or both ends of the file transfer, file compression is a good idea. Macs customarily use StuffIt (DropStuff and StuffIt Expander are shareware), and PCs usually use PKZIP. Both of these programs use the same types of lossless encoding used in image compression—LZW, Huffman, and so on. Compression is also a good way to keep all related files together until they reach their destination because all files compressed at the same time are bundled into one compressed archive file. This is convenient because you usually can't attach more than one file to an email message.

To make sure that files retain their file type information when they're done being transferred, several encoding methods can be used. Most email programs can perform this encoding, but file transfer programs may or may not have this capability. Mail attachments have to be encoded because Internet mail must be in ASCII format. Two of the most common encoding methods are MIME (all platforms) and BinHex (primarily Mac).

MIME (Multi-Purpose Internet Mail Extensions) is an encoding method specifically designed for mail attachments. If you receive a MIME-encoded attachment that your email program doesn't decode, you can unpack it using a program such as YA-Base64 (Mac), Mpack (Mac), or munpack (Mac, PC, Amiga, and Unix); these are shareware.

Note

The filename extension for MIME-encoded files is MME.

An alternative encoding method is BinHex (Binary Hexadecimal), which is primarily used on Macs for both email attachments and file transfer. DropStuff can perform BinHex encoding, and StuffIt

Expander can decode BinHex files; there are also a number of shareware applications to decode BinHex archives such as HQXer (Mac). WinZip can decode BinHex files as well as MIME and UUencode (another encoding method) files.

Chapter 17

PHOTOSHOP FOR THE WORLD WIDE WEB

In the beginning, the Web was not much more than a bunch of text files put together by scientists; Great information, but not very inviting to the general public. Along came evolution and POOF! The overwhelming amount of information, scientific and otherwise, could be presented in aesthetically enjoyable—and meaningful—ways.

Photoshop is a fantastic tool for preparing images for online use. It shines in all areas of the process—from compositing entire sites to creating custom graphic elements to converting file formats.

Of course, Photoshop is only one tool in the myriad that Web designers need to complete a project. With the many new features included in Photoshop 4.0, however, (such as GIF89a Export, the Web-safe color palette, and the Actions palette) that myriad has been reduced to half-a-myriad. ;-)

GENERAL CONCERNS FOR IMAGES ON THE WEB

One of the biggest difficulties Web designers face is not knowing what size, resolution, and bit depth an end-user's monitor might be set at. The difficulty lies in the way Web pages are displayed—the font sizes can change or the browser's window could be smaller than the screen. As a result, the Web designer must put the pages together in such a way as to allow for fluctuation in these variables, without the design's integrity falling into oblivion.

Bandwidth

Bandwidth is a measure of how fast information is able to travel from one point to another—the more bandwidth, the more information that can be transmitted. Web designers must concern themselves with bandwidth because of the diverse array of connections individuals have to the Web. Some are connected by lightening fast T1 lines (1.5 megabits/second). Others chug along on a 14.4 modem (14.4 kilobits/second) or even slower! Today, 28.8 Kbps modems are the norm. However, 33.6 Kbps modems are fast becoming reasonably priced and are bundled with many new home setups.

When designing a Web site, it's important to keep in mind how the majority of the end users are connected. Their connection speed influences just how graphic intensive a design can get. If the files are so large that they take more than a few minutes to download over an average connection, end users may get tired of waiting and visit a different, faster loading site.

Fortunately, there are tricks to reducing file sizes without compromising much image quality. These techniques are covered in the "Reducing File Sizes" section of this chapter.

A Bit on Bit Depths

Bit depth is a term referring to the number of colors that a particular image can contain. The higher the bit depth, the more colors that are possible, and also the larger the file size, particularly for GIF images (see Table 17.1).

TABLE 17.1

BIT DEPTHS AND THEIR RESPECTIVE NUMBER OF COLORS.

Bit Depth	No. of Colors
2	4
3	8
4	16
5	32
6	64
7	128
8	256
16	65,536 (Sometimes called "Thousands")
24	16,777,216 (Sometimes called "Millions")

GIF images can contain up to a bit depth of 8 (256 colors); JPEG, 24 bit (millions). PNG is reported to handle 48 bits, though not all of them are for color — they're used for the alpha channel, which dictates pixel transparency.

CHOOSING A FILE FORMAT

There are two major image file formats in vogue for Web designers— GIF and JPEG. Each of them have their plusses and minuses. And each have instances where they out-perform the other. When unguided, choosing which of these formats to use can sometimes feel like playing the lottery—if it works right, you feel extremely lucky. If not, you try again.

In addition, there's an up-and-coming format, PNG, that aims to knock GIF out of the ring and just might do away with JPEG, too. The format is not widely supported, however, requiring obscure plug-ins for Web browsers and custom tags in the HTML code. Photoshop is ready to grow with the popularity of PNG, as it already possesses an option to save images in this new format!

GIF

GIF (Graphics Interchange Format) is the most widely used image format on the Web and is beautifully supported in Photoshop 4.0. GIF is a lossless compression scheme: all the image information that was present before compression is retained after compression (unlike JPEG, which is a lossy scheme).

GIF has a few limitations that, at best, frustrate designers. The big one is the limited color palette. GIFs can contain up to only 256 colors (also know as 8-bit color). If an image has more than 256 colors, the lesser-used ones are dropped in favor of the more frequently occurring ones during the indexing process (see Figure 17.1). The indexing process attempts to compensate for this loss by dithering the colors it did keep to simulate the lost colors. Sometimes the results are negligible. But in the case of photographic images, it most often is not.

Figure 17.1

The original image for the example was an RGB file with a full-color rainbow on the bottom and the gray scale equivalent on top. This shows what happens when there are more than 256 colors in an image and it's indexed to 8 bit. Note the dithering effect performed by the indexing process.

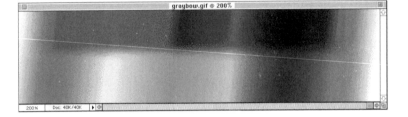

Note

Dithering is is a process in which the eye can be tricked into seeing more colors in the image than really exist. Dithering takes place when converting an image from one mode (RGB, for example) to Indexed mode. Dithering works its magic by placing two differently colored pixels in close proximity. Let's say, for example, that in RGB mode, the image contains a purplish color. But when it's converted to Indexed mode, red and blue were the only colors available because of the color limit in indexing mode. The purple would then be simulated by placing red and blue pixels next to each other. If dithering was NOT used in this case, bands or stripes of red and blue would be used instead of a speckles of red and blue — resulting in a less convincing representation of the purple.

For all its limitations, GIF gives Web designers some widely supported features that make other formats jealous. GIFs can do a primitive form of animation, for instance, letting Web designers add motion to an otherwise static page. GIFs can also have transparent areas that, when displayed in a Web browser, enable textured backgrounds to show through—the images don't have to look like a rectangle. Transparency for GIFs is an all-or-nothing situation — each pixel can be either entirely transparent or entirely opaque. There is no in-between.

Photoshop 4.0 can save GIFs in an interlaced format. Interlaced files, when loaded by a Web browser, do something similar to a fade to the image, giving surfers something to look at while the rest of the image loads. An interlace GIF first shows a rough, blocky representation of the final image, progresses to finer and finer detail, then appears in full detail. Interlaced GIFs can sometimes suffer from interpretation difficulties. An interlaced image may get half-way through showing full detail, then stop. Therefore, it's a good idea to avoid interlaced GIFs for navigation bars and other images essential to a Web site. Non-interlaced GIFs do *not* suffer from this interpretation problem.

There are two ways to save a GIF file from Photoshop. One is through the standard Save dialog box (see Figure 17.2). The other is through the File➡Export➡GIF89a Export plug-in (see Figure 17.3). The export plug-in is used for saving transparent GIFs. For more information about exporting to GIF format, see Chapter 16, "Saving and Exporting."

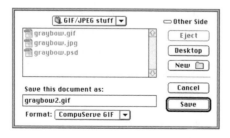

Figure 17.2

The standard Save dialog box, ready to save the file in GIF format.

Figure 17.3

Figure 17.3

The GIF89a Export plug-in.
This filter (under the File➡
Export menu) is used to save
GIFs with transparencies.

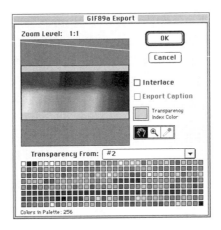

Indexed Color

For an image to be saved as a GIF, it first has to be indexed — a process that reduces the number of colors to fit in a specified bit depth (between 3 and 8 bits). An image is converted to indexed color via the Mode submenu on the Image menu. When converting an image to indexed color, you have the following options:

◆ **Exact.** This option is grayed out unless your image contains 256 colors or less. You encounter this if you convert a GIF file back to RGB for editing.

◆ **System (Macintosh).** This palette contains the 256 colors used by the MacOS. These are not the same colors used by the System (Windows) option.

◆ **System (Windows).** This palette contains the 256 colors used by the Windows operating system. These are not the same colors used by the System (Macintosh) palette.

◆ **Web.** These colors represent the 216 cross-platform colors used by Web browsers.

◆ **Uniform.** New in Photoshop 4.0, this is the same as the Web palette, but you have the flexibility to cut the bit depth from 8 bits (256 colors) to 3 bits (8 colors) while maintaining cross-platform legal colors.

- **Adaptive.** With this option, Photoshop analyzes the image and determines which colors are used the most. Then a palette is created to incorporate those colors, sacrificing the less-used colors for the chosen ones. This choice can be set to use bit depths between 3 and 8 bits per pixel — for reducing the file size of GIF images.

- **Custom.** This options enables you to load in a previously saved color palette.

- **Previous.** This option applies the last-used palette to the image being modified. This option is handy for when many images have to be set to use the same palette.

The Web Palette

A new feature to Photoshop 4.0 is the addition of the Web palette. This palette contains the 216 colors the major Web browsers recognize as being cross-platform. If you're concerned about the end users of the Web site having aged, low-end systems, use this palette for all of your images. See Figure 17.4.

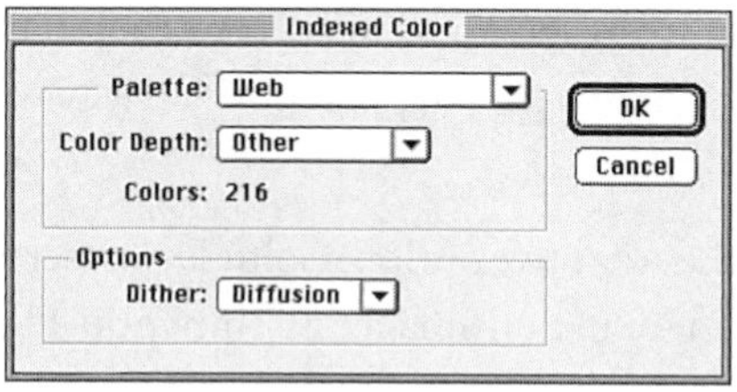

Figure 17.4

Using the Image➥Mode➥ Indexed Color dialog box to convert an image to the Web palette.

Unfortunately, this palette is severely short on grays and causes a lot of banding or noticeable graininess in many images. See Figure 17.5.

If you want to avoid the down-side of the Web palette and use an adaptive one, be sure to check the Web pages with your monitor set to 256 colors (in the Monitors control panel for Macs or the Display Control Panel for PCs). At that bit depth, Netscape Navigator and Internet Explorer use the Web palette for *all* images in a Web page, whatever format and bit depth they're saved at.

A sunrise in the colors of the Web palette. Note the graininess in the sky.

The Adaptive Palette

Using an adaptive palette results in a more image-specific, fine-tuned palette than the Web palette. The Adaptive palette, as its name implies, adapts itself to each image it processes. It analyzes the image, determining which colors best represent the image. This palette adds as many of these colors to the palette as the specified bit depth allows (see Table 17.1 for the number of colors available at each bit depth). The colors that cannot be added to the palette are done away with, their void filled by available colors.

By combining the Adaptive option, Color Depth settings, and Dithering options when indexing an image, as shown in Figure 17.6, you can avoid the pitfalls of the Web palette.

Figure 17.6

The Indexed Color dialog box, set for an Adaptive palette, using Color Depth of 4 bits/ pixel and a diffused pattern for Dither.

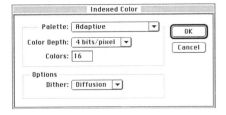

To Dither or Not?

When converting an image to indexed mode, you have the option of dithering or not dithering. The process of dithering tricks the eye into seeing more colors than are actually in the palette. This is accomplished by juxtaposing two or more similar hues to create the illusion of a color not available in the palette. Although this is great for preserving realism, the sacrifice is compression. GIF works best when the image contains long horizontal runs of a solid color. Dithering breaks up the lines with the varying hues, resulting in less compression and larger file sizes (see Figure 17.7).

Figure 17.7

This image was indexed with an adaptive palette set to 6 bits/pixel, using diffusion dithering. The final file size is 24k. The dithering is particularly noticeable in the sky. If you look closely you can see the little specs of color juxtaposed to compensating for dropped-out colors.

If an image is indexed with no dithering, then posterization, or banding, occurs. In images with fades and blends, banding becomes very noticeable (see Figure 17.8).

Figure 17.8

Again, an adaptive palette was used with 6 bits/pixel, but it was not dithered. Note the gnarly banding in the sky. Final file size is 22k.

Note

The images in Figures 17.7 and 17.8 are for illustrative purposes. Had it been necessary to put this image on a Web page at the size shown (300×206 pixels), I would have used JPEG, entirely avoiding the need to index the image.

JPEG

JPEG (Joint Photographic Experts Group) is another often-used image format on the Web. JPEG is a great method for transmitting photo images because it's not limited to 256 (8 bit) colors. JPEG can handle a full 24 bits (16 million colors). But, because of the overhead involved with the format, images under 100×100 pixels usually compress more with GIF. Of course, if your end user's monitor can only display 256 colors (also known as VGA settings, common on older computers), the extra quality is for naught. Many computers sold today, however, can display at least 16 bit color (thousands of colors).

JPEG also differs from GIF in that it uses a lossy compression scheme. That is, even at the highest quality settings, a JPEG image does not contain all of the information the original RGB image started with. Surprisingly, even images saved with the highest compression (most lossy) can be acceptable for online use (see Figure 17.9).

Figure 17.9

This JPEG file was created from the same original RGB file as in Figure 17.1. It was then saved as a JPEG with the lowest quality setting. Much more of the blends were retained, due to JPEGs being able to handle 24 bit color.

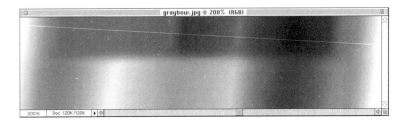

So, if it's a sizable photograph you need to include on your Web page, JPEG with a low- to medium-quality setting is the way to go—for now. (Insert dramatic intro music for the PNG format here.)

Tip

Remember this rule of thumb: If it's a photo-like image you're compressing, JPEG is usually the way to go. If it's a small piece of graphical text, incidental art, or button, go with GIF.

PNG

PNG (Portable Network Graphics, pronounced "ping") is an up and coming lossless compression scheme. It's designed to take on and replace the GIF format. PNG has several unique advantages over GIF: up to 48-bit color or 16-bit grayscale (GIF goes only as high as 8-bit), alpha channels with variable transparency (as opposed to on/off transparency of GIF), gamma correction (cross-platform control of image brightness), and two-dimensional interlacing (a method of progressive display). In addition, PNG, in most cases, compresses images 10 to 30 percent smaller than GIF — great for the bandwidth conscious!

Unfortunately, none of the most popular browsers yet support the PNG format without a plug-in and custom tags. In addition, Photoshop 4.0's support of the format is sketchy at best. There will undoubtedly be an export plug-in available in time, giving better control over compression settings. Updates and links to resources can be found on the PNG Home Page at http://www.wco.com/~png/.

REDUCING FILE SIZES

When designing Web pages, it's easy to overlook the issues of file sizes. Because the files being worked with are on your local hard drive or a connected server, they can load in the blink of an eye. On the receiving end of a modem, however, it's a different story. Large graphics, not properly compressed, can take an eternity to download.

Besides choosing the image compression method (GIF or JPEG) most appropriate for each image, there are other methods of getting the most out of each byte of data.

Alternating Stripe Method

By filling alternating lines of an image with runs of the same color, the file size of a GIF can be cut to nearly half! This works well for large background tiles and images that don't need to be particularly sharp or contrasty.

1. In an RGB image file, make a new channel.

2. Use the Pencil tool, set to white, to draw a short, horizontal line that is 1 pixel tall.

3. With the Marquee tool, select the white line and one row of pixels below it. This is detailed work, so zooming in is probably necessary (see Figure 17.10).

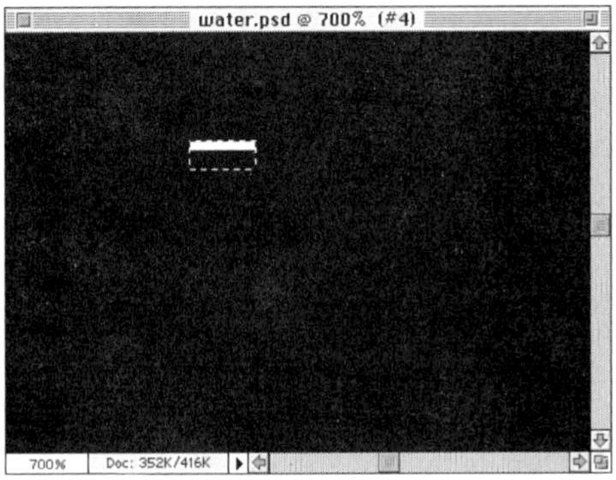

Figure 17.10

Selecting the short white line, 1 pixel tall and the adjacent row of black pixels.

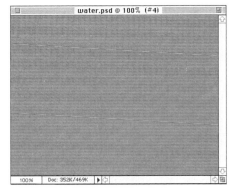

4. Define the selection as a pattern (Edit➥Define Pattern). Drop the selection and fill the entire channel with the pattern (see Figure 17.11).

Figure 17.11

The entire channel, filled with the striped pattern.

5. Return to the composite RGB channel. Set the foreground color to one that best represents the hues present in the image. Using a color toward the dark end of those present in the image tends

to be less noticeable. In this image of water, for instance, the dominant color is a medium blue, but a shade darker produced better results.

6. Load the selection channel and fill it with the new foreground color. Drop the selection (see Figure 17.12).

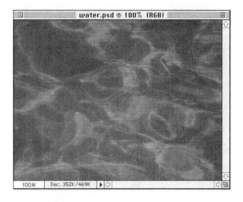

Figure 17.12

The image, striped with a medium color.

7. Delete the channel.

8. Change the image to Indexed color and save in GIF format. The file size should be 2/3 to 1/2 of what it would have been without striping. See Figure 17.13.

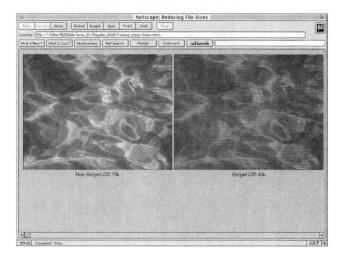

Figure 17.13

A comparison. The non-striped GIF weighs in at 75k. The striped GIF, 43k.

Reducing the Bit Depth

By trying various bit depths on GIF images, during the Indexing process, one can strike a balance between image quality and file size. The more uniform an image's color is, the lower the bit depth possible, and the smaller the file size.

Figure 17.14

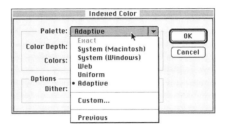

The Index mode dialog box. Bit depth is set by changing the Color Depth option.

Photographs usually contain a wide range of hues and tones. Because of this, they generally don't respond well to bit depths lower than 5 bits/pixel. If your image is monotone or grayscale, going down to 4 bits/pixel may yield acceptable results. The following images (Figures 17.15 to 17.21) can be used as a rough guide for determining the optimum bit depth for your images.

Figure 17.15

The original, 24 bit image of a rainbow of traffic cones. Image dimensions: 395 × 198 pixels

Figure 17.16

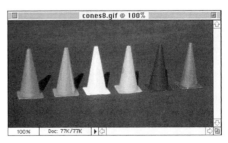

Photograph at 8 bits/pixel. Size: 57k

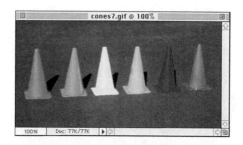

Figure 17.17

Photograph at 7 bits/pixel. Small amounts of dark grains develop around the blue cone (5th from left). Size: 49k

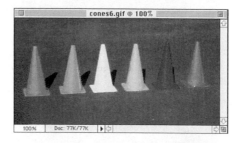

Figure 17.18

Photograph at 6 bits/pixel. Dark grains develop on the left side. Size: 41k

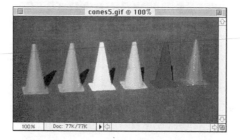

Figure 17.19

Photograph at 5 bits/pixel. Loss of subtle shades. Yellow cone (3rd from left) looks completely flat. Bright grains develop in purple cone (6th from left). Size 37k

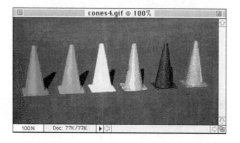

Figure 17.20

Photograph at 4 bits/pixel. Complete loss of cool hues. Grains run rampant. Blue cone (5th from left) has changed to black and gray. Size: 31k

Figure 17.21

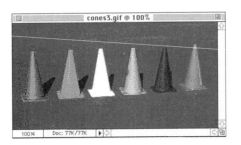

Photograph at 3 bits/pixel. Loss of yellow and orange hues. Mostly black and white, with some peach color. Size: 25k

Note

These images are on the CD so you can see them in living color. Drag the file "cones.htm" from the Examples folder on the Photoshop Complete folder to your Web browser's icon.

CREATING SEAMLESS BACKGROUND TILES

Background images and textures can set the tone for a Web page. The difficult part is matching-up the edges. If the edges don't match up, a jarring discontinuity can occur, but avoiding the mismatch can be tricky. Plug-ins exist that claim to produce seamless tiles and they do a fairly good job. They tend, however, to blur and/or dull the images at the seams. Doing the tiles by hand can help avoid this drawback of the plug-ins — and it's nearly as fast.

1. Open the image to be used as a tile. This image should lend itself to tiling — one that has more than a subtle hint of perspective is difficult to sew together. See Figure 17.22.

Figure 17.22

The beginning image.

Trick

Working with the image at about twice the size needed gives you room to be a little sloppy. When it's scaled down, your edits are less noticeable.

2. Select Filter➡Other➡Offset... to move the seams near the center of the image. The Wrap Around option should be selected. Set Horizontal to a number around half of the width (in pixels) of the image. Set Vertical to a number about half of the image height. See Figure 17.23.

Offset
Horizontal: 250 pixels right   OK
Vertical: 150 pixels down   Cancel
Undefined Areas   ☒ Preview
○ Set to Background
○ Repeat Edge Pixels
● Wrap Around

Figure 17.23

The Offset dialog box with Wrap Around selected.

Applying the filter shows how mismatched the edges are. See Figure 17.24. The seams where the image was wrapped around are pretty obvious.

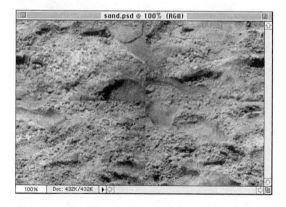

Figure 17.24

The mismatched edges in a tiled image.

3. Use the Rubber Stamp, Blur tool, Smudge tool, and any other tools necessary to do away with the seams. See Chapter 7, "Editing Images," for more information about using these tools.

Figure 17.25

Figure 17.25

The seams have been stamped, blurred, and smudged into oblivion.

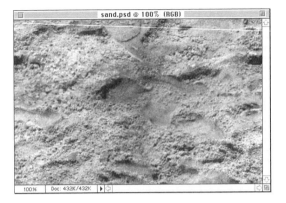

4. If necessary, scale and adjust the brightness/contrast of the image for use on the Web page.

5. Save the image in the appropriate format and incorporate in to the page using the tag

```
<body background="background.gif">
```

where "background.gif" is the name of the image to be tiled. Be sure to include other body definitions, such as text and link colors, in the tag as well. See Figure 17.26.

Figure 17.26

The image tiled on a Web page. Be sure to adjust the brightness/contrast of the image so text and other elements are easily distinguished.

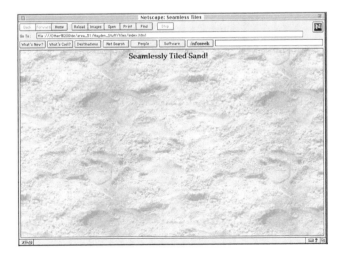

CREATING GRAPHICS WITH ANTI-ALIASING AND TRANSPARENCY

Here's the scenario: You've created a really nice patterned background for your company's Web pages and the logo, a separate image, is in a nice rectangle to be placed at the top of each page. Then your boss changes her mind. She doesn't like the box around the logo. She wants it freed from its rectangular prison. Changing the color of the rectangle won't help — it still obscures the background. What to do?

Anti-Aliasing and Transparency to the rescue! By combining these two techniques, oddly-shaped images can be put on top of patterned backgrounds without obscuring and without encountering jaggies!

Note

Anti-aliasing is a way of reducing the "jaggies"—those nasty bits that surround images with sharp changes in color and contrast. Anti-aliasing blends the two colors together, giving the object a smooth edge.

The key to avoiding halos is anti-aliasing the image or text to a background color that's close to the dominant color used in the pattern.

1. If it isn't already, place your graphic element on its own layer. Refer to Chapter 5, "Selections, Paths, and Masks," for ways to isolate elements. See Figure 17.27.

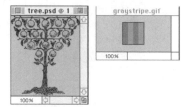

Figure 17.27

Here you see the company logo (the tree) on a light-colored field and the background for the Web page, medium gray stripes. The tree was cut from the background at a scale 3 times larger than shown here, then reduced for Web use.

Tip

When it's necessary to cut elements from a background, work with the largest dimensions of the file you can get your hands on. Reduce the image only after you get it on its own layer. This enables the image to be fine-tuned at a much more amplified scale, resulting in a cleaner end product.

2. Determine what the most common color in the background is. If there are two equally present colors, choose a color that falls between them. Set the background color to this color.

3. Create a new RGB file large enough to hold your graphic element. Fill the background layer with the background color.

4. Copy the graphic element and paste it into the new file. Crop the image to only as large as necessary. (Remember, keep those files as small as possible!) Flatten the image (see Figure 17.28).

Figure 17.28

The graphic element copied to the new file, cropped, and flattened.

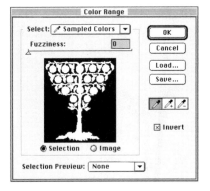

5. Use Select➡Color Range... to select the background color of the new image. Be sure Fuzziness is set to 0 and Invert is checked. See Figure 17.29.

Figure 17.29

Use Color Range... to select the area of the image to be visible. Fuzziness is set to 0 and Invert is checked.

6. Save the selection into a new channel. Drop the selection.

7. Convert the image to Indexed mode (Image➡Mode➡Indexed Color...) using the most effective bit depth. See Figure 17.30.

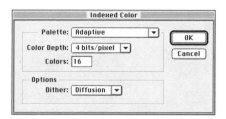

Figure 17.30

Convert the image to indexed color. This example used 4 bits/pixel.

8. Use File→Export→GIF89a Export... to save the image. The Interlace checkbox should be unchecked, and Transparency From should be set to the saved channel. See Figure 17.31.

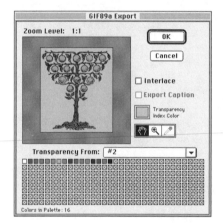

Figure 17.31

Export the image as a transparent GIF.

Warning

Interlacing is an option that, when used, causes Web browsers to load images progressively. That is, they do kind of a venetian blind effect — every fourth row is filled in, then every third row, and so on. This gives viewers something to look at while they're waiting for the page to load. Interlaced GIFs, however, are notorious for not completely loading. If this happens, the viewer sees only a representation of the final graphic. Much of the data is dropped out, leaving the image unreadable—especially if it contains text. Use interlacing with extreme caution. Or, better yet, avoid it altogether!

9. When the image is incorporated into the Web page, the edges are virtually undetectable. See Figure 17.32.

Figure 17.32

Two anti-aliased and transparent images are shown on a Web page. Note how the stripes in the background carry through the spaces in the letters and between the tree limbs.

Tip

The magic element of successful anti-aliasing is to render the graphic element to a background that blends into the pattern on the Web page.

CREATING DROP SHADOWS

In their primitive form, Web pages are flat — boring. Filling them with a lot of text doesn't help the situation much, either. One of the most often used techniques to break the single plane of Web pages is that of drop shadows.

Making Quick-and-Easy Drop Shadows

There are probably as many ways for adding drop shadows in this world as there are designers. This is the quickest, easiest way ever!

1. In a new file, place all elements that should have drop shadows onto *one layer*. If you have multiple elements, use the new Merge Down command in the Layers menu to put everything on one layer. Be sure Preserve Transparency is checked in the Layers palette. See Figure 17.33.

Figure 17.33

Figure 17.33

All elements to be shadowed are on Layer 1. Preserve Transparency is checked.

2. Duplicate the layer by dragging it to the Create New Layer icon in the Layers palette or selecting Duplicate Layer... from the Layer menu. The original layer serves as the shadow layer and the duplicate holds the actual elements. See Figure 17.34.

Figure 17.34

Layer 1 is Duplicated. The original layer becomes the shadow layer.

3. Set the foreground color to the desired shadow color. Black is the color most often used, but dark blues, reds, and greens can also produce good results — depending on your image.

4. Select the original layer and, checking once more to make sure Preserve Transparency is selected, press (Option-Delete)[Alt-Delete] to fill it with the chosen color. Note that this layer is hidden behind the duplicated layer and you won't notice any change. If you need to see what's happening, temporarily hide the duplicated layer. See Figure 17.35.

Figure 17.35

The original layer, with Preserve Transparency on, was filled with black. Layer 1 copy was hidden to illustrate the example.

5. Uncheck Preserve Transparency on the original layer.

6. Apply a Gaussian Blur to the original layer. Settings of 2.0 to 5.0 are the norm. See Figure 17.36.

Figure 17.36

The Gaussian Blur is applied to the original layer, giving the duplicate layer a sort of halo.

7. Use the Move tool and/or the arrow keys to offset the blurred layer. See Figure 17.37.

Figure 17.37

The shadow layer (the original layer) has been offset a couple of pixels, giving light direction and depth to the image.

8. Take down the opacity on the shadow layer if it's too dark. See
   Figure 17.38.

Figure 17.38

The opacity of the shadow layer has been adjusted to lighten the shadow.

9. Crop, flatten, and save the image in the desired format. See
   Figure 17.39.

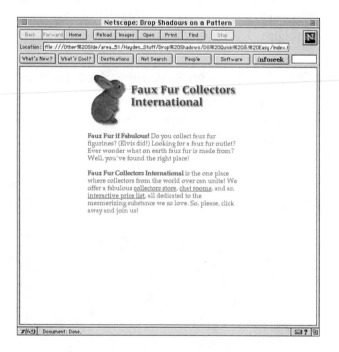

Figure 17.39

The final image, cropped, flattened, and saved as a GIF.

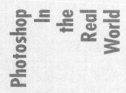

Drop Shadows at the Drop of a Hat

It must be some kind of universal aberration — corporate suits *love* drop shadows. I've been asked to redesign entire sites, adding drop shadows to every element! Although this is hardly an ideal situation, when the big-whigs call for it, it must be done. Fortunately, you can record the steps for "Quick-and-Easy Drop Shadows" into an Action. From there, you can assign it to a function key and create drop shadows for days with nothing more than a couple of button presses. A real time saver! See Chapter 19, "Automating Photoshop with Actions," for more information.

The example presented here assumes a solid-color background is used on the Web page. What if you don't have a solid background? The next section explains…

Creating Drop Shadows on Patterned Backgrounds

Patterns and textures can give added excitement to Web pages. They can also present a nightmare when trying to use drop shadows. The secret is to keep the patterns small and to use transparency wherever possible.

1. Start with a clean file and fill the background layer with the pattern to be used on the Web page. See Figure 17.40.

Figure 17.40

The starting image.

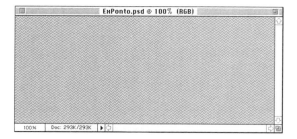

2. Add the elements needing drop shadows to a new layer. See Figure 17.41.

Figure 17.41

Add the elements to be shadowed.

3. Use the Quick-and-Easy method to create the drop shadows, but don't flatten the image yet.

Note

The less diffused and transparent your shadow is, the less noticeable any misalignment with the background is. A dark shadow Gaussian blurred only 1 pixel lines up better than a light shadow Gaussian blurred 5 pixels.

4. Merge the item layer down to the shadow layer. You should now have two layers — the background filled with the pattern and one with the element and its shadow.

5. Choose the Magic Wand, setting the Tolerance to 0 and unchecking Anti-aliased in the Options palette. If Anti-aliased is left on, a nasty halo surrounds the image when it's placed on the Web page.

6. On the combined shadow/element layer, click a transparent area (that is, an empty area of the layer) to select everything but the shadow and the element. See Figure 17.42.

Figure 17.42

The blank area of the shadow/ element layer is selected.

7. Invert the selection and save it to a channel. Drop the selection. See Figure 17.43.

Figure 17.43

The inverted and saved selection. This is used to set the transparency around the element and its shadow, minimizing mismatched patterns on the Web page.

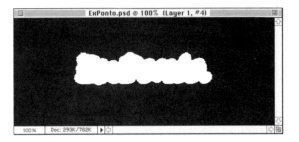

8. Crop, flatten, and change the image to Index mode, using whatever bit depth is appropriate.

9. Save the image as a transparent GIF by using the Export➡ GIF89a Export... function under the File menu. Turn off Interlace. Set Transparency From to the saved channel (#2 in this case). The area around the image is changed to a mid-gray, indicating transparency. Click OK to save the image. See Figure 17.44.

Figure 17.44

Set Transparency From to the selection channel (#2 in this example) and uncheck Interlace.

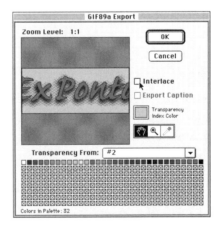

10. Add the graphic to your Web page. Note how the patterns appear to line up. Remember, the smaller the pattern and the less dispersed the shadow is, the better the chances of things lining-up nicely. See Figure 17.45.

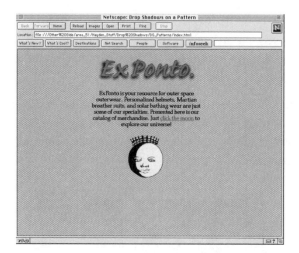

Figure 17.45

The final image on the Web page. The patterns on the page and those in the shadow are lined-up.

Note

When the PNG image format becomes supported by browsers, drop shadows will be much easier to do. PNG supports multiple levels of transparency, unlike GIF, which has only two states (opaque or transparent). With PNG, it will not be necessary to incorporate the background pattern into the image. Instead, the shadow's transparency can be set to enable the background to show through.

CREATING ANIMATED GIFS

An added feature of the GIF89a format is the capability to do simple animation. Animated GIFs enable Web designers to incorporate motion (although, a limited amount) on their pages, helping to break the static monotony. The animations are built by layering frames on top of one another. These frames are in the form of individual GIF files. Photoshop can help with building the frames by taking advantage of the Layers palette. Using multiple layers — each layer representing a frame — it's a simple matter of turning on the right layer to create each frame.

Photoshop alone cannot build the animations — a separate utility is needed for that. Macintosh users should check out GIFBuilder.

Windows users, GIF Construction Set. These utilities put together animations by importing individual GIF frames and layering them. The utilities can control the amount of delay between frames, as well as the number of times an animation repeats.

1. Open the image to be animated, sizing it as needed. In another file or files, place any items that will be moving onto individual layers as shown in Figure 17.46. After the animation is built, resizing isn't an option.

Figure 17.46

A comet moving across the sky is added to this astronaut image. The comet goes on its own layer so it can be moved easily.

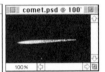

2. Put each element of change on a separate layer in the destination image. Each layer should be offset a couple of pixels to show motion. Kind of like the pages in a flip book. See Figures 17.47 through 17.49.

Figure 17.47

This image shows placement of the first comet on its own layer.

Figure 17.48

The second comet. It's been offset a few pixels to the left of the first comet.

Figure 17.49

Nine comets have been placed in the image, each on its own layer and spread evenly apart.

3. Save the layered file and *make a backup* — you'll be chopping-up the file a lot and don't want to lose all that layer work.

Warning

After building the initial layered Photoshop image, MAKE A BACKUP COPY! If you're as paranoid as I am, lock the backup file, too, so no changes can be made. Building an animation requires that layered files be flattened. I can't count the number of times I didn't make a backup copy and impulsively hit the quick save keys, loosing all of the layered work. Ug!

4. Hide all layers not needed in the first frame of the animation. See Figure 17.50.

Figure 17.50

The nine comets have been hidden because the animation should start with no comet visible.

5. Flatten the image, discarding hidden layers, and convert to Indexed color, using the most appropriate bit depth. Save the file as the first in a series. astro01.gif, for instance.

6. Before closing the first image, save the color palette by going to Image➥Mode➥Color Table. This color table will be applied to all other images associated with this animation. Not using the same color table for each image can result in unpleasant color shifts. See Figure 17.51.

Figure 17.51

The color table for the initial image. This palette will be applied to all images associated with the animation.

7. Re-open the original layer file, showing all layers. Use the rectangular Marquee tool to select only the area of the image that changes (see Figure 17.52). After saving the entire initial frame of the animation, it's no longer necessary to keep parts of the image that do not change — doing so increases the file size. If your selection does not span the entire width of your image, make a note of the coordinates of the upper-left corner, as displayed in the Info palette. You need the numbers for placement when building the animation.

Figure 17.52

The area around the nine comets has been cropped out.

Tip

To keep animation file sizes to a minimum, animate only the section of the image that contains motion. The entire image only needs to be drawn once. This speeds up the animation's download and play time.

8. Crop the selection and save the file. This is the working file for creating the animated frames.

9. Hide all layers except the first one and the background. Flatten the image.

10. Convert the image to Index mode, setting Palette to Custom... and using the palette saved earlier. Or, if you haven't interrupted your session, you can instead set Palette to Previous, which uses the last palette created. Save the image as astro02.gif or whatever sequential naming scheme you've decided on. See Figure 17.53.

Figure 17.53

*Applying the custom palette to
the second frame of the
animation.*

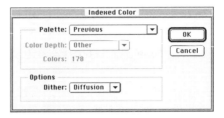

11. Repeat Steps 7 through 10 for each frame/layer of the animation, saving each resulting image as a different GIF image. In
the end, you should have a file list that looks something like
Figure 17.54.

Figure 17.54

*And then there were many!
The numbered files are used to
build the animation.*

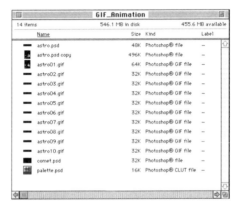

12. Now it's time to build the animation using the third-party
utility.

13. Open the first frame in the utility. The program may default to
a different palette than is used by your image. If the colors look
a little strange, set the utility to use the custom palette created
earlier. See Figure 17.55.

Warning

*When opening an image in a GIF animation utility, check it closely — many
of the animation programs default to a system palette, throwing off the
colors in your image. This is overcome by setting the program to use the
palette saved when the animation's first image was saved in Photoshop.*

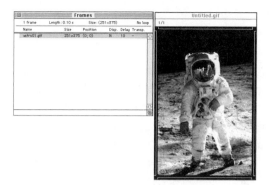

Figure 17.55

The first frame in the animation building utility.

14. Bring in the other frames, positioning them at the coordinates noted when the first image was cropped. See Figure 17.56.

Figure 17.56

All frames have been added to the animation. Note that the delay was increased on the astro01.gif. This causes a pause before the rest of he frames are shown. Each frame can be delayed individually. Also, a never-ending loop was applied so the animation repeats.

15. Save the image. To reference it in a Web page, it's treated just like any other image.

```
<img src="MyGif_Anim.gif" width="xx" height="yy">
```

"MyGif_Anim.gif" is the name of your file, and xx and yy are the width and height of the image. You can find the width and height of the animation in the animation builder utility, next to frame 1 (see Figure 17.56).

You can view the animation by opening the "astro.htm" file in your Web browser.

Note

I have to say something very loudly — MODERATION! That's the word to keep in mind when putting animated GIFs on a Web page. There are many, many Web pages out there filled with animated GIFs. They have buttons changing color, flashing title banners, little envelopes flying into a mailboxes —all at the same time! With that much movement on a page, it's impossible to concentrate on the content! One or two carefully placed, subtle animations are all that is needed to spice up a page. Your viewers will thank you!

SPEEDING UP IMAGEMAP CREATION WITH PHOTOSHOP

The focus of HTML is the ability to link documents to each other through the use of hyperlinks. These links can be accomplished using either text or images. An entire image can be linked to another document using a standard anchor tag. But what if different areas of the image need to lead to different places? The image could be chopped into several smaller images, then reassembled using HTML code with each piece hotlinked to a different locations. That, however, can get messy, especially if there are a lot of links to be made.

Enter, imagemaps.

Imagemaps enable specific areas of an image to be hotlinked to different HTML documents without breaking the image apart. Photoshop won't generate the code for you, but it can give you coordinates to plug into the code.

Note

There are stand alone utilities that can generate imagemap code for you. This is accomplished by using rectangle, circle, and polygon drawing tools to define hotlink areas right on the image. For the Macintosh, WebMap is a fantastic little utility. For Windows, Mapedit. The code they generate can then be copied and pasted into the final HTML document.

Specifying hotlinked areas is done by coordinate pairs. To define a hotlinked rectangle, coordinates for the upper-left and lower-right corners are needed; circles by their center point and radius; and polygons by the coordinates of each of their points.

1. Open the image you want to map.

2. Display the Info palette.

3. Choose the Marquee tool.

4. Position the cross hairs at the upper-left corner of the area to be hotlinked. Make a note of the X and Y coordinates shown in the Info palette. See Figure 17.57.

Figure 17.57

Finding the upper-left corner coordinates of the first rectangle. The coordinates are shown in the lower-left corner of the Info palette.

5. Move the cross hairs to the lower-right corner of the area. Again, make a note of the X and Y coordinates. See Figure 17.58.

Figure 17.58

Finding the lower-right corner coordinates of the first rectangle. Again, the coordinates are shown in the lower-left corner of the Info palette.

6. Repeat Steps 4 and 5 for each area on the image to be hotlinked.

The final code, including the line that displays the image, looks something like this. Each of the HREFs point to a different location — a Web page.

```
<IMG SRC="buttons.jpg"  BORDER=0 USEMAP="#buttons">
<MAP NAME="buttons">
<AREA SHAPE="RECT" COORDS="391,8,462,21"
HREF="mainmenu.html">
<AREA SHAPE="RECT" COORDS="471,8,524,21"
HREF="search.html">
</MAP>
```

Note

There are several standards relating to imagemaps, many of them requiring a common gateway interface script (CGI script) to be running on the Web server machine. The code presented here is for client-side imagemaps — a standard that does NOT require any CGI scripts and is supported by all major Web browsers. Client-side maps are also much easier to implement than other standards are. If asked to generate code for any other type of standard, check with your Webmaster for specifics.

Chapter · · · · · · · · **18**

ACCELERATING
PHOTOSHOP

Using Photoshop efficiently accomplishes two things: You
can perform essential tasks, such as opening large files and
performing complex operations, and you can work quickly
without waiting too long for the computer and Photoshop to
finish processing.

ADDING HARDWARE FOR SPEED

How Photoshop runs on your computer is directly related to the system on which it resides. It is now possible to use a souped-up computer running Windows or the MacOS and perform tasks that a few years ago could only be created on a workstation costing over $150,000.

Working on Computer Speed

A fast computer is a good place to begin to accelerate Photoshop. The processor speed controls how quickly information moves in your computer, and the faster the better. The faster microprocessor chips on the market today are the 604e processors in the Power Macs and the 586 Pentium processors with the MMX chipset in the PCs. These chips are moving at speeds of 200 MHz and faster in the newest computers. Slower computers can be made quicker, depending on the type of computer, by upgrading with a new processor chip, motherboard, or accelerator card.

Understanding RAM (DRAM)

Random Access Memory (RAM) is a critical component to help accelerate Photoshop. While the motherboard of a computer may offer high speeds, it is necessary to use large amounts of RAM to accelerate Photoshop and the computer system.

Consider, for example, a computer system with a clock speed of 150MHz with only 16MB of RAM. This computer is not powerful enough for Photoshop; Photoshop slows the system down or even stops the computer from processing instructions. Photoshop requires 16MB of RAM minimum and it is recommended to have at least 32MB of RAM installed in your computer.

Memory is the area of the computer that handles the instructions from the operating system and the programs. For each application to operate, there is a certain amount of digital information that must be loaded into the RAM. For this reason, each program requires a minimum amount of RAM to run. The bottom line is that Photoshop uses more RAM than most programs, and consequently more RAM accelerates Photoshop.

A number of different types of memory or RAM are in a computer. RAM, made of multiple silicon chips soldered onto a card, temporarily houses digital information. When you turn your computer off, the information contained in your RAM is lost. Compare this with your hard drive, which stores your documents and files in a more permanent fashion.

The most common usage of the term RAM refers to DRAM (Dynamic Random Access Memory, pronounced DeeRAM). DRAM is active, meaning that the information it houses is constantly changing. That is why DRAM is referred to as dynamic. It is DRAM that is meant when talking about adding memory or RAM to computers. Based on the number of elements and its circuit board structure, a DRAM module is either a SIMM (single in-line memory module) or a DIMM (dual in-line memory module).

RAM Size

The size of RAM is measured in megabytes (MB). In a computer a bit is the smallest unit of information. Eight bits equals a byte. Approximately one thousand bytes equals a kilobyte (KB). And approximately one million bytes (one thousand kilobytes) equal a megabyte. RAM is sold as 1, 2, 4, 8, 16, 32, or 64MB units. When buying RAM, you should know what sizes and what combination of sizes are possible for use with your computer.

RAM Speed

RAM speed is measured in nanoseconds (ns). Typically RAM runs at 60, 70, or 80ns. It is important to use the correct speed RAM for your computer. Using RAM that is faster doesn't have adverse affects on performance, but using slower RAM does.

How much RAM does Photoshop get?

Think of how you use Photoshop. What kind of operations do you perform on what size files? With this information you can get an idea of how much RAM you need to keep your computer from writing to your hard drive. Performance plummets if the temp files are written to the hard drive. As a rule of thumb, you want to assign Photoshop three to five times the amount of RAM as the size of your working document. That is because manipulating a file in Photoshop can often produce multiple variations of your original file.

For basic operations you only need a little more than double the file size. If, for example, you apply unsharp masking to a 5MB file, you would be using about 12MB of RAM. Photoshop holds your original document and the altered document in memory. The data from each of those versions have the same number of channels and each takes up 5MB of space. This enables you to undo your last action. The other 2MB is used for the application and the operation instructions.

continues

As your work in Photoshop becomes more complex, the data needs more space. If the operation involves a selection and copy of your whole image, that adds another 5MB temp file for clipboard storage. Now, if you apply a filter and paint onto the image, you may have expanded your memory needs to four times your original file size.

Sometimes a lack of RAM prevents you from working. Certain filters, such as Lighting Effects and Lens Flare, are so number intensive that they don't work if there is not enough RAM.

The motherboard manual or the manufacturer can give you information about the type of RAM your computer uses and how it should be configured. They may say use 70ns 72 pin SIMMs in pairs. It is important that this is exactly what you buy. The wrong RAM or bad RAM can often lead to computer crashes and lost data.

Tip

It is a good idea to stay consistent when you are adding RAM. If the computer is already using 70ns RAM, you can avoid problems by not buying faster RAM. Stick with the 70ns speed for all future additions.

Computer Architecture

The physical makeup of a computer limits the amount of RAM it can support. While 32MB was often the limit on older models, some computers now are capable of expanding to 1GB of RAM. The computer's slot architecture is further limited by the number of SIMM or DIMM slots available. Often there are only four or eight RAM slots on a motherboard. Adding memory takes some planning. Think of your future needs. If you are limited to four slots and you fill them all with 4MB SIMMs, you have 16MB of RAM and no room for future additions. Any expansions must replace rather than add to your RAM. Better planning would be to choose one 16MB SIMM and leave three open slots for the future.

Note

Some computers require that you add RAM two or four chips at a time. When you add RAM you must fill an entire memory bank. Motherboards have banks that need one, two, or four RAM modules. Look at the computer's specs or check with the computer's manufacturer to determine if this is the case. If so, it is important that each pair or set of four be matched. Buy them all at one time. These RAM modules should each have the same manufacturer, configuration, speed, and size.

SIMMs

Make sure that you buy the correct SIMMs for your computer. Although certain SIMMs are more common and others rarely used, there is quite a variety out there and new variations appear every year.

- SIMMs can be either 30 pin or 72 pin architecture. Many computers use the 30 pin modules but 72 pin SIMMs are almost exclusively used in the newer models.

- 30 pin SIMMs can be configured as either 2, 3, 5, 6, 8, or 9 chips to a module and they relay 8 or 9 bits of data to the CPU at one time. These modules are about 3 inches long.

- The 72 pin SIMMs are either parity and relay 36 bits or non-parity and relay 32 bits of digital information at a time. These modules are about 4 inches long.

- FPM (fast page mode) can refer to either parity or non-parity SIMMs.

- EDO (extended data output) is a newer non-parity SIMM that operates 15 percent faster than the FPM SIMMs. The EDO is recommended for Pentium computers running faster than 100 MHz. They are considered the faster 72 pin SIMMs.

Many mail-order businesses specializing in memory are familiar with what RAM matches what computers. It is never a bad idea to get a second opinion, so call two memory specialists and see if they agree. Most reputable dealers guarantee that their RAM works in your computer.

DIMMs

About 5 inches long, DIMMs are the newest advance in RAM modules. 168 pin DIMMs are used in the new generation of Power Macs. 168 pin DIMMs transfer 64 bits of data at one time to the CPU. This makes them, theoretically, two times faster than 72 pin SIMMs for transferring computer instructions and image data in the computer.

Two sets of DIMM modules are used to permit the computer to interleave the chips and transfer 128 bits at a time. This method began with the Power Mac 9500. This increases the performance.

There are also 144 pin DIMMs relaying 64 bits and 72 pin DIMMs relaying 32 bits. These are mostly used in notebooks.

Configuring RAM in Photoshop

RAM is the most important element in accelerating Photoshop. Run the program with as much RAM as you have available, meeting at least the minimum amount of RAM required to open the application. Most RAM responds in 60 or 70 nanoseconds (millionths of a second), and most hard drives take between 7 and 20 milliseconds (thousandths of a second). When the computer runs out of RAM for storage, it starts to use the hard drive, which slows response time. This performance reduction is most evident in the time it takes the computer to redraw screens.

To assign RAM to Photoshop on a Macintosh:

1. Close Photoshop but open all other applications (if any) that you would normally run while Photoshop is open.

2. Choose About This Macintosh from the Apple menu (see Figure 18.1). Note the size of the Largest Unused Block. Subtract 500K from that number for system use. This is the maximum amount of RAM that is available for Photoshop.

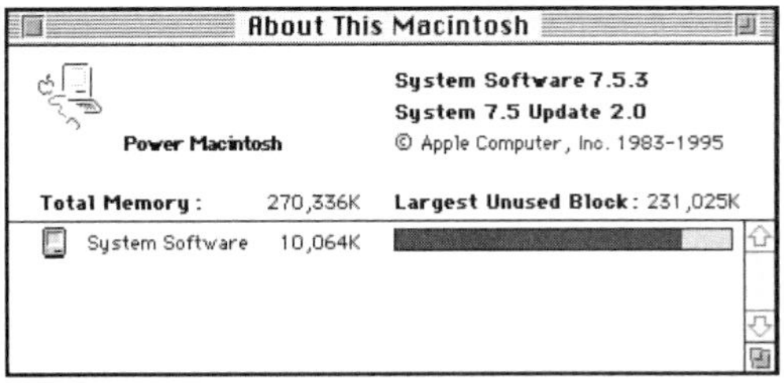

Figure 18.1

The About This Macintosh dialog box.

3. Select the Photoshop program icon and press (Command-I) [Control-I] (see Figure 18.2).

4. Under Memory Requirements in the Preferred size box, add the amount of RAM you want to assign to Photoshop. This number must be as large as the Minimum size box or Photoshop won't open.

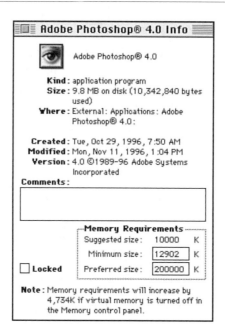

Figure 18.2

Assign RAM to Photoshop through the Adobe Photoshop 4.0 Info dialog box (Macintosh).

To assign RAM to Photoshop on a PC:

1. In Photoshop select File➥Preferences➥Memory & Image Cache. The available RAM is shown in the lower part of the window (see Figure 18.3).

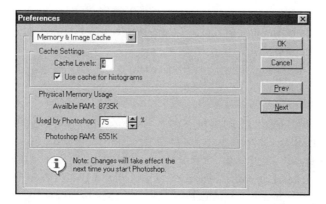

Figure 18.3

Assign RAM to Photoshop through the Preferences dialog box (PC).

2. Adjust the percentage of physical memory usage by Photoshop. If you are not going to open other applications while running Photoshop, you could put the percentage up to 95 or 100 percent.

Setting Virtual Memory for the PC

Windows uses virtual memory (swap file) to swap applications in and out of RAM. This should be set to a minimum of 16MB, but it would be best to set it equal to the amount of RAM installed. These settings have more to do with how RAM acts than how fast it operates. Windows 95 takes care of these settings and you don't have to make any changes.

To set the virtual memory in Windows:

1. Open the 386 Enhanced icon from the Control Panel.

2. Click Virtual Memory.

3. Click Change.

4. From the New Settings Type menu select Permanent.

5. In the New Size box type in the amount of virtual memory and click OK.

Configuring Mac Memory Control Panel

The Memory control panel is an important place to configure performance for your Mac. It is located in the Control Panels folder inside the System Folder (see Figure 18.4). The Memory control panel offers tools that increase performance by using RAM. Photoshop has its own methods of managing files, but the results can be poor when used in conjunction with these memory tools. It is here that you set your disk cache, virtual memory, and RAM disk.

Cache Settings

The disk cache sets aside RAM to store recent information. The assumption is that you are likely to return to that data. If so, you will see a speed improvement when your computer looks to your RAM cache instead of your hard drive. This is not a good use of RAM with Photoshop because Photoshop's file management system causes the cache process to slow down. Disk cache size should be set at the lowest setting, 32K (see Figure 18.4).

Virtual Memory Settings

Turn off Virtual Memory. The interaction of Photoshop's file management system and Virtual Memory causes conflicts because Virtual Memory is a file management system as well. Both file management systems are competing for the same RAM and drive space. With Virtual Memory, the computer uses hard disk space as if it were RAM. This is a way of getting your computer to recognize more RAM than you have. You must set aside part of your hard drive equal to the total memory that you want. The disk space you select includes the amount of RAM in your system. Because your hard drive is acting like RAM, your computer works slower. You also lose some valuable storage space.

RAM Disk

Keep RAM Disk off, as it limits the amount of RAM available to Photoshop (see Figure 18.4). If used, a percentage of your RAM is made available to the RAM Disk, acting as a separate drive. This makes poor use of Photoshop's file management system because it is not the most efficient use of the available RAM. Using RAM Disk, files can be loaded onto the RAM Disk like any hard drive. The data exists in RAM so it can be accessed quickly. RAM Disk is also temporary, and when the computer shuts off, the data is lost.

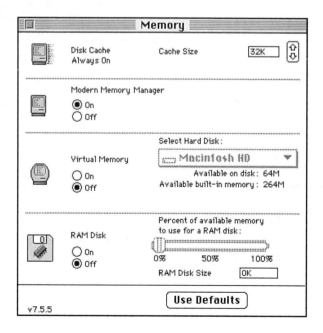

Figure 18.4

The Mac Memory control panel.

Selecting a Scratch Disk for Temporary Files

Photoshop has a file management system that is a type of virtual memory. Open documents are temporary because they are written to available RAM. When the RAM is full, Photoshop places temporary files onto the hard drive and uses it like RAM. As you perform operations, other temp files are created. Because information is written faster to RAM than the hard drive, operations in Photoshop slow down when the temp files start to write to the hard drive.

You must assign a scratch disk in Photoshop preferences. The scratch disk is hard drive space to which Photoshop temporarily saves files it generates while performing operations. When the RAM available is full, Photoshop writes temporary files to the primary scratch disk. And, when the primary is full, the secondary scratch disk, if you have one, is the repository of the temporary files.

To set the scratch disk in Photoshop:

1. In Photoshop select File➡Preferences➡Plug-ins & Scratch Disks (see Figure 18.5 for Mac, Figure 18.6 for PC).

Figure 18.5

Chose a scratch disk for the the Macintosh using the Preferences dialog box.

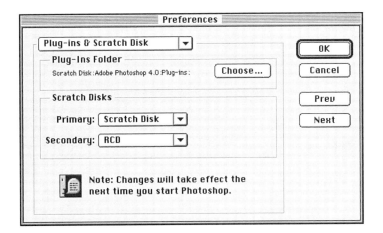

2. Consider space and speed. If you have multiple hard drives, choose your fastest drive as the primary scratch disk. If you have another drive, assign a secondary scratch disk.

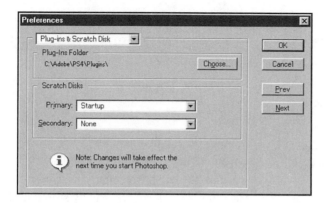

Figure 18.6

Chose a scratch disk for the PC through the Preferences dialog box.

3. Any changes you make do not take effect until the next time that you start Photoshop.

The amount of free space on the scratch disk must equal or exceed the amount of RAM assigned to Photoshop.

Tip

Don't use removable media, such as SyQuest cartridges, as a scratch disk. They are slower than a hard drive. This degrades Photoshop performance.

Cleaning Temporary Files off Your Hard Drive

When you exit Photoshop, the temporary files are deleted from your scratch disk. If a crash occurs or you leave Photoshop without exiting properly, those temporary files remain on your drive taking up valuable storage space. Get rid of those files.

On the Macintosh:

1. The unwanted files are on your scratch disk, but following a crash they are most likely to be found in the Trash after you restart your computer.

Partition Your Hard Drive for a Scratch Disk

If you partition your hard drive and isolate one section as a scratch disk, you can improve Photoshop's performance. This can be experienced both in terms of organization and how the drive responds.

♦ The scratch disk is empty. This means quicker read and write access.

♦ File placement is optimal, meaning files are more accessible.

♦ Photoshop spends less time searching.

continues

- The files are not fragmented.

- You can access a smaller section of a large drive more quickly than you can the whole unpartitioned drive.

- It is easier to find and delete temporary files that remain as a result of crashes.

The downside is that you cannot partition a hard drive without first deleting all the files that it contains.

Understanding Hard Drives

You might need a larger hard drive than you think. Photoshop requires file storage and scratch disk space. It is not uncommon to amass a large number of files while working in Photoshop. To complete one job you may need to store a number of scans, altered images, a layered work file, a flattened RGB version, and a CMYK version. If that job combined five 10MB RGB images, you possibly could end up with 170MB of files. Think of the storage space you require if you are working on multiple jobs. Consider your usage and then buy a larger hard drive than you think you need.

2. Sometimes it is necessary to restart your computer a second time to get your temporary files into the Trash.

3. Empty the Trash.

On the PC:

1. Go to the file manager and look for the unwanted *.tmp files left by Photoshop. The files are on the hard drive that you selected for your scratch disk. They are usually stored in the subdirectory /Temp. Or go to find in the file manager and look for *.tmp.

2. Delete the files when you find them.

Tip

Optimize or defragment your hard drive on a regular basis. This improves system performance and speeds up Photoshop. Writing and deleting files causes the drive to fragment. A hard drive is like an empty bucket. As files are added they are stacked side by side and one on top of the other. When files are removed, they leave gaps of different sizes at various locations throughout the bucket. These gaps are refilled when you add files. If a new file is larger than the available space, it writes part in one gap and finds other empty places to put the rest. This file is fragmented, and its physical placement on the disk may not be optimal. A severely fragmented disk slows down file retrieval and increases the possibility of lost data.

Accelerating Your Monitor

Photoshop is a 24-bit application. To properly view your documents, the screen should be set to 24-bit color. With this setting the screen displays 16.7 million colors. Using a large monitor makes working more accurate and much easier.

Adding VRAM

Increasing your Video RAM (VRAM) may be necessary for your computer to drive a larger size screen and display more colors. The VRAM is added to your video card if there are empty slots available. Not all video cards can support 24-bit color and large screens. You often need 4MB of VRAM to use a 21-inch monitor and get 16.7 million colors.

Accelerator Card Options

Waiting for an operation to finish or the screen to redraw can slow down productivity in Photoshop. Fast display cards and graphic accelerator cards can perform various functions that include faster screen redraws, quicker operations, and improved color accuracy. Some of these boards are quite expensive, up to $2,000. You must weigh the expense of these purchases against your increased productivity. Also, ask yourself where your money is better spent. New motherboard architecture that enables multiprocessing, increased processor speed, and physical changes in buses can make some of these cards obsolete. Faster processors can increase all functions while the DSP (digital signal processor) cards can only increase math intensive ones. Consider whether you will get more benefit from upgrading your processor, your motherboard, or your computer before spending thousands of dollars.

ACCELERATING PHOTOSHOP SOFTWARE

More than one way exists to do most tasks in Photoshop. Copying one image to another for compositing can be accomplished by dragging the selected document onto the other using the Move tool. You can use Duplicate Layer from the Layer menu or

---

Speed relates to the sustained transfer rate of data. This affects how fast files are loaded and saved. In Photoshop, any tasks that are not performed in RAM are written to the scratch disk on your hard drive. The quickness of your storage device affects Photoshop's performance. Drive speed is measured in access time in milliseconds and the throughput in megabytes per second. A fast hard drive needs a bus that can receive the data as fast as it can send it or the speed is wasted.

Photoshop DSP Cards

Digital signal processors (DSPs) are chips with numerous parallel processors that work to speed up math-intensive calculations. The hardware is proprietary and functions as an additional computer for certain operations. Some DSP cards are designed specifically to enhance Photoshop operations. Those DSPs are only effective on intensive, number-crunching functions. That includes a number of filters such as Gaussian Blur, Sharpen, and Emboss. It also includes image adjustments that tend to be slow such as rotate.

continues

Two companies, Adaptive Solutions and Radius, have designed DSP products specifically to accelerate Photoshop for the Macintosh. They have similar prices but offer different features.

- Radius offers the Thunder series graphic acceleration cards. These deliver DSP function acceleration, video acceleration, and improved color accuracy. They also have some graphic accelerators without DSPs and DSP-only boards.

- Adaptive Solutions makes the Powershop DSP accelerator. This product only accelerates with DSP math intensive functions. Powershop DSP does not do any video acceleration, but for what it does, it has been the winner in many reviews and comparisons published in trade magazines.

The utility of DSPs decreases as the speed of the CPUs increase. Fast processor chips can perform the calculations more quickly, so they take back control of the operations. Some DSP boards lose their effectiveness with processors running more than 150MHz, while others can still work

select all and then copy from one and paste to the other. Keyboard commands are available that duplicate actions with the mouse. Speed can usually be accomplished by knowing alternate ways of performing tasks.

Using Quick Edit

Quick Edit lets you open part of a document, perform operations and save that part back into the original file. The file size of the open section is proportionally smaller than the whole so it uses less memory. You can edit an image when you don't have enough RAM to work quickly or at all. The document must be saved as a TIFF to open in Quick Edit.

1. In Photoshop, select File➡Import➡Quick Edit. Open your TIFF file (see Figure 18.7).

2. Make a rectangular selection of the area you want to edit or click the Grid box. The Quick Edit screen divides your photo into grids. You may change the number of rows and columns. The Quick Edit window gives information about the size of the image and below that, the size of each section (see Figure 18.7).

3. Choose a section and click OK to open that part of the file.

4. Edit the image and when you are finished and select File➡Export➡Quick Edit Save. The section saves back to the original file.

Using Selections

Selections reduce the size of the temp files created while working in Photoshop. When you work on a file, Photoshop stores the original image data and the changed image data. You need both copies so that you can undo your changes. Instead of working on the whole image, make a selection of a small part of an image and work within that selection. Say you want to manipulate the eyes in a very large file of a woman's face, for example. Select the eyes and make the adjustments (see Figure 18.8). The image size is already being held in RAM or scratch disk. If the document is 20MB, a full copy takes up another 20MB in RAM or scratch disk. On the other hand, if you contain your changes within a 4MB selection, less of your RAM or scratch disk is used. Photoshop stores the changes in the selection instead of the full image.

productively up to 250MHz. If you don't have the RAM to perform operations in conjunction with a DSP card, the improvement in speed is greatly diminished.

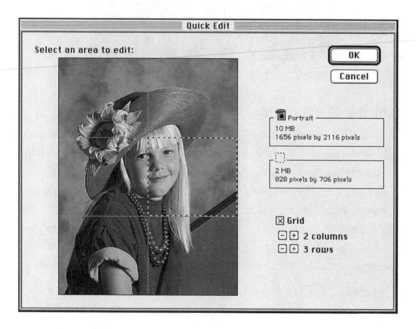

Quick Edit

Select an area to edit:

OK

Cancel

Portrait
10 MB
1656 pixels by 2116 pixels

2 MB
828 pixels by 706 pixels

☒ Grid
⊟⊞ 2 columns
⊟⊞ 3 rows

Figure 18.7

The Quick Edit window.

Figure 18.8

Selecting a small area of the image reduces the size of the temp files created.

Archiving Channels and Layers

Create a library document to store channels and layers that you are finished using but might want to use again. Working in layers, you can generate enormous size files. A 10MB file with 8 layers can become 80MB. This can fill your RAM and slow your productivity. If you merge your layers and delete your selection channels as you finish working with them, your document becomes a more manageable size. Save your discarded layers and channels in a new document before you merge and they are available when you need them in the future.

1. Choose a layer that you plan to merge and select Duplicate Layer... in the Layers palette menu (see Figure 18.9). The Duplicate Layer dialog box opens.

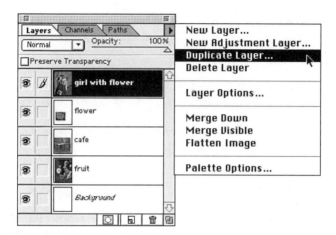

Figure 18.9

The Layers palette menu.

2. Put the name of your new file in the As space (see Figure 18.10).

Figure 18.10

The Duplicate Layer dialog box.

3. Choose New from the pull-down menu in the Destination Document box.

4. Click OK. This creates a new document that can be used as a library to store your layers and channels.

5. Choose the Move tool and drag other layers and channels that you want to store to the new document you created.

6. Save your new file to the hard drive and close it.

7. Merge layers on your original file and delete the selection channels you saved.

8. Keep working on your file and before you merge again, open your library file and drag the layers that you want to save to that file as you did before.

9. When you want to use files from the library, start by opening the library document.

10. Now select the Move tool and drag the layers and channels back to the original file.

Purging the RAM

Select Purge from the Edit menu to clear some of Photoshop's memory (see Figure 18.11). You may delete unwanted data from four different sources and free up RAM.

♦ When you copy a file, Photoshop places that data in the Clipboard. This information stays in memory until you make a new copy.

♦ When you paint with the Airbrush tool, Photoshop keeps your original file stored in RAM.

♦ When you choose Define Pattern from the Edit menu, the pattern is held in RAM.

♦ When you select Take Snapshot from the Edit menu, the snapshot of the selection or the image is kept in RAM.

These are valuable features, but they take up space in your memory. Copy, Undo, and Snapshot can each equal the size of your original file. Now you can remove them from memory when you no longer need the data.

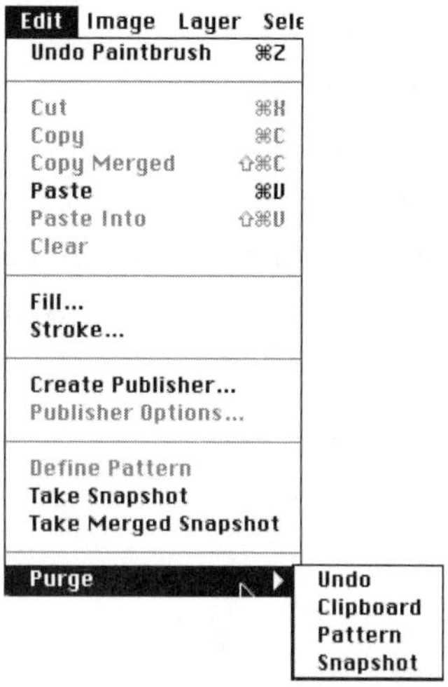

Figure 18.11

The Purge sub-menu.

Playing Repetitive Tasks with Actions

Actions records a series of editing steps that can be replayed and applied to different images or selections within the same image. This script also processes batches of images, a real time saver, and repetitive tasks can be automated and made to run unattended. Actions supports batch-acquiring of images from a digital camera, images that can be adjusted and saved automatically. The scripts are editable and can be reordered with drag-and-drop editing. Actions is also flexible, enabling selected steps to be disabled or displayed for user interaction. For more information about Actions, see Chapter 19, "Automating Photoshop with Actions."

Zooming In and Out with Navigator

The Navigator lets you move quickly to any part of your image by moving and then zooming in and out of a thumbnail of your document. Parts of the thumbnail can be selected with a box and the zoom levels adjusted with a slider control or a numeric field. For more information about the Navigator, see Chapter 7, "Editing Images."

New Faster Architecture

The new version of Photoshop supports symmetric multiprocessing on machines with multiple processors. This works in the Macs and PCs running Windows NT. Photoshop provides an MMX plug-in for the new Intel MMX chipset architecture, which enables 64-bit dual processing on the PC. This speeds up all actions in Photoshop.

Chapter

19

AUTOMATING PHOTOSHOP WITH ACTIONS

Using Photoshop often consists of repeating the same commands, functions, and techniques. So much so that various companies have tried to come up with methods to automate Photoshop. They use clever names such as PhotoMatic and AutoShop, but they always fell short.

Finally, an Actions palette has been included with Photoshop 4.0. While it's not the fully functional and scriptable automation engine that some high-end Photoshop users have dreamed of, the Actions palette's tight integration (and flawless reliability) with Photoshop makes it more than suitable for the majority of automation operations.

THE ACTIONS PALETTE

To become proficient in automating Photoshop you need to become familiar with the Actions palette, the nerve center of Photoshop automation. Actions (automatic sequences of events) are created, edited, and applied from the Actions palette.

Note

The Actions palette is a successor of sorts to Photoshop 3.0's Commands palette, which enabled you to assign one menu option to a button and key command. Unfortunately, command sets saved in version 3.0 can't be loaded into Photoshop 4.0's Actions palette.

Display the Actions palette by selecting Show Actions from the Window menu. Several actions are loaded when you install Photoshop on your computer: RGB to Indexed Color, Reduce Graininess, Drop Shadow (full image), Vignette (full image), Image Size, and Revert. Image Size and Revert are shortcuts to those functions. RGB to Indexed Color and Reduce Graininess are one-button methods for doing multiple-click actions. But Drop Shadow and Vignette are complex actions that do fairly intensive tasks.

Tip

You can also download several actions from Adobe's Web site (http://www.adobe.com).

Figure 19.1

The Actions palette. The checkmark indicates included (active) commands, and the dialog box icon indicates that the action contains a break point.

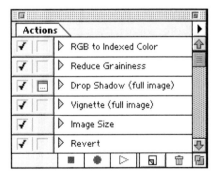

The checkboxes to the left of each action turn on and off the actions. This can be useful if an action's function key conflicts with another function or action. Unchecked actions can't be activated by pressing a function key (or shift-function), by selecting the action and clicking the play button, or by clicking the action while in button view. If you change any command in the action, the checkmark turns red to remind you that it has been customized.

The second column indicates whether or not the specified action stops to display any dialog boxes. When you record an action, you enter settings into dialog boxes to automate that task. If you decide later that you want to run that same action, but use a different setting, you can insert a break point. When you run the action, it stops so you can customize the action. A black dialog box icon appears in the Actions palette if the action contains a break point. If the action has been changed, that break point icon turns red.

A triangle is displayed to the left of each action. Clicking this triangle displays all the commands in the action (see Figure 19.2). Some of the steps in the action may also display a triangle, which can be clicked to display additional steps within that step.

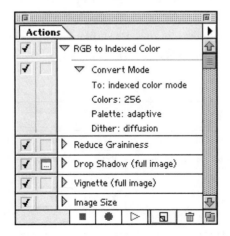

Figure 19.2

An Expanded Action: The convert mode command is the first step in the RGB to Indexed color action.

The bottom row in the Actions palette contains five icons, which are shortcuts for certain actions: Stop, Record, Play, New Action, and

Delete. There is also a pull-down menu accessed by clicking the triangle in the upper right of the Actions palette (see Figure 19.3). Additional commands can be found there.

Figure 19.3

The Actions palette's pull-down menu.

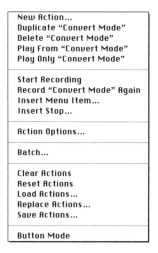

Using Button Mode

At the bottom of the Actions palette menu is an option called Button Mode. This changes the palette from the editable mess of actions and tasks into a simplified version, where only the names of the actions (and their respective F-keys, if any) are shown on large buttons. This makes activating an action as simple as clicking any of the buttons (see Figure 19.4).

Figure 19.4

The Actions palette in Button mode.

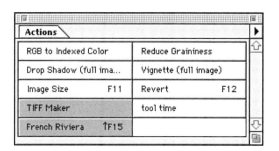

N o t e

You can't edit the Actions palette in Button mode. To return to the list view, select Button Mode from the menu again.

PLAYING ACTIONS

To play any action in the Actions palette, open an image, select the action you want to play, and click the play icon at the bottom of the Actions palette.

For the complex actions, it is important that you don't try to do anything while Photoshop is executing the steps within the action. This can stop the action before it has finished, resulting in something unusable.

Because many actions contain several different steps, you might not be able to undo an entire action. Photoshop is still limited to 1 undo, so only the last thing done to the image can be undone.

As a safety measure, you might want to save a copy of your Photoshop document *before* you run an action on it, just in case something happens that you didn't intend. This is especially true for actions that include Save commands.

Note

You can learn what an action does and exactly what is happening by clicking the triangle to show all the steps in that action (and resizing the Actions palette if necessary), and then playing that action. As each step is played, it is highlighted in the Actions palette.

INSPECTING THE DEFAULT ACTIONS

Photoshop 4.0 comes with a collection of default actions for commonly performed tasks. The following images show some of the default actions and the before and after image when applying each action.

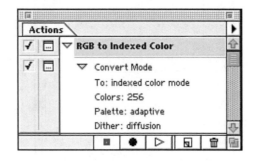

Figure 19.5

The RGB to Indexed Color action.

Figure 19.6

The Reduce Graininess action.

Figure 19.7

The Drop Shadow action.

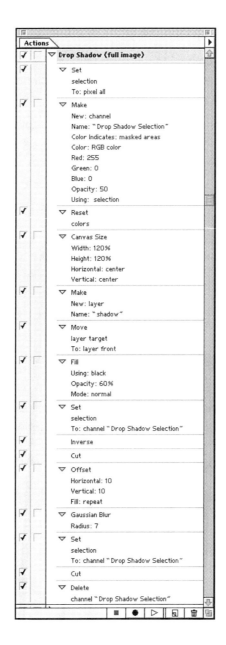

Figure 19.8

The Vignette action.

CREATING NEW ACTIONS

Adobe has gone to great pains to ensure that creating actions is almost as easy as playing them. This is readily apparent in the most common of creation methods, the "watch and learn" method. To have Photoshop create a new action by watching your actions, do the following:

1. Click the New Action button on the Actions palette

2. Name the action in the New Action dialog box (see Figure 19.9). You can select a color for the action's button to appear in (when the Actions palette is in button mode) and also a corresponding F-key that activates the action.

Figure 19.9

The New Action dialog box.

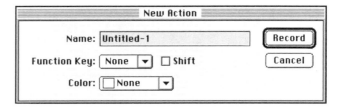

3. Click Record.

4. Perform the functions you want to automate. See the sidebar "Things You Can't Record with Actions" for information about commands that cannot be recorded.

5. Click the Stop button.

Your new action is created! To play it, highlight the action in the palette and click the Play button.

Tip

When setting up your action, it's a good idea to work with a copy of your image, especially if your action calls for any save functions.

EDITING EXISTING ACTIONS

You can tweak any action that's already been created by adding tasks, removing tasks, and changing the functionality of existing tasks within an action. You can also insert menu commands and stops within any action.

Before mucking about with an action that works correctly, you might want to make a duplicate of that action.

Duplicating Actions

1. To duplicate an existing action, select that action in the Actions palette.

2. Choose Duplicate "Name of Action."

You can also duplicate an Action by (Option-dragging)[Alt-dragging] it to the New Action icon at the bottom of the Actions palette. The duplicate has the same name as the original action, with the word "copy" after it.

Deleting Actions

1. To remove a task from the Actions palette, first select the task.

2. Click the trash can (delete) icon at the bottom of the Actions palette. A message appears asking you to confirm that you want to delete the task (see Figure 19.10).

3. Click OK.

If you wish to delete a task without seeing the confirmation dialog box, press (Option)[Alt] as you drag the task into the trash.

Things You Can't Record with Actions

None of the tool activities can be recorded. This includes switching between tools, changing tool options, and using tools within an image. Although this is a serious limitation, you can force an action to stop until you've done something that can't be recorded, and then click Play to continue (see the section on editing below).

Many of the other options that affect the way Photoshop behaves, but don't necessarily affect the file, can't be recorded either. Changing zoom levels, for instance, isn't an action that can be recorded. Nor are preference changes. You can access these dialog boxes by inserting a menu command (any item listed in one of Photoshop's menus) within an existing action; this is discussed below in the editing section.

Third-party filters such as Extensis PhotoTools, Intellihance, and Kai's Power Tools can be accessed, but none of the settings you use within those dialog boxes can be recorded. Instead, the dialog box appears when that task within the Action plays.

You can only do functions provided within Photoshop; activities within other applications are not supported.

Figure 19.10

The confirmation dialog box.

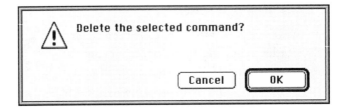

Adding Tasks to Actions

To add a task to an action:

1. Click the task *above* where you want the new task to be added.

2. Click the Record button.

3. Perform the tasks(s) you want to add to the action.

4. Click the Stop button.

Adding Stops to Actions

Stops can also be added within an existing action. A "stop" is a resting place for the action, so that you can do another type of activity, such as make a selection with a tool, sample a color with the Eyedropper, or sample an area with the Rubber Stamp tool.

To create a stop in an Action:

1. Click the task *above* where you want the stop to be added.

2. Select Insert Stop... from the Actions pop-up menu.

   Refer to the earlier section, "Things You Can't Record with Actions," for some ideas on when to use Stops.

3. In the dialog box that appears, enter the message you want to present at the time of the stop. These messages help remind you what you need to do during the stop. It is essential that your message be clear and understandable if anyone else uses this action besides yourself. Only check the Allow Continue checkbox (which is off by default) if you want to display a message; no activities can take place while the dialog box is up (see Figure 19.12).

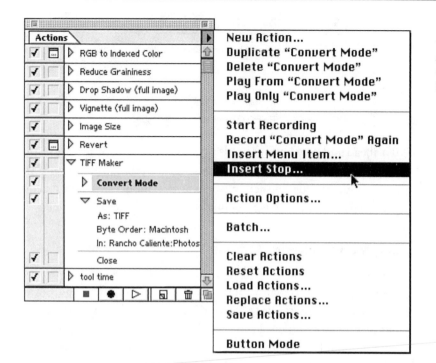

Figure 19.11

Adding a Stop within an action is done through the Actions pallette menu.

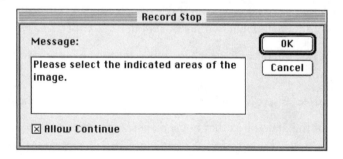

Figure 19.12

The dialog box that appears after selecting "Insert Stop..."

4. Click the OK button. The new stop is inserted within the action.

When an action reaches a stop, a dialog box appears with the message in it that you typed. Click the Stop button (see Figure 19.13).

Figure 19.13

A typical Stop message.

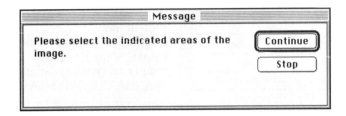

Go ahead and do whatever needs to be done, then click the Play button on the palette. The action continues from the point of the stop. If you are in button mode, the action's button containing the stopped action is colored bright red. Clicking that button continues the action.

Adding Menu Items to Actions

You can add any menu item to an action. This is useful for when you want to enter a different value in a dialog box each time you run the action. You might, for instance, want to rotate a selection in the action, but in some cases the rotation would be 90 degrees clockwise, other times it would be 90 degrees counterclockwise. The menu item, when inserted within the action, displays the Rotate dialog box at the point you define so you can pick the angle of rotation when the action needs it. To add a menu item within an action:

1. Click the task *above* where you want the menu item to be added.

2. Select Insert Menu Item... from the Actions pop-up menu.

3. In the dialog box that appears, enter the name of the menu item you want to access (see Figure 19.14). Instead of typing, it is often much easier to just go to the menu where the effect is located and select the menu item. The name is entered in the text field.

4. Click the OK button. The new menu item is inserted within the action.

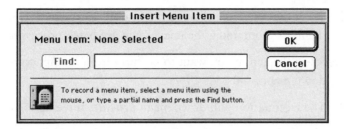

Figure 19.14

The Insert Menu Item dialog box.

This function is quite useful for inserting commands that can't be recorded, such as viewing functions, preference changes, and showing or hiding palettes. A snazzy effect to incorporate into a complex action is to display the Actions palette at the beginning of the action so you can watch it step through the actions by inserting a Show Actions Palette menu command, and then to hide it following the action by inserting a Hide Actions Palette command, all automatically.

BATCH PROCESSING

The Actions palette also provides a means for "batch processing" Photoshop files. Batch Processing means that one action can be used on an entire folder full of images, all with one keystroke. Place all the files to be batch processed in one folder and do the following steps:

1. Choose the Batch command from the Actions palette submenu. The Batch dialog box appears (see Figure 19.15).

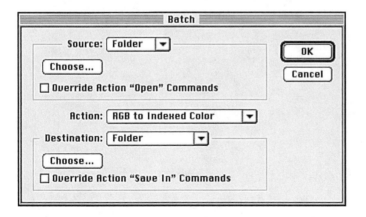

Figure 19.15

The Batch dialog box.

2. Select the source by clicking the Choose button and selecting the folder containing the images you are batch processing.

3. Select the action you want to perform from the Action pull-down menu.

4. The Destination pull-down menu provides three options:

   None—Leaves the affected files open and unsaved (unless a Save or Close was specified within the action).

   Save and Close—Saves and closes the file automatically.

   Folder—Lets you save the modified files to another folder.

5. Click the OK button, and the files are batch-processed!

Note

You can include batch processes in actions, so that you can apply several actions in a batch process with the click of a button.

Chapter 20

THIRD-PARTY PLUG-INS

Photoshop was the first program to popularize the use of plug-ins, add-on software that provides additional features within an application. Although Adobe provides dozens of plug-ins with Photoshop, third-party developers have created even more, offering features ranging from the obvious ("Why didn't Adobe include this?") to the obscure ("Who uses this?"). This chapter is intended to give an idea of the breadth of plug-ins available for Photoshop; it's not a complete listing, and some categorizations are rather arbitrary because many plug-ins are bundled in groups, each plug-in having a different function.

For more information about how to contact each plug-in vendor, please see Appendix B, "Photoshop Plug-In Vendors."

You can order from a wide-ranging collection of plug-ins for Photoshop and other Adobe programs at Adobe's Plug-In Source (http://www.pluginsource.com/).

Note

Many Photoshop plug-ins work with other programs, too. PageMaker and Illustrator support some plug-ins, letting you make image adjustments and apply filters without starting up Photoshop, as do paint programs such as Fractal Design Painter and ColorIt!. When you install programs that support Photoshop plug-ins, you're usually asked to locate the plug-in folder (or directory) within your Photoshop folder; this tells the other program where to look for plug-ins.

Commercial software developers aren't the only ones who create plug-ins; many freeware and shareware developers also release useful plug-ins, some near-professional quality. BoxTop Software, a commercial developer, maintains an archive of plug-ins for both Mac and PC users at http://www.boxtopsoft.com/plugpage, and more are available on online services and at other Web sites. As always, remember to pay your shareware fee if you come upon a plug-in you find useful.

One of the things you find at the BoxTop PlugPage is Plug-In Manager, a Mac shareware program that lets you enable and disable sets of plug-ins for any program that uses them, including Photoshop, Adobe Illustrator, QuarkXPress, Aldus PageMaker, Canvas, and Microsoft Word. Like Extensions Manager, Plug-In Manager lets you save sets of plug-ins for specific tasks, so you can load only the plug-ins you need (see Figure 20.1). This speeds up Photoshop's launch time and helps you keep from running out of RAM.

Tip

To find out what plug-ins you have installed and view additional information about them, such as their version numbers and creators, choose a plug-in from the About Plug-ins submenu of the Apple menu (Mac users) or select About Plug-In from the Help menu (Windows users). See Figure 20.2 for a sample of plug-in info.

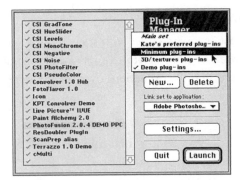

Figure 20.1

Plug-In Manager lets you load only the plug-ins you need for a given Photoshop session.

Figure 20.2

This splash screen provides information about Live Picture IVUE, a plug-in by Total Integration, Inc.

Note

We can't list prices here because we can't guarantee they won't change. We've included this coding system to give you a general idea of how much the package may cost.

$	under $50
$$	$50-$99
$$$	$100-$199
$$$$	$200-$500
$$$$$	over $500

ACQUIRING IMAGES

Although most scanners come with their own scanning software—usually a Photoshop plug-in—third-party scanning plug-ins may offer more control (or more automation) over the scanning process.

ScanTastic

ScanTastic works as a Photoshop acquire module or as a standalone application. It enables you to define sets of scanning parameters based on image type and intended output device; sets of parameters are available via a toolbar. Versions for Apple, Epson, and HP scanners are available.

Second Glance Software

http://www.secondglance.com

Platform: Macintosh (fat)

System requirements (Mac): System 7.01 or later

$$

IMPORTING AND EXPORTING IMAGES

Although Photoshop can import and export an impressive variety of file formats, there are still more it can't handle, such as proprietary formats used by medical imaging scanners. Other formats that Photoshop *can* handle include features not recognized by Photoshop; for these, there are third-party import and export filters that better utilize special features. Particularly useful in this group are plug-ins that offer precision control over GIF and JPEG color palettes, transparency, and interleaving for Web images.

AccuPress

AccuPress uses wavelet technology to provide high-quality compression at high ratios for 24-bit color and 8-bit grayscale images. A user-selectable compression ratio from 4:1 to 150:1 enables users to achieve high compression ratios while maintaining image quality.

Aware, Inc.

http://www.aware.com

Platform: Windows 3.1, Unix

System requirements (PC): Windows 3.1 or higher

System requirements (Unix): Sun OS 4.1.3 or higher, IRIX 4.0 or higher

$$$$

CD-Q Acquire

CD-Q Acquire expands the capabilities of Photoshop's included PhotoCD import plug-in; extracts and converts PhotoCD images into grayscale, RGB, or CMYK color separations; and offers GCR, UCR, color correction, cropping, rotation, and blending on the fly. (See Figure 20.3.)

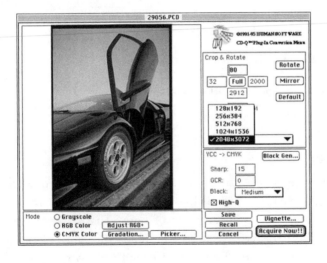

Figure 20.3

CD-Q Acquire lets you process PhotoCD images as you import them, applying color correction and filters like sharpening.

Human Software Company

http://www.humansoftware.com

Platform: Macintosh (fat)

System requirements (Mac): FPU

$$

Channel24

Photoshop's native file formats accommodate no more than four color channels (relegating all other channels to the status of alpha, or mask, channels). So images with extra color channels, such as those using spot colors or those destined to be printed in Hi-Fi color (which uses green and orange inks in addition to cyan, magenta, yellow, and black) can't ordinarily be opened and color-corrected in Photoshop. That's where Channel24 comes in. Channel24 lets users import and export multi-channel images, enabling manipulation of images that have more than four channels directly within Photoshop (see Figure 20.4.).

Figure 20.4

Channel24 lets you open images with multiple channels and assign colors to each channel.

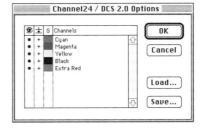

Visu Technologies

`http://www.vgm-visu.nl/visu/visu2.html`

Platform: Power Macintosh

Epilogue

Some images need to be created in Photoshop, others work best in drawing packages such as Illustrator and FreeHand—and others can best be created using features of both. That's where Photoshop's capability to rasterize vector EPS files comes in handy—it can turn them from stroke-and-fill PostScript data into bitmap pixels. A Level 2 PostScript rasterizer, Epilogue improves on the capabilities of Photoshop's native EPS rasterizer; it reads any PostScript file (as opposed to the native rasterizer, which only reads Illustrator files). Epilogue offers three levels of anti-aliasing (medium, high, and extra high), as opposed to Photoshop's one, and it lets you preview, crop, and select an area of an EPS or PostScript file to interpret (see Figure 20.5).

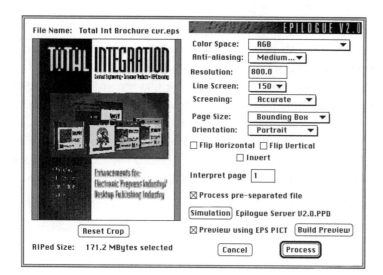

Figure 20.5

Epilogue offers much more powerful EPS rasterization than Photoshop's built-in EPS rasterizer.

Total Integration, Inc.

http://www.totalint.com

Platform: Macintosh

System requirements (Mac): System 7.1 or later

$$$$$

FASTedit/IVUE

FASTedit/IVUE enables Photoshop to acquire and export IVUE files and use Live Picture filters and effects from within Photoshop by previewing, selecting, and manipulating selections.

Total Integration, Inc.

http://www.totalint.com

Platform: Macintosh

System requirements (Mac): System 7.1 or later

$$

Genuine Fractals

Genuine Fractals encodes continuous-tone color images as scalable equations that can be rendered at any resolution with visually lossless results. Encoded high-resolution color files are small enough to transmit via telecommunications lines. Photographers, artists, and designers can start with an original image between 15MB and 25MB, compress it to 2–5MB, then print it at sizes greater than 450MB without compromising quality. Web designers can encode screen-resolution images to between 10KB and 150KB for quick display on the web.

Altamira Group, Inc.

http://www.altamira-group.com

Platform: Power Macintosh, Windows 95, Windows NT

$$$

Handshake/LW

Handshake/LW reads and writes files in Handshake linework (LW) format, which is used by Scitex systems. It also lets users edit, change color areas, and otherwise edit Handshake images in Photoshop and return the files to Scitex systems in Handshake/LW format. (See Figure 20.6.)

Figure 20.6

Using Handshake/LW, you can import linework files from Scitex systems.

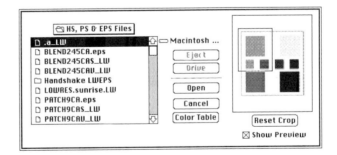

Total Integration, Inc.

http://www.totalint.com

Platform: Macintosh 68K, Power Macintosh

System requirements (Mac): System 7.1 or later

$$$$

HVS PhotoGIF

Offers advanced options for exporting GIF files, including extensive support for color palette reduction, alpha channels, and animated GIFs.

BoxTop Software

`http://www.boxtopsoft.com`

Platform: Macintosh (fat)

$

HVS ProJPEG

ProJPEG goes beyond the capability of Photoshop's built-in JPEG export by offering a live preview of the effects of the JPEG compression on your image—you choose a compression level and the preview is instantly updated to show any artifacts or other deterioration that occurs if the image is saved at that compression level. The plug-in also offers new mathematical algorithms that improve compression rates and image quality—ProJPEG files can be 2–5 times smaller than Photoshop's normal JPEGs, with similar image quality. The ability to save and load settings means you can easily apply the same compression rates to multiple images, saving time. (See Figure 20.7.)

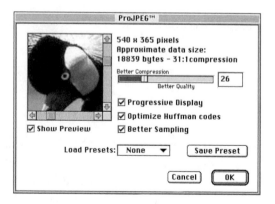

Figure 20.7

ProJPEG's dynamic preview window shows the results (in terms of image quality) of different compression ratios.

BoxTop Software

`http://www.boxtopsoft.com`

Platform: Macintosh (fat)

$

HVS WebFocus

A combination and expansion of HVS PhotoGIF and HVS ProJPEG, WebFocus enables users to create interlaced, transparent, and animated GIFs; export progressive JPEGs; and reduce image colors using adaptive or fixed palettes.

Digital Frontiers

http://www.digfrontiers.com/products.html

Platform: Macintosh (fat)

System requirements (Mac): System 7.0 or later

$$$

ImportAccess

This plug-in imports images created by radiology, nuclear medicine, and other scientific imaging systems into Photoshop; ImportAccess reads formats used by medical scanners and other applications, including the National Institutes of Health's NIH-Image application. Users can customize the filter to read images from their own scanning systems.

DesAcc

http://www.desacc.com

Platform: Macintosh

$$$$$

IrisFEP FeD

IrisFEP FeD acquires and exports Iris CMYK FEP (Front End Processor) image files. It also enables direct access to the Iris FEP by adding an Ethernet card or removable media drive to the FEP. Files that are downloaded can be pulled back into Photoshop for further manipulation.

Total Integration, Inc.

http://www.totalint.com

Platform: Macintosh 68K, Windows 3.1, Power Macintosh

System requirements (Mac): System 7.1 or later

$$$

PhotoCD Acquire Module

This plug-in enables users to import PhotoCD images into Photoshop. Users can select one of the six PhotoCD resolutions, crop the image, and adjust brightness, saturation, and color balance before opening the image. Provides 21 different conversion metrics for importing YCC color information, the color mode used by the PhotoCD format.

Eastman Kodak Co.

http://www.kodak.com

Platform: Macintosh 68K, Windows 3.1, Power Macintosh, Windows 95

System requirements (Mac): System 6.0.5 or later

IMPROVING YOUR PRODUCTIVITY

Although Photoshop is powerful, it's not always quick and easy to use. These plug-ins are designed to simplify your work in Photoshop; some offer such tools as macros and batch processing, while others make it easier to get to the commands and processes you use most.

Batch It!

Batch It! provides batch processing for Photoshop, enabling you to process all of your image files at one time. Tasks are represented by "tiles" that can be applied to image batches with simple drag-and-drop operations. More than 30 tiles are included that perform tasks such as cropping, adjusting colors, or activating Photoshop filters.

Gryphon Software Corp.

http://www.gryphonsw.com

Platform: Macintosh

$$$

FASTedit/Deluxe

FASTedit/Deluxe enables users to preview a file and edit one or more layers, portions of layers, or sections of images without opening the entire file. Because users are working with a much smaller file loaded entirely into RAM, changes can be made much faster. This plug-in is similar to the native QuickEdit feature, but it supports layers and more file formats, including Photoshop 2.5 and later, TIFF, EPS, Scitex CT, and DCS.

Total Integration, Inc.

http://www.totalint.com

Platform: Macintosh 68K, Power Macintosh

System requirements (Mac): System 7.1 or later

$$$$

FBI Writer

FBI Writer embeds an invisible, secure, and unique identifier or fingerprint within image data that remains in place after the file has been opened, edited, or copied. You can run the free FBI Detector on any image you suspect of unauthorized use to check for an identifying fingerprint.

HighWater Designs Ltd.

http://www.highwater.com

Platform: Macintosh (fat)

System requirements (Mac): System 7.0 or later

Priced per use

PhotoMatic

Free plug-in that adds a Record menu to Photoshop so users can record macro sequences. Macros are accessible from a menu; they can also be saved as stand-alone AppleScript files that can be edited with Apple's Script Editor. Also includes batch processing. Requires AppleScript.

DayStar Digital, Inc.

http://www.daystar.com

Platform: Macintosh (fat)

System requirements (Mac): System 7.5

PhotoTools

PhotoTools is a collection of eight tools including PhotoText (improved text formatting capabilities), PhotoBars (customizable toolbar that provides single-click access to menu commands), PhotoBevel, PhotoEmboss, PhotoGlow, PhotoShadow, PhotoTips (tips and expert advice from Photoshop guru Deke McClelland), and Intellihance Lite. From the makers of PageTools and QX-Tools (for PageMaker and QuarkXPress, respectively). (See Figure 20.8.)

Figure 20.8

This screen shows two PhotoTools modules— PhotoGlow, which applies a glowing halo to a selection, and PhotoBar, which adds custom toolbars to the edge of your screen.

Extensis Corp.

http://www.extensis.com

Platform: Macintosh (fat)

System requirements (Mac): System 7.1.1 or later

$$$

PROCESSING IMAGES

Even if you're not planning major changes to an image, chances are you want to fine-tune its appearance in Photoshop—sharpen it, smooth it down, brighten it, darken it, or whatever's needed to optimize its appearance. These plug-ins let you work efficiently with the colors and tones in an image, and they can help with output by providing pre-separated images or optimizing images for output on a particular device. Other plug-ins in this group help with masking and compositing (combining multiple images to create a composite image).

AutoMask

With AutoMask users can generate a mask around a subject using sophisticated density masking controls. This plug-in also drops out backgrounds; creates clipping paths; simplifies creation of drop shadows; and works in both RGB and CMYK. (See Figure 20.9.)

Figure 20.9

AutoMask lets you define masks based on the density of pixels in an image, and it can automatically create clipping paths from masks.

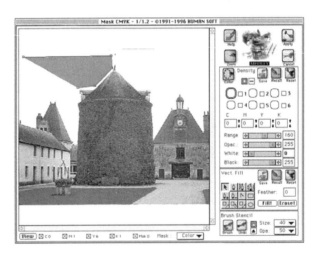

Human Software Company

http://www.humansoftware.com

Platform: Macintosh (fat)

System requirements (Mac): FPU

$$

Chromassage

Chromassage enables color table manipulation, palette rotations (alter hues according to their spectrum order), and color "injection" into 24-bit space. Chromassage provides an interactive preview of the image as it is being modified. It also displays current and modified color palettes and features sliders and an "injector" that adds a user-definable amount of color to an image.

Second Glance Software

http://www.secondglance.com

Platform: Macintosh

Chromatica

Chromatica consists of four tools that help in masking and replacing colors. ChromaMask selects objects with an intelligent magic wand, EdgeWizard blends edges in one step, ChromaPalette creates spectacular color effects, and ChromaColor changes or replaces colors while retaining image detail. (See Figure 20.10.)

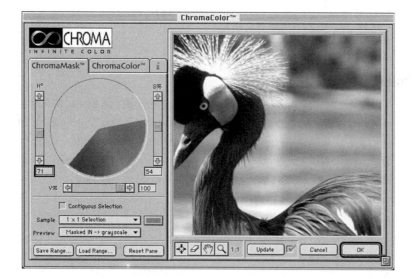

Figure 20.10

With ChromaColor, you can select and alter ranges of color in an image.

Chroma Graphics

http://www.chromagraphics.com

Platform: Macintosh (fat), Windows 95, (available March 1997 not included on *Photoshop 4 Complete* CD-ROM)

System requirements (Mac): System 7.1 or higher

System requirements (PC): 486 or higher

$$$

CoCo

There are two parts to CoCo: MC-P/CoCo and CoCo Multipoint. MC-P/CoCo is a color correction tool that enables corrections to be performed on images consisting of more than four channels. CoCo Multipoint enables you to correct up to sixteen colors in an RGB or CMYK image via one filter. In addition, the range function gives full control over the scope of colors to be corrected.

Visu Technologies

http://www.vgm-visu.nl/visu/visu2.html

Platform: Power Macintosh

ColorSynergy

This plug-in enables the creation of device profiles to be used in any of several color management systems; supports formats including International Color Consortium (ICC) compatible files for Apple ColorSync, Photoshop color separation tables, and PostScript Level 2 color rendering dictionaries (CRD). ColorSynergy can also be used to generate custom profiles.

Candela, Ltd.

http://www.candelacolor.com

Platform: Macintosh (fat)

System requirements (Mac): System 7.1 or later

$$$$$

ColorMatrix

ColorMatrix enables manipulation of images' color palettes using more than 90 included color tables. You can also swap separation plates, create black-and-white or duotone images from color images, enhance video images, reverse UCR/GCR to RGB devices, or create additional color plates or HiFi color separations. ColorMatrix works with both CMYK and RGB files. (See Figure 20.11.)

	Cyan	Mag	Yellow	Black
Cyan	0.10	0.29	0.52	0.65
Magenta	0.06	0.19	0.39	0.53
Yellow	0.06	0.20	0.38	0.51
Black	0.00	0.01	0.20	1.00

Active Table: Color to HQ B/W.CMYK

Description: Changes Color CMYK images to High Quality 4-color CMYK Black and White.

OK
Cancel
Load...
Save...
Reset

Figure 20.11

These ColorMatrix settings convert a color image to a four-color black-and-white image, which will have a very rich appearance.

Total Integration, Inc.

http://www.totalint.com

Platform: Macintosh

$$$$

HVS Color

HVS Color lets you convert 24-bit images to 8-bit color with little or no visible reduction of quality, producing much smaller files. This plug-in uses a patented algorithm that models the way the human visual system perceives and masks colors, enabling realistic photograph images to be saved in GIF format with as much as 70% greater compression.

Digital Frontiers

http://www.digfrontiers.com

Platform: Macintosh (fat), Windows 95

System requirements (Mac): System 7.0 or later

System requirements (PC): Windows 95 or NT

$$

Intellihance

For quick touch-ups to images, Intellihance provides automatic image enhancement, performing up to five image adjustment functions with one mouse click. Intellihance adjusts image contrast, brightness, saturation, and sharpness, as well as despeckling. A side-by-side preview shows before and after versions of the image; preferences let you determine how much or how little Intellihance will do to any image.

Extensis Corporation

http://www.extensis.com

Platform: Macintosh (fat), Windows 95, Windows 3.1

System requirements (Mac): System 7.1 or later

System requirements (PC): 386 or greater

$$$

Kwick Mask, Create B/W, Rotate Color

These shareware plug-ins, by Hugh Kawahara, perform a number of helpful tasks: Create B/W lets you control the way Photoshop mixes the RGB color channels to create a gray-scale composite that reproduces optimally on a black-and-white printer. Rotate Color changes image hues without producing artifacts, which can result from Photoshop's own Hue/Saturation command. Kwick Mask replaces Photoshop's Color Range command (which lets you create a selection based on image colors), adding much more precise controls.

Hugh Kawahara

http://www-leland.stanford.edu/~kawahara/photoshop.html

Platform: Macintosh (fat)

Charity-ware (author requests that you make a donation to charity if you use these plug-ins)

LaserSeps Pro

Exports CMYK-separated images without using halftone screens, thus reducing potential problems such as moiré patterns. Because separations are rendered in Photoshop, you can edit them before outputting them.

Second Glance Software

http://www.secondglance.com

Platform: Macintosh (fat)

System requirements (Mac): System 7.01 or later

$$$$$

Medley

Speeds the creation of composite images by rendering the assembled large RGB or CMYK images in one step at the end, enabling quick previewing of complex compositing and masking. (See Figure 20.12.)

Figure 20.12

Medley lets you quickly apply sophisticated compositing effects to images composed of several elements.

Human Software Company

http://www.humansoftware.com

Platform: Power Macintosh, Macintosh 68K

System requirements (Mac): System 7.1 or higher

$$$

PhotoFusion

PhotoFusion is an acquire module for creating naturalistic blue-screen image compositing, a video technique for substituting different backgrounds behind a foreground image. This plug-in automatically composites foreground and background images and generates a linear mask that maintains all the foreground detail.

Ultimatte Corporation

http://www.ultimatte.com

Platform: Macintosh 68K, Power Macintosh

PhotoLab

Based on traditional photographic color correction principles, CSI PhotoLab consists of eight filters controlling and manipulating exposure, contrast, color, and color casts. In particular, CIS PhotoLab enables accurate reproduction of traditional gel and lens filter effects, inversion of scanned color negatives, image colorization, and simulation of film grain. (See Figure 20.13.)

Figure 20.13

CSI Noise, which applies noise based on colors in an image, is one of the modules of PhotoLab.

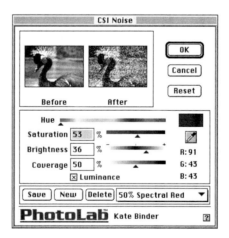

Cytopia Software, Inc.

http://www.cytopia.com

Platform: Macintosh (fat)

System requirements (Mac): System 7.0 or greater

$$$

PhotoSpot

PhotoSpot produces spot-color separations, exporting color-separated image files that can be output from Photoshop or imported into other programs. The package includes three color-reduction filters: Acetone, PaintThinner, and Turpentine.

Second Glance Software

http://www.secondglance.com

Platform: Macintosh (fat)

System requirements (Mac): System 7.01 or later

$$$$

PlateMaker

PlateMaker creates spot, custom, and HiFi color separations, as well as separate printing plates for varnishes, bumps, foil stamping, and other effects. This plug-ing also supports clipping paths, single or multiple Postscript files, low- or high-resolution composites, and previews, and lets you specify all screening information.

A Lowly Apprentice Production, Inc.

http://www.alap.com

Platform: Macintosh

$$$$

ScanPrepPro

This third-party plug-in automates image processing from initial scan to final output. It also uses an internal database of lithographic information to prepare images and files for commercial printing by automatically configuring the correct resolution, image size, dot gain, and tonal range. (See Figure 20.14.)

Figure 20.14

ScanPrepPro even warns you about possible copyright violations if you tell it you're scanning a previously printed image.

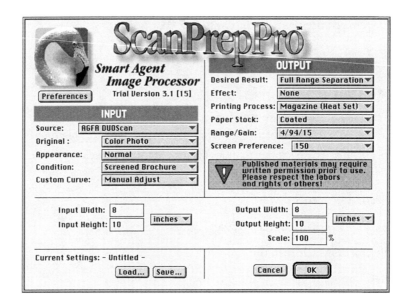

ImageXpress, Inc.

http://www.scanprep.com

Platform: Macintosh (fat)

System requirements (Mac): System 7.5

$$$$$

Select

Select enables you to perform selective color changes on up to six specific colors. You select and adjust specific colors without affecting other color densities and without masking. It can also use a CMYK gradation for global color correction, providing smooth cast removal. (See Figure 20.15.)

Human Software Company

http://www.humansoftware.com

Platform: Power Macintosh

System requirements (Mac): System 7.1 or higher

$$$

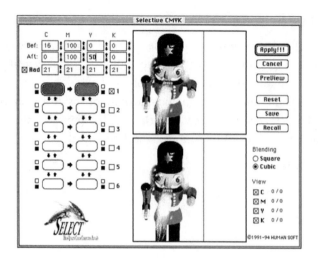

Figure 20.15

Change up to six colors in an image in one operation using Select.

Swap

Swap lets you combine colors much as you would on a high-end prepress workstation such as a Scitex system. With Swap, you manipulate a matrix of color percentages to multiply, add, subtract, or combine any colors or plates. This plug-in also lets you create casts and ghosted images quickly.

Human Software Company

http://www.humansoftware.com

Platform: Power Macintosh, Macintosh 68K.

System requirements (Mac): System 7.1 or higher

$$$

APPLYING SPECIAL EFFECTS

These plug-ins are the fun ones—they simplify the process of creating splashy special effects, both with type and with entire images. Most of these effects could be achieved using Photoshop's built-in filters and controls, but using these plug-ins can save lots of time and frustration, as well as let you try out effects in a preview window before applying them.

The A Plug-In Suite

This collection of plug-ins includes Shape Cutter (creates geometric shapes); Lightning (draws realistic lightning or electrical effects); Warper (enables stretching, distortion, and rotation of an area of an image); Halo (adds a glowing halo around or inside a selected area); Beveller (creates a beveled effect); Puddles (imitates fluid effects, including ripples and reflections); and Drop Shadow.

Almathera

http://www.almathera.co.uk

Platform: Windows 95

$$

Andromeda Series 1

This suite of plug-ins includes 10 optical-lens and photographic effects. The cMulti and sMulti filters create versatile circular or straight, multiple lens, kaleidoscopic effects. Designs has 100 single-bit textures and patterns that can be rotated, colored, bent and warped. Mezzo Line-Screen uses patterned screens within designs to convert your photo to black-and-white mezzotint line art. Diffract, Prism, and Rainbow have geometric controls to create color spectrum effects. Halo provides controlled highlight diffusion that can be adjusted for direction, spread, and intensity. Reflection provides instant clear pool reflections that can be adjusted for position, feathering, and opacity. Star adds bright glints, sparks, and glows. Velocity offers three different motion effects: multiple ghosting, highlight smears, and fade-outs.

Andromeda Software Inc.

http://www.andromeda.com

Platform: Macintosh (fat), Windows 95, Windows 3.1

System requirements (Mac): System 7.0 or later

System requirements (PC): 486 or Pentium

$$$

Andromeda Series 3

Andromeda Series 3 converts continuous-tone images to line art or mezzotints, using supplied patterns of various shapes and sizes: Mezzotints, Mezzograms, Straight Line Screens, Line Patterns, Mezzoblends, and Specialty screens. Because they result in a black-and-white image, these operations reduce file size dramatically. Can also colorize a screened image as a duotone. (See Figure 20.16.)

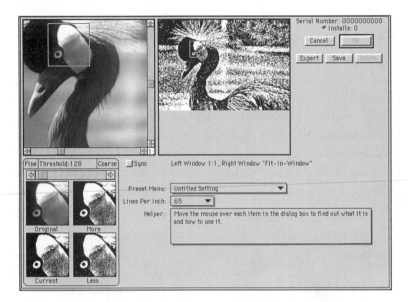

Figure 20.16

Series 3 from Andromeda applies different screening effects, including mezzotint patterns.

Andromeda Software Inc.

http://www.andromeda.com

Platform: Macintosh (fat), Windows 95, Windows 3.1

System requirements (Mac): System 7.0 or later

System requirements (PC): 486 or Pentium

$$$

Eye Candy v3.0

Eye Candy replaces Alien Skin's popular Black Box filters, which create sophisticated special effects; in addition to incorporating all of the

Black Box 2.0 filters, it adds 10 new filters, including Chrome, Fire, Fur, Polygon, Antimatter, Vibrate, Warpo, and Water Drops.

Alien Skin Software

`http://www.alienskin.com`

Platform: Macintosh (fat), Windows 3.1, Windows 95

$$$

Kai's Power Tools

Probably the most popular special-effects filter set, KPT includes the Gradient Designer, Texture Explorer, Fractal Explorer, and Gradients on a Path. New tools include KPT Spheroid Designer for sphere manipulation, KPT Interform for welding and animating multiple textures, and KPT Lens f/x for immediate previews of startling effects (such as showing your image through a simulated "fisheye" lens). KPT has an innovative and extremely non-standard interface (see Figure 20.17). Kai Krause is one of the world's leading Photoshop gurus.

Figure 20.17

The KPT Lens is just one example of the non-standard—but intriguing—interface in Kai's Power Tools.

MetaTools, Inc.

`http://www.metatools.com`

Platform: Macintosh 68K, Power Macintosh.

System requirements (Mac): 040 or faster with FPU; 8 bit video; System 7.1 or later

$$$

KPT Convolver

Convolver adds a spiffy interface to Photoshop's mysterious Custom filter, which enables you to achieve a huge range of effects by entering numbers in a matrix. Using precise controls and a dynamic preview, you can create custom sharpening, blurring, edge-detection, and embossing effects; the tweak mode lets you zero in on the precise level of each effect combination. Convolver provides a breakthrough in the way users work with many controls, such as hue, saturation, contrast, brightness, and embossing. Explore mode randomly generates effect combinations in the mutation grid. Users can creatively combine effects in real time; as you become more familiar with the plug-in, it adds five additional controls to reward you. (See Figure 20.18.)

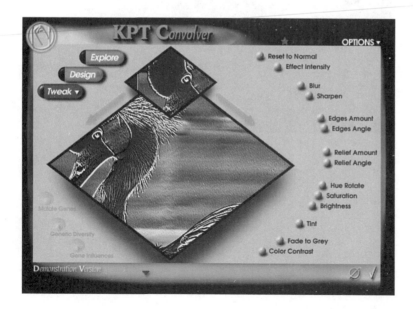

Figure 20.18

After you choose an effect from the Explore section of Convolver, you can make fine adjustments in the Tweak section.

MetaTools, Inc.

http://www.metatools.com

Platform: Macintosh 68K, Power Macintosh.

System requirements (Mac): 020 or faster with FPU; 8 bit video; System 7.1 or later

$$

Paint Alchemy

Paint Alchemy applies brushstroke effects to an image or selection in a wide variety of styles, angles, and sizes, automatically varying the strokes based on the image's hue, saturation, and brightness. Uses blend modes to mix overlapping brushstrokes. (See Figure 20.19.)

Figure 20.19

Dialog boxes within Paint Alchemy let you adjust brush angle, size, color, and other parameters.

Xaos Tools

http://www.xaostools.com

Platform: Macintosh 68K, Power Macintosh

System requirements (Mac): System 7.1 or later

$$$

Photo/Graphic Edges

This plug-in adds borders to images, letting you control the edge sizes, orientation, softness, feather, and borders. Effects can be previewed before they're applied, and different edge effects can be combined. You can also add colors to the borders and backgrounds behind the effect for different looks.

Auto F/X Corporation

http://www.autofx.com

Platform: Macintosh (fat), Windows 95

System requirements (Mac): System 7.0 or later

$$$/volume; discount for all three volumes

Power/Pac 1

This is actually a collection of 12 macros that work like filters, each using a series of built-in Photoshop features to achieve a special effect. The effects include embossing, soft focus, glowing, paths, recessing, saturation, screening, selecting, shadows, textures, and graphic edges.

Auto F/X Corporation

http://www.autofx.com

Platform: Macintosh (fat)

System requirements (Mac): System 7.0 or later

$$$

Sisnikk Pro

Create stereograms from your Photoshop images with this plug-in. Stereograms are repeating patterns masking a 3-D image that only appears when the viewer stares at the pattern for a while—they've appeared in dozens of popular books, posters, and calendars over the last few years.

Multimedia Marketing GmbH

http://www.mmmsoft.com

Platform: Macintosh

$$$

Squizz

Squizz creates distortion effects with a brush tool that lets you control exactly which portion of an image is distorted, as well as how it's distorted and how much. Works on images of any size, with unlimited undos. (See Figure 20.20.)

Figure 20.20

Use a brush to paint distortions into an image with Squizz.

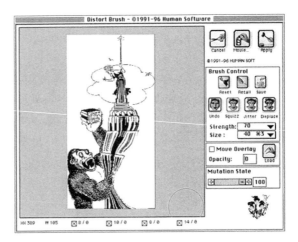

Human Software Company

http://www.humansoftware.com

Platform: Macintosh (fat), Windows 3.1

System requirements (Mac): System 7.0 or later

$$

Textissimo

Textissimo applies special effects such as drop shadows, bevels, carve, chrome, and glass using PostScript fonts or Illustrator drawings. This plug-in includes 150 effects and lets you create and save your own custom effects.

Human Software Company

`http://www.humansoftware.com`

Platform: Macintosh (fat), Windows 95

System requirements (Mac): System 7.1 or later

$$

WildRiverSSK Filters

This set includes 7 filters: DekoBoko (creates beveled rectangles), TV Snow (creates the illusion of television static), Chameleon (spectrum-based color manipulation), MagicCurtain and MagicFrame (use multipoint gradations to adjust the brightness of an image), MagicMask (apply built-in patterns to image elements), and TileMaker (creates tiled textures).

DataStream Imaging Systems, Inc.

`http://www.datastrem.com/`

Platform: Macintosh (fat)

$$$

CREATING 3D, ANIMATION, AND TEXTURES

These plug-ins enable you to use Photoshop for functions you'd ordinarily have to buy dedicated software to accomplish. Although the animation and 3D plug-ins listed here won't do as much as a stand-alone program would, they're great for Photoshop users who want to try their hand at animation or 3D modeling, as well as for images that don't require sophisticated techniques to create.

Andromeda Series 2

Series 2 is a 3D rendering plug-in that offers many features previously found only on expensive standalone programs, including the option to "fly around" the surface to alter your viewpoint and the object's appearance; a movable primary white light source; and adjustable ambient light that adds depth with shading. Series 2 performs 3D surface wrapping (map images onto a plane, a box, a cylinder, or a sphere), image and surface manipulation, shading, and 3D scene building. Images can be previewed in two modes, one quick and one more accurate. (See Figure 20.21.)

Figure 20.21

Andromeda's Series 2 plug-in maps images onto cylinders, boxes, angled planes, or spheres.

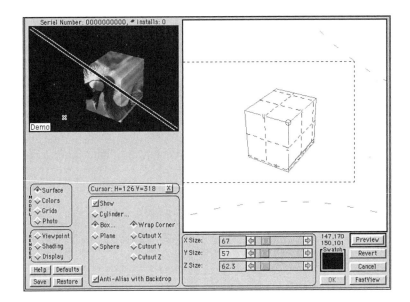

Andromeda Software, Inc.

http://www.andromeda.com

Platform: Macintosh (fat), Windows 95, Windows 3.1

System requirements (Mac): System 7.0 or later

System requirements (PC): 486 or Pentium

$$

Andromeda Series 4 (Techtures)

Series 4 makes textures and displacement maps. It also lets you use lighting effects, edit colors and transparency, and manipulate all pixels.

Andromeda Software, Inc.

http://www.andromeda.com

Platform: Macintosh (fat), Windows 95, Windows 3.1

System requirements (Mac): System 7.0 or later

System requirements (PC): 486 or Pentium

$$$

Velociraptor

Contrary to popular belief, this is not a meat-eating dinosaur that terrorizes Laura Dern. It is actually a motion-trail filter that creates smooth or broken trails behind objects; trails can loop, spin, or follow any path you want.

Andromeda Software, Inc.

http://www.andromeda.com

Platform: Macintosh

$$$

CyberMesh

CyberMesh enables you to convert grayscale images to 3D mesh models in DXF format, which is used by many 3D rendering programs. This plug-in also creates models by translating the brightness value of each pixel to a height value. Low-resolution images (which have fewer pixels) work better; high-resolution images end up with too many varying height levels. The resulting textures can be mapped onto a cylinder, a sphere, or a plane, and objects can be rotated. Written by one of Photoshop's original designers.

Knoll Software

Platform: Power Macintosh, Windows 3.1

HoloDozo

This plug-in lets you map any texture or image onto 28 unique 3D shapes. All 28 3D effects are completely customizable and can be previewed in real time in HoloDozo's interactive interface. (See Figure 20.22.)

Figure 20.22

By adjusting the projections from the three visible faces of the cube on the left, you adjust the dimensions and angle of the rendered toroid on the right.

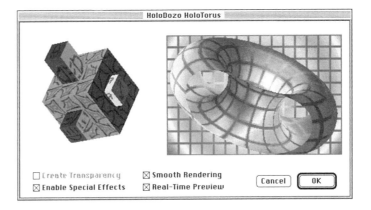

MultiMedia Marketing GmbH

http://www.mmmsoft.com

Platform: Power Macintosh

System requirements (Mac): System 7.0 or later

$$$

Terrazzo

Creating limitless tileable textures and patterns from any source image, Terrazzo makes geometrically complex patterns using a choice of 17 symmetries (tile shapes). Because Terrazzo uses supplied imagery as the source for its patterns, the results are a virtual kaleidoscope of color and pattern in harmony with the original image. (See Figure 20.23.)

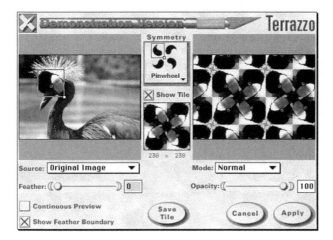

Figure 20.23

Terrazzo can use a dozen and a half different tile shapes to create patterns from existing images.

Xaos Tools

http://www.xaostools.com

Platform: Macintosh 68K, Power Macintosh.

System requirements (Mac): System 6.0.5 or later; 32-bit QuickDraw 1.2

$$$

TypeCaster

TypeCaster is a 3D type plug-in for Photoshop that enables users to create stunning 3D text without having to learn a difficult 3D interface. Text can be scaled, rotated, beveled, and extruded on the fly, and textures, bump maps, and lighting effects can be added. A bonus CD-ROM includes 200 free textures and bumps, as well as free fonts from Letraset.

Xaos Tools

http://www.xaostools.com

Platform: Macintosh 68K, Power Macintosh

System requirements (Mac): System 7.1 or later

$$$

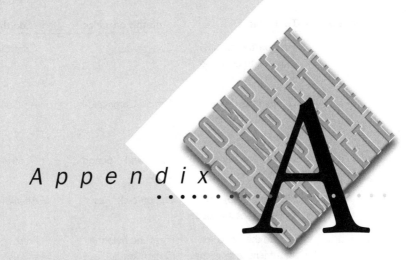

A p p e n d i x

KEYBOARD SHORTCUTS
FOR PHOTOSHOP 4.0

Keyboard	To do this...	...do this on a Mac.	...do this on a PC.
	To apply the last filter you used to an image or selection...	Command-F	Control-F
	To open the dialog box for the last filter you used...	Option-Command-F	Alt-Control-F
	To cancel an operation after it has begun...	Command-. (period), or Esc	Control-. (period), or Esc
	To reset a dialog box to the last setting used...	Option-click "Reset"	Alt-click "Reset"
	To load the last color adjustment settings that were used...	Press and hold the Option key and use the mouse to select Adjust (Levels, Curves, Color Range, and so on) under the Image menu.	Press and hold the Alt key and use the mouse to select Adjust (Levels, Curves, Color Range, and so on) under the Image menu.
	To return to the last preferences set...	Press and hold the Option key and use the mouse to select File > Preferences > General.	Hold the Alt key and use the mouse to select File > Preferences > General.
	To increase or decrease a value in a dialog box...	Press the Up or Down Arrow keys.	
	To make the Curves grid finer or coarser...	Press and hold the Option key and use the mouse to click in the Curves dialog box grid.	Press and hold the Alt key and use the mouse to click in the Curves dialog box grid.
	To display the Calculations dialog box with smaller fonts...	Press and hold the Option key and use the mouse to select Calculations in the Image menu.	Press and hold the Alt key and use the mouse to select Calculations in the Image menu.

MARQUEE TOOL

Keyboard	To do this...	...do this on a Mac.	...do this on a PC.
m	To create a rectangular selection...	Select the Marquee tool, move the tool where you want the upper or lower corner of the selection to be, then click down on the mouse button and drag until the selection is as large as you want it to be. Let go of the mouse button.	
	To select two or more separate areas of an image at once...	Hold the Shift key down while making your second selection.	
	To select only the area where two selections intersect...	Hold the Shift and Option keys while making the second selection.	Hold the Shift and Alt keys while making the second selection.
	To create a perfectly square selection...	Make sure there are no other selections and hold the Shift key down while making the selection.	
	To draw a selection from the center instead of from a corner...	Hold the Option key, click the mouse button, and drag.	Hold the Alt key, click the mouse button, and drag.
	To move the selection to a different part of the image...	Click the selection, and drag it where you want.	
	To copy a selection from one layer and paste it onto a new layer (turns the "marching ants" off)...	Command-J	Control-J
	To copy a selection from one layer and paste it into a new layer, bringing up the Make Layer dialog box (to adjust mode and opacity of the layer)...	Command-Option-J	Control-Alt-J
	To cut a selection out of one layer and paste it into a new layer...	Command-Shift-J	Control-Shift-J

continues

Keyboard	To do this...	...do this on a Mac.	...do this on a PC.
	To cut a selection from one layer and paste it into a new layer, bringing up the Make Layer dialog box (to adjust mode and opacity of the layer)...	Command-Option-Shift-J	Control-Shift-Alt-J
	To switch the Marquee tool to the Move tool...	Hold the Command key. To switch back, release the Command key.	Hold the Control key. To switch back, release the Control key.

CROP TOOL

Keyboard	To do this...	...do this on a Mac.	...do this on a PC.
c	To crop a portion of your image...	Select the Crop tool, move the tool where you want the upper or lower corner of the crop to be, then click the mouse button and drag until the area you want is within the selection. Let go of the mouse button. To finalize the crop, double-click inside the selection or hit the Enter or Return key.	
	To move the selected crop area...	After you make the selection and before you've finalized the crop, click anywhere inside the selected crop area and, holding the mouse button down, drag the selected area where you want it.	
	To rescale the selected crop area...	After you make the selection and before you've finalized the crop, click any of the eight handles along the outside of the selected area and, holding the mouse button down, drag the handle where you want it.	
	To cancel the crop and just start over...	Press the Esc key.	

MOVE TOOL

Keyboard	To do this...	...do this on a Mac.	...do this on a PC.
v	To move elements of your image such as guides, paths, the contents of a selection, or even an entire layer...	Select the Move tool, click the element you want to move, and, while holding down on the mouse button, drag the element where you want it.	
	To move an element on a 45-degree axis either horizontally or vertically...	Hold the Shift key while dragging the element.	
	To create a copy of the element...	Hold the Option key while dragging the element.	Hold the Alt key while dragging the element.
	To move a selection one pixel...	After the selection has been made, use the Arrow keys to move the selection.	
	To move a selection 10 pixels...	After the selection has been made, hold the Shift key and use the Arrow keys to move the selection.	

LASSO TOOL

Keyboard	To do this...	...do this on a Mac.	...do this on a PC.
l	To create an arbitrarily shaped selection by drawing...	Select the Lasso tool, click the mouse button, and draw the shape with the mouse. The shape completes when you release the mouse button.	
	To add to the selection...	Hold the Shift key and make an additional selection.	
	To select only the area where two selections intersect...	Press Shift-Option while making the second selection.	Press Shift-Alt key while making the second selection.
	To make the Lasso tool act like the Polygon Lasso tool...	Hold the Option key while making a selection.	Hold the Alt key while making a selection.
	To switch the Lasso tool to the Move tool...	Hold the Command key. To switch back, release the Command key.	Hold the Control key. To switch back, release the Control key.

POLYGON LASSO TOOL

Keyboard	To do this...	...do this on a Mac.	...do this on a PC.
I	To create an arbitrarily shaped selection by connecting the dots...	Select the Polygon Lasso tool and build the selection shape by clicking the mouse button around the part of the image you want to select. The selection builds between the points you create with the mouse button.	
	To add to the selection...	Hold the shift key and make an additional selection.	
	To subtract from the selection...	Hold the Option key while clicking the points you don't want.	Hold the Alt key while clicking the points you don't want.
	To select only the area where two selections intersect...	Press Shift-Option while making the second selection.	Press Shift-Alt while making the second selection.
	To force a segment of the selection to stick to a 45-degree angle...	Hold the Shift key while clicking the mouse button.	
	To make the Polygon Lasso tool act like the Lasso tool...	Hold the Option key and click your image to establish a starting point. Release the mouse button while making the selection (as you would with the Polygon Lasso tool) or else the Polygon Lasso tool does not take effect. Releasing the Option key while keeping the mouse button pressed returns the Lasso tool.	Hold the Alt key and click your image to establish a starting point. Release the mouse button while making the selection (as you would with the Polygon Lasso tool) or else the Polygon Lasso tool does not take effect. Releasing the Alt key while keeping the mouse button pressed returns the Lasso tool.
	To switch the Lasso tool to the Move tool...	Hold the Command key. To switch back, release the Command key.	Hold the Control key. To switch back, release the Control key.

AIRBRUSH TOOL

Keyboard	To do this...	...do this on a Mac.	...do this on a PC.
a	To paint on the screen as if you were using an airbrush...	Select the Airbrush tool, click the mouse button down and drag the mouse in the direction you want the painted line to go.	
	To paint a straight line between two points...	Click the mouse button and let go. Then hold the Shift key down and click somewhere else on the image. A straight line appears between the two points.	
	To just paint a straight line...	Hold the Shift key down, click the mouse button, and drag the mouse in the direction you want the line to go.	
	To fill a selection with the foreground color...	Press Option-Delete. To preserve transparency, hold the Shift and Option keys and press Delete.	Press Alt-Delete. To preserve transparency, hold the Shift and Alt keys and press Delete.
	To fill a selection with the background color...	Press Command-Delete key. To preserve transparency, hold the Shift and Command keys and press Delete.	Press Control-Delete key. To preserve transparency, hold the Shift and Control keys and press Delete.
	To change the size of the brush...	Select Show Brushes on the Window menu. Choose the brush size from the palette.	
	To display the Fill dialog box...	Press Shift-Delete.	
	To display precise cross hairs for brushes...	Press and release Caps Lock. To hide the cross hairs, press and release the Caps Lock again.	
	To set brush pressure or layer opacity...	With a Painting tool selected, press any number keys. Press two numbers quickly for two digits (50, for example).	
	To switch the Airbrush tool to the Eyedropper tool...	Hold the Option key. To switch back, release the Option key.	Hold the Alt key. To switch back, release the Alt key.
	To switch the Airbrush tool to the Move tool...	Hold the Command key. To switch back, release the Command key.	Hold the Control key. To switch back, release the Control key.

PAINTBRUSH TOOL

Keyboard	To do this...	...do this on a Mac.	...do this on a PC.
b	To paint on the screen as if you were using a paintbrush...	Select the Paintbrush tool, click the mouse button down, and drag the mouse in the direction you want the painted line to go.	
	To paint a straight line between two points...	Click the mouse button and let go. Then hold the Shift key down and click somewhere else on the image. A straight line appears between the two points.	
	To just paint a straight line...	Hold the Shift key down, click the mouse button, and drag the mouse in the direction you want the line to go.	
	To change the size of the brush...	Select Show Brushes on the Window menu. Choose the brush size from the palette.	
	To switch the Paintbrush tool to the Eyedropper tool...	Hold the Option key. To switch back, release the Option key.	Hold the Alt key. To switch back, release the Alt key.
	To switch the Paintbrush tool to the Move tool...	Hold the Command key. To switch back, release the Command key.	Hold the Control key. To switch back, release the Control key.

ERASER TOOL

Keyboard	To do this...	...do this on a Mac.	...do this on a PC.
e	To erase the current background color...	Select the Eraser tool, click the mouse button, and drag the mouse in the direction you want the background color erased.	
	To erase a straight line between two points...	Click the mouse button and let go. Then hold the Shift key down and click somewhere else on the image. A straight line appears between the two points.	
	To just erase a straight line...	Hold the Shift key down, click the mouse button, and drag the mouse in the direction you want the line to go.	
	To erase to the last saved version of the image...	Hold the Option key down then click the mouse button and drag the mouse.	Hold the Alt key down then click the mouse button and drag the mouse.

Keyboard	To do this...	...do this on a Mac.	...do this on a PC.
	To change the size of the Eraser...	Select Show Brushes on the Window menu. Choose the brush size from the palette.	
	To switch the Eraser tool to the Move tool...	Hold the Command key. To switch back, release the Command key.	Hold the Control key. To switch back, release the Control key.

PENCIL TOOL

Keyboard	To do this...	...do this on a Mac.	...do this on a PC.
y	To paint on the screen as if you were using a pencil...	Select the Pencil tool, click the mouse button down, and drag the mouse in the direction you want the line to go.	
	To draw a straight line between two points...	Click the mouse button and let go. Then hold the Shift key down and click somewhere else on the image. A straight line appears between the two points.	
	To just draw a straight line...	Hold the Shift key down, click the mouse button, and drag the mouse in the direction you want the line to go.	
	To change the size of the pencil...	Select Show Brushes on the Window menu. Choose the pencil size from the palette.	
	To switch the Pencil tool to the Eyedropper tool...	Hold the Option key. To switch back, release the Option key.	Hold the Alt key. To switch back, release the Alt key.
	To switch the Pencil tool to the Move tool...	Hold the Command key. To switch back, release the Command key.	Hold the Control key. To switch back, release the Control key.

RUBBER STAMP TOOL

Keyboard	To do this...	...do this on a Mac.	...do this on a PC.
s	To clone one part of an image to another part of the same image or to another image...	Select the Rubber Stamp tool. Select the portion of the image you want to be cloned by Option-clicking that part of the image.	Select the Rubber Stamp tool. Select the portion of the image you want to be cloned by Alt-clicking that part of the image. Release

continues

Keyboard	To do this...	...do this on a Mac.	...do this on a PC.
		Release the Option key. Then move the tool over the part of the image where you want the clone. Click down on the mouse button and drag the mouse in the direction you want the cloned image to appear. This process also works between two different Photoshop windows.	the Alt key. Then move the tool over the part of the image where you want on the clone. Click down the mouse button and drag the mouse in the direction you want the cloned image to appear. This process also works between two different Photoshop windows.
	To clone one part of an image to another part of the image in straight lines...	Select the portion of the image you want cloned. Then click the mouse button and let go. Then Shift-click somewhere else on the image. A straight line of cloned images appears between the two points.	
	To just clone in a straight line...	Shift-click the mouse button and drag the mouse in the direction you want the line of cloned images to go.	
	To change the size of the cloned area...	Select Show Brushes from the Window menu. Choose the clone size from the palette.	
	To switch the Clone tool to the Move tool...	Hold the Command key. To switch back, release the Command key.	Hold the Control key. To switch back, release the Control key.

SMUDGE TOOL

Keyboard	To do this...	...do this on a Mac.	...do this on a PC.
u	To smudge a portion of the image...	Select the Smudge tool, click the mouse button, and drag the mouse in the direction you want to smudge.	
	To smudge in a straight line between two points...	Click the mouse button and let go. Then hold the Shift key down and click somewhere else on the image. A straight, smudged line appears between the two points.	
	To change the size of the smudge...	Select Show Brushes on the Window menu. Choose the brush size from the palette.	
	To switch the Smudge tool to the Move tool...	Hold the Command key. To switch back, release the Command key.	Hold the Control key. To switch back, release the Control key.

BLUR/SHARPEN TOOL

Keyboard	To do this...	...do this on a Mac.	...do this on a PC.
r	To blur a portion of your image...	Select the Blur tool, click the mouse button, and drag the mouse over the section of the image you want blurred.	
	To sharpen a portion of your image...	Hold the Option key, click the mouse button, and drag the mouse over the section of the image you want sharpened. You can also click the Blur/Sharpen icon on the toolbox and hold it. The Sharpen tool appears.	Hold the Alt key, click the mouse button, and drag the mouse over the section of the image you want sharpened. You can also click the Blur/Sharpen icon on the toolbox and hold it. The Sharpen tool appears.
	To blur straight lines of your image...	Shift-click and drag the mouse in the direction you want the blurred line to go.	
	To sharpen straight lines of your image...	Press Shift-Option, click the mouse button, and drag the mouse in the direction you want sharpened line to go.	Press Shift-Alt, click the mouse button, and drag the mouse in the direction you want sharpened line to go.
	To blur or sharpen in a straight line between two points...	Click the mouse button and let go. Then Shift-click somewhere else on the image. A straight, blurred (or, if the Option key is held down at the same time, sharpened) line appears between the two points.	Click the mouse button and let go. Then Shift-click somewhere else on the image. A straight, blurred (or, if the Alt key is held down at the same time, sharpened) line appears between the two points.
	To switch the Blur/Sharpen tool to the Move tool...	Hold the Command key. To switch back, release the Command key.	Hold the Control key. To switch back, release the Control key.

DODGE/BURN TOOL

Keyboard	To do this...	...do this on a Mac.	...do this on a PC.
o	To lighten (dodge) a portion of your image...	Select the Dodge/Burn tool, click the mouse button, and drag the mouse over the section of the image you want lightened.	
	To darken (burn) a portion of your image...	Option-click the mouse button and drag the mouse over the section of the image you want darkened. You can also click the Dodge/Burn icon in the toolbox and hold it. The Burn tool appears.	Alt-click the mouse button and drag the mouse over the section of the image you want darkened. You can also click the Dodge/Burn icon in the toolbox and hold it. The Burn tool appears.
	To lighten straight lines of your image...	Hold the Shift key down, click the mouse button, and drag the mouse in the direction you want the lightened line to go. You can adjust the width of the dodge/burn by going to the Window menu, selecting Show Brushes, and choosing a brush size.	
	To darken straight lines of your image...	Press Shift-Option, click the mouse button, and drag the mouse in the direction you want darkened line to go.	Press Shift-Alt, click the mouse button, and drag the mouse in the direction you want darkened line to go.
	To darken or lighten in a straight line between two points...	Click the mouse button and let go. Then Shift-click somewhere else on the image. A straight, lightened (or, if the Option key is held down at the same time, darkened) line appears between the two points.	Click the mouse button and let go. Then Shift-click somewhere else on the image. A straight, lightened (or, if the Alt key is held down at the same time, darkened) line appears between the two points.
	To saturate the color of a portion of an image...	Select the Sponge tool, click the mouse button, and drag the mouse over the section of the image you want more saturated. You can also click the Dodge/Burn icon in the toolbox and hold it. The Sponge tool appears.	

Keyboard	To do this...	...do this on a Mac.	...do this on a PC.
	To desaturate the color of a portion of an image...	Option-click the mouse button and drag the mouse over the section of the image you want desaturated.	Alt-click the mouse button and drag the mouse over the section of the image you want desaturated.
	To saturate in straight lines of your image...	Shift-click the mouse button and drag the mouse in the direction you want the saturated line to go.	
	To desaturate straight lines in your image...	Press Shift-Option, click the mouse button, and drag the mouse in the direction you want the saturated line to go.	Press Shift-Alt, click the mouse button, and drag the mouse in the direction you want the saturated line to go.
	To switch the Dodge/Burn tool to the Move tool...	Hold the Command key. To switch back, release the Command key.	Hold the Control key. To switch back, release the Control key.

PEN TOOL

Keyboard	To do this...	...do this on a Mac.	...do this on a PC.
p	Draw paths...	Select the Pen tool and click and release the mouse button at points around your image. The path appears between those anchor points.	
	To force a segment of the path to stick to a 45-degree angle...	Hold the Shift key while clicking the mouse button.	
	To add anchor points along an existing path...	Select the Add-anchor-point tool, or with the Direct-selection tool selected, position it over the path and hold the Command and Option keys. Click the path at the place where you want the anchor point to be added.	Select the Add-anchor-point tool, or with the Direct-selection tool selected, position it over the path and hold the Control and Alt keys. Click the path at the place where you want the anchor point to be added.
	To draw a path in a straight line...	Shift-click the mouse button and drag the mouse in the direction you want the path to go.	

continues

Keyboard	To do this...	...do this on a Mac.	...do this on a PC.
	To hide or show a path...	Press Shift-Command-H.	
	To switch the Pen tool to the Convert-anchor-point tool (Macintosh only)...	Press Control-Option and move the tool over the point. To switch back, release the keys.	
	To switch the Pen tool to the Arrow tool...	Hold the Command key. To switch back, release the Command key.	Hold the Control key. To switch back, release the Control key.

DIRECT-SELECTION TOOL

Keyboard	To do this...	...do this on a Mac.	...do this on a PC.
p	To select and manipulate anchor points on a path...	Select the Direct-selection tool, move the mouse over the path you want to manipulate and click the mouse button to select the path. Your points become hollow and you can manipulate the points by click-and-dragging them.	
	To select more than one anchor point...	After selecting the first point, hold the Shift key down and select additional points.	
	To select the entire path at once...	Option-click somewhere on the path.	Alt-click somewhere on the path.
	To create a copy of the path...	Select the path and then hold the Option key while dragging the path with the mouse.	Select the path and then hold the Alt key while dragging the path with the mouse.
	To switch the Direct-selection tool to the Convert-anchor-point tool...	Hold the Command key and move the tool directly over the point. To switch back, release the Control key.	Hold the Control key. To switch back, release the Control key.

ADD- DELETE-ANCHOR-POINT TOOL

Keyboard	To do this...	...do this on a Mac.	...do this on a PC.
p	To add an anchor point to a path...	Select the Add-anchor-point tool, move the mouse over the section of the path you want to add a point to, and click and release the mouse button.	
	To delete an anchor point from a path...	Select the Delete-anchor-point tool, press and hold the Option key, move the mouse over the point you want to delete, and click and release the mouse button.	Select the Add/Delete Anchor Points tool, press and hold the Alt key, move the mouse over the point you want to delete, and click and release the mouse button.
	To switch to the Arrow tool...	Hold the Command key. To switch back, release the Command key.	Hold the Control key. To switch back, release the Control key.

CONVERT-ANCHOR-POINT TOOL

Keyboard	To do this...	...do this on a Mac.	...do this on a PC.
p	To toggle anchor points between smooth and corner points...	Select the Convert-anchor-point tool, move the mouse over the anchor point you want to change, and click and release the mouse button. If the point was smooth it becomes the corner, and vice versa.	
	To force the movement of the handles of the anchor point to stick to a 45-degree angle...	Press the Shift key while clicking the handle and dragging the mouse.	
	To switch to the Add/ Delete Anchor Point tool...	Hold the Option key. To switch back, release the Option key.	Hold the Alt key. To switch back, release the Alt key.

TYPE TOOL

Keyboard	To do this...	...do this on a Mac.	...do this on a PC.
t	To add text to your image...	Select the Type tool and click and release the mouse button. The Type dialog box appears. Your text always appears on a new layer.	
	To create text as a selection rather than solid type...	Select the Type tool from to the tool palette and hold the mouse button down until the Type Mask tool appears. Then create type as you would with the regular Type tool.	
	To switch from the Type tool to the Eyedropper tool...	Hold the Option key. To switch back, release the Option key.	Hold the Alt key. To switch back, release the Alt key.
	To switch from the Type tool to the Move tool...	Hold the Command key. To switch back, release the Command key.	Hold the Control key. To switch back, release the Control key.

LINE TOOL

Keyboard	To do this...	...do this on a Mac.	...do this on a PC.
n	To draw a simple line...	Select the Line tool, click the mouse button, and drag the mouse in the direction you want the line to go.	
	To create a line that is on a horizontal or vertical axis...	Hold the Shift key while dragging the mouse horizontally or vertically.	
	To switch from the Line tool to the Eyedropper tool...	Hold the Option key. To switch back, release the Option key.	Hold the Alt key. To switch back, release the Alt key.
	To switch from the Line tool to the Move tool...	Hold the Command key. To switch back, release the Command key.	Hold the Control key. To switch back, release the Control key.

GRADIENT TOOL

Keyboard	To do this...	...do this on a Mac.	...do this on a PC.
g	To create a gradient...	Select the Gradient tool. Click the foreground and background colors in the toolbox to select your colors. Then click the mouse button and drag the mouse in the direction you want the gradient to go. If you have a shape selected, do not deselect. The Gradient tool puts the gradient only within the confines of your selection.	
	To create a gradient in Gradient Editor...	Double-click the tool to open the Gradient Tool Options palette, then click the Edit button.	Double-click the tool to open the Gradient Tool Options palette, then click the Edit button.
	To easily browse colors in the Gradient Editor...	Open the Gradient Editor and press the Tab key. Each time you press the Tab button, the selection jumps one color to the right. To jump one color to the left, hold the Shift key down while pressing the Tab button.	
	To save a gradient permanently in Gradient Editor...	Press Shift-Command while using the mouse button to click Save.	Press Shift-Control while using the mouse button to click Save.
	To save a gradient as a Curves map file...	Press Option-Command while using the mouse button to click Save.	Press Option-Control while using the mouse button to click Save.
	To draw a gradient that is on a horizontal or vertical axis...	Hold the Shift key while dragging the mouse horizontally or vertically.	
	To switch from the Gradient tool to the Eyedropper tool...	Hold the Option key. To switch back, release the Option key.	Hold the Alt key. To switch back, release the Alt key.
	To switch from the Gradient tool to the Move tool...	Hold the Command key. To switch back, release the Command key.	Hold the Control key. To switch back, release the Control key.

PAINT BUCKET TOOL

Keyboard	To do this...	...do this on a Mac.	...do this on a PC.
k	To fill a selection or layer with color...	After making your selection, select the Paint Bucket tool, and click the selection.	
	To switch from the Paint Bucket tool to the Eyedropper tool...	Hold the Option key. To switch back, release the Option key.	Hold the Alt key. To switch back, release the Alt key.
	To switch from the Paint Bucket tool to the Move tool...	Hold the Command key. To switch back, release the Command key.	Hold the Control key. To switch back, release the Control key.

EYEDROPPER TOOL

Keyboard	To do this...	...do this on a Mac.	...do this on a PC.
i	To select a color from someplace else on the image...	Select the Eyedropper tool and click the color you want.	
	To switch from the Eyedropper tool to the Move tool...	Hold the Command key. To switch back, release the Command key.	Hold the Control key. To switch back, release the Control key.

HAND TOOL

Keyboard	To do this...	...do this on a Mac.	...do this on a PC.
h	To pan the image around the screen...	Select the Hand tool, click the mouse button, and drag the mouse in the direction you want the image to pan.	
	To fit the image on the screen...	Double-click the Hand tool.	
	To switch from the Hand tool to the Zoom tool...	Hold the Command key. To switch back, release the Command key.	Hold the Control key. To switch back, release the Control key.

ZOOM TOOL

Keyboard	To do this...	...do this on a Mac.	...do this on a PC.
z	To zoom in on some part of your image...	Select the Zoom tool and click somewhere on the image. To zoom in on a particular element of an image, click near that area and drag the mouse until a selection appears. When you let go of the mouse button, that part of the image appears in the window.	
	To zoom out...	Option-click your image.	Alt-click your image.
	To switch from the Zoom tool to the Move tool...	Hold the Command key. To switch back, release the Command key.	Hold the Control key. To switch back, release the Control key.

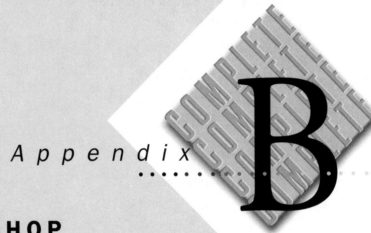

Appendix B

PHOTOSHOP
PLUG-IN VENDORS

Here is a listing of the plug-in vendors whose products are described in Chapter 20. For more information about those products, please refer to that chapter. This is not a complete listing of plug-in developers.

A Lowly Apprentice Production, Inc.

5963 La Place Court

Suite 206

Carlsbad, CA 92008-8823

(619) 438-5790 (phone)

(619) 438-5791 (fax)

support@alap.com

http://www.alap.com/

Plug-in: PlateMaker

Alchemy Mindworks, Inc.

P.O. Box 500

Beeton, Ontario L0G 1A0, Canada

(905) 936-9501 (phone)

(905) 936-9502 (fax)

alchemy@mail.north.net

http://www.mindworkshop.com

Plug-in: GIF Construction Set

Alien Skin Software

800 St. Mary's Street

Suite 100

Raleigh, NC 27605

(919) 832-4124 (phone)

(919) 832-4065 (fax)

alien-skinfo@alienskin.com

http://www.alienskin.com/

Plug-in: Eye Candy

Almathera

Southerton House, Boundary Business Court

92-94 Church Road

Mitcham, Surrey CR4 3TD

United Kingdom

+44 181 687 0040 (phone)

+44 181 687 0490 (fax)

almathera@cix.compulink.co.uk

http://www.almathera.co.uk/

Plug-in: The A Plug-In Suite

Altamira Group, Inc.

1827 West Verdugo Ave.

Suite C

Burbank, CA 91506

(818) 556-6099 (phone)

(818) 556-3365 (fax)

webmaster.alt@altamira-group.com

http://www.altamira-group.com/

Plug-in: Genuine Fractals

Andromeda Software, Inc.

699 Hampshire Rd.

Suite 109

Thousand Oaks, CA 91361

(805) 379-4109 (phone)

(800) 547-0055 (toll-free)

(805) 379-5253 (fax)

orders@andromeda.com

http://www.andromeda.com/

Plug-ins: Andromeda Series 1 through 3

Auto F/X Corp.

Black Point HRC 73

P. O. Box 689

Alton Bay, NH 03810

(603) 875-4400 (phone)

(603) 875-4404 (fax)

webmaster@autofx.com

http://www.autofx.com/

Plug-ins: Photo/Graphic Edges, Power/Pac 1

Aware, Inc.

One Oak Park

Bedford, MA 01730

(617) 276-4000 (phone)

(617) 276-4001 (fax)

sales@aware.com

http://www.aware.com/

Plug-in: AccuPress

BoxTop Software

One Research Blvd.

Suite 201

Starkville, MS 39759

(601) 323-6436 (phone)

(601) 324-7352 (fax)

info@boxtopsoft.com

http://www.boxtopsoft.com/

Plug-ins: HVS PhotoGIF, HVS ProJPEG

Candela, Ltd.

1676 East Cliff Road

Burnsville, MN 55337-1300

(612) 894-8890 (phone)

(612) 894-8840 (fax)

candela@candelacolor.com

http://www.candelacolor.com/

Plug-in: Color Synergy

Chroma Graphics

577 Airport Blvd.

Suite 730

Burlingame, CA 94010-2020

(415) 375-1100 (phone)

(888) 8CHROMA (toll-free)

(415) 375-1118 (fax)

http://www.chromagraphics.com/

Plug-in: Chromatica

Cytopia Software, Inc.

1735 E. Bayshore Road

Suite 30b

Redwood City, CA 94063

custerv@cytopia.com

http://www.cytopia.com/

(415) 364-4594 (phone)

(800) 588-0274 (toll-free)

(415) 364-4592 (fax)

Plug-in: PhotoLab

DataStream Imaging Systems, Inc.

P.O. Box 2148

Lexington, KY 40595-2148

(606) 255-6686 (phone)

(800) 889-7781 (toll-free)

(606) 259-1541 (fax)

info@datastrem.com

http://www.datastrem.com/

Plug-in: WildRiverSSK Filters

DayStar Digital. Inc.

5556 Atlanta Highway

Flowery Branch, GA 30542

(770) 967-2077 (phone)

(800) 962-2077 (toll-free)

(770) 967-3018 (fax)

http://www.daystar.com/

Plug-in: PhotoMatic

DesAcc

2502 N. Clark St.

Suite 204

Chicago, IL 60614

(773) 404-7888 (phone)

daccess@interaccess.com

http://www.desacc.com/

Plug-in: ImportAccess

Digital Frontiers

1019 Asbury Avenue

Evanston, IL 60202

(847) 328-7789 (phone)

(800) 328-7789 (toll-free)

(847) 869-2053 (fax)

info@digfrontiers.com

http://www.digfrontiers.com/

Plug-ins: HVS Color, HVS WebFocus

Eastman Kodak Co.

343 State Street

Rochester, NY 14650

(800) 235-6325 (toll-free)

http://www.kodak.com/

Plug-in: Photo CD Acquire Module

Extensis Corporation

55 SW Yamhill, 4th floor

Portland, OR 97204

(800) 796-9798 (toll free)

(503) 274-0530 (fax)

info@extensis.com

http://www.extensis.com/

Plug-ins: Intellihance, PhotoTools

Gryphon Software Corp.

7220 Trade Street

San Diego, CA 92121

(619) 536-8815 (phone)

(888) 8GRYPHON (toll-free)

sales@gryphonsw.com

http://www.gryphonsw.com/

Plug-in: BatchIt!

HighWater Designs Ltd

6 Bedford Farms

Bedford, NH 03110-6532

(603) 669-7466 (phone)

(603) 669-7456 (fax)

info@highwater.com

http://www.highwater.com/

Plug-in: FBI Writer

Human Software Company

P.O. Box 2280

Saratoga, CA 95070

(408) 399-0057 (phone)

(408) 399-0157 (fax)

102474@compuserve.com

http://www.humansoftware.com/

Plug-ins: AutoMask, CD-Q Acquire, CyberSquizz, Medley, Select, Squizz, Swap, Textissimo

ImageXpress, Inc.

1121 Casa Nova Court

Lawrenceville, GA 30244

(770) 564-9924 (phone)

(770) 564-1632 (fax)

websupport@scanprep.com

http://www.scanprep.com/

Plug-in: ScanPrepPro

Hugh Kawahara

kawahara@leland.stanford.edu

http://www-leland.stanford.edu/~kawahara/photoshop.html

Plug-ins: Kwick Mask, Create B/W, Rotate Color

Knoll Software

P.O. Box 6887

San Rafael, CA 94903

(415) 453-2471 (phone)

(415) 499-9322 (fax)

Plug-in: CyberMesh

MetaTools, Inc.

6303 Carpinteria Avenue

Carpinteria, CA 93013

(805) 566-6200 (phone)

(805) 566-6385 (fax)

MetaSales@aol.com

http://www.metatools.com/

Plug-ins: Kai's Power Tools, KPT Convolver

MultiMedia Marketing GmbH

Germany

+49 511 317221 (phone)

+49 511 317203 (fax)

info@luxussoft.de

http://www.mmmsoft.com/

Plug-ins: HoloDozo, Siznikk Pro

Yves Piguet

piguet@ia.epfl.ch

http://iawww.epfl.ch/staff/yves.piguet

Plug-in: GifBuilder

Second Glance Software

7248 Sunset Avenue NE

Bremerton, WA 98300

(360) 692-3694 (phone)

(800) 682-3110 (toll-free)

(360) 692-9763 (fax)

info@secondglance.com

http://www.secondglance.com/

Plug-ins: Chromassage, LaserSeps Pro, PhotoSpot, ScanTastic Control

Total Integration, Inc.

334 E. Colfax Street

Suite A1

Palatine, IL 60067

(847) 776-2377 (phone)

(847) 776-2378 (fax)

http://www.totalint.com/

Plug-ins: ColorMatrix, Epilogue, Fastedit/Deluxe, Fastedit/IVUE, Handshake/LW, Iris/CT

Ultimatte Corporation

20554 Plummer Street

Chatsworth, CA 91311

(818) 993-8007 (phone)

(818) 993-3762 (fax)

http://www.ultimatte.com/

Plug-in: Photofusion

Visu Technologies

Anthony Fokkerweg 61, 1059 CP

Amsterdam, The Netherlands

+31 (0)20 669 37 01 (phone)

+31 (0)20 669 37 01 (fax)

visu@vgm-visu.nl or Visu1@aol.com

http://www.vgm-visu.nl/visu/visu2.html

Plug-ins: Channel 24, CoCo

Xaos Tools

600 Townsend Street

Suite 270 East

San Francisco, CA 94103

(415) 487-7000 (phone)

(800) 833-9267 (toll-free)

(415) 558-9886 (fax)

http://www.xaostools.com/

Plug-ins: Paint Alchemy, Terrazzo, TypeCaster

A p p e n d i x · · · · · · · ·

ONLINE REFERENCES

AMERICA ONLINE

AOL has always had top quality Photoshop information available. To find it, search keyword: Photoshop.

Included in the list:

Photoshop SIG (Special Interest Group)

- ◆ About the Photoshop SIG
- ◆ Windows, Photoshop Plug-ins
- ◆ Adobe Systems, Inc.: Company, product information, and tech support

Digital Artist's Chat that includes more than 10,000 postings broken down into 31 topics.

Mac Software Libraries

- ◆ Photoshop tools
- ◆ Photoshop images
- ◆ Kai's Power Tips for Mac

MAILING LIST

Index of PHOTSHOP Digest—This is a searchable index of the PHOTSHOP mailing list. The list is maintained by the Fine and Performing Arts Department of Governors State University in University Park, Illinois.

```
http://kells.vmedia.com/cgi-bin/wais-phshp.pl
```

NEWSGROUP

Newsgroups are discussion groups for certain topics on Usenet. For Photoshop, check out the following.

```
comp.graphics.apps.photoshop
```

FTP SITES

Adobe Photoshop FTP Archive at Adaptive Solutions—This FTP site includes downloadable KPT tips, other Photoshop tips, files, and Photoshop filters for Mac, PC, and Sun systems.

```
ftp://ftp.asi.com/pub/photoshop
```

General FTP Archive—Downloadable Photoshop files organized by date (1993–1996). There is also a link to a subdirectory of Photoshop goodies. Warning: This is a long text list and takes a while to load into your browser.

```
ftp://uxa.ecn.bgu.edu/pub/archive/photshop/
```

WEB SITES

Mother Lode Sites

These sites are rich in tips and tricks for using Photoshop, as well as downloadable software.

Alf's Photoshop Page—A Web site put together by Alfredo Mateus that is extremely complex, deep, and devoted to Photoshop.

```
http://www.fns.net/~almateus/
```

BoxTop PlugPage—Download plug-ins for both Mac and Windows Photoshop.

`http://www.boxtopsoft.com/plugpage`

The Plug Page—Links to an FTP site with recent Mac and Windows Photoshop plug-ins.

`http://www.aris.com/boxtop/plugpage/welcome.html`

PC Resources for Photoshop—The intent of this Web page is to collect and maintain information on Adobe Photoshop for use on the PC platform *only*. There are links to FAQ lists, mailing lists, newsgroups, personal Web sites, commercial Web sites that develop and support software for Photoshop, plug-ins, reviews of books, seamless tiles, and artwork.

`http://www.netins.net/showcase/wolf359/adobepc.htm`

The Photoshop Mail-List World-Wide Web Page—The home page for the Photoshop mail-list includes links to other Photoshop sites, a tips and tricks area, and an area for subscribers to submit their work, as well as a way to subscribe to the list.

`http://WWW.CSUA.Berkeley.EDU/~kima/photshop/`

Photoshop Web Reference 4—Although the site for Photoshop 4 isn't up yet as of this writing, the section for Photoshop 3 (`http://www.duke.edu/~ac10/photoshop/three/index.html`) is rich with tips and ideas.

`http://www.duke.edu/~ac10/photoshop/four/index.html`

Commercial Sites

These sites have been created to help market products as well as provide customer service. They are a great way to get information about particular plug-ins or to get help making them work.

Adobe Photoshop Product Information—This is the official Adobe Systems information page on Photoshop—a good way to get the official line on what's new for Photoshop.

`http://www.adobe.com/prodindex/photoshop/main.html`

983

Color Reproduction—QMS has contributed an excellent primer on digital imaging and the science of color.

http://www.qms.com/www/products/color_paper/

Color Separation with Adobe Photoshop Software—A quick tutorial about how to prepare Photoshop to create color separations from Colorite, a service bureau in New York City.

http://www.aols.com/colorite/separationinps.html

ColorBlind and the ICC Standard—Another color management system. In 1993, Adobe Systems, Agfa, Apple Computer, Eastman Kodak, Microsoft Corporation, Silicon Graphics, Sun Microsystems, and Taligent, Inc., formed the International Color Consortium (ICC) to develop a profile format that could be used on any computer platform by any operating system to handle the color translation between device gamuts. This page describes what they came up with and offers several pieces of software that use this system.

http://www.color.com/CB/cb_and_icc.html

MetaTools: GIF Animation Tutorial—Part of a series of multimedia and Web publishing tips, this tip is on animated graphics for the Web.

http://www.metatools.com/webtips/anitip/what.html

MetaTools/HSC Software/Kai's Power Tools/Live Picture/Bryce— The company formerly known as HSC is now MetaTools, Inc. If you want to keep up on what's happening with Kai Kraus, watch this site. This is a rich, complex site with lots of good information. To make it easier to navigate, we've included some other MetaTools pages here.

http://www.metatools.com

♦ **MetaTools: Kai's Power Tips**—An index of the classic set of Kai's Power Tips on Macintosh.

   http://www.metatools.com/kptips/mactips.html

♦ **MetaTools: Multimedia/Web Publishing Tips**—Tips for using MetaTools products to create art and effects for use in multimedia environments. Learn nuances about creating and laying out Web pages, create graphics using MetaTools products, view background and button libraries, and follow step-by-step text treatment examples.

http://www.metatools.com/webtips/webtips.shtml

◆ **MetaTools: Transparent GIFs Tutorial**—A good explanation of transparent graphics for the Web with a list of cross-platform transparent GIF tools linked to the tools' home sites.

http://www.metatools.com/scott/tip2.html

◆ **MetaTools University**—A good collection of resources related to MetaTools products and tips from Kai. The original 23 Photoshop Power Tips are updated here for Photoshop 3.0. Also there is a growing collection of Web and Multimedia Tips, as well as a gallery of art from the Corcoran School of Art.

http://www.hsc.com/metatoolsuniv.html

Microtek: Best Scans—Tips and techniques for scanning into Photoshop using Microtek scanners.

http://www.mteklab.com/best.html

Photoshop Central—A section of the Thunder Lizard Productions training group Web site devoted to Photoshop. It includes a live Q&A, links to HSC, a Photoshop newsgroup, a filter compendium, and sample images.

http://www.cyweb.com/~misc/ps.html

Photoshop f/x Tutorials Page—In addition to the description and the links, there are tutorials on creating GIF 89a files, quick drop screens, and quick glow effects as described in the Photoshop f/x book.

http://www.vmedia.com/vvc/onlcomp/phshpfx/tutorial/

PowerShop and Photoshop Tips—Includes tips for using layer groups, creating spot colors through layers, and creating halftoned text and overprinting one-color drop shadows.

http://www.asi.com/powershop/tips.html

UMAX FAQ for Photoshop PC—A section of the UMAX (scanner) site, this FAQ has a good Q&A section about scanning into Photoshop.

`http://www.umax.com/support/pcfaq.html`

RBGtoHex: an RBG to Hexidecimal Color Converter—UNIVOX has developed an online conversion calculator. Just put in your value and go!

`http://www.univox.com/rgb2hex.html`

Individual Sites

There are some individuals online who have taken it upon themselves to collect and distribute information on Photoshop. These sites are well worth looking at.

Chris Cox's Home Page—Among other things, this hotlist home page includes several great links to Photoshop resources on the Web.

`http://www.teleport.com/~ccox/LocalHome.html`

CPK Designs Plug-in Page—Chris Kendall put together a package of Photoshop plug-ins for PCs you can download right from the page.

`http://www.the-wire.com/usr/cpk/plug.htm`

Greg's Factory Output Page—Greg's Factory Output filters are sets of filters created by Greg Schorno with Adobe Photoshop Filter Factory. The filters work on any RGB format image as long as enough memory is available. Most of the filters are available for both Windows and Macintosh.

`http://mars.ark.com/~gschorno/gfo/`

H+S Chart—Color Depth for GIF Files—A set of GIFs of a logo showing the effects of reducing bit-depth to decrease file size.

`http://www.shore.net:80/~hsdesign/tips/bitdepth.html`

List of Known Photoshop Plug-ins—A simple list of Photoshop plug-ins, including the name of the company (for third-party plug-ins) and platforms. This list does not include hyperlinks to the companies, but it's still a good reference.

`http://www.teleport.com/~ccox/plug-ins.html`

Laurie McCanna's Photoshop Tips Page—This page has a great series of tips for simple Photoshop effects. Particularly good for Windows users is a discussion of Photoshop gotchas on Windows (`http://www.mccannas.com:80/pshop/pshop8.htm`).

`http://www.mccannas.com:80/pshop/photosh0.htm`

Steve Mockensturm's Web Page: Custom Photo Illustration and Design—A collection of custom Photoshop plug-ins, custom Photoshop brushes, 3D model library, 3D EPS drop cap font, and tutorials on clipping paths. There is also a nice collection of Shockwave buttons.

`http://www.primenet.com/~mock/`

Naeem's Adobe Photoshop page—A good page for Photoshop beginners, it includes links to resources, online FAQs, pictures, and so on.

`http://www.cyweb.com/~misc/photo.html`

Charles A. Poynton—A specialist in digital video and high definition TV (HDTV), Poynton has several articles here about digital video, gamma and color, typography and information design, and the Mac on the internet.

`http://www.inforamp.net/~poynton/`

PC Resources for Photoshop—My Tips—An excellent collection of tips and links for Photoshop for the PC.

`http://www.netins.net/showcase/wolf359/pcrptips.htm`

Photobooks—Written by a senior support specialist at Adobe, the primary goal of this Web site is to provide information about Photoshop books for those folks who are shopping for additional reading material.

`http://www.aa.net/~davidh/PSBooks/PhotoBooks.html`

Photoshop FAQ—An extremely complete collection of questions and answers about Photoshop.

`http://www.cybercomm.nl/~muller/photoshop/`

Raytracing in Photoshop—Kevin Björke developed a raytracing effect for Photoshop and put the details in this online article. There are also links on the page for other uses of Photoshop.

`http://www.rahul.net/natpix/RayPS.html`

Magazines

These sites are online magazines with great information about Photoshop and what people are doing with it.

Get Info Newsletter: Photoshop Techniques—A short, to-the-point monthly newsletter by Jeffrey M. Glover on Mac graphics techniques, this newsletter includes a lot of good information on Web graphics. Also be sure to see the June 1995 issue: the special Photoshop issue (`http://getinfo.asap.net/getinfos/lib/9506.html`).

`http://getinfo.asap.net/getinfos/getinfos.html`

GRAFICA Obscura—This online publication from SGI covers all sorts of topics from Japanese English advertising slogans to checking Your Monitor Gamma (`http://www.sgi.com/grafica/setup/index.html`).

`http://www.sgi.com/grafica/index.html`

Kai's Power Tips and Tricks for Photoshop—The classic Microsoft Word files converted to HTML by the Pixel Foudry. While they are a bit dated now, if you are a Kai Krause fan you shouldn't miss them.

`http://the-tech.mit.edu:80/KPT/KPT.html`

ImageSoup at emedia.net—A publication for New Media arts professionals. Tips and tutorials on Photoshop, Macromedia Director, Fractal Design Painter, and countless filter packages.

`http://www.emedia.net/imagesoup/`

Photoshop Techniques—This publication offers tips and tricks for Photoshop available in downloadable PDF format.

`http://the-tech.mit.edu/KPT/Techniques/`

Organizations

The PC Graphics Web—The PC Graphics Web is a campaign aiming to make users of PC computers in advanced graphics production more visible. You can join the group, download samples, or even contribute graphics to the site.

`http://members.gnn.com/MissMary/PCGW.htm`

Index

• • • • • • • • • • • • • • • • •

B

D

F

H

J

K

M

S

X-Z

Other MACINTOSH—
Design/Graphics & Multimedia Titles

Adobe Illustrator for Macintosh: Classroom In a Book, Second Edition

Designed and tested in Adobe's classrooms, this comprehensive, up-to-date guide covers thirteen tutorial lessons demonstrating how to maximize the power and sophistication of Adobe Illustrator.

- CD-ROM contains sample lessons and projects, including an advertisement, an annual report, and a poster
- Designed to work as a set of self-paced tutorials or within an instructor-led program

Adobe Press
1-56830-234-7 ■ $45.00 USA/$61.95 CDN
320 pp., 8 1/2 x 11, Covers Version 6.0 for Macintosh, Casual - Accomplished
Available Now

Adobe Illustrator Creative Techniques
1-56830-133-2 ■ $35.00 USA/$47.95 CDN
Available Now

Adobe Photoshop Creative Techniques
1-56830-132-4 ■ $40.00 USA/$54.95 CDN
Available Now

Advanced Adobe PageMaker for Macintosh: Classroom in a Book
1-56830-261-4 ■ $50.00 USA/$68.95 CDN
Available Now

Advanced Adobe Photoshop for Macintosh: Classroom in a Book
1-56830-117-0 ■ $50.00 USA/$68.95 CDN
Available Now

The Amazing PhotoDeluxe Book for Macintosh
1-56830-266-5 ■ $30.00 USA/$40.95 CDN
Available Now

The Color Mac Production Techniques, Second Edition
1-56830-126-X ■ $50.00 USA/$68.95 CDN
Available Now

PageMaker Scripting
1-56830-318-1 ■ $45.00 USA/$63.95 CDN
Available October 1996

Adobe After Effects for Macintosh: Classroom in a Book
1-56830-267-3 ■ $50.00 USA/$68.95 CDN
Available Now

Adobe Premiere for Macintosh: Classroom in a Book, Second Edition
1-56830-119-7 ■ $49.95 USA/$67.95 CDN
Available Now

Macromedia Director Design Guide
1-56830-062-X ■ $29.95 USA/$39.99 CDN
Available Now

Macromedia Director Lingo Workshop for Macintosh, Second Edition
1-56830-287-8 ■ $45.00 USA/$63.95 CDN
Available Now

Visit your fine local bookstore, or for more information visit us at http//:www.mcp.com/hayden

Other DESIGN/GRAPHICS Titles

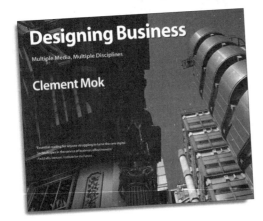

Designing Business
Provides the design/business communities with a new way of thinking about how the right design can be a strategic business advantage. It is the definitive guide to presenting a business identity through the use of traditional media vehicles and emerging technologies.

- CD-ROM (dual-platform) exhibits interactive prototypes of multimedia brochures, interactive television, and Web sites as developed by Clement Mok designs Inc., one of the most sought after interactive design agencies in the world
- Shows how effective communication is one way to out-think, out-plan, and out-perform the competition

Clement Mok
1-56830-282-7 ■ $60.00 USA/$81.95 CDN
264 pp., 8 x 10, Covers PC and Macintosh, New - Expert
Available Now

Adobe Persuasion: Classroom in a Book
1-56830-316-5 ■ $40.00 USA/$56.95 CDN
Available Now

Learning Adobe FrameMaker
1-56830-290-8 ■ $60.00 USA/$81.95 CDN
Available Now

Adobe Illustrator for Windows: Classroom in a Book
1-56830-053-0 ■ $44.95 USA/$59.99 CDN
Available Now

Adobe Pagemaker for Windows: Classroom in a Book
1-56830-184-7 ■ $45.00 USA/$61.95 CDN
Available Now

Adobe Photoshop: Classroom in a Book
1-56830-317-3 ■ $45.00 USA/$63.95 CDN
Available Now

Advanced Adobe PageMaker for Windows 95: Classroom in a Book
1-56830-262-2 ■ $50.00 USA/$68.95 CDN
Available Now

Advanced Adobe Photoshop for Windows: Classroom in a Book
1-56830-116-2 ■ $50.00 USA/$68.95 CDN
Available Now

The Amazing PhotoDeluxe Book for Windows
1-56830-286-X ■ $30.00 USA/$40.95 CDN
Available Now

Branding with Type
1-56830-248-7 ■ $18.00 USA/$24.95 CDN
Available Now

The Complete Guide to Trapping, Second Edition
1-56830-098-0 ■ $30.00 USA/$40.95 CDN
Available Now

Design Essentials, Second Edition
1-56830-093-X ■ $40.00 USA/$54.95 CDN
Available Now

Digital Type Design Guide
1-56830-190-1 ■ $45.00 USA/$61.95 CDN
Available Now

Fractal Design Painter Creative Techniques
1-56830-283-5 ■ $40.00 USA/$56.95 CDN
Available Now

Photoshop Web Magic
1-56830-314-9 ■ $45.00 USA/$63.95 CDN
Available Now

Photoshop Type Magic 2
1-56830-329-7 ■ $39.99 USA/$56.95 CDN
Available November 1996

Adobe PageMaker 6.5 Complete
1-56830-331-9 ■ $45.00 USA/$63.95 CDN
Available Now

Production Essentials
1-56830-124-3 ■ $40.00 USA/$54.95 CDN
Available Now

Stop Stealing Sheep & find out how type works
0-672-48543-5 ■ $19.95 USA/$26.99 CDN
Available Now

Visit your fine local bookstore, or for more information visit us at http//:www.mcp.com/hayden

WHAT'S ON THE CD-ROM

The *Photoshop 4 Complete* CD-ROM is pretty simple. There are three folders/directories: Books, Examples, and Software.

BOOKS

Included are techniques from Hayden's newest, hottest Photoshop 4 titles: *Photoshop Type Magic 2*, by Greg Simsic, and *Photoshop Web Magic*, by Ted Schulman (http://www.tspi.com), Renée LeWinter (http://www.911Gallery.org/911/), and Tom Emmanuelides.

EXAMPLES

The Examples folder contains items that are referenced throughout the book, divided by chapter. These are examples, animations, or practice images to work with.

The image "Portrait.psd" (Chapter 9) is ©Michele Clement.

The images "Sandleaf.psd" (Chapter 9) and "Flower.psd" (Chapter 8) are ©Karen Tenenbaum.

The image "Cafe.psd" (Chapter 8) is ©Gail Blumberg.

SOFTWARE

The Software folder contains demos of Adobe software and other related products. We have made every effort to include the most updated versions of software, and on both platforms, whenever possible. Adobe did not have a demo of Photoshop 4.0 ready at the time we went to press, so we were unable to include that. If you cannot find a product, it was not available on your platform at the time we compiled the CD. Many companies are in the process of porting from Mac to Windows or vice versa, so you might contact the company to check on the status. (See Appendix B, "Photshop Plug-In Vendors," for plug-in vendor contact information.)

Applications that are not shareware are generally save-disabled: you will be able to open and work with all the functional features of the application, but you may not be able to save or print the software. If a product is shareware, please register and support the shareware concept. Follow the guidelines set forth, including, if required, forwarding a modest shareware payment. Your purchase of this book and accompanying CD-ROM does not release you from this obligation. Refer to the READ ME and other information files that accompany each of the programs.

Notice: The GIF Construction Set software included with this publication is provided as shareware for your evaluation. If you try this software and find it useful, you are requested to register it as discussed in its documentation and in the About screen of the application. The publisher of this book has not paid the registration fee for this shareware.

MACMILLAN COMPUTER PUBLISHING USA

A VIACOM COMPANY

Technical ---- Support:

If you cannot get the CD/Disk to install properly, or you need assistance with a particular situation in the book, please feel free to check out the Knowledge Base on our Web site at **http://www.superlibrary.com/general/support**. We have answers to our most Frequently Asked Questions listed there. If you do not find your specific question answered, please contact Macmillan Technical Support at **(317) 581-3833**. We can also be reached by email at **support@mcp.com**.